ACKNOWLEDGMENTS

Since putting it all together has been more like working a Jigsaw puzzle with pieces missing than exploring on a tranquil lake in a comfortable canoe, we are more thankful to those who have encouraged us than apologetic for our shortcomings. Wallace Gray of Southwestern College, Kansas, and Connie Hager, have generously given assistance and encouragement. Wallace Gray has become an occasional co-author and really deserves a place on the title page. Besides some very competent textual editing, Connie Hager has also blessed us with her indominable enthusiasm for value. We also thank Len Evan Goodman and the entire philosophy department at the University of Hawaii, Madhev Deshpande of the University of Michigan, Russell Hatton of the University of Delaware, as well as the librarians at Hawaii and Michigan, and especially the wonderful librarians at Marshall University, Huntington, W. Va. A personal note of gratitude goes to Hideo Murakami and Hossein Bombedad, whose assistance has been profoundly appreciated though seldom rewarded. And finally a special thanks to Margaret O'Neill, who exemplifies so well the interplay between adventure and tranquillity in the human quest for this world and any other. To all these and the many unnamed, we extend onr deepest gratitude for their various but always invaluable assistances.

CONTENTS

INTRODUCTION

It was intially hoped that the Period of Scholasticism (800-1350) could have been treated in one volume as the other periods have been. That not being possible due to length and circumstances, the period will be presented in two volumes. Admittedly we have not been able to find subdivisions for this period which are to our satisfaction. Therefore we have used those subdivisions which seem to fit the history of philosophy, although by no means do we propose that periodizing only according to philosophical developments is desirable. Thus, for the Period of Scholasticism (800-1350) we suggest the following divisions : the Earlier Period of Scholasticism or "Monism in Many Moods" (800-900); the Middle Period of Scholasticism or "Exfoliation and Elaboration" (900-1150); and the Later Period of Scholasticism or the "Great Summas" (1150-1350). What we intend by "Monism in Many Moods" and "Exfoliation and Elaboration" should not necessarily be taken in any strict technical sense, but rather as indicating the dominating *trend* in contrast with the architectonic structuring of the "Great Summas" of the Later Scholastic Period. The reader is referred to Volume II of this study for an overview of our periodization scheme, "The Problem of Periodization".

The basic problem for the ninth century is that implicitly set by St. John of Damascus, namely the Formlessness or Indescribability of God and His relation with nature and man. In Erigena, this relation is basically contingent on God's drawing all things back to Himself ; in Saadia, it rests primarily on the Semitic doctrine of God's transcendent position as Creator; in al-Ash'arī, primarily on the Unicity of the Godhead; in Śaṅkara, on the unavoidable inference that since everything experienceable must be within *māyā*, there must be That upon which all rests as *adhyāsa*, superimposition; in Kūkai, on the experience of mystical enlightenment or that level of consciousness wherein all things and all possible ideas are seen as fragmentations of a single Continuum of ever-changing Process. A completely synoptic view of these together is our end.

The temper of the ninth century throughout Eurasia was basically monistic. There may have been variations on the same theme, but there was the will to see all things from a God-like perspective, to see all things as not separated from God. Our thesis is that the rallying point for the ninth century throughout the world was that of the absolute Unity of God and the nondeparture from that Unity of all things natural and human. Scotus Erigena manifests this through the theology of theophany; Saadia does it through the moral sphere, emphasizing the moral injunctions given to man in prophetic revelation; Śaṅkara does it through his strict ontology of nondivision, even the nondifference of being and becoming; and al-Ash'arī through his emphasis on Predestination. The monistic tendency and its counter-balances are always in a delicate position. Complete equilibrium would mean *pralaya*, dissolution of the whole of the cosmological panoply, and that we do not yet see—history still moves on.

Al-Ash'arī's reaction against "rationalism" may be best taken as a neo-orthodox re-establishment of the absolute dependence of man on the Will of God, insofar as He can be said to "have" a "will" without compromising his non-anthropomorphic transcendence. This neo-orthodox tendency is manifest also in Śaṅkara, to whom the Buddhists are the 'heretics', and in Saadia against the overmuch Hellenizing tendency of those who were following Philo's precedent, and in Scotus Arigena in his assistance to Charlesmagne in establishing the Holy Roman Empire. This same tendency towards neo-orthodoxy is found in China in the beginnings of Neo-Confucianism in the persons of Han Yü and Li Ao. This does not mean, however, that innovations ceased; neo-orthodoxies also have a way of getting broken open and having rivals.

By the close of the ninth century we have at best qualified monisms and often openly dualist and pluralist trends. Out of the unification of Islam in the external world emerged a new metaphysics of unity which was almost monolithic; but as the political and theological unity of Islam became fragmented, so the monist trend was soon lost in proliferation of distinctions and subtleties of scholastic argumentation until we reach the "Great Summas" (1150-1350). This trend from monistic simplicity through elaboration to excessive complexity and ornamentation is remarkably paralleled in architecture in the transition from Romanesque to elaborate Gothic in Europe and in Dravidian India from the solidity of Tanjore to the filigreed fragrance-in-stone of Belur and Halebīd. In Islam likewise we can see essentially the same transition from the early puritanical unadorned mosques to the elaborate and even gaudily ornate mosques of the later centuries. In the Buddhist world the halo begins with the pure simplicity of the early Gupta style, but eventually in China, Japan and India it encompasses the entire universe. Similar developments of the halo motif transpire also in Byzantium and even in Gothic Europe. During the Later Period of Scholasticism the greatest works of Bonaventura and Aquinas, al-Ghazālī and Ibn Rushd, Rāmānuja and Madhva, Lu Hsiang-shan and Chu Hsi, Dogen and Nichiren, emerge systematically out of previous seminal insights and formulations such as the *Sentences* of Peter Lombard, the *Brahma Sūtras*, and the speculations about the Great Ultimate. They mark without doubt the culmination of that cycle of systematization in a way that has seldom been achieved.

Complexity of argumentation soon becomes the chief characteristic of the whole Scholastic Period equally in the Islamic, Christian, Indian and Chinese fields. One needs much patience indeed, although he who acquires this virtue will be plenteously rewarded. Not till Ockham and his contemporaries is there a trimming down of the multiplication of "arguments". Logic as well as faith leads to extremes; but it is just this that the best were trying to avoid. The Middle Way must be inclusive, whether it easily does so or not, or else it must resort to a "somehow" or an "as if" or a multiplication of "neverthelesses" in order to avoid disjoining man and nature and God. One is again and again tempted to return to the Zen Buddhists or the Taoists and abandon logic altogether: but this dichotomizing will never do. The One is always in need, so to speak, of logical as well as trans-logical presentation.

The scholastic philosphers ideologically as well as geographically were very much involved in multi-dimensional encounters between civilizations, which is reflected in the supposed conflict between reason and revelation and the efforts at rendering the scriptures consistent in the way that systematic philosophy and theology demand. This basic problem in the traditions entailed the exploration of the limits of reason as well as the full employment of the rational faculty in defending a supra-rational foundation and/or orientation for philosophizing. This age-old controversy was certainly not peculiar to any particular century. But it is difficult to understand any philosophy in any culture during the Scholastic Period without some appreciation of this problem, which again perplexes many minds, especially among Existentialists and those who are fascinated with Zen.

There is always the temptation of "reading history backwards". One may not rightly judge Aristotle a dolt because he did not invent the microscope, or condemn Śaṅkara for not including a treatise on advanced mathematics, nor condemn any of the Byzantine or Islamic scholastics for not inventing symbolic logic. Likewise, one may not historically condemn any of the scholastic philosophers for not questioning the authority of their canon of scriptures. There are always things which human beings take for granted. One may rather marvel that the critical spirit did get as far advanced as it did (indeed, one sometimes wishes that modern philosophers could show the same keenness of dialectical skill that these thinkers did).

The most important point historically to understand is that from the ninth century tradition becomes so firmly established and the problems so set and the possible solutions so exhaustively explored that only commentaries follow and not original discoveries. Not the *individual* but the *tradition* itself becomes the important thing. This cannot be overstressed.

Through the history of philosophy and religion one must be cautious in either affirming or refuting the positions of those who gained the epithet "heretic". Often it is only historical accident or the struggle for political or military power which determines heresy and orthodoxy, whether in Hinduism, Buddhism, or Christianity. The important thing for any of us concerned with the history of ideas, and especially the global history of ideas, is the recognition of what was considered important enough to become controversial.

Although one may not yet point to many great advances in the empirical sciences, the time of "retreat" which may be noted in Gregory the Great, for example, is at an end. Still, the chief difference between this and the post-Humean world-view is that here nature is a field of reflection of the Glory of God, a matter of contemplation more than an area for investigation. For most scholastic philosophers the whole of human existence is pointed toward transcendence; this world is the *preparation* for the world to come. Some think the ideal did not quite succeed. But that is not the important thing, for "success" is not the criterion of judgment until the advent of American Pragmatism. The establishment of the God-given goal—everything depends on that, and on that alone. If the goal has not yet been attained, it remains to the credit of the scholastic philosophers that they helped to set it clearly.

That *yin/yang* polarizations should occur historically in the drama of development should not be surprising to those familiar with our previous volumes. Philosophies just do not appear in isolation from each other. Normally they develop in contexts of historical controversies—controversies which more often than not continue through many centuries and even down to the present time. That realization involves us in the more general problem of typology of philosophies and the sociology of knowledge question as to whether or to what extent certain types of philosophies occur in particular types of circumstances. For example, do materialisms come from proletarian movements or rebellions? Are all mysticisms "escape mechanisms" or "opiates" as the orthodox Marxists say; and do they prevail in "Times of Troubles" (to invoke Toynbee)? Under what conditions do fanaticisms become historically effective even though open-minded humanisms seem to be more desperately needed? Do we yet have something to learn from the distinction made by Ibn Sīnā and others between prophetic types of philosophies and 'merely' rational metaphysical systems ? Should one make still further distinctions between philosophic mysticism and esoterics; and what of the history of philosophies that claim to be trans-historical !

But these are only a few *questiones disputandae* which arise, and often as not remain unanswered in our *explorations*—for that is all that they can thus far claim to be, and no more. No doubt many specialists will complain that our estimation from their particular point of view is out of focus. To them we appeal for corrections, for we hope to present challenges to others to put it all together as it actually transpired in history.

MONISM IN MANY MOODS
(800-900)

1. Jābir

The emergence of Islamic law in its four schools, the Mu'tazilite-Qadarite controversy, the emergence of Ṣūfism, the definite beginnings of Hellenizing philosophy commonly referred to as the *Falsafah*, the emergence and development of the natural sciences (the field for which Geber, as Jābir was known many centuries later in Latin Europe, achieved some fame as an innovator)—all of these currents in Islamic intellectual, spiritual and cultural life seem to conform to a sort of entelechy which begins in the eighth, takes on definitive form in the ninth century, and flowers in the tenth. Many of the eighth century pioneers, especially those who unlike Jābir did not have the fortune of getting Latinized, are only beginning to be rediscovered even by Muslims themselves in some cases, especially those whose "westernized" education has alienated them from their own heritage. Many of those working in mathematics, astronomy, medicine, alchemy and the like have not received due attention, partly because much of the information is extant only in fragments but also because of the strange prejudice of keeping the history of science in Islam separate from the history of Islamic philosophy.

The corpus of the works ascribed to Jābir ibn Ḥayyān (fl. 776) is much more varied than the ordinary textbook designation "alchemist" indicates, including cosmology, astrology, mathematics, and music.

> The large number of works bearing the name of Jābir has cast some doubt upon the authenticity of some of them.... By and large, most of what is not by Jābir himself is by later alchemists, who followed his teachings closely.
>
> In fact there was very probably a kind of "society" or "fraternity", which used his name for all of its writing. The name Jābir, therefore, not only refers to a historical person, but is also (like that of Vyāsa in Hinduism, or of Hermes in

> Hermeticism) a symbol for an intellectual function and a point of view. It is in this sense both the proper name, and the name of the "archetype", of the Muslim alchemist. Consequently, one can safely refer to a Jābirian corpus, which expounds a particular intellectual perspective of specific origin, even if all the works in it are not by Jābir himself.[1]

In this Jābirian corpus "we can see the merging of certain esoteric aspects of Islam with Oriental Pythagoreanism, Hermeticism and even elements from the Far East."[2] This much can be said although only a fraction of the texts in that corpus has been studied.

To the same extent as al-Rāzī, Jābir was also a philosopher. He was both a Shī'ite and a Ṣūfī, a fact which reminds us that mysticism, philosophy and science have not always been at odds with each other as the modern secular prejudice would have us think. Jābir himself claims nothing original, saying that he is simply passing on what he had gained from his tradition as a disciple of the sixth Shī'ite Imām, Ja'far al-Ṣādiq (d. 765), who was the founder of the so-called Twelver school of law in Shī'a Islam. Jābir was born at Tuṣ in Khurāsān, and enjoyed patronage as court physician of Hārūn al-Rashīd. He was not only celibate but a vegetarian and generally an ascetic.

> No two figures are better known in the annals of Islamic alchemy than Jābir ibn Hayyān and Muhammad ibn Zakariyā al-Rāzī, the Latin Geber and Rhazes. Both men were celebrated masters of alchemy. Both are believed to belong to the same school by later generations of alchemists in the Islamic and Western world. Yet, study made of the writings of both men clearly reveals that although Rāzī employs the language of Jābirian alchemy, he was in reality dealing not with alchemy but with chemistry. ...
>
> Jābir, while also interested in natural occurrences, never divorced the facts of the natural world from their symbolic and spiritual content. His famous balance (*mīzān*) was not an attempt to quantify the study of nature in the modern sense but "to measure the tendency of the World Soul". His preoccupation with numerical and alphabetical symbolism, with

> the study of natural phenomena as determinations of the World Soul, with specifically alchemical symbols, all indicate that Jābir was applying the process of *ta'wīl* to nature, in order to understand its inner meaning. ...
>
> Applied to nature, *ta'wīl* means penetrating the phenomena of nature to discover the noumena which they veil. It means a transformation of fact into symbol and a vision of nature, not as that which veils the spiritual world, but as that which reveals it.[3]

Most well known in Jābir's philosophy is his doctrine of balance, which had much influence in Islamic tradition after him. It is basically a matter of chemistry but was extended in application even to general cultural matters, such as jurisprudence. The concept has metaphysical as well as historical roots, and has to do with the harmony of the World Soul, which is related to music. Here we may again reflect that, as with the *Sphoṭavāda*, if we equate vibration (music) with the harmonics of energy-transformations from gross to subtle in a series of qualitative leaps, then we get a very stimulating participative sense of reality, since that's what we also really are. This is not to say that Jābir had the equipment or techniques of the modern scientific outlook of the Einsteinian revolution, but he may have had the right notion basically in proto-scientific form.

The doctrine of the balance seems to work on a *yin-yang* dynamic principle rather than merely a static mathematical formula. Those interested may do well to consult Joseph Needham's researches again for he does have some references to Jābir in comparison with alchemy in China as well as the alchemy of the later Roman Empire. An indirect connection with Leibniz's "pre-established harmony" is not only possible but definitely plausible, although Leibniz also may have derived it from Chinese sources.

> If the Jābirian corpus contains chemical texts which are easily understood in terms of modern chemistry, it also contains several cosmological treatises which, along with the purely alchemical writings, belong to quite another type of knowledge. In them, the various orders of cosmic reality are explained in terms of the masculine-feminine or sulfur-and-mercury

> principles. His scheme of cosmology is based upon the relation of a number of states of being with each other, a relation that is dependent upon the effect that a lower state derives from the action of a higher one, and in turn transmits to the state lying below it in the chain of Being. He describes the descent from the world of the Intellect, through the Soul to the world of the elements.... The elements of alchemy, therefore, form a part of the great unity which is the universe, just as the science of alchemy forms a branch of the more universal science of cosmology.[4]

Thus it may be claimed that Jābir did have a total philosophy with a relatively advanced cosmology for his time.

Jābir held that everything in the physical world was some balance or other between sulphur and mercury. Now this theory is a little fanciful, but the important thing is not the theory as such but Jābir's very scientific complaint that no one has found an adequate *method* of separating out the components of natural compounds in order to reduce them to their primordial nature and thus find out *experimentally* the nature of matter and the material world.

As was the case with his teacher and friend Imām Ja'far, it was from the Ismā'īlian heritage that Jābir received the tradition of an esoteric interpretation of the alphabet as a "science of letters"—which again sounds to us, although evidently unknown to him, like Hindu *Sphoṭavāda* or like the esoterics of the sounds of the mantras according to Tāntric practice. This "science of letters" influenced others long after Jābir such as even Ibn'Arabī and his school, and was used as an esoteric explanation of the true meaning of the Divine Names (a theme reminiscent of John of Damascus and behind him of Pseudo-Dionysius).

There is strong evidence that Jābir had borrowed the theory of the philosopher's stone from the Chinese and improved upon it by introducing sulphur as well as lead and mercury as basic elements. The esoteric numerology that is associated with Jābir's alchemical or Hermetic system can also be traced back to Chinese rather than Greek or Syriac sources. To say the least, Jābir emerges as a figure important historically, not just as the Geber of Latin Scholasticism but as another and rather unique "missing link" in the chain of trans-Eurasian communications, which by the ninth century, centering in Baghdad, had ceased to be a single chain and was fast becoming a complex net (indeed one may quip that it was a pretty good net to catch Hegel's "Absolute" in and tie it down to concrete factual history).

The important thing is that, whether one looks to Jābir or to Zakariyā al-Rāzī as really the first chemist that began to move away from the esoterics of alchemy to truly experimental method, what did transpire in Baghdad in the ninth century was no less phenomenal than what was done by Paracelsus in the much-vaunted Italian Renaissance. Not a few authorities who know both Jābir and Paracelsus seriously question whether the latter made any radical improvement from what he had derived, howsoever indirectly, from the Arabs.

2. Nara Buddhism

The Japanese assimilation of Chinese Buddhism in its already confusing varieties had a close resemblance to what had happened only few centuries previously in China itself, with the notable exception that in China, in spite of the *ko-i* syncretism with Taoism, there continued to be strong opposition from the Confucian orthodoxy (strengthened, if anything, by the strong Legalist philosophy), whereas in Japan during the Nara period (710-794) there was virtually no opposition at all. That all of this contrasted very sharply with the military advance of Islam and of Christianity scarcely needs pointing out. Japan was not without its military aristocracy already, but if anything Buddhist influence softened this somewhat as a peace-giving faith and philosophy being welcomed into a relatively peaceful country. No wonder that the aesthetic component could flourish as it did in the Nara period.

There were not only adaptations of the Chinese sects to the Japanese scene but various degrees of mixture with indigenous

Shintō and with what had been assimilated long since of Han Confucianism. The syncretistic mixtures between Buddhism and indigenous Shintō were definite enough even in the Nara period to become almost another separate cult, namely the *shinbutsu shūgō*. This *shinbutsu shūgō*, which literally means the unification of gods and Buddhas, was especially popular in the circles of the royal government. The government positively encouraged this emergence by building *jingūji* (shrine-temples), the first certain instance of such a construction being about 698.

Patronage also figured, as we might expect. As Buddhism became the official state religion (or philosophy, it might still be claimed), those in the Shintō shrines wanted some share in that means of support, so naturally they would adapt their ways to accommodate. Shintō up to that time was not a very clearly defined practice and had little theoretical underpinning, being primarily aesthetic with the *kami* notion (really not a concept but a "felt presence") as the key to it all. And there were a large number of local Shintō deities, so that chanting of Buddhist sūtras at the shrines of these various deities became a common practice; and reciprocally, these Shintō gods and goddesses naturally got assimilated into Japanese Buddhism as indigenous Buddhas, since everything is supposed to partake of the Buddha-nature according to most of the Mahāyāna sūtras.

Buddhism permeated the whole society to such an extent that not only did most varieties receive generous patronage from the throne but even became the normal milieu for adjudicating law suits and keeping vital statistics of births and deaths. Indeed there seems to have emerged a rather harmonious relationship between the government and the Buddhist saṅgha on the whole, although of course there were exceptions. Not only at first but continuing for some time, Buddhism was adopted and patronized by the state for definitely superstitious reasons, as had happened with Northern Buddhism even well into the T'ang Dynasty. The emperors wanted the Buddhist monks because they believed that by patronizing them the nation would be saved from calamities and aided against its enemies.

The Seventeen Article Constitution of Prince-regent Shōtoku in 604 is of supreme importance to Japanese cultural historians not only because of its demonstration of early Chinese influence

(Confucianist for the most part), but it is the first known codification of Japanese law. It certainly does not compare with the Code of Justinian as far as details and legal technicalities are concerned, or even with much more elaborate codes in China. But it does stand in the history of Japanese civilization in a similar position to such codes in other civilizations; and what interests us keenly is that it is basically an ethical code rather than merely a legal document and therefore has considerable philosophical import.

Although Buddhism had been made the state religion as early as 594, it was under the Emperor Temmu in the years 676-685 that Buddhism was more vigorously propagated in Japan. Rather than one of the standard classsic Mahāyāna sūtras such as a *Laṅkāvatāra Sūtra* or the *Lotus Sūtra* later imported by Saichō, not to mention the *Prajñāpāramitā* literature and the simple codes of Buddhaghoṣa's variety of Buddhism or the logical expertise of Dignāga, it was the definitely esoteric *Sūtra of the Sovereign Kings of the Golden Light Ray* which appealed to the Emperor Temmu because it promised (in his interpretation) magical protection for the Holy Nation of Japan, which was already having conflicts with Korea. This infatuation with the esoteric was also a strong current in Kūkai's teaching, and not entirely absent from Saichō's form of Buddhism. Nevertheless, there was in Japan, as in the late T'ang Dynasty in China and with full force in Sung China, a Confucian countercurrent to the esoteric. However this Confucian reaction did not develop fully until the early tenth century, though as a result of the reform of the universities at the very outset of the Heian period the Confucian classics were required of all students.

With Saichō (Dengyō Daishi) and Kūkai (Kōbō Daishi)—these being titles of the highest respect combining the concepts of national hero and of saint—and the others such as a Ennin in ninth century Japan, we have what is commonly known as the full flowering of the Heian period (794-1192). Although Tendai and Shingon, associated with Saichō and Kūkai respectively, are historically to be placed in the Heian period, virtually all the other basic sects of Japanese Buddhism (still current today for the most part) took shape in the Nara period (710-794). These Six Sects of Nara Buddhism are Kusha, Jōjitsu, Ritsu, Sanron, Hossō, and Kegon.[1]

The Kusha sect was brought to Japan by two Japanese 'priests' Chitsū and Chitatsu about 657. The canonical text which they brought back from China and translated into Japanese was the *Abhidharmakośa* of Vasubandhu, which may translate as the *Book of Metaphysical Treasure*. By this time this text had probably received some not necessarily essential esoteric and syncretistic interpretations. "The *Abhidharmakośa* provides an ideal forerunner for Vijñānavādin philosophy and undoubtedly this is one of the principal reasons why the Kusha school was brought to Japan in conjunction with the Hossō (Vijñānavāda), becoming a permanent appendage of that sect in 793."[2] Thus as such this school did not continue independently for long, but its indirect influence was considerable.

The Jōjitsu was imported about 625 by the Korean monks Ekwan and Kwanroku. The canonical text is the *Satyasiddhi Śāstra*, translated in Japanese as *Jo-Jitsu-Ron*, which reads *The Book of the Perfection of Truth*. This *Sūtra* came into China through Kumārajīva and continued during the *ko-i* assimilation with Taoism through Seng-tao and Seng-sung. Aesthetic and somewhat esoteric, its emphasis is on non-ego/no-self and meditation on the Two Nothingnesses in an attempt to transcend mere intellection. The teaching originally with Harivarman (third century) seems to have been somewhat like Patañjali Yoga, being strongly rooted in, if not a continuation of, the original Abhidharma heritage. However, interpretation in terms of 'nothingness' or 'emptiness' had glossed over the original realist orientation until it had become typically esoteric and other-worldly, or even illusionistic. The Four Noble Truths have been expanded by this school into a very elaborately schematized set of twenty-seven stages of spirituality.

> One unusual feature of these twenty-seven stages that Mahāyānists notice is the fact that only one form of ignorance is overcome (clinging to self). Mahāyāna Buddhism recognizes two forms of ignorance, which correspond to two of the attachments the Jōjitsu sought to eliminate: the clinging to self

> and the attachment to the dharmas. Here, in the important stages of religious awareness, the Jōjitsu only mention emancipation from the hindrance of human ignorance (clinging to self) but do not discuss the release from clinging to the dharmas. Such an inconsistency is a further reason why critics believe this school did not reach the complete level of Mahāyāna thought, for their theory was not clearly correlated with practice.[3]

Shōtoku's teacher Eji is said to have had some association with this Jōjitsu as well as with Sanron. By 806 Jōjitsu became incorporated into Sanron.

The Ritsu or Vinaya school was concerned with the precepts of the Buddhist *saṅgha.* This aspect of Buddhism had been one of the three basic parts of the *Tripiṭaka,* the three-fold 'basket' of authentic Buddhist canonical scriptures. This discipline was considered as an ethical propaedeutic necessary before undertaking comprehension of the metaphysical and spiritual aspects. It was the only sect that took this very essential aspect of Buddhist inheritance as primary and "placed these rules before meditation, devotions or philosophy as the means of attaining Enlightenment "[4] Long since in China it had become a separate school also rather than being incorporated, as one might expect, as a normal part of all varieties of Buddhism.

There was already a confusing proliferation of different sects in Japan along with the aestheticism of original Shintō and something of the adapted Confucianism of Prince Shōtoku and the Taika Reforms. "The teaching of the various sects as they arrived in Japan was primarily philosophical and not related as yet to the practical matters of religion such as the behavior and discipline of the clergy."[5] Thus there were not enough authenticated initiates into the Buddhist *saṅgha* to carry on proper 'ordination' since the rules called for ten *vinaya* experts to perform the ceremony in a "civilized" country like China, and in a less civilized country at least five such persons were necessary. Even the Emperor Shōmu (724-748) had become concerned about the matter and had sent two priests to China to receive training and proper initiation. As things developed, Ganjin, one of the best known Chinese Vinaya masters, himself came to Japan even though he had to do so in disguise to escape government interference since travel abroad was at that time forbidden in China. After his arrival in Japan he found that the Japanese had already devised their own way of doing things; and, having difficulty with the language and not gaining the patronage that he had expected, he resigned in 758 and placed his disciple Hosshin in charge of official ordinations. The proper ceremonies for ordination were what the Japanese at this time were most concerned about, much fuss being made over the *kaidan*, the platform erected for the ceremony. It seems that the Ritsu had some functions interdenominationally, governing ordinations for the other sects as well.

Besides being another of the Six Sects of Nara Buddhism, the Ritsu played a very important role in the historical development of Buddhism in Japan generally.

> The vinaya plays a crucial role in Buddhism representing the tangible application of Buddhist doctrines to create and maintain a society (sangha) dedicated to the pursuit of Enlightenment. Although the interpretation of individual regulations for monks and nuns naturally differed in accordance with the social environment of a given society, the transmission of the vinaya represented the actual establishment of the Buddhist sangha, for without proper standards for ordination the clergy could not properly exist. This is why the transmission of the Ritsu sect to Japan was an essential step in the development of Japanese Buddhism. The rules later were modified to suit Japanese needs and eventually, during the Heian period, other sects gained the right to conduct their own ordinations in keeping with their vinaya regulations, but the precedent and basis had been established by the Ritsu sect.[6]

By comparison almost in the same years, from Augustine and Dionysius on the theories about the Church were major themes of philosophers and theologians in Christianity. The chief difference is that in the Japanese Buddhist traditions there seems not to have been the claims toward the supernatural asserted for the *saṅgha*. By and large the Buddhist *saṅgha* in Japan remained just that, the community of monks and nuns governed by rules and rituals both practical and devotional with the laity participating as material supporters and recepients of blessings in return, whereas it was claimed of the Christian Church that it was the Body of Christ continuing on earth, dynamized by the Holy Spirit, for the purpose of effecting not only a transformation of individuals but the redemption and virtual if not actual recreation of all things natural and human.

All through the medieval periods throughout Eurasia such disciplines as are found in the Ritsu school were typically practiced, not only in the Buddhist world but in Hinduism (at least after Śaṅkara's organization of his monastic order), in Christianity, and to a very great extent in Ṣūfī Islam; and moreover, we should not forget that there were in these centuries very few who could be called philosophers who were not monks or nuns.

The Sanron or Mādhyamika sect goes back to Nāgārjuna with transmission into China through Kumārajīva and others. The three canonical texts are (1) the *Mūlamādhyamika-kārikā* and commentary by Piṅgala, known in China as the *Chung-lun* or *Treatise on the Middle*; (2) the *Treatise of One Hundred Verses* attributed to Āryadeva; (3) the *Treatise of Twelve Categories* attributed to Nāgārjuna. Chi-tsang (549-623) systematized the Chinese version of this school under the designation of San-lun, which nevertheless eventually came to an end in China.

> The principle philosophy of these texts was the refutation of views believed to impede the attainment of Enlightenment and the revelation of the true meaning of Buddhism by means of the middle way of the two levels of truth. They attempted to refute all views establishing either the existence or nonexistence of the dharmas, maintaining that conceptual ideas such as "this is truth', 'this is good' or even 'this is Buddha' were false insofar as Absolute truth (*paramārtha satya*) transcended both speech and thought.[7]

Although the Sanron does not survive today, it was "one of the most influential of the Six Sects and its philosophy dominated the early Nara period."[8] The school became divided into many subsects, not to mention a still further variety of "new" Sanron or Betsu Sanron which supposedly arrived directly from India about 747 looking to Bhāviveka as founder. They were all rivals evidently, arguing and fighting about 'nothing'.

Moreover they all ended in 'nothing', for the last remnant is reported to have disappeared with the death of Echin in 1169.

Sanron is noted for such themes as the two levels of truth and the famous eight-fold negation of Nāgārjuna himself (which is currently enjoying a fresh popularity), and for its justification for claiming to be the 'middle' way. "The Sanron, in keeping with the Mādhyamika viewpoint, are not willing to cease with the experience of Enlightenment, but insist that the application of Enlightenment be made to the conventional world . . . ."[9] This is symbolized by the Boddhisattvas which they recognized. Sanron tried, as Chih-i to some extent and Tsung-mi very earnestly had done, to make sense out of the proliferation of canonical literature by classifying it into three divisions. "This classification was an effort to demonstrate that the various teachings of Buddhism do not lead to different goals, but ultimately are embraced within the one vehicle of the historical Buddha's teaching, in essence the realization of inner Enlightenment."[10]

> The Sanron sect played an extremely important role in the history of Japanese Buddhism since it crystallized the essence of Nāgārjuna's philosophy. This thought, in conjunction with Yogācāra, had formed the basis of Mahāyāna Buddhism and it was natural that it play a significant role in Japan and become, in conjunction with the Hossō school, a major foundation in the development of Japanese Buddhism. The Sanron presentation of the constant denial of conceptualized reality also served as a reminder to succeeding Buddhist sects not to fall into the error of becoming unduly attached to their own doctrine and thereby losing the spirit of Buddhism."[11]

Sanron did have the merit of challenging all dogmatism, which is perhaps the most basic and central teaching of Buddhism at its best anywhere.

The Hossō sect was indebted to the school of Hsüan-tsang in China and was primarily Vijñānavāda, following the teachings of Vasubandhu and Asaṅga. Other Indian patriarchs recognized by the Japanese inheritance include Dharmapāla (c.570) and Śīlabhadra (529-645), under whom Hsüan-tsang studied at Nālandā. Among the Chinese patriarchs are K'uei-chi (632-682), the chief disciple of Hsüan-tsang, and his disciple Hui-chao (649-714). The Hossō sect was founded in Japan in 653 by the monk Dōshō after his return from China where he had been taught by no less than Hsüan-tsang. The numerous texts used by Hossō had been compiled into a comprehensive canon known in Japan as the *Joyuishikiron* (*Vijñāptimātratāsiddhi*). That in the course of time there was some measure of syncretism with Shintō should not surprise us, for this historically became more or less true of virtually all traditions in Japan.

As was done variously by Chih-i and Tsung-mi in China and by most of the other Nara sects, there was an attempt at classification of the various canonical and semi-canonical texts. The Hossō classification does not attempt any historical periodization and does not so sharply separate the higher esoteric teachings from what were considered to be teachings for the masses, as was the case with the Sanron/Mādhyamika classification.

The Sanron/Vijñānavāda never really believed in "scientific objectivity" but in a sort of phenomenological 'intentionality', as may be seen from the following explication, which also emphasizes how the teaching was not only adopted but adapted to the Japanese milieu :

> Of the different Buddhist sects issued from India and China which established themselves in our territory, those alone subsist which, without losing anything of their universal value, modelled their philosophic teaching upon our racial and psychological exactions, and assumed, if I may express myself thus, the light and color of our country. After this study of the Kusha, Jō-Jitsu and Sanron sects, too redolent with Hindu mentality, we might have foreseen that Japanese thought would reaffirm its contours, like Fuji after a fog. Effectively we are going to see the Hossō doctrine emerge from the clouds and reinstate an Absolute : *Thought*. It is said that nothing exists. Indeed something does exist : Thought. But as Thought creates the world, the latter being a projection of Thought, is nevertheless only a dream. ...
>
> The Hossō doctrine . . . teaches that the whole universe, all that we perceive by the senses and by the spirit, or the Three Worlds, the world of desire (*Yoru*), the world of form (*Shiki*)

> and the world that has no form(*Ma-shiki*), exist only in thought and that nothing exists outside of thought. Life is but a dream. All is illusion. The Ego is certainly mere illusion but the universal illusion has a spiritual support. The Hossō doctrine is a spiritual axis which affirms itself in the vanishing of things—the subject creating its own object and its own concepts. You will learn that there are seven kinds of thoughts or faculties, which all proceed in last analysis from an eighth thought—pure and primitive—which is precisely that subject, that ideal support called the *Araya-shiki* (in Sanskrit, *Ālaya-vijñāna*). This projects like a shadow upon a transparent blind the illusion of reality . . . (the sense impressions and mental constructs). . . in short, the world. The Hossō doctrine is idealism.[12]

No wonder that beginning somewhat even before the Meiji, the Japanese found German Idealism and German Phenomenology the most compatible of thoughts with which to reinterpret their own heritage —at least to the outside.

An element of predestination slipped into the Hossō teachings, for the idea is there that some people have such bad *karma* that they will never become true Buddhas. The Hossō school was severely criticized for this negative predestination doctrine, which does seem rather un-Buddhistic, the historic Buhdha himself being pretty much a radical humanist. In particular the Tendai sect criticized the Hossō since they, taking the *Lotus Sūtra* as their chief canon, believed that everyone has the inherent Buddha nature—as most Ṣūfīs also believed and not a few Christians outside the influence of the Augustinian tradition, especially in Byzantium. Nevertheless, the teaching of universal compassion, embracing all beings from the lowest demons to the highest deities or angelic beings, figured very prominently, although it may have become too much mixed with the Confucian filial piety, allowing for more hierarchical deference in society than the Buddha seems to have envisaged.[13]

One might get the impression that the notions of *nirvāṇa* and the illusoriness of the world constituted really a religion of consolation, perhaps somewhat paralleling the cult of the Sorrows of the Blessed Virgin Mary. But from the historic and systematic point of view this is far from the truth. In the first place in all varieties of Buddhism the Four Noble Truths teach that there is a way to end suffering, and in the Eight-fold Noble Path we find that effort is needed, rather than taking refuge in emotionalistic other-worldliness. In the second place, given the right connotation of the term *vijñāna* in both Hinduism and Buddhism, the practice and teaching prevails that "by mere thought" the adept at yoga—and the other name for Vijñānavāda is Yogācāra—can perform what the masses would call miracles, or can exercise his *siddhis* secretly for the positive benefit of all mankind. Hence the *Dharmamegha-mahākaruṇā* teaching : "By mere thought" the Boddhisattva is supposed to benefit all suffering beings, but secretly.

> The uniqueness of Hossō thought lies in its attempt to explain the plight of man in terms of the analysis of the human mind, and by demonstrating how the condition of ignorance can be transformed into Enlightenment within the mind. In this respect, its approach slightly differed from the Sanron but both philosophies clearly emphasize that in essence, *saṃsāra* and *nirvāṇa* occur within the same locus. Hossō philosophy became dominant during the latter half of the Nara period and its study has continuously played a significant role in Japanese Buddhist history.[14]

In spite of its method of contemplation, which is supposed to have taken the whole of the universe into its conscious grasp, it evidently did not quite succeed in the world any more than the Christian Church succeeded in bringing the Kingdom of Heaven down to earth unsullied and unscathed.

The nominal founder of the Hua-yen (Japanese Kegon) sect in China was Fa-shun (557-640). Chih-yen is recognized as the second patriarch af this school, but the most well known was Fa-tsang of "Golden Lion" fame.

> Hua-yen teachings spread to Korea during the lifetime of the third Patriarch, Fa-tsang. At the time when he was still studying under Chih-yen, a monk from Silla, I-hsiang (625-702) was a fellow disciple. Upon returning to Korea (Silla), I-hsiang founded the Hua-yen sect in that country. ...Another

> student from Silla, Shen-hsiang (?-742) later came to China and received instruction from Fa-tsang. Upon completion, instead of returning to Korea, he went to Japan and arrived during the early Nara period.
>
> Prior to the arrival of Shen-hsiang, scriptures related to Hua-yen had already been brought to Japan by Vinaya master Tao-hsüan in 736 but had not been studied. When Shen-hsiang arrived, the influential Japanese priest Ryōben, or Rōben (689-773), sought to hear his lectures and in 740 persuaded Emperor Shōmu to invite Shen-hsiang to deliver an Imperial lecture on the *Kegongyō*.[15]

Three years after this the great Buddhist image at the Tōdaiji was cast. Moreover, it was this form of Buddhism which then became the official religion of Japan.

Kegon claimed to be the Ekayāna or Single Vehicle, reconciling and transcending the Mahāyāna and the Hīnayāna. It taught that all beings in the universe will gain salvation or enlightenment. In spite of its extremely monistic metaphysics, it developed a very elaborate symbolism, contributing to the development of aesthetics. The *Avataṃsaka Sūtra* (*Kegongyō*) is the chief if not the only sūtra really used in this tradition.

> According to the *Kegongyō* . . . everything, be it thought or matter, is derived from one source, which is 'unconditioned state' or absolute nature. Buddha and men are of one and the same essence. We call this common essence *Buta-Thātat*, and we compare it to the calm ocean whereas the world of sense may be compared to the passing waves of the rough sea. Below there is unity and identity. On the surface, the ephemeral phenomena of life.
>
> The thought of the Buddha reflects and repeats itself infinitely eternally, in all parts of the world, and even in the minutest specks of dust. . . . In the cosmic ordering of things, every atom reflects the whole and the whole reflects every atom.
>
> Each one of the grains of dust forming myriads of worlds contains myriads of Buddhas . . . which eternally inculcate wisdom to men. Each particular thought of Buddha is the

> whole truth and is at the same time the thought of all the Buddhas. . . .
>
> The moral and the human aspect of the Kegon concept... is to bring hope to the living and an easier possibility of salvation. ...We Buddhists always consider life as admitting of suffering. In the *Kegongyō,* however, we see the Buddha, by reason of his great love for all humanity, trying to deliver us from this suffering. ...Human beings are surrounded by a force of Sympathy of which the *Kegongyō* has striven to express the marvellous spiritual and moral mechanism.[16]

Kegon also recognizes the ten stages (*bhūmis*) towards Bodhisattvahood, these stages of the Bodhisattva's enlightenment being derived from the *Daśabhūmika Sūtra,* which is a commentary on a chapter in the *Avataṃsaka.* Again, this sort of philosophizing is not just sentimental indulgence in pious feelings but a systematic attempt at regularizing an aspect of potential human existence that too many modern secularists have ceased to pay any attention to (with the potential loss of their complete humanhood and to the detriment of spiritual power for making this planet a peaceful place to live). This sort of philosophizing, we would like to reiterate, was very common in the centuries between about 325 and 800 all across Eurasia and not merely among these Nara Buddhists.

Kegon is a panpsychic or pantheistic philosophy with structure and not just an amalgam of esoteric or mystical ways to achieve "sudden" enlightenment as was the case with the later Chinese versions of what became Rinzai Zen. (Just as the Hua-yen in China had rather close relations with Ch'an, especially in the case of Tsung-mi, so in Japan it continued to influence Zen.) One could develop a detailed apologetic for Kegon in terms of Whiteheadian process philosophy with its emphasis on the kaleidoscopic multi-dimensional interrelationalities such that the All (the Totality) is 'surrelationally' related to each part. We have hinted at such reinterpretations of the Buddhist *kṣaṇavāda* in general, but with Kegon it does seem to be particularly apt.

There is a need to study the much neglected societal implications of the development of the many varieties of Buddhism in Japan as a corrective to the still widespread impression that they were all completely other-worldly if not escapist pseudo-mysticisms without any concern for political reform or social justice (even if we do not list "democracy" at this juncture since that would be a gross anachronism). The original Shintō cult had laid the foundations for what could well have emerged into a full-fledged theocracy; even the *vinaya* rules for monks and nuns became modified to suit this trend, such that violation of the more serious rules became a state offense (as had been somewhat the case already in China).

In some respects there is an analogy between the *ko-i* period of adaptation and translation and the situation in Nara Japan; however, the Japanese did not at first make translations but simply learned to read the Chinese texts. It follows that their comprehension and awareness of the logic and systematics in the Indian sources was minimal. Everytime anyone went to China in search of the "true *dharma*" he returned with a different variety of the mixtures there, for by this time in China there were many varieties of Ch'an alone, not to mention the Pure Land and T'ien T'ai and all the mixtures with the many varieties of Tantra—all of this being largely due, one may conjecture, to the fact that each monastery was autonomous except for certain licensing for taxation purposes by the civil government. All of these Nara sects had done their best to unify the proliferation of Mahāyāna sūtra literature by eclectic schematization; such schematizations were not limited only to Chih-i, Tsung-mi and Kūkai. Nevertheless it remains true that they were evidently the only ones who introduced a sense of history into their reasons for eclectic preference.

In summary, the Nara period was an important stage of Japanese Buddhism. The imported seed was planted that eventually would ripen and mature into a unique native fruit during succeeding generations. The grandiose temples fell into stagnant corruption and the era ended upon the note of reform, but the Buddhist institutions had learned from their initial mistakes and the need for independence from the government was painfully obvious, although not easily achieved. The reforms had restored some vitality, at least in the Hossō sect, and basic preparations had already been made for the evolution of Heian Mikkyō (esoteric) Buddhism; in short the stage was set.[17]

3. Rābi'ah

All through the history of philosophy in any civilization until very recently (and there is reason enough for the complaint in the present century still), the profession of being a philosopher has been almost exclusively a male-dominated enterprise, quite universally. There were some exeptions in the late Hellenistic period; and in the early Greek Patristic period the teacher of St. Basil of Caesarea and his brother was a woman philosopher; and occasionally one finds passing mention of some famous Buddhist nuns. In the centuries we have covered thus far no doubt there were women of talent besides the Empress Irene and the Empress Wu who may well have made some contribution to philosophy but have remained in obscurity. Later in the Latin West there were some famous Christian nuns, most of whom were of the ecstatic and often erotic mystical type such that they are usually treated only in the history of religions and not in the history of philosophy.

The fact that Islam has traditionally been a religion with strong male domination makes it all the more remarkable that Rābi'ah (d. 801) as a woman could not only achieve considerable fame in the history of Ṣūfism but that she had disciples of both sexes. However, the male dominance in Islam has been grossly exaggerated. The daughter of the Prophet Muhammad had long since played a very prominent role in the shaping of Islamic tradition in almost every aspect; the veil, now taken as so controversial, was originally a device for protecting women when they appeared in public, not for suppressing them; women, almost uniquely in the ancient and medieval worlds, could inherit and own property in their own right; they had a large say in matters of divorce; and finally, they had almost equal rights to education, so that Islam produced not only many famous women singers but many important poetesses and dramatists.

'Aṭṭār gives the following answer to objections to his including a woman in his hagiographical work :

> My answer is that the Prophet himself said, " God does not regard your outward forms". The root of the matter is not form but intention, as the Prophet said, "Mankind will be raised up according to their intentions." Moreover, if it is proper to derive two-thirds of our religion from A'esha, surely it is permissible to take religious instruction from a handmaid of A'esha. When a woman becomes a 'man' in the path of God, she is a man and one cannot any more call her a woman.[1]

A'esha was the Prophet Muhammad's favorite wife who was much involved in the dispute after the Prophet's death over who should assume the leadership of the burgeoning Islamic community.

Like so many famous prophets and saints before and since, Rābi'ah spent some time in the desert doing *tapas* (ascetic discipline), but with the pure motive of pleasing God for His own sake rather than for the sake of securing any divine assistance. Her pattern of ascesis might be comparable to that of others who were contemporary with her, such as John of Damascus for example. However, we are rather struck by her colorful wittiness and the fact that, although she always stressed interior contemplation, she seldom taught by word alone but by dramatizing some significant action. In this respect she more resembles Āṇḍāḷ, the early Vaiṣṇava Ālvār woman saint in the Tamil *bhakti* tradition, and one might mention Teresa of Avila later on.

Rābi'ah points to a supra-rational way rather than a merely 'existentialist' irrational cultish indulgence in oddities as such. A bit of apparent anti-intellectualism does occasionally shine through, although the emphasis probably should be on the matter of pride rather than the 'intellectualism' as such. Most emphatic all through the anecdotes about her seems to be her utter detachment from worldly possessions and even from what we would like to think of as merely material conveniences.

> A leading scholar of Baṣra visited Rābi'ah on her sickbed. Sitting beside her pillow, he reviled the world.
>
> "You love the world very dearly," Rābi'ah commented. "If

> of it so much. It is always the purchaser who disparages the wares. If you were done with the world, you would not mention it because, as the proverb says, Whoever loves a thing mentions it frequently."[2]

Fakhry gives the following summary of Rābi'ah's teachings :

> She introduced for the first time in the history of Islamic mysticism the concept of divine love (*al ḥubb*). Earlier mystics had spoken of yearning (*shauq*) or friendship (*khullah*), but Rābi'ah went far beyond them by speaking in passionate terms of the believer's love of God. In this regard she ran counter to the whole religious tradition in Islam, in which man dare not approach God except in a spirit of devotion, piety, or awe. Asked once whether she loved God and hated the devil, she replied, "My love of God has barred me from occupying myself with the hate of satan." On another occasion the Prophet appeared to her in a dream and asked, "O Rābi'ah, do you love me?" Her answer was, "O Apostle of God, is there any one who does not love you ? However, my love of God Almighty has filled my heart so completely that there is no room left in it for the love or hate of anybody else."[3]

Concerning this love of God, Margaret Smith writes :

> To sum up Rābi'ah's teaching on Love, that is the love of the servant to his Lord : she teaches, first, that this love must shut out all others than the Beloved, that is, the saint must turn his back on the world and all its attractions, he must cut himself off from the creatures of God, lest they should distract him from the Creator, he must even rise above the claims of the senses and allow neither pleasure nor pain to disturb his contemplation of the Divine. To Rābi'ah God seemed to be a jealous God, Who will suffer none to share with Him that love which is due to Him alone.
>
> Then, secondly, she teaches that this love, directed to God to the exclusion of all else, must be disinterested, that it must look neither to hope of reward, nor to relief from punishment, but seek only to do the Will of God and to accomplish

that which is pleasing to Him, that He may be glorified. So will the love of the servant be transmuted into that higher-love, which is truly worthy of the Beloved. Only to the servant who loves thus, can God reveal Himself in His perfect Beauty and only by treading this Way of self-renouncing love, can the loving soul at last be united with its Beloved and in His Will find its peace.

By means then of Love and all the stages which have passed before, the Ṣūfī attains to the mystic gnosis and "the heart becomes filled with its grace". That knowledge comes directly as a gift from the Lord and from it the gnostic proceeds to contemplation of the unveiled Essence of God. With the enlightened eye of gnosis, the mystic gazes upon the Vision, and thus beholding, is rapt up into union with the Divine, and the final Goal of the Quest, the End of the Path, is attained, not by annihilation, but by absorption and transmutation, so that the soul transmuted into the Divine Image, and become itself part of God, in Him abides and lives forever.[4]

The following prayers by Rābi'ah have become universally classic as being very typical of Ṣūfism :

O God, whatsoever Thou hast apportioned to me of worldly things, do Thou give that to Thy enemies; and whatsoever Thou hast apportioned to me in the world to come, give that to Thy friends; for Thou sufficest me.

O God if I worship Thee for fear of Hell, burn me in Hell, and if I worship Thee in hope of Paradise, exclude me from Paradise; but if I worship Thee for Thy own sake, grudge me not Thy everlasting beauty.[5]

In spite of the brevity of the written record, Rābi'ah's influence was such that, for example, her known prayers such as the above probably influenced al-Ghazālī as much as anything he ever encountered. One may even wounder if it might have been the influence of Rābi'ah that led al-Ghazālī to renounce his favored position of philosophy professor, teaching logic and other routine matters, and go into complete retreat among Ṣūfī

Concerning fear of hell and hope of heaven, Rābi'ah is known mostly through her influence on al-Ghazālī who wrote a famous book on the subject which, as we might say in the modern European context, is downright Kierkegaardian in its 'leap of faith', total abandonment or surrender to God, having left behind anything like the Aristotelian Golden Mean or the Theravāda version of the Middle Way or the Confucian teaching of composure and observance through propriety. For Rābi'ah, instead of the Hellenic *meden āgan* (do nothing to excess), nothing was too much in her devotedness to God.

Another anecdote tells of Rābi'ah carrying fire and water through the streets saying that she was going to put out the flames of hell and burn paradise completely so that people would worship God for His own sake instead of out of fear of hell and hope of heaven. This was not untypical of general Ṣūfī teachings, for they almost always denied any literalistic interpretation of heaven and hell and instead accepted the symbols as indicating enjoyment of the presence of God (heaven) and alienation from God (hell).

Rābi'ah's cult of Holy Poverty, like that of St. Francis of Assisi, is not just peripheral to some systematic deontology but at the very core of her ethical and spiritual teaching and example. One might term her 'otherworldliness' differently in order to get past some emotional twitches attached to certain words. For Rābi'ah did not delight in poverty as such, and it was not proposed as an ethic for everyone. Rather, it was a matter of removing all physical obstacles and the purgation of all attachments, leaving only her ecstatic devotion to God. Spiritual poverty (*faqr*) means far more than mere detachment from earthly possessions; rather it should be taken in terms of dependence upon God and total surrender to His Will, whether in terms of consolation or dejection, grief or even ecstatic joy.

The denial of pantheism, which is shared by orthodox Jewish, Christian and Islamic theologians universally, is not peculiar even among the extreme Ṣūfīs, like al-Bisṭāmī for example, who were often accused of this sort of heresy. It seems that pantheism is often considered a "dangerous" word, even though simple observation without obligation to make apologetics for anyone's particular views reveals that historically varying degrees and types of pantheism were actually not uncommon. Margaret Smith claims that Rābi'ah did not share the pantheistic attitude that later on became very common among Ṣūfīs. For example, the pantheistic note which dominates the whole harmony of Jāmī's verses would never have met with Rābi'ah's approval. An oft-repeated anecdote illustrates the point :

> Once in spring, she was in the house, giving praise to God, and her servant-maid came to her and said, "O mistress, come out to behold the works (of God)," but Rābi'ah replied, "Come you inside that you may behold their Maker. Contemplation of the Maker has turned me aside from contemplating what he has made."[6]

Rābi'ah insists that God is to be found within the human heart even more than in the mosque or in all the wonders of nature. The inference that may easily be drawn then is that Rābi'ah remains theistic and not pantheistic, since if she had been consistently pantheistic she would have regarded all of nature as also divine and might have drawn the conclusion, as some extreme Gnostics had done, that asceticism was not necessary.

Some insist that Ṣūfism is not only compatible with the Qur'ān but that its origins are therein only and can be traced back to the Prophet himself. Others insist that what may be called Ṣūfism even in the Qur'ān itself, not to mention subsequent developments, shows influence from Neo-Platonism and/or Gnosticism. There is also a heated dispute about the relations between Ṣūfism and the Vedānta, not to mention the Vijñānavāda and erotic Tāntric Buddhism of Central Asia which was prevalent in areas both geographically and chronologically close to Rābi'ah's Baṣra. The controversy about the origins of Ṣūfism is not just a modern phenomenon since it can be traced back at least to the time of al-Qushayrī (1072) if not even to al-Mubārsk of Merv (d. 797) on the traditionalist or Qur'ānic line and/or to Dhu al-Nūn Miṣri (d. 861) on the esoteric score. Certainly Neo-Platonic influence on early Ṣūfism is there and can be traced rather easily through the Christian Neo-Platonists in Alexandria and Athens. But the important factor is not the 'historicism' involved but the actual experience of mystical union, which was much more common in the Middle Ages if not earlier throughout Eurasia than is often understood by modern psychologists and philosophers.

Within the emergence of Islamic civilization at Baṣra, not to mention Baghdad, there was a very fertile and seminal variety of traditions emerging. Surely Rābi'ah could not have been ignorant of these, even though we have little factual record of her attitude towards them. It is known that even Ḥasan al-Baṣrī, a sort of forerunner of the Mu'tazilite persuasion, was a close associate of hers. Likewise she probably was not ignorant of the scientific achievements of her age, but she was so absorbed in her interior world that either she condemned them or she did not think them so important.

The channels of communication were sufficiently open during Rābi'ah's lifetime for possible influences from India among the ecstatic mystics, just as we know for certain that there was influence in mathematics, astronomy/astrology and medicine if not also in metallurgy and the other applied sciences. This is not to claim that there actually was influence, and certainly speculations about Ṣūfism and Vedānta—especially Advaita, except perhaps for Gauḍapāda—during Rābi'ah's lifetime should definitely be carefully qualified since at the date of her death Śaṅkara was only thirteen years old! Although there could have been influence from Mahāyāna Buddhism, and although Vijñānavāda was certainly flourishing in Kaśmir and Central Asia right down to and after the Muslim conquest, here mysticism was of an entirely different type. As in the case of al-Ḥallāj, there was probably quite a bit of mutual exchange between Ṣūfīs and Hindu *sādhus* and yogīs later on; but Rābi'ah's roots are in other soils.

Unfortunately we do not know about the nuns in Byzantium even during Rābi'ah's lifetime who might have been very much like her—or even if not in Constantinople proper, no doubt in the convents among the Coptic Christians in Egypt and Ethiopia or even in the deserts near Jerusalem and/or Damascus. As for possible comparisons with some Ch'an nuns, influences here are as improbable as influences from Latin Europe, though again we must await further research. Also, Rābi'ah's mysticism

Bodhisattvas Amitābha, Avalokiteśvara or Maitreya, which were much more devotional than Ch'an ever dared to be.

The early Ṣūfīs certainly manifest in several moods the "monism in many moods" that seems to characterize the ninth century almost completely. Admittedly Rābi'ah was not much inclined towards systematic philosophy as such, even though she had an uncanny way of unnerving those who were proud of "Knowing all the answers" concerning reason and faith. In the Islamic perspective and certainly in the larger Eurasian perspective Rābi'ah belongs more to the history of religions than to the history of philosophy, but with this very strong proviso : she probably influenced more philosophers than many of those who claimed to be philosophers. She is indeed near the source out of which Ṣūfism grew and continues to flourish even today.

4. Liu Tsung-yüan

There were a goodly number of reform parties and not only the two which Han Yü and Liu Tsung-yüan (773-819) belonged respectively at the beginning of another "time of troubles" toward the end of the T'ang Dynasty. We may generalize in the light of similar situations all through world history, including our own time, that in times when radical reform is really needed, the major conflicts are not between the "old order" and the reformers but between the rival reform parties. After acknowledging that Liu's travellogues, metaphorical satires, and other works have figured very highly in the history of Chinese literature, Hou Wai-lu states that the "materialist and atheist" aspects of his thinking have been left in obscurity.[1] Though others had rejected the old concept of the Mandate of Heaven, both Liu Tsung-yüan and Liu Yü-hsi (772-842) brought this rejection to its fullest expression. Hou writes :

In his writings Liu Tsung-Yüan criticized Han Yü for his

accordance with laws. In his essay entitled "Heaven Answers" he replied to questions concerning the universe and history posed by the famous ancient poet Chu Yüan in his prose poem "Heaven Asks". From a materialist standpoint he pointed out that the universe is made of original matter, it is presided over by no monstrous creature of any kind and there is nothing mysterious about its beginning. Liu Tsung-yüan quoted the achievements in natural science in his time. He said that natural laws are knowable and denounced all the false theories of theology and idealism. With great insight he also saw that the interaction between positive and negative forces is the sole cause of motion in nature, which was an elementary form of dialectics.[2]

In 805 there was a dynastic transfer of power with the usuat factions and intrigues and counter-intrigues with the result that the emperor was forced to abdicate; the opposing reactionary party prevailed and put its emperor on the throne so that the Liu party was not only out of favor but ignominiously demoted and its attempted reforms completely abandoned. Needless to say, the conservative record-keepers had little praise for these reformers, but even Wang An-shih and many centuries later Fu-chih wrote of them with approval. Liu took advantage of his political banishment to study and write. The basic theme of his work, as of so many works of the period, was the relation between Heaven (T'ien) and man (usually stated in terms of the classic triad Heaven, Earth, and Man). His opponent here as in other matters was Han Yü, who himself had some rather interesting naturalistic tendencies. According to Han Yü, the Will of Heaven is so high and exalted that it is virtually sacrilegious to question it; what may superficially appear to be only natural phenomena actually transpire according to the Will of Heaven operating through the *yin/yang* principle. Liu Tsung-yüan rejected this aspect of Han Yü's explanation. Liu may or may not be technically "materialistic" in his view, but certainly he is naturalistic, rejecting any supernatural aspect of "Heaven" and tending to recognize everything "as it is" without any need of fancy theorizing or appeal to a supernatural theologized *T'ien*. Thus Liu records his opinion against Han Yü: "That which is successful is successful through itself; that which suffers calamity suffers calamity through itself. To hope for that which rewards and punishes is a great error. And to blame and decry those who long for its sympathy and benevolence is an even greater error !"[3]

Of course Liu was limited by the science of his time (as no doubt we are limited by ours); but at least he did have a notion that from the original Primal Matter—not anything like the *ex nihilo* controversy that plays such a pivotal role in Judeo-Christian-Islamic scholasticism—Heaven emerged out of the *yang* and Earth out of the *yin*. All the living creatures on Earth came through the interaction between these, with man of course as the ultimate result of this interaction. Through knowledge man "can know, utilize and conquer nature and can also create in social life things which did not exist originally in nature ; and it was a general system which he could comprehend."[4] Hou Wai-lu continues :

> In the work *Heavenly Dialogues* Liu Tsung-yüan, with comparative exactitude, related, from the point of view of naturalism, a broad system of materialist monism of "primal matter" and strove mightily to expose the errors of the idealist viewpoint.
>
> Liu Tsung-yüan's monistic philosophical thought of the materialism of "primal matter" obviously entailed a certain factor of naive dialectics, but he was far from thoroughly developing evidence for it. This also confirms he was limited by the level of natural science of his time . . . . Because of this, when he ran into relatively difficult problems, he could not but dredge up knowledge of the character of ancient "theories" to make forced explanations, even sometimes seeking help from accidentalism and he got on the wrong road.[5]

For Liu, Heaven and Earth are not beings created by gods or a God but are a function of the "unbounded, ever-extending illimitable nature of the universe." In the global perspective there is no great need historically of making much fuss over this, because the old classical Greek view was still well known, and there were those scholastics who had very similar conceptions, only conforming to the orthodox theology enough to keep out of trouble; and moreover, if anything the Hindu and Jaina theories in Liu's time put even more stress on the vastness and agelessness of *Prakṛti*. Classical Confucianists just did not bother very much if at all with such questions since they were such ethical humanists that they put all their attention on social reality in the here and now, although always appealing to antiquity as the ideal model. Hence Liu must have got this idea through the Buddhists primarily, although Taoist naturalism also influenced him.

Liu advances the idea (which did not reach Western Europe until many centuries later) that matter and nature, both individually and as a whole, are self-moving and not made to move from the outside, externally. Now no doubt Liu is not outright advancing a theory of physics but laying a realistic foundation for his rationalist ethics. Nevertheless he does advance a theory of strictly naturalistic, or, as Hou claims, materialistic, theory of causation. Among his contemporaries this would put him in sharp contrast with such as Scotus Erigena, who thought of God as the only Uncaused Cause, and hence the only Unmoved Mover; and with Śaṅkara, who virtually if not actually denies causation altogether to *nirguṇa*-Brahman, relegating that at best to *saguṇa*-Brahman, if not to *Prakṛti* as an evolute of *saguṇa*-Brahman. Thus it might at first appear that Liu is a major exception to our theme of "monism in many moods" as the dominating trend in the ninth century. But materialist monism is still a monism, for monism as such does not necessarily have to be *māyāvādistic*. Hou writes :

> The problem resides in this : Is the essential substance of movement nature itself, or does it turn out to be an exterior force beyond nature ? If one approves the latter, in actuality one tends to idealism. Opposite to this, Liu Tsung-yüan inherited and developed the tradition of Wang Ch'ung and affirmed the uninterrupted movement of the two inexhaustible material forces *yin* and *yang* in the universe, which of necessity manifested all sorts of configuration (like "movement" and "rest", "piling up" and "circulating", etc.) ; they do not obtain from any outside force, but are "self-movement and self-rest, self-piling up and self-circulating,

> self-struggle and self-exertion, self-collapse and self-deficiency."[6]

Hou asserts that Liu did make definite advances over Wang Ch'ung in that he was not satisfied with interpreting phenomena in nature as simply the operations of *yin* and *yang* but attempted a naturalistic or even materialistic explanation of those forces in his discussion of the forms, shapes, or patterns of the transformations of matter.

> Of course, these topics still dealt with forms and had not progressed to an explanation of the inner lawfulness of the various changes among shapes of the narural world and to an evaluation of them from the viewpoint of materialistic historicism. This was the limit of understanding that Liu Tsung-yüan's age could attain. However, he made a large dent in a numbed and deadened natural world, absorbed the accomplishments in natural science of his time, and climbed even somewhat higher than the scientists.[7]

In the commentary on Liu's theory by Liu Yü-hsi essentially the "materialist monism" (as Hou calls it) is further reduced so that the traditional term "Heaven" is interpreted as the "objective existence of nature and ... self-motivating."

In a very advanced way by comparison with the other theoreticians of his era all across Eurasia, Liu was a demythologizer. He believed in the objective existence of time, quite in opposition to the idealist Buddhist view and consonant with the Vaiśeṣika or Jaina view, and that, like space, it was limitless. Of course Liu still had some relatively crude notions about the sun, moon and the planets; but then few in Eurasia of that era had a more sophisticated view. At least he had the view that the Earth is floating in the heavens, even though he still had somewhat of a geocentric view of it; but he had the notion that they were real physical entities and not gods or supernatural beings and as such can be investigated rather than worshipped or feared. In short, he had one of the essential aspects of a truly scientific attitude, namely radical questioning of traditional views.

Hou Wai-lu observes that, almost uniquely among these early Neo-Confucians, Liu Tsung-yüan does not bother much about refutation of Buddhism. This is somewhat of a puzzle since as a materialist or even a naturalist of a realistic sort it might be expected that the idealism of Chinese Mahāyāna, much less the superstitious practices that had crept into popular Buddhist religion, would be his major point of attack. Actually he attacks rather Han Yü for accusing him of being a "fellow-traveller" with the Buddhists, and objects to Han Yü's opposition to Buddhism as being too superficial.

> What T'ui-chih (Han Yü) disparages are its objective manifestations; he talks of making the head bald and the drab black silk robes (of the Buddhists), its absence of marital and filial (relationships), and the fact that it does not encourage sericulture among the peasants and is not active on man's behalf. However, I also do not like these things. ...Buddha's truth has something which should not be condemned, for it often corresponds to the *Changes* (I) and the *Analects* (Lun-yü), which love truth; the nature and circumstances of its fulfilment are not doctrines unlike those of Confucius.[8]

A major aspect of Liu's "materialism" was simply a sharp critical faculty, exposing untruth wherever he found it, and that with a remarkable open-mindedness. His taunting of Han Yü's even stereotyped criticism of Buddhism was evidently more a matter of rebuke of Han Yü for his lack of thoroughness in his refutation than an approval of Buddhism as such. Again we should remember that the monasteries had grown unimaginably wealthy such that they used slaves to do the manual work which the monks were supposed to do themselves. Thus the condemnation of Buddhism in the late T'ang was really a purge which tended to restore the *dharma* and the *saṅgha* to its true intent, unmixed in political intrigue, and again paying attention to the original humanistic teachings of the historic Śākyamuni Buddha instead of speculating and arguing endlessly about the indefinability of *Śūnyatā* and *Tathatā*.

Liu's philosophy of history compares very favorably with any of his contemporaries' views. According to Hou, the following citation from Liu on the origin of civilization shows a strong influence from Han Fei-tzu, at least in respect to the 'natural' origin of the state as opposed to the more orthodox Confucian view that the state was divinely ordained so that the emperor had some divine charisma under the traditional Mandate of Heaven.

> Now in man's beginning everything was new; forests covered everything ; snow, frost, wind and rain, thunder, and hail came suddenly from without, and so he learned to build dens for himself and clear out the caves, pull up vegetation and obtain leather; hunger, thirst, and the (animal) desires of male and female drove him from within, and so he learned to bite into birds and beasts, to suck and chew the fruit of the valley, to cohabit, and to have social intercourse; the latter led to contention, the strange or unusual aroused him, those whose strength was great pounced upon others, those whose teeth were sharp bit (others), those whose claws were hard ripped at (others); conglomerates of people formed; those with good soldiers killed their enemies; disorder spread and there was slaughter in the plain. Afterwards, those with greater strength emerged to rule ; always the words of command arose in times of duress, and so the law of the prince, the minister and the (lesser) ranks was established. ...From this it appears that the beginning was not without great disorder, but afterwards there was seldom the possibility of disorder.[9]

There is a note of stark realism if not of outright materialism in this, almost as much so as that of Machiavelli or Hobbes in Europe many centuries later. Struggle with nature is the basic drive. Disorder came first, and the state became a practical necessity in order to establish order. This is diametrically opposed to the views of Lao Tzu and Chuang Tzu, not to mention the orthodox Confucian doctrine as interpreted by Mencius.

In Liu's interpretation of the development of "feudalism" what we find is a strong reliance on Hsün Tzu's realist interpretation of "circumstances" or "necessity" over against Mencius' more idealistic interpretation. Liu here tends to demystify the term *Te*, which in the *Tao Te Ching* does have some metaphysical and even mystical connotations as that which brings Tao out of undifferentiated primordiality so that the unknown can become known. But here it is interpreted as simply finite human political and economic power exercised by the feudal lords over their serfs as well as in contention with each other. Liu writes : "From the Son of Heaven to the country géntlemen, their power resides in man; with the inevitability of death (upon them) they search out their heirs and make bequests to them; therefore, feudalism is not the will of the Sage, but comes from circumstances "[10] In Liu's review of the Chin Dynasty this sort of feudalism was abolished, he says, not through any "mandate of Heaven" but simply due to *circumstances.*

According to Hou, Liu Tsung-yüan's literary expressions are even more outspokenly anti-orthodox. He reports how vehemently Liu "hated the powerful nobility who acted evilly and did wrong. He refined model instances from the raw material of real life or secret parables of a very general nature, which graphically disclosed the deep contradictions of the time." In a very universal literary idiom he uses animals in parables to make his point, as in the following.

> The ox was described in this way : "With the coming of the noble light of day, he daily plows a hundred *mou*; back and forth he cultivates straight rows for the planting and growing of millet; he plows and cultivates by himself, goes to the granary for his accounting, making contributions to the officials' granaries; he never accommodates his own palate; rich or poor, satisfied or hungry, without any benefit to himself, he sinks in the mud, kicking up lumps of earth; he is always in the countryside. People have no shame and they seek their own advantage in the world; his skin and horns are used, neither the buttocks nor the shoulder is saved; more than likely he will be bound up, and more than likely made to serve as a sacrifice." This was regarded as a symbol of the broad masses of exploited working people. Thus, they were diligent and long-suffering, but in the end had such a sad finish.[11]

Hou gives us this conclusion :

> In summary, Liu Tsung-yüan was a great thinker, literary artist, and politician. The theoretical criticism which he carried

in philosophy, the chastisement of the real world in his political and literary works, and his orientation toward a good and beautiful life, were significant as an extension of the political struggle he engaged in : after the political reform movement which he participated in was defeated, this was simply the only form of struggle that he could adopt.

In history there is no lack of phenomena of this kind : in a progressive social movement, certain of the movement's thinkers or leaders have the ability to go even further than this movement itself, and see even further ahead. When we evaluate the social and political thought of Liu Tsung-yüan, we cannot forget this point because this outstanding thinker ought properly to be restored to the ranks of this kind of historical figure.[12]

In world history as well as in the history of social thought in China, Liu-Tsung-yüan needs to be better known as ranking among the "creative minority" (as Toynbee calls them) who do real thinking even when that does not lead them to success, fame, or fortune in this controversial world.

5. Śaṅkara

Just as one cannot philosophize without Kant in the modern European context (whether for or against him), so in Indian philosophy as a whole one cannot philosophize without Śaṅkara (788-820). His works have become the basis of a nearly inexhaustible corpus of commentaries and reinterpretations. Virtually every philosopher after him in India wrote either to clarify the many ambiguities left in his work, or in opposition to his Advaitic interpretation of *māyā*, his way of treating the *nirguṇa*-Brahman as the only possible way of dealing with *saguṇa*-Brahman, and his insistence on the ultimacy of indefinability (*anirvacanīya*), as well as in opposition to what is often a strained if not distorted interpretation of the *Gītā*.

Śaṅkara's position historically is so important that it has become the fashion to include Gauḍapāda and others as "pre-

Śaṅkara Vedānta" and all Advaitins after Śaṅkara, at least from Vācaspati Miśra to Śrīharṣa if not down to Madhusūdana Sarasvatī, as "post-Śaṅkara Vedānta". This is the source of the misconception that the term Vedānta means purely and simply Advaita Vedānta. That notion, popular though it is in many circles, has no historical or factual foundation. The *Brahma Sūtras* of Bādarāyaṇa and all the non-Advaitin commentaries on those *Sūtras* are also Vedānta or "the end of the Vedas."

Śaṅkara came from the region of present-day Travancore, although he was also very active in what is now the region of Madras. By no means are all the legends about him true historically ; but he did travel throughout India, and as a debater his brilliance was even more luminously manifested than in his various writings. Indeed in some places even today, as in Maithili in Bihar, there are folklore legends about him. His charisma, in short, even exceeded his brilliance of intellect.

Although Śaṅkara's formal work dealt with the *Upaniṣads* and the *Brahma Sūtras*, he lived in the midst of a very rich literary milieu, as is reflected in his poetry. The *Purāṇas* were being cultivated by the masses as were the Sanskrit classics among the higher classes. During the ninth century North and South India were culturally united though distinct political units. Buddhism, although dominated by the Tāntric cult, was still flourishing in what is now Bihar and in Kaśmir. Kaśmiri Śaivism was emerging. North India was being threatened and invaded by Muslims. South India was the center of an expanding empire in Southeast Asia with which there was extensive trade even with China and to some extent with Byzantium. Relations with Śri Lanka and Burma where Theravāda Buddhism prevailed were not always peaceful. Within South India a rivalry between the Sinhalese and the Tamils often led to conflict, with intermittent periods of accommodation and assimilation. There were pockets of Buddhists, both Mahāyāna and Theravāda, and Jainism thrived.

We do not yet have adequate information about the condition of scientific developments in ninth century India ; but all indications show that India was well ahead of Byzantium and China, and Muslims in present-day Persia were still borrowing from India. Political philosophy had also made considerable advances, although Śaṅkara seems to have remained aloof from both of these developments.

Śaṅkara's success in converting Buddhists by sheer wit in debate has been exaggerated. Buddhism survived for some time after him in Nālandā, Vikramaśilā and Kaśmir as well as in South India. We have no record of any encounter with the Muslims, but such a meeting might not have been a very happy one in the ninth century. The Islam of al-Kindī or Bāyazīd Bisṭāmī would have been more agreeable to Śaṅkara. On the question of whether Śaṅkara was a "crypto-Buddhist", Bhattacharjee writes :

> The Buddhist theory of extreme idealism and the doctrine that all is ultimately a void (*śūnya*) influenced the philosophy of the great Vedāntist, Śaṅkara, to such an extent that later critics of Śaṅkara did not hesitate to dub him as a 'Buddhist in disguise', even though he had criticised the Buddhists in his commentary on the Vedānta-sūtras.[1]

And C.D. Sharma writes :

> He too is considerably influenced by Buddhism. He preserves the best that was in Mahāyāna in his own philosophy. He uses many words, especially in his Upaniṣad-Bhāṣyas, which were commonly used in Mahāyāna literature. But outwardly he is an enemy of Buddhism. Gauḍapāda had love and respect for Mahāyāna. Shaṅkara has nothing but strong and even bitter words for it. It is very important and interesting too to note that Shaṅkara does not at all criticize the two most important schools of Mahāyāna, the Shūnyavāda and the Vijñānavāda. What he criticizes under the name of Vijñānavāda is in fact Svatantra-Vijñānavāda; and he summarily dismisses Shūnyavāda as a self-condemned nihilism which is below criticism.[2]

There are many who insist that the sharp difference between the Buddhist *kṣaṇavāda* and the Brahmanic triad *advaitam-anantam-ānandam* as a reaffirmation of permanence over change, of being over becoming, renders Śaṅkara's Advaita *totally* different from the various forms of Buddhism except in some points of method.

Śaṅkara was not completely unique in the field of philosophy in his era. Not only had there been commentaries on the *Brahma Sūtras* but the other *Sūtras* and the schools that cultivated them were still very much alive and flourishing.

> The intellectual war that was waged found expression not so much in new writings as in exegeses on old ones. It was now the period of *bhāshyas* or expositions of the Sūtras. Less important commentaries and expository summaries were also written and bore titles of *vrittis*, *kārikās*, etc., besides the general name of *ṭīkā*.[3]

Śaṅkara's work is done in the form of commentaries on the *Upaniṣads* and on the *Vedānta Sūtras*. After an exposition of the chief theses of his own system, he follows with a critique of the other philosophical systems available to him. These critiques in turn are punctuated by virtually interminable citations and exegeses of the Upaniṣadic texts and the *Bhagavad Gītā*, all of which are handled in such a way as to reconcile them with his systematics.

As with most of the classical philosophies of India, but perhaps even more than any of them, Śaṅkara's system is so dependent on his technical terminology that it is not easy to translate either his manner or method. His method is at best exhaustively dialectical and astutely scholastic. The technicalities of his sources also prove to be a barrier to many students. Śaṅkara belonged to an age that had time to philosophize, and attempts to streamline even the basics of what he has to offer risk betraying the very spirit of exhaustive thoroughness in detail wherein his genius is most manifest. The *Brahma Sūtras* also pose problems for textual interpretation, and the various commentators often take liberties in the division of the *Sūtras*. For instance, what is intended to be the *pūrvapakṣa* and the *siddhānta* differs sometimes radically. When they disagree on such points, most of the commentators agree with Rāmānuja against Śaṅkara because Śaṅkara does frequently bend the text to suit his logic of pure identity, denying consistently the validity of any difference.

Śaṅkara's philosophy claims, like Mādhyamika, to have no position of its own but rather to afford a perspective from which all other views can be refuted at the level of dialectics. It is at the *pāramārthika* or *nivṛtti* level that it can claim to absorb all other apparently contradictory viewpoints as operative only at the *vyāvahārika* or *samvṛtti* level. In short, it claims to be the all-inclusive and all-absorbing system of no system. The typical attitude is, "We have no disagreements with anyone. All are welcome under our shelter regardless of the welter of confusions that may have engrossed them." Advaitins deny or try to circumvent the logic of contradiction altogether. A key term in this context is sublation, whose semantic burden is that if one appears to be encountering a contradiction, one must reduce it to the nexus of larger unity or non-duality within which the points may seem to be contradictory but ultimately are not.

It is typical of Advaitins to relegate all who do not agree with them to the 'empirical' level (the *prātibhāsika* or at best the *vyāvahārika*), claiming that they alone have the *pāramārthika* level as their all-engulfing range of operation. If anyone else has reached that level of *sādhana*, then he has perforce become an Advaitin! And the *pāramārthika* level is carefully guarded with the sometimes almost magical word *anirvacanīya* or "indescribable", which is an (exaggerated) invocation of the *via negativa*, the *neti neti* of the *Upaniṣads*.

Although in the technical sense Śaṅkara condemns *tarka* as sophistical juggling of arguments in order to gain a point, in actual practice he resorts to the same device in order to undermine his opponents' positions (just as Kant claimed that he had used reason only in order to show the limits of reason and thereby to make room for faith). In regard to the inadequacy of *tarka* as such, Devaraja writes :

> Śaṅkara's condemnation of reasoning is based on commonsense considerations. 'In the case of right knowledge,' he says, 'a conflict of opinions is impossible. But it is well known that cognitions based on reasoning contradict one another. It is notorious that, what one logician establishes to be right knowledge, is demolished by another who, in his turn, is ousted by a third.... Nor can all the logicians, past, present and future, be gathered together at one time and in one place and their agreed opinion regarding the uniform object (i.e., the

> real) ascertained so as to yield right knowledge.' Śaṅkara feels . . . that there is some sort of arbitrariness about the so-called purely logical knowledge. The battle of wits or the warfare of words seems to have no connection whatever with the realities of experience. *Tarka*, therefore, being based on mere speculation, is *apratiṣṭhita* or unfounded. For speculation (*utprekṣā*) is absolutely unfettered.[4]

But there are other places where Śaṅkara not only admits but asserts the utility of reasoning "in ascertaining the correct sense of scripture" :

> Criticising the Sāṅkhyas . . . he remarks : 'A (metaphysical) scheme cannot be accepted simply because it is desirable. There must be adequate reasons for commending a particular scheme.' In the commentary on *Gauḍapādīya Kārikā* attributed to Śaṅkara it is promised that the truth of non-dualism could be established through reasoning unaided by the Scripture. In the *Kaṭha-Bhāṣya* Śaṅkara asserts that 'reason alone is our authority in matters relating to the essential nature of the real and the unreal'.[5]

This apparent inconsistency has plagued Śaṅkara's later Hindu critics and European Indologists alike, giving cause for some to ponder the idea that Śaṅkara may be an agnostic or even an outright skeptic.

A more adequate explanation lies in the realization that *tarka* is not a *pramāṇa*, although it might easily be confused with *anumāna* (inference) or *arthāpatti* (presumption). Dialectically, however, Śaṅkara insists that the latter are dependent on *pratyakṣa*, sense perception or common sense experience. Devaraja summarizes :

> *Tarka* in its conventional sense of a hypothetical argument usually operated without reference to experience. It was natural, therefore, that it should sometimes lead to conclusions which defied empirical verification and which were wholly speculative in character. Śaṅkara, who was anxious to assert nothing which could not be supported either by experience or by Scripture, was very sceptical with regard to the utility of

this sort of reasoning. But he was not a disbeliever in the efficacy of *anumāna* or inference, for this latter depended for its working on experience itself.[6]

Apte gives the following epitome of the irreducible basics of Advaita—if indeed it can be reduced any further than Śaṅkara's own method of dialectical reduction, for it is a reductionist philosophy *par excellence* :

> There is only one Ultimate Reality viz. Parabrahma (Nirguṇa Brahma) which is the only one without a second. It is also described as the Sat or the Paramātmā, which is pure Being, pure Consciousness, and pure Bliss (Sachchidānanda). Sat, Chit, and Ānanda, however, are not the attributes of Parabrahma but its very constitutive essence. It is eternal and Aja, i.e., it has not originated as an effect from a cause. It is an incorporeal Being and is indivisible, spaceless, sexless, passionless, changeless and perfect. It is all-pervading (Vibhu) and is the substratum of everything, and while it is immanent in everything, yet it transcends all things. The attributes of goodness, justness, all-powerfulness, being the internal regulator (Antaryamī), and being one whose desires are just and are already fulfilled, etc., are applicable to what on a lower plane of thought is understood to be the Lower Brahma (Saguṇa-Brahma) for the purpose of contemplation, devotion, prayer and propitiation. It is through its own power of Māyā that Brahma in its aspect as the Īshvara has projected all the phenomenal world in which human beings and others exist, move and have their beings. ...The phenomenal world according to rigorous Advaitins is not real in the extreme real sense, yet they concede that prior to the actual realization of Brahma, one has to understand the phenomenal world practically as real as one finds it during one's condition of being under the binding and blinding influence of Nescience, i.e., Avidyā or Māyā. The Advaitins hold that the moment a man realizes Brahma, i.e., realizes his own identity with it, he knows that the phenomenal world, which he so far fondly, but all the same erroneously, believed to be real, is not so in fact and is but merely an illusion (Vivarta).[7]

From the Pūrva-Mīmāṁsā Śaṅkara inherited the sense of the objectivity of the phenomenal world, and this could not be safeguarded unless *Māyā* is itself cosmic, as if individual consciousnesses bathe in it without creating it themselves. Even so, he could not conceive of any way of explicating this concept of *māyā* without relating it to an *Īśvara*, a sort of Supreme Consciousness of the phenomenal world which, fully conscient and directing the order of everything, projects the illusory world of names-and-forms (*nāmarūpa*) Without resorting to the dialectic procedures of Nāgārjuna, Śaṅkara rejects the world of "difference", multiplicity and diversity in order to attribute being only to a Single Brahman—a Being which has nothing to do with our experience of differentiated being. Pure Being without any trace of multiplicity or of relation, Śaṅkara's *nirguṇa*-ness, which is wholly and absolutely undifferentiated, is the only 'Whatever-it-is' (for it cannot be 'known' except negatively) that is the 'isness' of Everything. Included of course is *Īśvara* as *saguṇa*-Brahman and all that is (falsely) distinguishable from non-differentiation.

With Śaṅkara it is difficult to find anything quite corresponding to the *ex nihilo* doctrine. Although in some of the earlier schools there is occasionally something resembling it, by the time of Bādarāyaṇa it had been almost completely discredited. Instead, arguments concerning the cosmological question, at least as far as causation is concerned, range around the difficulty of the infinite regress and the necessity of finding an ultimate mode of self-causation. But even more important is the sense in which all causation turns on itself in such a way that, in the last analysis, it is almost impossible to distinguish with certitude the difference between cause and effect. For example, the question is often posed, What happens to the cause ? Is it exhausted in the effect; does it disappear into the effect; is it absorbed into the effect; or is it changed/transformed into the effect; and given any of these, what is the cause of that ?

In the end all of the arguments virtually cancel each other out and one is left with something rather the reverse of the *ex nihilo* doctrine. Causation is demonstrated to be a pseudo construction as a rationale for the consideration of things in their (falsely assumed) individuation. After the false film of error is removed it is seen that the "nihilo" is superimposition on the necessary ground of unchanging Being (*sat*). This Being is identical with the Self (*ātman*), which is in turn identical with absolute consciousness and bliss which is Brahman, Reality-as-such. The problem for Śaṅkara then becomes how, within this complete and undivided and indivisible and partless Self-identity, there *appears* to be sequences of events in such patterns of conformity to law that one may say with practical certainty that, for example, unrefrigerated milk will turn to curd.

For Śaṅkara there is a perspective within which, from which, and/or not apart from which, cause, causer and caused are inseparably One. The Mādhyamika system had tried to go further than this and deny the ground of this Unity also, leaving the 'nothing' at the foundation, arguing in effect that though you try to argue in terms of superstructure and superimposition, there is still no reason to suppose that the mental constructions themselves should have 'more' than 'nothing' behind them. But for Śaṅkara this last step is going too far, or, more aptly, not far enough. For him there is a Consciousness which is not a 'nothing' and which is aware of both the 'nothing' and that which appears as the infinite maze surrounding it. And we must speak in a meta-language about it for the simple reason that we *are* that ! The 'transformation' of causation, therefore, is no more than a pseudo-logical function within that Consciousness, which is all-pervasive.

It is much more important for Śaṅkara to disassociate Brahman from all relation to the world of phenomena than to explicate what the world itself really is in itself. To the example of Nāgārjuna, thus, he voids *māyā* of all true reality, and he repeats emphatically and often in many contexts that Brahman in itself has no power by which it might manifest itself in the world of phenomena. Brahman is absent from phenomena in so far as they are not sustained in appearance except by Ignorance, which is itself inexplicable. Nevertheless, if there are appearances more than nothing, it is because Brahman *is*; and one can say that appearances reveal it by transparence at least as much as they conceal it. This concept of Brahman differs, for example, from Nāgārjuna's *Śūnyatā*, of which one cannot say that it is or that it is not. It is in this sense that Brahman is the material cause of the world (or rather, the cause of Ignorance) just as much as it is the Object of all knowledge, which is however illusory. In itself Brahman could not become the object of knowledge since it is beyond the subject-object dichotomy.

One can thus say of *māyā* that it neither is nor is not, since it is altogether different from the one or the other. The fact that *māyā* is not a pure and simple non-being, and yet that it is not Brahman, the Unique Being, obliges Śaṅkara to attempt to define its relation to Brahman, a relation which cannot be in itself any other than a mere appearance since Brahman cannot be said to sustain any relation with anything whatsoever of any sort whatsoever. Relationality involves duality, which Śaṅkara consistently denies outright. Thus the phenomenal world even in its entirety is conceived as a pseudo-manifestation of Brahman as *vivarta*. This notion intervenes in the polemic of Śaṅkara against the Sāṃkhya: Brahman is, like *Prakṛti* of the Sāṃkhya, the material cause of phenomena, but there can be no question of any real causation in the sense of a real transformation of Brahman.

One of the most basic points in Śaṅkara's and in all Advaitic if not all Vedāntic philosophy is the *ātman*-Brahman equation. This has been one of the major difficulties with most Eurameri-can critics who are mortally afraid of pantheism in spite of virtually the same trends in Neo-Platonism (as demonstrated rather vividly in Staal's *Neo-Platonism and Advaita*). The *ātman* or Self is asserted by some to be objective. Śaṅkara, however, does not hold to this *asmatpratyaya* concept of *ātman* but to the idea that *ātman* is the self-luminosity of the pure *cit* or Consciousness-as-identical-with-Being.

One of the chief difficulties encountered by neophytes is the confusion between ego (*ahaṅkāra*) and self (*ātman*). In Śaṅkara's commentary on the *Bṛhadāraṇyaka Upaniṣad* the *pūrvapakṣin* objects that even though it be argued that the *ātman* also is known only through revelation, nevertheless there must be an ego, an 'I', with all its faculties which must be the knower.

> Not so, replies Śaṅkara; the contention is refuted by the fact that the *Ātman* is the witness of the notion of the "I". 'Only the ignorant, who mistake the senses, *manas* and *buddhi* for

> *Ātman*, believe the *Brahman* to be known. ... What is really known is the limiting *buddhi* which produces the illusion of the *Brahman's* having been known.'[8]

Padmapāda insists that the *manas* and *buddhi* are such that one may be aware that "that was *my* thought, *my* interpretation, as a matter of fact *I* think differently now, etc.", so that the inference is very obvious that there must be that observer-consciousness that is irreducible or transcendent even as these other levels of intellection and thinking are not. That, however, is the *cit*, which is usually associated with the *sākṣī*, observer-consciousness. Here again we are in the realm of the *svalakṣaṇa*, self-validating autologous level which needs no justification since therein all other justifications have their irreducible orientation. In short, *cit* has no *pramāṇas* because it could not have any, being neither subject nor object but the point of convergence or of transmergence of both subjectivity and objectivity.

How is this *sākṣī/cit* related to the *ātman* as distinct from the *jīva*? Again Śaṅkara's answer is simple: by denying the (ultimate) reality of any and all differences. Indeed in some texts we get the continuous equation *jīva-ātman-Brahman-sat-cit-ānanda*. Devaraja writes :

> ...the self is the knower not by virtue of any activity in it but by its mere existence. The self is merely the principle of revelation in experience, and there can be no experience without revelation or illumination. Just as there is no meaning in speaking of vision without light, similarly it is meaningless to speak of experience without consciousness. The self is the light of all seeing, the breath of all knowledge. It is coextensive or coterminus with experience. The *content* of experience changes, but consciousness, the core of experience or knowledge, does not change. The knowable fails knowledge, but knowledge itself can never fail the knowable. In other words, consciousness as the revelatory principle in experience is never known to be sublated.[9]

The objection follows that since consciousness-as-such may be reduced to *suṣupti* (dreamless sleep) when in its purest form, it is sublatable. To this objection Śaṅkara has a very plain and direct answer which Devaraja quinticizes as follows : "...the self whose essence is consciousness is an ever-present reality in experience. *Its sublation is unthinkable, since its absence can never be made a datum of experience.* In other words, the self satisfies the test of reality..."[10] (Husserl's attempt at the transcendental reduction may be the best modern European basis for apologetics; and the objections of Sartre and Merleau-Ponty and others to Husserl's attempt at arriving at consciousness-as-such without content are paralleled in those who object to the same attempt by Śaṅkara.)

That all Indian philosophies consider the world as illusion is still an all too popular generalization. Actually only Advaita has this kind of conception of the (phenomenal) world. A proper interpretation of this idea in Advaita is possible only if one clearly sees what is really meant by "illusion". Apte writes:

> It should be clearly understood that when it is said that the phenomenal world is merely an illusion and is really not existent, it is so in the sense in which a non-existent snake is wrongly imagined in a rope, or non-existent water of a mirage is wrongly imagined on a hot desert land, and not in the sense of total non-existence in the sense of a hare's horn or a non-existent flower in the sky or the non-existent son of a barren woman or the non-existent phantom city, because in the former cases there is always a substratum on which the illusion is perceived, while in the latter cases there is no such substratum at all. In the case of the phenomenal world appearance, Brahma always is such a substratum.[11]

At this point one should bear in mind that, according to Śaṅkara Brahman is both the material and the efficient cause of the world. In fact, of the controversial points in the *Brahma-Sūtra-Śaṅkara-Bhāṣya,* the foremost is the interpretation of *māyā.* Śaṅkara writes :

> This potential power of the seed is of the nature of Nescience (Avidyā) and it is indicated by the word 'undeveloped' (Avyakta) and has the Highest Lord as the basis, and is of the nature of an illusion (Māyā) and is the great sleep in which

> transmigratory Jīva-Selfs, unaware of their own true nature (Rūpa) continue to slumber on. (I.iv.3)[12]

And in another place Śaṅkara explains *māyā* as follows:

> It is declared by both the Scriptures and the Smritis, that the names and forms which are imagined through Nescience, and which are as it were the Self of the omniscient Lord, and about which it is impossible to say either that they are one with, or that they are different from Brahma, and which are the seeds of this entire expanse of transmigratory existences, are the illusory power of the Lord. (KK. i. 14)[13]

Māyā is beginningless (*anādi*) though unlike Brahman not endless (*ananta*). *Māyā*'s association with Brahman can be explained according to the orthodox exposition as "Brahma in association with its power of Māyā that creates as it were the illusory world-appearance (Prapancha)."[14] *Māyā* is the power of Brahman as Īśvara, that is, Brahman in its qualified (*saguṇa*) aspect.

What follows is the inevitable paradox which has provoked interminable controversies ever since that both Brahman and *māyā* are *anirvacanīya*, indescribable, inexplicable. Sinha suggests the weakness in the *māyā*/Brahman paradox:

> Śaṅkara's indeterminate and unqualified Brahman and indefinable Māyā, the individuating principle, are the targets of criticism. The relation of Brahman to Māyā is the crux of his philosophy. But Śaṁkara dismisses it lightly as an illegitimate question (atipraśna). Māyā is not real. Brahman alone is real. So the question of the relation of Brahman to Māyā does not arise.[15]

Likewise Sinha epitomizes the paradox of the relation of *Īśvara* as usually identified with *saguṇa*-Brahman which is already in the realm of *māyā* :

> God is subordinate Brahman (apara Brahman). Indeterminate Brahman appears to be determinate, qualified, personal God to the intellect which is infected with avidyā. Brahman is Absolute. God is relative. Śaṁkara sometimes speaks of

> Īśvara as identical with Brahman. Sometimes he clearly distinguishes them from each other. Brahman is the ontological reality of Īśvara. He has no reality distinct from that of Brahman. He is identical with Brahman in essential reality. But still Brahman is the ontological reality while Īśvara is an empirical reality. Brahman is conceived by intellect to be personal Īśvara for the sake of religious communion. The distinction between Brahman and Īśvara, the Absolute and God, is indefensible and irrational. If they are identified with each other, Śaṅkara's absolutism becomes rational and acceptable. If Īśvara be regarded as an empirical appearance of Brahman due to its adjunct, māyā, cosmic nescience, His role as a Creator, Preserver, and Destroyer of the world, and Moral Governor of the jīvas and the world becomes a magic play devoid of real worth and meaning.[16]

A major problem is how it is that Ignorance arises from Brahman if Brahman *is* Knowledge as indeed Śaṅkara claims. And when *māyā* is brought in, how does that solve the problem or save Śaṅkara from sheer absurdity? Sinha writes:

> Māyā is avidyā. It is nescience. Is it subjective or objective ? Does it abide in consciousness or outside consciousness? Brahman is the only ontological reality. It is Absolute Consciousness. Its Being is Consciousness. Nescience cannot exist in it. There is no reality outside Brahman. So nescience cannot exist outside Absolute Consciousness...The legitimate conclusion of Śaṅkara's philosophy is that Brahman contains within itself the principle and explanation of plurality, that it is not an undifferentiated unity.[17]

How in the midst of all this does Śaṅkara manage to insist on a rational construction, all the while insisting that the only source of the knowledge of Brahman is the Upaniṣadic revelation? Of all the *pramāṇas* he retains only the *śabda*, the revealing word, in direct line with the Mīmāṃsā, which also claims that the 'Veda' is eternal, destined in the end to make us know what is absolutely inaccessible to human perception, and even to yogic perception, which to Śaṅkara is also limited to the phenomenal world. As a matter of fact, there is really no proof whatsoever of the existence of Brahman. Śaṅkara prohibits us from thinking that the world is the work of non-spiritual Nature, as the Sāṃkhya affirms; but in turn this does not necessarily constitute a proof of the existence of his Brahman since emphatically Brahman cannot be known in any ordinary sense as the *ordonnateur* of the things of creation.

According to Devaraja, "Scores of passages can be quoted from Śaṅkara showing that he believed the world to be an *ordered whole*, possessed of a *definite* nature which could be *known*."[18] No doubt there are those who may not agree with Devaraja when he concludes that Śaṅkara denies not the *possibility* of knowledge of the world but its *desirability*. But, given the kaleidoscopic situation thus indicated, he may be considered correct just as other views may also be held as correct, as this ultimate paradox entails in infinite number of such facets or 'peep-holes' into reality. Perhaps like the Kṛṣṇa-līlā in the *Bhāgavata Purāṇa*, Kṛṣṇa multiplies himself by his ineluctible *māyā* so that each of us thinks, like the *gopīs*, that he is dancing with each of us alone. For one of the most telling but baffling things about reality as *anirvacanīya* is not that it is unavailable but that there is so much of it ! This may be yet another key to Śaṅkara's intention: both Brahman and *māyā*, whatever be the relation between them, are infinitely available !

Śaṅkara asserts the autonomous self-validating character of *śabda* (the authority of revelation or the Vedas) and denies the ultimate, though not the proximate or pragmatic, validity of the other *pramāṇas*.

> In his ultra-orthodox moods Śaṅkara insists that *Brahman* can be known only through Scripture, and through no other *pramāṇa*, i.e., perception, inference, etc. 'The statement that, because *Brahman* is something existent, other *pramāṇas* may apply to it, is gratuitous. For, being devoid of colour, form, etc., it cannot become an object of perception; and having no characteristic mark, etc., it is not amenable to inference and other *pramāṇas*. Like duty, it is to be known solely through the Scripture.'[19]

And on self-validation, Devaraja writes:

> Knowledge according to the *Advaita* Vedānta is not only self-revelatory but also self-validating. It is impossible to obtain a truly serviceable criterion of truth without granting self-validity to knowledge. On this point the *Advaita* Vedānta of Śaṅkara finds itself in complete accord with the Mīmāṃsā system.[20]

The claim of self-validation (*svataḥ-prāmāṇya*) ultimately cannot be explained since it is a matter of *sādhana* or enlightenment which constitutes a different dimension of reality than that of our ordinary experience. However, the claim was by no means accepted by all the other schools. By way of apologetics one could insist that the only alternative to some point of autonomous or autologous truth as the basic orientation from which other truths may be derived is an infinite regress, or else something like the "Net of Indra" which symbolizes an unlimited interconnexity of hypotheses so linked together that if one of the knots of connexity is untied the whole realm of (demonstrable) truths would come unravelled.

> 'All empirical knowledge', says Śaṅkara, 'is true until the *Ātman* is known to be one with *Brahman*, just as dream-experiences are true before one awakes to consciousness.' While refuting the Mādhyamika Śaṅkara remarks: 'This world whose reality is attested to by all the *pramāṇas*, cannot be negated without the knowledge of a higher reality.'[21]

The beginning of true knowledge then is really that realm of wisdom whereby one realizes the radical insecurity of any possible attempt at constructive systematizing.

The knowledge of Brahman could not be of the conceptual order. All the world of phenomena is of the *vikalpa* order, of the relational and discursive. *Vikalpa* is not exactly a "mental construction" since it has an objectivity at least insofar as *māyā* and *avidyā* are its source. It is moreover the multiple and diverse insofar as it is that which gives place to a differentiated knowledge by opposition to Brahman, which is undifferentiated. The knowledge of Brahman cannot even be intuitive, for intuition would still allow a subject-object relation to subsist, whereas Brahman *is* knowledge and not merely the object of knowledge. Thus *nirvikalpa* knowledge of Brahman is purely and simply mystical identification, the realization that individual knowledge or awareness-*conscience* rather than *connaissance*—is nothing other than Brahman itself and that it is just this which is at once *sat-cit-ānanda.*

The access to this *nirvikalpa* knowledge requires meditation, and for that the *Upaniṣads* furnish a multitude of symbols of Brahman which can aid the *sādhaka.* On the other hand, the negative formulations of the same *Upaniṣads* denying everything that can be applied in or to the phenomenal world also equally prepare the *sādhaka* for the approach to absolute transcendence, acting as a sort of detour away from everything which resembles discursive thought. Advaita above all constitutes a yoga, a discipline. In fact it presupposes all the other yogas, *hatha, bhakti, karma* and *jñāna,* asserting the supremacy of *jñāna* over all the others. But it also presupposes that one has gone through the traditional Hindu rituals and classical forms of meditation. For this reason a transported Advaita may be a new development, as different from its original as Alan Watts' Zen differs from the rigorously strict and monastic discipline of Dōgen.

The teaching of the identification of the individual subject with the All—*Tat Tvam Asi,* That Thou Art—is too often lifted out of context; and other interpreters of the *Upaniṣads* put quite a different stress on it than Śaṅkara does. Rāmānuja insists (as Mādhava does not) on the *essential* unitive relation between the *ātman* and Brahman, but he does not see why it should be necessary to twist the texts in order to prove that the *adjunctive* differences are to be denied right along with any possible assertion of *essential* difference (which Mādhava maintains) between the individual *jīva* or *ātman* and Brahman.

This *Mahāvākya* should not be taken in isolation from the other three basic ones, so that one's meditations over many years of patient practice should go progressively from the *Aham Brahm Asmi* (I am of the nature of Supreme Reality) to the *Tat Tvam Asi* (That Thou Art) on through the *Sarvavijñātman Brahmaḥ* (Everything is of the nature of the mergence of consciousness and Selfhood) and finally to the *Ekam Advaita*

Brahmaḥ (There is that which is, the One-and-Only non-dual Supreme Reality). Śaṅkara, of course, attempts a complete obliteration of the *Tvam*, the Thou, the Otherness that is clearly expressed in that *Mahāvākya*, and stretches everything back into the *Tat*, the Supreme Identity.

Śaṅkara makes every possible effort to interpret these key phrases in such a way that they deprive or even deliver Brahman of all positive knowledge. For him the *Mahāvākyas* have nothing to do with intellectual knowledge, which remains in the realm of Radical Ignorance; they directly introduce us to the mystic realization by contemplative communion which is quite distinct from discursive communication or careful calculation. Seeking support from Kumārila's theory of language, Śaṅkara thinks in common with Tantra that each word and sound has its own sense even before coming into relation with the others. But Kumārila does not resolve the problem of knowing how several terms can concur in giving an undifferentiated *nirvikalpa* nature such as Śaṅkara insists on. Hence it is necessary for him to explain this at great length; and by repeated emphasis on the *sat-cit-ānanda* triad, Śaṅkara makes the solution appear to be very simple. Each of these terms is appropriate solely to Brahman and to nothing else; for Brahman is all that there is, and there is nothing in the nature of Brahman which can allow it to be constrained in the realm of finitude. In other words, these terms are related with each other not as subject and predicate, but in a relation of pure identity. The *Mahāvākya* is not a general description of Brahman, nor an affirmation about things that remain in the conceptual order. It indicates Brahman by a sort of pointing the finger, expecting recognition more than knowing. This is indeed the reality even of the individual to whom the words are addressed.

Each of the terms in the *Tat Tvam Asi* ought perforce to be disassociated from every empirical content. The Thou, the *Tvam*, is no more the thou as limited and individuated; and likewise the *Tat*, the That, loses all its otherness in order to become that which is the most possibly immanent in the *Tvam*. Śaṅkara resorts to a traditional distinction between the first sense and the secondary sense of words (which he really ought to have condem-

meanings to suit their systems). Thus it is necessary to appeal to the secondary sense of the words *Tat* and *Tvam* in order to put them into a relation of identity. His critics accuse him perhaps not unjustly of sophistically attempting to do the impossible.

Śaṅkara's prescription for the *jīvanmukta* does not follow the rituals prescribed by the Vedas. The *jīvanmukta*, who has already achieved enlightenment, is exempted from strict conformity to ritual procedures. Śaṅkara leaves the ritual texts to others as appertaining to the realm of ignorance; the rites cannot but continue to engender new karma which determines still other new rebirths. Among modern Advaitins these rituals are advised "for the sake of others" since not to follow them would set an improper example for the unenlightened. And in actual practice strict Advaitins do follow them, perhaps more rigorously than any other Hindus, no doubt because the actual texts are not as permissive as Śaṅkara would have them. On the other hand, Śaṅkara does prescribe strict conformity until that knowledge dawns, even to the extent of forbidding women and non-caste Hindus from access to this discipline. Many later critics, Rāmānuja in particular, are actually much more democratic and open-mindedly liberal.

Every place where Śaṅkara insists on *vairāgya* and such like, or at every turn where he gives any explication of *māyā*, he will insist that the dawn of the knowledge of Brahman *is* available to all who have the aptitude and inclination according to previous karma and present attainments. Moreover, just as beatitude, especially in the tradition of Erigena, is considered in the Christian system as a restoration of the pristine *Imago Dei* and the removal of all hindrances to perfect union with God, so in Śaṅkara the final reward is a restoration of identity with God, all hindrances of ignorance being removed. The concept of release (*mokṣa*) is further expanded by the different subschools which follow Śaṅkara according to whether one prefers the *pratibimba* (reflection) or the *avaccheda* (nescience) or the *bhrānti* (error) or the *adhyāsa* (superimposition) interpretation of the relation of Brahman and *māyā*. According to the Bhāmatī of Vācaspati Miśra, which still enjoys the most popularity, there never was any 'fall', the redemption being really an *eternal* re-

If it be charged that in his consummate dialectic in which the total engagement is focused on the Ultimate Śaṅkara neglects the doctrine of man, the answer should be relatively simple : in his interpretation of the *Tat Tvam Asi* is contained all that is really needed : *all that is not divine in man is māyā.* The true self (*ātman*) in man *is* Brahman, is supreme Tautology from which one need never depart and over against which any attempt to construct a second, whether by theological speculation or by empirical investigation of nature, is only a superimposition of an epiphenomenological superstructure. Such are not false in themselves for even such attempts must be included in the Supreme Identity, but they are simply unnecessary.

It is this attainment of *mokṣa* which is most unduly neglected in the study of Śaṅkara's system, largely, no doubt, because most scholars have not the metaphysical inclination (*adhikāra*) nor the ascetic patience to completely explore the difficulties of the last two *adhyāyas* of the *Brahma Sūtras*. Vedānta is an heroic philosophy, certainly not an escape into self-delusion as some missionaries have tried to claim. The prerequisite discipline requires complete and final self-purification and the spirit of uncompromising renunciation of everything, including, at the final stage, the intellect itself, which, in theory at least, will no longer be needed once the *Aham Brahm Asmi* has been authentically attained. But true *jīvanmuktas* are not readily available, and one will not even meet one until one is ready for it even though one lives in close proximity to such a person—at least, such is the claim.

The "journey into the Absolute" wherein alone is true repose and the Way of no return, though found in its germinal form in the *Bhagavad Gītā*, finds its full implications only at the terminus of the *Brahma Sūtras*. In the last section of the *Brahma Sūtras* the way of speculation and of dialectical refutation has been exhausted. One must meditate : this is axiomatic. Meditation as distinct from the usual way of philosophizing is essentially the achievement of complete identification of the subject/object of the meditation. The way these may be seen to coalesce by this discipline is not easily demonstrable by other disciplines.

the usefulness of symbols. Here Śaṅkara rather fully anticipates the post-Hegelian attempt at "demythologizing", and herein is also a radical departure from the "sacramental universe" *Weltanschauung* of Erigena which will be further expanded in the Victorines. In Erigena all reality is contemplated as a symbolic theophany, the "outward and visible sign of an inward spiritual grace." At the practical level Śaṅkara has no objection to this. In his commentary on the *bhakti* sections of the *Gītā* Śaṅkara explains that the masses still need the symbols for the sake of edification and provocation of ecstatic devotion. However, this remains for the true Advaitin not an alternative way but a halfway house, a *dharmashālā* on the Himalayan Pilgrimage.

After various instructions on the regularity of meditation right up to the point of death and on non-clin ing to the fruit of meditation even though it increase merit infinitely, Śaṅkara concludes the first *pāda* of the fourth *adhyāya* with a discussion of the controversial issue of the usefulness of ritual observances, both before and after enlightenment. Just as symbols are not necessarily to be discarded altogether (only the obligation toward their use is dispensed with in the later stages of spiritual growth), so it is with other observances and doings so long as *gnosis* is promoted. One is not obligated to "do" anything so long as one is bent on realization, for it is not the "doer" that is the true self so much as the observer (*sākṣī*) of what is done. If and when all gain *Brahma-vidyā*, the *karmakāṇḍa* will itself become no longer necessary. The realized sage or saint is above the ritual prescriptions because, having *become* that which has ordered them for the masses in the various levels of society and stages (*āśramas*) along life's way, he is no longer a distinct ego. His whole person is only a place of the presence of God in the world—a *jīvanmukta*. The classical Hindu law (Manu) allows a place for such a noble ideal and for such souls in society without expecting that all will attain that degree.

The second *pāda*, following the pattern set in the *Upaniṣads*, describes the final departure of the soul from the body: speech to mind, senses to mind, mind to breath, breath to the individual soul,

departure is therefore preferably when the sun is on the increase.

The third *pāda* continues the same pattern on the macrocosmic scale. Herein the chief argument is whether the *saguṇa*-Brahman is correspondingly reabsorbed into *nirguṇa*-Brahman, and the parallel argument whether the individual soul may go directly into the *nirguṇa* condition or whether it must tarry in the *saguṇa* for a season. To this of course Śaṅkara replies in the negative, although others disagree with him. Here is where Śaṅkara's position concerning the relation of the *saguṇa* and *nirguṇa* comes out most clearly. There is also a further discussion as to the usefulness and effectiveness of actions as against knowledge in this final "going". Śaṅkara holds to the primacy of knowledge because this alone is appropriate to the *nirguṇa*-Brahman.

The fourth and last *pāda* is the most important, for here Śaṅkara's beliefs about the relation of the human soul to God become most vivid. The *Sūtras* demand a consideration of what the beatified soul must really be after it attains its own form stripped of its adjunctive accumulations of merit and demerit. The most tempting answer is that it is of the nature of light, especially since in the case of many saints at the time of their departing from the body a peculiar spiritual light is perceptible on the part of their devotees. Śaṅkara, however, replies that this is not its true nature but only its manifestation. The true nature of the soul is really the *ātman*, which is absolutely formless and identical with the formless Godhead, Brahman. He quotes, for example, the passage in the *Chāndogya Upaniṣad* where it is said, "Just as pure water poured into pure water remains the same, thus, O Gautama, is the Self of a thinker who knows." Śaṅkara says that the soul who comes into complete union with God shares all His nature except the power to create and destroy the universe. This seems to be the only place where his insistence on the 'Single Principle' does appear to break down. But advisedly we say "appear" because we may not understand him here.

The whole ends with a summary interpretation of the "no return" in the *Gītā* and *Chāndogya Upaniṣad* in which the Hindu version of *nirvāṇa* is explicated. According to the Adavaitic view, those who insist on individual immortality simply have not reached true enlightenment; they still cling to their little egos (although admittedly that last hurdle is not so easy). The concept of no return is based on metempsychosis, which theory is based beautifully on the analogy of the cyclic nature of experienceable reality. *Nirvāṇa*, final release, is deliverance from the endless chain of cyclic causation, and for the Vedāntin there is no other freedom.

Those who charge Śaṅkara with pantheism, illusionism, oriental mysticism or the many other epithets that compromise his critical acumen have not begun to understand him. T.R.V. Murti says, "... as opposed to naive realism, the Vedānta shows that the true object of knowledge is beyond empirical experience, and what we empirically know is appearance of the real, not the real itself. The Vedānta has greater affinity with Kant and the Mādhyamika than with Idealism." But Sinha levels this criticism regarding Śaṅkara's ethical position :

> Morality and religion are real and ultimate. They are not empirical. Śaṅkara does not discard morality and religion, but he degrades them to a lower plane of avidyā. But morality is real and absolute and grounded in God .... Śaṅkara's indeterminate Brahman is neither philosophically satisfactory nor adequate to moral needs and religious aspirations.[22]

Of course the Advaitins claim that they have answers to such objections ; and as a matter of fact, as seldom we see in conventional textbooks on the history of Indian philosophy, there continued to be constant dialogue between the Advaitins and their opponents well into the eighteenth century and even to the present day. After the coming of the Europeans the form of the debate changed although essentially the content remained and remains the same.

Devaraja is not uncritical as many modern Advaitins are, his chief objection to Śaṅkara's system being that it does not sufficiently allow for change and further development of mankind. In a word, it is too 'absolutistic' and does not encourage the great potentialities of human nature to make cultural advances of historical importance. But in that regard Śaṅkara is certainly not alone ; and in spite of that defect, he remains among the greatest of all philosophers in world history.

A sociology of knowledge approach would be most useful in sorting out the reasons why Advaita has come to dominate most Euramerican interpretations of what is considered at the textbook level to be "Indian philosophy" over against the factual interplay in history of the various and *very different* systems of Indian philosophy, of which Advaita is only one among many. Was it because Radhakrishnan popularized it and made it acceptable in non-Indian circles ? Perhaps; but then there is Sri Aurobindo, who is by no means an Advaitin. Was it because of Vivekānanda's popularization? But there is also the Ārya Samāj whose interpretations are diametrically opposed to Advaita. Was it because of Ram Mohan Roy and the Brāhmo Samāj ? But there were also modernizing reformers, accused of heresy by almost all of the unwesternized schools. Or was it because those Brāhmins who were the first to learn English and come into the employ of the British Raj were predominantly Advaitins since the centers famous for the other traditions were not so completely penetrated by Westernization ?

Regardless of the manner in which it happened, until very recently Advaita predominated, especially in the universities set up according to the British style, and in spite of the work of Thibaut, Lacombe, Tilak, Deussen, and other Indologists. Mādhava's *Sarvadarśana-saṃgraha* seems to have set the pattern for what was thenceforth to be considered as Indian philosophy. It is often forgotten that he was an Advaitin. But then Śivaji of Poona and the Maharashtrians were anything but Advaitins. Every indication points to the predominance of the *non*-Advaitin schools in the literature in the vernacular languages of India. Thus again the predominance in the first two quarters of the twentieth century remains quite a puzzle. Nevertheless this imbalance is beginning to be rectified as more and better translations of the basic texts become available. The work of B.N.K. Sharma in the Mādhava Dvaita school is a healthy effort in that direction, and there are many others.

Another warning that must be given to the neophyte concerns the manner in which even Śaṅkara's Advaita has been misinterpreted in terms of British Hegelianism, which happened to be fashionable when the British were first discovering that "the natives" of India did have something that might be called philosophy. This was only natural, by way of apologetics, and was good as far as it went. It is only now that British Hegelianism has been replaced by the Analytic tradition that apologetics for Indian philosophy are beginning to be recast in terms of such things as comparisons of Bhartṛhari and Wittgenstein.

In a very radical sense Advaita in general and Śaṅkara's seminal version of it, like Zen, can be characterized as supra-historical or para-historical ; nevertheless, it cannot be divorced from its historical milieux nor from the history of its own development. Yet because Advaita is so adaptable to so many interpretations, it may be that it can serve as a rallying point for many of the various controversies in the modern world. These interpretations vary from the view that it is the "self-refuting philosophy" and therefore opens the way for whatever else one wishes to assert (not ultimately but as judgment), to the "self-affirming philosophy" that appeals to the sense of Identity which is the natural remedy or counter-assertion for widespread Alienation in the confusion of ideologies superimposed on almost all of the cultures during the Colonial Era. In a world where people increasingly experience a sense of lostness, Advaita becomes that Transcendent Something which puts all else in a properly *phenomenal* perspective. (Asked about comparisons between Heidegger and Śaṅkara, Olivier Lacombe replied : "Śaṅkara *rests* in Being; Heidegger does *not* !")

According to most critics the place where Śaṇkara may be most assailable is in his refutation of Nāgārjuna's Mādhyamika. It is not easy, without having come to complete enlightenment or the Beatific Vision, for anyone to choose between (1) a system in which the Dialectic is taken as the most that any human can become engaged in for the very reason that there may not "be" anything beyond it, the *śūnyatā* being so inexpressible that it is better not to try to bind it even to the designation of "being", which sooner or later is contra-distinguishable from becoming and/or non-being, and (2) a system wherein Brahman as Absolute, as Being-beyond-becoming-and-non-being, is asserted to be of such a nature that it "asserts itsef as self-illuminating" (*svayaṃprakāśatva*), the *śūnyatā* being considered as simply impossible because we may not speak of an 'emptiness' that in some sense or other does not have being.

But perhaps the final judgment is that of history. Nāgārjuna's system did not survive in India, and Śaṅkara's did. Although there is a revival of the study of Nāgārjuna in the twentieth century, to a very great extent all that Nāgārjuna taught (and for that matter, Vasubandhu and all the Buddhists before Śaṅkara) was incorporated by Śaṅkara. Unfortunately Śaṅkara died rather young before he could remove the inconsistencies in his system, and his followers had much work to do in further enlarging and defending his system against various assailants, especially among the Vaiṣṇavas, e.g., Rāmānuja and Mādhava. But that belongs to a different period, a period in which we shall find to a great extent the same movement away from the more strictly monistic tendencies almost equally in China, India, Islam, Christianity, and somewhat among the later Jewish scholastics also.

6. Padmapāda

The four varieties of first generation post-Śaṅkara Advaita are distinguished by their theories of *māyā* as indicated in the following semi-stereotypic characterization:

Sureśvara: mistake theory of *māyā*
Maṇḍana Miśra: *avidyā* simply taken
Vācaspati Miśra: *adhyāsa*, superimposition
Padmapāda: Pratibimbavāda, reflection theory, coupled with the *mithyā* level as the lowest of the four levels of the better type of Advaita, the other three being *prātibhāsika, vyāvahārika* and *pāramārthika* (a good pattern for *sādhanā* any time by the way); *vivaraṇa* comes in later with Prakāśātman as transformation theory to explain reflection (the very universal mirror metaphor, or another metaphor might be the prism individuating colors).

Factual biography for Padmapāda (c. 820) is almost completely absent, although there is a rather fanciful legend related by Deutsch and van Buitenen as follows:

> According to tradition Padmapāda (ca. 820 A.D.), the founder of the Vivaraṇa school of Advaita, was, along with Sureśvara, a direct pupil of Śaṁkara. Tradition has it that after completing a commentary on Śaṁkara's *Brahmasūtrabhāṣya* Padmapāda traveled on a pilgrimage to Rāmeśvaram in the South. On the way he stopped at the house of an uncle who was an ardent supporter of Prabhākara—one of the leaders of an important school of Mīmāṁsā. The uncle was entrusted with the safety of the mansuscript while Padmapāda continued on his journey, but the uncle, upon reading Padmapāda's attack upon Prabhākara, set fire to his own house in order to destroy the manuscript. Padmapāda later related to Śaṁkara how the manuscript had been destroyed whereupon Śaṁkara dictated to him from memory Padmapāda's commentary on the first five parts of his own work, hence the title *Pañcapādikā* for Padmapāda's work...
>
> The Vivaraṇa school, as founded by Padmapāda, refined a number of important doctrines of Advaita (e.g., the notion of *mithyā*, falsehood) and elaborated a few themes in somewhat new directions (e.g., the theory of perception). As indicated previously, the question of the locus or support of *avidyā* became an important problem for post-Śaṁkara Advaita, with the Vivaraṇa school arguing quite clearly that Brahman must be the locus. In connection with this, it elaborated a theory of "reflexionism" for working out the relation that obtains between the individual self (*jīva*) and Brahman, arguing that the *jīva* is a mere reflection (*pratibimba*) of its prototype (*bimba*) and that hence, in essence, the individual is identical with Brahman. The Vivaraṇa school also held that an encounter with any of the "great sayings" (*mahāvākyas*) of Advaita such as *tat tvam asi* ("thou art that") is sufficient for the attainment of enlightenment, of the realization of the identity between the self and Reality.[1]

Although the term *pratibimba* (*vāda*) is definitely associated with Padmapāda himself, it seems to fall out of the picture later and *vivaraṇa* (*vivartavāda*) then characterizes the school after the work of Prakāśātman. This impression, however, is subject to further research; and it may be devoid of any profound significance since ultimately they mean essentially the same thing. The basic meaning of *pratibimba* is simply reflection. *Vivarta* and *vivartavāda*, however, have a much richer connotation historically. The basic meaning is simply modification or conversion. As a *vāda*, a theory, it is more conveniently defined as "illusory-appearance theory".

Historically there was through many generations and many centuries an ongoing controversy between the Vivarta school of Padmapāda and the Bhāmatī school that stems from Vācaspati Miśra and puts the emphasis on the *adhyāsa* theory of *māyā*. The Vivarta school thinks of the realm of *māyā* as a sort of modification of reality such that we never really get the "real thing" but only a poor copy of it. The realm of pure ideas remains 'over there', so to speak, though to some extent we construct models of ideal situations. This applies in everything from macro-astronomy to the circle one draws, which is never absolutely the ideal circle. Hence it was that Plato himself in his later life had to realize that, with detachment, we have to be pragmatically content with the "second best". Vivartavāda is something like that, and it would be therefore asking too much to expect a *perfect* definition of it. Nevertheless, we must keep striving at all levels to produce, if it is not already there, the best possible existentialization of the ideal.

However, those of the Vācaspati/Bhāmatī school do not have the same attitude, because their theory is different. They believe that all of our model-construction approach to reality is unnecessary, and often as not even a snare and delusion. It is only after long reflection that we often realize that we have just been floundering around with unnecessary theorizing, since all of that is *adhyāsa*, superimposition of our wrong notions on the actualities of the world as it really is—not to mention the ultimate reality of Brahman, which is nothing more but nothing less than the *principle* of reality that is not-*māyā* rather than any particular reality as such. So, according to this tradition, just get rid of your stupid notions about everything and the reality of whatever you are dealing with (or is dealing with you) will take care of itself. Such at least is one way of attempting to communicate what is intended by the word *adhyāsa*. Of course the other two schools also have their theories, but it seems they did not have the same degree of development and popularity historically as these two (who still argue it out endlessly).

Concerning Padmapāda's view of *avidyā*, Das Gupta summarizes as follows:

> It is this entity that obstructs the pure and independently self-revealing nature of Brahman, and thus, standing as the painted canvas (*citra-bhitti*) of ignorance (*avidyā*), deeds (*karma*) and past impressions of knowledge...produce the individual persons (*jīvatvāpādikā*). Undergoing its peculiar transformations with God as its support, it manifests itself as the two powers of knowledge and activity...and functions as the doer of all actions and the enjoyer of all experiences... In association with the pure unchangeable light of Brahman it is the complex of these transformations which appears as the immediate ego (*ahaṁkāra*). It is through the association with this ego that the pure self is falsely regarded as the enjoyer of experiences. This transformation is called *antaḥkaraṇa*, *manas*, *buddhi* and the ego or the ego-feeler (*ahaṃ-pratyayin*) on the side of its cognitive activity, while on the vibratory side of its activity (*spanda-śaktyā*), it is called *prāṇa* or bio-motor functions. The association of the ego with the pure *ātman*, like the association of the redness of a *japā* flower with a crystal, is a complex (*granthi*) which manifests the dual characteristics of activity of the *avidyā* stuff and the consciousness of the pure self...[2]

Such are the *vivartas*, the transformations. Vācaspati believes that *avidyā* has Brahman as its object (*viṣaya*) and the *jīva* as its support (*āśraya*) whereas Prakāśātman argues that Brahman is both support and object of *avidyā*, thus defending his master against Vācaspati. However, this is a question which Sureśvara deals more with whereas Padmapāda is more concerned with other matters. Das Gupta says that on this question "Padmapāda's own attitude does not seem very clear. He only says that *avidyā* manifests itself in the individual person (*jīva*) by obstructing the real nature of the Brahman as pure self-luminosity and that the Brahman by its limitation (*avaccheda*) through beginningless *avidyā* is the cause of the appearance of infinite individual persons."[3]

According to Das Gupta, Padmapāda was probably the first to interpret *ajñāna* or *avidyā* "as being of a material nature (*jaḍātmikā*) and of the nature of power (*jaḍātmikā avidyā-śakti*), and interpreted Śaṅkara's phrase "*mithyā-jñāna-minttaḥ*" as meaning that it is this material power of *ajñāna* that is the constitutive or the material cause of the world-appearance."[4] Again Prakāśatman elaborates on this later, but that need not concern us during the present century except to suggest that it was *defensively* that these later elaborations took place and developed. In regard to the process of perception from the Advaita point of view, Padmapāda was again an innovator, and it was his interpreters who had to defend his position against the others and thus elaborate on it. Basically Padmapāda asserts that perception is an activity of the ego, the *ahaṃkāra*, as well as the *antaḥkaraṇa* (the 'sensus communis' or the faculty that integrates perceptions into conceptions). Das Gupta writes:

> Describing this process, Padmapāda says that, as a result of the cognitive activity of the ego, the objects with which that is concerned become connected with it, and, as a result of that, certain changes are produced in it, and it is these changes that constitute the subject-object relation of knowledge...The *antaḥkaraṇa*, or psychical frame of mind, can lead to the limited expression of the pure consciousness only so far as it is associated with its object. The perceptual experience of immediacy (*aparokṣa*) of objects means nothing more than the expression of the pure consciousness through the changing states of the *antaḥkaraṇa*. The ego thus becomes a perceiver (*pramātṛ*) through its connections with the underlying consciousness.

On the one hand Śaṅkara insists on *anirvacanīya* (indescribability) and the primacy of *nirguṇa*-Brahman over *saguṇa*-Brahman; but on the other hand he has to acknowledge the minimum of attributes such as eternal, pure, etc. in conformity with the Upanisadic literature. But Padmapāda evidently does not minimize the role of Īśvara as Śaṅkara usually does. Sinha writes: "Padmapāda opines that Brahman of the nature of bliss cannot be the cause of the world of the nature of non-bliss, that therefore the attributes of being the cause of the world, and the like, are the indicating characteristics (*upalakṣana*) of Brahman, and that they are the essential characteristics of the omniscient and omnipotent Īśvara."[6] In a modern apologetic this could possibly be used as a pretext for surveying the controversy about the "symbolic forms" such as Cassirer and opened and Tillich applied in religion. But that might be building too much on too little foundation. It could also and more appropriately introduce a fresh review of the problem of attributes of Allah between the Mu'tazilites and al-Ash'arī, not to mention al-Fārābī and other Muslims, and that joined with the Jewish scholastics of the same period such as Saadia.

Like all other commentators and sub-commentators on the *Brahma Sūtras* Padmapāda invokes *śruti* as the final authority —even though seldom if ever is there complete agreement in any case, Abrahamic or Vedic, when it comes to *interpretation.* Sinha writes :

> Padmapāda avers that Brahman known from the Vedas is not established by them as an object of the act of knowledge. When the immediate knowledge of the identity of the self with Brahman dawns, Brahman is not known as an object of knowledge. The distinction of a knower, a means of valid knowledge, valid knowledge, and an object of valid knowledge due to *avidyā* is simultaneously annulled, when the intuition of Brahman dawns. Yet the apprehension of Brahman as limited by this distinction is due to Vedic testimony.[7]

The expression "when the intuition of Brahman dawns" is left unexplained because there may be no rational finite explanation of how and when and to whom this 'dawning' happens, short of a doctrine of grace and election such as the Vaiṣṇava critics of Advaita affirm.

To Padmapāda the world-appearance is relatively real and not a totally false appearance, as a limited and even limiting re-tion school in Islam whose representatives roughly contemporary with Padmapāda were Ibn Masarrah (d. 931) and al-Wāsiṭī (d. 942), both in Spain. Padmapāda evidently holds a more reasonable and common-sense position in the midst of the increasingly (and sometimes almost obsessively) subtle and supersophisticated dialectics which typifies positions and traditions that are on the defensive, since patchwork seldom gets back to the basic issues, to which it seems that Padmapāda prefers to remain faithful. Padmapāda puts much less stress on superimposition than the others, notably Vācaspati and his followers. Even though we do get wrong notions about realities not to mention Reality as such, this does not mean that ontologically the whole "phantasmagoria of existence" is a false superimposition on the one indescribable, ultimate, qualityless, whatever-it-is, *nirguṇa*-Brahman. Sometimes admittedly Śaṅkara seems to believe this, but typically at the cost of a radical inconsistency which these four sub-schools are in dire straits to reconcile (or attempt to explain away).

7. Sureśvara

Sureśvara, who was a direct disciple of Śaṅkara (d. 820), is one of the major figures in the field of post-Śaṅkara Advaita along with Vācaspati Miśra, Padmapāda, Prakāśātman, Sarvajñātman, Vimuktātman, Śrīharṣa and Citsukha. As often happens in the second generation of a new tradition there developed subvarieties of Advaita, the chief point of division among them ranging around their different interpretations of the locus and nature of *māyā*. Each of the sub-varieties may well have developed in response to challenges from other schools contemporary with them, although the standard textbooks give the impression that they developed quite independently, and indeed that they were all that there was of Indian philosophy until Rāmānuja. Some interpreters do not so sharply distinguish the post-Śaṅkara Vedāntins but simply attach their interpretations as really an enlargement of Śaṅkara's system outright, especially in regard to the *adhyās* interpretation of *avidyā* and *māyā*. Other interpreters might disagree in detail, but basically this is true since all they do is to enlarge on it by commentaries instead of critical examination of its presuppositions or original application of it to existential human and historical situations.

Mahadevan states that "although Sureśvara follows Śaṅkara closely and interprets him faithfully, it does not mean that he does not differ from his master in certain points of doctrine."[1] He adds, however, that these differences are of minor importance, at least in the *Saṁbandha-vārtika*. A *vārtika* is technically only a commentary in the stricter sense the purpose of which is to examine what is said, what is not said and what is well said in the original text, whereas a *bhāṣya* is a form of commentary which gives the author much more freedom of interpretation, while a *ṭika* is only an explanation of the text for the sake of clarification. The *Saṁbandha-vārtika* is part of Sureśvara's commentary on Śaṅkara's commentary on the *Bṛhadāraṇyaka Upaniṣad* and deals primarily with a refutation of the ritualism of the Pūrva Mīmāṁsā, but it is also done in defence of Śaṅkara's system against his opponents. Sureśvara's differences from Śaṅkara are probably best exposited in the *Naiṣkarmya-siddhi*, which was an independent work and not a commentary of any sort.

One feature of Śaṇkara's Advaita which is bothersome not only to modern secularists but also to other commentators on the *Barhma Sūtras* and the *Upaniṣads* is his insistence on the *nirguṇa* attributeless nature of Brahman at the expense of the *saguṇa*-Brahman. And Sureśvara like a true disciple if anything stresses the *nirguṇa* even more than Śaṅkara (if that were possible), claiming that this *nirguṇa* "featureless feature" of Brahman extends also to the *jīvātman*. Not only is the *ātman*-Brahman equation affirmed by Sureśvara as with all Advaitins, but he is also an *ekajīvavādin* by virtue of affirming non-difference also between *ātman* and *jīva*. In other systems this is seen as unreasonable and fraught with many difficulties ; but in trying to eliminate all logistics of difference Sureśvara counts himself with those who evidently side-step these difficulties.

In Sureśvara we find the famous *neti neti*, for which we have often pointed out parallels with the *via negativa* in the Neo-Platonic heritage in Christianity and Islam and to a great extent in Jewish Scholasticism as well. To this extreme version of the *via negativa* Rāmānuja, Mādhava and others object that all the *Upaniṣads,* quite aside from any valid logic that any human knows, do have very numerous texts describing Brahman as having all sorts of marvelous attributes.

> . . . Sureśvara says : How can we ignore Scripture which repeatedly asserts the attributeless Brahman and denies everything other than the seeing consciousness as insubstantial, by saying "not this not this". If any description of the indeterminate non-relational, non-dual Self is possible at all, it can only be a negative description as 'not this not this' as stated in the Bṛhadāraṇyaka. A spiritual aspirant who fulfills the requisite conditions attains directly the non-relational knowledge from the śruti text, 'Tat Tvam Asi'.[2]

Evidently in this respect Sureśvara had nothing to add to Śaṅkara's own version of the *nirguṇa* concept. Nevertheless, he seems to specify the term *avicārita* more than Śaṅkara's own favorite *anirvacanīya* (indescribability). In discussing *avidyā*—the usual term for "ignorance", although in some texts one occasionally finds the term *ajñāna* as virtually equivalent in connotation though their etymological derivations are different, *a-vidyā* indicating "not seeing" and *a-jñāna* indicating "not-knowing"—Balasubramanian writes:

> Though Sureśvara has not used the neat expression anirvacaṇīya in describing the nature of the primal ignorance, he does bring out its full significance in his writings. He characterizes it very frequently as *avicārita-siddha* with the view to how that it exists only so long as it is not scrutinized . . . "The name Māyā", says Sureśvara, " is given to an appearance which cannot be accounted for." Again, "This harlot which is māyā appearing only so long as not scrutinized, does deceive the Ātman by her false affection of coquetry". In another place he says, "He who desires to see avidyā through the knowledge gained by pramāṇa could as well certainly see the darkness in the interior of a cave by means of a lamp".[3]

Anirvacanīya is a very pivotal term in Śaṅkara's system and is used quite frequently—or according to Rāmānuja and Mādhava later on, overused to his own peril. Although in a sense *avicārita* and *anirvacanīya* have the same general connotation, the root denotation is somewhat different. For *avicārita* means that which cannot be verbalized but that which denies dialectically the ultimate value distinctions ; though for practical purposes distinctions still remain useful and therefore have a qualified validity at their own level, they are sublatable by the logistic of reduction.

Since Reality/Brahman as such must ultimately be One and undivided (*a-dvaita*), the 'appearances' (*Ābhāsas*) of it as phenomena are better termed pseudo-appearances. Markandeya Sastri states :

> The supreme contribution of Sureśvara to Advaita doctrine is his own interpretation of the illusory nature of the world and the utmost possible approximation of personal soul to the impersonal One. He considered both the world and the personal soul as pseudo-appearances—Ābhāsas of the Supreme—but not delimitations or transformations. The essence of such a doctrine is that not even a transitory reality and utility is acceptable to this appearance . . .
>
> According to him the whole universe is only an appearance of Brahman disguised as it were. The disguising factor is Avidyā, which serves as a flimsy curtain. The Brahman when apprehended through this curtain, is cognized as the world with its multiple facets and activities. The curtain, as it were, gives its own form and name to the Brahman and without the basis or illumination of the latter, the curtain... has no existence at all.[4]

There is a sort of process of degrees and graduations within the *Ābhāsa* ranging from the grossest *avidyā* to the omniscient and omnipotent Īśvara, Deity, which he calls *cidābhāsa* because the veil there is very thin. Parallel with *cidākāsa* as the rarest material element, evidently *cidābhāsa* is the rarest manifestation of reality in religious form, with only a thin distinction between reality as such and reality as religious-consciousness.

Similar to Plotinus' pattern in the *Enneads*, Sureśvara traces the 'evolutes' of this *Ābhāsa* of Brahman, although there is evidently that difference from Neo-Platonism since all the 'secondary' *Ābhāsas* are derived through the first or Īśvara. The third stage in the Manifestation-*Ābhāsas* is *Hiraṇyagarbha* or the Universal Soul. We might also find a parallel with Sureśvara's contemporary John Scotus Erigena :

Uncaused and Uncausing	*nirguṇa*-Brahman
Uncaused and Causing	Īśvara
Caused and Causing	*Hiraṇyagarbha*
Caused and Uncausing	*māyā*

The following is a schematic summary of Sureśvara's cosmology or pattern of manifestations :

1. Avidyā exists intrinsically in the Supreme Consciousness.
2. The Supreme Consciousness evolves itself as an appearance and thus the Kūṭastha is formed. The primordial Avidyā has not a clear place or function in this stage of evolution of the Supreme into Kūṭastha.
3. The first projection through the primordial Avidyā is called Īśvara and the Avidyā that persists at this projected stage is called Māyā.
4. A further creation of appearance is that Īśvara through his Māyā assumes the form of an all pervasive individual soul when the Māyā is thickened, as it were, into ignorance (Ajñāna).
5. This individual soul entangles itself in the multiple world through the ignorance when he gets the name of cogniser and the ignorance is called as the intelligence (Buddhi or Antaḥkaraṇa).
6. A further projection is in that the Jīva becomes doer and the ignorance the organ of sense and action.[5]

Markandeya Sastri further explains the *Kūṭastha* consciousness :

> This all-pervasive absolute cognitive consciousness has its summum bonum and full purpose in the pure consciousness, freed from all cognitions which is simply another way of expressing the Supreme Reality of Existence. In other words, Kūṭastha consciousness itself is generated, as it were, from

> the absolute consciousness. The latter is a plenum and the former is continuum both being "beyond the ripples of multiple, discrete and finite expressions or appearances".[6]

And in considering the relation of the *Kūṭastha* to the *jīva* the well-known metaphor of the spider and its web is invoked :

> The spider stands in the place of *jīva*, and the world, the web. From the view-point of Kūṭastha, the creation is false but from the view-point of jīva it is partly real. The individual soul is capable of consisting of these two phases of existence, i.e., reality and falsity at the same time only on account of this nature of partial reality.[7]

Behind the *Kūṭastha* concept is the metaphor of the summit of a mountain such that one should keep on climbing until reaching the top; and hence all hierarchies must be determined by virtue of the highest 'summit' which is their focus. Thus in a sense what is involved in *sādhana* according to Sureśvara may not be so much distinctive levels of reality as the continuum of *upāsanās* or even constancy of meditation on the *Aham Brahma Asmi* and the *Tat Tvam Asi* until one "gets there"—and stays there ! *Kūṭastha* has the connotation of permanence since the summit remains the constant goal even though the paths to reach it are many and often changing.

"Sureśvara explains that if the Self identifies itself with this Supreme cognitive consciousness, i.e., the stage of Kūṭastha, it is the essence of realization and then it attains salvation automatically."[8] According to Advaita in general and Sureśvara himself, in a sense all knowledge that is valid is really a co-participation in the knowledge that God has. This doctrine, although not very popular today even among Neo-Scholastics (not to mention Whiteheadians, who have not developed enough the notion of the Primordial as distinct from the Consequent nature of God) is not unique to the Vedānta. It also can be found in many who have continued in the Augustinian tradition, and one might find something not completely foreign in such as Li Ao when enlarging on Mencius' version of the relation between microcosm and macrocosm.

The Advaita doctrine of the ultimate identity (or reduction to identity) of knower, known and knowledge was denied by other schools of Indian philosophy even during Sureśvara's own epoch to some extent and vehemently denounced by others later on. It must be remembered that instead of a logic of equations linking subjects and objects, Advaita uses a rigorously reductionist logistic—an implosion, as it were, rather than an explosion, a sort of 'black hole' philosophy rather than a spiritual nebula in full blossom. Sinha writes of Sureśvara's views on that 'reductionist' equation :

> Sureśvara avers that the knower (pramātṛ),the means of knowledge (pramāṇa) and the object of knowledge (prameya) are concerned with external objects alone, and cannot prove the existence of the Inner Self or spirit. Perception and other pramāṇas are directed towards external objects, and so cannot prove the existence of Ātman—Inner Self. It can be proved by the scriptural sentence "That thou art" or the like. It is known as the eternal witness (sākṣin) of all changing mental modes. The eternal Ātman is the presupposition of all cognitions of objects. Ātman is different from all objects of knowledge. It is known from scriptural testimony alone, which destroys nesciene (avidyā), the cause of all evils—the distinction of the knower, knowledge, the means of knowledge and the object of knowledge, as the manifester of the real nature of things. The knowledge of Ātman is not produced after the extinction of avidyā. It depends upon the scripture which points to the existence of Ātman, the supreme Reality, the true knowledge of which destroys avidyā and its products——the knower, the means of knowledge, knowledge, and the object of knowledge. Ātman is self-proved, and cannot be proved. So it must be admitted to be real. It is the presupposition of all proofs, Scriptural testimony merely reveals the nature of the self-existent Ātman. It cannot be perceived even by gods as another object. It is self-existent and self-proved. It is self-luminous. It is the inner light of eternal consciousness. It transcends intellect and its modes, and is eternally free.[9]

Perhaps most interpretations have exaggerated the traditional Vedāntic insistence on the permanent inalienable self (*ātman*) as identifiable with Brahman, as though the *ātman*-Brahman were some ghostly actual existing entity which could be perceived if only one had sufficiently spiritual faculties. Perhaps an approach from linguistics might get us further, as was done by Bhartṛhari and others. What is meant, for example, by *sva-lakṣaṇā*, self-proved, needing no other explanation since it is that by which one explains other things; or *sva-dharma*, one's own *dharma*, irreducible to anything else than just what one ought to do oneself regardless of circumstances or activities. This is perhaps the best approach to what is really intended by *ātman*. It is the irreducible point of reference of identity. As locus of perspective or node of identity it is nothing in itself but rather *that by which* all that is something is identifiable. Thus in that sense *ātman* could not be disproved since it would be the self that is trying to disprove itself.

All this being the case, how then can there be anything else but Supreme Identity ? But there is still the problem of what is *not* That, and that is Ignorance, which to Sureśvara is *māyā*. The basic problem is the locus of individuation and the related problem of how much is encompassed by this *māyā*, and from what 'existence' this 'non-existence' derives its orientation, i.e., in the traditional language, what is its *āśraya*, its abode or its locus. Since negation cannot be just negation of a vacuum, it must be a negation of something. Of what are we ignorant; or, in other words, what is *māyā* the 'negation' of ? The answer to this question (insofar as there can be an answer to questions involving such undefinable indeterminacies) constitutes one of Sureśvara's most distinctive interpretations of Advaita, although others do not agree with him at all.

> Sureśvara proves that Brahman or Ātman is the abode and the object of avidyā. Not-self is insentient by nature. What is devoid of knowledge by nature cannot be related to nescience. Supposing nescience exists in not-self, it cannot produce any excess (atiśaya) in itself. Nor can not-self acquire knowledge, whose negation is nescience, because not-self is produced by nescience. Nor does not-self exist already, and then becomes devoid of knowledge, and then becomes the locus of nescience, because it is devoid of any nature without nescience. So not-self cannot be the object of nescience. Nor is it the

locus of nescience. Being unconscious, it cannot have nescience. So Ātman is the locus of nescience. Ātman is not of the nature of nescience, because Its nature is consciousness. It can have a peculiarity (atiśaya) in the form of lapse of knowledge. It can also acquire knowledge. Ātman is unchanging in nature. It is independent of nescience (ajñāna) and self-existent. Ātman Itself becomes ignorant owing to lapse of knowledge. It becomes ignorant of Itself. It becomes ignorant of Its real nature.[10]

In most treatments of Sureśvara, whether for the simple reason that it was Sureśvara's own omission or whether due to his modern expositors, we do not find the full range of the four classical *Mahāvākyas* but only the first two, namely the *Aham Brahma Asmi* and the *Tat Tvam Asi*. At least in the Rāmānuja tradition, however, one should by no means stop there but go on to the other two, namely *Sarvavijñātman Brahmaḥ* and *Ekam Advaita Brahmaḥ*. This it seems to us is terribly important since the greatest temptation for Advaitins as distinct from the other interpretations of the *Gītā* and the *Brahma Sūtras* is to emphasize the first to the exclusion of the others, and thus in attempting to reach the goal of selflessness absolutely to the *jīvan-mukti* state they risk developing an impenetrable EGO instead of the warm human-hearted humility that the *bhakti* tradition developed. Concerning Sureśvara's treatment of the *Aham Brahma Asmi*, Maximilien writes : "The *Aham* is the most inert and gross (*brut*) of all objects. It is thanks to a reflection in it of the Self, the Ātman, in which is summarized the order of knowledge, that there can be this existence of intermittent knowledge, fragmentary and complex as it is, characterized by subject and object and their relation."[11] Sureśvara would have us realize that the ego acts and makes mistakes by fragmenting what is inherently integral. The ego gets in the way of proper perception, not to mention proper conception. Nevertheless it is not completely devoid of value :

> The I (the Ego) thus enjoys some privilege of being the point of transparence to the Self, whence the aptitude of its notion to indicate the Self. The 'I' can be of service to the Self because it is a misconception of the Self and the Vedāntic

> proposition can be made to provide access to the Self because it (the Self) suppresses our misconception. It abolishes the 'I' and precisely it does so in putting it in proper relation with the object of Brahman. The object of Brahman is also a misconception of the Brahman in so far as it is that which the subject poses outside of itself as distinct from the Self.[12]

The *Taittirīyopaniṣad Bhāṣyavārtikam* is Sureśvara's sub-commentary on Śaṅkara's commentary on the *Taittirīya Upaniśad.* As in the other works the chief theme throughout is that of removing ignorance so that we may "become aware of the identity of our Self with Brahman and this very becoming brings release. These three coincide: the way to knowledge—Brahman-Self-identity—and release ..."[13] The method is that of *anvayavyatireka,* which is the dialectic of knowing the ultimate identity by becoming aware of distinctions from the 'lower' point of view. As for the famous *Tat Tvam Asi,* Van Boetzelaer writes :

> This is not an empirical knowledge, but a mystical intuition through which one is released. As to the locus of ignorance, which ignorance itself is the cause of non-Self, Sureśvara holds the view that this is the Self, whereas Maṇḍana Miśra on the other hand thinks the *jīva* to be the locus of ignorance.[14]

Van Boetzelaer claims that at least in this commentary Sureśvara does not differ in basics from Śaṅkara, although he does give some "radicalization" of Śaṅkara's constant insistence on the identity of *jīv-ātman-Brahman* through *jñāna.*

Of course Sureśvara deals with the age-old problem of the relation of body to soul and self, including the distinction, so all-important in almost all Indian systems, between the gross (*sthūla*) and the subtle (*sūkṣma*) bodies. Sureśvara writes : "(The Self) has (no more) originated along with the origination of the body than space (has originated) through the production of a pot. Hence 'to be' etc. do not exist (properly speaking) for they (would only exist) if there (really) were production."[15] The sub-commentary explanation makes a distinction of six modes of "to be" : production, existence, growth, maturity, decay and death—for which there are innumerable parallels in the Aristotelian, the Augustinian and the Byzantine Neo-Platonic traditions. Considering the confusion of body and self, Sureśvara writes :

> So if the body is burnt, the fool thinks "Iam burnt"; (thinking) "I am black" he identifies with the blackness of his body.... ...Through the erroneous identification with the possession of cows, etc. (one thinks) on account of Ignorance : "I possess this". As a consequence of attachment one identifies himself (erroneously) with the consecrations of the body and the subtle self, (thinking) "I am a chaste student, a householder, an ascetic or a hermit".[16]

Indeed even attachment to the subtle body can be a snare. This may be taken as a warning to those first getting involved in esoterics since there may be considerable confusion between the *jīvātman* and the *sūkṣma śarīra.* The remedy is not non-identification with anything but, as ever in all varieties of Advaita, identification with Brahman, the right application of the *Aham Brahma Asmi.*

A pivotally important contribution from the *Taittirīya Upaniṣad* which all Vedāntins virtually take for granted—and which could and perhaps should become a basis for those modern psychologists who are interested in more than the behavioristic sensor-motor arc and such—is the five 'sheaths' or *koṣas.* These are in ascending order or in order of interiority, *annamaya koṣa, prāṇamaya koṣa, manomaya koṣa, vijñānamaya koṣa,* and *ānandamaya koṣa,* or respectively, the level of food, the level of breath or breath control (the sheath of 'vitality'), the level of (discursive) mind, the level of subconscious mergence of mind and will, and the level of serenity or bliss. In the *Brahma Sūtra Bhāṣya* as well as in his commentary on the *Taittirīya Upaniṣad* Śaṅkara tends to neglect the lower *koṣas* and comments at great length on the controversy whether the *ānandamaya koṣa* itself is equatable with *nirguṇa*-Brahman. Sureśvara does not disagree with his guru but rather enlarges on the text in considerable detail. The final conclusion to Sureśvara's opinion is given by Balasubramanian as follows :

> Ānanda is free from specifications and distinctive forms. It is nirviśeṣa. And so it is identical with the Highest Brahman.

> But the ānandamaya...is described as a differentiated entity with joy, enjoyment, and the like, as its limbs. So it cannot be the Supreme Brahman.[17]

There is somewhat of a logical discrepancy here if one takes strictly and literally the basic assertion of Advaita monism that *all* is identifiable if not already identical with the *nirguṇa*-Brahman. But this seems to be Sureśvara's chief contribution, allowing a more dynamic dialectic between the manner of keeping that basic ultimate realization and the distinctions at the 'lower' levels which 'appear' to be different. Thus he acknowledges that all of the *koṣas* are merely psychological and belong to the individual *sādhaka* and not directly to the Brahman.

A very advanced yoga is presupposed here which may require long and arduous years of practice, and the penetration of these *koṣas* is a good guide. In most expositions dealing with the *koṣas* and the other yogas that are presupposed in these Vedāntic texts, there is mention of a sort of "breaking through the knots of the heart" so that the *suṣumṇā* is opened and both lobes of the brain are brought into full operation. But these things are not easily available without an accomplished guru. Unfortunately such gurus are very rare even in India since there the authentic tradition has been watered down and often alienated by confusion between secularization, Westernization, and modernization. Thus it is even more important now than it was for Sureśvara's generation—which evidently had experienced some degree of decadence thanks to corruption by the wrong kind of Tāntric practice, and as a result of increasing inroads by the Muslim raids of destruction—to reinvestigate these classics, not just as "divine revelation" in the literalistic sense, but as the fruits of centuries of experience and training. Incidentally, there should be a correlation between the *koṣas* and the *chakras* (psychic centers), which remain far too dormant in most humans but can be brought under conscious control in proper yogic discipline. And these in turn could perhaps be correlated with the centers known to the Chinese in their practice of acupuncture. No doubt there is an entirely new science to be developed interculturally here alongside modern medical technology in terms of non-introspective neurology.

All commentators on the *Brahma Sūtras* take *mokṣa* as very important; but the different interpretations of those *Sūtras* vary rather widely, from the strictest Advaita assertion that nothing is really gained by *mokṣa* but rather that it is at best merely the sloughing off of all karma, bad and good, to the interpretation by Rāmānuja that the *jīvan-mukti* is not the ideal and that *mokṣa* is not self-merited by effort but a free gift of God's grace, to Mādhava's insistence on the radical difference between the *mukta* and Brahman and the *mukta* and one who has not reached that far. Sureśvara does affirm the *jīvan-mukti* concept, though according to some critics his view is excessively 'gnostic'. Sinha writes :

> So works cannot generate emancipation; they produce desires alone. They can never bring on liberation. The Śruti inculcates renunciation of actions and acquisition of the right knowledge of Ātman as the only means to release. So whole-hearted performance of specific duties in all orders of life does not lead to liberation, but knowledge alone achieves the supreme end. It is suprarational intuition of Ātman.[18]

Such a position is certainly a challenge to ritualism at least. Sureśvara writes : "Because every kind of activity, secular or sacred, is (performed) here with an end, therefore just (that end) gives rise to the activity."[19] This leads to the requirement of desireless action (*niṣkāma karma*) according to non-Advaitin texts and the Gandhian ideal, but with Sureśvara the *ātman*-Brahman realization implies deliverance from all kinds of activity—a 'quietist' monism in the extreme indeed ! Sureśvara writes :

> Because the one who knows Brahman attains the objects of all his desires, which are the causes of activity, therefore the knower of Brahman is not active, for there is no reason (to be active).... Desires are caused by ignorance, activity is caused by desire, merit and demerit have their cause therein (i.e., in activity), from that (originates) the body, the seat of evil.[20]

In the modern world this would seem rather exaggerated since *avidyā* is taken to include all the computerized sciences including mankind's entry into the space age. It might be argued that it would be better to spend one's energies in that direction instead of digging back into these "medieval obscurantisms". The reply to that *pūrvapakṣa* should be rather obvious : Certainly meditation of any sort is not a substitute for realistic application of *ko wu*, extension of knowledge, by any and all means available. Nevertheless is it not more painfully vivid now than perhaps in any previous period in world history that no matter how much we learn there is always that Infinite Residuum of Radical Ignorance for mankind. If there is any one distinctive feature of the twentieth century "knowledge explosion" it is the realization that all we have learned is only a reminder of how ignorant we really are since every new discovery seems only to open another infinity of unknowns. May it not be argued that whether or not S. Radhakrishnan, U Thant or Gandhi had reached the *jīvan-mukta* stage, we certainly need such persons more desperately than any one other thing. As a matter of fact this removal of avidyā probably should be interpreted today not in terms of infinite knowledge of finite particulars but as the spiritual wisdom of knowing where to direct one's efforts such that mankind as a whole, or at least creative minorities who are struggling for a renewal of *Dharma*, can be benefited.

Balasubramanian gives this estimate of Sureśvara :

> Being a direct disciple of Śaṅkara, Sureśvara has thoroughly imbibed the spirit of his master. As the author of the *Vārtika*, he has played the distinguished role of an accredited spokesman of Śaṅkara. His role was more than that of a commentator of Śaṅkara. By his massive writings which touch every aspect of Advaita, he has enriched the literature of Advaita. He is an inexhaustible fount of inspiration and ideas for later Advaitins who have drawn heavily from him. His authority has been invoked by Vimuktātman, Sarvajñātman, Prakāśātman, Vidyāraṇya, Ānandabodha, Citsukha, Madhusudanasarasvatī, Brahmānandasarasvatī, and Appayyadīkṣita in support of some view or other. Just as the important features of the Bhāmatī school can be traced to the *Brahmasiddhi*, so also the important features of the Vivaraṇa school can be traced to the writings of Sureśvara.[21]

Sureśvara's spirit of reconciliation may be seen in his statement that "Whatever be the mode of explanation through which people attain the firm knowledge of the inward Self must be treated as valid. But it is (in itself) not valid." Balasubramanian comments :

> One may, for example, adopt the limitation theory (*avaccheda-vāda*) or the reflection theory (*pratibimbavāda*) or the semblance theory (*ābhāsa-vāda*) in order to bring out the non-difference between Brahman and the *jīva*... But all these different modes of explanation, which converge on the same point, are equally valid, though none of them can claim any privileged position over the others. Keeping in view the final perspective, we have to explain the differences between the Bhāmatī school and the Vivaraṇa school, or between any two Advaitins. Sureśvara wants us to understand that Advaita, far from being a house divided against itself, is the Rock of Ages.[22]

But is this *historically* true? Or once again are we up against the paradox that, as with Zen and most other monisms, the claim to rise above history is difficult to vindicate since all varieties of philosophical systems do have a history. A corollary to that observation is the rather safe generalization that once a new seminal system emerges it will inevitably foster many sub-systems by virtue, not of its inadequacy, but because of its historical fertility. Nevertheless such fertility should not serve as a pretext for uncritical syncretism—or is Advaita by its very nature inevitably syncretistic? In Sureśvara's case not so much so, though this may be somewhat true of Vācaspati Miśra.

We wonder what Sureśvara would have said to the Muslim scientists who had incorporated all of Aristotelian and Hellenistic science and Indian mathematics and astronomy as well. Could that have made any difference? Probably not. For as a very high-caste Brāhmin Sureśvara's education would have included mathematics and at least enough astronomy to enable him to cast astrological horoscopes as well as the basics if not more of Āyurvedic medicine. But as an Advaitin, in contrast to his Nyāya-Vaiśeṣika contemporaries, these were not considered as philosophy and not of ultimate value; therefore, for the sake of the "inquiry into Brahman", they should be left behind like everything else that pertains to this world. The same applies to political philosophy. That discipline was not neglected in South India, and indications are that the works compare favorably with Byzatine, Islamic and Neo-Confucianist works of the period. But they are not generally included in what is usually taken to be Indian philosophy, no doubt due to the dominating influence of modern Advaitins, who likewise have little sense of history and consider such matters the responsibility of other castes.

To say the least, in Sureśvara we find very astute dialectical logic and not mysticism in the popular sense that still is ascribed to 'Oriental religions' or 'Wisdom of the East' and such like. In fact Sureśvara's work presupposes many centuries of refinement in the logic of the varieties and degrees and loci of negation, from which perhaps even the best of experts anywhere today might have something yet to learn.

8. Saichō

Although Saichō (767-822) is the real founder-organizer-transmitter of the authentic historical Tendai sect in Japan, by tradition Prince Shōtoku is often given the honor of having been the first promulgator of this heritage, which comes down through Chih Taolin and Chih-i in China. Dōsen (Tao-hsüan) arrived in Japan in 736, and his disciple Gyōhō (722-797) became the master of Saichō. Dōsen brought some of the writings of Chih-i with him; he had also had some connections with Ch' an Buddhism in China, though his primary affiliation was with the Vinaya/Ritsu heritage. Essentially the same can be said of Ganjin and Gyōga (729-803), the latter having gone to China with the express purpose of studying Fa-hasiang (Hossō); but during his seven years in China he had studied T'ien T'ai also. Thus the foundation work of Tendai in Japan had already been done in the Nara period so that Saichō was free to build soundly and completely in the Heian period.

Saichō obtained permission to promote his interpretation of the Buddha's teaching from the emperor in 805. Saichō's intention was to effect a virtual revolution as great as any since the establishment of Buddhism in India. He also had travelled to China to gain contact with the authentic tradition, but seems to have inaugurated a way that was somewhat his own interpretation, enforcing strict discipline in the community, which included a continuous study of the *Lotus Sūtra.* Other Tendai leaders were Ennin (794-864), whose diary has fortunately been translated, and Enchin (814-891), who also had travelled in China.

Saichō was born in 767 of the Mitsuobi family, who may originally have been immigrants from China. His father was such a devout Buddhist that he had virtually converted the whole house into a Buddhist temple. Hence it was only natural that Saichō himself entered a monastery at the age of twelve for training. Soon after taking his full vows he made a retreat in a small hermitage on Mt. Hiei where evidently he came into full realization of his true vocation. There is some speculation as to initial motives, since it was a time of political instability, and the confusion for a youth concerning all the rival claims of the Six Sects of Nara Buddhism may have led him to go in search for spiritual foundations. At the end of this retreat he founded the Hieizanji temple and himself carved an image of Yakushi, the healing Buddha, as the central image. He found what he was searching for in the Tendai tradition, which seemed more warm-hearted and less theologically controversial than bickerings of the Six Sects, which up to that time were all rather limited to the decadent aristocracy.[1] It was the T'ien T'ai of Chih-i (538-597) that attracted Saichō the most. It might be well to recall that even by the time of Chih-i there had already been a lot of syncretistic mixtures between Ch'an, the Pure Land, and T'ien T'ai, especially in regard to the Bodhisattvas they revverenced and their respective theories of the hereafter.

A Naigubusō (Imperial Court priest) who made a pilgrimage to the mountain to visit the hermits there prevailed upon Saichō to become himself one of the ten court Naigubusō in 797. It was this connection that eventually led to Saichō gaining not only permission but a commission by the Emperor himself to go to China after more authentic Tendai sources and to receive authentic training in that practice. Indeed, Saichō did not go alone, for Kūkai was on board the same ship. While Kūkai went directly to the capital, Ch'ang-an, Saichō with different interests went directly to the place most famous for the tradition in which he wished to receive training, namely Mt. T'ien T'ai. The T'ien T'ai sect had undergone a revival under Chan-jan (711-782), the sixth patriarch of the school. Saichō received instruction from two of his leading disciples, Tao-sui and Hsing-man, as well as training in meditation from Hsiu-jan. After nine and a half months in China, Saichō returned to Japan loaded down with 450 volumes and 230 sections of Buddhist scriptures.

Many interpreters put stress on some of the differences between the 'purer' Chinese version of T'ien T'ai and Saichō's own Japanese adaptations, which were partly due to his own genius and partly due to his being influenced even before going to China by Ganjin and his disciples who belonged to the Ritsu sect, which was primarily devoted to stricter observance of the *vinaya* rules of monastic life. But he had also come into Zen meditation somewhat, and had adopted the Pure Land *nembutsu* practice of rhythmic repetition of the Holy Name of Amida. And like virtually all the other Japanese sects since the time of Shōtoku, Heian Tendai as established and regularized by Saichō took on a nationalistic flavor. In this regard Saichō might well be compared to Nichiren.

> Another distinct difference between Saichō's version of Tendai and its Chinese parent was in the realm of nationalism. Chinese T'ien Ta'i tended to be universalist and quite apolitical in nature, but in Japan in keeping with the Nara heritage, the Tendai sect played an important role devoted to the protection of the nation...In his *Kenkairon* (Treatise on Mahāyāna *śīla*), Saichō repeatedly wrote, 'for the sake of the nation chant the sutra, for the sake of the nation, lecture and expound the sutra.' He was also the first to use the stirring nationalistic phrase '*Dainipponkoku*' (Great Country of Japan). The ideal was to preserve and protect the nation and make it into a Buddhaland.[2]

movement, but Saichō, somewhat in keeping with the later trend that dominated Hōnen and Shinran, but less so than Kūkai, allowed more participation of the laity in his reforms. However he required a vow from his novices to the effect that they would not leave Mt. Hiei for twelve years, after which they could go down and risk corruption by the laity. The question remains as to whether Saichō achieved a systematic synthesis or whether his was another syncretistic mixture characteristic of the age.

The T'ien T'ai in China had already undergone some syncretistic mixture with the Hua-yen tradition, thus becoming extremely metaphysical and mystical rather than zealous about social and ethical much less political affairs. But such influences had become common, and Chih-i had tried to elucidate the confusions ; and again, it was Chih-i's writings that influenced Saichō perhaps more than any other. Saichō conceived of his work in a spirit of reform, "fighting the corruption of the Nara Sects and for revolutionary establishment of a Mahāyāna *kaidan*". Japan had by this time finally "received the Buddhist scriptures in practically complete form. They had an overall view of the philosophical development and could afford to be eclectic both in doctrines and attitudes."[3]

One of the chief differences between Kūkai and Saichō may be that Kūkai had too many connections with the previous Nara aristocracy, who welcomed his extremely esoteric ways which carried less challenge for moral reform, whereas Saichō was more in line with the new aristocracy which was attempting a fresh start at Kyōtō. Esoteric traditions seem to flourish greatest in times of affluent decadence as an escape from social, economic and political reform and moral discipline. But also perhaps esotericism flourishes when a low level of spirituality renders people incapable of understanding anything else. In Saichō's day the popularity of esoterics across the water in China was due to patronage from the declining phase of the T'ang Dynasty, soon to be purged by the fresh cycle of Neo-Confucianism. Although Saichō considered the esoteric tradition as only a subordinate discipline for training his novices, Kūkai earnestly, zealously, almost fanatically, believed that it was the highest crown of all philosophical and religious endeavors.

Saichō wrote the *Shōgun jitsukyō* (*Mirrored Reflection of the Provisional and True*) in 817. This was a systematic attempt at establishing the basic unity of all Buddhist teachings —the famous Ekayâna, One Vehicle, reconciling and combining Mahāyāna and Hīnayāna. Through such efforts Saichō established Tendai as independent and comprehensively the most authoritative interpretation of Buddhism in Japan—or at least so it may be claimed, to the great chagrin of Kūkai. By contrast to the genocides that had been committed in suppressing 'heresies' by the Roman and Byzantine 'Christian' churches (not to mention similar things in ninth century Islam), the jealousies between the various Japanese varieties of Buddhism were only polite games. Later there was some violence on Mt. Hiei, but that was between the monks and the government at Kyōtō, not a *jihād* to exterminate those one disagreed with.

Saichō attempted to establish the Tendai as independent of government sanction, much less control, thereby impliciting putting the Nara sects out of business, as it wẹre, since they all had intimate connection with Imperial patronage and authorization. This entailed a veritable purge of his *saṅgha*, somewhat comparable to what Hsüan-tsang had done in China when he returned from India. Saichō thus made departure from Mt. Hiei easy for all those who were not utterly sincere about their specifically religious vocation apart from all éclat and prestige connected with government or other worldly ambition. Nevertheless, government sanction for Saichō's independence from government was necessary, and this was not gained until after his death. In attempting to gain this sanction there had been an erudite debate between Saichō and a priest named Keijin who had listed twenty-eight 'errors' committed by Saichō. Thus Saichō's masterpiece of writing, the *Kenkairon*, answering all the charges against him.

The primary text for the Tendai was the *Lotus Sūtra*, which traditionally (and perhaps actually) Kumārajīva had translated into Chinese alongside the Mādhyamika texts. Its primacy within the T'ien T'ai early became the chief feature of that Chinese variety of Mahāyāna. According to Saichō's interpretation (and Chih-i's before him) the most central teaching in the *Lotus*

tion of the historic Śākyamuni Buddha, not necessarily with the *Nirmāṇakāya* (as with Mahāyāna generally), but with the *Dharmakāya* itself, the cosmic, supernatural, theistic Buddha, the Tathatā. However, the esoteric influence became historically very storng among Saichō's followers, almost driving out the influence of the *Lotus Sūtra*.

In considering the teachings of the Tendai under Saichō, Nakamura gives the following quintessential summary :

> The most remarkable characteristic af Tendai is its comprehensive and encyclopaedic character. It finds a place for all scriptures, regarding them as a progressive revelation, gradually disclosed by the Buddha during his life, as he found that the intelligence of his listeners ripened.
>
> According to our common sense, it seems that parts depend on one another and all depend on the whole. But the so-called complete or perfect teaching (*En-gyō*) of this sect goes beyond this. It seems that the whole and the parts are identical. The Whole Cosmos and all the Buddhas are present in a grain of sand or on the point of hair. A celebrated maxim says ; One thought is the three thousand spheres (that is, the whole universe) and the three thousand spheres are but one thought. That is to say, the relations involved in the simplest thought are so numerous that they imply the existence of the whole universe, our perceptions and thoughts being identical with absolute reality. This leads to the doctrine of ontology. There are three forms of existence : the void, the temporary, and the middle. That is, all things which exist depend on their relations. If we try to isolate them and to conceive of them as entering into no relations, they become unthinkable and in fact non-existent.
>
> But as temporary formative parts of the whole they do exist and the whole could not realize its true nature if it did not manifest itself in particulars. So in that sense all things exist as phenomenal beings. Things exist or do not exist according to our view of their relations to it, but the middle exists absolutely. Phenomena and the one absolute truth are, if rightly regarded, synonymous. When the significance of each of the

three is properly cognized, this is the enlightenment as obtained by the Buddha himself.[4]

Typical of Saichō's effort towards catholicity or comprehensiveness rather than a sectarian bias is the fact that he encouraged veneration of virtually all the Bodhisattvas, according to the needs of each *sādhaka*. Emphasis, however, fell on the following four, with Amida for the most part taking first place : Amida (Amitābha), Monju (Mañjuśrī), Fugen (Sāmantabhadra), Kannon (Avalokiteśvara).

Although Kükai was also influenced by Chih-i, it was Saichō who carried on the master's work of studying the pattern of periodization of the multifold accumulation of sūtras. Saichō shared Chih-i's life work of ascertaining the historical arrangement of the sūtras, a field in which Kūkai showed little interest. However, Saichō's amalgam of the sūtras almost exactly reduplicates that of Chih-i.

Saichō was the first person in Japanese history to be granted the posthumous title of Daishi (Great Master). It was conferred by his admirer the Emperor Seiwa. Thus even today all over Japan Saichō is reverenced and known as Dengyō Daishi. Saichō's status was such that he received a place in the 'apostolic succession'. Virtually all Japanese varieties of Buddhism trace their ancestry back to Nāgārjuna, who by this time had become a sort of mythological figure, a Boddhisattva indeed, much as the Christian saints had become objects of veneration rather than of historical verification. After Nāgārjuna, according to the schematic arrangement of Saichō, the order goes as follows :

Sūryasoma Kumārajīva	(transmitters and translators of Nāgārjuna's writings and the *Lotus Sūtra*)	
Hui-wen	(550-?)	technically the first Chinese founder
Hui-ssu	(514-77)	
Chih-i	(538-97)	popularly considered the founder and first patriarch since he was responsible for systematizing the doctrine of the sect.

Kuan-ting	(561-632)	who compiled the three great works of Chih-i and is considered the second Chinese patriarch
Chih-wei	(?-680)	third patriarch (Dark Ages
Hui-wei	(634-713)	fourth Patriarch of T'ien T'ai)
Hsüan-lang	(633-754)	fifth patriarch
Chan-jan	(711-82)	sixth patriarch and reviver of the school
Tao-sui	(dates unknown)	seventh patriarch and Saichō's master
Saichō	(767-822)[5]	

Saichō established a monastic institute on Mt. Hiei which was at first a very humble and unassuming place, but which later grew into a "priestly city of some 3,000 temples". Ennin, who became a disciple of Saichō at the age of fifteen, was one of his most trusted followers. It may have been at Saichō's behest that Ennin attempted a pilgrimage to Mt. T'ien T'ai, perhaps with the intention of restoring the denizens of Mt. Hiei to a greater purity of Tendai discipline. But the cult had waned in China, and the more esoteric types of Buddhism were what Ennin encountered and brought back to Japan. Ennin was a rival to Enchin (814-889), who is associated with the growth on Saichō's Mt. Hiei of influence from Kūkai's Mt. Koya. This rivalry had already led to a schism within the Tendai, and animosity ran so high that the emperor had to intervene. But the schism was never healed with the result that Ennin's following remained on Mt. Hiei and the rival faction under Enshu migrated to another place. Saichō's Tendai came to have more influence in Japan's history than Kūkai's Shingon, although both sects (we might say both Mountains) went through all the temptations and near-corruptions that similar monastic institutions in world history have undergone in their second and third generations. As for Saichō's system itself, it was "sufficient to offer a theological challenge as well as ample room for development by future scholars. Such eclectic freedom in conjunction with the stimulating intellectual atmosphere of Mt. Hiei, allowed the Tendai sect to become the mother of Kamakura Buddhism. Eisai, Hōnen, Shinran, Dōgen and Nichiren all were scholars on the mountain before initiating their own schools of Buddhist thought."[6]

Philosophy as an exclusively analytical, strictly logical matter is found in Saichō's contemporaries among the Nyāya-Vaiśeṣikas and the Byzantine and Islamic Aristotelians. But historically these were definitely in the minority in the ninth century all over Eurasia. If one takes a philosophy of values as equal if not primary to the analytico-logical scientific enterprise, then there may be much to learn from Saichō and his contemporaries, virtually all of whom had one sort of monism or other as their basic metaphysical position. In dialectics Saichō could hardly have competed with Śaṅkara or his Kaśmir contemporaries—at least those who had not 'gone under' in infatuation with Tantra. Evidently the expertise in dialectics that had developed in India in the preceding centuries had not come to Japan through the Chinese filter. Saichō emphasized ethical disciplines in addition to thoroughness in the contemplative method probably more than any of his Japanese Buddhist contemporaries; and by comparison in the larger Eurasian perspective with such as al-Ḥallāj, for example, he was very moderate and well-balanced indeed. Given his basic temperament and intentions, if he had had access to the Nyāya-Vaiśeṣika or even the Jaina texts, no doubt he would have incorporated them into his comprehensive Ekayāna.

9. Han Yü and Li Ao

Although during the T'ang Dynasty (618-907) poets generally fared better than prose writers Han Yü is more remembered for his excellent prose style; indeed, both Han Yü (768-824) and Li Ao (d. 844) are probably more important historically as stylists and *littérateurs* than as philosophers. They are universally discussed together, some authorities claiming that Li Ao was initially a disciple of Han Yü. They are initiators of a neo-orthodoxy, a post-Buddhist return to the Confucian classics in China, parallel with the post-Buddhist return to the Hindu classics in India and with a return to the Greek sources in Europe (Aristotle in the thirteenth century and Plato in the fifteenth). Although Han Yü and Li Ao were the first of a wave of opponents of Buddhism during the T'ang and later dynasties, we must be on the alert against the exaggerated stereotype that after the rise of Neo-Confucianism Buddhism ceased to play a significant role in China. This was by no means the case, even though some textbooks inadvertently give that impression. Although Neo-Confucians consistently rejected Buddhist popular religion with its dazzling pantheon of Buddhas and Bodhisattvas as well as Buddhist monasticism with its rejection of familial and societal obligations, they nevertheless continued to be profoundly influenced by Buddhist philosophy.

Nor was influence between Buddhism and Neo-Confucianism a oneway road. The reverse current was also running very openly and uninterruptedly. For example, during the Northern Sung Dynasty the Buddhist monk Chih-yüan (976-1022) was so much influenced by Confucianism that he took the title *Chung-tzu* (Master of the *Doctrine of the Mean*). The monk Ch'i-sung (1007-72) even wrote a commentary on the *Doctrine of the Mean*, a work which along with the *Analects*, the *Great Learning* and the *Mencius* was designated by Neo-Confucians as the equivalent of sacred scripture for the Confucian tradition. Of course we must remember that after the fourth century any Buddhist who came from Confucian family would have been exposed to the Confucian classics, or at least their essential ideas, almost from the day of his or her birth—for this applies to Buddhist nuns also, Buddhism thereby giving more opportunity for ladies of intellect to have a less subordinate role in society. Moreover, if one was to secure a government. job, the Civil Service examinations were a *sine qua non* ; and these were on the Confucian, not the Buddhist, classics. Thus Confucians might peruse the Buddhist classics and / or visit a Buddhist monastery out of curiosity; but Buddhists, unless they came from the lower classes and unless their families had been devout Buddhists for many generations, were required to know the Confucian classics.

In 819 A.D. the Emperor Hsien-tsung, who was a fervent and

Buddhism by arranging for the exhibition of a finger-bone of the Buddha in the Imperial Palace as well as at various temples around the land. Such a cult of relics continues to have parallels all over the world. Students of Buddhist philosophy tend to forget that much popular Buddhism has very little to do with the Four Noble Truths, the Eightfold Noble Path, or the *pāramitās.* Han Yü was disgusted with such antics and submitted his famous Memorial, which contains what were to become the standard criticisms of the Buddhist religion by Neo-Confucians : (1) since the Buddha was a barbarian, he could not have taught anything of much value (2) the sage-kings managed quite well with no knowledge of Buddhist teachings; (3) there has been much disorder within the empire since the arrival of Buddhism; (4) the Buddha taught the neglect of familial and societal obligations. Thus, "If he were living now and came to your Court, Your Majesty might accord him one audience in the Hsuan-cheng Hall, invite him to a banquet at the Li Pin Office, bestow gifts upon him, and escort him to the frontiers of the empire, without permitting him to have any contact with the people."[1]

Some of these criticisms are obviously a manifestation of the profound ethnocentrism that characterized China's response to outsiders for millenia. However, the criticism of Buddhist monasticism is a reaction to what Confucians viewed as a profound threat offered by Buddhism. For monasticism struck at the heart of the entire Confucian tradition with its this-worldly emphasis upon obtaining good government. However, in spite of these general criticisms, one finds admiration for individual Buddhists in the writings of Han Yü. In particular, he (and succeeding Neo-Confucians) was impressed by their philosophical abilities and the state of mind which they had achieved through their meditative discipline—unattached to material goods, indifferent to worldly affairs, and unafraid of death.

The Buddhist Emperor, not liking Han Yü's Memorial at all banished him to South China. But there the Buddhist and Confucian accounts of what transpired are not consistent. The Buddhist claim is that in the South Han Yü came under the influence of a famous Buddhist monk by the name of Ta-tien, who taught him more by silence than by words, with the result that Han Yü, moved by a quotation from the *Mahāparinir-*

vāṇa Sūtra, became suddenly enlightened, or at least attained the realization of the truth of Impermanence. Be that as it may, later on Han Yü did return to court to serve in a position of higher honor under the next emperor, Wu-tsung.

As it turned out, the Confucian disgust with Buddhism so effectively given voice by Han Yü eventually resulted in a persecution of Chinese Buddhists by the Emperor Wu-tsung (845) sufficiently effective that according to some sources it was necessary to import Buddhist monks from Korea to restore the *Dharma.* This is of critical importance since it shows how historically effective philosophers can be—sometimes even more so than they originally intended. Perhaps Han Yü would have viewed the emperor's reaction as an overreaction. Certainly his Mencian *Dharma* would never have sanctioned all that transpired. Surely he would have preferred a heavy program of rectification by re-education rather than all the violence that actually ensued.

Making Mencius the primary focus is perhaps Han Yü's most important contribution to the emerging Neo-Confucian tradition. This is not to say that Hsün Tzu was completely rejected, for Han Yü also emphasized the *Great Learning,* a product of Hsün Tzu's school, and sought to reconcile Mencius and Hsün Tzu as both being true Confucians. Thus it was not Hsün Tzu's pessimism about human nature so much as his method of self-rectification that was adopted by the Neo-Confucian tradition. It was viewed as an activist alternative to Buddhist contemplation. The goal was essentially the same—serenity. Although Neo-Confucians borrowed much from Buddhist meditative practices, for them the state of mind thus attained must be properly utilized. This could certainly not be done by withdrawing from the world into a monastery. Rather, the Confucian *arhant* must continue to be active within the world, even while psychically transcending it. Such attempts to "domesticate" Buddhism is a hallmark of Neo-Confucianism. Also, Han Yü stresses the direct line of transmission of Confucian wisdom from the sage-kings of remote antiquity through Confucius and Mencius right down to his own revitalization of the Confucian *Dharma,* this evidently in rivalry to the claims of apostolic succession or direct transmission from patriarch to patriarch (and ultimately from the Buddha) so imporant to Chinese and Japanese Buddhists.

In his essay entitled *Inquiry into Tao* Han Yü presents a traditional synopsis of classical Confucianism. He actually devotes as much of the essay to criticism of the rivals to Confucianism as he does to an exposition of his own views. In the critical portions most of his attention is directed towards Taoism, while the critical references to Buddhism are quite brief and seem to be included almost as a formality. Han Yü writes :

> Lao Tzu belittled humanity and righteousness not because he destroyed them but because his viewpoint was small. If a man sits at the bottom of a well, looks up at the sky, and says, "The sky is small," it does not mean that the sky is really small. Lao Tzu considered little acts (of kindness) as humanity and isolated deeds (of good) as righteousness. It is no wonder that he belittled them. What he called the Way was only the Way as he understood it and not what I call the Way. What he called virtue was only the virtue as he understood it and not what I call virtue. What I call the Way and virtue always involve both humanity and righteousness, which is the opinion shared by the whole world. What Lao Tzu called the Way and virtue was devoid of humanity and righteousness, which was the private opinion of one man.[2]

Han Yü's stressing of *Te* alongside of Tao is perhaps significant also since this can be taken as a punctuation in his realistic 'grammar of interpretation' over against the trend toward esoteric and syncretistic pseudo-mysticism into which most of Chinese Buddhism had degenerated since Hsüan-tsang's unsuccessful efforts to instill a logically disciplined metaphysics into various sectarianisms that had emerged, largely out of asssociation with esoteric Taoism.

The philosophy of human nature has been the *chef d'oeuvre* of Chinese philosophizing. Even in the classical Axial Age all the possibilities had been proposed. Han Yü tries to reconcile them all by his notion of "grades" which he presents in his essay *Yüan Hsing* (*An Inquiry on Human Nature*) :

> The nature of man comes into existence with birth, whereas

> things. There are three grades of human nature, and what constitute that nature are five. There are three grades of feelings, and what constitute feelings are seven. What are these ? I say : The three grades of nature are; superior, the medium, and the inferior. The superior is good, and good only. The medium may be led to be either superior or inferior. The inferior is evil, and evil only. Human nature consists in five virtues, namely, humanity (*jen*), propriety (*li*) , faithfulness, righteousness (*i*), and wisdom. In the superior grade, one of these five is the ruling factor while the other four also are practiced. In the medium grade, there is more or less of one of the five while the other four are not pure. In the inferior grade, one rebels against one of these and is out of accord with the other four. The relation of nature to feelings depends on its grade.
>
> Similarly, there are three grades of feelings : the superior, the medium, and the inferior, and what constitute the feelings are seven : pleasure, anger, sorrow, fear, love, hate, and desire. In the superior grade, when any of these seven becomes active, it abides by the Mean. In the medium grade, some of the seven are excessive and some are deficient but there is an effort to be in accord with the Mean. In the inferior grade, whether they are excessive or deficient, action is directed by whatever feeling happens to be predominant. The relation between feelings and nature depends on their grade.[3]

This passage highlights what was to become a key disagreement among Neo-Confucians about the most desirable state of mind. In particular, the debate centered upon the moral status of the *ch'ing* (feelings, emotional responses). Those most influenced by Buddhism tended to insist that the state of mind to be attained was one in which emotional response had been eradicated. Those truer to their own tradition insisted that it was one in which all of one's emotional responses were "proper". The ideal was the proper feeling expressed to the proper degree in a given situation.

Han Yü cites from the *Great Learning* the traditional Confucian counsel that one should begin with oneself and then extend one's virtue to one's family, until it is ultimately extended to the whole empire, with implicit condemnation of those who do not follow this pattern of cultivation since each neglect simply reduces the person to the condition of the barbarians.

The basic concepts in Li Ao's major work, the *Fu-hsing Shu* (*The Recovery of the Nature*), are by no means new; but again, that is not the issue. Rather we must observe how he handles them. According to Carsun Chang :

> If one reads (the) ...essays of Li Ao carefully, one may see that all the fundamental concepts of the Neo-Confucianism philosophy of the Sung Dynasty are there—such concepts as *Tao*, Truth, Enlightenment, Emptiness, Calmness, the idea of the sage, watchfulness in time of solitude. They are all there, in Li Ao's essays, although he does not elaborate on them as the Sung philosophers did afterwards.[4]

Li Ao's views on the feelings are problematic. On the one hand, the feelings are evil; and

> That whereby a man may become a sage is his nature (*hsing*). That whereby a man may betray his nature are the feelings (*ch'ing*). Joy, anger, pity, fear, love, hate, and desire; these seven are all the operations of the feelings. When the feelings cause obscurement, the nature is thereby drowned. This is not the fault of the nature, but is because, owing to the ceaseless revolutions and interminglings of these seven, the nature is unable to gain its fulfillment.[5]

Sincerity (*ch'eng*), the state of silent immobility which is devoid of the feelings, is the mental condition of the sage. However, Li Ao also holds that the feelings and the nature cannot exist without one another. This being true, not even the sage could completely eradicate the feelings. He could only hope to minimize them. Thus the saint or the sage is not without the feelings, but he is not blinded by his emotions like the *natur-mensch*.

Li Ao's method recommends "realization of the absence of (discursive) thought in the mind", which is similar to Buddhist methods of meditation. In short, the mystical base is undisguised; and the ultimate goal of sincerity (*ch'eng*) may not be attained without the classical disciplines of control of the senses, desires, and effections, and the conscious purification of the subconscious mind by elimination of all unwanted images in that center where dreams take place. However, Li Ao remains after all a Confucian rather than a Quietist (whether Ch'an or Taoist). For he does not condemn action at all; rather he commends action in accordance with propriety (*li*).

Li Ao, like Confucius and Plato in the Axial Age, recommends music. He writes in his *Fu-hsing Shu* :

The sage knows that all men's natures are good, and that by following them, they (these men) may themselves become sages. Therefore he institutes the rules of propriety (*li*) to keep them under proper restraint, and creates music to keep them in harmony. Rest amidst the harmony of music is the foundation of music. Activity in accordance with propriety is the foundation of the rules of propriety.

Therefore when he (the sage) is in his carriage, he listens to the harmonious sounds of the (carriage) bells, and when walking on foot, he listens to the tones of the pendant jades. He does not abolish the music of the lute unless there be proper reason. In hearing, seeing, speech, and conduct, he acts ever in accordance with propriety. In this way he teaches men to forget indulgence and desire, and to return to the Way (*Tao*) of the nature and of Destiny (*Ming*).

This Way is that of sincerity in its utter perfection. This sincerity, if uninterrupted, leads to 'vacuity' (*hsü*) ; vacuity, if uninterrupted, leads to enlightenment (*ming*); enlightenment, if uninterrupted, leads to an all-embracing illumination of Heaven and Earth. This, and nothing else, is the Way whereby to develop to the utmost one's nature and Destiny. Alas! All men are capable of reaching this state, yet, though no one stops them, they do not do so. Is this not indeed because of delusion?[6]

The Ṣūfīs used music as a major method of achieving their highest spiritual and psychic states, though the ultimate state, according to both heritages, is silence and emptiness. Li Ao said, "When Emptiness remains forever, one is enlightened"; and correspondingly, "right thinking means no thinking and no deliberating". Carsun Chang observes that even though Li Ao is using Confucian language its content is clearly Buddhist.[7]

Li Ao and the other Neo-Confucians were offering an alternative to the Buddhist way of attaining Buddhahood. "In other words, their aim was to induce men to follow a Confucian type of training which would make of them 'Confucian Buddhas.' "[8] The chief factor of difference seems to be in the active dimension of Confucian Buddhahood. Li Ao recommends that instead of fasting and other ascetic practices, even though times of reflection are definitely needed in order to clarify the mind and purify the spirit, the right observance of the classical Confucian virtues in worldly affairs is the key. This typically practical emphasis is illustrated by his reply to the question concerning his own interpretation of the "investigation of things" :

> By things is meant the myriad things, and by *ko* is meant arriving or reaching. When things come before one, his mind clearly sifts them and yet he does not respond to (or is not affected by) them. This is the extension of knowledge. This is the perfecting of knowledge. As knowledge is perfected, the will becomes sincere. As the will is sincere, the mind becomes rectified. As the mind is rectified, the personal life becomes cultivated. As the personal life is cultivated, the family becomes regulated. As the family is regulated, the state will be in order. As the state is in order, the world will be at peace. This is how a person can form a trinity with Heaven and Earth.[9]

In his interpretation of *ko wu* (investigation of things) Li Ao's emphasis is on the unity within which these things have their place. Indeed, he stretches this to an almost mystical microcosm-macrocosm perspective that is remarkably like that of his contemporaries throughout Eurasia : Śaṅkara's Advaita with its complex involvement in *māyāvāda,* Scotus Erigena's Neo-Platonic hierarchy of causation, or Bāyazīd al-Basṭāmī's dissatisfaction with orthodox Islamic transcendental theism.

Some emphasis might be put on Li Ao's *darśan* of the Ch'an monk Yao-shan wei-yen from whom he learned the meditative discipline of the "Sudden Southern" school (in *preparation*, we may well say, for *sudden* enlightenment). However, it was by no means uncommon for Buddhists, Taoists and Confucians to learn from each other; and we scarcely need remind ourselves how much syncretism was prevalent in the late T'ang Dynasty. Li Ao remained definitely a Confucian, and even opposed building Buddhist monasteries and the practice of prayers for the dead. Monasteries were an essential part of classical Buddhism, and still remain so. No *saṅgha* without the *dharma*, but also conversely, no *dharma* without the *saṅgha*. Buddhism was always and still is basically monastic with only secondary discipline for the laity. But prayers for the dead, requiem masses indeed, belong to popular cultic practice and suggest Nestorian or Monophysite Christian influence, having very little to do with Buddhist philosophical teaching. So Li Ao may have been doing Buddhism a service by this restriction.

Even so, the Buddhist records differ considerably from the official Confucian records, the Buddhists making much more out of that *darśan* with Yao-shan wei-yen. Li Ao was also interested in and no doubt influenced by T'ien T'ai as well as Ch'an, since he cultivated an intimate friendship with one Liang Su, the author of *General Principle of Samādhi,* which was an exposition of the T'ien T'ai *dharma.* Carsun Chang takes the position that Li Ao was not opposed to Buddhism but neither was he a convert.[10] Although privately he did use Buddhist methods of meditation, in public life he seems to have followed the classical or typical Confucian sense of duty and of propriety and acceptance of public responsibility without compromise of integrity, rather than the ethics of renunciation.

When one has been deeply involved in the profound obscurities of modern Phenomenology or the extremely technical methods of the latest developments in symbolic logic, and then returns to the classical cultivation of "sincerity" (*ch'eng*) in Li Ao as the key to sagehood, one must wonder whether this is really somewhat trivial. But perhaps we have become so completely engrossed in complexities and technicalities that we seldom ever think of sagehood/wisdom as really important, if indeed we ever think of it at all. Of course in his own time Li Ao was by no means unique in that such concern for virtues was quite universally uppermost all across Eurasia and remained so right down to the impact of the Industrial Revolution and the development of the exploitative colonial system that supports it. Whatever his sources, Confucian, Taoist, or crypto-Buddhist, in syncretistically mixing them all together he expresses this ideal in a pure and simple way, re-emphasizing the *philosophia parennis*.

By this time even in India Buddhism was on the way out as Neo-Hinduism was on the way in. The question of why Buddhism from the ninth century on had so much less influence everywhere remains unanswered, unless it is simply that it had become as a popular religion something quite different than what its original founder had intended. But that in turn raises the more basic question of why traditions tend to follow cycles of initial vitality, flourishing and spread, popularization, decadence and decline, only to be replaced by other similar cycles.

10. Theodore of Studium

Very few have studied Theodore of Studium (d. 826) at all, and those who have studied him have not done so from the standpoint of the history of philosophy but rather from the standpoint of Church history or some other theological or semi-theological point of view. As was the case with his contemporary Photius, Theodore was an ecclesiastic and was also very much involved in politics, for in Byzantium generally and especially in the Iconoclast controversy, political and ecclesiastical matters were difficult to separate. His asceticism, more or less monist and certainly in the Christianized Neo-Platonist heritage, constituted a certain mysticism. No less than Photius, he had the whole of Plato and Aristotle at his disposal and very much more, including the texts of Proclus' commentaries on Plato's dialogues and the literature of the Greek Fathers from Origen down to his own time. As for the basic types of philosophy, Byzantium had virtually all of them just as did the Islamic world, India and China, though it still seems that the monist trend dominated in the ninth century.

Theodore's famous *Catechism* of monastic life should be relevant to those who are experimenting today with varieties of communities dedicated to renunciation and seeking ways to help toward world peace; but it also gives us a vivid basis of comparison with Ṣūfī ways of the same period, for the similarities on the whole seem to outweigh the differences, whether or not they are both rooted in Neo-Platonist tradition and heritage. If we take the Holy Rule of St. Benedict or the Augustinian Rule as our basis of comparison, or for that matter specific *vinaya* rules for the Buddhist *saṅgha*, we might be impressed by Theodore's simplicity since it is highly desirable in any ethical code to reduce complication in application to irreducible basics in theory. Historically his *Catechism* is representative once again of the basic monist trend all across Eurasia in the ninth century. In that perspective Theodore is probably better placed in the heritage of Pseudo-Dionysius and Maximus Confessor to whom he is deeply indebted. The purpose and motive behind this rather definitely ascetic way, as was also the case in Ṣūfism, Mahāyāna and Vedāntic circles, was preparation for and progress towards the experience of mystical union.

Theodore is a figure of the late eighth and early ninth centuries when *vairāgya* was considered a necessary prerequisite for philosophy, hence we should compare Theodore's *Catechism* with some of the opuscula Śaṅkara, the ethical treatises of al-Kindī, such codes as we might find in Kūkai or Saichō, or even with the *pāramitās* of Mahāyāna. Parallel with Theodore, by the way, one of the great achievements of Śaṅkara was the organization of a monastic order within Hinduism pretty much on the model of the Buddhist *saṅgha* although *vairāgya* is only a propaedeutic prerequisite for philosophy for Śaṅkara, he nevertheless *acted* and set an example in spite of his extreme insistence on *jñāna* over *karma*.

As for Theodore's education we are left largely to speculation. Constantinople had great libraries in which the works of classical antiquity were all readily available; and the fact that Photius did make use of these classics leads to the real likelihood that Theodore also had exposure to them. The direct evidence is limited to the citations from Theodore's pious biographer, who states simply that Theodore pursued studies in grammar, dialectic ("which those skilled in it call philosophy"), and rhetoric. Of course "dialectic" was based largely on Aristotle, and we may well infer that the works of John Philopon were his guide to rhetoric since we do know that Photius made full use of Philopon's work in that and other fields. Nevertheless, there are no explicit references in Theodore's extant writings to Plato and Aristotle. But his frequent citations of the Greek Fathers of the Church, such as Basil of Caesarea, are not devoid of realization that these Fathers were not only influenced by the Greek classics but advocated studying them critically and assiduously.

As an aristocrat Theodore would sooner or later expect some position among the officialdom of the Empire, which with its so-called Caesero-papism did not distinguish very sharply between church and state. It is not completely clear as to when Theodore first conceived the intention to try the monastic vocation; but it is known that his revered uncle Plato became disgusted with the vascillations and vanity of political intrigue and left family and fortune to join the monastery in Symboli in Bithynia on the other side of the Hellespont which was famous for its austerity. However, as political fortune swung to the other side Plato did return to Constantinople, although without abandoning his vows. This is not the place to review the character and career of the Empress Irene, who was so much like the Empress Wu of T'ang China; but we must note in passing that as an Athenian she did favor images, and it was for this reason that Theodore's family was again restored to favor. But restoration to imperial favor did not lessen their religious zeal, for the whole family then renounced the world—Thoctista, Theodore's mother, being very strong in her will to renunciation even to the point of breaking up the normal pattern of family life. Actually this act of renunciation on the part of the whole family was facilitated by the fact that the family owed a country estate in that region of Bithynia where other monastic establishments were common. Thus it might be said that their renunciation was somewhat more similar to the Chinese pattern of retiring to the family country estate when the going was not so smooth at the imperial capital. Still, such was universal in Eurasia in the ninth century.

Although in name all Byzantine monasteries were following the Rule of St. Basil, things had become lax, as had become the case among Buddhists in India and in China also to a great extent, not so much by reason of lack of interior discipline as by involvement in politics. Thus Theodore's uncle, although he was obliged to take part in the Second Council of Nicea, broke precedent and set an example for his nephew by refusing to accept higher ecclesiastical office, which would have involved him in political affairs, including involvement in the controversy with the Papacy which eventually led to what has come to be known as the "Photian schism".

Theodore had taken the side of the Iconodules (the "imagists") against the Iconoclasts, and had accepted ordination in 794 only reluctantly, as a matter of holy obedience, his uncle Plato being his abbot and guru; and probably as reluctantly did he accept the abbotship of a monastery, so that uncle and nephew were then joined together as co-abbots of important monastic houses. Then in 799 Theodore became abbot of the famous monastery of Studium which was known for its rule of combining study with ascetic piety, whereas some other monasteries, more like the Zen monasteries of the later T'ang Dynasty, were definitely anti-intellectual. Incidentally, the aging uncle Plato also transferred to Studium along with Theodore. Traditionally it was founded about 454 by one Studius who came from Rome, and it was originally simply a church. But around this foundation there grew a community of monks with the appellation of Acoemeti, which literally means "the sleepless ones"; their practice was to engage in praise of God by shifts so that praise would never cease—a practice still common today in Vārāṇasī and Vṛndāban in India. The community was organized by a certain Alexander, a member of the nobility who had first fled to the desert to escape from the world and avoid being appointed Bishop of Edessa. This establishment was further developed by his successor Marcellus. It was then that this community of monks became associated with Studius, who had enough wealth to become its patron.

Differing from other monastic institutions, this community was not obligated to manual labor but rather devoted its energies to studious research concerning theological issues of the day. When the first breach with the Papacy occurred, it was one of these monks who represented the 'orthodox' position, which at that time was very zealously anti-Monophysite and in full support of the decrees of the Council of Chalcedon. During the intervening centuries this community had been involved in almost all of the then current theological disputes in varying degrees of intensity; but when the Iconoclast controversy flared up it became involved in a major way. Byzantium in these days was terribly entangled in affairs . dealing not only with the Papacy and the successors of Charlesmagne of France, but with the Bulgarians, and with the equally sumptuous if not quite so proud court of Hārun al-Rashid of Baghdad. The Iconoclast controversy became involved in relations with all these external as well as with internal affairs.

With this Iconoclast controversy in mind we suggest that the most important issue at the minimum in any aesthetics may be, To what extent may good art appeal to the senses? But at the maximum one may ask, Can truly spiritual reality be manifested, much less incarnated, in sensible form ? To what extent is that possible ? What canons of spirituality and/or of technique (not to mention *sādhana* on the part of the "incarnating" artist) are necessary; and can he depend only on "inspiration" or does the Holy Spirit also work in and through regularized forms, and if so, what forms ? Not to mention such issues as political censorship and patronage. Perhaps never in the whole of world history did aesthetics become so politically, religiously, sociologically, well, universally important as in this Iconoclast controversy. But strange as it may seem no one seems to have regarded it as a problem in aesthetics !

In his writings Theodore treats of the virtues meant for the monastic community, but they are applicable in varying degrees to any and all; and to say the least they add to our repertoire of schemata of asceses in a very valuable way. It is rather strange that so few contemporary Euramerican philosophers have dealt in any major way with specific sets of virtues. Too many of our traditional ethics textbooks look merely to the standard works of Aristotle, Bentham and Mill, John Dewey, maybe something from Gandhi and maybe even something from Descartes, Spinoza and Kierkegaard ; the more radical textbooks on the other hand cluster around the ethics of revolution or the pressing problems of the day dealing with psychosis, political crises, class struggle, and so forth. Even Sartre, although he treats afresh and vitally the emotions, seems not to examine adequately any particular virtues ; and perhaps as a misinterpretation, since Nietzsche the tendency is to deal with "ethical values" rather than working out a set of virtues that can be consistent internally and applicable as standards of judgment. Few take seriously enough those sections of the *Second Critique* where Kant does consider particular virtues in considerable detail.

Theodore's list of virtues is simple enough, the monastic state with its vows constituting the basic orientation. Then follows the spirit of martyrdom as the motivation for total submission of the will in a selfless following of one's abbot or spiritual mentor. Then follows obedience, humility, poverty, chastity, laughter, affection, mortification, comportment and power of the will. One might speculate whether Theodore would have proposed other virtues if he had been familiar with the classical Confucian virtues, for example, or with the *niṣkāma karma* ideal of the *Bhagavad Gītā*, or even more saliently with the Buddhist Eight-fold Noble Path and/or the *pāramitās*. Certainly he would have approved of the Jaina vows of non-possessiveness as almost the same as his virtue of voluntary poverty, and for the most part he could embrace Jaina and Buddhist precepts of non-violence as quite in harmony with Charity. It is surprising that Theodore does not formulate what emerged eventually in Latin Scholasticism as the combination of Aristotle's four virtue system with the Christian virtues of faith, hope and charity since the sources for such a scheme were plainly available to him.

The problem of free will and determinism was prominent in the Mu'tazilite-Ash'arite controversy and among the Ṣūfīs; and the Confucianists of all varieties had always put ethics in the foreground above epistemology or aesthetics. Even if it might be claimed that relatively Scotus Erigena and Śaṅkara by comparison are not voluntarists, it is not surprising, even if he were not necessarily involved in the Monotheletite controversy, that Theodore put problems of the will in first rank. For him the will is that by which the soul advances on the path of perfection in the ascetic way. Much depends on Theodore's attempts at definition of the term *autexousion*, which reminds us of Saṁskṛt terminology like the *svayaṃ-prakāśa* the self-revealing or self-sh'ning of truth after enlightenment has removed the veils of *māyā*. For to Theodore, once the will is free man can do anything. Indeed there seems to be something of a Promethian drive in his interpretation of Christian freedom : "We have only one thing to do, and that is to will and to achieve everything." "It is possible for anyone to will to live well, to arrive at perfection and to practice the virtues."[1] Asceticism is necessary in order to arrive at this authenticity or almost that *jen* which is intended in the term *autexousion,* self-validating, intrinsic in its essence sort of transvaluating will that follows the Christian vocation (as we found in Maximus Confessor) of the *kainon ktisma,* the new creature, in which everything is transformed under the new Dispensation, which the New Testament claims displaces and replaces the old law of both the Levitical code and the Greek *nomos* concept. Even allowing more leeway for Pelagianism than Augustine did, such claims would be downright Faustian and certainly dangerous if it were not that the virtue of humility must guard and preserve this freedom.

Theodore follows John Chrysostom's doctrine of grace in that it is only by the operation of grace that the will is made free to pursue the path of perfection. There is of course a theoretical paradox here, for if the will to perfection is inherent in man by virtue of the image of God in his nature, then why is it not free inherently to pursue that path, without need of grace ? It is almost like needing a will to have a will to perfection, which entails a will to will the Will of God. Since we know that even Byzantine laymen were fond of arguing endlessly about such conundrums as long as they had a few theological overtones, we marvel that Theodore does not deal more directly with the problem in such a manner. But perhaps there is something in him of the Zen master after all : Such speculations and intellectualistic puzzlements, where do they get you ? It is quite enough if one corrects faults and performs his own duty in the daily monastic round as selflessly as possible—not an easy counsel to the brilliant youth who is just discovering the sovereignty of the reign of ideas in human affairs, but salutary nevertheless. The will must become wholly clear, unhindered by desire, much less selfish desire, and undistracted by conflicting motives. Hence one need not speculate about where one's faults come from or how it is that, given the will to perfection and given the doctrine that God's Will is already and always perfect, there should be imperfection in the first place.

There are many notes in Theodore concerning advancement along the path of mysticism in typical Christian Neo-Platonic themes. In these, which often follow the theological controversies about the two natures of Christ, Theodore for the most part follows Maximus Confessor " in acknowledging three kinds of future restoration : of each individual, according to his merits; of the whole physical creation, which is to be made incorruptible and immortal; and of the whole moral creation, when sin is to be made to disappear, as the soul of man retruns to the Infinite God. For sin has no real existence, since it is not a creature of God, and in the fullness of time it will perish, and he who has committed sin will be 'saved as by fire'."[2] Theodore nevertheless wanted to avoid the 'heresy' of Origenism; but to us it still sounds typically monistic in keeping with the trend of the century. One could almost read Śaṅkara's doctrine of *māyā* into it, while we would not have to search very far among his Ṣūfī contemporaries, al-Bisṭāmī or Junayd for example, to find rather close parallels, even if the Mu'tazilites, some Nestorians and most Manichaeans might object.

Not so much to fight the evil as to strive constantly toward the good, such seems to be Theodore's spirit. And as such he is fully aware that dedicated community life is the easier and healthier way. Given the troubled times and tangled career of Theodore, it is not surprising that we find not so much metaphysics and epistemology as ethics and expressions of piety. Most of his letters of counsel simply try to instill courage, in spite of difficulties, in following the example of Christ, to endure grief and suffering with the consolation of promise of Final Reward, and even hint that martyrdom should be the ideal of any true Christian. In spite of his lack of adequate theory, Theodore is not alone either in his own century or in world history at large in appealing to the basics, teaching by example, and emphasizing practice over theory.

11. Nicephorus

The Iconoclast controversy is central in the life, career and extant writings of Patriarch Nicephorus (758-828), the contemporary of Theodore of Studium and perforce roughly of al-Kindī, Śaṅkara, Scotus Erigena, Han Yü and Li Ao. Once again we register our continuing complaint that with him as with so many Byzantine thinkers little attention has been given from the definitely philosophical point of view, even though some theologians and Church historians have become aware of his historical importance, and of course historians as such cannot avoid him because of his role in this controversy whose implications in political and even economic and social affairs were very intense, extending even to Byzantium's relations with Latin Europe and with the growing Muslim power at Baghdad, Antioch, Egypt and elsewhere.

As we have mentioned in connection with Theodore of Studium, the philosophical aspects of the Iconoclast controversy constitute a major problem in aesthetics. Aesthetics is a field difficult in our study since most histories of philosophy neglect this altogether, putting virtually all the emphasis on epistemology and/or ethics. There are some very salient issues in the Iconoclast controversy such as the problem of essence and manifestation through the aesthetic medium, or in other words how spiritual reality can be manifest in sensuous form without compromising its true intent. Nicephorus' aesthetics is fascinating comparatively since it is not too far removed from that of the Rāmānuja school under the caption of arch-avatār. It is, in short, incarnational aesthetics, true beauty being not a matter of entertainment but a direct communication of being equal with the good and the true.

Nicephorus was born in Constantinople about 758 under the Emperor Constantine V 'Corronymus' (741-74) whose religious policy Nicephorus was to combat almost all his life. Nicephorus was from a rather highly-placed aristocratic family, his father, Theodore, having been Imperial Secretary under Constantine V. Theodore had been condemned for worshipping images of Christ, the Virgin Mary and the saints, with the result that he was banished and forced into exile, although this exile did not last long, evidently because his services were far too valuable but also because it had been hoped that the exile had cured him of his 'evil' ways. But not so, with the result that he was tortured, banished and forced to live under great hardships until his death about 767.

The sources of information about Nicephorus' life are traditional hagiology. Hence little information is available about his childhood and education, except that it was according to the usual Byzantine pattern in Constantinople, including music (for chanting the psalter, not the 'pagan' kind inherited from Pythagoras of Samos), grammar, poetry, rhetoric, and perhaps a little history (ecclesiastical history, no doubt, such as that by Eusebius) and of course the Greek Fathers of the Church, whether or not Plato and Aristotle and the Stoics and Epicureans were studied directly or through those early Christian (Neo-)Platonists. But also there were minima of mathematics, astronomy and philosophy and theology. At any rate evidently Nicephorus was raised in the imperial entourage, in spite of his father's banishment.

While still relatively young Nicephorus grew weary of the formalities and corruption in high places and became anxious about the salvation of his soul. So he crossed the Bosporus, as Theodore of Studium had done, and underwent a period of voluntary rigorous asceticism. But not long solitary, he soon gathered a monastic community about him. The sudden and complete transformation of his style of life astonished everyone who knew him; and although such things are usually exaggerated in lives of saints everywhere, there is objective evidence that his renunciation was very real.

But Nicephorus' period of *vairāgya* and *tapas* did not last long since he was forced to return to Constantinople and accept the directorship of the largest poorhouse in the imperial capital (evidently only a nominal office which would lead to promotion whether in state or church). The promotion to the Patriarchate came in 806, immediately after the temporary suppression of Empress Irene by the Emperor Nicephorus I (802-811), even though there was considerable objection to the election of a layman to the Patriarchate directly, for Nicephorus was still that.

After the death of the Emperor Nicephorus in a battle with the Bulgarians, the Patriarch Nicephorus not only had a freer hand but increased responsibilities, including coronation of the new emperor. But the succession was a typically Byzantine affair of fantastic entanglements resulting in the rightful heir (Stauracius) taking refuge in a monastery. But even then it was not that simple since rival empresses, not to mention the Papacy and Charlesmagne, also had a role in such affairs. Truly nothing in Byzantine history is simple and straightforward, even as the same is true of the late T'ang Dynasty in China. Out of the tangled tale, however, one factor emerges which is very significant for Patriarch Nicephorus' place and policies in it all : Emperor Leo V espoused the cause of the Iconoclasts.

Nicephorus and Theodore of Studium were in the same camp as far as the Iconoclast controversy is concerned. However, Nicephorus was more willing to negotiate the controversy by calling an impartial assembly to undo the unfair workings of the assembly in which all iconodules were roundly anathematized. Theodore being adamant and unwilling to compromise at all, they both suffered persecutions although they escaped capital punishment (or were denied the privilege of martyrdom) and ultimately Nicephorus was forced to abdicate.

The Iconoclast controversy was really a revival of an old issue which went back at least as far as the days of John of Damascus and might be traced at least in germ still further back to the rivalry between the Antiochian and the Alexandrian/Athenian traditions of the early post-Patristic period. The Iconoclast period stretches between 726 and 843 essentially, although its fruits extend right down to the present day, not only in Greece but in Russia also, the Byzantine Ikon being the most characteristic feature to even the casual observer of the Eastern Orthodox Church. The initial attack was quite sudden, under the reign of the Emperor Leo III (717-40), and its severity was continued under Constantine V (740-75), long before Nicephorus and Theodore became involved.

The typical Byzantine practice of using paintings (icons) rather than carved three-dimensional images goes back at least to the fourth century when mosaic floors began to be common. Omission of the shadow also followed the demand for less sensuous representation at that early date. Even Gregory of Nyssa had

> stated that the painter, with his colors, could play a very useful role in the propagation of the faith, for paintings on the walls of churches constituted a visual book of Christian teaching, while St. Nilus, in the fourth century, said that scenes from the Old and New Testaments should be depicted on the body of the church so that those who could not read could follow the Bible story; but he added that in the sanctuary the cross only should be shown.[1]

The masses began to worship the pictures in and for themselves as though there were a unity or even identity between the image and the prototype, and miracle-working icons began to come into prominence. However, it was not just correction of these extremes that provoked Leo, for he and also his successor Constantine V were both very superstitious and were persuaded that natural calamities and military failures were acts of the Wrath of God because of this sin of idolatry.

Iconoclasm was also tangled up in the condemnation of the Monophysites and Nestorians :

> ...A new council was summoned in 753 to examine the problem and another in 815 reiterated its findings. The most essential of its decisions appears to have been that, to attempt to depict Christ as the Godhead mingled with manhood savored of the Monophysite approach, while to depict him in his (natural) human character alone was to adopt a Nestorian outlook. The two outlooks were condemned as equally heretical. So argued, any representation of Christ clearly tallied with espousing a heresy rather than true Orthodoxy.[2]

As for the question of Muslim influence on Iconoclasm :

> Detailed analysis...shows that the introduction of various intermediaries between Yazīd and Leo—migrating Jewish soothsayers, Leo's confidant Beser (a former Muslim captive), the Phrygian bishop Constantine of Nacolia—is only a series of literary attempts to provide a causal link between two dis-

> parate and unrelated events. In fact, it cannot be proved that eighth-century Islam was solidly iconoclastic, though such tendencies were doubtless present. As is well known, the Qur'ān offers no directives on images, and the earliest pertinent *hadīṯ* and legal material cannot be shown to have existed before the middle of the eighth century. The Muslim dominions were a haven for iconophile refugees; the earliest Christian evidence for Muslim opposition to Christian image worship is given by the bishop Theodore Abu Qurra (late 8th cent.). Iconoclastic cross veneration squarely militates against the thesis of Muslim influence; the specific Muslim injunctions for mutilating representations of living beings (e.g., decapitating an image, or making a large enough hole in its abdomen to "kill" it) plainly do not correspond to iconoclastic practices. (Incidentally, scratching out the eyes of an image was not enough, according to the medieval legal experts, to render the image harmless.)[3]

There had been an iconoclastic Council of Hiereia-Blachernae in 754 concerning which we have the following summary:

> The earlier council had rejected religious images on three grounds. They were said to be idols in the sense that their worshippers substituted worship of created things for the worship of the Creator ('argument from idol worship'). Icons of Christ in particular violated christological doctrine inasmuch as they either separated Christ's human nature from His divinity or confused the two natures ('argument from christology'). Finally, the Council of Hiereia-Blachernae had used a third line of reasoning which is of considerable importance in the present context and will be referred to henceforth as 'argument from holiness'. According to the Council, paganism with its practice of making and worshipping images was the source of Christian image worship. Since it had no hope for a resurrection from the dead 'it thought up a toy (the making and worship of idols) worthy of itself in order jestingly to present what was absent as if it were present' (i.e. the dead as if they were alive). The Christian Church rejects this because 'the Saints...enjoy eternal life with God'. It is blasphemy against God to attempt to portray

the Saints 'by means of an art which is dead, hateful, and never life-giving'. These remarks mean that the bestowal of true life is God's prerogative, that the portrayal of a dead person constitutes an attempt to make him 'live' again and is consequently an encroachment upon God's domain. The artist offends likewise against the Theotokos or the Saints whom he wishes to portray, 'for it is not permissible for Christians who possess the expectation of the resurrection... to insult by means of inglorious and dead matter the Saints who will be made bright in such glory'. The Council clearly implies that the artistic portrait of a Saint can do no more than portray the Saint's mortal body and can hope to represent neither his soul nor his incorruptible and glorified body after the resurrection. Artistic portraits consequently 'insult' the essential holiness of the Saint, to be revealed (rather than brought about) by the future resurrection.[4]

As we finally extricate ourselves from the controversies which surrounded Nicephorus and begin to look for his philosophy, we may be forced to stretch the meaning of that word a bit or else admit that only in a derived sense can he be called a philosopher. If, for example, one expects a thorough treatment of the *pramāṇas*, the categories, problems of cosmology and cosmogeny, causation and the relations of matter with mind, soul and spirit; or even if one expects doctrines of freedom and necessity or determinism in relation to human nature; or if one expects a definition of the True, the Good and the Beautiful in their interrelationalities; then one will be sorely disappointed. But if one looks from the standpoint of such as Dilthey who wanted us to work towards overall *Weltanschauungen* in terms of historical lived-through situations-in-the-world, and/or from a higher Neo-Buddhist cultivation of awareness and expansion of horizons as a function of the *Ālaya-vijñāna*; or if one takes a Neo-Confucianist attitude or a Marxist or pragmatist demand that theory and practice must go together, and that the value of ethical stamina is of the highest that can be demanded of man; then we may call Nicephorus a great philosopher indeed. The same may be said of Theodore of Studium.

In an opusculum whose long descriptive Greek title has been

abbreviated to the *Adversus Iconomachos*, Nicephorus argues that the prohibition of images was only for those under the Mosaic law, but Christians, having been delivered from that Covenant, are free to use images. His *Refutatio et Eversio* is a refutation of the pronouncements of the Council of St. Sophia of 815. Nicephorus' method in this work is twofold : either to discredit quotations from the Church Fathers used by the opponents, or to counter every quotation with a counter-quotation supporting his point of view instead of theirs. Nicephorus uses definitely Aristotelian logic in forming and framing his definitions, in addition to using the dialogue form of composition. Theodore also used the same method, although he was more inclined to spice his logic with invective. The definitions are concerned with the distinction between identity, sameness and likeness, including the key term "prototype", but also with what is meant by worship, veneration, etc. Even the question of univocity and ambiguity comes into play, and the question whether it is any different to venerate a simple cross, a mere symbol, or an image of Christ.

The key term in his discourse evidently is whether Christ is "circumscribable". Ever since the Athanasian Creed every member of the Blessed Trinity is indicated as incircumscribable (*perigraptos*), i.e., unlimited to any possible human definition. Historically indefinability or incircumscribability was typical of the *Trikāya* of Mahāyāna, not to mention that Nicephorus' contemporary Śaṅkara also bases his whole non-dualist system on the indefinability/incircumscribability of Brahman. But, of course, an image is definable—at least to a certain point, although when any work of art reaches that perfection or power so that we spontaneously exclaim that it is indescribable, we are inadvertently admitting that it approaches or even embodies definitely spiritual qualities. Thus there is a wide range of possibilities between worship of an unworthy image, worship of the indescribable Christ with the image of only an aid to concentration, worship of Christ through veneration of the image, worship of Christ (though indescribable in Himself) as manifested finitely through a spiritualized work of art, and worship of Christ as actually forthgiving His Presence in the Image sacramentally in the same sense that He is communicated (or at least His grace is freely given) in any other sacramental operation; and finally, worship of the Image as though it were Christ Himself. Here we could review Vaiśṇavism wherein the dedicated image becomes the arch-avatār, an *actual* incarnation of the deity, and not merely an artistic symbol, in contrast to the Buddhist and Jaina practice of using the images only as an aid for meditation and not for worship.

Nicephorus was familiar with the classics of Greek philosophy, which were not available in the ninth century in Latin Europe, although they were known and used in Baghdad. Ever since Leontius of Byzantium at least, Christians had been using the technicalities of Aristotelian logic; and it is likely that Nicephorus did rely on Leontius for much of his terminology, whether directly or indirectly. Historically Aristotelian arguments had been used in the Iconoclast controversy even by John of Damascus. Nicephorus accuses his opponents of violating a rule of proper use of 'specification by generalization' and thus denying Christ's human nature by refusing to allow images of Him.

> What, I ask you, gives you this power to disregard the other specific properties (*idiōmata*) of body, namely that of being shaped, tridimensional, tangible, provided with organs and the others from which its being circumscribable is being inferred...? For if a man would not retain his property of being rational he would not be a man. Similarly if his mortality, or his erect walk, or his moving, or his being animate, or any of the other properties which combined constitute the nature and definition of man, were lacking he would not be a man. And if somebody take away the ability to neigh from a horse, or that to bark from a dog, there will be neither horse nor dog. Therefore the humanity of Christ if bereft of one of its properties is a defective nature, and Christ not a perfect man, or rather not Christ at all, but is lost altogether if He cannot be circumscribed and represented in art.[5]

Nicephorus is very specific about the important distinction between definition and description, to which one could readily find parallels in the Nyāya tradition of his own time if not in other Indian systems as well. In order to be precise as possible Nicephorus gives us three definitions of what an *eikōn* is :

> The pattern (archetypon) is an existing beginning and exemplar of a form shaped after it, and the cause of the likeness of the similitude. Of the Image, however, the following definition says what one might say about objects produced by art : an image is a likeness of an archetype (archetypon) which reproduces in itself by way of resemblance the entire form of what is impressed upon it, and which differs from it merely by the difference of a substance with respect to matter. Or, an imitation and similitude of a pattern differing in essence and substratum. Or, an artifact shaped in imitation of a pattern but differing in substance and subject; for if it does not differ in some respect, it is not an image nor an object different from the model. Thus an image is a likeness and a figuration of things being and existing.[6]

One might find in these things some adumbration of the realist-nominalist-conceptualist controversy in Latin Europe soon after Nicephorus' century, or for that matter even in Peter Damien or Saadia ben Gaon, and certainly in John Scotus Erigena; but as far as technique of definition as such is concerned, it would not be difficult to make him sound very modern. The fact that he applied his technique to what became a controversy that engulfed not only theology in the technical sense but politics and ecclesiastical discipline should not blind us to the fact that he was applying it to art with a clarity seldom found even in the most astute modern aestheticians or even in definitions of *rasa* and *dhvani* in Abhinava Gupta and his predecessors who were Nicephorus' contemporaries.

It is not only in technique of definition as such that Nicephorus manifests his Aristotelianism but also in his use of Aristotelian categories. Concerning the category of relation (*to pros ti*), relatives are "such as they are from their being *of* some other thing, and through their relations that are mutual correlatives." He gives the father-son relationship as a paradigm example, and insists that likeness is such a relation, an intermediate relation that bridges the gap between the extremes of person and (artistic) representation in that it "unites and connects (them) through the form even though they differ in nature; for although they are different objects according to their nature they are not different subjects and the image is another self (*allos de autos ekeīnos*)."[7] Then having established the relation of likeness he goes on to deal with differences, this culminating in the following expression :

> Now since on the basis of both reasoning and definition, the difference is thus realized to lie in these points, and as pictorial representation is an external factor, and has nothing in common with the definition of the essence, why do our opponents stir in vain and boast that henceforth there will be separated what is naturally united ?[8]

Similarly Nicephorus uses the other Aristotelian categories with complete ease and remarkable astuteness. For example, quality and substance are invoked to disprove the Iconoclastic view of the identity of essence between original and image.

In applying Aristotelian methodology to the Iconoclast controversy, Nicephorus also enlarges on the concept of change, relying heavily on John of Damascus. Technically he criticizes the view of Eusebius, who claimed that "the form of a servant was changed completely into His light".

> . . . If Eusebius meant that change took place *kata to poion* (i.e., qualitatively) or by alteration (*alloiōsis*) this would not change Christ *completely* as Eusebius claimed, 'for alteration is a transfiguration of some characteristic, or a separate or associated variation concerning some feature of the substance'. The same holds true for quantitative change, as it does not represent complete change either. The remaining alternative, essential change, i.e., coming-to-be and passing away, would imply a complete annihilation of Christ's human form. This would be a complete change, but it would do away with Christ's humanity.[9]

In a similar context he invokes the consideration of place and time as essential to the definition of "body"—*place* and time being a distinction that became common many centuries later in the Italian Renaissance. Again Nicephorus is attempting a definition of circumscription:

> For as a body does not exist without place or time, thus does it not exist without circumscription. For place circumscribes and contains the body, if it is ture that 'space is the limiting surface of the body continent, in which it contains the body contained'. Now to say that the body is not circumscribed is identical with saying that it is not in a place. What, however, is not in a place, is not a body.[10]

If one takes Nicephorus' treatment of the argument about circumscription in comparison with Śaṅkara's *anirvacanīya* (indescribability of the Brahman-*ātman* linkage), then something emerges historically which has been neglected until very recently with such as Nishida Kitaro's and Heidegger's reinstatements of the problems stemming from the concept of nothingness. Certainly one admires the clear-headedness of nineteenth century French rationalist philosophy and the attempts at comprehensiveness of German philosophy of the same period; but sooner or later one has to admit that such efforts also have their limits and are bounded, circumscribed, whether by the way one is dealing in straight metaphysics as such or in ethics or in aesthetics. In aesthetics (as was the case with Abhinava Gupta more than with Śaṅkara) this matter becomes critically acute. If spirituality is *anirvacanīya* or incircumscribable or indefinable—there the Taoists could also be invoked, and we should not forget that aesthetic Taoism had not disappeared from T'ang China—then art becomes almost by definition a crass indulgence in *māyā* and delusion, even more than Plato had taught. But if spiritual reality is manifestable or at least approachable in certain aesthetic manners and modes, then art becomes critically significant, so much so that one can claim that no art without a high degree of spirituality of some sort can be really authentic. Art should in a sense really 'be' its object as far as possible, or at least it must be the *tao* of that object, metaphysically and not just sensuously. For if there is anything that really great art does do or at least tries to accomplish it is to unite the apparent antinomies of finite and infinite, manifestation and essence, spiritual reality and physical reality, form and content, inspiration and technique.

The final outcome of the Iconoclast controversy is a beautiful example of how thesis-antithesis-synthesis works in history: from use of graven images through the denial of all artificial representation by the Iconoclasts, we come after a long struggle and not a few executions to the synthesis of the Byzantian-Russian *Ikon,* which has such restrictions imposed that it cannot become a merely sensuous misrepresentation of heavenly spiritual values or presences (such as for example did come forth in the late Italian Renaissance, in Rococo Latin American churches, or in those images of Kuan-yin whose face is rather luscious to be true Bodhisattva).

In this entire Iconoclast controversy one hears echoes of that zeal for orthodoxy that led to the massacre of so many 'heretics, in the whole history of Byzantine and Roman Christianity. As observed in previous treatments of this theme, the relatively peaceful penetration of Buddhism into China, Tibet, Korea, Japan and Southeast Asia, and the corresponding relative lack of persecution of heresies in the Buddhist world, make noteworthy contrasts. Of course in the late T'ang Dynasty there was a rather devastating purge of the Buddhist monasteries which had become wealthy places of refuge for political conspirators more than places of piety and contemplation; and the state did need the gold that had been used for the images for financing other projects, including defense against the Western 'barbarians'. True enough also, the monks of Mt. Hiei in Japan did get into armed battle with the court at Kyōtō, and not always was there harmony between the followers of Kūkai and those who espoused Saichō's way. But scarcely did the "two mountains" (Hiei and Kōya) anathematize each other with such violent zeal as was the case in this Iconoclast controversy in Byzantium, which more resembles the Protestant Reformation and the wars of religion in later centuries in Western Europe, or the time of troubles that followed after the Sikhs in India tried to find a middle path between the bibliolatry of fanatical Muslims (who were arch-iconoclasts) and the idolatry of the Hindus.

Another of our recurring themes is that throughout the centuries and in virtually every civilization philosophers and philosophies come in pairs. The *yin-yang* principle of polarization (as may be seen in Chou Tun-i) constitutes a philosophy in itself. And in a sense it also constitutes a sort of meta-philosophy since it does give a partial explanation of how it is that the histories of philosophies are not exempt from laws of historical dialectics, even supposedly meta-historical philosophies also having a history.

> In many periods can be found a pair of historical figures who approached identical problems on the basis of diametrically opposed sets of principles and with different temperaments. ...In such situations the key to the understanding of the period lies in a comparison of the 'parallel lives', their standards and their characters. This is also the case in the early decades of the ninth century when the Patriarch Nicephorus and Theodore the abbot of Studios were the recognized leaders of the Eastern Church.[11]

And it is a long list that turns up in our studies, in this volume including such as Nichiren and Ippen, Dōgen and Eisai, Chu Hsi and Lu Hsiang-shan, Ibn Rushd and Suhrawardī, Aquinas and Bonaventura, Citsukha and Mādhava.

It remains unfortunately true that our standard textbooks in aesthetics, even the few available in comparative aesthetics which include introductory hints concerning the canons of excellence in India, China, Japan, and elsewhere, completely ignore Byzantine art in general, not to mention the canons for spirituality in art as manifested in the icons that resulted from the Iconoclast controversy. Here again we may reflect on the difficulty not only of keeping philosophy in the different civilizations in proper balance and proportion, but of keeping philosophy at the dynamic center between political and economic theory, epistemology and scientific developments, religion, art, ethics and moral codes, mysticism and materialism, and all the other polarities that range around the *Śūnya*-zero center that philosophy is or ought to be. All the way through our study we wish that the world history of art were more prominently in the background than thus far has been possible, since certainly the true, the good, and the beautiful, *sat-cit-ānanda*, *jñāna-karma-bhakti*, are all equally philosophical and it is wrong to let any one dominate the others.

12. Kūkai

Of Kūkai (774-835) it has been written, "His memory lives all over the country, his name is a household word in the remotest places, not only as a saint, but as a preacher, a scholar, a poet, a sculptor, a painter, an inventor, an explorer, and—sure passport to fame—a great calligrapher."[1] After studying Esoteric Tāntric Buddhism in China, Kūkai established the Shingon (True Words) sect in Japan. His influence was immediately felt, especially by the Tendai sect.

> Saichō (767-822), the founder of Tendai, received instruction in Esoteric Buddhism from Kūkai. His successors increasingly stressed Esoteric Buddhism over the Tendai teachings proper. ...Under the impetus of Kūkai's Esoteric Buddhism, the most eminent successors of Saichō, such as Ennin (794-864), Enchin (814-91), and Annen (841-915); busied themselves adopting and assimilating Esoteric Buddhist elements into the Tendai teachings. Consequently, about a century after Kūkai, Mt. Hiei and Miidera, a temple near the shores of Lake Biwa became centers of Esoteric Buddhism, and Taimitsu (Tendai Esotericism) came to contend with Tōmitsu (Shingon Esotericism, that of the Tōji) for supremacy in Japan. "The contest between Tendai and Shingon for recognition as the center of esotericism resulted in victory for the Hiei monks. Their success was due partially to the failure of Shingon to produce great leaders in the generations after Kūkai, and partially to the advantage which geographical proximity to the capital gave to Hiei over the more distant Kōya." Paradoxically the triumph of the Tendai monks also meant their defeat, for the Esoteric Buddhism advocated by Kūkai virtually overwhelmed them.[2]

Tāntric Buddhism seems so far removed from what is known of the original teachings of the historic Buddha Śākyamuni that it might be questioned whether it authentically should be called Buddhism at all, even though it had become very popular at Nālandā and certainly in Kaśmir and Central Asia, as well as in Tibet where it appears to have originated as an amalgam with Central Asian Shamanism or even with the Bon cult in pre-Buddhist Tibet.

Obviously it is difficult to trace the history of traditions which do not put much emphasis on history, as is the case with most esoteric brands of thought and practice since for the most part they claim to transcend history. Although elsewhere we may have over-emphasized its heritage at its worst, the range being very wide, Tāntric Buddhism at its best can be traced back even to the Vedas wherein the word *dhāraṇī* is used in reference to the use of *mantras*. But such remote ancestry in this case is not so significant as what we have traced in volume three of this study, how that Tāntric Buddhism really took root in India at Nālandā where the Vijñānavāda was strongest with the Mādhyamika running close second. It was probably in the sixth and seventh centuries that the specifically Tāntric sūtras took shape, such as the *Mahāvairocana*, the *Guhyasamāja* and the *Sarvatāthagata-tattva-saṃgraha*. The use of *mantra, dhāraṇī, mandala* and other characteristic Tāntric practices from the Indian sources were brought to China in the eighth century or so—rather late as a matter of fact, and we may infer that they came there from Kaśmir where Tantra became even more common in practice than at Nālandā.

The Indian masters Śubhākarasiṃha, Vajrabodhi and Amoghavajra came in person to China. Śubhākarasiṃha (636-735), coming originally from central India, had studied Tāntric Buddhism at Nālandā after having been the ruler of a small principality. He finally arrived at Ch'ang-an in 716, already eighty years old, and went to Loyang where he translated the *Mahāvairocana Sūtra*. He died in China at the age of ninety-nine, after being refused permission to return to India. Vajrabodhi (671-741) had studied both Mādhyamika and Yogācāra at Nālandā and had gone to South India for further studies under Nāgabodhi. Thence he came to China, arriving at Canton in 720. He translated, among other things, the *Vajra-śekhara*. Amoghavajra (705-774) was a native of Siṃhala (Sri Lanka or Ceylon) and arrived in China at the age of ten, becoming a disciple of Vajrabodhi at the age of fifteen. "After the death of his master, Amoghavajra travelled to India and Ceylon, where he received national honors. In Southern India, he met Nāgabodhi and was able to bring back many Tāntric texts to China, which he subsequently translated."[3]

The seventh and eighth centuries were the golden age of Esoteric Buddhism both in India and China and elsewhere, including emphatically Tibet. But since patronage (which too often has played the deciding role rather than inherent excellence or defect of a system) ran out for Tāntric practices, and since along with the other varieties of Buddhism it suffered considerably in the purge of 845, it virtually died out in China except as a popular cult among the masses. "The doctrine of the Esoteric School never became wholly acceptable to the Chinese but it spread in Japan and exists to the present day."[4] For better or for worse, the texts and practices central for Tibetan Tantra never got into Japan. It was Hui-kuo (746-805) from whom Kūkai got his initiation, Hui-kuo having been a direct disciple of the famous Amoghavajra.

The Vajrayāna that Kūkai and generally the whole Shingon school of Buddhism in Japan inherited was pretty much a systematic monism; but whether it was a syncretism of many elements or a synthesis of them might be debated. Esoteric heritages generally and certainly newly emerging (or as is usually the case in world history, re-emerging) esoterics tend to be terribly unsystematic and extremely syncretistic, not even aware of logical or moral inconsistencies. The word *vajra* in the term Vajrayāna (which is almost synonymous with Tantra) simply means "diamond". The proponents of Vajrayāna usually advertize it as a third way or alternative to both Mahāyāna and Hīnayāna.

There was a gradual transition from the lower to the pure form of Esoteric Buddhism, the problem of enlightenment taking a much more exalted position in the pure form rather than the use of magic for mere worldly material ends. Moreover, the pure form had a much more ascetic discipline than the lower Tantra. From a very early time many *mantras, mudrās* and *mandalas* were used in various ways, no doubt superstitiously as magic by many uneducated and ill-trained devotees, but with very definite psychological effects by those who knew the philosophical, indeed metaphysical, intention of their use. The higher morality and the higher meditation and wisdom is the true intention of Vajrayāna.

Tantra at its best with its *mantras* is really very intimately interrelated with Śabdavāda : Brahman (or Buddha or Logos, it really doesn't matter) is Sound or Vibration, as we have attempted to explain in other contexts; and this becomes almost identical with the Vijñānavāda, which has somehow become scarcely distinguishable from Śūnyavāda. But the real inge of difference from these others is the emphasis on practice rather than theory. "The outstanding characteristic of Esoteric Buddhism is not philosophy; rather it is the ability to experientially grasp by means of complicated rituals and practices the abstract philosophical concepts of Mahāyāna Buddhism."[5] One would have to be specially trained, in some instances for many lives, so to speak, in the proper way to resonate the sounds. If properly used so that the sounds actually resonate in the heart in such a way as to activate the ganglia there, OM RAM LAM is a very useful mantra for restoring recollection in times of distraction, and the sound RHIM can be very destructive of unwanted thoughts and even of things. But the attainment of *siddhi* or the super-normal powers, even as in Patañjali Yoga, is only incidental to the more ultimate end.

In the *Mahāvairocana Sūtra* as in almost all Mahāyāna as well as Vajrayāna texts, the Buddha is regarded as the *Tathatā*, the Undefinable Thatness, equatable perhaps with the Hindu *nirguṇa*-Brahman, or remotely with the Ṣūfī concept of "beyond the Beyond", or even distantly with the Mu'tazilite rejection of attributes in their definition of Allah. And in the vast bulk of the other Mahāyāna and Vajrayāna sūtras likewise this monistic *Tathatā* is identical with the *Dharmitās* of the Mahāyāna Trinity. *Prajñā* moreover remains the chief of the *pāramitās* in this practice, rather than magic for lower ends. Somehow in this system as distinct from the others, *upāya* and *prajñā*, means and end, are not only commensurate but identical. Monism emphatically!

The *Mahāvairocana Sūtra* is devoted first of all to the theoretical basis, and later to the practice. The theory is essentially the same as in most of the Mahāyāna sūtras, namely the emphasis on the *pāramārthika* level of reality and the identity of this to Consciousness; and, of course, the stages of attainment leading up to this ultimate realization of unity of microcosm and macrocosm.

In a word, the essence of Kūkai's Esoteric Buddhist meditation is simply "imitating". This is technically called the practice of "entering self into Self so that the Self enters into the Self (*nyūga ga'nyū*)". The Self is the individual existence and the Self, Mahāvairocana. To practice the samādhi of Mahāvairocana is to imitate through one's total being—physical, mental, moral, intellectual, and emotional—like an actor acting alone on stage. The stage is the sacred ground (*mandala*; *dōjō*). This can be anywhere as long as it is ritualistically consecrated, but it is usually the main hall of temple where a principal Buddha or bodhisattva or any other manifestation of Mahāvairocana is enshrined. Here the eternal and cosmic drama of the samadhi of self-enjoyment (*jijuyō sammai*) of Mahāvairocana is performed through rigidly prescribed activities of body, speech, and mind, every step exactly as prescribed : how to move one's fingers (mudra); what to think or visualize or feel; and which mantra to recite at what moment and how many times. On performing the rituals of purification and consecration of the ground and of the ten directions, the circle where the student meditates is transformed into the center of the universe. Then begins the invocation of the presence of Mahāvairocana, or of any of his manifestations, as the object of meditation confronting the subject, followed by a conscious effort to imitate the object through symbolic activities of body, speech, and mind. The climax is reached when the subject, while performing the acts of imitating, loses the awareness that he is imitating—the subject is transformed into the object, and the separation between the subject and the object disappears. In the end, as the actor withdraws from the stage, the subject returns to the imitating self, and the object, to where it came from, by means of ritual acts. The entire process is regulated by rules, that is, the process of time is punctuated by prescribed activities so that the student will not lose himself in timelessness; step by step he returns from unconscious imitating to his conscious self by counting beats, striking a hand bell, and so forth.[6]

Kūkai's understanding of true awareness of reality and the means of attaining it certainly differed radically from modern secular and scientific views. For Kūkai "appreciated direct samadhi over all other experiences. Life unaccompanied by aesthetic and ecstatic experience of samadhi seemed to him devoid of real value and purpose."[7]

In his work *The Difference between Exoteric and Esoteric Buddhism*, Kūkai wrote : "The doctrine revealed by the Nirmanakaya Buddha (Shakyamuni Buddha) is called Exoteric; it is apparent, simplified, and adapted to the needs of the time and to the capacity of the listeners. The doctrine expounded by the Dharmakaya Buddha (Mahâvairocana) is called Esoteric; it is secret and profound and contains the final truth." Hakeda comments on this in his study of Kūkai :

> His assertion that Esoteric Buddhism was not the doctrine expounded by the historical Buddha was a radical one : everyone believed that literally all the Buddhist sutras had been preached by him. According to Kūkai, the historical Buddha is but one manifestation of Mahâvairocana, who exists in history and yet at the same time transcends it. Mahâvairocana in his samadhi is timeless and eternally present in a state of bliss. The Esoteric teachings contained in the *Mahāvairocana* and *Vajraśekhara Sutras*, Kūkai says, unconditionally reveal the inner-most secrets of that eternal samadhi of Mahâvairocana; and by practicing Esoteric Buddhist methods of meditation, one can quickly experience the samadhi of Mahāvairocana. In other words, one can attain enlightenment.[8]

"Attaining enlightenment in this very existence" became the best known characterization of Kūkai's Buddhism.

> Kūkai meant that the practice of Shingon Buddhism enables the devotee to attain enlightenment here and now without having to wait for rebirth in this or in another world. This motto reflects both Kūkai's affirmative attitude toward this phenomenal world as the very realm in which the highest enlightenment is to be attained and his basic belief in man's potential for enlightenment. Indeed, Kūkai held that, even in the lowest level of mind, the highest "glorious mind, the most secret and sacred" is fully present.[9]

Kūkai's emphasis on attainment of enlightenment in the present body could be interpreted by Advaitins and even by Kaśmiri Śaivas as parallel if not identical with the *Jīvan-mukti* ideal, which later Rāmānuja will criticize rather intelligently. It could also be equated with the Bodhisattva ideal as such by other Mahāyāna Buddhists, and modern Christians of the sort who emphasize the interpretation of the Incarnation as sanctioning of embodiment could find a parallel, although we must remember that the Monophysites and Nestorians did not quite go along with this.

The classification of teachings in Kūkai's formula is directly parallel with the similar formulae used by the Six Sects of the Nara period immediately preceding him and is therefore not so unique or original with him. Of course in the face of the others he has to vindicate his eclectic arrangement, naturally claiming superiority for his own. He puts them into ten stages of spiritual advancement, only the last one being "all there", the other nine being still in the realm of *saṃsāra* or *avidyā*. He had recorded these in two writings, the *Jūjūshinron* (*Ten Stages of the Development of Mind*) and the *Hizō Hōyaku* (*Precious Key to the Secret Treasury*), both done in the year 830. The tenth stage is called "The Glorious Mind, the Most Secret and Sacred".

> In the *Ten Stages* Kūkai begins his presentation of this mind with the following definition : "The glorious mind, the most secret and sacred is, ultimately, to realize one's own mind in its fountainhead and to have insight into the nature of one's own existence." He conceives man as "body-mind", not as mind or body, nor body and mind, and holds that this "body-mind" is grounded in the "Body-Mind", the secret and sacred living Body-Mind of all, the Dharmakaya Mahāvairocana. His premise is that our mind in its essence is united with the Mind of Mahāvairocana and that our body, so long as it is in the universe, is part of the Body of Mahāvairocana; all men as well as all other sentient beings are particular "body-mind" beings participating in the "Body-Mind". It is this "Body-Mind" that is represented in the Shingon mandalas, which describe various aspects of Mahāvairocana.[10]

Kūkai had placed Tendai at the eighth stage, but of course Saichō did not at all agree with Kūkai that Tendai was an inferior way. In fact, these two were rivals, exemplifying another of our continuing themes that ordinarily in the whole range of world history philosophers come in pairs.

Although Buddhism continued to be the official state religion in the Heian period as it had been in the Nara period, there were also Confucianist elements in it, as of course had been the case long since in China. Kūkai was not only interested in both Confucianism and Taoism (even though he was definitely a Buddhist) but he openly advocated official adoption of all three traditions as useful for Japanese life. Kūkai had, however, a deep conviction of the superiority of Buddhism rather than a mere preference in a syncretistic way. He used a rather rigorous analysis of all three heritages, concluding that Buddhism demonstrated a better pattern of filial piety ! In China that was a major issue until the decision was finally made by the government to treat every Buddhist monastery as though it were a Confucian "family" or clan, so that it could be brought under government supervision and taxation.

The *Sangōshiki* is actually a novel written by Kūkai and constitutes one of the earliest pieces of literature in that form known in the history of Japan (although such works had become fairly common in China long before this time). It is composed of three major sections, the first being a sort of preface in which Kūkai presents his motives; the second being a presentation of the case for Confucianism, Taoism and Buddhism respectively, each of which is represented by a separate character; and the conclusion is a poem in which the main points in the trialogue are pulled together with Buddhism coming out in the forefront.

The Confucianist character takes the position of a reformer-teacher who tries to improve the ethical standards of his wayward nephew; but the Taoist character wins out with his teachings about the Taoist methods of attaining longevity. Then enters a Buddhist mendicant monk (Kūkai's mouthpiece) whose arguments succeed in the end on the basis of insisting that Confucianism is all right for the present life, but not for other lives yet to come, nor for the attainment of anything like ultimate truth. Moreover, Confucianism and Taoism are concerned only with external duties and ritual performances, whereas Buddhism teaches that one's efforts should extend if necessary even to the sacrifice of this life in order to attain the higher realizations.

No other civilization has made filial piety the cardinal virtue *par excellence* as China has done; but the Japanese adaptation of this to the bushido code of loyalty continued to such an extent that even in the twentieth century the American philosopher Josiah Royce was profoundly impressed by it and made it a major factor in his own philosophy of Community. Kūkai's contribution lies perhaps not so much in his arguments against the Confucian version of it and the Taoist attitudes alongside that, but in the fact that before him basically loyalty had been associated historically with the Shintō heritage rather than the Buddhist *saṅgha* discipline as such. In his *Sangoshiki* Kūkai writes :

> When you are at home, you must keep smiling, studying the moods of your parents, so that you may do what they want done before you are asked to. ...By reading their faces, provide the things they need and give them satisfaction. Such is filial piety. ...When the time comes to serve your Master, transfer your devotion from the practice of filial piety to loyalty; exert yourself to the fullest extent and give advice to your master when he is wrong, even if, by offending him, you may lose your life. Know well both astronomy and geography. Think of past events and compare them to the present situation; pacify the people in distant areas and control well the people nearby. Govern the world with order and assist your king to be righteous. Then your fame and success will be transmitted to posterity. Such is Loyalty.[11]

Among Buddhists both filial piety and loyalty were applied to the four basic Buddhist meditations, viz. the body, the Buddha, the *Dharma* and the *saṅgha*. Renunciation of the world does not entail lack of concern for its welfare; quite the contrary, intercessatory prayers for the welfare of the people, the security of the nation and prosperity for all, as well as protection in calamities, were evidently as common in Kūkai's Japan as in

Christian, if not Ṣūfī also, monastic practice not only in the medieval past but continuing right down to the present.

Given the already strong nationalistic identity of the Japanese people even during the Nara period, it is not surprising that Kūkai's interpretation of filial piety was not centered so much on the family as such as was traditionally the case in China, but on loyalty and obedience to the State. Hence Kūkai's significance in strengthening and partially moulding the Japanese cultural nexus. Kūkai's fervor and zeal for reform in the political realm as an extension of his concept of loyalty may have something to offer for our own time with the very emphatic proviso that what he conceived as loyalty to his own Japan in a naturally limited way must be extended to the United Nations or some other global, non-nationalistic symbol. Incidentally, the fundamental concept of loyalty may be seen in Japanese business today where the company provides everything needed by the workers who in return pledge their loyalty to the company, which thereby becomes a human community living and growing together. This is only a modern application of what in Kūkai's time applied to the Buddhist monastic establishments.

That Kūkai was concerned with the monastic community should not be ignored since it was one of the most basic of his many concerns. Celibate communities do become corrupt and/or oppressive and can even become political instruments of suppression, as did happen in Byzantium and in China, for example before Kūkai's time. Nevertheless, many of the most effective reforms of society and culture as a whole have come about through monastic reforms and innovations. Kūkai's career is only another paradigm example of that, comparable to Benedict and Basil in a previous cycle, or perhaps even to Photius in his own time, or to the monks of Iona in Ireland with whom Scotus Erigena had close association, or in the Islamic world to Bayazid Biṣṭāmi and the great al-Ḥallāj—to name only a few besides Śaṅkara, who established a monastic order that virtually replaced the Buddhist *saṅgha* in India, an establishment that is even today very often important in political as well as religious and philosophical circles.

Kūkai was not concerned with personal *sādhana* alone but made quite an issue of conducting esoteric rites, such as chanting the sūtras for the welfare of the nation. In fact at times that seems to be his major concern. Universally patriotism a d religion are almost always mixed and very often in world history become identical. The Qur'ān and the Bible likewise, not to mention the four Vedas, were also chanted for purely magical purposes without necessarily paying much heed to the meaning. Esoterics of all brands tend towards monism, even at the price of syncretism; and it might be said that Kūkai's concern for the unity and prosperity of Japan as a whole was only a ripening fruit of his monist vision of unity in all things.

More critical examination into the tenets and practices of the Shingon sect might lead us to some conclusion other than what Kūkai claimed for it. It too seems to have taken on a lot of unnecessary esoteric paraphernalia; and yet much of the world at that time was involved with this sort of thing—which almost always seems to accompany an exaltation of female figures, the Theotokos in Byzantium having her Indian, Chinese and Japanese counterparts. The Vajra tradition also fits with the almost universal if not axiomatic observation that when the ultimate deity is conceived as female, art flourishes more than when male domination prevails, as in pure Confucianism or Islam or prophetic Protestant Christianity. After returning from the fabulous T'ang capital of Chang-an which even exceeded Rome or Byzantium in splendor and layout, Kūkai taught such things as the following:

> The law (dharma) has no speech, but without speech it cannot be expressed. Eternal truth (*tathatā*) transcends color, but only by means of color can it be understood. Mistakes will be made in the effort to point at the truth, for there is no clearly defined method of teaching, but even when art does not excite admiration by its unusual quality, it is a treasure which protects the country and benefits the people. ...The various attitudes and mudras of the holy images all have their source in Buddha's love, and one may attain Buddhahood at sight of them. Thus the secrets of the sūtras and commentaries can be depicted in art, and the essential truths of the esoteric teaching are all set forth therein. Neither

> teachers nor students can dispense with it. Art is what reveals to us the state of perfection.[12]

This reminds us of the Iconoclast controversy in Byzantium which resulted, no less than in Buddhist Japan, in the development of a canon for religious art of a very high spiritualized sort, not merely imitating ordinary human figures, but presenting saints, angels, demons, the Blessed Virgin, and God (Himself) in forms that could not be confused with secular values. The Buddha no less than the Christ had ceased to be earthly figures at all, and their cosmic roles were stressed over their historic appearances, missions, and teachings on earth. Geometric designs (*mandalas*) with esoteric meanings began to develop equally in Tibet, Japan, China, Byzantium and in the "rose" windows of Gothic churches, and gargoils as well as angels guarded all human enterprises. Hymnology was keeping full pace with the graphic arts, and not unlike his near-contemporary Saint John Damascene, Kūkai sings very beautifully of the vanity of this world.

> From the deep, dim, most distant past,
> A thousand thousand tomes we hold
> Of sacred texts and learned lore.
> Profound, abstruse, obscure and dark,
> Teachings diverse and manifold—
> Who can encompass such a store?
>
> Yet, had no one ever written such,
> And if no one read what they have told,
> What should we know, what should we know ?
> However hard they strove in thought,
> The saint today, the sage of old
> Would still be lost, have naught to show.
>
> The ancient god with herb and balm
> Took pity on the stricken host
> Of suffering, sore humanity.
> And he who made the compass-cart
> Showed them the way whose way was lost,
> A guide in their perplexity.
>
> Yet senseless dawdlers in this world,
> The three-fold realm of fantasy,

Mad, their madness do not perceive;
And all the four-fold living things
Are blinded so they cannot see
How blind they are, the self-deceived.

Born, reborn, reborn and reborn
Whence they have come they do not know.
Dying, dying, ever dying
They see not where it is they go.[13]

13. Vidyānanda

Although Jainism as in the previous period lacked patronage in the North, in the South it continued to hold a prominent place (and still thrives at Udipi, the center made famous by Mādhava and his following). Rāmānuja, as is well known, converted a Jaina king; but the famous shrine at Śravanabalagola in Mysore is a definite testimony to the importance of Jainism in the history of that area, even though there is little evidence today of its continuation in the extreme South where once it had not only royal patronage but some new developments in the dialogues and controversies with the Buddhists and Nyāya-Vaiśeṣikas. During the ninth and immediately following centuries as much as one-third of the population of the Deccan may have been following the gospel of Mahāvīra.

Vidyānada (fl. 795-840) worked in unbroken continuity with the work previously done by such as Akalaṅka, Sāmantabhadra, and Haribhadra Sūri.

> Akalaṅka had conducted his thought-experiment on three different levels, and in each case he was some sort of a pioneer. But Vidyānanda had received in heritage all that Akalaṅka was able to achieve. So the first task before him was to integrate into one whole the different strands of Akalaṅka's legacy and then there was the obvious task of augmenting the riches received by way of inheritance. Vidyānanda performed these tasks by composing two immortal works, viz.,

Tattvārthaślokavārthıka which is a commentary on the Tattvārthasūtra, and Aṣṭasahasrī which is a commentary on (Akalaṅka's) Aṣṭaśatī.[1]

Vidyānanda's *Satyaśāsana-parīkṣā* is a critique of all the other systems current in India in the period. It reviews from the Jaina point of view the Vedāntic monism, the Buddhist idealism, the Cārvāka materialism, the Sautrāntika fluxism, the Sāṃkhya evolutionism, the Vaiśeṣika categories and theism, the Nyāya salvation, and the Mīmāṁsā realism.

As far as present scholarship goes there is no verification that Vidyānanda knew Śaṅkara, but geographically and chronologically it would not be difficult to believe that he did. Nevertheless there were other interpreters of the *Vedānta Sūtras* before Śankara, some of whom had "advaitic" leanings. Vidyānada's refutation of Advaita in his *Satyaśāsana-parīkṣā* is done in detail, point by point. First, to the Advaitic claim that all pluralism and change is only due to *avidyā*, the Jaina position is clearly stated that "plurality is not capable of being repudiated as false appearance. Absolute unity and absolute plurality are both contradicted by experience. Differnce is as clearly given to experience as identity."[2] Nathmal Tatia in his study of the *Satyaśāsana-parīkṣā* summarizes Vidyānanda's position thus:

> The Vedāntist in despair refers to indeterminate (nirvikalpa) cognition, which cognizes bare existence, as the proof of the existence of Brahman which is unity, pure and simple. But the Jaina philosopher refuses to believe in the possibility of such undifferentiated experience. What we immediately perceive on opening our eyes is specific existence determined by space, time, otherness and the like. We never perceive what is not determined by space and what is not other than the knowing self.
>
> Our perceptual experience thus is found incapable of proving the Absolute Brahman. On the contrary, it proves difference to be as integral to reality as identity.[3]

Vidyānanda reviews the standard list of classical *pramāṇas* with which we have long since become familiar. The Advaitin places an inordinately heavy stress on inference from the Jaina realist point of view, inferring that *all* knowledge being inferential it is the mind of the cognizer rather than the object cognized that is all-important. The Jaina refutation of this is relatively easy:

> The unreality of an independent objective world is deduced from an analysis of even an ordinary empirical judgment. Take for instance the trite experience 'I see the pen'. What is the status of the pen? The pen is felt as an object no doubt. But it is felt as the content of, that is, coincident with its cognition. Now, by the application of the principle 'whatever is coincident with cognition is inside, i.e., identical with it' it follows that the pen, being coincident with its cognition, is inside, i.e., identical with the cognition. For instance, the character of cognitionhood, being coincident with the cognition is identical with the latter. All things can similarly be shown as coincident with cognition, and as such identical with it. There is thus nothing outside consciousness which alone exists.

But the Jaina considers the argument suicidal. The Vedāntist infers 'identity' from 'coincidence'. But how can the inference be valid unless both 'identity', the probandum, and 'coincidence', the probans are admitted as two distinct facts existing in their own right?[4]

The argument continues to show the ridiculousness of the Advaitic assertion that there is absolute identity between probandum and probans, since obviously if that were so in every case thought would be impossible as well as useless.

There is, nevertheless, a point of qualified agreement between the Jaina and the Vedāntin that sense perception alone is not adequate since this necessitates inference, i.e., putting two or more perceptions together (sight and touch) to make a concept (white silk). But then for the Vedāntin to attempt to deny the reality of the object thus perceived and inferred involves too many difficulties, including the 'self-shiningness' of the concept, i.e., the assertion or expression, "Why of course this is white silk ,"as though one had known white silk from eternity and only needed the perception-*cum*-inference to recognize its eternal essence (that being likewise tautologous with the eternal, undifferentiated, indescribable *nirguṇa*-Brahman). Such a reduction to tautology is really an admission of ignorance, which is just the opposite of the Advaitin's claim. Tatia summarizes as follows:

> With the collapse of inference as the proof of monism, the Vedāntist in the last resort falls back upon revelation(Āgama) in support of his position. But the question arises whether revelation is ontologically different from the Absolute or not. If it be absolutely different from the Absolute, this will prove the dualism of revelation and Brahman at any rate. If on the contrary it be absolutely identical with the Absolute Brahman which it seeks to establish, then the revelation will be as much an unproved fact as the monistic Absolute which is yet to be established. Certainly the means of proof and the object of proof cannot be absolutely identical as in that case the two will be on the same level so far as they are not established facts.[5]

This is reinforced by the recognition that as soon as the Advaiti uses any grammatical form, such as "*sarvaṃ vai khalvidṃ brahma*" (all that exists is the Absolute), he is involved in subject-object relationality, and in order to assert his anti-relationality he has to become involved in it. So his assertion is self-refuting.

Vidyānanda argues that the Advaitin claim to self-validity or self-intuition as proof for the Absolute is also self-refuting, or else it is no proof, since once again there is the distinction between that which is to be proved and the proof proffered in its behalf. Indeed, one might add, if it were truly self-proved then it should be obvious to everyone, even the most stupid or the most wicked or the most miserably bound to *saṃsāra*, which is very obviously not true. Or again, in Tatia's words, "nor can the Absolute be taken as self-proved for why not then plurality or voidity or the doctrine of universal illusion be accepted as the ultimate truth."[6]

No Advaitin will ever admit a distinction between consciousness and content of consciousness. Hence he has no way of refuting the assertion that there is that difference since he cannot even admit that there is difference between contradiction and contradictor. Moreover, such a pure consciousness could not prove the invalidity of ordinary experience since it cannot really know any ordinary experience, if indeed it 'knows' anything at all. The negation of dualism is such an important factor in the whole history of Indian philosophy that it might be well to follow Vidyānanda's way of dealing with it. Tatia explains:

> Furthermore, monism can be established only by the negation of dualism. In fact, Śaṅkara, the founder of the school of monistic Vedānta, has called his philosophy the doctrine of non-dualism. The expression 'non-dualism' can convey an intelligible meaning only if dualism be understood. Now 'dualism' is a whole (akhaṇḍa) expression and stands for a whole concept. It can be asserted as a universal proposition that the negation of a whole concept presupposes the reality of the concept in some other context. Of course, there are such expressions as 'a square-circle' which do not stand for anything real, and its negation by such a negative expression as 'a non-square-circle' cannot be thought to presuppose the reality of the negatum. But this does not invalidate the universal proposition: 'The negatum is always real'. The rule holds only in the case of whole world and whole concepts. A square-circle is only an attempt at combination of square and circle, and it becomes a fiction because the two concepts are mutually repellent. It is for this reason that the rule is propounded to hold good of whole concepts *qua* negata. Now monism *qua* negation of dualism is possible only if dualism be a false appearance. But dualism being a whole concept, its negation will necessarily presuppose the reality of the negatum (*sc.* dualism) in some context or other.

The Vedāntist however is not convinced by such linguistic arguments. Even if dualism is regarded as a concept, its negation cannot be made the ground of its ontological reality. The negation of dualism does not in reality belong to the Absolute. The whole logical apparatus which is the creation of the professional logician is possessed of a provisional value. It is valid until the ultimate truth is realized. But what is the necessity of negation of dualism and what again is the reason for the adoption of the logical apparatus

> for the establishment of monistic position by the Vadāntist? The Vedāntist answers that the whole order of plurality is an unreal show which has deceived the dualist and the pluralist into the belief of its ultimate reality. When the Vedāntist tries to convince the dualist of his error, he has to adopt the logical apparatus invented by the logicians of the realistic persuasion. The distinction of self and not-self is necessitated by avidyā and is not to be mistaken as possessed of ultimate validity. So the charge of self-contradiction urged against the Vedāntist is the outcome of misunderstanding.[7]

Such, however, from the Jaina standpoint is the *pūrvapakṣa*, not the *siddhānta*. Tatia states Vidyānanda's position thus:

> The Jaina frankly confesses his inability to appreciate the argument of the Vedāntist. In the first place, the postulation of nescience which the Vedāntist himself admits to be incapable of any proof strikes him as an unphilosophical position. It is extremely puzzling that a philosophy should subscribe to a position which is not amenable to test by any accredited organ of knowledge. Whatever may be the subject of dispute call it truth or untruth, science or nescience, the matter can be finally decided by means of the accredited sources of knowledge available to us. The Jaina does not dispute the existence of nescience, but he insists that this is also a matter of proof.[8]

It is not an easy task to refute a philosophy which even denies the validity of all refutations as such, and the Advaitin will remain convinced of his *darśana* even though every possible logical peg is removed from his scaffolding. It sometimes seems that the Advaitin claims to be already established in divine omniscience, though it is difficult to find in the whole of human history any evidence whatsoever that any sane human being of that sort can be found. Even al-Ḥallāj in his most extreme moments would not make such an exaggerated claim.

As we consider Vidyānanda's refutation of the Buddhist idealism, we might recall that there were the parallel refutations of the Chinese Mahāyāna schools by the early Neo-Confucianists. Han Yü, who was almost exactly the contemporary of Vidyānanda, appealed as much to the naturalism of Taoism in his refutations of Mahāyāna as to the strictly Confucian classics. Very often, especially when there is a sort of neo-orthodoxy in the making, what is refuted has a major influence on the refuter. Thus we get a thesis-antithesis-synthesis situation such that what actually comes out in this century is a sort of Larger Monism rather than outright objections and rejections. Vidyānanda does have to give some concessions to the Advaitins, so that perhaps he becomes more definitely metaphysical than his predecessors, who were more ethically ascetic, logical and matter-of-fact realists. Likewise, Han Yü is a pioneer in metaphysical rather than merely ethical Neo-Confucianism; and it might even be argued that his appeal to Taoist naturalism makes him more parallel to the Jaina opposition to Buddhism and Advaita than to the continuing Nyāya-Vaiśeṣika school.

Vidyānanda's refutation of the Mahāyāna idealism already had a long history behind it in India. It is the *vijñāna* basis of Yogācāra Buddhism that he attacks first, following Akalaṅka, after reviewing their own rejection of the epistemologies of the Sautrāntika, the Yangas (Naiyāyikas and Vaiśeṣikas), the Sāṃkhya, and the Jainas.

> The Jaina philosopher observes that the subjectivist establishes his position by means of inference, and refutes the validity of all instruments of knowledge in the same breath. This is nothing but blatant self-contradiction. Without the support of an organ of knowledge, the Buddhist cannot prove the falsity of the theories of rival philosophers who believe in extra-mental reality. Not only this, the subjectivist cannot prove the falsity of the differentiation of cognition into an act and content. He holds that our cognitions are momentary and self-intuited and that there are other epistemic subjects. Certainly all these facts cannot be proved by our intuitions. The service of inference as a valid instrument of knowlege must be requisitioned. A cognition may be felt by itself, but it is not felt as momentary, or as not cognized by another. Moreover, if the cognition has no veridical reference to a real extra-subjective fact, how can the subjectivist believe in

> the existence of other subjects ? The denial of genuine extra-subjective reference must end in solipsism.[9]

The refutation continues from there basically according to the same technique applied in the case of Advaita, namely the arguments against the subjectivity of the assertion of no difference between knower, known and knowing, and against the subjectivist manner of trying to avoid apparent self-contradiction. Dignāga is cited in this context, and of course the *pūrvapakṣa* in his behalf appeals as ever to the distinction between the pragmatic *samṛtti* and the *nirvṛtti* levels. Dharmakīrti also is refuted in the following way:

> The Jaina philosopher observes that his charges could be ineffective if the Buddhist idealist succeeded in proving that his conclusion was established by an unimpeachable logical ground. Dharmakīrti asserts that the 'identity' of cognition and content follows from the 'necessity of their being known together'. But what is the meaning of the expression the 'necessity of being known together' and of the term 'identity'? The former may possibly be interpreted as the 'absence of separate cognition' and 'identity' may be understood to mean 'absence of numerical difference'. In other words, the 'negation of separate cognition' may be made the ground for the inference of 'negation of numerical difference'. But this is not possible because there can be no necessary relation beween two negations.[10]

This is further supported by the traditional smoke and fire on the mountain paradigm instance, Vidyānanda implicitly taking sides with the Naiyāyikas, especially in terms of the negative instances of *absence* of cause, i.e., whether an absence of a cause can have causal effect on an absence of the effect, etc., Vidyānanda asserting that obviously there can be no valid syllogism where both premises are negative.

> There is no independent relation possible between two negations. The Buddhist argument could be effective if the positive concomitance between 'separate cognition' and 'numerical difference' were possible. To be explicit, the Buddhist is the last person to assert that a separate cognition of the content

> from that of the cognition concerned is possible by means of which the numerical difference of the cognition and content can be established; for the admission of the possibility of the content, separate and numerically different from that of the cognition, will knock out the Buddhist position of identity of cognition and content. The Buddhist therefore is precluded from asserting a logically necessary relation between their corresponding negations as negations have no independent logical relation apart from that of their opposite positives. The result will not be different even if either of the terms be given a positive interpretation. Thus if the probandum be asserted to be positive identity, it cannot be proved from negative probans, because there can be no relation between a positive and a negative term. Causality and identity of essence are recognized to be the two types of necessary relation. But these two relations are found to obtain between positive entities and not non-entities, nor between an entity and a non-entity. The same difficulty will stand in the way if the probans is supposed to stand for a positive fact. But let us see if the Buddhist can establish his position by making the probans and probandum both positive. Thus it may be interpreted that the 'necessity of being known together' means 'identity of the cognition' and the probandum is 'identity of the two'. But this interpretation would make the inference a case of tautology because the probans will not be different from the probandum.[11]

These technicalities of logic are increasingly being translated into modern symbolic logic in present-day explications. Suffice to note that here we certainly do not have any appeal to anything remotely resembling F.S.C. Northrop's famous "undifferentiated aesthetic continuum". Quite the contrary, just as in the previous centuries in India logical expertise became the criterion *par excellence* for genuine philosophizing—as it did only abortively with Boethius, not to be revived until Abelard in the late eleventh and early twelfth centuries in Latin Europe—so even in the basically monistic ninth century this expertise continued to develop. And in this particular instance it is used specifically as a refutation of any possible appeal to any "undifferentiated" stance whatsoever !

Tatia explicitly states in Vidyānanda's behalf : "The Jaina avers that the necessity of compresence of two or more contents in one cognition proves neither the identity of the contents *inter se* nor the iden ity of the contents of the cognition."[12] Of course he illustrates this with particular examples. We might again cite Han Yü's appeal to Taoist naturalism and Confucianist realism as at least loosely parallel to Vidyānanda's position when he further insists :

> Moreover, we do not find any logical absurdity in the supposition that things may be perceived together and yet be different from one another. Thus, for instance, when any subject is seen, it is seen together with light. But nobody will conclude from this that light and the jar or the pen are identical. It is quite possible to argue that the relation between cognition and its content is one of illuminer and illumined. And that they are felt together is due to the fact that without the cognition of the one the other cannot be cognized. In other words, the relation may be one of means and end, condition and conditional.[13]

From this sequence Vidyānanda looks to the opposite pole of the continuum of types of philosophies, namely to the Cārvāka materialism. We do not know whether there were any philosophers around who were openly espousing this position, though in the time of Buddha and Mahāvīra it was not uncommon. As in later times in Latin Europe and continuously in Byzantium, it was never completely forgotten and waș inherently a sufficiently strong possible position that everyone felt obligated to give some sort of at least nominal refutation. We may speculate that Vidyānanda's refutation of materialism follows immediately after his refutations of Advaita and the Vijñānavāda/ Yogācāra because he wan ed to be careful, having refuted one extreme, not to fall in any way into an opposite extreme. This seems an especially sensitive point with Jainas since their realist metaphysics could well come under attack as being too materialistic; and their theory of karma likewise, being on the borderline of a materialist-realist view, might well be attacked.

Vidyānanda attacks the Cārvāka's denial of a non-material *jīva* or *ātman*: for the Jainas, unlike the Buddhists, never denied the existence of etiher the *jīva* or the *ātman*. Vidyānanda's argument is not in an illusionist or other-worldly manner but in terms realistically of the argument from causality.

> The Jaina philosopher observes that the materialist's denial of soul as an independent principle of consciousness goes against the law of causality. The nature of consciousness is radically different from matter and so it cannot be the product of material elements. The effect must be essentially homogeneous with the cause and reducible to the latter in turn. The law of causality demands that the cause and its effect must be mutually reducible. Consciousness is not reducible to matter and hence cannot be a material product.[14]

Vidyānanda makes the standard assertion of the distinction between internal and external experience (both of which are real but really distinct), for the strict materialist would have no basis for making this distinction. Similarly the distinction between intellectual and ethical faculties would be difficult to explain on a merely mechanist basis.

The next argument involves the distinctly Jaina doctrine of the possibility of an omniscient soul such as the Jaina Tīrthaṅkaras are supposed to have been and which is the ultimate goal of Jaina *sādhana*. Again the argument is as devastating for the Cārvāka materialist as it is simple; since he will not accept any *pramāṇa* except sense-perception, he can have no logic of negation at all. All he can assert is what he does perceive through his five senses; and for him to deny the existence of what he does not perceive would involve the other *pramāṇas*, notably inference if not *anupalabdhi* also.

> ...Perception, being capable of cognizing positive objects alone, cannot cognize the absence of omniscience. Even if perception is admitted as capable of cognizing the absence, the materialist should clarify whether it is capable of cognizing the absence of omniscience in a particular soul at a particular moment, or in all souls at all times. The first alternative will not refute our position, while the second would

prove the omniscience of the materialist himself, and land him in self-contradiction.[15]

The next school Vidyānanda considers is the Sautrāntika. Perhaps there were some Theravādins of the Sautrāntika persuasion still around in South India then since we know that something very similar was thriving in Ceylon during his era. The Sautrāntika position like the Jaina position is realist in its orientation and believes in material atoms in addition to psycho-intellective factors.

> The Jaina philosopher considers this Buddhist view of things to be opposed to experience and logic. The objects that we perceive are massive, permanent, and composite. We never perceive the atomic, momentary and simple objects. The Buddhist philosopher cannot dismiss this perception as illusory unless he succeeds in pointing out a perception which cognizes the momentary simple atom.[16]

The theme of part-whole relations is treated next in a relatively traditional way, emphasizing the view that even where atoms are joined together in a whole, that whole is perceptible as such and therefore might as well be accepted as just as real as the parts that make it up. After this comes Vidyānanda's view on the reality of universals, a topic which becomes increasingly strategic in all of Eurasia during the succeeding centuries even as it had already been treated quite exhaustively in India in the preceding centuries and with relative thoroughness in Byzantium, but not so much as yet in the Islamic world and Latin Europe.

Then comes, as we might expect, the *anātman* (no-self) doctrine, which is also universal among all schools of Buddhism. The Jainas have their own realist interpretation of the distinction between the *jīva* (soul) and *ātman* (Self), tending to emphasize the former whereas the Hindus with the Advaitins in the lead emphasize the latter. Of course the Jainas never will admit the *ātman*-Brahman equation, even when it is asserted by the non-Advaitin Hindus to be only that and not sheer identity. Given this age-long controversy between the Buddhists on the one hand and the Hindus and Jainas on the other, we may easily anticipate how Vidyānanda is going to deal with it. These arguments are quite universal, and evidently Vidyānanda does not have so much that is notably distinctive to offer about them.

The basic arguments might be broken down into the following simplified outline : (1) argument from the nature of time, which the Buddhist considers ungraspable and which the Jaina takes as real, substantially so ; (2) argument from causal relation, the Buddhist, according to the Jaina, committing a *reductio ad absurdum*, since if each momentary cause is exhausted in its particular momentary effect, then what is this momentary connection between them, and how can it be real enough to have causal power ? and (3) the argument from the very nature of the flux (*kṣaṇavāda*) itself. The first argument concerning flux is in terms of universal experience. We all normally experience a certain continuity of the experiencer, which we may most readily refer to as the continuing self. How then could the Buddhists claim that this is not the case but that there is only a continuity of momentary impressions ? The argument is put forth that if all that happens is only a succession of flashing moments, then by what means could one succession of flashing moments become aware that there is such a myriad of other flashing moments ? This argument needs careful examination in terms of modern Process philosophy also (Whitehead himself was bothered by it and managed to compromise somewhat by positing his doctrine of 'Eternal Objects'). To a great extent essentially the same objection was made by the realist branch of the Neo-Confucianists against the Buddhists, although in that case the argument was put more in ethical than in ontological terms, i.e., if there is no "true original human nature", then how can the Confucian virtues have any validity ?

Vidyānanda reinvokes the argument from the nature of time as additional support against the radical *kṣaṇavādin* view. For how could we as only a subtle series of flickerings ever have any sense of the passage of time; indeed, how could anyone ever know the difference between past, future and present ? Although Dignāga and Dharmakīrti took this difficulty as a basis for proving the unreal nature of time, as realists the Sautrāntikas would not go quite that far since this might entail that even the 'moments' of time themselves were also illusory, and this being conceded they would have to abandon their realism concerning atoms and the rest of their philosophy of nature. The Jainas are quite content to share with the Sautrāntikas all of their *realist* orientation, so the argument must remain in that context : if the 'moments' are real then the time not only of their occurrence but the continuum of time in which these 'moments' occur must be equally real, as the Jainas believe.

The heterodox schools now disposed of, Vidyānanda turns to the orthodox Hindu schools, and naturally Sāṃkhya comes first. Here the *pūrvapakṣa* is stated in the familiar dualism of *puruṣa* and *prakṛti*, evolution taking place in the latter while the former has only the role of observer and enjoyer. Expositions given more typically by modern apologists with Advaitic leanings usually minimize the plurality of the *puruṣas* in favor of the *Parama Puruṣa* so that plurality lies in the dynamism of the *prakṛti* while the *Parama Puruṣa* is identified with *nirguṇa*-Brahman. Here, however, the emphasis is put quite the other way around : "Prakṛti is one but the puruṣas are infinite in number. Both are ubiquitous. The prakṛti evolves in a definite order and the evolutes are twenty-three in number. ..."[17] The rest follows in more traditional order : the three *guṇas*, the sense organs, and the gross elements, etc., with *mokṣa* as the comprehension of the radical difference between *puruṣa* and *prakṛti*.

As with the Sautrāntika realism, there is much that original Jainism and original Sāṃkhya have in common as two of the oldest traditions in Indian civilization. Tracing the Jaina refutations might give us a better clue as to the nature of the original Sāṃkhya than the usual tracing back through the Advaita interpretations, which had been originated even in extreme form by Gauḍapāda. Both Jainism and Sāṃkhya posit a dualism between matter as non-living (*jaḍa*) and spirit or soul as living and conscious; both are realistic as far as their philosophy of nature is concerned; both put more emphasis on *jñāna* than on *bhakti* or *karma*; their concepts of the ultimate goal for man are very similar, *kevalajñāna*; and both in their original forms were technically atheistic although later Sāṃkhya became theistic.

In stating the refutation the following point is perhaps most basic : "The Sāṃkhya doctrine of unchanging puruṣa also does not commend itself to the Jaina. The puruṣa should be conceived as permanent-cum-changing."[18] In the Jaina case the *jīva* changes, quite distinct from the Advaita interpretation of *jīva-ātman,* for there is a sort of transformation that takes place as the gross *karmans* are purified, the *jīva* thus experiencing purification and therefore change. The Jainas insist on the *jīva* having consciousness of change and therefore disagree with the Sāṃkhya about the *puruṣas,* which supposedly have no connection with the material real world. The Jainas also insist that there can be radical novelty in the cosmic evolution, over against the Sāṃkhya's assertion that *prakṛti* is permanent, eternal and all-containing.

The rest concerns the radical dualism of classical Sāṃkhya, which the later Sāṃkhya tried to modify by making it theistic. The Jainas link up their quasi-dualism of matter and spirit by admitting a 'scientific' interplay between these two distinguishable factors : the *karmans* are material but they do infuse and infect the spiritual soul until they are purified and made ineffective. From this position, which is consonant with experience, it seems passing strange that anyone could insist that there is no connection between them, or if any at all, merely that of observer and enjoyer.

In Vidyānanda's refutation of the Vaiśeṣika system it is again not their realism or their doctrine of categories as such that he opposes but their theism and their particular system of categories (especially the distinction between the *saṁyoga* and *samavāya* relationships). Buddhism classically was not anti-theistic, as the original Jainas were and as systematically in philosophy the later Jaina *ācāryas* were also, but somewhat agnostic, avoiding theological bickerings as a source of suffering. But in popular Jainism even during Vidyānanda's time a sort of theism had developed in the *bhakti* mode, for the Jaina Tīrthaṅkaras had been deified for all practical purposes quite as much as the Buddha himself and all the panoply of Bodhisattvas with him. One development characteristic of the period was the custom of singing devotional hymns to the Jaina Tīrthaṅkaras. The *bhakti* atmosphere among Vaiṣṇavas and Śaivas had developed to such a high degree of artistic fervor and perfection that in spite of the Jaina formal commitment to *kevalajñāna* as the chief if not the only ultimate goal for man, a considerable amount of *bhakti* literature became quite popular and a certain degree of syncretism was inevitable, almost amounting to a sort of popular henotheism parallel with other sectarian tendencies of the period. This was characteristic not only in India but throughout Eurașia during this period, perhaps just beginning in the ninth century but continuing to become increasingly elaborate everywhere alongside the increasing elaboration in art and architecture.

Vidyānanda cannot see how an eternal material world could come out of an equally eternal but non-material deity. He probably would have raised the same objection against Aristotle's Prime Mover that he does against the Vaiśeṣikas and for essentially the same reasons. What Vidyānanda advances is a uniquely Jaina argument concerning the inherent causal power of the *karmans*, the difference here from the Mīmāṁsakas being that according to them *karma* is inexorable, affording virtually no remedy "even for the gods", whereas for the Jainas the *karmans* can be made ineffective by proper *sādhana*.

> Now God, though possessed of intelligence, is devoid of bodily organism and so does not satisfy the full condition of creation. Karman, though unconscious, makes up a composite material body according to the Jaina, and so it is on a par with God in this respect. Karman therefore is as much the satisfactory condition of creation as God of the Vaiśeṣika philosopher. ...But the Jaina submits that God also, being devoid of bodily organism, is incapable of knowing, willing and effort, and hence of performing the function of creation.[19]

The moral argument advanced against the Vaiśeṣika theism with only a minimum of modernizing interpretation could be made to sound almost like some of those proposed by Bertrand Russell, Julian Huxley, M.N. Roy or other atheist humanists—for the Jainas are first and foremost definitely humanists in their ethics, even though other humanists might not go so far in their asceticism or their metaphysics.

> The Vaiśeṣika believes in God as the dispenser of justice in accordance with the merits and demerits acquired by the

person. In other words, God grants the fruits of our own karman. The Jaina thinks karman is the sole and sufficient condition capable of producing the results of good and bad moral acts.[20]

The Nyāya system being virtually identical with the Vaiśeṣika as far as these matters are concerned Vidyānanda gives it only passing mention. He concludes with a refutation of the Mīmāṁsā, which arguments as not essentially new or different from those discussed we need not follow.

14. Haribhadra

The ninth century Buddhist philosopher Haribhadra should not be confused with the better-known Haribhadra Sūri, the famous eighth century Jaina *ācārya*. We may readily infer from the case of Haribhadra that there was no lessening of the dialectical expertise among Buddhists in India in the ninth century even though the stereotype still prevails that there were no Buddhists left in India after the beginnings of Islam and the supposed conversions effected by Śaṅkara.

For our present discussion we shall be following Obermiller's article entitled "A Study of the Twenty Aspects of Śūnyatā" with the explanatory sub-title, "Based on Haribhadra's *Abhisamayālaṃkāra-ālokā* and the *Pañcaviṃśatisāhasrikā-prajñāpāramitā-sūtra*". The translation of *śūnyatā* as "relativity" will raise a lot of disturbing waves on the supposedly mirror-like lake of contemplative reflection usually associated with the Mādhyamika tradition. Although through the centuries the term *śūnya* has accumulated a heavy burden of connotation, its original denotation was simply "zero". Hence the now more traditional translation as 'emptiness' is probably preferable, even though it must be granted that around this zero-emptiness all the possible relativities could and did accumulate during the centuries since Nāgārjuna himself and continue to do so afresh in our own time, interpretations ranging from the sheerest other worldly mysticism to rigorous dialectical logic of negation and interpretation as radical scepticism. Certainly this text fits superbly into our designation of the ninth century as the century of "monism in many moods".

The first aspect of *śūnyatā* is "subjective relativity" and is interpreted in terms of the unreliability of the senses, especially the faculty of vision.

The second aspect of *śūnyatā* is "objective relativity". The first being accepted, the second follows : scepticism at best concerning the reality of the external world, much less the particular external elements, visible matter, etc.

The third aspect of *śūnyatā* is "both subjective and objective relativity". We might add the further refinement interpretatively that instead of the Kantian *ohne begriffe* in which the percepts and the concepts complement each other, or the external and the internal put together correct each other as some might claim, here they actually cancel each other out—or would if they could be taken as reliable singly, which according to Mādhyamika negative-eliminative-reductive dialectics is not allowable since this would simply be like adding two zeros or multiplying zero by zero.

The fourth aspect of *śūnyatā* is "relativity of (the transcendental wisdom cognizing) relativity". It might well have been translated "the emptiness of emptiness" since the intention is that one may not make a dogma out of anti-dogmatism. Obermiller explains that "the understructure or the foundation of relativity is considered to be the principle of relativity itself."[1] The intention is to avoid the logical fallacy of infinite regress, the emptiness of emptiness of emptiness, etc.

The fifth aspect of *śūnyatā* is "the great relativity". Here the metaphor is used of how the points of the compass are relative to each other as well as relative to the full 'round' of the horizon. Though the full horizon is all-embracing, nevertheless it also has no *svabhāva*, no self-subsistence, except in so far as it is related to the points that compose it. This is analogical to a certain stage of spiritual development of the Bodhisattva, i.e., once one realizes that there is no "absolute reality" as such apart from the particulars that compose it, and that the particulars have no definite reality except relationally, then there will be detachment from any dogmatic views.

The sixth aspect of *śūnyatā* is "relativity of the ultimate reality". What is intended is no less than *nirvāṇa*, which in its original Abhidamma formulation simply meant the extinction of desire in the simple psychological sense as a result of proper discipline according to the Eight-fold Noble Path and the *pratītya-samutpāda*. But in the centuries since then *nirvāṇa* had taken on not only mystical overtones but had become, quite contrary to the Buddha's original intentions, the subject of endless metaphysical disputations. This was probably why Nāgārjuna, as an effort at trimming off this superfluous pseudo-philosophizing, had also called *nirvāṇa śūnya*. With an historical approach to these matters in mind we may here recall the dictum, paradoxical as it seems to be, that *saṃsāra* is *nirvāṇa* and *nirvāṇa* is *saṃsāra*. But as far as spiritual discipline is concerned, the intention is the stage of "renunciation of renunciation" or the "discipline of no discipline", which is just as dangerous to adopt for the neophyte as it is necessary for the adept.

The seventh aspect of *śūnyatā* is "the relativity of conditioned existence". This seems to begin the path of transdescendence, or of the Bodhisattva Vow and its implications, for the renunciation of *nirvāṇa* in the previous "aspect" has that implication as the highest attainable spiritual state in this life. Even in Plotinus many centuries before one finds both the ascending and the descending orders. Obermiller writes : "The Three Spheres of Existence which are a product of causes and conditions...are devoid of a separate essence of their own."[2] In other words, evidently it is only after gaining complete detachment that we realize the complete contingency of the world.

The eighth aspect of *śūnyatā* is "the relativity of the unconditioned". This "unconditioned" is further defined as "that which is beginningless, endless and not liable to change. It is relative, inasmuch as origination etc. (which are denied in) the beginningless and so on, do not exist, being the contradictorily opposed parts, the mere foundation of a name."[3] This beginninglessness or unconditionedness was taken as belonging to God in the Judeo-Christian-Islamic nexus of Scholasticism ever since John Philopon's "corrections" of Aristotle's and Proclus' notion that matter is beginningless and unconditioned. But here no doubt is the same claim essentially of the Sāṃkhyas and the Vaiśeṣikas alike, and the Jainas as well, that matter is eternal and uncreated even though subject to natural laws or *dharma*. Whereas in the ascending order of gaining spiritual detachment one has to penetrate this "veil of matter", so in the transdescending order one sees the material universe as it really is, which is that there really is no such thing, according to Mādhyamika, as a permanent and unconditioned, uncreated "stuff"—whatever it might be, material or not—that is not changing and literally unsubstantial; it is only a *nāmarūpa*, name-and-form, a manner of speaking, an "as if".

The ninth aspect of *śūnyatā* is "the absolute relativity". It is the sort of position that all in India but the Advaitins both before and long after the ninth century rejected outright or else refuted with considerable expertise as well as zeal. Having seen the non-ultimacy of any spiritual absolute paralleled by the non-ultimacy of the opposite end of the hierarchy, now we see here the non-ultimacy of the whole range in between—the *metaxù*, to use Plato's term—almost in anticipation of Bruno's famous three infinities. In fact, one might well translate *śūnyatā* as "infinity" rather than "relativity". It is only after considerable discipline of detachment that we get the vision of the infinitely great, the infinitely small and the infinity of mediation in between them, much less the realization that even this is only another way of looking at the world. This infinity of mediation too is unsubstantial, a *nāmarūpa*, a *śūnyatā*.

The tenth aspect of *śūnyatā* is "the relativity of degree". This means that "'the beginning', 'the middle' and 'the end' are ideas that are correlative and have consequently no real essence of their own...(There is consequently no differentiation of good and bad, high and low, etc.)".[4] Sooner or later all monist philosophies have to deal with the dualities and/or pluralities whether by ignoring them or undermining them or transcending them, or simply, like the typical Advaita tendency and to some extent also this Śūnyavāda tendency, by absorbing them like a sponge, or like water puddles being evaporated in the sun.

The eleventh aspect of *śūnyatā* is "the relativity of the points that are not to be rejected". This means that "rejection, etc., which has the character of action is connected with an enunciation of non-rejection".[5] In other words, rejection and non-rejection in true Mādhyamika style tend to cancel each other out. Nevertheless, it is not exactly clear in what sense, given the by then age-old adage that *nirvāṇa* is *saṃsāra* and *saṃsāra* is *nirvāṇa*, *nirvāṇa* is not to be rejected, even though it is to be regarded as also a *śūnyatā*.

The twelfth aspect of *śūnyatā* is "the relativity of the ultimate essence". It is unclear what the ultimate essence might be in this ultra-Buddhist context that rejects all essences and substances. Even though not to be rejected, again all such notions are also *śūnyatā*; so perhaps what is meant is that having acquired the discipline of complete detachment, we can now deal with non-Buddhistic concepts in a sort of pragmatic "as if" or instrumental way. The famous Dignāga had done essentially the same in the Vijñānavāda heritage.

The thirteenth aspect of *śūnyatā* is "the relativity of all the elements of existence". This means that "every separate element is devoid of a real essence of its own. Indeed, all the elements, those belonging to the categories of the conditioned as well as the unconditioned, are mutually dependent and have consequently no ultimate existence."[6]

The fourteenth aspect of *śūnyatā* is "the relativity of essence". The term "essence" here is intended to indicate the "general and specific characteristics (which are put forth as the essences of things)", these, of course, being considered as merely nominal and not substantial. The emphasis could be put into the historical context of the attempts at refutation of the Jaina and Vaiśeṣika theories that not only are there substances which are real, impenetrable, unaltering and unalterable, but that the relations between them can be categorized systematically and realistically.

The fifteenth aspect of *śūnyatā* is "the relativity of the present, past and future which cannot be perceived (all of them at once)". This means that "if we take the elements relating to the past, etc. separately, it is impossible to perceive (within each of these categories) other elements which are dialectically opposed. Indeed, (time is a property) which can be only nominally attributed to a thing"[7]. We may here recall that whereas the Brahmanical schools considered time or temporality as a substantial characteristic of substantial things, the Buddhists considered time as no more than a pragmatic notion. Yet not all the Buddhist schools agreed in detail about the relation between one *kṣaṇa* and another, some even denying any continuity altogether, each event, each moment, being unique. One is here easily tempted to bring in the controversy about the nature of time between Kant and Bergson; but that being anachronous we must rather guard against reading Bergson into the Buddhist theories and Kant into the Brahmanical ones. The temptation is also there to bring in Meister Eckhardt's concept of the Eternal Now. Haribhadra would say of Eckhardt's view that it is also a *śūnyatā*, an indefinable. And if anything it is even worse than the Momentary Now. For if even that cannot be considered as really real, then how could stretching it out to something else completely unknown called "eternal" or "eternity" solve the problem. Rather it would only magnify it infinitely. We begin to suspect that what these Mādhyamikas are really trying to get us to understand is not the reality or unreality of the things in the world as such (including ourselves), but rather the assertability of views as such, since any view, positive or negative or even neutral or any combination of the three, sooner or later can and will become a dogma.

Passing over the next four aspects, the twentieth aspect of *śūnyatā* is "the relativity of a foreign origin". This means that "the Ultimate Absolute of the elements is everlasting and exists independently from the appearance or the non-appearance of the Buddhas. It is relative being viewed in its (negative) relation to an agent from without. Indeed it is said:—Human effort that is directed upon the Ultimate Monistic Essence will have for its result only a useless toil".[8] This last sentence may sound terribly pessimistic if not even fatalistic, but in the historical perspective it is only another way of expressing the *via negativa*. Since the Mādhyamika never will admit any essence as such, much less any ultimate absolute essence, we might re-read the intention as something like this: In so far as any ultimate absolute essence could be posited, it would still be only a *śūnyatā* from the standpoint of any attempt to understand and/or approach it, much less —and here is the crux of the radical difference between Śūnyavāda and Advaita—any possibility of becoming identical with it !

Monism strictly speaking asserts the supreme unity, but here we are reminded that this also is another *śūnyatā*. Is the Mādhyamika or Śūnyavāda then not a monism? It is certainly not a pluralism or dualism, or even a pseudo-dualism like Advaita with its inescapable antinomy between *māya* and *nirguṇa*-Brahman. Seemingly one can go on endlessly listing what it is not, but one can never say what it is. We might take Śūnyavāda as a type of philosophy completely unique, neither idealism nor realism, neither monism nor pluralism, but at best a high scepticism in the sense that it counsels suspended judgment in every possible situation and dialectical detachment. But we may still for all practical purposes classify it as a monism of an extreme type—the most extreme "mood", just as zero (*śūnya*) in the number series is neither plus nor minus but rather the nonsubstantial point of orientation, there being no true unity without it for it is the only non-dual concept which has no opposite.

15. Vācaspati Miśra

With Vācaspati Miśra (c. 850) and the other sub-varieties of Advaita belonging to the first generation after Śaṅkara it may well be posited that we are in a new cycle, which we may designate as the "exfoliation and elaboration" of the ninth century monisms and their refutations. "Scholasticism" may be used to designate the whole of Eurasia after the late ninth century, for the method is essentially the same in all the geographical regions, as is the substance of the basic themes treated. Most of the major works are in the form of commentaries on the charismatic or revealed texts.

Of the post-Śaṅkara Advaitins, Vācaspati is certainly one of the most important. In fact one gets the definite impression that it was he who made Advaita a dominating philosophy rather than Śaṅkara himself. Śaṅkara is certainly the more charismatic figure, but he died too young to remove all the inconsistencies in his commitments. That job was left to his immediate successors, among whom Vācaspati is certainly the most comprehensive and versatile. Given his continuing popularity in India within the orthodox Advaita tradition, it is strange that he is not better known in Euramerica. His *Bhāmatī*, for example, is a standard text for every student of Indian philosophy working in the traditional Saṁskṛt medium, yet it is very difficult to get a copy in the United States.

Vācaspati was extremely prolific. There is scarcely any variety of philosophy in India up to his time that he did not take in stride, writing commentaries on them all. Those in India who are still in the authentic Saṁskṛt tradition regard him as *the* Indian philosopher *par excellence*, rivalled only by Śaṅkara himself; and from the standpoint of comprehensiveness and thoroughness of treatment of every theme in its proper proportion it might well be claimed that he is even greater in stature, even if not in charisma, than Śaṅkara. At least these claims may be made within the Advaita heritage, although there are those in the heritage of Rāmānuja, Mādhava, Nimbarka, Vallabha and other Vaiṣṇava philosophers, as well as those who look rather to Abhinavagupta and other non-Advaitin Śaiva traditions, who would not accede to such an unbiased valuation.

Vācaspati is a super-eclectic, for virtually all that we have as far as established opinions are concerned has been filtered through him. Indeed, if he should have a single epithet no doubt he should be dubbed "The Commentator" since he wrote commentaries on virtually every school of philosophy before him, even though what we have that is independently his own is very little. Vācaspati is most remembered as a commentator of such faithfulness to the text that many even in other camps than the Advaita persuasion resort to him in order to reconstruct texts before his time. His famous commentary on the Sāṃkhya *Sūtras* became so popular that the original as formulated and commented on before him evidently was virtually forgotten. This was so with many if not most of the pre-Śaṅkara *sūtras* and commentaries, but it seems that this was especially true of the Sāṃkhya tradition; much of its terminology was fully incorporated into the Advaita tradition and to some extent implicitly in the *Brahma Sūtras* themselves without commentary.

Almost every interpretation of Śaṅkara's Advaita can be traced back to Vācaspati's *Bhāmatī*, which is his commentary on Śaṅkara's *Brahma-Sūtra-Bhāṣya*. But there are also the other works of almost if not equal importance from the standpoint of his expertise in dialectical critique and refutation, especially of the Nyāya-Vaiśeṣika school, Vācaspati being the chief rival of Jayanta Bhaṭṭa. These include the *Nyāyakaṇikā*, based on Maṇḍana Miśra's *Vidhiviveka*; the *Nyāyasūcīnibandhu*, based on Gautama's *Nyāya-Sūtras*; and the *Tātparyaṭīkā* based on Uddyotakara's *Nyāyavārttika*. The *Tattvakaumudī*, based on Iśvarakṛṣṇa's *Sāṃkhyakārikās*, contains his critique of the Sāṃkhya system and is probably the most studied next to the *Bhāmatī*. Then there is also the *Tattvabindu*, which includes a critique of the Sphoṭavāda variety of the Mīmāṁsā school, as well as the *Tattvavaiśāradī*, based on Patañjali's *Yoga Sūtras*.

In any variety of Advaita the topic of *māyā* comes to the fore. "Vācaspati Miśra regards the world as false appearance of Brahman associated with indefinable twofold avidyā. ...According to Vācaspati Miśra, Brahman is the independent creator of the world, and avidyā is its instrument which does not compromise its independence."[1] This position is fraught with difficulties, but the difficulty is really inherent in the problem itself, no matter how one approaches it; and Vācaspati's contemporaries were by no means unaware of this. Otherwise it would not have occupied so many minds with such intensity for so many centuries. Moreover, solution or no solution, the problem of radical ignorance (*avidyā*) is still surrounding us whether we are aware of it or not. Modernizers and apologists to those in the Western European heritage are very fond of pointing to Kant's "thing in itself" as the modern correlate; but more recent apologists may well re-examine Heisenberg, for example, in the light of Vācaspati's position.

The interpretations of *māyā* vary after Śaṅkara between (1) the reflection theory (*pratibimbavāda*) of Padmapāda, (2) the 'mistake' theory (*bhrāntivāda*) of Sureśvara, (3) the superimposition theory (*adhyāsa*) of others and to some extent also of Vācaspati, and (4) the radical ignorance theory (*avidyā*) of Vācaspati. It must not be assumed that this radical ignorance is a simple matter like the ordinary everyday realization of ignorance. It is the metaphysical impossibility for finite minds to encompass not just the myriads of affections and facts but the various levels which must be penetrated before the *pāramārthika* perspective is attained and maintained in virtually total detachment. Through the 'veil' of radical ignorance, nevertheless, the *nirguṇa*-Brahman is revealed by concealing itself, as it were; in short, here is the *āvaraṇa-vikṣepa* paradox that Brahman reveals its true nature by concealing itself behind this screen of *māyā*. That is almost like saying that in every controversy God will be in the opposition—lest one become proud!

In so far as anything participates in reality there is that echo, at least, of Reality-as-such, which really is no more but no less than Brahman. Thus it is that everything in itself, in its own true nature, is indeed indescribable. This does at first admittedly seem exasperating. Even Proust in the modern world is an example on the one hand, and perhaps Einstein and his critics on the other. For literally, no matter what you are describing, there is no limit to what you can say about it, not to mention what you must admit you cannot say about it. *Anirvacanīya*, then, remains the key word for the whole system. Illustration is also illusion since it can only represent, but not be, the object described. For such is the inextricability of *māyā* : we cannot get out of it because we can do nothing without it !

According to strict Advaita any claim to knowledge of particular things must perforce be in the realm of *māyā*, which, by definition, is indefinable. But there is the question which bothers Rāmānuja profoundly in the next century, namely whether "indefinability" can be a "definition" at all since we are here caught in a paradox that is too nearly an outright contradiction. In the Advaita formulae the only indefinables are *māyā* on the one hand and *nirguṇa*-Brahman on the other; but that leaves nothing out, with the result that *a priori* any attempt at definition of anything less than *māyā* or Brahman will only lead into further difficulties. Opponents can and do taunt Advaitins about their own disagreements since, on the one hand, if the popular Advaitin remark holds good in any sense that it really doesn't make any difference since it is *all māyā* or ignorance, then why all the fuss and botheration; but, on the other hand, since the system seriously claims to have access to *The* truth as the all-embracing unity, which must be *ad-vaita,* undivided, "one only without a second", how is it that there are so very many 'seconds' in the interminable arguments even within the fold ?

In a word, everything else is *māyā* or within the realm of *māyā* except the consciousness that this is so. But that (level of) consciousness has no proof or disproof, since in itself it scarcely exists in its own right, for rather it is a *perspective* from which all else is viewed. The key term is *sva-prakāśatā* : "Vācaspati defines truth and reality as immediate self-revelation (*sva-prakāśatā*) which is never contradicted (*abādhita*). Only the pure self can be said to be in this sense ultimately real. He thus definitely rejects the definition of reality as the participation of the class-concept of being, as the Naiyāyikas hold, or capacity of doing work (*arthakriyā-kāritva*), as the Buddhists hold."[2] Some Advaitins and implicitly Vācaspati among them claimed to have already incorporated into their perspectives the Buddhist *prajñā* and its correlates, including the *Prajñāpāramitā* literature, claiming in essence that *jñāna mārga* is inclusive of the *prajñā* perspective, and not the other way around. That both heritages are in a definite sense varieties of *māyāvāda* is fairly clear (although the Buddhists do not necessarily call it that). Certainly the *Buddhatathatā* concept is very similar to the *nirguṇa*-Brahman of the Vedānta in that they both 'indicate' what cannot be expressed much less explicated except in negative terms. Indeed the two systems are virtually identical in so many ways that one too easily forgets the basic difference (which Advaitins seem more prone to try to ignore than the Buddhists). The Buddhists retain a dynamic orientation, emphasizing the changeability and transciency of literally everything, whereas the Advaitins—and without this, pointedly Vācaspati does appear to be a sort of chamelion, changing colors according to the topic at hand—insist on the substantiality and permanency of *nirguṇa*-Brahman.

Each fine point concerning *avidyā* has been debated almost threadbare, for the very nature and proof of *avidyā* is the fact that we do not know the true answer to these questions and hence argumentation about them can be, as it has been, literally endless and inexhaustible. "Like Maṇḍana Miśra, Vācaspati Miśra regards an empirical self as the abode of avidyā, and Brahman as its object. Avidyā is indefinable, and does not abide in Brahman. That is eternal and pure. A jīva is Brahman limited by limited indefinable avidyā. Identified with the subtle body, the gross body, and the sense organs, it is the object of I-consciousness."[3] The chief ignorance after all is the nature of the ego as distinct from our true "region of identification" (if we may call it that) which distinguishes the *ātman*-Brahman relation, which is really limitless. This snag of the ego receives considerable attention from Vācaspati. But the Vaiṣṇava critics of Advaita and others may still be correct that, lacking *bhakti*, one can never get liberation from fascination with one's own ego. Having nothing outside of themselves to be devoted to, namely Bhagavān, God, no wonder they spin around endlessly in the same place instead of going somewhere with all that energy !

Adhyāsa is the doctrine that we superimpose our wrong notions on the truth such that the way to correction is simply to remove the untruth so that the truth may shine in its own brilliance—a very inviting view indeed. Sinha writes :

> Inner Self is pure consciousness and bliss. Buddhi and ahaṁkara are unconscious, active, and painful. They are opposed to each other. But because of nonapprehension of difference between them, their attributes are superimposed on each other. Superimposition of not-self on Inner Self is the root of all evils. It is the nescience (avidyā). Because of this superimposition the pure, blissful Inner Ātman appears to suffer misery. The nonapprehension of difference is terminated by the apprehension of difference between them through hearing, reflection and meditation. Then the comprehension of the nature of Reality—the true knowledge (vidyā) of Ātman of the nature of consciousness dawns, which removes superimposition.[4]

There are endless quibbles about which really comes first, the illumination that removes the *adhyāsa* or the removal of *adhyāsa* in order for the illumination to take place, as well as whether it happens gradually as in Sōtō Zen or suddenly as in Rinzai

Zen. For the Vedāntins of all varieties took the matter very much in earnest, and still do today.

The Advaitic complete identification of *ātman* and Brahman makes even the most extreme Augustinians and Neo-Platonists look like crass materialists by comparison. While some varieties of Taoism might find rough parallels, all of the Vaiṣṇava Vedāntists take exception or else object outright. Ṣūfīs often as not are so similar to Advaitins that it is rather frequently asserted that they must have influenced each other. Vācaspati's view is that "when a jīva is liberated, it realizes Ātman's purity and the like. It is, in its essence, devoid of birth, old age and death. Ātman is eternally free and transcendent, and appears to be bound because of avidyā."[5]

The status of the object is a terribly crucial theme for any variety of Advaita, which, *pace* Radhakrishnan's brilliant apologetics in terms of the then prevailing British idealism, is neither idealism nor realism, neither subjectivism nor objectivism, but a third type, unique in itself, transcending by sublation that bifurcation—at least according to its own claims, even though to the outsider it may appear to be more like a hydra: cut off one head and another appears somewhere else; or like a chamelion, changing color according to circumstances. Sinha writes :

> Vācaspati Miśra follows Śaṁkara faithfully in admitting externality of an object of perception. He avers that the witness (sākṣin) perceives an apprehension as apprehending an external object, which as different from an internal cognition cannot be denied. A cognition cannot cognize itself as an object, since it involves self-contradiction. It cognizes an object distinct from itself. A knower knows an object (e.g., blue) through knowledge. It does not know knowledge through another knowledge. Nor is knowledge a knower. So Vācaspati emphatically asserts the existence of an external object.[6]

A related question is the relative ontological status of the world, as mixed in *māyā* and yet depending ontologically, though not actively, on Brahman :

> Vācaspati Miśra avers that Ātman or Brahman Itself is the ontological reality of all phenomenal appearances. The world appearance and empirical selves are shown by the beginningless nescience. They are ontologically unreal. It is contended that the Śrutis assert Brahman to be the omniscient, omnipotent, cause of the world, Supreme Self of all, all-knowing, all-experiencing, all-desiring, all-tasting, all-smelling and the like, and that therefore the world is real.[7]

Needless to say, the matter does not remain fixed at that point in subsequent commentators, perhaps because, as often happens in history, one question being finally surrendered as unanswerable, other questions move in and take their place. In any case, quite as much as in Christian, Islamic or Jewish scholasticism, the last appeal is to scripture; and if the scriptures contradict each other—well, Advaitins are not Mu'tazilites !—too bad for the contradiction !

Very closely allied with the *saguṇa-nirguṇa* dispute is the question of the relation between Brahman and *Iśvara*, the Brahman-*ātman-jīva* relation of identity being established. Implicitly, by this very question being posed, we must recognize that in India the right and duty of philosophers to establish criteria for claims of religious phenomena was commonly accepted long before Vācaspati, as was not necessarily the case with the Byzantines or the Latin world of the same time, and this of course was vehemently denied by most orthodox Muslims. Śaṅkara himself did not ignore this question but left it inadequately and almost ambiguously answered. Among Śaṅkara's commentators Vācaspati is generally the clearest and most reliable. Sinha gives Vācaspati's position as follows :

> Īśvara is Brahman limited by avidyā, and omniscient and omnipotent. He is the cause of the world. Eternality, purity, consciousness, and freedom are the essential form of Brahman, not due to limiting adjuncts. But omniscience and omnipotence are the adventitious form of Brahman due to the limiting adjunct (avidyā). Īśvara's omniscience and omnipotence are due to the beginningless avidyā. He is the source of the Vedas. Īśvara is "all-acting, all-desiring, all-tasting,

> all-smelling". These determinate qualities are due to the limiting adjuncts, and are superimposed on Brahman. Brahman is indeterminate, uniform, homogeneous consciousness and existence. Its determinate qualities are really indeterminate, but are attributed to It because of its limiting adjuncts. Īśvara is Brahman limited by avidyā, and has determinate qualities. Brahman is indeterminate and attributeless. The determinate form of Īśvara is superimposed on Brahman because of the limiting adjuncts for meditation or prayer. Omniscient and omnipotent Īśvara is the creator of the world, which is an effect limited by objects in the nature of names and forms or appearances, that are neither real nor unreal but indefinable, and that are, in reality, unlimited, indeterminate Brahman.[8]

That later Latin scholastics were eventually faced with essentially the same problem has been clear ever since Rudolf Otto published his comparative mysticism book on Śaṅkara and Eckhardt.

Inevitably any treatment of virtually any traditional Indian philosophy or philosopher must deal with the problems related to *mokṣa*, variously translated as salvation, enlightenment, liberation, release. Likewise any treatment of Advaita of any variety must sooner or later come to terms with the Advaita version of the *jīvanmukta* doctrine, i.e., whether *mokṣa* is possible in the present body, or "embodied liberation". Other commentators on the *Brahma Sūtras* later, especially those of Vaiṣṇava persuasion, had considerable reservations about this, but Śaṅkara makes the most of it. Śaṅkara insists that it is a matter of *jñāna* alone rather than the saving grace of the Lord freely given in response to *bhakti* as the Vaiṣṇavas and some Śaivas later teach. After Vācaspati there begins to be a very involved discussion of all the fine points, such as whether *mokṣa* is a cause or an effect of *Brahma-vidyā* and the removal of *adhyāsa* and *avidyā*. Typically Vācaspati intends to give clarifying exposition of Śaṅkara's own thinking rather than his own.

Correspondingly, as to the means of reaching *mokṣa* there is by no means homogeneity among the different Advaitins. This is a matter on which most secularized philosophers today remain silent either through lack of personal experience or else in order to pretend that such intensive personal experience really does not 'count' in the external world. It is in the details of the technique of meditation (*upāsanā*) that the difficulties arise, as indeed they do also in the Latin scholastics' treatment of what has come to be called "mystical theology" as well as in the vast corpus of the many varieties of Buddhist literature on meditation ranging from the 'emptiness' *zazen* sitting of Rinzai to the ecstatic or even orgiastic rituals of extreme varieties of Tantra. Advaita, as Uttara Mīmāṁsā, must treat as the most important the *hearing* of the Vedas, comparable almost to the "hearing of the Word of the Lord" in Calvinist Christianity later on, or to the almost magical importance of the punctiliously correct chanting of the Holy Qur'ān. By Vācaspati's time the Vedas were regarded with no less reverence (almost to the point of superstition) than the Qur'ān. Hence the avid controversy whether hearing alone might be sufficient for *mokṣa*. Vācaspati leans towards the affirmative, treating the others as subservient to the 'hearing' or even as part of it. Other aspects of the meditation technique are important only insofar as they are enjoined by the Vedas, for the divine Authority of the scriptural texts is to be obeyed without question. Most modern interpreters are inclined to tone down this Mīmāṁsā aspect of Advaita. But from closer study of the *Brahma Sūtras* with whatever commentary this cannot be avoided; and in a very definite sense Advaita just does not make sense in any of its subvarieties without it.

Vācaspati really did nothing else but commentaries, even his famous *Bhāmatī* being a sort of super-commentary. One remains puzzled why he did these and nothing else. The usual answer is that, like the best of the Śūnyavāda Buddhists, Advaita claims to be nothing in itself, the "position of no position" it is sometimes said, since in the position of total transcendence which it claims as its ultimate orientation everything else can and must be taken in and assigned its proper place and function in the vastness of the great possibilities in and around and transcending the universe. That may be the reason (so we may speculate) that instead of being satisfied with Bādarāyaṇa's summaries of the other systems Vācaspati must have come out of some profound meditation one day with the simple but devastating challenge : Now what happens if we go behind Bādarāyaṇa and re-examine all of those systems without single tool of detachment ? And, essentially, that is what he did all of his life so that we have very little of the pre-Śaṅkara systems that has not been filtered by his great encompassing. For that reason, although it has long been the custom to speak of pre-Śaṅkara and post-Śaṅkara Vedānta, what we really have is pre-Vācaspati and post-Vācaspati Vedānta for the most part.

Vācaspati is one of those rare philosophers who has the *śakti* of interpreting others' philosophies without distortion by inserting his own ideas and values into them or overlooking salient points because of cultural blindness. It might even be said of Vācaspati that he really has no philosophy of his own in his confidence that ultimately *all* philosophies are only parts or aspects or manifestations of Ultimate Reality, the One True Brahman.

16. Mu'tazilites

One God, one world, one humanity—regardless of the variations and elaborations of this simple theme and the theological quibbles over all sorts of things from the proper position of the hands in performing the *namaz* to the various possible solutions or nonsolutions of the problem of evil, this radical creed has been enough to move history in a way that is virtually unique in the saga of man's civilizations and systems. Soon after the death of al-Ash'arī (d. 935) Islam was to stretch from the borders of China to the citadel of Timbuktu and from the banks of the Ganges to the wandering waters of the Danube. While comprising a great attempt at the unification of humanity and a bridging of East and West, still Islam itself remained only one of the world faiths into which humanity still remains divided. Each version of the Vision of Unity has had its prophets, its seers, its saints, its politicians and statesmen, and its philosophers, all of whom in the end must point to some End beyond the present ken of man. In the ninth century, far from being a period of "dark ages", this Vision seems to have been quite intense. But again it tends to become crystallized and needs to be broken open again. This happens only two and a half centuries later, again from an unexpected quarter, from Genghis Khan, an entirely unphilosophical source invading from the outside with a sense of destiny that is unaccountable from any system.

It seems to take at least two hundred years for the full range of possibilities to be explored and adjusted to the fresh inspiration before definite schools or 'heresies' are established independently in a form in which they survive until they in turn are replaced by a new cycle that follows the same essential pattern. As elsewhere, there was in the Islamic world the full development of the 'heresies' aside from the well-known split between the Sunni and Shī'a rival orthodoxies—for such they must be called from a third-party point of view, even though each regards the other (even today in many parts of the world) as arch-heretical and schismatic. The rivalry is even stronger than that between the Mahāyāna and the Theravāda Buddhist schools, or between the Greek and Latin Churches. By the ninth century Islam had already split between the Shī'as and the Sunnis, the former claiming that a blood relative of the Prophet should be the leader of the new movement, the latter following Abū Bakr and 'Umar who claimed that the Prophet had chosen them because of their executive skill and had never intended (for this was a fault in the pre-Islamic tribal organization of Arabia) that the succession should follow a hereditary pattern. In regard to the sects of Islam, it was said that the Jews had 71 sects, the Christians had 72, but the Muslims had 73. Obviously this saying cannot be accepted historically as accurate, but of the development of sects and subsects there seems to be no end regardless of the origin, whether it be on the Yangtze or the Sindh.

Prophethood is to be distinguished sharply from Avatārhood or Bodhisattvahood, but the Prophet Muḥammad was considered to be no ordinary sort of man, especially in Shī'a Islam, since his miracles are considered to be evidence of his divine mission in virtually the same way as was the case with Jesus, the various Mahāyāna Bodhisattvas, and even Buddha. Moreover, the views that grew around this point varied controversially through about the same range as in the Buddhist and Christian cases, classifiable according to philosophical presuppositions, from docetal idealism or mysticism to realism of an almost naturalistic sort. The "eastern" Shī'a branches tended more toward the docetic extreme, and the "western" Sunni toward the realist extreme. Officially there never was any cult of the Virgin or Goddess of Mercy in Islam, but the role of the wife and the daughter of the Prophet also varies in the different traditions considerably. As for the cult of saints, the Shī'a branch in time sanctioned this practice much as the Byzantine and Roman Churches did, but for the most part the Sunni branch was much more like the Arians, the Theravāda Buddhists and Protestantism in discouraging adoration of the saints and prayers for intercession. There is also considerable literature on angelology in Islam. Again the Shī'a shows much more emphasis on this field, probably reinforced from Zoroastrian sources; but the Qur'ān itself has many references to angels, even more than the New Testament. This of course is primarily a theological matter rather than a philosophical one, except that this might be said to be the area in which the principle of hierarchy developed in Islam, even though at its outset that principle was not very evident since it was a radically democratic movement, indeed a democratizing one, and allowed no mediators between man and God.

The seventh and eighth centuries as far as Islamic philosophy is concerned are developmental, transitional centuries in which rationality emerges out of illiteracy even before Hellenization has begun in earnest. Out of this rationality comes not only theology but philosophy, as in previous and subsequent cycles. Within a century after Muḥammad, contact with and influence from Greek learning from Byzantine, Alexandrian and Antiochian scholars, as well as Syriac learning from the Armenians and others in Basrah, Baghdad and Edessa, had begun to influence the formulation of doctrines. Many Muslim thinkers, even some of the earliest ones, had been influenced by Stoicism, largely through the Syrian Christians. This influence was exerted through Stoic writings which had been translated into Arabic under the Umayyad Dynasty and through contact with monks in the monasteries, as well as through the commentators on the organon of Aristotle who were filled with allusions and references to Stoic interpretations, Alexander of Aphrodisias and Galen being among the most prominent in this list. From all of these contacts we might well expect even more syncretistic tendencies in Islam than we do find.

Even before the beginnings of systematic theological formulations or *Kalām,* opinions based only on the Qur'ān and the Tradition inevitably became more and more rationally treated; but as time went on, roughly parallel with the transition from purely intellectualistic attempts at solutions in Christianity, the earliest Muslim thinkers also transferred their field of endeavor from the intellect as such to the will. Even in matters of the doctrine of Creation, speculation based almost entirely on the Qur'ān and the Tradition began to focus on the Will of God and its nature in the Act of Creation. It is interesting that this transpired about the time of the Monotheletite 'heresy' in Christianity. As with the Christian Fathers, the Muslim Fathers in the *Kalām* or strictly theological period seem to have given little attention to Aristotle's doctrine of the eternity of matter as a point for controversy for there was rather in both cases an adaptation of Neo-Platonic (and to some extent Stoic) doctrines, Plato's *Timaeus* already playing a prominent role in this development even as later in Latin scholasticism it became an almost canonical text. The problem of Creation is so important during the *Kalām* period that no orthodox or traditionalistic Muslim writer on philosophy or theology can ignore it, no matter how much he may be influenced by the later developments among the *Falsafah* (philosophers influenced to a major degree by Aristotle and other Greek philosophers).

The Mu'tazilites are important not only because of their numbers and their influence on the later development of Islamic scholasticism, and through that influence on Jewish (Maimonides) and Christian scholasticism, but also because they mark the true beginning of Greek rationalism within Islam. Because they are known almost entirely through reports of their opponents, it is difficult to get a comprehensive picture of what the Mu'tazilites as a whole believed. Fakhry gives us this list of names of the leading representatives :

The Basrite Branch

Wāṣil b. 'Aṭā' (d. 748)
'Amr b. 'Ubaid (d. 762)
Abu'l-Hudhail al- 'Allāf (d. 841 or 849)
Ibrāhīm al-Naẓẓām (d. 835-45)
'Alī al-Aswārī (contemporary of al-Naẓẓām)
Mu'ammar b. 'Abbād (contemporary of al-Naẓẓām)
Hishām al-Fuwaṭī (flourished during al-Ma'mūn's reign, 813-833)
Al-Shaḥḥām (d. 847)
'Abbād b. Sulaymān (d. 864)
Al-Jāḥiz (d. 868)
Al-Jubā'ī (d. 915)
Abū Hāshim, son of al-Jubā'ī (d. 933)

The Baghdadī Branch

Bishr b. al-Mu'tamir (d. 825)
Abū Mūsa al-Murdār (d. 841)
Ja'far b. Mubashshir (d. 849)
Thumāma b. Ashras (d. 828)
Al-Iskāfī (d. 855)
Aḥmad b. Du'ād (d. 855)
Abu'l-Ḥusain al-Khayyāṭ (d. 902)
Abū Qāsim al-Balkhī al-Ka'bī (d. 931).

According to the traditional account, the founder of the Mu'tazilite school was Wāṣil b. 'Aṭā' (d. 748), originally a pupil of al-Ḥasan al-Baṣrī, who was a central figure in the history of Islamic jurisprudence, asceticism, and theological dogma. His differences with his master are said to have centered around the vexed question the Khārijites had so dramatically raised : whether a Muslim who committed a grave sin (*kabīrah*) could still be rightly regarded as a Muslim. The Khārijites had answered this question in uncompromising negative terms, the Murji'ites in a liberal, if noncommittal, manner, and Wāṣil, now, in a new, but subtle, fashion. The grave sinner, he urged, must be placed in an interme-

> diary position between infidelity (*kufr*) and faith *īmān*. Indeed such a sinner, Wāṣil appears to have contended, is what he is semantically acknowledged to be, a grave sinner (*fāsiq*), no more and no less.[1]...

All of the Mu'tazilite philosophers were much vexed about the condemnation of unbelievers and others. This is a doctrine we do not encounter in the Indian philosophical tradition until Mādhava, and although there are traces of it in Augustine, in the Latin Christian world it does not become a vital issue until the time of Calvin. It seems not to occur at all in China or Japan except in a mitigated form, for there the hierarchy of heavens and hells are provided *of their own accord* for the punishment and reward of life as lived here without the judging decree of an autocratic deity. But in Islam all must acknowledge that God does both reward and punish. The problem is whether hell is for the good of the inhabitants or for the sake of safeguarding other from further contamination. And even if the former be the case, is it more in punishment from what had already been done or to prevent them from further wrongdoing—or misbelief, for heresy is as great a fault here as in Byzantium.

Fakhry gives us the following summation of the general positions held by these Mu'tazilites :

> Almost all authorities agree that the speculation of the Mu'tazilah centered around the two crucial concepts of divine justice and unity, of which they claimed to be the exclusive, genuine exponents. Although other propositions were debated by them, it is noteworthy that many could be logically reduced to the two fundamental ideas of justice and unity. Thus, according to a leading Mu'tazilite authority of the end of the ninth century, five basic tenets make up the strict Mu'tazilite creed : justice and unity, the inevitability of God's threats and promises, the intermediary position, the injunction of right, and the prohibition of wrong. Of these five, the latter three will be shown to follow logically from the Mu'tazilite doctrine of the all-pervasive justice of God. It was doubtless their interest in vindicating this justice that led the Mu'tazilite

> doctors to resolve rationally the problems raised by the Koran's doctrine of God's unlimited sovereignty, and to engage in those ethico-theological polemics concerning their assertion of free will. ...
>
> What set the Mu'tazilah apart, from the outset, was their revolutionary vindication of what might be called the rationality of God's ways, which they sought to substantiate intellectually without necessarily repudiating the authority of Scripture. Especially significant in this regard was their contention that good and evil are not conventional or arbitrary concepts whose validity is rooted in the dictates of God, as the Traditionists and later the Ash'arites held, but are rational categories which can be established through unaided reason. From this as a major premise the Mu'tazilah proceeded to argue that God cannot enjoin what is contrary to reason or act in total disregard for the welfare of His creatures, in so far as this would compromise His justice and His wisdom. Unlike the Traditionists, those ethical rationalists could not reconcile themselves to the concept of an omnipotent Deity who could act in total violation of all the precepts of justice and righteousness, torture the innocent, and demand the impossible, simply because He was God.[2]

According to Maimonides and Ibn Khaldūn, the problem of atomism also concerned them considerably. We have scarcely heard anything about atoms since Lucretius and the Vaiśeṣika and the early Jaina systems; so why do they come back into the picture here ? There has been far too little interest in tracing the doctrine of atoms even through the Christian Patristic field, and the usual twentieth century studies of the history of the concept of atoms do not give adequate space to the Muslim treatment of this doctrine. Neither the Bible nor the Qur'ān has any overt reference to the doctrine of atoms; therefore there must have been influence, howsoever indirect, from 'pagan' or Christian Greek or Syriac, if not Indian, thought even before the Muslims had reliable translations of the classics thereof.

Along with the problem of reason versus revelation, the problem of attributes is of major concern and reflects the general monistic tendency of the ninth century. The Ash'arites insisted on seven attributes, namely, Power, Will, Knowledge, Life, Hearing, Seeing, and Speech, in opposition to the Mu'tazilites who accepted the negative attributes but either reduced the positive ones to negation or identified them with the Divine Essence:

> They do not deny that God knows, wills and does things, but deny that His knowledge or will or action is different from and coeternal with His Essence. They are all identical with the Essence. To assert the separate existence of the divine attributes which are eternal because they belong to God is to assert a plurality of eternal beings, which is contrary to the oneness of God. The Mu'tazilites went so far as to deny all positive attributes. To say that God knows such and such a thing, they say, means that He is not ignorant thereof, and the same with the rest of the attributes.[3]

The first to take this position was Wāṣil b. 'Aṭā', who also concerned himself considerably with refuting the Christian doctrine of the Trinity.

It is not quite clear what their political and social theories were. We may infer that they were at least the better organizers, and that one reason for the success of the Muslim Empire may have been their departures from the strict and absolutely literal following of the Qur'ān which the Qadarites (and even today in Pakistan the strict Malwis, for example) would insist upon.

As true Muslims accepting the authority of the Revelation of the Qur'ān, the Mu'tazilites, though admitting the rational analysis of human experience, could not in the least compromise the omnipotence of Allah. However, the Basrah school did not come to terms directly with the problem of the relation of reason as such to God, and the Baghdad school also failed to do this directly although they (notably al-Mu'tamir) evidently incorporated more Greek philosophy in determining distinctions between substance and accident. This, however, did not entail any compromise in the doctrine of God's omnipotence; God, says al-Mu'tamir, is not *obliged* to do what is best for man. After the time of al-Jubā'ī the rationalistic tendencies of some of the Mu'tazilites forced a separation of some, e.g., al-Naẓẓām, Ja'far b. Ḥarb and al-Ash'arī, who put the primary emphasis on revelation.

In conclusion, Valiuddin gives us this summary and estimation of these Mu'tazilites:

> Ibn Ḥazm says in his *Milal w-al-Niḥal* that whosoever believes (1) that the Qur'ān is uncreated, (2) that all the actions of man are due to divine decree, and (3) that man will be blessed with the vision of God on the Day of Judgment, and (4) admits the divine attributes mentioned in the Qur'ān and the Tradition, and (5) does not regard the perpetrator of a grave sin as an unbeliever, will not be styled as one of the Mu'tazilites, though in all other matters he may agree with them.
>
> This statement of Ibn Ḥazm shows that Mu'tazilities were a group of rationalists who judged all Islamic beliefs by theoretical reason and renounced those that relate to all that lies beyond the reach of reason. They hardly realized the fact that reason, like any other faculty with which man is gifted, has its limitations and cannot be expected to comprehend reality in all its details. The point does not need elaboration. As Shakespeare puts it, "There are more things in heaven and earth, Horatio, than are dreamt of in your philosophy." Some modern thinkers have recognized that there is a place for intuition in the field of comprehension and, as a corollary to this, have admitted the claim of revelation or *waḥi* as a source of knowledge. That is why Iqbāl exclaimed:
>
> "At the dawn of Life the Angel said to me:
> 'Do not make thy heart a mere slave to reason.' "
>
> And probably on a similar ground Iqbāl's guide, Rūmi, offered the following meaningful advice:
>
> "Surrender thy intellect to the Prophet !
> God Sufficeth. Say, He sufficeth.
> Beware of wilful reasoning,
> And boldly welcome madness !
> He alone is mad who madness scoffs,
> And heeds not the agent of Law !"[4]

Theology, it seems, is full of blind alleys regardless of which religion maps it out. It is curious that "rationalism" should be most closely associated with man's effort while revelation as God's own affair should, until the later period of Ibn Rushd and Aquinas, be considered as antithetical to reason for the most part.

17. al-Muḥāsibī

Although some mystics seem not to think that history is important, mystics nevertheless do occur in historical milieux and at least in form and manner of expression are definitely conditioned by their cultural environments. Al-Muḥāsibī (781-857) is no exception.

Although we know that communications were open between India and Baghdad and Baṣra, and although we have very definite information about the influence of Indian science on Islamic science and therefore would expect some influence in philosophy also, it appears that this is not very likely in Muḥāsibī. Even if he had been influenced from Indian sources, the argument can be put rather forcefully that it would not have been anything like Śaṅkara's *māyāvāda* even though Śaṅkara was his contemporary, since evidently the lines of communication were stronger between Kaśmir and Baghdad than between South India and Baghdad (although adventurous traders had begun to ply the ocean route even to Canton, necessarily stopping and trading for supplies at Cochin or other ports in Travancore, not far from Śaṅkara's place of origin; the earliest on record, however, are not until the mid-ninth century).

There were many conflicts and controversies in Muḥāsibī's milieu, such as the Mu'tazilite-Ash'arite controversy, the controversy between the ultra-orthodox theologians (the Mutakallimūn) and the specialists in jurisprudence (the fuqahā), the conflicts between the Persians and the Arabs and both of them with the Byzantines, not to mention the Sunnīs and Shī'as. Almost everyone was in controversy with more than a few opponents. Muḥāsibī was a controversialist also, and seems to have disagreed in some respect or other with virtually all the sects that were active in his time, including the Khārijites as well as the Shī'ites. Among the Shī'ites Muḥāsibī was especially opposed to the Rāfiḍites, who were somewhat fanatical in their denial of the authority of 'Ali; and likewise the Zaidites, who seem to have been at the other end of the spectrum of varieties from the rationalistic Mu'tazilites.

Given any basic seminal tradition, sooner or later it will generate heresies and varieties embracing the full spectrum from scepticism and realism to mysticism and idealism, from strict determinism to complete freedom, from strict asceticism to ornate aestheticism. And such was the case in Baghdad and Baṣra during Muḥāsibī's lifetime. Recluse though he overtly was, through his writings Muḥāsibī seems to have been much engaged in all the controversies ranging along the spectrum. From a wider perspective we may speculate that after all he had a sort of Mādhyamika perspective on all these bickering controversies, his apparent engagement in them all being only to point out that they were not operating at the truly spiritual trans-intellectual level, even though he certainly did use his intellect adroitly to refute them all, himself as Ṣūfī after all retaining a sort of neutral monism.

Evidently Muḥāsibī gained quite a following in the midst of the remarkable intellectual and spiritual ferment that was characteristic of his time. The fact that he was an active polemicist belies the possible claim that his mysticism is of the completely escapist or quietist variety. Indeed, he was very active evidently all his life, not only writing but teaching. He did not teach anything like abandonment of reason in favor of 'mysticism', often engaging in controversies with the Mu'tazilites by using their own methods. He also belonged to the Shāfi'ī school of canon law, having studied under Shāfi'ī himself.

Apart from a relatively meagre collection of anecdotes, we have very little information about his life. The biographers are agreed that Muḥāsibī's father was considered a heretic, a Wāqifī or Rāfiḍī, or else a Qadarī and a 'Magian' (probably of the Mazdakite brand of Zoroastrianism). Though his father left him a substantial fortune, he refused to accept it and had the whole sum donated to the state treasury. One might infer, after the example of Rābi'ah and other Ṣūfīs before him, that this was a matter of a vow at an early age to voluntary poverty; but whether or not that might have been his internal motive, his external reason was that the Qur'ān had forbidden true Muslims from accepting fortunes from non-Muslims, in this case his Zoroastrian father.

There is the anecdote of how once early in his career Muḥāsibī had written a book on *gnosis*, concerning which he could not help being a little proud. But a young dervish came along—rather uncannily, as is not uncommon in the lore of classical mysticism—and, after quipsical exchange, Muḥāsibī burnt the book he had written since this nameless Ṣūfī had convinced him that his practice was not up to his theory. Nevertheless in his more mature years Muḥāsibī did write another book essentially on the same theme but with much greater humility about it, for that, rather than the actual details of the book, seems to have been the burden of his intention. There are many other anecdotes like this, one of the most famous being that concerning Aḥmad b. Ḥanbal, the founder of the Ḥanbalite school of the orthodox Sunnī type, who arranged to witness Muḥāsibī's teaching secretly. Supposedly this publicly acknowledged authority in Islam was moved to tears, even to exhaustion and unconsciousness ! But after he recovered (even though later he is supposed to have repented of his own hypocrisy), he warned others against associating with such Ṣūfīs since he could not consider them as strictly orthodox.

Muḥāsibī's mysticism has the perspective of intense personal relations between the soul and God. As we might expect, he puts the unity or unicity of God first and foremost. The argument for the unicity of God in Muḥāsibī's works was substantiated and enlarged with the realization of the overall harmony of nature, entelchy included, each factor in nature serving some divinely inspired and directed trend towards the harmony of the whole, which he viewed as a sort of reflection of the Perfection of God. As for the need for a theodicy in the face of the problem of evil in the world, he is somewhat orthodox in saying that such evils are indeed not illusory but are real Judgments visited on the peoples of the world in order to make them believe in God and follow His Prophet.

As for the attributes of God, there is not much trace of

Muḥasibī's involvement in that controversy. Though he was not in sympathy with the Mu'tazilites here or with their rationalist interpretation of the "uncreatedness" of the Qur'ān, this is not to be taken to indicate that he allowed the extreme opinions either. Indeed between the literalistic anthropomorphists and the fanciful allegorizers as well as the strict rationalists, he seems to attempt a middle path. In other similar issues, such as the attributes of omniscience, omnipotence and omnipresence, as almost all mystics in all faiths he comes rather close to pantheism—or again perhaps we should rather say panpsychism, leaving God, as it were, in complete transcendence. For Muḥāsibī expressly denied the presence of God in his creatures. Only God is perfect, although He has given man the ability to work towards perfection, and the Divine Command to do so as well as the means to accomplish the needed purifications leading towards God's perfection. Muḥāsibī would say to such seekers-perfectionists that they should remember that we are God's possession, not the other way around. He put all the stress on God's justice, omnipotence and omniscience in a transcendent theistic perspective which is basically Sunnī after all, Ṣūfī though he definitely was. His interpretation of the predestination doctrine seems to be that God simply gives grace whereby the individual soul, without losing its individuality or freedom, is enabled to transform its will in such a way that the choice of means for accomplishing the rightly willed end is left to that individual. Thus Muḥāsibī counters the quietist tendencies found in Rābi'ah and others.

Concerning the *ex nihilo* controversy, Muḥāsibī takes the stand that the contingency of the world is demonstrated by the non-eternity of movement. The createdness of man is stressed alongside the assertion that even the Prophet Muḥammed was definitely human and not an incarnate *Logos*. He even tends to minimize the importance of miracles, since mankind will demand those as such instead of acknowledging the exaltedness of God in His own nature. Muḥāsibī wrote :

> He who pretends that he has seen things which come from the Beyond, or that are related directly to God on His throne, is only a liar. He who says that he has been elevated even

> to Heaven or that he has talked with God, or who pretends to have received revelations (from Him) is a charlatan or a show-off wishing only to get attention. He who pretends that he has seen angels or the *houris* is only a liar. We need to avoid all men who pretend to such things.[1]

Following this Muḥāsibī puts all the stress on the uniqueness of the revelation through the Qur'ān in a very orthodox Sunnite perspective.

Although Muḥāsibī was a prolific writer his works remained only in manuscript form and mostly unpublished until recently. Margaret Smith looks on Muḥāsibī primarily as a precursor of al-Ghazālī, although she is convinced that his chief work, the *Ri'āya Liḥuqūq Allāh*, "well known to Orientalists in both East and West, is perhaps the finest manual on the interior life which Islam has produced"[2]—and that is making a very heavy claim. The factors involved in the more advanced disciplines are very specific, involving such terms as the following which assume a somewhat technical meaning in Ṣūfī tradition *'tawakkul'*, confidence in God; *war'a*, scrupulousness in observance (suggestive of the mindfulness of Buddhist discipline or the "recollection" of Benedictine, Basillian and other Christian monastic practices); *zuhd*, renunciation; *tafwīḍ*, submission to God; *riḍā*, satisfaction (we might infer that this also carries a warning of detachment lest spiritual gluttony come in where physical appetites have left an empty house, as it were); *maḥabbah*, love of the faithful for God alone.

In the broader scale we have seen many similar patterns of *ascesis*, not least in this case that of John of Damascus, who had bathed, as it were, in the same stream, although of course not in the same water for even the history of mysticism never stops.

Mahmoud explains *tawakkul* as follows :

> Tawakkul signifies absolute confidence on the part of the faithful (individual) in God, and the certitude that no activity deployed in this world could change what ought to happen. That is an idea applying in all circumstances and which constitutes the Faith among Muslims in theory at least universally.

> When one talks about Tawakkul in the writings of Muslims, one usually treats it in a larger context, and also in all details, especially in reference to wealth and to licit gain. Are wealth and licit gain not in contradiction with Tawakkul? If the faithful (soul) has complete confidence in God and if he believes in his destiny, that is, if he is certain that whatever happens infallibly is because from all eternity God has chosen it to be so, whether that be poverty or wealth or good fortune or bad, . . . if the faithful soul, we may well say, is convinced of these truths, then there will be no lack of confidence in regard to God, and correspondingly no neglect of adoration of Him as is His due, nor anxiety in searching out in all activities what God has guaranteed to him.[3]

For Muḥāsibī *tawakkul* is not merely a matter of detachment in the face of possessions but of not having any wealth to tempt one or distract one's attention. In short, *tawakkul* to Muḥāsibī leads to *zuhd* (renunciation) sooner or later, which discipline represents much of Muhāsibī's character.

> Closely connected with abstinence as a means of mortification is asceticism (*zuhd*), the renunciation of this world and its goods, of the pleasures of life, sensual and even spiritual, preference of hunger to satiety, of wakefulness to sleep, of poverty to riches; indeed, for the sake of God, the ascetic is prepared to renounce all save Him. "The believer who is seeking for godliness," writes al-Muḥāsibī, "renounces all that is destructive to him in this world and the next, and leanness is manifest in him, and mortification and solitude and separation from the companionship of the pious, and the appearance of grief and absence of joy, and he chooses all that, hating to indulge in pleasure which may incur the wrath of his Lord and make him worthy of His chastisement, and he hopes that his Lord will be well pleased with what he does."[4]

To be occupied with the things of this world is to be alienated from God ; and to be freed from the world, that is the means to become consecrated entirely to Him alone. This basic theme, prominent in all monastic and semi-monastic traditions, supports many variations and implications, from promise of reward in the afterlife to simple pragmatic considerations. As may be very clearly seen in the wider framework of the history of monastic movements universally, wealth does bring corruption, whether it be in Byzantium, China, Nālandā or Baghdad.

Tafwīḍ (total submission to God) resembles *prapatti* in the Vaiṣṇavism of Rāmānuja and has very close parallels in Byzantine monasticism, especially during Muhāsibī's time whan the seeds of the later Hesychast controversy were beginning to germinate. The Prophet Muḥammed himself is reported to have said, "Commit yourself entirely to God and you will be tranquil." One may recall St. Augustine's "My heart was restless until it found Rest in Thee"; but the cultivation of serenity in China among both Buddhists and Taoists during the T'ang Dynasty may offer closer comparisons. The commitment to God should be in a *niṣkāma* manner, selflessly and with no ulterior motive, and then the result will be peace and tranquillity to body and heart. This reminds us of his predecessor Rābī' ah who even engaged in some strange antics to dramatize the need to love and serve and praise God with no ulterior motive, not even for the sake of avoiding hell or going to heaven. In the larger perspective parallels can easily be found in Mahāyāna Buddhism and with such as the *niṣkāma-karma* of the Bhagavad Gītā (on which Muḥāsibī's contemporary Śaṅkara wrote an important commentary).

Tafwīḍ being so important, one must ask about finding a person who lives according to such discipline. The answer is that it is not difficult, though no amount of academic study, money, or action will help very much. Simply if one's submission or surrender is complete, God will arrange for such a meeting: but if one is tainted with motive in the face of God defiantly to "show me such a man !", then he is unlikely to get the guru demanded. And even if one should find such a man, one should not attribute his attainments to that merely human, ignorant, fellow-mortal but to God outright. There is the common taunt that if one went all the way with this *tafwīḍ* or *prapatti* one would not need to do anything in this world since to such a saint God does everything anyway. Such extremes were not unknown in the Mahāyāna world as well as among the Byzantine Hesychasts, a few Taoist hermits, and some Advaitins. Quietism, in short, is a common 'heresy'.

In her chapter on the inner life of the mystic, Margaret Smith writes of *riḍā* (satisfaction) :

> Al-Muḥāsibī was asked how this state of satisfaction was attained, and he replied that it was through the knowledge of the heart that the Lord is just in all His decrees, without any doubt that the choice of God for His servant is better than his own. It comes when the understanding of men is enlightened and their hearts attain to certainty and their souls to knowledge, and knowledge bears witness that God's Will is carried out, and they know that He does what is best for His servant in His choice for him and His love towards him, and the hearts of men know that He Who has no compeer is just in all He decrees, there is no doubt of His sovereignty, and the heart of His servant rejoices in accepting it.[5]

After stressing the intimate connection between *riḍā*, *tawakkul*, and *tafwīḍ*, Mahmoud gives this explanation :

> ...When man is taken into the presence of his Destiny, fixed by God, he can have then one of the three following attitudes : (a) he can revolt; that, naturally, is reproved by Islam ; (b) he can bear with it patiently; that is for man, according to Muḥāsibī, at least obligatory, as obligatory in fact as *war'a*; and (c) he can accept the divine decree with satisfaction (*riḍā*).[6]

This *riḍā* is the quietude of the heart when man finds himself placed before the divine will. There are those who generalize *riḍā* as merely ordinary well-being as the opposite of misery. But Muḥāsibī demands more than that of us : *riḍā* is concerned with misery alone, so that if true and authentic it comes in the midst of misfortune. Even before man encounters misery *riḍā* should already be with him. This means that those who have *riḍā* will be desireless—so much so that even though Muḥāsibī does sanction asking favors of God even in the highest states, he should never ask for deliverance from his misfortunes and miseries but might even ask God to increase them ! Such exaggerated sentiments later became poetically very common even to the point of stereotype among later Ṣūfīs; but with Muḥāsibī it was no mere poetic embellishment but very earnest advice. Such a basic attitude can be found in virtually all the classics of mature and authentic mysticism regardless of place and time in history and may even be taken as a test against inauthentic pseudo-mystic shortcuts which seek all delights without discipline.

Concerning *maḥabbah*, the love of the faithful for God, Smith reports Muḥāsibī's experience and counsel thus :

> The lover is filled at all times with yearning for the Beloved, "the soul being so on fire with love of God that she is ever thirsting after His presence"; and of this all-absorbing love al-Muḥāsibī wrote, "Love to God is intensity of longing, because longing, in its essence, is the heart's remembrance of the contemplation of the one longed for." ...If those who were filled with longing did not force upon themselves exhaustion and humility, they would be deprived of the sweet influences which God bestows upon the hearts of His lovers. Al-Muḥāsibī was asked what was his view of longing, and he replied, "Longing, in my view, is a lamp kindled from light of original love, but greater than the light of original love." Asked what was "original love," he said, "The love (born of) faith, for God has borne witness that the faithful love Him, saying, 'Those who believed were the strongest in love to God,' and the light of passionate longing is derived from the light of love, and that which makes it exceed that light comes from the love which is attachment (*ḥubb al-wadād*, i.e., that which is based on experience, not merely faith), and longing arises in the heart only from the light of this love which is attachment. And when God lights that lamp in the heart of one of His servants, there is no radiance kindled in the heart which is not derived from it, and that lamp is not extinguished except by looking upon one's actions with the eye of self-confidence, which turns the lover aside from the love of God."[7]

Mahmoud accompanies his treatment of this most intimate and

most difficult theme with a warning which he gives after descriptions of the more Pleasant states :

> There is nevertheless withall a danger which tints this illumination of the heart which is the love towards God. This danger is that of abandoning the fear of God, and that he regard his actions with a certitude that they are agreeable to God completely. That leads to neglect of constant purification. Love for God ought always to be, thus, accompanied with the fear of being abandoned by Him, but also the hope which puts man at a distance from the unhappy effects of this fear, that is to say, despair.[8]

Parallels can easily be found in the many *bhakti*-type expressions common throughout Eurasia during this period.

Muḥāsibī has probably been underestimated, and probably for the simple reason that he did not get translated into Latin like Jābir ibn Ḥayyān (Geber) or Zakariyā al-Rāzī (Rhazes) or al-Kindī. Given his character as a controversialist, it is unfortunate that evidently little attention has been given to his relations with the scientists and the *Falsafah*. It would be premature to conclude that he had become, like his predecessor Rābi'ah, such a recluse and so engrossed in the "world within" that he did not care for those things and simply neglected them deliberately. If this be the case, then he is certainly an exception to the rule among later Ṣūfīs that there was no gap between mysticism and science (Omar Khayyam, to cite only the most famous example later on, did not appear suddenly but had a long history behind his versatility, which was really only one aspect of his Ṣūfī heritage).

The account of Muḥāsibī's last days is rather typical of many of the world's greatest spiritual giants; for he died as he wished, voluntarily : "'If I see what I desire, I will smile at you and if I see what is otherwise, you will perceive it in my face.' An hour later Ja'far looked at him and al-Muḥāsibī smiled and passed away."[9] Like so many contemplative souls, his life was one more of interior rather than exterior adventure. Though censored almost to the point of persecution, his writings reveal that external fame meant nothing to him. The name ascribed to him, "Muḥāsibī", means "one who examines his conscience constantly". He would no doubt have preferred obscurity.

18. Ennin

For historical perspective we may follow Reischauer's book *Ennin's Travels in T'ang China*, especially since he uses Ennin's diary along with other sources. Reischauer begins his study of Ennin (794-864) with a comparison with Marco Polo as a gesture to establish a connection of familiarity; but he moves quickly on to the famous Chinese pilgrim to India, Hsüan-tsang, as a more apposite base of comparison. He also brings in Jōjin, who died in China in 1081 and stems from Enchin's branch of the Tendai. Jōjin did not leave Japan until he was already sixty-two years old; his travels included pilgrimage to Mt. T'ien T'ai and also to the holy Mt. Wu T'ai in the North. Although his diary, like Ennin's, is full of fascinating details faithfully told, it has not become so famous because in his period of East Asian history there are many other sources from which the general historian can gather sufficient information. Ennin's diary, however, furnishes some information that is not available from other sources at all, and his was a personal record whereas the official documents at the court in China were always in a very formal, stilted style and of course not always unbiased.

Ennin's work has the title *The Record of a Pilgrimage to China in Search of the Law*, that "Law" being Tendai Buddhism. He wrote it in classical Chinese, just as a monk from the British Isles, Ennin's contemporary Scotus Erigena, would use Latin. Ennin's is a case where his philosophy is more readily demonstrated by his life than by his formal teachings. Along with his fame as a diarist, we must emphasize that Ennin was after all a Tendai monk and one of Saichō's most trusted immediate disciples, and that it was a doctrinal dispute that caused the rift with Enchin (814-889) and eventually the schism in the Tendai which has never been healed to this day. Indeed, the rivalry between Ennin's and Encnin's followers eventually became so intense that violence erupted and the government had to intervene. Kūkai's Shingon sect was also having similar troubles. Other-worldly monasticism does not necessarily guarantee this-worldly stability it seems.

There are the typical stories accruing to Ennin's charisma. Saichō introduced him even at the early age of fifteen into special study of the *Mahā-shikan* by Chih-i. He excelled his fellow novices in his studies and monastic regularity, and was soon selected by Saichō for the responsibility of being a 'transmitter', as a consequence of which he received special training in the *Lotus Sūtra*. Ennin became famous for his preaching and teaching far and wide, and retired into solitude at the age of forty. Then he was appointed by the court to become a member of an ambassadorial group to go to China. From the Chinese point of view ambassadorial relations with the surrounding countries were primarily of a tributary nature, confirming the Chinese image of themselves as the Central Kingdom. Of course the Japanese did not like this treatment as a lesser nation or civilization, but they were able, and had been since long before the time of Prince Shōtoku, to accommodate themselves to it in such a way that it was to their own advantage more than to the advantage of China.

Providentially or not, Ennin was never allowed to go to Mt. T'ien T'ai. Among other unplanned events, he contacted and actually stayed for a good part of a winter at a Korean monastery. In the spring he visited Mt. Wu T'ai, which was regarded as of equal importance for Buddhist studies and of course miraculous wonders. But this mountain was not a place associated with T'ien T'ai Buddhism devoted as it is to Amitābha and Avalokiteśvara; rather here was the more esoteric cult of Monju (Mañjuśrī), the Bodhisattva of (Esoteric) Wisdom. Evidently not much of systematic Buddhism was practiced there, though one might well suspect there was quite a bit of popular Taoism and, given its location in the North, no small amount of Central Asian Shamanism mixed in with what Buddhism was there.

When Ennin reached the capital Chang-an he did receive sufficient patronage to study the most substantial works. Reischauer reports that the diary indicates a shift of form travellogue to more earnest matters at this point. He also reports that here Ennin made contact with Indian as well as Chinese scholar-monks. Reischauer claims that "the Buddhist church (was) then at a peak of prestige and intellectual vigor in China",[1] though we definitely have the impression that ever since the death of Empress Wu (whose corruptions were not really cleaned up till after the end of the dynasty) things had gone from bad to worse as far as internal discipline was concerned, though Buddhist art and architecture were externally flourishing in a "bath of Gold".

The Purge of 842 remains a controversial matter. It seems to have been motivated by a fresh wave of xenophobia in which Taoist and Neo-Confucianist fanaticism—not to mention intrigue within the court by Taoist necromancers who were not well known for unselfish motives—had full sway, driving out all 'foreign' religions and philosophies, including Nestorian Christianity and Manichaeanism, while the Buddhist Church "was dealt a blow from which it never fully recovered."[2] Persecution or purge? It may depend on one's point of view. For far too many in the monasteries and nunneries were there for political or economic reasons, to escape taxation, for example, rather than for reasons of scholarship and monastic discipline, not to mention philosophizing.

During the Purge it is recorded that there were as many as eighteen "other foreign clerics...including one each from Ceylon and Kucha in Central Asia and several from India and Korea."[3]

> We hear of a "learned doctor Ratnacandra", described as a scholarly foreign cleric (who) rashly presented a petition to the Emperor asking to be allowed to return to his homeland without first consulting Ch'iu Shih-liang, who as the commissioner of Good Works of the Streets of the Left had direct supervision over him...(Ratnacandra) was detained by the military for five days charged with the crime of going over the heads of the officials. As a result, Ratnacandra's three disciples were each sentenced to seven strokes or ten strokes of the rod, but the Learned Doctor was not beaten nor was he allowed to return to his home-land.[4]

Unfortunately we know nothing more about this Ratnacandra,

but such bits of information are significant as accumulating evidences of very wide trans-Eurasian communications in this period contrary to some still prevailing stereotypes.

Sectarian divisions in China had grown increasingly wider ever since Kumārajīva's translations; and the efforts even of Hsüan-tsang to rectify the situation by bringing back from India more authentic texts (at least of the Yogācāra/Vijñānavâda variety) had not been very effective. Ennin had ample opportunity to contact many if not most of these sects, especially since others in his party represented other varieties of Japanese Buddhism. Although it was Han Yü's famous Memorial about Bnddhism that was a major motivating factor in the Purge, it is not completely clear whether Ennin had any direct contact with him or with any other (Neo-) Confucianist philosopher, although he had to deal constantly with government officials who no doubt nominally were Confucianist. He did nevertheless have some minor contacts with Taoist monks and included reports of several Taoist ceremonies conducted with Imperial patronage, noting, for example, that often both Buddhist and Taoist monks would be commissioned to pray for rain (the former wearing black and the latter yellow, curiously). Reischauer reports very little about the philosophical import of Ennin's adventures, even though we can well infer that his studies at Chang-an were of a substantial philosophical nature. Reischauer says they were theological, but for this ninth century nexus in Eurasia we must again remind ourselves that there had not anywhere been any rift between theological and philosophical study and thought.

With the Purge in full blast, Ennin and his associates were defrocked and deported. "As Ennin rather wryly records in his diary, he had unsuccessfully applied more than one hundred times for permission to return to his homeland, but now, because of the intensification of the persecution, he was suddenly ordered home, and he comments, 'There was both sorrow and joy.' "[5] Ennin had spent nine years in China. Saichō and Kūkai had not stayed a fraction of that time but upon return had become the most charismatic figures in Japanese Buddhism to date. With his return in 847 Ennin received an official royal welcome by the court as well as by the *saṅgha* and was appointed court priest. The official records mention mostly the ceremonies he conducted for the remaining sixteen years of his life, many if not most of which were at that time new to Japan, including, incidentally, a baptism ceremony for the new Emperor Montoku in 854. Soon after appointing his successor to the temple-monastery Enryakuji on Mt. Hiei, he died at the age of seventy. In accordance with the customs of the times, many posthumous honors were conferred upon him equal to or even greater than those conferred on Kūkai and Saichō before him. Ennin's posthumous title, Jikaku Daishi, means Great Teacher of Compassion and Understanding.

Ennin's additions to the Tendai were mostly more of the esoteric type rather than systematically doctrinal. "With the return of Ennin, the Tendai sect no longer had any feelings of inadequacy and they were able at last to equal and surpass the Shingon in esoteric Buddhism."[6] Of course Ennin had learned Saṁskṛt, the lack of which "had also been an added source of Tendai inferiority."[7] Among the esoteric texts Ennin brought back and put into practice, many were of the Tāntric sort left at Mt. Wu T'ai by no less than Amoghavajra. Though both Ennin and Enchin introduced a very large measure of Tāntric esotericism into the Tendai heritage, this was not systematized until much later under Annen (841-889), who based his work on the notion that after all there is only One Buddha (Dainichi Nyorai) with Whom everything else can be identified monistically. The monist trend that was dominating virtually all of Eurasia in the ninth century came intensively to dominate Japan along with the rest, even in the Tendai, which had been more comprehensive under Saichō.

Ennin rose from a lower class family to the very highest honors. In spite of his fame in his own time, Ennin has almost been forgotten in Japan even within the Tendai denomination of Japanese Buddhism. Evidently his teachings were not of the sort to be studied by posterity even though his influence was very great. Ennin did discuss doctrinal disputes, but his work definitely reflects much more interest in rituals and relics and miraculous things no less than similar chronicles by Christian monks of the same period from Edessa to Iona.

19. al-Kindī

Al-Kindī (c. 801-c. 866) was born at al-Kūfa and was among the few in that area who were really Arabs, which gave him some minor prestige; however there was also jealousy and conflict which almost split the Islamic community even as once it almost split the early Christian community when some thought it was necessary to have been of Jewish rather than gentile extraction in order to really become a Christian. His family, who were in high government employ, moved to al-Basra where he received most of his education. In order to advance his chances for patronage, al-Kindī later moved to Baghdad where he spent most of the rest of his career. Baghdad by this time had become a major *entrepôt* both of trade and culture. The so-designated "Hellenization of Islam" took place in Baghdad but also at Damascus, Antioch and Cairo/Alexandria. It was the Calif al-Mutawakkil (847-861) who later censored al-Kindī because of his supposed association with the Mu'tazilites. The court favorites were typically suspicious and envious of al-Kindī's superior learning and great library, even persuading the Calif to confiscate that collection; later it was returned to him, but he never recovered his patronage or position in the court. Al-Kindī died at Baghdad in solitude, like so many philosophers for whom truth was more important than patronage. "His death must have been a quiet one, noticed only by those nearest to him. It was the death of a great man out of favor, yet at the same time that of a philosopher who loved solitude."[1]

Al-Kindī was not the very first to pay attention to the Greek heritage, but he does represent the divide between the purely Qur'anic *Kalām* and the tradition of the *Falsafah.* The *Falsafah* were the philosophers who had been influenced heavily by the Greek heritage, whether through the Syriac translations (chiefly of John Philopon) or by direct translation from Greek into Arabic. The Hellenizing philosophers were always suspect by the ultra-orthodox, more or less similar to the way the Confucianist orthodoxy was always suspicious of those who were influenced by or had even gone completely over to the 'foreign' religion and philosophy of Buddhism. Nevertheless there is scarcely any philosopher in Islam after al-Kindī who was not indebted to him, including even those in opposite camps such as al-Ghazālī and Ibn Rushd.

Not only was al-Kindī an initiator of what became known as the *Falsafah*, the Hellenizing philosophers whom we refer to as Muslim or Islamic Scholastics, but he was a humanist and scientist as well as a philosopher-theologian.

> Regardless of what one thinks of al-Kindī, there is no doubt that he challenged Arab-Muslim thought into new alleys. His raising the problems of the relation between philosophy and religion, his delving into the problem of the One, his attitude towards the epistemological and ethical problems single him out as the founder of Arab-Muslim philosophy.[2]

Such is true even though there had been Mu'tazilites before him and he was even imprisoned because of association with them in the minds of some.

The only 'Aristotle' they all had access to was the Neo-Platonic interpretation, including the historically famous and influential (pseudo) "Theology of Aristotle". Al-Kindī also had access to translations of Ptolemy's *Geography* and part of Aristotle's *Metaphysics*. The following are al-Kindī's six dfinitions of philosophy:

1. Philosophy is composed of two words, philo, friend and sophia or wisdom. Philosophy is the love of wisdom. This definition is based on the Greek etymology of the word.
2. Philosophy is the human emulation of divine excellence as far as such emulation is possible. This is a functional definition.
3. Philosophy is the practice of death. Death means the separation of the soul from the body. Moreover, death involves the suppression of material concerns, which are inimical to the virtuous life or, what is its practical equivalent, the activity of the intellect. Another functional definition.
4. Philosophy is man's knowledge of himself.
5. Philosophy is the science of sciences and the wisdom of wisdoms.
6. Philosophy's proper subject-matter is defined as the

> science of haecceity, the essence and causes of things to the limit of human power.[3]

Al-Kindī seemed to prefer the last definition over the others, thus showing to what extent he had become a sort of Aristotelian.

Al-Kindī deserves perhaps more credit than most of the later *Falsafah* because he was the actual innovator in Islam of the attempt at synthesizing or at least reconciling Qur'anic religion with Greek philosophy, most of the others simply following suit with variations and various emendations. According to al-Kindī, "the utterances of Muḥammad the truthful and the message that he transmitted from the Almighty are ascertainable by intellectual arguments. Only people deprived of sound reason and enshrouded in ignorance would reject it."[4] His accommodation of the Qur'anic heritage is done largely by allegorical interpretation. Atiyeh summarizes al-Kindī's interpretation of the verse from the Qur'ān, "But His command when He desires a thing is to say to it, 'be' and it is" (XXXVI : 81) :

> The problem which this verse raises is both linguistic and metaphysical. How can one order "something" to be which has no being? Al-Kindī justifies the linguistic use of the imperative 'be' by the fact of its being metaphorical. Metaphors, similes and allegories are of common usage among the Arabs, he maintains, and it is completely justifiable to describe a thing by using qualities which that thing does not possess.[5]

Al-Kindī takes this as justification of the *ex nihilo* doctrine inherited from John Philopon and the other Christianized interpretations of Aristotle's *On First Philosophy* or (as it is now called) the *Metaphysics*. He goes into detail reconciling the whole causational sequence in the Aristotelian-Ptolemaic cosmology with the Qur'anic expression that the whole of creation bows before its creator :

> ... The outermost sphere and consequently the heavenly bodies bow, that is obey, voluntarily. Al-Kindī, like Aristotle,

> believes that the heavenly bodies are endowed with life and reason. To prove his assertion, he uses self-evident principles such as the following : the cause pertains to a higher order than the effect. Now, if the life and reason of human beings are properties immediately caused by the heavenly bodies, then these bodies, as causes, must likewise be endowed with life and reason or they would be inferior to their effects.[6]

Curiously like the two-level theory of truth that had been asserted by various Buddhists, but with the exception that for al-Kindī the higher level is a matter of prophetic revelation rather than a metaphysics of *māyā* or preference of one sūtra over another, he teaches that ordinary human beings

> who are not prophets have no way of attaining to the higher knowledge of the secondary true substance or to the primary sensible substances and their accidents without research of the help of logic and mathematics. ... But the prophets attain to this knowledge without recurring to anything of that kind but through the Will of Him Who sent them.[7]

This is historically very important since this distinction becomes pivotal later on in Ibn Sīnā and Ibn Rushd.

Within the realm beneath revelation there is very wide room in al-Kindī's House of Reason. Just how many of Aristotle's strictly logical works were available to him is not absolutely certain, but the basic principles therein were familiar to him. From these he inherited a genius for classification which would have pleased even his Jaina and Vaiśeṣika contemporaries, although some of his Ṣūfī, Ch'an ond Tendai contemporaries would have seen these things as unnecessary if not even a hindrance. Thus in this regard :

> ...There are four different classes of beings into which all that exists can be reduced. Three of these classes are substances (a'yān) which include the individual, the species and the genera; the remaining class is a notion (na'nā) consisting of the differentiae, which distinguishes the different species from others of the same genus.[8]

Atiyeh concludes that "al-Kindī's only deviation from the Stagirite's classification is simply linguistic and almost unnoticeable."[9]

We need a specialized study of al-Kindī's metaphysics of being in comparison with Śaṅkara's treatment of the same problem along the lines of Olivier Lacombe's excellent researches in fields related to the Christian Scholastic milieu and Vedānta in general. Here we note Atiyeh's summary of al-Kindī's basic but after all basically simple, for ultimately universal, principle:

> To sum up, we may say that al-Kindī conceives of duality of beings. On the one hand there is God, whose being is beyond our descriptive capacity and to whom the definition of substance as self-subsistent does not apply. On the other hand, there are the three kinds of beings...which fall under the category of created being. This kind of dualism is closer to that of Aristotle, whose Unmoved Mover occupies a separate category, than to that of Plato who assigns to God the highest place among His Likes, the Ideas. ...Kindī's is a duality between the absolutely eternal and the created-out-of-nothing, between God and His creation. ...Al-Kindī's God is the only Being who possesses absolute Eternity. Al-Kindī believes that some created beings such as the soul are indestructible, but the soul's eternity is *a parte post,* and it is by the Will of God that this is so.[10]

It might appear that al-Kindī does not fit so well into our framework of "monism in many moods" in the ninth century, but there might be a slightly "Thomistic" twist to this interpretation since other interpreters put more stress on the Neo-Platonic monistic flavor of al-Kindī's 'Aristotelianism'.

The "problem of creation" became pivotal in Jewish, Christian and Islamic Scholasticism ever since John Philopon critiqued Proclus' exposition of the "eternity of matter" by positing the *ex nihilo* doctrine, which then became no longer an alternative hypothesis (Philopon thought it was simply more scientific) but a basic dogma in which not to believe was heresy. According to al-Kindī, the world could not be infinite since then it would be equal to God, who is Single. All matter by definition must occupy real time and real space, and therefore could not possibly be eternal or infinite. Al-Kindī got almost all of his arguments from John Philopon, the only "difference between the two being one of methodology rather than content."[11]

Al-Kindī must prove that God is *Creator* and not merely Aristotle's Prime Mover. The Cosmological proofs later found in Aquinas and other Christian Scholastics are already pretty well explicated by al-Kindī, as also the teleological argument, which held a special fascination for the Muslim Scholastics since it more than the other arguments emphasizes the contingency of the universe and also explains beauty and awesomeness.

Al-Kindī gives an exposition of the ambiguity of the term "One", which later we shall also find even in Bonaventura and still later in such as Pico della Mirancola, and which might be shown to be not completely unlike Śaṅkara's arguments for his "non-dual" metaphysics. Here is where al-Kindī does fit into our theme of "monism in many moods". It is the doctrine of the Unicity of Allah from which all other doctrines in Islam stem and to which they must return in the end. For al-Kindī this is not just a matter of piety but a matter of necessary metaphysics. Oneness may be taken as simplicity in nature or as number, but "it cannot be attributed to any being except God. All 'single' beings are composite in themselves, that is, divisible into component parts. Only God is indivisible."[12] Of this Śaṅkara would heartily approve, along with the Kaśmir Śaivas and even some varieties of Mahāyāna Buddhists, especially those associated with Tendai and the Pure Land 'theistic' traditions, not to mention Scotus Erigena and Photius and indeed most of al-Kindī's ninth century contemporaries.

> He is one in essence as well as in number. Oneness is essential in God, but in single objects it is accidental. In the case of God, Oneness is absolute unity; in the case of all other beings, it is relative and dependent on God.
>
> Everything other than God, then, is in some way composite which means it is multiple. ...Ultimately, then, everything that acquires material and temporal existence must emanate from that One which preceded all other "ones", and which is, therefore, the eternal cause of all coming to be. The One

is the cause of all other "ones"; He is the Creator by whose actions everything lasts as long as He wills it to last.[13]

With the problem of the attributes it is not difficult to find many parallel controversies in the varieties of Vedānta and in those varieties of Mahāyāna which spoke of the Buddha as only the undefinable *Tathatā* on the one hand, and those varieties which emphasized not only the *Trikāya* doctrine but the thousandfold attributes of mercy and compassion as symbolized in the Bodhisattva Avalokiteśvara (Kwan-yin or Kanon), the Goddess with as many arms as an artist could possibly attach to an otherwise human figure. In Islam this issue produced no less than seventy-two varieties of sects which professed different sets of attributes.

> However they (these seventy-two sects) are all varieties of three main schools: (a) the Anthropomorphists, (b) the Mu'tazilites, and (c) the Ash'arites. The first group maintained that the attributes of God are similar to those of man. ...The majority of the Mu'tazilites upheld the theory that the attributes of God are identical with His essence. They reject any positive attributes on the ground that they would do away with God's Unity. ...Others among the Mu'tazilites such as Abū Ḥāshim predicated for the attributes a state between existence and non-existence (aḥwāl); according to this theory, the attributes cannot be known independently of God. The third group did not admit that the attributes are identical with the essence of God...but these attributes although different from the essence of God are not similar in any sense to those possessed by men. Hence we cannot assume that they destroy God's unity.[14]

It was this matter wherein al-Kindī's sympathy was strongly on the "liberal" side with the Mu'tazilites and which got him in trouble with the reactionary authorities.

Al-Kindī follows Aristotle closely in regard to his definition of movement as change and being changed. Here, as we have observed in the case of other Aristotelians, the Buddhists of all brands might have challenged him considerably since few if any Aristotelians went as far as they in their universalization of the principle of change as *kṣaṇavāda* to the extent of denying any permanent substance. But then again the Aristotelian refutation of that notion would probably be very similar to the Vaiśeṣika attempts at vindicating permanence of substances, rather than the Advaita way of insisting that it is only the spiritual *ātman*-Brahman equation that is really permanent. Thus it might be debated whether al-Kindī would have sided with the Vedāntins here or with the Vaiśeṣikas (and we should also mention the Jainas in this regard), or whether he would have derived something of a middle position between them. For he admits that everything in creation does change, whereas God uniquely does not change but is the supreme Changer or Agent of change—but with the curious exception that he thought that the celestial bodies do not change because their motion is circular.

Although evidently al-Kindī did not get into such points that Augustine emphasized so much, namely that one must distinguish between 'created' time and the 'timeless Time' of God before creation began (later on al-Ghazālī does come to something closely resembling that view), he does have the following view (again probably following Philopon):

> As to the nature of time, al-Kindī maintains that it is the *now* of our consciousness which links the past with the future. The present *now*, however, is nothing by itself—it passes away even before we think of it; consequently in itself it cannot be time. Time can be known only in relation to a *before* and *after,* and as such it is nothing. That is why there is no time without movement and no movement without a moving body.[15]

For the rest al-Kindī follows almost every detail of the Aristotelian classification of types of motion, and differs from Aristotle only in that he does not think, as Aristotle and the Buddhists do, that motion is eternal.

Al-Kindī's writings on the soul are neither numerous nor comprehensive. He is not purely an Aristotelian here but also looks back to Plato, and there is an element of Neo-Pythagoreanism as well. Among many of his contemporaries human nature and its transformation had long been the central theme for what was considered philosophy. True Muslim that al-

Kindī was he would scarcely have sanctioned the ideal of gynandromorphy or hermaphroditism that was latent and sometimes overt in pre-Christian Neo-Platonism and Neo-pythagoreanism, Gnosticism and Tantra; but on the other hand as a physician he might have been very keen to learn more about Sāṃkhya psychology and Patañjali yoga, which might be correlated with Aristotelian psychology (e.g., the three *guṇas* and the vegetable, animal and rational souls). He might have admitted that the hatha yogīs (and maybe some aspects of Ayur Vedic medical practice) probably had in practice even better expertise in neurology than the inheritors of Galen such as he was. Likewise in terms of classical distinctions in Saṃs-kṛt terminology between *manas*, *citta*, *sākṣī*, etc., he might have agreed that some of these distinctions supplemented rather than conflicted with the Aristotelian hierarchical ordering of human faculties. But when it comes to the classical Buddhist *anātman* doctrine on the one hand and the *ātman*-Brahman equation of Advaita on the other, he could scarcely have found much common ground at all, even though in al-Bisṭāmī and al-Ḥallāj and other Ṣūfīs there are some remarkable similarities.

In his psychology al-Kindī departed more radically from Aristotle than in any other work. That he tried to reconcile Aristotle and Plato in these matters suggests a Byzantine source, whether Philopon again or not, since such efforts had been going on there since antiquity and was a basic theme with Photius, al-Kindī's contemporary. Needless to say, he opposes any materialistic conception of the soul, although it is not clear who in this respect his supposed opponents might be, unless perhaps the Epicureans in the background or such as al-Rāzī his younger contemporary whose theories did border on materialism. There is controversy as to whether al-Kindī believed in the pre-existence of the soul, though definitely he did believe in the Qur'anic concept of heaven and hell even interpreted in terms of the Ptolemaic cosmology. There was a work, now lost alas, with the title *On the Reminiscences of the Soul in the Intelligible World before its Descent to the Sensible World*, but the contents of this could have been a refutation of the 'pagan' view even though Plato held it.

Many of al-Kindī's works were no more than exploratory commentaries and/or attempts at adaptation of the rich fund of Hellenistic ideas and viewpoints to the Qur'anic exegesis. For example, in his treatise *On the Definition of Things* he records the three different definitions of the soul given by the Aristotelians and the Pythagoreans without voicing any personal opinion, while in the *Discourse on the Soul* he tries to reconcile Plato and Aristotle. Too many interpretations of late have looked back to al-Kindī through later developments, not all of which were necessarily improvements on his own discernments. Al-Kindī is not an Averroist nor even an Avicennist, and above all he is certainly not a Thomist much as some Christian Neo-Scholastics would like to make him one. Much of al-Kindī's own text was not necessarily an affirmation or denial or even critique of the Aristotelian canon but simply commentary by which he is trying to learn what the experts of the past really thought.

In his account of the faculties of the soul al-Kindī follows Plato in distinguishing the passionate, the intellectual and the concupiscent faculties as found in the *Phaedrus*; the universal designations of the functions of the various sense organs are considered; memory and imagination also take their hierarchical positions; likewise the functions of nutrition and growth are assigned their due place; and all through these considerations the problem is the relation of the soul as a spiritual, non-material entity to the material world and to its own embodiment in a very physical organism.

After the less controversial 'natural' faculties, we come to al-Kindī's *Treatise on the Intellect*. Mind is defined as a "simple essence cognizant of things in their true realities." Atiyeh gives the following commentary:

> There are four intellects, the first of which is separate and seems to be constructed in the image of Aristotle's Active Intellect. It exists outside the human soul; it is divine and always in actuality. And although al-Kindī, like al-Fārābī and Ibn Sīnā, believed that the celestial spheres possess intellects, there seems to be no indication that our philosopher ever thought of the First Intellect as the intellect of the moon,

better known as the "Donator of Forms" and maintained by the above-mentioned philosophers.[16]

The other three intellects are the Potential Intellect, the Acquired Intellect and the Demonstrative Intellect. One might find rather close parallels between these four levels or types of intellect and the classical Indian distinctions (including Buddhism, Jainism and most varieties of Hinduism) between *manas*, *buddhi*, *citta* and *sākṣī*. There is also a possible parallel with the four-level structuring of the best of the Vedānta and the Mahāyāna traditions :

Pāramārthika	First Intellect (linking divine and human)
Vyāvahārika	Second Intellect (comprehension of Forms)
Prātibhāsika	Third Intellect (integration of perceptions)
Mithyā	Fourth Intellect (operation of senses as such)

Not that this does not raise more questions than it may settle, but it may help get us out of the rut of traditional endless rehashing of the age-long controversy that culminated in the European perspective only in the Averroist heresy in later Latin Scholasticism, and may suggest other angles of possible interpretation that are more universal and more universally philosophical and not merely confined to the technicalities of theology as such.

The Potential Intellect resides in the soul as that faculty which has the disposition of receiving sense impressions or percepts and correlating them or "in forming" them into concepts. This might be well parallel with the *antaḥkaraṇa* in Saṃskṛt terminology or what later Latin Scholastics called the *sensus communis*.

Apparently it is just not clear what al-Kindī thought the relation of the Acquired to the Active Intellect really is. Atiyeh says that the "identification of the Acquired Intellect with universals smells of Neoplatonism"—contrary, we might add, to the Thomistic interpretations. Al-Kindī refers to the Acquired Intellect as the "form which is not material nor of the nature of imagination...and is given to the soul by the First Intellect which is the species of the things that are always in actuality."[17] The burden here seems to be a caution against emanationism, such that the Active Intellect, evidently like *Parama-Puruṣa* of

Sāṃkhya or the *sākṣī* of Śaivism or Vedānta, remains not in need of direct contact with the intelligible material 'stuff' of the world lest contamination result therefrom. But when on the other hand al-Kindī says that the First or Active Intellect is *not* the perfection of the soul whereas the Acquired Intellect is, there is confusion, since the Acquired Intellect is in the soul and the Active Intellect is not, and yet those two, somehow, have to come into contact in order for the Potential Intellect to become actualized as the Acquired Intellect wherein perfection of the soul resides. We are left only with a metaphor which sounds terribly trans-Eurasian if not definitely Mahāyānistic or Vedāntic even though historically it could have come from Neo-Platonist sources : "...As the rays of the sun which illumine a dark place turn the darkness into light without the sun suffering any change, so do the universals turn the state of readiness into a state of perfection without the First Intellect suffering any change."[18]

There is less ambiguity concerning the Demonstrative Intellect. Atiyeh offers this summary :

> The Acquired Intellect refers to an effect of the union of the intelligible form with the human intellect. The Demonstrative Intellect, on the other hand, refers to a *process*, the process of bringing out the intelligibles into open action. To use the analogy of writing, the Third Intellect would be equal to the positive ability which one acquires by learning how to write. The Fourth (Demonstrative Intellect) would be equal to the process of writing when one is actually writing.[19]

In these as in so many other matters al-Kindī's importance lies in his historical position as a pioneer whose pattern of exposition has been followed by virtually every Muslim, Jewish and Christian Scholastic and/or Neo-Scholastic ever since. Many things are left in ambiguity and many questions unresolved, and many controversies have arisen from these obscurities ; but al-Kindī "set a model for later Muslim philosophers by introducing a fourth intellect and establishing the bases for the theory of abstraction."[20]

In his contribution to ethics al-Kindī has the same difficult job of reconciling or effecting a synthesis between the Qur'anic heritage and the Hellenistic heritage which was at his disposal. The Ṣūfīs were very much involved in essentially the same difficulty of synthesizing what actually was the Neo-Platonic *via negativa* with the Sunni and even the Shī'a orthodoxies (even though the Neo-Platonist aspect is still often denied and modern Ṣūfīs insist that their way is strictly in conformity with the Qur'ān and the *ḥadīth*). The difficulty in either case is essentially the same as that encountered by the Jewish and Christian Fathers, namely adjusting the 'naturalistic' humanism of Socrates, Plato, Aristotle, the Stoics and Epicureans(not to mention Plotinus and Proclus), which was based on rational calculation within human faculties, with the *revealed commands* of the Bible and the Qur'ān, disobedience to which was sin and punishable by God in His own way (this concept of sin as disobedience being virtually foreign to the Greeks, who acknowledged error due to ignorance but who had little or no concept of original sin). There resulted a legalism of strict observance, but at least there was no separation between political philosophy and personal ethics. Since all and sundry were subject to the same Final Judgment, all were equal before God no matter what their state and responsibilities might be in this world. Hence one finds Islamic democracy at least at the mosque, which unlike the Greek, Christian or Jewish ways never developed a sacramental sacrosanct priesthood.

In the Abrahamic heritages it was consistently held that without the authority of revelation the Hellenic and Hellenistic ethical codes were inadequate. Man unaided by grace and fait h was left floundering inexorably in *saṃsāra*, never enabled to transcend the natural forces that condition his behavior by his own faculties and the experience of his forebears alone. By way of comparison we could again review what had emerged in the Sinic, Indic and Japanese civilizations, from the legalistic interpretations of the inexorability of the law of karma in the strict Mīmāṁsā to the easy-to-attain grace of Amida and the Great Compassion of Kwan-yin, not to mention the alchemistic ethics of Neo-Taoism or the strict observance of *ahiṃsā* by Buddhist and Jaina monks in sharp contrast to the difficult-to-hide *jihād* and crusading ethics of Islam and the various varieties of Christianity (which strangely were so often engaged in military combat in the name of the Prince of Peace and Savior of Mankind).

Along with Plato and the purely Islamic bases there is also a strong Aristotelian element in al-Kindī's ethical system—for systematic ethics it is, as is the rest of his philosophizing, and not mere moralizing. Thus the four cardinal virtues (wisdom, courage, continence, and justice) take a prominent place, the first three being considered as within the soul subjectively and the last as exterior or objective. The secret of ethical life is the harmonization of the interior and the exterior, the subjective and the objective, virtues. Al-Kindī has a special term for this harmonization, *'adl'* which may also be rendered as 'equilibrium'. Thus he is not a conflict philosopher but definitely a humanist advocating the golden mean and moderation. Evidently al-Kindī had a very Hellenic confidence in the inherent goodness of man's nature and little if anything of the notion of total depravity that is found in some of the Latin Patristics. Evil to al-Kindī was essentially what it was to Plato : allowing the passions to dominate the intellect.

Only one ethical work of al-Kindī's has survived in complete form, *On the Means to Drive Away Sorrow.* While we infer some influence from Galen in this text, Buddhist influence of course is highly unlikely even though there are some parallels in a broader context. For example, the fact that sorrow is caused by desire is the first point stressed in this work, and of course psychological pain is acknowledged as being of more importance than physical pain. But as the discourse develops it begins to sound more Epicurean and/or Stoic than Buddhist. Relief and/or prevention of sorrow comes from elevating the mind as well as limiting harmoniously the desires so that a "spiritual equilibrium" may be maintained. Also, realization that all things are subject to generation and corruption should ease anxiety, for misfortune cannot last forever any more than good fortune. So, rationally, one should be as content as possible under all circumstances, for sorrow comes from irrational extremes.

Again this could also be Buddhistic or Stoic: and the anecdote told about the mother of Alexander the Great sounds very much like the story of the woman who came to the Buddha weeping because her child had died. The Buddha told her to go to so many houses looking for a family that had not experienced death. Of course not finding any she realized that suffering was universal, became enlightened and joined the *saṅgha*. The story here is that Alexander's mother was requested by Alexander himself to invite to his funeral only those who had not suffered any disgrace, for the funeral was to be a great celebration of joy over Alexander's accomplishments, and no one can be joyful who has suffered disgrace. No one came, for no one had not suffered some disgrace; hence his mother was no longer saddened by his death. The chief point here is that it is just good practical advice to remember others' situations when one is troubled, or at the other extreme, excessively overjoyed. In other words, evidently much of al-Kindī's ethics is just good mental hygiene, not striving for the transcendental perfection of a Bodhisattva vow or heroic asceticism, but, again and again humanist moderation.

There is another work known as the *Maxims of Socrates* concerning which Atiyeh informs us that al-Kindī was the first Muslim to take Socrates seriously. The Islamic Socrates gives a slightly different picture than the one we have from Plato, but it may well be that this tradition has some elements in it that are authentic since recent scholarship throws some doubts on the picture of Socrates we have from Plato alone as too much idealized. In Hellenistic tradition there was some confusion between Socrates and Diogenes; but given the variety of Socrates' disciples, of whom Plato was only one, it may well be that the Diogenes-Socrates is, as it were, the other side of the coin. Al-Kindī himself accepts only the image of Socrates as a great moralizer rather than as the sort of ascetic that Diogenes was. Indeed he looks to Socrates as the champion of moderation.

Al-Kindī's works in the natural sciences far outnumber his works in metaphysics and theology. Along with the influence in philosophy, Greek science such as it was also came in, with Galen's medical treatises in the forefront. The scientists (and Ṣūfīs, as in the case of al-Ḥallāj) also began to absorb all the best from India and not a little likewise from China—paper, for example, and navigational science and porcelain, for which Iranian Islam soon became famous. Knowledge of medicine and astronomy were considered as essential for purely practical reasons. The califs were naturally always anxious about their health, and they needed experts not only to get the calendar straight but also as astrologers since there were very few then who did not believe in it. Hence somehow those trades or professions were acceptable without theological qualm except by the most fanatical extremists. Most of the *Falsafah* followed one or another or all of these professions in order to get patronage and to escape censorship. In most cases they probably made no separation of Plato, Aristotle and the Stoics from Galen and the Ptolemaic cosmology and saw no discrepancy in their role as scientists. The (perhaps) false separation of science, religion and philosophy in the modern secular world has made that seem strange, with the odd result that although al-Rāzī is usually listed as important only in the history of science, al-Kindī is usually remembered almost exclusively in the history of philosophy. But both were both.

Al-Kindī was known in his own time as much if not more for his scientific achievements as for his work in philosophy in the more limited sense. He was a pioneer and not just a transmitter in mathematics, geometry, spherics, astronomy, engineering, medicine, chemistry, meteorology, and other sciences. He was also the first Arab writer on music. While one may find some Indian influence in his scientific works, it is not impossible that influence from India might have come into his philosophical works also. To say the least, if so many products were imported from India and China, then commerce and communication must have been much more open than generalists have heretofore suspected. And if such products, why not ideas, even if in garbled guise. While we cannot say that Śaṅkara had any influence on al-Kindī or vice versa, communications were sufficiently open to account, at least in part, for the concomitant variation in basic themes of philosophizing if not in actual attitudes. And while al-Kindī was primarily if not almost exclusively concerned with Greek sources, it would be difficult to believe, polymath and prominent in state affairs as he was, that he would have been ignorant of the many intercultural contacts which were going on during his time.

Certainly a comparison of al-Kindī with Scotus Erigena

would bring out their indirect common heritage in the *via-negativa* from Maximus Confessor (since it is doubtful whether Philopon could have been in Erigena's lineage). The humanist manner and basic attitude in the face of opposition in Photius is such that it is indeed a pity that he and al-Kindī could not have had some direct communication or personal contact, for they might have mitigated some of the bitter strife and unnecessary bloodshed between Baghdad and Byzantium. Al-Kindī's emphasis on unity is shared with Śaṅkara and the Kaśmir Śaivas and Buddhists, if not even with the Chinese and Japanese Buddhists who were insisting on the Ekayāna one-vehicle approach to the plethora of Buddhist sūtras. The expertise in logic in al-Kindī is also found in the Nyāya-Vaiśeṣikas right along with their realistic insistence on atoms and definite and definable categories (which we have long since noted are amazingly similar to Aristotle's). However, the Advaitins and the Mahāyāna Buddhists of all brands as well as the Jainas would have vehemently disagreed with the *ex nihilo* cosmology.

Al-Kindī shares with Li Ao and Han Yü basic humanist attitudes and (qualified) reservations about the other-worldliness of non-systematic religious practices that border on superstition. In their case there is the problem of adjusting the metaphysics of Buddhism to Confucian ethics, and in al-Kindī's case, of incorporating Greek metaphysics to the almost exclusively ethical teachings of the Qur'ān and *ḥadīth*. Al-Kindī's broad-mindedness and rationalist humanism are expressed in the following :

> We should not be ashamed of recognizing truth and assimilating it from whatever source it may reach us, even though it might come from earlier generations and foreign peoples. For him who seeks truth there is nothing of more value than truth itself. It never cheapens or abases him who searches for it, but ennobles and honors him.[21]

Besides taking this as a possible mild condemnation of Han Yü's scarcely concealed ethonocentricity and zenophobia, it certainly applies today even more than ever (such as in the aim of UNESCO, not to mention departments of philosophy, which should not be limited to Euramerican perspectives only).

Al-Kindī is not just a philosopher but an encyclopedic mind, as becomes the case with almost all of the great Islamic thinkers after him. Poetry, medicine, jurisprudence, astronomy, biology—all after him became virtually prerequisites to the study of philosophy. Al-Kindī insists that mathematics is a *sine qua non*, being more important even than the study of Aristotle. He also contributed to the science of music and in this as well as other things was followed by al-Fārābī (who seems to have eclipsed al-Kindī in virtually every respect although he was influenced almost solely by him).

Al-Kindī tried to follow at the same time two paths, that of philosophy and that of religion, and never does he claim that one has absorbed the other. He seems to think that they lead to knowledge of the same realities.

> The thought of Kindī offers thus an example of the difficulties which one encounters in wishing to be at once a philosopher and theologian.... He is not a mystic; one does not count him among the Mutakallimūn. The first undoubtedly in the whole history of Islam to have held to the attempt to construct a philosophical system, he distinguishes himself nevertheless from the *Falsafah* who came after him; for more than they he wants to maintain the rights of religion, and he does not try to absorb it into philosophy. He is the most theological among the philosophers of Islam, and the most Greek of the Mu'tazilites. What he makes is not a synthesis but a design tracing an effort, characteristic of his personality, and reflects—with an appetite for universality which nothing can astonish, and a speculative ambition richly nourished—the vigor of the first century of the Abassid Califate.[22]

Although al-Kindī has been called the most original of all Muslim thinkers, it might be charged that he only imitated the Greeks, integrating them into Islamic tradition much after the pattern that the Christians had followed some centuries previously. At any rate he represents the other pole from al-Ash'arī in giving a firm ground to the rationalist school; in this he greatly influenced al-Fārābī, Ibn Rushd, and Ibn Sīnā, who of course influenced Christian Scholasticism very much indeed.

At long last we are getting translations of Islamic materials from the original texts directly into Euramerican languages and no longer have to rely on the Latin translations, which in not a few cases were biased and inadequate. Fortunately there is a fresh Neo-Scholasticism in Islam which parallels the recent emergence of Christian Neo-Scholasticism (though unfortunately the needed parallel development of Neo-Byzantine studies is lagging far behind these currents). Certainly al-Kindī and the other Muslim Scholastics can and must be studied no longer as merely relevant to the emergence of Latin Scholasticism but in their own right and in their own milieu.

20. Erigena

John Scotus Erigena (810-870) was from Ireland, which had already had a relatively rich cultural tradition for several centuries and had been the chief center from which Christian missionary work on the northern part of Europe had been quite active. He arrived in France at the Court of Charles le Chauve about 846-7, and taught at the Palatine School. Erigena's *De Devisione Naturae* and Śaṅkara's *Commentary on the Brahma Sūtras* are two of the greatest works in philosophy the world has ever known. Basically they are both varieties of monism. But that is far too simple, for monism itself contains many varieties and subheads and is always in need of a multitude of distinctions in order to uphold itself. On first reading Erigena may seem pretty much an Advaitin sort of monist; but another reading may show him more of a Viśiṣṭādvaitin or panentheist. But in a sense this would be true also of virtually all Muslim philosophers who also continue the theophany theme, and many Byzantine conferres as well. Even so, this is what we mean by our theme of "monism in many moods".

When Erigena makes the three-fold distinction of the orders that create and are not created, that create and are created, that do not create and are created (the fourth, not created nor creating, being almost inadmissible as a pseudo form without a demonstrable existent), it might be argued that he is not setting up a mere calculus of logical possibility but is coming rather close to the sort of *pariṇāmavāda* that Śaṅkara had to deal with : a continuum of transformation which somehow does not depart from the Ground of Being which is God prior to manifestation in external Nature, sustaining that manifestation in all of its cosmological wonder, and drawing it back to Himself in one eternal constancy which ineffably belies our finite necessity of thinking in discrete individuations. The triad, in other words, even more vividly than with Maximus to whom he is most indebted, never ceases to be monad. We tentatively suggest the following scheme :

pāramārthika	That which creates and is not created
vyāvahārika	That which creates and is created
prātibhāsika	That which does not create and is created
mithyā	That which is neither creating nor created

This parallel would fit better with those varieties of the Vedānta which take the theistic interpretation of Brahman, minimizing the *nirguṇa* and emphasizing the *saguṇa* aspect as Īśvara (often identified with Śiva), since the Godhead therein is considered as Supreme Creator and/or Preserver and/or Destroyer ('destruction' being omitted in the Judeo-Christian scholastic schematizations for the most part, even though there are passages, especially in the Old Testament scriptures, which would justify such an inclusion). But there would be a difference between Erigena and Śaṅkara here if we take the interpretation of Śaṅkara's system as he seems to wish us to do, that the supreme *nirguṇa*-Brahman is more like the *Parama-Puruṣa* of non-theistic Sāṃkhya : neither created nor creating—in just the opposite sense of Erigena's fourth which is at the bottom of the hierarchy which the Indian systems would identify as simple *jaḍa*, 'dead matter'. Of course very similar schemata can be derived from most of the pre-Śaṅkara Mahāyāna Buddhist systems, although most of them seem to prefer merely a two-fold division between the *pāramārthika* (*nirvṛtti*) and the other three lumped together as *pravṛtti* or *samvṛtti* (as a matter of fact many post-Śaṅkara Vedāntins, even Advaitins, seem to have the same tendency).

Apparently Schopenhauer thought that Erigena received Indian influence through Pseudo-Dionysius, who, having lived in Alexandria, had come to some knowledge of Indian thought. According to Schopenhauer, relying on Colebrooke, the third *śloka* of the "Kārikā of Kapila" can be found again in Erigena's scheme in the *De Divisione Naturae.* Martin presents the scheme somewhat as follows :

Sāṃkhya	*Erigena*
1. *Prakṛti* with the three *guṇas*.	Nature which is uncreated but creates.
2. The seven derivatives of *prakṛti*, i.e., *citta* and *ahaṅkāra* and the five purely material elements (earth, water, fire, air and ether).	Nature which is created and which creates.
3. The sixteen modifications which are only products (created or evolved): faculties of sense perception and agents of action.	Nature which is created and does not create (*Natura naturata*), which provokes man to seek to return towards nature which is not created and does not create.
4. *Puruṣa* (Spirit, Person); Martin suggests that this could be analogized to the Person of Christ (as Logos) or Personhood as distinct from the otherwise undifferentiated 'Father'.	Nature uncreated and not creating.[1]

Nevertheless Martin adds that the comparison is necessarily limited since classical Sāṃkhya is dualistic, realistic and atheist. Still, as Martin suggests, such comparisons do challenge our limitations to ethnocentric perspectives and even "suggest a revelation of a universal mode of archetypical thought beyond the socio-cultural contingencies".

The typical charge by the Western Church of "pantheism" or "emanationism" is a gross misinterpretation of Eastern Orthodoxy, according to Duclow. He invokes the distinction that

Dionysius himself makes between God's Essence and His Presence : it is the Essence that is ineffable (*anirvacanīya,* to use the Advaita term), but His Presence is everywhere as Theophany, as communications, as uncreated energies—too bad these Byzantines and Erigena and Nicholas of Cusa did not have the Saṃskṛt terminology, because for energies they could substitute *śakti,* and of course they could have distinguished the *nirguṇa* from the *saguṇa* aspect of Deity, as well as distinguish between *antarātman* and *antaryāmin*, etc. But the concepts are so similar, so parallel, that they would have found themselves pretty well in the same camp over against the Aristotelians on the one side and the Arians and Ash'arites on the other. Duclow writes :

> Within the traditions of Eastern Orthodoxy, for which Dionysius is both witness and formative influence, creation is interpreted as the self-manifestation of the divine. There being no distinction between nature and a supernature conceived as intermediary between God and creation, creation is itself grasped as an on-going revelation of its uncreated Lord. Hence, for Dionysius "all creation is 'theophany'"—theophany, that is, the disclosing or showing forth of God himself. There is, therefore, a radically active presence or immanence of the divine in creation, in the things of the earth themselves. Within Eastern Orthodoxy we may thus speak of a radical interpretation of the *analogia entis* as the condition for theological-philosophical speculation, for the *analogia* is given in the very structure of creation as theophany. Stating this doctrine most strongly, John the Scot—claiming the authority of Dionysius—states that "He is the Essence of all things Who alone truly is." This "essential" inherence of the divine in creation establishes the condition for God's possessing "the names of all things"—that is, the condition for there being any validity to the cataphatic way of affirming creaturely names of the uncreated Lord of creation. It is by the presence of God within the earth, understood as the self-manifestation of the divine, that it becomes possible to speak of God as "Sun, Star, Fire and Water, Wind or Spirit, Dew, Cloud...and All Creation."[2]

Of course John the Scot is John Scotus, since in the ninth century the Irish were known as *Scoti* and Ireland as *Scotia Maior*.

The *ex nihilo* dogma introduces an otherness of a pseudo-nature as the Creation which is opposed to God, 'outside' of Him even though 'made' by Him, in such a way that His Nature does not include it within His Being. Erigena was often accused of rank pantheism by later scholastics because of his softening of the *ex nihilo;* and he seems to lessen the emanation theory of the Neo-Platonists, to whom most writers acknowledge that he is most indebted. There seems to be some source other than Neo-Platonism responsible for his sense of God in everything, or rather for his sense that nothing has ever really departed or been "sent out" from God. A fascinating hypothesis here would be that he had absorbed something of the pre-Christian Irish culture, but this would be difficult to prove since it has been lost in such obscurity. Another hypothesis equally difficult to prove is that there is some sort of *Weltgeist*, a panpsychic unity, that guides and permeates the destiny of mankind, and that this *Weltgeist* "explains" the ninth century monisms while our empirical methods at best only "describe" the historical movement.

For Erigena the things of nature in their multifariousness are not a compromise of the Oneness of all things in God but rather a manifestation of it. The *ex nihilo* is simply their right to be a part of this Oneness and not apart from it. It is here that one may understand God's superessential nature vis-a-vis the *ex nihilo* : the things, which would be nothing without being given existence according to the essence of God, are preserved from non-being by His superabundance of being, which is so self-reduplicating that there is, as it were, a surplus which necessitates a certain theophany in and through them. In His super-essence all ambiguities of affirmation and negation, being and non-being, all the Pythagorean opposities are superceded. The better criticism that might be made against this is not that commonly given, namely that this pushing all the dialectical interplay of negations and affirmations into the superessential or supernatural runs the risk of a confused naive pantheism that becomes oblivious of distinction and individuation, for Erigena glories in those, reiterating that this is the theophany. Rather the criticism might be that he did not push the limit of this field of nondistinction back far enough, as, for example, Nāgārjuna did.

Erigena is striving to express a reciprocative action in his distinction of the three modes of creating and created, specifically in his emphasis on the theophanic aspect of the reciprocating interconnexity of the three. There are many connections in which this becomes clear, whether one is considering the primordial causes, or the necessity of pushing everything back behind all dichotomies, or trying to show that this can be done only by the trans-positive manner in which the ultimacy of interreciprocation (as distinct from mere progressional transformation of essence to substance and such like) must be recognized as obtaining within the nature of God, as self-originative in the Father, as self-generative in the Word, and as self-reciprocative in the Holy Spirit. These are *hypostases*, not transformations; and that is the definition, all emotional fixations aside, of hypostasis : *distinction of operation without compromise of essence;* not emanations, but rendering emanation possible, and in a mode even necessary from the self-generating surplus of Being which is the Divine becoming as distinct from the phenomenological becoming-in-transformation in Nature, which is a compromise of Being as the Buddhists rightly argued. It is a Divine becoming because it does not go out of its Divine origin but always leaves open the way of inseparable Return (for want of a less paradoxical mode of expression).

An important question in our comparison is whether, from Śaṅkara's point of view, Erigena really reached as far as the *nirguṇa*-Brahman. His constant reiteration of all forms is within this perspective, and Śaṅkara would have no objection to that; but he would enjoin, no doubt, the further question whether and from what perspective this also can be 'bracketed', seen as either included in or transcended by the Absolutely Formless. This is not easy for most moderns, except perhaps for such as Husserl, Scheler and Jaspers; but it is all-important, for until this 'opening' becomes available one is still subject to the realm of illusion, of *māyā*, of unfreedom, of subjection to the world-process. One has not come, in terms of the Christian tradition, into the

Vision of the Glory of God; one has not allowed onself to be taken up into the completion of the *via negativa.* And the discipline leading to Śaṅkara's *vidyā* is commensurate with the consideration of the end itself in such a way that it is perhaps better to treat the question in a purely historical fashion lest one get trapped in the desire to 'get it', to be there (although the Buddhists should have long since cleared the ego out of the way !).

At any rate it does seem that Erigena did come into this same 'nirguṇa' perspective, and perhaps in such a way as to even get a critical appraisal of it. Not only anticipating Anselm in substance (if not in form) in the burden of the ontological argument, but as it were going beyond this, Erigena asserts that there is even a mode in which not only is it impossible to "give a definition" of God but it may even be said that God must be ignorant of His own nature, at least of that whereby, even as Creator, He is related to creatures. "From then on nothing else is seen" is to be equated quite closely with that 'ignorance' above 'knowledge' which is the Field beyond all possible distinctions. Thus, when he is trying to demonstrate the distinction between essence (*ousia*) as generically and universally applicable in all things, and the superessential nature of God considered in relation only to Himself, it seems to us he is making basically the same distinction that Śaṅkara constantly insists upon between *saguṇa* and *nirguṇa*-Brahman. The relation between them constitutes a third 'motion' in a way that is not a mere category of relation universally applicable but an absolutely irreducible aspect of the self-identity (even in the 'ignorance') of the Godhead. This threefold motion is also reflected in the human soul or self in Erigena in almost the same way as it is within Śaṅkara.

This "ignorance of God" of His own incapacity of being subjected to definition entails, dialectically, His nature of being a mode of Knowledge, or rather of wisdom (*prajñā*) of the sort aimed at in Kūkai and the Chinese Buddhists, which is far above every normal human attainment apart from mystical enlightenment—a matter dangerous indeed to meddle with unless one has a guide, as Śaṅkara among others is careful to give warning about. But without meddling, as historians at least we may observe that there is a strange convergence here of the knowledge *of* God, *by* God, *in* God, that really *is* God : it is a state of consciousness then rather than a "knowledge". We may also note that this is not unique with any particular school in this century.

After the "descent" in Erigena comes the "remounting" as in all varieties of Neo-Platonism and virtually all Indian systems, but especially the Vedānta in all its varieties—and even in Neo-Confucianism under the caption of 'cultivation of the Original Mind'. So here we have nothing unusual but basically universal, indeed so much so in these previous centuries that it is passing strange that it has fallen so much into neglect in recent years in Euramerica, with the notable exception of Scheler and in a certain measure Whitehead. But the most salient exceptions are Aurobindo and Teilhard de Chardin.

With Erigena, just as the Goodness of God is the *ratio* for His creating things, so it is the entelechy toward which all things must perforce tend in the final consummation of Nature in the Return to God. Erigena accepts the traditional scheme of redemption wherein the Fall of Adam is over-compensated by the Resurrection and Ascension—he seems to emphasize these more than the Crucifixion and the Atonement, which later Anselm will stress. The doctrine of *theosis,* which he takes from Gregory Nazianzen and Maximus, becomes a vivid expectation with him. It is true that Erigena has to accede to the Church's doctrine that not all will be saved, though he seems to do so unwillingly. But this much is certain, that the Return to God is a matter of deifying vision, of knowledge of the sort given only in perfection of contemplation, which is possible only after all the veils are removed. And the veils are removed by the theophanies, not by the merit of effort of the meditator. Just as in Zen, "there is nothing done". With Śaṅkara and Erigena, but with the paradox removed, the whole moral realm is taken up into the dawn of the Vision of the Goodness of God, which is identical with His other aspects in such a way that even the distinguishing between them is allowed rather than prescribed for the sake of contemplation on the part of the weaker souls. But the end is the same. One possible distinction between Śaṅkara and Erigena, however, is that Erigena ends in praise whereas Śaṅkara considers this more appropriate to the *saguṇa*-Brahman.

In Erigena we find what amounts to another version of the microcosm/macrocosm doctrine, which Gracia in his study puts under the more relevant metaphor of 'containment' : "Man is said to 'contain' everything in the created universe."[3] This was derived from Maximus Confessor, to whom Erigena openly acknowledges his indebtedness and from whom he even makes frequent quotations, especially from Maximus' *Ambigua*. This indebtedness is well known though some others would rather emphasize Erigena's sources, direct and indirect, in the Patristic literature. Erigena summarizes by quoting Maximus as follows : "There is no creature, from the highest to the lowest, which is not found in man; hence he is correctly called the workshop of everything. In him converge everything made by God, in the way many different sounds make up a song. ..."[4] This transformer role is carried further into the one-and-many problem since man uniquely—as far as we know, and here we are no more but also no less ignorant in our time than Erigena was in his—has the *śakti* or power not only to find and explain unities and analogies in nature but to bring things as well as ideas together into new unities. Gracia continues :

> The view of Maximus revealed by these texts portrays man as a connecting link in created nature. It is because man contains everything that he constitutes the basis of unity and harmony in creation. He is in fact a workshop, a place where everything comes together and is fashioned into a new order, the place where creation is unified into a whole. Erigena's glosses on Maximus's texts emphasize these points. ...He explains that the multiplicity of nature—what he calls "the extremes represented by the sensible and the invisible"—are mediated by human nature; for it is in human nature, according to him, that the diversity of things is made one...Man, created in the image and likeness of God, is the end of the differences between all things, for there is no creature, visible or invisible, that is not in him.[5]

Certainly this "Byzantine" interpretation of the Image of God in Man leaves little room for the gloominess of the doctrine of total depravity in some Western Euramerican versions of Christianity, and for that matter likewise little room for the extremes of predestination and inexorability of karma or mechanistic determinism in Erigena's own or our own century. If this view of human nature—not unlike that, by the way, even of Li Ao, derived from Mencius—were more common today there would be more hope for deliverance from the demon of war just as we have been largely delivered from the devil of legalized slavery..

Gracia states that the metaphor of 'containment' cannot easily be translated into ontological language. This difficulty is not the fault of Erigena but of those who are not sufficiently open to Erigena's 'vision', for Erigena did not intend his teaching to be taken as a mere metaphor but was much more serious about it. He insists that, in short, we should rather marvel at the number of things that man contains instead of entertaining doubts and quibbling about such a notion. This almost reminds us of the controversy about the interpretation of the *ko wu* investigation of things in Erigena's contemporary Neo-Confucianists.

> ...Eriugena states unambiguously that nothing whatsoever among created things is excluded from this containment; and from what other texts suggest, this seems to mean not only that the number of things man contains is very great but also that their variety is astonishing. Indeed, the things man contains range from creatures superior to him, such as angels, to creatures of an inferior kind, such as animals; from substances...to the properties and accidents of those substances; and from causes, such as the primordial notions, to effects of those causes.[6]

Thus there is nothing in the created universe, corporeal or incorporeal, that is not somehow contained in man. Hence man's excellence as being made in the Image of God.

Erigena explicates this 'containment' through the 'notions', which is a translation for the Latin term *notitae* or *notiones*, which Gracia tells us Erigena uses almost interchangeably. *Notiones* in turn is a very poor translation of the Greek term *en-noiai* with the rich Neo-Platonic connotation of something like the operation of *Nous* as the hypostasis of the Divine One in things such that as plural they are Exemplars of the primordial relation of natural laws as expressions of order and therefore of intelligence both in our little minds and in the universe at large. Thus they resemble the *li* concept in its plurality in Neo-Confucianism.

> First, Eriugena shows how notions constitute a type of reality different from and superior to the accidents and substances of which they are notions and that it is these notions that are said to be "created in" man. In a second step, he demonstrates that the notions of the created universe, except that of man himself, constitute an essential part of man's nature. Finally, he points out how things may be said to be in man through their notions.[7]

Erigena invokes Augustine for his authority in regard to the difference between things themselves and the notions of things, the notions constituting a higher order of excellence (from Augustine, *De Trinitate*, 9:2) : "Reason teaches that what understands is better than what is understood." The *notiones* are perhaps like the model concept in recent philosophizing and scientific hypothesis building, for as Gracia puts it, the notions are logically and axiologically prior to the things of which they are notions. "It is because they are prior that notions are not to be understood in terms of the things of which they are notions but the reverse, for the knowledge (*a rtes*) of things is formed from notions, not notions from the knowledge of things."[8] Gracia explains further :

> Notions differ from things in being incorporeal, better, and older. ...That notions are better and older than things does not imply a fundamental ontological rift between the two, since "better" and "older" indicate only differences of degree, not substance. Moreover, it is clear that the incorporeality of notions is regarded by Eriugena as a basic ontological distinction either, since in *Periphyseon* 1 he explained in great detail how the corporeal is in fact the result of the union of incorporeal notions and, consequently, is only accidentally different from the incorporeal. Indeed, visible matter itself,

> according to Eriugena, is nothing other than a composition of invisible accidents; substantially, the corporeal is equivalent to the incorporeal.[9]

Such a notion about the notion of matter differs rather radically from the Aristotelian-Thomistic concept and resembles more what we find in Giordano Bruno and later in Leibniz, and even echoes of it can be found in Whitehead.

Erigena applies this metaphysics to the nature of man through his conception of 'art' (*disciplina*), by which he does not mean the more limited sense that is the usual theme of modern secular aesthetics. Art here is very much involved in the *notiones*, and Gracia tells us that the two terms are used by Erigena almost interchangeably : "Art is nothing other than the notions of things considered as models or archetypes of things."[10] Erigena uses geometrical figures as a paradigm example :

> The learned man, he tells us, understands without difficulty that sensible geometrical figures subsist naturally not in themselves but in the notions (*rationes*) of that very art of which they are imitations. The true triangle for example, is that after which triangular figures (i.e., sensible representations) are fashioned; it is the cause of all sensible triangles, and, since its ontological repository is the mind, it is part of the art possessed by the mind.[11]

The primary sense of 'art' is the "divine art" wherein the primordial *notiones* are at once that by which God manifests the notions phenomenally and at the same time infuses in man the concepts of models whereby he can recognize these principles or laws operating in things, rather than being limited to knowledge of the individual things themselves. As Gracia writes : "Art, then, is nothing other than the notions of things present in the knower and considered as models of those things. Consequently, the problem of the relation between man and his notions may be passed as that of the relation between man and his art."[12]

Man is essentially an "artist" as well as merely a knower; that is, he has the inborn capacity to recognize order and general principles, and, under the operation of the Holy Spirit, even to deal with them directly, for just as the Godhead is triume so is man a lesser trinity of mind, 'art' and skill (*peritia*) such that man can even conceive how that by the operation of the *notiones* the Idea of Man exists eternally in the 'Mind' of God.

Erigena applies the *via negativa* not only to the nature of God but to human nature as well in a very close parallel: a man can know *that* this *notio* is in the Mind of God, but he cannot know *what* it really is or contains—or whether it might even be contentless. Duclow writes :

> Within the context of the *imago dei*, cannot this self-ignorance of man be interpreted as an analogue of the impenetrable unknowability of the divine nature subsisting by itself ? As John the Scot writes,
>
> "The divine likeness in the human mind, therefore, is recognized most clearly in that it is known only to be; but what it is is unknown. ... If it were known to be some certain thing, it would be circumscribed certainly in something and, by that fact, it would not express in itself wholly the image of its Creator who is entirely uncircumscribed and is understood in nothing because he is infinite, above all that is said and understood, super-essential."
>
> Within man's very self-ignorance, therefore, is constituted a relatedness to his origin in the absolutely transcendent Lord of creation. In this sense, our ignorance emphatically is not without purpose : it is a fundamental ground for the *Via Negativa*. ...[13]

Gracia quotes Erigena to the same effect : "The (human) mind understands through...its art and it is understood in its...art, not in terms of what it is, but that it is; otherwise it would not be a coessential and coequal trinity."[14] Thus man is both 'contained' and 'container' just as he is both a caused and a causing/ creating being. But, as in the Vedānta, apart from his knowledge of God he really knows nothing, not even himself.

In the following Gracia points to a possible comparison with Berkeley, but a comparison with Erigena's Kaśmir Buddhist or early Kaśmir Śaiva contemporaries might be even more appropriate.

> Man possesses the notions of all sensible and intelligible things. It is this fact, according to Eriugena, that makes man to be almost everything. Indeed, he writes, "What is there astonishing, then, if the notions of things which the human mind possesses because the notion was created in it, be understood as the substance of the very things of which it is the notion, that is, in the likeness of the divine mind in which the notion of the whole created universe is the incommunicable substance of the whole ? " In a passage that sounds much like Berkeley, Eriugena asks : "Just as we call the notion of all things which are understood and are perceived by the corporeal sense in the whole of things, the substance of the things which fall under the understanding or the sense, so shall we also say that the notion of the differences and properties and natural accidents are the differences themselves and the properties and the accidents?" In short, to be is to be understood, "for where (things) are understood, they are, and in fact they are nothing more than their being understood." Accordingly, the substance of things is none other than the notion found in the human Mind, and man's own substance is none other than the notion through which he knows *that* he is and God knows *what* he is. Although these two notions —man's notion of himself and God's notion of man—appear to be different, they are substantially the same, understood in one way in the primordial causes and in another in the effects of those causes, where they are endowed with accidents.[15]

It might well be said that here he is operating in the *Vijñānamayakoṣa* as far as man is concerned ; and as far as God is concerned, or the 'Mind' of God, we suggest the *Alayavijñāna* wherein the functional divisions between knowledge, knower and known are reduced back into their primordial nondifferentiation. In other words, if Erigena were using Saṁskṛt terminology, he would probably agree that from the lower *samvṛtti* and/or *pravṛtti* point of view there is a sort of discrepancy in that paradox; but that can be sublated back to the *nivṛtti* or *pāramārthika* level in which the differentiation is "no yet" or no longer, as it were, for that dimension is timeless or even dimensionless.

Of course the doctrine of the convergence of knower, known and knowledge is by no means unique to any school or any civilization, although it does seem chronologically to receive more attention during the centuries under review in the present volume. We have this expression of it from Erigena :

> The angel...is made in man through the understanding of the angel which is in man, and man in the angel through the understanding of man constituted in the angel. For he...who understands purely is made in that which he understands ... when I understand what you understand, I am made your understanding and in a certain ineffable way I have been made into you. In the same way, when you understand clearly, you have been made, constituted by that which we both...understand.[16]

And so it might be argued that indeed he is a sort of *Vijñānavādin*. But on the other hand, he seems almost to be quoting the *Mahāvākyas* from the Upaniṣads and notably the *Tat Tvam Asi* in an Advaitin sort of way. Listen to this, for example, and compare it with Śaṅkara or Sureśvara :

> Hence, by the process of understanding, the different parts of nature are made one : "I am made into you and you are made into me. For we are not one thing and our understandings another, but our true and supreme essence is the understanding made specific in the contemplation of truth."[17]

Gracia reminds us that this doctrine was nothing new or original on Erigena's part since it can be traced through a very rich history stemming back not only to Boethius (not to mention Augustine) but even more to Gregory of Nyssa. Gracia notes, however, that in others before Erigena it had been only incidental whereas in him it is central and even emphatically so. Gracia continues :

> Given the ontological character of the doctrine, it is only by uncovering its ontological bases that we may hope to understand it. These...are two : first, Eriugena's rejection of any substantial difference between individuals and their

> notions or universals: second, his commitment to a metaphysical monism in which created reality is seen as all of the same kind. The first commits Eriugena to a view in which the individual differs from the universal only in accidents; the former is nothing but the notion of man as it is accompanied by accidents of place, time, color, and so on—in short, what contemporary philosophers are fond of calling "a bundle". As such, the relation between the universal and the particular is not one of participation, as Plato would have it, but one of identity. In fact, there is no relation, for a relation would necessitate substantial distinction, which in this scheme does not appear. The individual is the same being, essence, or substance (terms Eriugena interchanges frequently) with the universal, although considered as encrusted with various accidental features.[18]

Any monism of any breed sooner or later has to deal with these problems and paradoxes. But as with many if not most of those monisms the answer is not in systematic metaphysics as such but in a realm of experience (apparently rather rare nowadays) wherein by meditation/yoga one actually experiences things happening "by mere thought" as we find in Upaniṣadic literature evidently as a result of entering a sort of field of consciousness. And we should not forget that Erigena also recommended meditation or 'yoga' rather than divisional analysis as the way back to the Primordial or the Archetypical.

Those who still hold antipathy to 'mere' commentary on the Bible are forgetting that those done in the centuries now under review are certainly parallel to such commentaries as those of Śaṅkara on the Upaniṣads, for example, and even of al-Kindī, Bisṭāmī or Junayd on the Qur'ān, not to mention such other parallels as the commentaries on Mencius by Li Ao and Han Yü. Concerning the relationship between faith and intelligence, Erigena like Anselm is extremely keen to understand what is to be believed. Certainly he is poles apart in this matter from such as Peter Damien, who was almost a medieval fundamentalist like the Ash'arites in Islam and some extremist Mīmāṁsakas in Hindu India. If anything it is intelligence that is accorded the higher place in Erigena, though it would be an exaggeration to say that he minimized faith.

The theme of the two sources of knowledge, namely nature and the scriptures, is the very heart of Erigena's *De Divisione Naturae*; but one might wonder how he gets this commentary on the Gospel of St. John. The answer is relatively simple : by allegorical interpretation. For example, in commenting on the passage where John the Baptist says he is not worthy to touch Jesus' foot-wear, Erigena sees the two worlds there conjoined. For allegorically the whole of nature can be treated as the 'foot-wear' of the *Logos*, leaving footprints (*vestigua*, a metaphor found even in Plato) in all the natural world, but symbolizing the divine in action therein. Erigena appeals a great deal to what is not uncommon among those who are accustomed to allegorical interpretation, namely that a single text can suggest or stand for or communicate symbolically a veritable plethora of spiritual significances. It could be suggested that this might be a test as to whether a piece of writing has reached the canonical level of communication, namely that its fertility primordially is the reason for its universal significance. That this is certainly true of the Upaniṣads, the Confucian and Taoist classics and the Qur'ān is obvious, and no doubt it applies to the Buddhist Mahāyāna canon and much of the Pāli canon as well.

This is where Erigena's aesthetics comes out in full blossom, as for instance when he uses the Mountain of the Transfiguration of Christ as signifying that in climbing up from the valley of literalism one has to pass through the spiritual, the moral, the intellectual, natural knowledge, and the theological stages in the ascent. Each stage is beautifully embellished with poetic sensitivity rivalling that of Bernard of Clairvaux and Bonaventura later on. We might submit that the method of allegorical or symbolic interpretation is still good. Modern philological expertise and historical research have indeed given us better texts and translations, but these should not be ends in themselves but only a broadening of the base for more 'meta-scientific' interpretations.

As in other *sādhanas* or yogas, Erigena counsels purification and dedication in service to the path towards *theosis*, although this can be done only under and with the help of the grace of God, which Erigena says is the final "ornament" of the spiritual life in the same manner as the cosmos can be spoken of as the ornament of God as Theophany—all in all a challenging vision, profoundly and not just superficially aesthetic, in spite of the prejudices of some modern secular aestheticians that the Latin Middle Ages had no aesthetics. This concept of *theosis* is parallel with the *fanā'* and *baqā* idea in Ṣūfī ways and the *jīvanmukti* idea in Advaita and Kaśmir Śaivism. Based on the text of John I : 18, "no man has ever seen God", Erigena says that no creature, not even the angels, has knowledge of God's Essence ; and yet there are the records of various types of revelations in the Scriptures as even in the lives of some saints. The answer lies in Saṁskṛt terminology in the *āvaraṇa/vikṣepa* paradox of revelation through 'veiling'. All the theophanies are that short of veiling. They do not give knowledge of God's Essence but only, like the parabola, suggest or point towards the Infinite.

Again, Erigena's commentary on the Fourth Gospel is in a profound sense a philosophical work in the full flower of Neo-Platonic tradition, and not, as most commentaries on the Gospels have become, merely sentimental piety. It is really unfair to read, for example, Śaṅkara's commentaries on the Upaniṣads and Li Ao's commentaries on Mencius while neglecting works such as this one by John Scotus Erigena.

There is also the question how it should be that the Celestial Hierarchy should contain, at least symbolically, so many extremely strange creatures with multiple faces, such as are found in the Visions of Ezekial in the Old Testament and the Book of the Revelations Of St. John in the new Testament, when one would expect that the Divine would contain nothing but regularities. The answer must be posed in the realm of aesthetics rather than in epistemology or ontology. In short, in the realm of symbolism we need not be limited to Apollonian clarity and regularity ; for in attempting to symbolize the Divine, anything may evoke wonder and astonishment. In short, the imagination should be stretched, as it were, in our efforts to understand what must be beyond symbolism. Natural things are usually poor symbols for supernatural reality. Thus we are confronted with a paradox : in dealing with the *via negativa*—and we might subjoin that this certainly applies also to Hindu and Tibetan Buddhist art as well—since we know very well that the Divine cannot be described directly, we are completely free to attempt to symbolize it 'fantastically'. In fact such a tendency should be encouraged lest we be tempted to absolutize some naturally beautiful object and to become idolaters, as it were, in reference to it.

> To deny these perfect and eternal natures, to contest their internal structure, to deform them, to devise them according to the aberrations of the imagination, to make them enter, mutilated, deformed, and all mixed up in such absurd and unreal representations in order to signify God and the divine realities,—that is to render the best possible homage to a transcendency which defies all expression and all symbolization. From that point of view, it is perhaps paradoxical, but it is not rash to affirm that Erigena's thought associates the Negative Theology with the most radical vision of the most optimistic sort as far as those natures are concerned, as well as their internal consistency and their destiny.[19]

Concerning the *via negativa* and symbolization, needless to say words are also 'symbols', attempts at expressing or describing the ineffable, a finite means of pointing to the infinite. Hence any monist who affirms that 'negative' way is confronted with a dilemma of silence or else paradox. Extreme Śūnyavādins, some Advaitins, some Zen masters, and for that matter some of the Ash'arites in Islam, admit that *Śūnyatā*, God, Brahman, Tao, *Dharmakāya*, *Tathatā*, Allah, or whatever, is beyond description, and even affirm that the ascription of any attributes whatever is only for the sake of praise or else by way of pointing at best rather than descriptive or even indicative. If they write or speak at all—for many of them spend long times in silence—it is usually in metaphors or mind-boggling puzzles like the Zen koans. There are two types, those who say the least, and those who believe it best to use the maximum number of "divine names". Rāmānuja and the author of the *Shāhnāmeh*, Firdausi, and some of the *bhakti* Buddhists in Japan like Ippen later on, instead of using the minimum of expression pour forth praise and glorification with unlimited superlatives. Scotus

Erigena, following Dionysius and followed by Nicholas of Cusa (and to some extent even Hegel), belongs to this type also.

Erigena needs to be re-examined also from the standpoint of the history of science, although the sciences in Latin Europe were not very advanced as yet by comparison with what was transpiring in India, China, the Islamic world and even in Byzantium. Certainly he manifests a genuine active interest in the natural sciences such as were available to him (as the other 'book' for theophany along the Scriptures). In this respect he is quite on par with his Byzantine and Vedāntic but also with his Muslim contemporaries, such as, for example, what we find in al-Kindī, although not quite as advanced as the work of al-Rāzī and others in the following century. Erigena is perhaps the most astute in the field of astronomy and cosmology between the Hellenistic period and the Italian Renaissance—at least as far as Latin Europe is concerned, though we have yet to see whether somehow Erigena was indebted either directly or indirectly through the Byzantines to the Muslim astronomers, who were largely indebted to the Indian theories as much if not more than to the Greek sources. Nevertheless, according to Erhardt-Siebold, "the repeatedly uttered belief in Erigena's anticipation of Tycho Brahe's system ... is refuted as untenable. The generally adopted heliocentric interpretation of Erigena's famous passage is shown to be irreconcilable with other astronomical teachings of the philosopher."[20]

General stereotype opinions of John Scotus Erigena warn us of his tendency towards pantheism and treat him as a 'dangerous' mystic. On the other hand there are romanticizations of him as an almost unique philosopher of nature for his time and place in the history of Western civilization who was, even more than his predecessor Isidore of Seville, a shining light in the obscurities of the so-called "dark ages". In our perspective he remains one of the most outstanding figures in our ninth century of Monism in Many Moods.

21. Bāyazīd al-Basṭāmī

Ṣūfism philosophically is a variety of monism which had its most dramatic developments in the ninth and tenth centuries. It is above all, like Zen, a trans-historical tradition that depends on personal transmission of a high order of esoteric spiritual discipline from guru to disciple. There was by no means complete harmony of beliefs among the Ṣūfīs, although as a loosely organized tradition within tradition they tended to be more monistic, especially in regard to the distinction between "I" and "Thou" which is supposed to be removed in the experience called *fanā'*. That sub-varieties have developed through the centuries is only natural, even though like all monist traditions its chief emphasis is on unity. Ṣūfism, like Zen, is still a very vital force, now beginning to attract proselytes from all around the world.

The controversy continues as to what extent the Ṣūfī tradition is rooted in the Qur'ān. Circumstances such as we have investigated in the previous volumes of this study certainly open the possibility of considerable influence from Neo-Platonisn on Ṣūfism, comparable to that influence among Jewish and Christian mystics from Philo and Augustine right down to Gilson and Thomas Merton. But influences, especially where oral tradition is concerned, are very difficult to determine, for influence may be dialectically defensive or offensively provoking, or it may be an almost imperceptible blend of cultural currents that are inherently similar and harmonious. Origin, however, is a much more sensitive matter than influence, and much acrimonious writing bolstered by considerable erudition can be found in the literature not only about origins of Ṣūfism but about the origins of many traditions. At minimum Ṣūfism may be seen as a legitimate outgrowth from Qur'anic revelation and a constant reminder that the Qur'ān itself does insist on intensive personal experience and condemns conformity to the externals of religion only.

It seems that Ṣūfism had a rather early start in the history of Islam, beginning soon after the split between the Shī'as and the Sunnis. But to say that Ṣūfism comprises a distinct sect is not completely correct since there were Ṣūfīs among both Shī'as and Sunnis. Its first full-fledged emergence and flourishing was in Iranian territory, but to the question of possible Zoroastrian or Manichaean influence the answer is usually negative. The fact that Buddhism had become established in eastern Iran makes one wonder afresh whether the Ṣūfī concept of *fanā'* was influenced at all by the Buddhist doctrines of *anātman* and *nirvāṇa.* But the differences there for the most part outweigh the likenesses, for the Buddhists believed that the concept of an immortal self or soul was an illusion, whereas no Ṣūfī would assert this. *Fanā'* is a union of soul with Allah rather than the 'extinction' of soul or self. Moreover, Ṣūfīs as Muslims are first and foremost theists, whereas even the most ardent Amida devotee could be designated as theistic only in a derived sense. The influence of Christianity is a much more delicate matter, both among Christian and secular authorities. Since Jesus certainly figures prominently in the Qur'ān itself, one is sometimes amazed that the Crusades against the infidel Turks ever took place in the first place. The types of Christianity that could have influenced Ṣūfism were Nestorian and/or Monophysite, not Augustinian or even Arian or Athanasian in the strict sense.

It seems that Ṣūfīsm was primarily a protest against the legalism and formalism that had already crept into Islam. Affifi quotes one Ruwaym of Baghdad (d. 915) as saying, "All people hold fast to external appearances (of religion), but this community (the Ṣūfīs) holds fast to realities. All people consider it their duty to observe the external aspect of the religious law ; the Ṣūfīs consider it their duty to strive after piety and unremitting sincerity."[1] Affifi adds that, according to the Ṣūfīs, "Islam is *haqiqa,* a reality hidden behind words and forms, while for the rest of the Muslims it is principally words and forms."[2] *Haqiqa* is the counterbalance for *shari'a,* the religious law, which has given Islam as a theocracy such power in history. The ideal situation, of course, is that in which the two are in proper balance. According to al-Ghazālī,

> He who says that haqiqa is contrary to shari'a, and the internal (side of religion) is contrary to the external is nearer to infidelity. Every haqiqa that has no root in shari'a should

be rejected. Shari'a is the law enjoined upon people ; haqiqa is seeing the work of Divine Providence. Shari'a is worship of God ; Haqiqa is to behold Him. Shari'a is to obey the Divine Command : haqiqa is to know by mystic vision what God has predestined, what He has revealed and what He has concealed.[3]

Concerning the Ṣūfī conception of God, Affifi writes :

> The barren speculations of the Muslim rationalists deprived the Godhead of its positive content, and God was reduced to a logical abstraction. The orthodox theologians made of Him a despot whose absolute power could do everything, even the impossible and the irrational. The philosophers, in their attempt to reconcile Islamic dogmas with Greek philosophy, were obliged to abandon many of the theological attributes of God, or explain them away, and put an active or final cause in place of a creator of the world. To the majority of the Ṣūfīs, God is essentially a personal being endowed with attributes which determine His relations with the world in general and man in particular. ...
>
> The early Ṣūfīs had an exaggerated sense of guilt and of the terrible torments that awaited the sinners in Hell. Consequently an overwhelming fear of God and His wrath seized their hearts, and their pious devotions were regarded as a means of escape from the judgment to come.[4]

But as more Manichaean and Neo-Platonic influence came in, and perhaps influence from India also, these extremes were counterbalanced by extremes of the opposite sort, and an extreme eroticism began to work some havoc, as exemplified by a woman saint of Basra, Rābi'ah (d. 801). Affifi writes :

> From the third century onward (in the Islamic calendar), the doctrine of divine love became the dominant feature of Ṣūfism. God was the Beloved of the Ṣūfīs, and loving Him for His own sake was the end of all their endeavor. It was no longer the fear of Hell or the hope of Paradise, but the hope of obtaining a glimpse of the everlasting beauty of God which motivated the Ṣūfīs. Rābi'ah says in one of her prayers, "O God! if I worship Thee in fear of Hell, burn me in Hell, and

> if I worship Thee in hope of Paradise, exclude me from Paradise. But if I worship Thee for Thine own sake, withhold not Thine everlasting beauty."[5]

"Pardon me, since loving God makes me forget to love Him" —such is a typical and favorite sentiment of Ṣūfīs. This emerging erotic mysticism has some parallels in the Amida variety of Buddhism and in the Tantra, but most, in the *bhakti* tradition in both Vaiṣṇavism and Śaivism in South India which already has some roots in the ninth century and comes into full flower about the mid-eleventh, continuing variously until its exaggerated forms with the Bengal Vaiṣṇavism of the Chaitanya heritage, which is now beginning to spread worldwide right alongside of Ṣūfism and the Baha'i faith. Likewise in Europe, we do not have to wait many centuries to see the same outbursting of Franciscan romanticism and the eroticism of the medieval women mystics of Germany and Italy, culminating in the classics of John of the Cross and Teresa of Avilla.

The ancestors of Bāyazīd al-Basṭāmī (d.874) were Zoroastrians. He was first a jurist following the school of Abū Ḥanīfah, and only later turned to Ṣūfism. His first teacher in this tradition was a Kurd ; later he received instruction from one Abū'Alī al-Sindī, who evidently had incorporated something of hatha yoga into his Ṣūfī practice, including breathing exercises. During his days as a jurist al-Basṭāmī had Mu'tazilite tendencies, but he was converted away from this much in the same manner that several centuries later al-Ghazālī was converted to this supra-rationalist way after a long career of expertise in rationalist logic, and still more centuries later Chaitanya was converted from the Navya Nyāya school to his ecstatic mysticism.

Al-Basṭāmī is one of those seminal charismatic figures who left no known writings in his own hand, although his disciples reported very much. One of the collections of his sayings and reports of his experiences received a commentary by no less than al-Junayd, and Ibn 'Arabī's monism may have been influenced by al-Basṭāmī's life and teachings. Al-Basṭāmī spent most of his time (thirty years) wandering in the deserts of Syria leading a typical ascetic life. But his asceticism did not allow him to depart from strict observance of the orthodox Islamic injunctions.

Above all, Bāyazīd would never allow the monist tendencies inherent in Ṣūfī ways to lessen his transcendental theism. B. A. Dar writes :

> Bāyazīd is the first Ṣūfī who gives a detailed description of his mystic experience and calls it by the name of ascension (*mi'rāj*), a practice which was later followed by ibn 'Arabi and others. We give below a few passages from the account as given by 'Aṭṭār in his *Tadhkirah* :
>
> "When I attained the stage of indifference (*istighna*) towards the things of this world and was lighted up by the light of God, several mysteries were revealed to me. I looked from God towards myself and found that my light was utter darkness in comparison with God's light, my loftiness was utter lowliness; it was all purity there and all darkness here. But when again I looked, I found my light in His light, my loftiness in His loftiness, and that whatever I did I did through His power. His light shone in my heart and I discovered that in truth all worship was from God and not from me, though all the time I had thought that it was I who worshipped. I felt perplexed and received the explanation : All that is, is I and not not-I... I looked from God towards God and saw Him as the only reality. I remained in this stage for long, left all efforts and all acquired knowledge. Grace from God began to flow and I got eternal (*azli*) knowledge. I saw that all things abide in God."[6]

Certainly the monist tendency in Bāyazīd is very strong. Indeed, Bāyazīd and other Ṣūfīs in the ninth century, with only minor differences, would have been equally at home in some Monophysite Christian monasteries, among Hindu yogīs, and among many varieties of Mahāyāna Buddhists. Deny it as one may as a possible *source*, at least the *parallel* is very evident; for even today Śaiva yogīs meditate on the mantra *Om Śivo-hum*, "I am Śiva" ; and in the Christian milieu, although we do not know of any famous stigmatics like Francis of Assissi during this century, there were many others who, following after Simon Stylites, went to all sorts of extremes in their "imitation" of Christ, the whole *via negativa* inherited from Neo-Platonism being intensively focussed in that direction. Dar writes :

> In Bāyazīd's utterances we notice a distinct tendency towards monism. He tries to reach the divine unity by the process of abstraction (*tajrīd*) till he is devoid of all personal attributes and feels himself as well as others submerged in the One. In this state of unity he gave expression to his experiences which remind one of the *an al Ḥaq* of Ḥallāj. "I went from God to God, until He cried from me in me, 'O thou I.'" "Glory to me! How great is my majesty." "When I came out of my 'self', I found the lover and the beloved as one, for in the world of thought, all is one." "For twelve years I treated the self (*nafs*) in me as a smith does with his material, heating and beating alternately in the fire of penance and with the hammer of blame (*malāmah*) till it became a mirror. For five years I was busy in polishing this mirror with different kinds of religious practices. For one year I looked within myself, and discovered a girdle of infidelity (*zunnār*) round my waist. For another five years I tried to remove that girdle till I recovered my true faith. Then I found everything dead before my eyes and God alone living." What is '*arsh* ? It is I. What is Chair (*kursi*) ? It is I. What is the Table or the Pen ? It is I. What are prophets like Abraham, Moses and Muḥammad ? They are I. Explaining it further, he remarked that whoever becomes annihilated in God finds that whatever is, is God. His negativism (*tajrīd*) is illustrated by the following quotation : "Nothing is better for man than to be without aught : having no asceticism, no theory, no practice. When he is without all, he is with all." A mystic should be in a domain where neither good nor evil exists; both good and evil belong to the phenomenal world ; in the presence of unity there is neither command (*amr*) nor prohibition (*nahi*).[7]

According to Massignon, Bāyazīd's strict adherence to monotheism makes it difficult to assert that he was fully a pantheist or any other sort of monist. Moreover, Massignon puts Bāyazīd in the category of *jñāna*, not that of *bhakti*, for intelligence takes priority with him over love. Therein, we take it, he differs somewhat from his other Ṣūfīs. Fakhry writes of al-Basṭāmī's mysticism :

> But despite the unquestionable pantheistic implications of these utterances, the culmination of the mystical experience remains suspended, as it does in some forms of Hindu mysticism (e.g., Patanjali) between the I and the Thou, the Self and the Absolute, which have both been annihilated. A statement ascribed to him speaks of the station of nonbeing (*laisiyah*) which he reached and continued to hover in for ten years until, he says, "I could pass from the No (*lais*) to the No, through the No."[8]

This certainly sounds like the *Śūnyatā* rather than the Neo-Platonic One or anything strictly Qur'anic. Concerning a parallel with Patañjali *Yoga Sūtra* rather than the *Śūnyatā* of Mahāyāna Buddhism, geographically the latter is more likely since we know that Buddhism was still in eastern Iran right down to the Muslim conquest. If Bāyazīd had been in the Sind, however, he could have come into contact with both heritages, and no doubt with some syncretistic mixture of the two such as was emerging in Kaśmir even before the appearance of Abhinavagupta's work. Fakhry continues :

> The Hindu influence on this type of mysticism has been shown by Zaehner to be unmistakable. There is a clear link to Vedantic metaphysics not only in the case of al-Basṭāmī's Indian master, al-Sindī, who taught him some "ultimate truths," but also in the very complexion of his thought and its "nihilistic" implications. Al-Basṭāmī lived at a time in which the revival and systematization of Vedantic thought itself was being actively pursued by Shankara (d. 820) and his school. His ecstatic utterances, such as the already quoted "Glory be to me" (*Subḥāni*) or "I am I", all purport to assert his total self-identification with the divine and have numerous parallels in the *Upanishads* and the *Vedanta*. Perhaps the wildest of all his utterances is the one in which he speaks of his search for God : he could not find God and therefore took His place on the Throne. "I plunged into the ocean *malakūt* (the realm of Ideas), and the veils of divinity (*lāhūt*),"

he writes, "unitl I reached the Throne and lo ! it was empty; so I cast myself upon it and said : 'Master, where shall I seek Thee ? and the veils were lifted up and I saw that I am I, yea I am I. I turned back into what I soguht and it was I and no other, into which I was going."

How a Muslim could make such extravagant claims that placed him almost above God and yet go unscathed in the ninth century is truly surprising. However, a note made by later authors gives us the clue to this problem. When al-Basṭāmī was accused of laxity in the performance of his ritual duties, we are told, he resorted to the expedient which other *Ṣūfīs* also employed : affected madness. This device apparently saved his life as well as the life of numerous fellow *Ṣūfīs*.[9]

Most of the reported sayings of al-Basṭāmī must remain puzzling to the modern secularist, such as his telling a disciple that it is "better by far to see me one time than to see God a thousand times." In other of his extravagant utterances Bāyazīd asks to ravish him so that when other creatures see him they may say, "We have seen Thee". Al-Junayd's criticism of al-Basṭāmī is to the effect that he had not completed his spiritual progress; he had not arrived at a clear-headed serenity with a vital sense of reality beyond all the intensive ecstacies which tend to vascillate between self-immolation and self-exaltation in the presence of the divine glory. He had been limited to the *imaginative* way and had not achieved, beyond the function of mere ideas, the authentic union; he had not really been ravished, he still wanted to be. In his defense it might be argued that Bāyazīd was after all concerned not so much with the divine essence as with the attributes, not claiming mystical union with the former but identification with the latter. If al-Basṭāmī was concerned with identification with attributes or virtues of God, al-Ḥallāj was concerned with complete self-transformation in and by and for the Divine Essence itself, and that not as a goal to be attained but as something he actually realized. In his extreme asceticism it seems that Bāyazīd explored to the nth degree the *via remotionis*, the way of negation and of realizing his distance from God in order to increase his ardor for union with Him; whereas al-Ḥallāj was more 'inebriated' by the complete erasure of all distance between himself and God.

In keeping with the best of orthodox Islamic practice, Bāyazīd al-Basṭāmī made his prayers not in terms of himself but in terms of intercession for all humanity. This suggests to us a sort of Bodhisattva vow, which may have been misunderstood by his later critics like al-Junayd. Perhaps monism becomes perverse only when it is limited to the first person singular but is not so when it includes otherness, and especially other people. This was perhaps a saving grace with Bāyazīd.

22. Jayanta Bhaṭṭa

There is no reason to believe, contrary to popular prejudice in our own time, that a master logician could not also be a master poet. We may well remember the same controversy about Bhartṛhari and several in India during the long period of controversy between the Nyāya-Vaiśeṣikas and the Mahāyāna Buddhists, especially in Kaśmir where the Kaśmir Śaiva tradition with its advanced aesthetics was vivaciously emerging. H. G. Narahari in his article "Jayantabhaṭṭa : Poet-Philosopher of Kashmir" has no doubt about the poet and the famous logician being the same person, and Satkari Mookerjee writes :

> He was a poet of no mean order and his mastery of a facile diction is evidenced in his prose style, which for its grace and easy flow has not been surpassed except by Śaṅkarācārya and Vācaspati Miśra. His poetry is pithy, graceful and what is more, is rich in its aesthetic appeal. Rightly could his son aver that the Muse of learning found her fulfillment in poetry and eloquence in the person of our author. Jayanta was not only a poet in himself, but his appreciation of Kālidāsa and Bāṇa Bhaṭṭa shows that professional philosophy and aesthetic culture can be combined in one person.[1]

As we might expect of a Kaśmiri, Jayanta (fl. 890) was also a master of prose style and is often rated as on par even with

Patañjali, Śabara, Śaṅkara and Vācaspati Miśra. "The range of his vocabulary is vast, his diction profound, and his expression most mellifluous."[2]

It is the *Nyāyamañjarī* for which Jayanta is most famous. As a defense of the Nyāya system in the face of criticisms from the Buddhist schools and as a continuation of that 'dialogue' which had been going on for several centuries, this work does present somewhat of a notable exception to our generalization that the ninth century was universally a century of "monism in many moods". It also punctures the myth that Śaṅkara defeated *all* adversaries, whether Buddhist or Nyāya-Vaiśeṣika, establishing Advaita once and for all as *the* Indian philosophy.

> Very great care is taken in the work to remove, on the defensive side, all loopholes in old definitions. They are all fortified by the fullest set of qualifications calculated to make them withstand the sharpest attack of the strongest adversary. On the offensive side the author assesses very carefully the strength of the position of his adversaries individually and has a particular way of attack meant for each of them. The least important of these adversaries seem to be the Cārvākas (Materialists) while the Buddhists are admittedly the most powerful. As heretics they need not be considered at all, feels Jayantabhaṭṭa, while axpounding the orthodox doctrine. But, since they have pretensions to ability in the art of reasoning and have their own view in almost every matter, their theories need to be referred to frequently for purposes of refutation. The Jains come in rarely for any serious criticism.[3]

Actually Mīmāṁsā and Sāṃkhya come under attack almost as severely as the Buddhists, and it seems that not only dialectic but even *ad hominem* ridicule if not outright abuse is resorted to in these refutations. The Grammarian school, which no doubt was still strong following the ingenious work of Bhartṛhari, also comes in for a substantial critique. Narahari insists that even Advaita (although not mentioned by name) does not escape his rational analysis, especially in regard to that school's doctrines of nescience (*avidyā*), superimposition (*adhyāsa*) and false transformation (*vivarta*). Narahari also claims that Jayanta's description of the four classical schools of Buddhist philosophy is "perhaps the most accurate among those attempted by a Brahmin philosopher in Sanskrit, an account which would be acceptable to the Buddhists themselves."[4]

That Jayanta is thorough in his refutations is not surprising considering the expertise of those he had to refute, such as Dignāga and Dharmakīrti, much less Śāntarakṣita and Kamalaśīla : but Mookerjee insists that he was never unfair to his opponents, whether the topic be concerned with the techniques of negation or *abhāva, kṣaṇavāda*, or the controversy over universals. The Mīmāṁsakas receive the same sort of treatment : fair, complete, thorough, but politely devastating.

Jayanta himself does not claim any originality but rather says of his work :

> No original matter forsooth ! We have not the requisite gifts to conceive any original theory. The learned will have to content themselves with only a novel plan of arrangement of the old matters. Even the same old flowers, that have been used more than once in personal embellishments, do not fail to rouse the curiosity of experts when presented in a garland of unique plan of arrangement.[5]

Nevertheless Jayanta has been compared to the very greatest of Indian philosophers, such as Kumārila Bhaṭṭa, Dharmakīrti, Śāntarakṣita and Vācaspati Miśra; but whereas most of the others had the good fortune of royal patronage, Jayanta "was the victim of the cruel tyranny of a royal despot". Concerning the circumstances of the writing of the *Nyāyamañjarī*, Jayanta writes : "As for my poor self, I have been thrown by the king as a prisoner in this cavern where no human voice can enter and I have beguiled my days here by this diversion of writing a book."[6] Many other classics of philosophy have been written under similar circumstances (Mookerjee reminds us that Lokamanya Tilak wrote his famous Gītā Rahasya while he was in prison thanks to the "democratic" British).

Humor is a trait all too rare among philosophers, necessary though it is in order to keep a healthy-minded detachment. In introducing this topic, Mookerjee says that what we have with Jayanta is like the live-voice lectures of a witty philosopher addressing his students in vivid language that will keep them awake even when the substance of the topic is highly technical.

> In another place where the debate proceeds on the uncreated character of the *Vedas*, which is the Mīmāṁsā position, the Mīmāṁsaka argues that the Vedic texts are eternal verities and this is plainly deducible from the peculiar form of nouns and verbs, prefixes and suffixes found in the *Vedas*. "All who study the *Vedas* understand their uncreated character from their very nature, but the fame has been drunk by the Mīmāṁsakas alone." Jayanta's reply contains a biting sarcasm. "Well, let the Mīmāṁsakas drink fame, or let them drink milk, or to remove the dulness of their intellect they may drink *Brāhmī* ghee (a well-known medicine to stimulate memory and intelligence); we shall not grudge. But there is absolutely no error in the fact that the *Vedas* are composed by a personal author.[7]

About the same time there was a very heated controversy going on about the Holy Qur'ān and to some extent about the Bible also, not to mention the controversy about the role of Confucius in regard to the pre-Confucian classics in China. Just as the Mu'tazilites had asserted reason above authority, so Jayanta Bhaṭṭa argued that even the Vedas had to have some author, even if it be claimed that the author was God Himself. We cannot help wondering again whether this theological defense of the Vedas was not at least in part a counter-claim to that made by the Muslims, who were increasingly in evidence in Kaśmir during Jayanta's lifetime as rivals to the Buddhists, especially among the masses.

> Again after animadverting upon the Buddhist doctrine of momentariness of all reality, Jayanta bursts forth into a characteristic sarcasm against the Buddhists. "These Buddhists do not believe in the existence of a permanent self, but they will worship at the altars (*caityas*) for a residence in heaven. All realities have a momentary existence according to their philosophy, but they have built these monasteries (*vihāras*) which will last for centuries. They maintain that all is void,

but they constantly exhort the laity to make gifts to them, their teachers. This is in short the character of the Buddhists, what else can it be if it is not hypocrisy *par excellence*."[8]

Other authors seem to be of the opinion that the Jaina theories were not so important to Jayanta, and we may conjecture that this is because he would have been at least partially in sympathy with their realist metaphysics. Mookerjee says of Jayanta's critique of this major 'heresy' :

> Jayanta has a fling at the Jainas too. "These Jainas," says Jayanta, "are really conversant with the secrets of ultimate reality. They have discovered a short-cut to salvation and they prescribe these recipes, which they themselves practise, true to their words. 'Tear out all hair from the head, clothe your person with the sky (be nude), and mount up the high mountains and tramp on and around the wide earth. Bald-headed persons are to be envied, because they have no hair on their heads; and birds and beasts, which have no care for clothes, sky-clad as they are like the Jaina ascetics, will have an instantaneous cessation of rebirth. All these blessed hill-men, who make a profession of constantly climbing up the mountains, will have an easy walk-over to salvation. Who else but the sapient Jainas could teach of this easiest and nearest road to salvation?"[9]

Although Jayanta gives thanks that he was born into a family whose specialization was *vyākaraṇa* (grammar and the philosophy of language), he expresses disapproval of those who are limited by this discipline. In the following summary we have a very advanced philosophy of language and a controversy on the nature and function of language quite as vital as that in our own epoch :

> The doctrine of *Śabdabrahman* has been strongly criticised by Jayantabhaṭṭa in his monumental work, the *Nyāyamañjarī*. He opens his criticism by saying that the Absolute can never be the Word-Principle, which is the very thesis of the grammarians. He makes bold to opine that the Word-Principle is neither eternal nor ubiquitous for the obvious reason that it is limited by time and space. The indivisible character of the Word-Principle also is strongly denied by Jayanta and he

makes no secret of his conviction that there is no logic in the argument that whatever is permanent should be called the Word-Principle. He subsequently reviews the argument of the grammarians who state that every cognition is associated with a verbal form and that any cognition which is free from a verbal association cannot manifest itself and is not on that account materially different from a cognition which has not arisen at all. The grammarians have said that each and every cognition is determinate (*savikalpaka*) and that it should at least be specified in a manner that 'this is such,' in order to justify the fact that it is born. A cognition which cannot be so described should not unnecessarily be called a cognition at all. Even the young boys, who are as yet ignorant of the relationship subsisting between a word and an object, communicate their cognition through the medium of such vague, indefinite and general words as 'this' or 'that'. It is for these reasons that the grammarians contend that if a cognition becomes destitute of a verbal association, it ceases to shine and manifest itself. Hence they urge that a cognition does not present as its content an object in its naked form but an object couched or determined by word. Advancing further they point out that when we enquire about the substantive-element in the content of a cognition we have no other means but to describe it with the help of word or comprehend it through such a cognition as has not forsaken its verbal association. From this they draw the conclusion that the substantive, namely, the object, is of the form of word and that word appears only as an attribute of the former. Under the circumstances, as the substantive cannot be described or comprehended separately from its determinant, the grammarians insist that the former is the transformation of the latter. Word or *Śabdabrahman* is thus the only reality which under the influence of *nescience* appears in diverse forms which we are wont to call objects and as soon as the veil of *nescience* is removed, the reality shines in its purest form, in its undimmed lustre and gtory. This is how Jayanta understands and explains the grammarians' doctrine of *Śabdabrahman*.[10]

The notion of the Grammarians that objects are transformation of Word is not too remote from the Neo-Platonic emendation of the Stoic interpretation of the Logos doctrine wherein every particular logos or word is no less than an instantiation of the General Principle of Communicability in such a way that the monism of ultimate reality is not compromised while at the same time allowing an explanation of the pluralism of ordinary non-visionary experience. Thus it is claimed by the Grammarians not only that all words and particular realities are manifestations of the same principle, but each individual instance of the operation of this principle is only an instantiation of the General Principle, the basic metaphysic of the Grammarian-Vyākaraṇa school being that *Śabda* Brahman is the Principle of Communicability itself rather than some Supreme Ultimate of an incommunicable sort such that any attempt at communication inevitably traps us in *māyā*.

Jayanta is not only a realist (Śabdavāda might be called a realist monism) but a pluralist also. As Shastri puts it : "Every object is endowed with many an attribute and it is word which helps us in understanding only one such attribute. There is, therefore, no justification for the belief that word is superimposed on object or that word assumes transformation in the form of object."[11] As illustrating this contention he insists that sunlight or lamp light is normally not seen as such but is the medium *through* which we see objects, so the notion of *adhyāsa* or superimposition is not justified. Just as light is not superimposed on the objects-there but is only the instrument of our perception of the object-as-such, so with words : they are instruments, means, not ends. Translated into the Graeco-Latin idiom, Jayanta is denying the Platonic forms and is much closer to the more radical Aristotelians among his Islamic contemporaries.

In the doctrine that the Word is transformed into objects (which Jayanta critiques) one may recognize something parallel with the notion in Neo-Platonism that the Platonic Ideas or Forms actually do 'incarnate' themselves. Jayanta's refutation of this likewise loosely parallels the typical Aristotelian realist refutation. Jayanta uses the tactic of refuting the *adhyāsa* (superimposition) way of supposedly supporting that doctrine, namely that we superimpose our notions of individuated 'real' objects on the Great One Undifferentiated Ultimate Brahman, whether that Brahman be of the *Śabda* nature of the Mīmāṁsakas or the *anirvacanīya* nature of the *nirguṇa*-Brahman of the Advaitins.

The Grammarians' theory is very much like that of the Advaitins in their extreme monism, even though a distinction can still be made between the concept of *Śabda* Brahman and *saguṇa*-Brahman. For in either case the 'reality' resides not in the things referred to by the words but in what they 'instantiate', the general or generalizable Reality with which they are concerned. In this context Jayanta simply asserts the reality of objects as such as the point of orientation for any reasonable epistemology. Matter may be eternal, but words do change; and therefore words are less real than the things they refer to. Transformations of forms of matter may render old words obsolete since they in that case no longer have any object to refer to; but likewise when a new form arises, we need a new name for it, so that we have to admit the transiency of words. But there is a warning against the opposite extreme that just because words and the objects they refer to are recognizably separate and distinct does not necessarily entail that there can be no relatedness between them. Rather, against the idealist positions, Jayanta would argue that the relations are just as real as the objects and words related, whereas his opponents would insist on the non-substantiality of relations as such and therefore of their 'ideal' nature if not their illusoriness as superimpositions.

Further than this, his opponents even argue that words rather than things have causal power. In the Hindu *śruti* and *smṛti* alike one may easily find parallels to the Biblical and Qur'anic texts that speak of God "speaking" as the primal act of creation. Hence they argue easily for the ultimacy of that Word, *Śabdabrahman*.

The answer that he gives to this is that if the creative principle of the world is believed to be Word or Śabdabrahman, it would obviously be on a par with God; but as Word is not ragarded as a conscious principle we are hardly justified in identifying it with God. If, however, it is maintained for the sake of the argument that Śabdabrahman is not only ubiquitous but also conscious, Jayanta smiles and says that then there is no utility whatsoever in having a separate Śabdabrahman which is only another name for God.[12]

Jayanta seems to have been rather prominent in the controversy about universals. Although it had received some attention in Byzantium following the neo-Aristotelianism of John Philopon and was copied with varying varieties of interpretation among the Muslims indebted to Philopon, it seems to have reached a much higher peak among the Kaśmiris and those before them in Nālandā in India long before it became the dominant controversy among Latin scholastics. It was only weakly echoed in China however.

Jayanta summarises the Buddhist objection in connection with the subsistence of the universal in its particulars thus : "Does the universal subsist in its particulars in its entirety or by parts? Both the positions are impossible. If the universal subsists in one of its particulars in its entirety, it will be exhausted there and will not be found in other particulars. If it subsists only by parts, the universal *gotva* 'in its entirety' will not be found anywhere, and there will be no idea of a *cow* with reference to individual cows. Moreover, the universal being partless has no parts by which it can subsist in every individual. Nor can it subsist in an individual in entirety, because then it cannot subsist in entirety in other individuals. For, that which is exhausted cannot have another entirety without being born again." Jayanta meets the objection thus : "A universal subsists in every individual in its entirety. As for the objection that it should not be found in that case in other individuals, what are we to do and with whom should we find fault ? It is, indeed, found in other individuals. When it is present there, how can we conceal it? (It is so in the nature of things.) Parts of a universal, of course, do not exist by which its subsistence could be averred. As to the question whether such a phenomenon is found elsewhere, we indeed appreciate your cleverness in asking for a similar instance even when there is a direct experience. A similar instance should be asked only in the case of an inference."[13]

We turn to Jayanta's exposition of the *samavāya* relation, which is almost uniquely characteristic of the Nyāya-Vaiśeṣika tradition. First and typically Jayanta states a strong *pūrvapakṣa*, then his reply is stated thus :

> There is certainly a difference (between parts and the 'whole' of a substance and its qualities, etc.) which is proved on account of its being cognized by us, but the difference of the space (occupied by two such things as parts and 'whole', or a substance and its qualities, etc.) cannot be accepted, and therefore, the relation of substance called *samavāya* must be assumed in such cases.[14]

Certainly any part-whole or substance-attribute relation pertains to things that occupy the same time and/or place; but they are not identical with each other. The parts inhere in the whole, even though they are distinguishable from each other. One may think of the example of life in a living body, which becomes a corpse when that relation of subsistence or inherence is absent. This aspect of Jayanta's philosophy is still very relevant today in any scientific or metaphysical situation. Indeed, a fuller exposition might well examine in some detail Bradley's theory of internal vs. external relation as a basis of comparison. At any rate, the distinction between *saṁyoga* and *samvāya*, a basic aspect of the Nyāya-Vaiśeṣika school, continued to be in controversial coflict with the Buddhist schools.

There was also the continuing dialogue concerning *abhāva* (non-existence or absence) as *real* existence of something that is *not there*, rather than non-existence of whatever is involved in privative situation. Jayanta argues against Prabhākara on the one hand and against Dignāga and his interpreters on the other.

> Jayanta refers to the refutation of the reality of non-existence by writers of Dignāga school also. According to them, non-existence is a mere mental construction (*vikalpa*), and not an external reality. Jayanta points out that it cannot be held to be pure imagination because "like the mental construction

of a positive reality (*vidhi-vikalpa*), it also follows in the wake of a pure sensation." If, therefore, external reality is held to be the source of positive mental constructions, likewise, a corresponding reality should be accepted in the case of negative mental constructions as well.[15]

But the matter does not rest simply with the affirmation or denial of the reality of *abhāva*. Rather the consideration of the *varieties* of *abhāva* also comes under Jayanta's scrutiny :

> In earlier works such as those of Jayanta, Śrīdhara, and others, however, we find a good deal of divergence of opinion with regard to the four-fold classification of non-existence. According to some ancient writers, 'non-existence of a jar on the ground', which can be effected by removing the jar and destroyed by bringing it back, is not an instance of absolute non-existence. They hold it to be another kind of non-existence which has a beginning and end. The absolute non-existence (which is eternal) is found in such instances as 'the non-existence of colour in the air'. There are other points of divergence in the account and classification of non-existence, some of which may be noted here. Jayanta, for instance, thinks that the two principal kinds of non-existence are : (i) antecedent non-existence (*prāg-abhāva*) and (ii) consequent non-existence (*dhvaṁsābhāva*). Besides these two, he refers to two more kinds of non-existence, but he says that the principal *abhāvas* are only the first two, all other kinds depend on particular conditions. In fact, Jayanta thinks that all other *abhāvas*, i.e., 'absence of identity' (*anyonyābhāva*) and 'absolute non-existence' (*atyantābhāva*) are included in the *prāg-abhāva*. All this would look strange to a modern student of the Nyāya-Vaiśeṣika who is acquainted only with the theories of the later manuals.[16]

Whatever attitude one may take towards, or apologetic one may make for, the doctrine of revelation as such, the fact remains that it was accepted almost without question all across Eurasia during the whole of the medieval centuries. The burden by the ninth century was not on the doctrine as such but on rational interpretation of the holy texts, which contain so many contradictions that to systematize them into a consistent corpus or code is a lifetime work for every generation. Although officially from time immemorial one spoke of the four Vedas, the *Atharva* somehow had fallen out of use, probably because of lack of utilitarian value, its hymns being more of the aesthetic sort than intellectual or moral. In his apologetic Jayanta appeals to the great authorities of antiquity such as Jaimini, Kaṇāda and Akṣapāda, and he cites quotations from the *śruti* and *smṛti* demonstrating that all four Vedas are always intended as equal in authority. Moreover he argues that the *Atharva* contains the great *Mantra* with which Brahma performed his primeval *praṇava* whereby the universe came into material manifestation or "creation", and hence if anything it should be preferred above the other three. One may speculate that Jayanta enjoyed the *Atharva* perhaps even more than the others simply because it is more poetic, more detached from utilitarian ends, and even more realistically historical than the other three.

Jayanta's orthodoxy might even be termed a counter-neo-orthodoxy to that of Śaṅkara. This should be of interest to modern Hindus trying to make intelligent adjustment between what is obviously obsolete in the Vedas and what is still valid, beautiful and primordially relevant to universal human existence. Historically essentially the same thing was going on in other parts of Eurasia. In Byzantium (as with Photius), in China (as with Han Yü and Li Ao), and elsewhere there was a radical fertilizing of the roots in order to support the increased flowering of intellectual and religious activity. Jayanta spends much time in defense of the *Atharva*; but a critique of 'heresy' as such seems to be implicit when he deals with the Buddhists and Jainas. Jayanta seems to accept the position that at least one should be familiar with the Buddhist classics as well as Vedas; but that they should replace the Vedas is as utterly unthinkable as it would be for a Muslim of the same period to go over to Aristotle without the Qur'ān.

Mookerjee probably has exaggerated Jayanta's spirit of tolerance in the face of his pronounced Vedic orthodoxy; still he puts the matter this way :

> Jayanta ultimately winds up this discourse by an appeal to all persons of unbiased judgment to accept his finding that there is truth in all the various scriptures held sacred by the different sects and creeds and whether this truth is derived from the respective prophets and teachers or from their affiliation to the *Vedas* or from their origin from God Himself in His various incarnations, any one of these theories, he believes, should satisfy the fanatic that there is no monopoly of truth in the sphere of religion.[17]

It is premature to reach any final conclusion about Jayanta Bhaṭṭa since our materials are far too scattered and fragmentary. He must have been a very colorful character since his original metaphors and other figures of speech are far from traditional and are often very vivid, sometimes indeed on the border of being risqué. Nevertheless he was a master of style, balancing originality and colorfulness of content with classical form. In keeping with the norm of his era, in his refutations he is often more expert in stating his opponents' positions than they are themselves. This is of course an old trick which Jesuits in later centuries will use ; but it was then as it remains today perhaps the most effective as the most devastating fashion of debate.

Jayanta certainly deserves a much more respected place in our histories if not also in our classics of instruction for systematic philosophizing as such. Even if we could ignore his role in the Logic school, Jayanta would deserve a very notable place because of his scholarly work on the Vedas. Mookerjee makes a salient observation to the effect that the "craze for specia ization" has deprived modern India of encyclopedic mind like that of Jayanta. We certainly concur ; not only India but most countries in the world have forgotten these classical demands on what it should really mean to be a philosopher, Leibniz being perhaps the last in European civilization to approach the ideal of being an encyclopedic polymath as a propaedeutic to engaging in philosophical pursuits.

That Jayanta was a realist and even further developed some of the tenets of the Nyāya-Vaiśeṣika heritage may constitute one reason why he has not received proper attention in Euramerican languages, since what is known outside of India as

"Indian philosophy" has thus far been dominated by the Advaitins. Unfortunately, in some cases there may be emotional investment in vindicating Vācaspati by comparison with Jayanta, since Advaita has had the limelight in the field of Indian philosophy since the last of the nineteenth century, thanks in part to the work of Vivekānanda, Radhakrishnan and even Das Gupta, all of whom were writing in English during the period when Hegelian idealism was in the harness in England. That "pressure" being now removed, we may find less biased views on Jayanta forthcoming in the near future.

Certainly along with his contemporaries who were Buddhists and Kaśmiri Śaivas, knowledge about Jayanta is a good corrective to the myth that all of India was won over completely by Śaṅkara. Once he is better known, he may be rated as the equal as well as the rival of Vācaspati Miśra, whose fame rests partly on his basking in the sunshine of Śaṅkara's charisma. But Jayanta Bhaṭṭa had to vindicate himself in his own right, and against every sort of opponent. We may expect therefore a radical re-evaluation of his role in the history of Indian philosophy when that is more adequaterly put together, because he is both a transmitter between such as Praśastapāda and Śrīdhara and Udayana, and a developer of his heritage, but most of all because of his comprehensiveness.

23. Photius

Photius (810-891) is known in Latin Catholic circles best for his association with the schism between the Greek and Latin Church; but of equal importance are his other contributions, including philosophy which he inherited from the Greek classics. Like most of the famous Patriarchs of Byzantium, Photius came from an aristocratic family. There was scarcely any aristocratic family in Byzantium that did not get involved in politics and ecclesiology, which were intricately related and finally became such that the political pendulum was the most decisive factor over one's life and career. This dramatically influenced Photius' own career, not to mention that his parents had been exiled by the Emperor Theophilus because of their opposition to his Iconoclast policy. Photius was very early attracted to the monastic vocation, but the attraction of secular learning inspired him even more. This culminated in his active participation in founding the University of Constantinople, whereupon he was appointed to the chair of philosophy by Theodosius II. While increasingly drawn into public responsibilities, beginning with a directorship of the Imperial Chancery and membership in the Senate, Photius nevertheless persevered in his love of philosophy.

Owing to a factional dispute over his election to the Patriarchate, Photius convened a synod in 859. The opposition, however, not content with logomachy, stirred up a riot to prevent its functioning properly. Thus Photius was late in contacting Pope Nicholas I in this matter, and when he did so in 860, the Pope objected to his having been elevated directly from lay status to the Patriarchate and so sent a delegation to investigate. Subsequently Photius was excommunicated in a Roman synod in 863 and the rival Ignatius chosen as the legitimate Patriarch. Needless to say, this provoked a lively dispute between the Pope and Emperor Michael III. A synod of the Eastern Patriarchs in 867 resulted in the famous Filioque controversy which became the official line of division between the Latin and the Eastern Churches.

> In the year 867 Photius had summoned a council at Constantinople : the obsequious prelates listened to the arraignment, and joined in the counter excommunication of Pope Nicholas. Photius drew up eight articles inculpating in one the faith, in the rest the departure, of the see of Rome from ancient and canonical discipline. Among the dreadful acts of heresy and schism which were to divide forever the churches of the East and West were : (1) the observance of Saturday as a fast; (2) the permission to eat milk and cheese during Lent; (4) the restriction of the chrism to the bishops; (6) the promotion of deacons at once to the episcopal dignity; (7) the consecration of a lamb, according to the hated Jewish usage; (8) the shaving of their beards by the clergy. The fifth only of the articles objected to by Photius, the procession of the Holy

> Ghost from the Father and the Son, was an error so awful as to deserve a thousand anathemas. The third, condemning the enforced celibacy of the clergy, was alone of high moral or religious importance. "From this usage we see in the West," says Photius, "so many children who know not their fathers." These, however, were but the pretexts for division. The cause lay deeper, in the total denial of the papal supremacy by the Greeks; their unequivocal assertion that with the empire that supremacy had passed to Constantinople.[1]

Although Photius was reinstated upon the death of the rival Ignatius, the net result remained, i.e., the complete and thus far still permanent split between the Greek and Roman Church. And Photius' bad reputation at Rome has only recently begun to be rectified.

Later Photius was accused of treason and again expelled from his throne; and though exonerated, he then went into retirement. "Though the schism of thirty years, properly speaking, expired in his person, and again a kind of approximation to Rome took place, yet the links were broken which united the two churches."[2] Of Photius' role in the schism, Barker writes :

> It was not until two centuries later (in 1054) that the breach between the Greek and the Latin Church began finally to widen; but it was Photius who, during his two patriarchates, raised the issues and struck the blows which were ultimately to be decisive. He sought generally to vindicate the independence of Constantinople from the primacy claimed by Rome, which was the final and fundamental issue at stake : he sought in parlicular to defend, in his treatise 'on the mystagogy of the Holy Spirit', the main doctrine of the Greek Church, on the procession of the Holy Ghost, which was the formal and overt issue debated between the two Churches. He fought for himself and for his own ambition as well as for the Greek cause and the independence of 'Hellenism'; but it may be that he fought all the better, and served that cause all the more, because he was also fighting for his own hand.[3]

It must be emphasized that Photius was not alone responsible for the schism which had such bearing upon him. The differences in the church politics of these two areas were evident long before, but surfaced during Photius' career. The Eastern Church is one of solemn tradition, deeply rooted in rituals, hierarchies, and a certain rigidity in matters of doctrine, reinforced by zeal for orthodoxy. In contra-distinction to this was the lack of profundity and subtle thought which typified the spokesmen in the Western Church. Though excelling in administrative matters and in a certain spontaneity which allowed popular cults to prosper, there was exhibited most abundantly the distinct flaw of substituting dry dogmatic formulae for dialectical appraisals of authoritative opinion. As for Photius' personal responsibility for the schism, let us bear in mind that though a polemicist, he could not have constructed a viable theology for the opposition due to his over-extension in other more expedient activities. Also, it would be difficult to maintain that he wanted to construct a Church of New Rome since he seems to have ultimately identified with the original Church of Old Rome. It can be claimed that the Roman Church was at fault because it identified itself as independent from the start of the breach whereas the Greek Church did not. At any rate, the Carolinian Church, in spite of the efforts of John Scotus Erigena and others, was really pretty much in a state of decadence whereas the Byzantine Church was not.

In contrast to the prevailing pattern in Rome, where the monks were supposed to remain apolitical, in Byzantium, the "cross-roads civilization" of diverse cultures and languages, in order to merit community recognition one had to be politically responsible. It has been said that the Empire was 'in the Church' rather than the other way round, which was similar to the situation in China about the same time, whereas India's turn of events proved somewhat similar to the pattern of Rome. The purveyance of all aspects of cultural life in Byzantium, which was the Church's ambition, included the preservation of the Greek classics. The Church was filled with a mission to transform the pagan culture of old. In this light it is understandable that the Iconoclast controversy was as much a political as a theological issue. Under the Empress Irene and her son Nicephorus, that controversy had virtually worn itself thin; Photius happily escaped its extremes, so that it was possible for him to bypass the monastic life and enter the Patriarchate directly.

From the point of view of philosophy rather than ecclesiastical politics, it is Photius' humanism which needs to be emphasized. In working for the greater integration between the sacred and the secular orders within society, Photius has been commended by Ostragorsky and others as an educator and master political theoretician. Barker praises him as no less than

> ... a scholar and a paragon of Byzantine polymathy, taking all learning to be his province.... He was not a notable theologian; but he was at once a genuine scholar (with some touch of pedantry) and an ecclesiastical statesman who could do battle with one of the strongest of Roman popes. His chief title to fame is his scholarship; he was one of the leaders of a Byzantine revival of study which was parallel to the Carolingian renaissance in the West. He made his house a school and a salon where young men regularly met for reading and discussion; and the record of his 'Academy', as it may not unjustly be called, survives in his MYRIOBIBLION, which gives an account and appreciation (sometimes brief, but sometimes full and exhaustive) of the 280 books which had come under review in the course of the various sessions. But even after he became patriarch, and while he was immersed in affairs, he still collected books and still continued to study. He leaned to Aristotle, as Greek scholars and the Greek Church generally did down to the days of Psellus and the eleventh century, when Plato began to come into his own.[4]

Frequently one encounters the mention of a ninth century renaissance generally and sometimes mention of a "Photian Renaissance". Arnold Toynbee in his book on Constantine Porphyrogenitus is among the first to fully appreciate Photius' many contributions. Authentic Hellenism colored the humanism on the crest of which Photius rode, and this phenomenon had its parallels elsewhere in the world. The ninth century, which is almost another Axial Period, rang in a renaissance of classical roots in the post-Buddhist Neo-Confucianism of China and the post-Buddhist classicism of Neo-Vedānta. Notwithstanding the

Carolinian renaissance as represented by John Scotus Erigena and the Hellenization of Islam, we can venture to say that Photius himself represents a humanist re-Hellenization of Christianity. This reconciliation, which is the point of departure for a long and brilliant period of Graeco-Byzantine civilization, finds its incarnation in Photius. Whether or not he fits in snugly with our theme of monism in many moods for his century; with him we witness a Christian faith harmoniously blended with a revival of the *profane* Greek classics, which, again, parallels a return in China to the pre-Buddhist Confucian classics under the guidance of Han Yü and Li Ao as well as Śaṅkara's return to the pre-Buddhist classics in India in search of fresh vitality.

Dvornik gives us this summary of Photius' contributions to the ninth century Byzantine Renaissance :

> Photius was one of the leading figures in the Byzantine intellectual renaissance of the 9th century, and his learning commanded the respect of his bitterest enemies. His scholarly reputation is established through his MYRIOBIBLION (Bibliotheca), giving criticisms of and extracts from 280 works that Photius had studied, many of which are not preserved today. The other of his main works, the AMPHILOCHIA, contains answers to more than 300 questions of a theological and profane nature. His writing against the filioque (Mystagogia Spiritus Sancti) was exploited by anti-Latin polemicists from the 12th century on. His 200 extant letters and his HOMILIES are written in an elegant style.... He reorganized the patriarchal academy for the education of the clergy and brought philosophical and theological speculation back to the foundation established by Aristotle. He manifested interest in philology by composing a LEXICON and an ETYMOLOGICUM.[5]

Many of Photius' Hellenistic ventures were met with little appreciation in his own day, however, and, for example, in the controversy between him and Symeon the Neo-Theologian, he was accused of many trivial vices in addition to blasphemy and forgery. But another of his many successful contributions lies in his role in the historic mission to Kiev. Toynbee maintains that at least partial motivation for the mission was the ambition to provide a counter-offensive against the Rhos, a Scandinavian people. More important was the transfer of Byzantine culture into the Slavonic world through St. Vladimir of Kiev (972-1015). Photius, Cyril, and Methodius laid the groundwork for his opportunity to choose the Byzantine Church, a decision he made after weighing its advantages against those of several other faiths, including Islam.

Photius founded at Constantinople a circle of intellectuals, of which his own brother Tarasios was an assiduous member, and we can say that the *Myriobiblion* was in fact *their* special project. Modern scholars who reproach Photius do so largely from the choices made in this traveller's library; there are some uncomfortable lacunae in it, including all the notable classical authors, and there is scarcely a single poet. Other criticisms, such as the following, suggest a lack of thoroughness in the treatment of some authors :

> Byzantine education and scholarship shows not so much originality as enjoyment of the accumulated intellectual wealth of centuries. Men such as Photius and his friends must have had a real appreciation and a literary background that would have been impossible without a tradition of education and learning. It is the same with John Geometres, whose poems are full of references to classical authors, Xenophon, Sophocles, Homer, Aeschylus, Euripedes, to mention only a few. The difficulty is that it is often little else but names that are mentioned, and that apart from reading of Plato 'the teacher of immortality', or Aristotle 'the definer of the bounds of mind and nature', there is often no means of probing the depths, or otherwise, of the author's knowledge of these writers.[6]

Based upon individual lectures from either Photius or from his companions, the *Myriobiblion's* inclusive works could not have all been read by Photius. The procedure for admitting a work into the *Myriobiblion* probably was along the following lines : one of his companions would comment or summarize a work which Photius had entrusted to him; the others would listen, discuss, and then allow Photius to conclude. Then there remained the most difficult step, that of transmitting the oral work into writing. The style of writing adopted for the *Myriobiblion* resembles the modern book review form, which was unknown in the Latin West until the time of Ficino. It bears a marked resemblance to the Neo-Confucianist authors in Photius' time.

The *Amphilochia*, written between 867-872, was dedicated to the metropolitan of Cyzicus, after whom it is entitled. On the whole there are fewer questions of the profane category than others, and of these Plato and Aristotle are the main targets, Photius' answers revealing a partiality to Aristotle. Plato's theory of Ideas is dealt with severity, whereas Aristotle is found to be most *useful* for Christians. Excessive enthusiasm for these 'pagans' is guarded against however, and at times he resorts to putting them in their places : "Our noble (Christian) muses differ as much from the hellenic muses as free natures differ from slaves, and truth from trumpery."[7] Evidently Photius underwent an evolution in his thinking, being more involved with the 'profane' subjects in his youth. His insatiable appetite for knowledge of all kinds never diminished, but these subjects increasingly became subservient to theological considerations.

Photius once gave advice to Michael Prince of Bulgaria (Boris I) on the theme 'What is the function of a Prince?' The advice which Photius offers in this document is modelled as much on Isocrates, the Greek classicist, as on the Bible. Michael is advised, among other things, to study history :

> It is your duty to cultivate practical wisdom (*phronēsis*) through all the course of your life. Such wisdom is acquired from the recollection and memory of old achievements; from the conversation and company of men of wisdom who are still living; and from actual experience of the business of life. It is action itself which—gathering strength from imitation, from counsel, and from the handling of affairs—leads to good and useful results if the influences that are above be not adverse.[8]

He further advises that appointments be made on the basis of merit, and warns that the proper function of the court is to provide a check against tyranny. On this point he adds :

> Tyrants often overlook offences against community and wrongs done by citizens to one another; but they visit harshly offences committed against themselves. The policy of a king and of constitutional government is different : it is a policy of tolerating offences against themselves in a humane spirit, and of justly correcting and pursuing offences against the community and wrongs done by citizens to one another.[9]

He then counsels for a mean between the extremes of laxity in law-making and law enforcement, and excessive rigidity, the latter of which prompts resentment and rebellion. The ruler must rule by educating the people in "gentler and more humane methods". His warning against ambition to increase the size of the state to the neglect of its cultural quality and public welfare remains sound advice for modern nation-states.

All of this advice offers striking parallels to the Confucian code. This becomes even more evident in Photius' exhortation that the ruler's virtue must begin with himself, and from there should proceed to his family, and from there proceed outward to the more externalized institutions, culminating in the dominion as a single entity. Photius counsels a foreign policy of peace, stating that the laying down of arms and seeking peace is superior to military exploits, the latter being signs of weakness while the former is a sign of confidence and respect for all parties involved. In another chapter he advises that if one must have weapons, good will may still be the more powerful as instrument of peace. (In our own time it has become axiomatic that since the invention of nuclear weaponry the only insurance agaist mutual obliteration is a policy which obviates the formation of mankind into enemy camps, i.e., that we are not each the other's enemy, and therefore even that one has no enemies.)

That Photius had a following of sorts there is no doubt. His disciples' attitude toward him is reflected in the following :

> Arethas of Caesarea, a disciple of Photius, goes still further in his veneration for his master, when he places him in paradise next to St. Chrysostom and St. Nicephorus. On another occasion, Arethas replies in unrestrained terms to the Armenians 'Among them there was recently found one holy by his family

ties and holier still for his wisdom, both human and divine. Who is he? Photius, the one raised today to the highest in heaven.' This is frank canonization, and another disciple of the Patriarch, Nicholas Mysticos, goes still further in his letter to the Emir of Crete : 'The most eminent of God's high priests and the most famous, Photius, my father in the Holy Ghost, has likewise written to your Excellency's father....' In another letter, this time addressed to a Christian king, the ruler of Armenia, Nicholas calls Photius 'the very saintly patriarch.'[10]

Photius' place in the Byzantine tradition has been summarized as follows :

> He remains, along with Psellus (of the eleventh century) and Plethon (of the fifteenth) one of the great figures in the history of Byzantine thought; and in some ways—not indeed as a scholar, but as a personality and an influence—he was the greatest of the three. Legend recorded of him that he had sold his soul in youth to a Jewish magician, and thus made him a precursor of Faust. He was not a precursor of Faust; but he deserves to be remembered as a parallel, in the East, of the great medieval popes of the West who were canonists, theologians, and statesmen all in one.[11]

Photius expressed in his correspondences a longing to be left alone for his scholarly work. His duties threatened to keep him endlessly involved in jealousies and intrigues, to which he felt the necessity of responding in a *niṣkāma karma* manner, i.e., selflessly accepting, although unwillingly, the responsibilities of public life. Unifying Photius' polymathic versatility and humanism is his perception of himself as a teacher ; as Photius Patriarch, he saw himself as a teacher of the Church and the Empire, steering his pupils through the narrow straits between the Scylla of neo-pagan heresy and the Charybdis of sterile and stagnant literalism.

24. al-Sarakhsī

When great masters are innovators, as were al-Kindī and Zakariyā al-Rāzī in Islam, Śaṅkara in India, Photius in Byzantium, Scotus Erigena in Carolinian France, Li Ao and Han Yü in China, Kūkai and Saichō in Japan—the ninth century was almost as great an Axial Period in all of Eurasia as was the fifth century B.C.—do their disciples of the second or even first generation tend to interpret them correctly and faithfully, or do they elaborate to such an extent that they distort or even sometimes pervert the original teaching? There are numerous comments to this effect. Marx is said to have complained that he was not a 'Marxist', and we have previously noted the discrepancy between the historic humanist Śākyamuni Buddha and the manifold varieties of Buddhism, as well as between Jesus' own teaching and the very strange things that have been done in the name of Christianity. One can readily quip that Aristotle was not an Aristotelian nor Plato a Platonist—much less a Neo-Platonist—and so on till one wonders whether Śaṅkara was really an 'Advaitin', much less one of the modern Hegelian variety!

Aḥmad b. al-Ṭayyib al-Sarakhsī (833-899) was a disciple of al-Kindī. One very seldom finds in the broad historical scope any thinker of great importance who was not at some time or other the disciple of someone ; the phenomenon of multiple 'gurus' is, however, a strictly modern, secular development of our universities. Al-Sarakhsī did some outstanding work in geography and many of the other sciences as well as in philosophy as such, much as his teacher had done. Evidently no cult accumulated around al-Kindī, who was really only a sort of crest-wave in the wide sea of the general enlargement of Islamic thought through Hellenistic, Syriac, Indian, Persian, and probably a bit of Chinese influence. Not only the disciples of al-Kindī but many others were also carrying on in the new developments, not only in philosophy but in science and the literary arts as well.

Probably Kindī's most important disciple in the domain of

philosophy was Aḥmad b. Ṭayyib al-Sara*kh*sī from *Kh*urāsān, who was born between 218/833 and 222/837 and died in 286/899, according to some sources by suicide. Although well-known in his own lifetime, having been the instructor to the 'Ab-bāsid prince al-Mu'taḍid, even becoming his boon campanion (*nadīm*) when the prince became caliph and being given charge of some state duties by him,he fell from favour late in life and was imprisoned. This fact may have contributed to his becoming rapidly forgotten ; even his works, of which there were many, were mostly lost or neglected. Enough has been recounted of them, however, to enable us to reconstruct an image of him. He wrote in nearly every field, following the example of his teacher. His writings embraced religion, philosophy and the sciences and ranged over fields as far apart as music, in which he wrote a major work, and politics, in which his *Ādāb al-mulūk* still survives. In geography and especially literature (*adab*) he had many original ideas while in philosophy he followed cloesly the teaching of Kindī. His tragic life coincided with the period when the intellectual climate of Baghdad was changing, preparing the way for the spread of philosophy beyond the inhospitable atmosphere of the capital to the cities of Persia and especially *Kh*urāsān, which were soon to become its new home. One of Sara*kh*sī's students, Rāzī, was in fact to carry the transformation to an extreme, by not only shifting the centre of intellectual activity away from Baghdad but also opposing completely the Peripatetic school of thought established by Kindī and followed by Sara*kh*sī.[1]

Khurāsān in the present-day frontier between Iran and Russian Turkestan was an area where virtually every religion and philosophy and science up to that time was in a state of constant encounter and syncretistic mixture. There Manichaeans, Nestorians, Buddhists, perhaps a few Confucianists, and most likely some off-brand Taoists were not unknown, not to mention men familiar with Hindu science and philosophy. As for the Baghdad of Sarakhsī's time, one might compare it with the 'Enlightenment' period in the history of Paris. There were many 'salons' where feasts of poetry and displays of refinement had become an art, and wit was often valued more than wisdom. All this despite the orthodox *'ulamā'* whose control of public opinion, not to say literary taste and openness to heresy, had lessened considerably, at least for a season.

The impression is that Sarakhsī was not as religious as his teacher and might even be termed a 'secularist'. Even though the accusations are often discordant, the general tenor of them is against Sarakhsī's lack of interest in the petty theological squabbles in process in Baghdad (as in Byzantium, Kaśmir, Japan, and South China); thus accusations of heresy were as easy to make as they were difficult to prove conclusively. Sarakhsī was a Shī'ite, or at least passed for one. He wrote a treatise (now lost) on the religion of the Sabaeans. The Hermetic heritage he had learned from al-Kindī. His work on the Sabaeans was intended to lead to their conversion to Islam based on the claim that they did not have any revealed scripture like the Muslims; but either they did not read it or, if they did, it had little effect on them. Not only did Sarakhsī contribute considerably in making the Arabic language more adequate to handle Greek philosophy, but he invented a phonetic alphabet to facilitate the correct transcription of technical terms from Persian, Syriac and Greek. He is also a major source of information about Stoicism in Arabia, which was somewhat influential in Islamic tradition.

Evidently one stimulus to Sarakhsī's interest in geography came when he accompanied his princely student to northern Syria on a military expedition of a remarkable sort called the Battle of the Mills. Neither side won, both retreating in mortal fear of the other's might. The journal Sarakhsī kept of the journey and return, as we know from fragments which have survived, was mere travellogue. At each place visited Sarakhsī investigated all available historical documents to see how much change had come about since the days of the Roman Empire and even further back into antiquity. Thus history and geography were intelligently bound together even as they never should have been separated.

About three years after al-Mu'taḍid became calif, Sarakhsī naturally was promoted to a responsible government post, evidently something concerning market regulations, including the flourishing slave market. Slaves were brought in from Central Asia, many having a syncretistic mixture of Nestorian Christianity, Manichaeanism and Tāntric Buddhism, some probably having some mixed Chinese ancestry. Slavery under Islam then involved no racial or caste status but was merely a financial arrangement more like a liberalized endenture system in which the slave could own property, accumulate wealth, and, as in some cases he had sold himself into bondage in order to get out of a financial difficulty, he could buy his freedom back.

Sarakhsī's fame did not last long after his death ; only the genius of later Muslim historians like Yāqūt rescued him from complete oblivion. Censorship can be very effective in obliterating genius, just as lack of adequate patronage can often prevent it from flowering. This of course is a warning to our own time in history.

It is unfortunate that we have so little explicitly dealing with systematic philosophy from Sarakhsī, for we get the impression that whereas al-Kindī his teacher had been a very deep-hearted and earnest worker, polymath though he certainly also was, Sarakhsī may have been more of a dilettante than a truly earnest philosopher. By comparison with the disciples of Śaṅkara, notably Vācaspati Miśra, certainly Sarakhsī was more versatile, but no doubt less systematic. If we had more detailed information about those who studied under Photius we would probably find some very similar figures since the aesthetic component of Constantinople's cultural life was very similar to that of Baghdad. In Baghdad the Greek, Persian and Indian materials were still considered as innovations and were therefore doubly under suspicion as heterodox; regard in Byzantium for the 'pagan' philosophers was a matter of cultivation of antiquity, and they had less impact on the theological orthodoxy since adjustment to the Biblical heritage was nothing new or exciting. Indeed, there was probably less original thinking in Byzantium than in Baghdad.

We know little of the disciples of Scotus Erigena, although if we take Godisalc as typical it might appear that what was original in Erigena was more ignored than followed, and the much more 'orthodox' theology (in that case, Augustinian) continued to have a negative effect on free philosophical thought, much less scientific investigation. As for those who immediately followed after Li Ao and Han Yü, since China entered a time of troubles in the transition between the T'ang and the Southern Sung Dynasties we might find, especially in North China, syncretism of a much more esoteric sort than was evident in the works and career of Sarakhsī, while in South China no doubt some of the literati were more of the dilettantish sort, although the polymath ideal, as also in Byzantium, prevailed. As for parallels in Japan, with only a slight chronological discrepancy Kyōtō could well be compared to Baghdad and Constantinople in that it became the center of everything from ribaldry and foppishness to serious and very earnest attempts at reform. Discussions often concerned what ought to be considered truly Japanese, even though imported from foreign sources. The polymath ideal was surviving after Kūkai and Saichō, but more frequent were imitators of previous masters than solid systematic innovators. Dilettantism, in short, had set in there as in Baghdad, while the serious minds were increasingly engaged in what might be considered as more petty if more intense theological quarrels. In Baghdad, India and Byzantium the natural sciences along with systematic metaphysics and logic had wider circulation and received much more devoted attention than in Japan. As to Tibet, the new materials were the highly developed systematics of Śūnyavāda and Vijñānavāda Buddhism, but with only a minimum of the natural sciences. Instead of prophetic religion the base was the Shamanism which was increasingly getting syncretized into Tibetan Tantra of an extremely esoteric sort perhaps comparable to the Hermetic tradition which fascinated Sarakhsī even at the expense of further advancement in logic, mathematics and scientific astronomy.

Although evidently Sarakhsī was somewhat peripheral to it, Baghdad did have, as with al-Rāzī and Thābit b. Kurra, more original and systematic scientific work advancing than anywhere else. The basic monist trend that prevails through al-Kindī's work had begun with Sarakhsī to be diluted into elaborations through fascination with greater details of exposition, as was basically the trend all over Eurasia after the Axial Age that the early ninth century really was.

EXFOLIATION AND ELABORATION (900-1150)

1. Somānanda

From our previous survey of the milieu in which Śāntarakṣita (705-762) and Kamalaśīla (715-763) worked we know that Vijñānavāda Buddhism had been flourishing in Kaśmir for some time, and that it was from Kaśmir that this variety of Mahāyāna Buddhism was transmitted to Tibet. The great Ṣūfī al-Ḥallāj Manṣūr visited Kaśmir, confirming other reports that the Muslims were indeed vying with the Tibetans for hegemony over the region. Politically and militarily Kaśmir was not in a very stable situation, and it seems that this instability stimulated intercultural communications. We may look on the emergence of Kaśmir Śaivism as a unique synthesis of the dynamism of the Buddhist heritage with the sense of system and structure from the Hindu systems, including Nyāya-Vaiśeṣika. There was influence from the later Mīmāṁsā with its exhaustive analysis of the *pramāṇas* alongside the 'illusionism' (*māyāvāda*) Gauḍapāda, and perhaps some influence from the theism of Islam.

In his study of the *Śivadṛṣti* of Somānanda (fl. c. 900), Gnoli informs us that this work was not a great success, Utpaladeva's shorter work on the same being more popular. Somānanda is a sort of prelude to the full development of the Pratyabhijñā school of Kaśmir Śaivism later on with Abhinavagupta. The "apostolic successions" of the Spanda and Pratyabhijñā schools are given as follows :

> According to Bhāskara (Daivākari, Divākaravatsa) the *saṃpradāya* of *Spanda* school is as follows : Vasugupta, Bhaṭṭa Sūri, Kallaṭa, Pradyumna Bhaṭṭa, Prajñārjuna, Mahādeva, Śrīkaṇṭha, and Bhāskara. Bhāskara, alias Divākaravatsa, is quoted by Abhinavagupta and was probably one of his masters. The *saṃpradāya* of the *Pratyabhijñā* school is as follows : Saṅgamāditya, Aruṇāditya, Ānanda, Somānanda, Utpaladeva, Lakṣmaṇagupta, and Abhinavagupta.[1]

Śaṅkara does not refute the Pratyabhijñā school of Śaivism probably for the simple reason that it had not yet emerged historically; and whether his works were known in Kaśmir by the time of Somānanda we do not yet know—probably not since the indications in terms of general trends are that the influence was rather in the opposite direction, Kaśmir Śaivism having some influence on South Indian Śaivism, which remained fairly independent (and still does even today) of Śaṅkara's Advaita.

Gnoli emphasizes the difference between Buddhism and Kaśmir Śaiva tradition as follows :

> Kashmirian Śaivaism, as is well-known, is opposed to Buddhist thought, according to which reality is absolutety ineffable and, in other words, the void, the zero of discursive thought. According to Śaivaism, the fact that reality is, in its essence, ineffable, does not prevent reality unfolding conceptually in the images (and therefore in the words), I, knowledge, thought, light, energy, etc., and, in the religious and devotional moment, God, Īśvara, Bhairava and so on. In other words, in the very moment in which the philosopher issues from the compact body of reality in its living concreteness and, moved by pity for others, seeks to conceptualize this experience, the most adequate images for this purpose which come to his mind and in which, as it were, reality seems to solidify, are the images of light, thought, consciousness, etc. Reality, there fore, which strictly is unpredicable and ineffable, takes on, in the very moment in which it comes into contact with our thought, an inevitable noetic colouring.[2]

This again reminds us of how the bold monisms of the previous cycles manifested in Śūnyavāda, Vijñānavāda, and Śaṅkara's Advaita, etc., are already under necessity of unfolding themselves in differentiating forms of manifestation. Gnoli continues :

> As with Buddhism, the realisation of reality does not detract from, or impoverish, life but is, really, another way of seeing it . ... The saint sees things—and here we come back to a Buddhist or rather a pan-Indian conception—independently of any association with the 'I' or the 'mine'; that is to say, independently of his practical interests. This vision is a direct perception or experience, precedent, thereby, to the activity of

> discursive thought, which rests on the shadow of the thing and not on the thing *'in se'* in all its concrete plenitude. All that exists is thought, consciousness : reality is reality in the very measure in which it is thought, in which it rests in our 'I'. Time, space—in short, all the multiplicity of things—are simply the fruit of the division of reality into the modes of conceptual knowledge. The division of reality into multiplicity and becoming is not determined by any extrinsic agent, but by an intrinsic force, indivisible from the proper nature of reality itself. This force—*māyā*—is the self-same expression of the absolute liberty and autonomy of consciousness, which creates and dissolves, obscures and retrieves itself ceaselessly its original plenitude.[3]

Even in the interpretation of *māyā* according to Kaśmir Śaivism we have something significantly different from any of the four sub-interpretations in the post-Śaṅkara Advaita school, to whom *māyā* is something we want to get beyond since it is nothing marvelous or positive but that unyielding X of unwanted negation in all things, the principle of limitation. In Kaśmir Śaivism, however, *māyā* is a cosmic power, the supreme *śakti* of Śiva whereby He does all the wonderous things in the vast incomprehensible universe. To almost all Hindu systems, and certainly to Advaita and even to some later Mahāyāna thought, movement, change, and alteration are not really real since reality as such is identified with permanence—but a permanence which is unattainable in any finite, material manifestation and therefore radically ineffable. But not so with Kaśmir Śaivism. Dynamism is not only included in the Divine but is the major manifestation of it.

> Reality, from this point of view, is vibration (*ghūrṇana*), movement (*spanda*), continual ebullition (*ucchalattā*). This aspect of reality was emphasized above all by Vasugupta and by Kallaṭa. Consciousness, in its pristine force and limitlessness, can be caught in any *moment-limit*, of anger, fear, love : when it would seem, that is, that the external world, the world of our habits and of our normal thought, disintegrates, bit by bit, to flow back into an incandescent matter, full of

indeterminate potentiality. This moment may be caught in reality in any form of knowledge. Every movement we make, of a physical or psychic order, is born, originally, of a species of tension, or urge which unfolds inside us. One of the aspects peculiar to this school is, indeed, this observation, in all our activities, of an element of 'drive', of 'urge', of an inner conation. ... which, directed towards a given end, contains within itself the image of the things to come. This tension represents, as it were, the heart, the most intimate and central activity of consciousness. All forms of knowledge—in short, all our psychic activity—come from this inner impulse, which—one takes good care—is not determined by any extrinsic cause, but is the expression of the very nature of consciousness. This moment of our inner life is called the 'first moment' (*prathamā tuṭi*) of will. It develops, successively, in a given idea, in a given sound (thought and language are indivisible according to this school) and thus already contains potentially within itself the image to come, is, in other words, determined by it : otherwise it would be impossible to explain why an act of will unfolds in one given product (e.g., a vase) and not in any other. The effort, the initial will to remember a stanze, for example, is enough, of itself, to call up in their fixed and immutable order, all the letters and words of which it is composed, without, that is, any new effort being required of us by the birth of each letter. This act of will, this initial tension which contains potentially all the intermediate letters, is the first stage in any form of thought, of language.

In the measure in which consciousness is liberty, autonomy, it is also beatitude. Beatitude presupposes the absence of every desire directed towards an otherness which opposes us. From this point of view, beatitude is, therefore liberty, freedom from all things. Thus it coincides with a perfect *autarcheia*, self-sufficiency : it is rest, resolution, lysis in one's own being to the exclusion of any extrinsic influence. In the very moment in which reality is thought, consciousness, it is also language, word. Reality, from this point of view, is the word, the supreme language, the verb that divides itself in the words and in the sounds that populate the horizon of consciousness.[4]

The *Śivadṛṣṭi* is done in the traditional *sūtra* style in the most condensed language possible such that without commentary it is difficult indeed to know the true intention. Such texts were intended for memorization and for commentary. Right at the outset in the Invocation of the *Śivadṛṣṭi* we find an assertion of the identity of Śiva and oneself, a concept traditional in Śaiva practice from antiquity, the typical mantra being simply *Om Śivo hum* ("I am Śiva") : "Let Śiva, who is co-penetrated with my own being (identified with me), praise Śiva in his extended form through his own power, Śiva who obscures Himself by Himself!"[5] This "obscuring Himself by Himself" should not seem strange to anyone familiar with the *āvaraṇa-vikṣepa* paradox in the Advaita tradition.

> Somānanda defines māyātattva as the Lord's sportive power of concealing His nature as one universal consciousness, and of assuming the stage of the impure principles. Māyātattva is also defined as the knowledge of difference among its modifications and among all individual souls, which veils the Lord's absolutely free spiritual wealth. In creating impure states He conceals Himself and generates the knowledge of difference of the principles from Himself and from one another for the experience of bound souls by His māyāśakti because of His power of doing the impossible.[6]

Of course Abhinavagupta and others enlarge on this interpretation of *māyā* considerably. But this interpretation of *māyā* as a sort of *līlā* of the Lord whereby He sometimes reveals Himself just enough to allow his devotees to become infatuated with Him, and at other times removes His Presence in order to increase their devoted-ness-in-longing for His consoling and enlightening sense-of-unification, will persist in both Śaiva and Vaiṣṇava traditions as a major feature for many centuries now. Whether one finds it personally acceptable or not, one must observe that it has been since before Somānanda's time a major factor historically in moulding both religious and philosophical traditions in India. But it is also significant as an elaboration of the stricter monist formulations of the previous century. These remarks are likewise applicable to the concept of God praising Himself through us.

The second and third aphorisms emphasize perfect union of will, knowledge and action in Śiva, although later it is explicated dialectically how that they do get separated outside of Him (in so far as there is any "outside" of Śiva who is the supreme, all-encompassing Unity as such). This union is possible only because there is asserted to be His all-pervading Consciousness in things. What we know in things is really not their thinghood but the degree of operation (hence *action*, in contrast to strict Advaita) of consciousness in them. In a modern interpretation we might say that we really do not know things-in-themselves but what we call the "natural laws" governing their development and activity. For we do realize now that there is no such thing as completely "dead" matter. All reality is really activity ($e = mc^2$). Our 'knowing' is only a sympathetic vibration with the 'thing' we 'know', and this activity is only a small part of the totality of Vibration that constitutes the universe—and that is the Dance of Śiva !

Although Śiva remains unelaborated in Himself, in his manifestations he becomes supremely elaborated; and it is both within these elaborations and through them that we exist, make distinctions, and seek understanding and wisdom. As to how the tendency towards impurity arises, the answer may seem naive to some moderns; but perhaps it is no less plausible than the more usual kinds of theodicies : "Śiva...unfolds at his pleasure in all that exists. This impurity therefore has no reason to exist (since the whole is none other than Śiva himself).... What reason is there then to look for the motives (which cause Him to act in this way)?"[7] Any monism with whatever qualifications must make some such assertion. In the commentary there is the further explanation, typical of the Śaiva tradition : "Śiva, by his own nature (*svarūpa*), becomes all that exists. The whole is Śiva himself and is thus 'pure'. Śiva, by his own nature, completes ceaselessly five operations : emission (*sṛṣṭi*), preservation (*sthiti*), re-absorption (*saṃhāra*) grace (*anugraha*) and obscuration (*tirodhāna*)."[8]

There is mention in the *Śivadṛṣṭi* of the usual faculties of the senses and the mind in the act of knowing; but this is qualified heavily in the case of the act of creating anything. For in other activities the three activities of willing, knowing and acting may remain separate; but in the act of creating they converge—or re-converge, since in Śiva's own nature they are never completely separated, for He allows in the finite world only temporary separation in order to effect greater creativity by this sort of pulsation. It follows that every knowing is a sort of creativity, perception of a vase being given as the paradigm example : "If there were no tension, the knowing-subject (or knowledge) would cease to exist. Without the tension (literally *lysis*) one would be unable to turn towards that which one hates (i.e., that which one wishes to leave)."[9] This hatred is explained in Gnoli's commentary as hatred of *limited* knowledge which is associated with *saṃsāra*.

There comes the objection that this knowing activity can be only an activity of matter, and that therefore knowledge itself is just another instance of the extremely complex inter-system of the psycho-physical organism. Somānanda's very need to answer this objection gives us a hint that indeed materialist philosophy had not completely died out in India.

Śiva as Supreme Self is not just the Supreme Knower, for Willing, which Advaita does not acknowledge, is also involved. Somānanda writes :

> Thus God, who comes forth in this way, sometimes appears through the power of will in the form of power alone; sometimes He calls forth the power of knowledge and appears in the form of Sadāśiva; sometimes He emphasises the power of action and appears in the form of Īśvara; while sometimes His knowing continues to solidify further and He appears in the form of Vidyā-s, of Vidyeśvara-s, of Mantra-s and of Mantreśvara-s. Sometimes it pleases Him to hide His own self and He appears then in the form of māyā and of the thirty-three orders of reality, taking on the nature of each of these. With this ends His activity as it is known and recognised by all. The last form which He assumes is the earth, solid, insentient, resistent and compact.[10]

The parallels or similarities here to un-Christianized Neo-Platonism are unavoidable. Archaeologists have begun to suspect that there was some relation between the Greek cult of Dionysius and the Hindu cult of Śiva, though this point has not been proven. We again wonder whether those 'pagan' Neo-Platonists who had fled to Persia when Justinian closed the Academy at Athens had shifted further east as the Muslim conquest moved across Iran.

Even as a great Chakravartin, "king over the whole earth", could take delight in going *incognito* among his lowliest subjects, so with Śiva, even to the extent of forgetting His own Śivahood. For although He is Knowledge itself and not just the Supreme Knower, He is also the Radical Restlessness in all reality, although during times of *pralaya* He appears as though he were quiescent, sunk in sleep with the sensory organs inactivated. A basic problem is how the *Paramaśiva* can become an individual soul without losing His Godhead, and how the individual soul, who is really Śiva Himself ultimately, can forget its divine nature. The solution, however, seems to lie not in intellectualistic propositions but in proper *ascesis* leading to that realization. The basic monistic pantheistic assertion is still there that all is Śiva; but the assertion becomes increasingly intense as the problem becomes increasingly acute that it is Śiva *in manifestation*, and there seems to be a sort of glorying in the idea that the more concrete, indeed the more *material* is this manifestation of the supremely spiritual reality, the more complete.

Quite contrary to what might be expected, namely that this Kaśmir Śaiva tradition would be heavily idealistic or even illusionistic by virtue of its admission (howsoever reinterpreted) of the importance of *māyā*, it turns out to be definitely realistic in its concluding note and therefore quite something else than the type of monism found in any of the Advaitins. Somānanda writes :

> Thus Śivahood is in the same proportions, in all things (from Śiva to an earthen-ware vase). The distinctions in half-way state, etc. (purity, impurity, etc.) are created solely by human opinions.
>
> The reality Śiva is thus eternal, infinite, inseparate from that which is distinct....The proper nature of Śiva is to manifest itself in all things; the whole, in all its multiplicity, is therefore real.[11]

This fits very well our general interpretation of the trend after the ninth century of elaboration and exfoliation of the previous basic monist trend.

The emanational scale prevails throughout Somānanda's realistic qualified monism. He extends the same principle not only as the bridge over the gap between the spiritual and the psychic and the material or somatic levels of existence, but even within the realm of spirit itself. This, of course, Muslims were unwilling to do, even over against the Christian concept of the Trinity, the Mahāyāna *Trikāya*, and the Brahma-Śiva-Viṣṇu Trinity. Even in Zoroastrianism and thence into Judaism to some extent and certainly into much of Christianity and even indirectly into Iranian Shī'a Islam, the doctrine of the hierarchy of angels and archangels fills that need. But whereas the other trinities are not hierarchical, the Śaiva concept of the levels within the Divine of Sadāśiva, Īśvara, Śiva-Śakti, etc., do seem to be basically hierarchical, thus much more closely resembling 'pagan' Neo-Platonism with its distinctions between the One, the Mind, and the Soul. Nevertheless this similarity must be rather heavily qualified, especially when it comes to the place of the I-consciousness (*ahaṅkāra*) in this system which is not found in any form of Neo-Platonism.

The following is Sinha's presentation of the differences be tween the Pratyabhijñā school of Śaivism and Śaṅkara's Advaitavāda :

1. Śaṁkara regards Brahman as the ontological reality while Somānanda regards Śiva endowed with divine power (Śakti) as the ontological reality. Śiva and Śakti are inseparable from each other. Śiva is endowed with the power of consciousness or illumination, self-illumination, bliss, volition, knowledge and action. Brahman is infinite existence-consciousness-bliss. They are Its essential characteristics. 2. Śaṁkara regards God (Īśvara) as a phenomenal appearance of Brahman limited by nescience (avidyā). God is the omniscient and omnipotent creator, sustainer and destroyer of the world, while Somānanda regards Śiva as the omniscient and omnipotent creator, sustainer and destroyer of the world. Śiva is not a phenomenal appearance. 3. For Śaṁkara, māyā is

neither real, nor unreal, nor both, nor either, but indefinable, while, for Somānanda, māyā is a real power of Śiva, a principle of self-limitation whereby He produces the world. 4. For Śaṁkara, the world is a false appearance (vivarta) of Brahman due to māyā, while, for Somānanda, the world is created by Śiva by His power of volition and by His power of action without any extraneous material; it is the product of His volition. Śaṁkara advocates absolute idealism while Somānanda advocates absolute ideal-realism or voluntarism (svātantryavāda). The former regards the world as an unreal appearance while the latter regards the world as real : all are Śiva. Somānanda regards the diverse objects of the world as created or projected outward by Śiva, and sustained and dissolved by His volitions.... 5. For Śaṁkara, the individual soul is an unreal appearance, a reflection of Brahman in nescience, while, for Somānanda, the Jīva is real in that Śiva limits Himself by māyāśakti and becomes the Jīva. 6. For Śaṁkara, the soul's bondage is due to its nescience or ignorance of its identity with Brahman, and its liberation is due to the destruction of nescience by the knowledge of its identity with Brahman. But, for Somānanda, bondage is due to the taints due to nescience, and liberation is due to the destruction of the impurities and nescience, the acquisition of omniscience and omnipotence, and the recognition of the soul's Śivahood. 7. For Śaṁkara, Brahman is mere infinite knowledge, while, for Somānanda, Śiva is the unlimited Knower. 8. For Śaṁkara, the jīva, in its real nature, is mere knowledge, while, for Somānanda, the jīva is a limited knower, doer and enjoyer; it derives its consciousness or illumination (prakāśa) and 'I'-consciousness or self-illumination (vimarśa) from Śiva, and is a limited self-conscious knower of its cognitions, feelings and volitions. 9. For Śaṁkara, Brahman is transcendent of the false world-appearance unreal empirical selves, while, for Somānanda and Utpaladeva, Śiva-Śakti is both transcendent and immanent. 10. For Śaṁkara, Brahman as pure identity is real, while, for Somānanda, Śiva is real as unity, plurality, and unity of plurality.[12]

By comparison with the clarity of some of his predecessors in the Nyāya-Vaiśeṣika or even the Mīmāṁsā, Somānanda shows a sort of syncretistic ignoring of inconsistencies; and by comparison with the apex of brilliant dialectics achieved by Śāntarakṣita and Kamalaśīla (which had been continued by Dharmottara and others), Somānanda must have been trying to reach a synthesis by other than strictly logical means. Many of the apparent inconsistencies still evident in Somānanda were later removed by Abhinavagupta. We are, in short, dealing with a newly developing tradition which does not come to full maturity until later on. At any rate, Somānanda does fit into the general pattern of the predominance of monism in the ninth century, which is then elaborated into gradually increasing complexities, leading into and beyond the Great Summas of the thirteenth century.

2. Bhāskara

Bhāskara is well-known in the field of objections to Advaita. Evidently he was one of the first to reject Śaṅkara, although that is somewhat controversial since there is in his *Brahma Sūtra Bhāṣya* no overt refutation as such as with Rāmānuja; but implicitly his *bhedābhedavāda* (difference and nondifference or identity) is either an unspecified alternative or refutation, or else it is possible that there were non-Advaitin commentators on the *Brahma Sūtras* and he was simply carrying on that tradition independently of Śaṅkara. Sinha agrees with those who place Bhāskara's dates around 900, although there is considerable uncertainty about his life as well as about his dates.

> He criticises Śaṁkara's views of knowledge only as the means of liberation, of the world as a false appearance due to nescience, of an individual self as an unreal reflection of the Brahman in nescience or in an internal organ, its product, of an effect as an unreal appearance of a real cause, of an individual self as identical with the Brahman, and of the Brahman

> as indeterminate and unqualified. He does not criticise Somānanda and Utpaladeva's (1000 A.D.) Śaiva monism. Nor does he criticise Rāmānuja's view (1200 A.D.). His view is criticised by Udayana....Udayana wrote 'Lakṣaṇāvalī' in 984 A.D. Hence it is certain that Bhāskara flourished in 900 A.D. He refers to Śaṁkara as a crypto-Buddhist. Many other Vedāntists follow him in branding Śaṁkara as a disguised Mahāyāna Buddhist.[1]

Bhāskara is also keen on refuting the Vaiśeṣikas in many points, really almost as much as he is dedicated to refuting Śaṅkara's *māyāvāda* and all others of that sort. Thus it may be inferred that Bhāskara was seeking for a commonsense middleground between the Vaiśeṣika over-emphasis (at least in his viewpoint) on difference and the extreme of nondifference of the *māyāvādins.*

Sinha treats in a very traditional way the systematics of this variety of anti-Advaita philosophizing, conforming generally to the basic "scholastic" outline, proceeding from the nature of Brahman and cosmology to philosophy of causation; thence to the nature of the self (including a standard refutation of the Buddhists from the Hindu point of view); then the theme of human nature, including Bhāskara's making the most of identity-and-difference as on par with each other rather than one being engulfed by the other; then comes Bhāskara's criticism of Śaṅkara's view of the individual self and of *avidyā*/nescience, especially as to its relation to Brahman, Bhāskara's position being a rather common-sense balanced view of "conditional difference and essential nondifference from Brahman"; the critique of *satkāryavāda* then follows, and this must entail a view of the reality of the world and a refutation of Śaṅkara's doctrine of the falsity of the world-appearance; finally, considerations leading to *mokṣa*/liberation. Such in basic outline is Bhāskara's treatment of the perpetual themes of traditional Indian philosophies, especially those based on the *Brahma Sūtras* and on the *Gītā*.

In spite of the traditional unexciting way that he is usually presented, Bhāskara was indeed an original thinker. However, this does not mean that he rejects revelation or the absolute authority of the Vedas. But that is no hindrance since it had by that time become a matter of 'pre-text' rather than text as such and the commentaries often contain only loosely related interpretations. Concerning the authority of the Vedas, the *pūrvapakṣa* is placed in the hands of the Mīmāṁsakas who argue that it is imperative to make the supreme inquiry into the ultimate nature of reality that Brahman is, but that such an imperative really takes second place behind the multiple imperatives of the rules and regulations of ritual performances, which regulate the operation of karma automatically, as it were. Bhāskara replies that the Vedas are very explicit in pointing to the ultimate inquiry as the sole and all-encompassing single injunction; but in addition to the merely moral injunctions which Mīmāṁsā prescribes, the Vedas also deal with the epistemological aspects of the inquiry, including the proofs of the existence of Brahman, since that cannot be proved conclusively except as relying on revelation.

Next must be considered the nature of the object of this inquiry. In that, as with all varieties of the Vedānta, the controversy over attributes comes immediately into focus. Bhāskara does not hesitate to list and discuss the traditional attributes instead of trying to explain them away as the Advaitins do. Such attributes are omniscience, omnipotence and omnipresence as well as Creator, Maintainer, and Destroyer of the universe. But also the moral aspects are included, as well as Providence. Not surprisingly he puts emphasis on the *antaryāmin* (the Holy Spirit idea) much more than the Advaitins do, or for that matter more than the Mādhavas later on.

Brahman is the Guide in matters of ethical situations, Brahman being also the Highest Good and the One who pardons sins ("Consumer of all sins"), and the Giver of fruits of actions, since freedom is supposed instead of the inexorability of karma as in Mīmāṁsā. Attainability or accessibility is also a basic attribute since any Ultimate that is not accessible or knowable in some sense would be a contradiction in terms. If accessibility were not true then there could not be any inquiry or even curiosity or controversy about the existence of Brahman. Nevertheless, accessibility does dot entail denial of the 'negative' attributes such as "the unseen Seer, the unheard Hearer, the unthinkable Thinker, the unknown Knower" since these indicate only transcendence, not inaccessibility. Śaṅkara denied the validity not only of these attributes but also of the *saguṇa*-Brahman, insisting exclusively on the *nirguṇa*-Brahman. But for Bhāskara, Brahman is always to be interpreted as *saguṇa*-Brahman. As Sinha writes : "The Brahman is always qualified. He is never unqualified. He is always the omnipresent, omniscient, omnipotent, infinite, eternal, blissful, adorable, pure, holy Lord."[2]

As for the attribute of creatorship of the world, the *pūrvapakṣa* is put in terms of the Vaiśeṣikas since they do not accept the notion that the world is the effect of Brahman as modified in order to become, as it were, His own creation, but rather insist that Īśvara is only the efficient cause of the world and completely separate from it. One might think that as a theist this would satisfy Bhāskara as such; but that is not the case since he is not merely a theist but after all a Vedāntin. Hence Bhāskara argues for the notion that God is rather the material cause of the world as the correct interpretation of the text, "From the Brahman these creatures are born, by Him they are maintained, and in Him they are dissolved."

Bhāskara's position of Brahman modifying Himself into the world is known as *Brahmapariṇāmavāda*. The basic metaphors here are milk turning to curd, water turning to ice, and a spider spinning a web from its own body. For Bhāskara what comes forth is just as real as its Source, whereas Śaṅkara would like to claim that it is not and only the Undifferentiated Source is really real. Bhāskara holds that

> the Brahman modifies Himself into the world without losing His nature, that modification is transformation of His powers, that His power of experiencing is modified into the conscious individual souls which experience insentient objects, and that His power of being experienced is modified into the insentient elements and gross objects. He creates the conscious souls and the unconscious objects by expanding His powers and then withdraws them into Himself. His creation is the expansion of His powers, and dissolution is the withdrawal of them.[3]

Needless to say we do not have here anything like the *ex nihilo* controversy in the Judeo-Christian-Islamic scholastic sense but something much more similar to the emanational pattern of Neo-Platonism.

The Advaitins tend too much, in the Bhāskara perspective, towards a gnosticism that tends to subordinate or even to explain away the ethical and the aesthetic values in preference to the epistemic ones. But not so with Bhāskara; Brahman is to be *worshipped.* In answer to the Advaitin claim that it is the *saguṇa*-Brahman that is to be worshipped (if any worship at all) even though that is already in the realm of *māyā*, Bhāskara again resorts to a common-sense view that the split between the *saguṇa* and the *nirguṇa* is strained and arbitrary, and such worship would be artificial and at best made into a burdensome duty instead of being a spontaneous activity. As undifferentiated, Brahman is indeed above all possible conceptualization on the part of finite man; but as differentiated, Brahman is a marvel evoking awe and wonder as the Ultimate Reality manifesting Itself in all the forms of Creation. Bhāskara may not be as eloquent as Rāmānuja in expressing that sense of marvelling or wonderment, but his perspective is relatively similar. The Upaniṣadic texts can be taken to mean just what they say, without any sophistical manipulations of pseudo-contradictions; the *neti neti* texts cannot be advanced at the expense of those that emphasize the manifestation.

Nevertheless, crass pantheism which runs the risk of worshiping the effect instead of the Supreme Cause of all effects must be avoided, as well as the opposite extreme of worshipping a Vacuum, as it were. Indeed it is the 'formless form' that should be the focus for devotion, but that for the reason that this same Reality is manifest in all the forms, and apparently so for whoever has the spiritual eyes and intellect to realize that. And it is in this perspective that again Bhāskara puts the major emphasis on the *antaryāmin*, the "inner controller", the "That of God in every man" (to invoke the Quaker expression), but in every *thing* also, as the Guarantor of its Reality.

From these considerations Sinha then guides us through Bhāskara's concept of the individual self. The Vaiśeṣika *pūrvapakṣa* is that consciousness is no more than an activity of the *jīva* rather than of its essential nature. "But Bhāskara holds that an individual self is a knower by nature, and that consciousness is its essential nature....Knowledge exists in the self so long as it exists. It can never be divested of its essence of knowledge."[4] But is knowledge alone enough? Obviously not, according to Bhāskara, since that in modern parlance, or even in Hellenistic terminology with its many Islamic parallels, would be gnosticism, the kind indeed that led al-Ḥallāj into trouble. Bhāskara is not a 'quietist', for although some varieties of Advaita and some extremes of Ch'an/Zen did have hesychast tendencies as much as the Byzantines later on, Bhāskara insists that the self is a doer; and therefore *karma yoga* is just as important as *bhakti* or *jñāna*. Hence a refutation of strict Sāṃkhya is rather obvious : if *jīv-ātman* is to be identified with the *puruṣa* then activity is not of its nature, but rather all activity is material, belonging to *prakṛti*. But this, ontologically inviting in its way, puts no responsibility or obligation on the individual soul or self. Moreover, freedom would be denied, whereas it is certainly experienced, especially in accepting or rejecting different actions to be done or not to be done. Sinha summarizes Bhāskara's position :

> The self is endowed with limited freedom, and is, consequently, under moral obligation to do right or wrong actions. But its freedom is limited by its own merits and demerits acquired by it in the past births by its free actions. God limits its freedom by impelling it to do those actions which make it experience the fruits of its merits and demerits. If it has no freedom, scriptural injunctions and prohibitions are meaningless. If it is absolutely free and not under the necessity of experiencing the consequences of its actions, the demands of the Moral Law of Karma are not fulfilled. So its freedom is limited by the will of God who makes it suffer the consequences of its actions in accordance with the Law of Karma.[5]

Thus the freedom of the individual *jīva* is not swallowed up in predestination, nor its responsibility. In general, Bhāskara seems to put much heavier stress on the ethical side of reality than most of the other commentators.

On the relation of the self to the Brahman we find a very extended controversy typical of all the different commentators on the *Brahma Sūtras* ranging around the multiple possible variations on the *Tat Tvam Asi mahāvākya* (Bhāskara also tends to neglect the other *mahāvākyas*). A panoply of metaphors come into play in justifying one or another position. Among others, Bhāskara himself relies on the reflections of the sun in the water : Brahman is the sun and the reflections the *ātmans*, the limiting adjuncts thus not hindering Brahman. There is a similarity here to Padmapāda's interpretation of Advaita as far as reflection is concerned; but whereas Padmapāda stresses the single sun at the expense of the many reflections, Bhāskara stresses both the single sun and the plurality of the reflections, involving both difference and nondifference together without compromising either. Sinha writes :

> When a jar is destroyed, the ether enclosed in it becomes ubiquitous ether; so when the limiting adjunct, the mind-body-complex, is destroyed, an individual soul becomes one all-pervading self or God. There is natural nondifference between an individual self and the Supreme Self or God as well as conditional difference between them due to a limiting condition. When the limiting condition is destroyed, the conditional difference between them is destroyed.[6]

Thus somehow—and Bhāskara is not so meticulous as some of the later commentators on the *Brahma Sūtras* in regard to that somehow but deliberately leaves it an open question—Brahman is not affected by the *jīva*'s fluctuations between joy and grief, or between genius and stupidity, or even between merits and demerits. Brahman is never free from the three *guṇas*, eternally pure and unlimited, and not subject to any prohibitions or inhibitions that characterize the individual (who is here characteristically referred to as the *karmātman*). But for the individual, as all of us experience painfully much of the time and some saints and Bodhisattvas and prophets no doubt most of the time, embodiment is a limitation (as in the modern European context Merleau-Ponty was fond of reflecting about).

"That Thou Art", according to Bhāskara's view, "declares an individual soul's natural and eternal identity with Him and its conditional difference from Him due to a limiting adjunct which endures during bondage."[7] Perhaps Bhāskara's greatness lies in his unsophisticated simplicity. He simply states the simplest position, the most common-sense, with only the minimum of explanation, without all the overlay of sophistical intellectual gymnastics which typify the later commentators, notably the later Advaitins, or even Vācaspati Miśra, his contemporary. *Mokṣa,* or the possibility of *mokṣa,* at least, does illustrate the basic *bhedābheda* relation : before *mokṣa,* difference; after *mokṣa,* identity. It's just as simple as that.

It is in Bhāskara's interpretation of the *satkāryavāda* philosophy of causation that his *bhedābheda* position becomes most prominent. The Vaiśeṣika is selected for the first *pūrvapakṣa,* again by way of critique more than outright refutation. The Vaiśeṣikas affirm the *asatkāryavāda,* that the effect is different from the cause as something really new and unique, as in the case of a jar made by a potter from clay. The jar is quite a new and different thing from the clay it was made from. But Bhāskara does not accept that. Sinha explains :

> An effect is dependent on its cause in the past, the present, and the future. An effect is a state of its cause, and is not perceived as different from its cause in space and time. It is real like its cause, and becomes unmanifest in its cause when it is destroyed. The world is real, and its cause, the Supreme Self, is real. An effect is both different and nondifferent from its cause. It is nondifferent from its cause in its essential nature, but different from the latter in its form and function. The world is nondifferent from its cause—the Brahman—in its essence, but different from Him in its physical form and in being experienced by individual souls.[8]

As might be expected, Bhāskara spends considerable effort in refuting the *māyāvāda* aspect of Advaita. We may well speculate as to which of the post-Śaṅkara Advaitins he might have had contact or communication with or from—probably Vācaspati Miśra, with whom he shares the term *upādhi* and several characteristics, although in some other contexts there are hints that the *vivartavāda* of Padmapāda might have been in mind. At any rate, Bhāskara's attempts at refutation of māyāvāda are familiar and will be increasingly common with future commentators who are critical of Advaita in the long history of the refutations and counter-refutations that actually continue right down to the present time.

Bhāskara argues that empirical knowledge of a real world is not contradicted by sublating knowledge, and that experience is universally common. The argument from dream experience does not hold good since everyone can discern the difference between dream experience in which unreal objects prevail and real waking experience. The argument from *śruti* does not hold good either :

> The Māyāvādin avers that the falsity of the empirical world is known from the Śruti 'There is no plurality in the Brahman'. Bhāskara interprets it thus : there is no plurality in the causal state of the Brahman; but there is plurality of effects in His effected state; hence there is no contradiction in this. He interprets the Śruti 'Ātman is not this, not this' as follows : the self is different from the mind-body-complex which is not self. 'The Brahman devoid of difference appears to be different'. This text means that in the causal state of the Brahman there is no difference or plurality, but that it does not deny the existence of plurality altogether, because appearance is an appearance of what is known to be real.[9]

In short, for Bhāskara the world is real as a real manifestation of a real Brahman.

All commentators on the *Brahma Sūtras* are obliged to give a critique of the Buddhist systems, especially the Vijñānavāda and the Śūnyavāda. In Bhāskara's exposition the Vijñānavāda receives the greatest attention as closest to Śaṅkara's position. As far as the critique of the Buddhist *kṣaṇavāda* is concerned, Bhāskara does not differ very radically from the other commentators. Essentially they all agree that it is a gross exaggeration if not a fallacy of hasty generalization to say that *everything* is only change and flux, since all the changes can be observed, and that *capacity for observation* (in both the internal and the external worlds) is the basic function of the permanent self. Therefore the Buddhist doctrine of *anātman*/no-self cannot hold. Parallel loosely with that one might point to Whitehead's difficulty in establishing categories for a process philosophy, since one cannot but question whether these categories also do not change along with the things or events of which they are supposed to be categories. Or again one might point to Bergson's philosophizing about memory as the minimal guarantor of continuity through change. Especially in moral situations, how can any legal action be justified if the person who commits a crime, or becomes worthy of reward, has no permanent self. Moreover, metempsychosis cannot be explained at all if there is no continuity of selfhood of some sort or other. Refutation of the Buddhist realist position deals with the *asatkāryavāda* espoused by that system. The refutation is relatively simple and is framed in terms of the metaphor of the seed and sprout. The Buddhist notion that every event is a matter of momentariness leaves the problem of causation unexplained since it denies all continuity as such. If every entity "just happens" in its own uniqueness, then there can be no causation involved at all, and anything or anything else could happen in the same sequence.

According to Sinha, "Bhāskara thinks works (karma) and knowledge (jñāna) combined as the means to liberation. He is opposed to Śaṅkara's view that knowledge alone is the means to release, and that knowledge and works, like light and darkness, cannot be combined with each other."[10] For those familiar mostly with the modern European context it should be easy to read into this the controversy between the Lutherans and the Calvinists and the Counter-Reformation concerning the operation of grace and faith and good works or salvation by merit. Actually what we have here is a perpetual problem that is quite universal, extending down to the present era in the revolt against the German Idealists by both Pragmatists and Marxists. In the Euramerican context the best reference might be that of the New Testament and the Neo-Platonists against Gnosticism. But more nearly contemporary with Bhāskara were the hesychasts of Byzantium, who soon were to figure as a major controversy. Likewise and still closer at hand, one might well invoke the controversy between the followers of al-Ḥallāj and al-Junayd, al-Ḥallāj being much closer to Śaṅkara whereas

Bhāskara might find some support from al-Junayd. In China we might point to the Neo-Confucianists' objections to the "non-action" of the Ch'an cult as well as most Taoists. To say the least, what Bhāskara is here dealing with is not just another of those esoteric issues peculiar to the internal controversies of a religion rather than being of a philosophical nature, but indeed a very universal problem. Even in the light of recent work in the philosophy of action as such Bhāskara might make some fresh contribution.

Again Bhāskara frames his arguments in terms of difference and nondifference. Sophistically he could have taunted Śaṅkara (and implicitly so he does) by arguing that Śaṅkara stays consistently with his logic of pure identity, then he could not distinguish between *jñāna* and *karma*. But more explicitly Bhāskara, with manifold support from *śruti* and common-sense logic, holds that *jñāna* and *karma* together effect *mokṣa*. They are different in operation but similar in purpose. Again the argument of Śaṅkara that works lead only to perishable ends but that knowledge alone yields the permanent imperishable end of *Brahmavidyā* evokes a lot of typically detailed dialectics, but the basics Sinha reports very clearly :

> The Śruti says, 'The works of a person who meditates on the Brahman do not perish.' Works are perishable in themselves, but they are not so when they are combined with knowledge. Works combined with knowledge are the cause of the attainment of the highest good. Works combined with the knowledge of the Brahman lead to liberation which is imperishable. If they cannot yield liberation, an ascetic's knowledge of the Brahman also cannot do so because he performs the unavoidable bodily, vocal and mental acts for the preservation of his life. Works uncombined with knowledge lead to the attainment of heaven. But works combined with knowledge lead to the attainment of liberation. The renunciation of all works is a vain pursuit. Offering all works to God is true renunciation of works, and brings about the realisation of Him.[11]

The Advaitin belief in *jīvan-mukti* or complete Brahma realization or enlightenment in this life is rejected by Bhāskara. As long as the body lasts it must act or die, so obviously action is necessary. Thus both knowledge and action are necessary as long as we are here.

On the theme of *mokṣa* the first *pūrvapakṣa* is that of the Vaiśeṣika, which system holds that *mokṣa* consists simply in, as we might say today, scientific passionlessness. But this is not enough for Bhāskara, who holds the view that the individual souls when released from the bondage of karma and embodiment will enjoy union with Brahman and therefore positive bliss, very much as Rāmānuja will later teach. Essentially the same argument is given in refutation or critique of the Sāṃkhya claim that *mokṣa* is simply a state of consciousness unaffected by the fluctuations of the *guṇas*. Bhāskara is not satisfied with this either since it has no positive note, and who would strive for such a condition. Omniscience might be of *mokṣa*, but what is the use if we could not *enjoy* it.

As to the state of the soul after release, "Bhāskara holds that a soul remains nondifferent from god in release. There is natural or essential nondifference or identity between a soul and God, but there is a conditional difference between them due to a limiting adjunct. When the limiting adjunct is destroyed, a soul becomes nondifferent from God."[12] Bhāskara holds that this is not an acquired state but one that has been potentially there inherently all the while. And this seems the more universal view. Even the Neo-Confucianists were appealing to the concept of "returning to one's original nature"; and in the Judeo-Christian-Islamic heritage, though some overstressed the Fall of Adam, most claim that in spite of that the divine nature of man, the Image of God in man (not to mention of operation of the Holy Spirit), is never destroyed. Thus salvation consists in restoration of that primal nature before the Fall rather than a new gift.

What sort of consciousness can be expected of such a perfect state of release? The Advaitin gets caught in a trap of his own design here, since if he admits that there is difference in the objects of consciousness here or hereafter (i.e., difference in the objects themselves and between them and the knower), then his claim of nondifference is compromised. But if he does not admit of difference, how could anyone be Consciousness Itself without any content or locus of operation or individuation? Hence, in conclusion, Bhāskara insists that his *bhedābheda* persists in *mokṣa*, both in terms of relation to Brahman and in terms of knowledge of other things. "A liberated soul may associate or not associate itself with any body or sense as it likes. It is as omniscient, omnipotent and as one with all souls as God Himself."[13]

3. Thābit ibn Qurra

In the late ninth and early tenth centuries at Baghdad, and increasingly not only at Baṣra but Balkh, Khorasan, Ispahan, and many other centers "east of Suez", there were very few intellectuals who were not equally versed in mathematics, medicine, philosophy, comparative religion, philology, etc. We see something of this in the case of al-Kindī, whose scientific endeavors have been neglected in our standard textbooks because he was a philosopher, while the stereotyping of al-Rāzī as a scientist (or merely as a medieval alchemist) has unfortunately minimized his unique contribution to the global history of philosophy, not to mention his genius and originality in virtually everything he attempted.

Thābit ibn Qurra (836-901) is only representative of the very impressive list of Islamic savants from the early eighth century on through to the time of Ibn Sīnā and al-Ghazālī in the eleventh and twelfth centuries ranging in and around Baṣra and Baghdad—but also east of Baghdad and hence left in obscurity as far as Europe is concerned until the very recent researches of such as Henri Corbin. Others were as significant historically, such as al-Khwārazmī (d.c. 863), who is generally credited as the first seriously to merge Hellenistic and Indic concepts and techniques in mathematics and astronomy.

The Central Asian region had become a melting pot of all the basic traditions, religious and philosophical. There were constant encounters between Confucianists and Taoists (mostly of a messianic character), Nestorian Christians, Manichaeans (probably of descent from the Mazdakite heresy from Zoroastrianism that had been forced to leave Persia proper about the same time as the Nestorians), and Buddhism also was still very strong in many centers, although it had become rather syncretized with Shamanism indigenous to Central Asia and Tibet, whence Tāntric Buddhism took a more definitive shape that later migrated through China to Kūkai's Japan. Islam entered sporadically, at times welcomed, especially by the poorer classes, and at other times gaining converts by *jihād*, holy war, but also at least in one famous instance simply by the Muslim army through utter sincerity converting a 'pagan' ruler. Political boundaries were extremely unstable since the Chinese were still trying to gain support from peoples on the western side of the Uighur Turk region but not always succeeding; and Tibet was expanding enough to have become a menace to all the older establishments until, among other factors, China regained its own strength for a while on the one side and Islam posed a threat on the west and north. Kaśmir, along with Kasgar, Bukhara, Sogdiana, Tashkent, and other Central Asian centers which at various times became almost rivals to Baghdad, was certainly a cross-roads of conflict, oftentimes of confusion, occasionally of attempts at systematic, though more often syncretistic, mixtures of all the then-known religions. Khurasan was indeed a rival to Baghdad and produced some first-rate thinkers who have never become famous in our textbooks because they did not influence Latin Scholasticism. Nevertheless, one very critical event transpired as a result of this "total encounter" stretching between Mesopotamia and Loyang which revolutionized intellectual life at Baghdad perhaps more than any other material factor : paper.

It appears that while Indian science previously had been stimulated by a modicum of Greek influence, and Chinese science likewise by Indian influence, by the eleventh century there were very few new developments even though further improvements on the old materials were attempted. Also in Baghdad, by the mid-tenth century, there were few notable innovations even though there were attempts at improving on previously gathered materials. As time went on and Baghdad entered its decline due to decadence, even before the Mongol destruction, communications with the rest of the world may have lessened. The general hypothesis suggests itself that when a new center first is established communications are eagerly opened and influences from all possible quarters not only filter in but are welcomed and even solicited, whereas as that center becomes 'mature' it tends to become self-satisfied and proud if not even eventually decadent due to lack of external stimulation. The classical Chinese philosophy of history had this pattern in terms of dynasties, and this appears to apply also to the Islamic dynasties generally, not to mention Byzantium and India. But this seems to be critically the case with Baghdad as later it was with Cordova, Toledo, Fez and other places in Islamic Spain, even if we omit Cairo as an obvious example.

Fakhry introduces Thābit as

> ...the great pagan astrologer-philosopher ...who hailed from Ḥarrān in north Syria, settled in Baghdad, where he was attached to the service of the famous patrician family of Banū Mūsā. He subsequently became astrologer-royal and companion of the caliph al-Mu'taḍid (892-902). He was the sire of a long line of distinguished scholars, who like their great forebear, devoted themselves to the study of astrology and mathematics. His extraordinary mathematical-philosophical output, which was by no means limited to translations from Greek and Syriac, includes a commentary on the *Physics* of Aristotle, treatises on the *Nature of the Stars and Their Influences*, *Principles of Ethics* and *Music*, paraphrases of *Analytica Priora* and *Hermeneutica*, as well as numerous mathematical-astrological works. His translations included a medical compendium and an Arabic version of *Almageste* of Ptolemy and the *Elements* of Euclid, which were definite improvements on the earlier versions.[1]

And Nasr gives us this introduction :

> Thābit hailed from the community of Sabaens in Harran, where there was a religious cult centered around the symbolism of the planets. This cult, much interested in the Pytha-

> gorean mathematical and mystical tradition, survived well into Islamic period. Like many members of this community Thābit was well versed in mathematics and astronomy. Due to religious differences with his community he set out for Baghdad and was fortunate in meeting on the way the influential mathematician, Muḥammad ibn Mūsā ibn Shākir, who recognizing his ability, took him under his patronage. Thābit soon gained fame in Baghdad and became the court astronomer.
>
> Thābit was a major translator, almost as important as Ḥunain, and, like him, he wrote lasting works in medicine and philosophy. In addition he wrote many treatises on mathematics that exercised an immense influence on Muslim scientists. The echo of his scientific views, especially regarding the theory of "trepidation," was heard throughout the Middle Ages in the West.[2]

Thābit had virtually all the resources from Hellenistic authorities in mathematics, astronomy and medicine that were also available in Byzantium. Though later on the Byzantines did make some advances, during the centuries up to the time of Thābit there had been little improvement upon their Alexandrian forebears. Thābit made improvements over Aristotle and his experimental approach to astronomy, though that led him to a theory of the "trepidation" of the equinoxes which was later proved erroneous. But his improvements in Euclidian geometry and in algebra were such that some authorities claim that he even anticipated Descartes in some aspects of mathematics. Much of Thābit's fame rested on his work with the moon, especially eclipses. His work on the time of the appearance of the new moon was of sufficient importance and detailed enough to merit a semi-popularized condensed version later by al-Hāzinī, and some authorities claim that Thābit's work was far more advanced than that of al-Battānī.

Harran had been famous for many centuries as a stronghold of the Hermetic esoteric tradition, which included astrology and alchemy, there being little discrepancy between science and esoterics in that period of world history. Thābit was no exception to the general fascination with astrology still prevailing, and even incorporated something of the ancient Mesopotamian lore in this field. He is known to have translated and commented on works on talismans, magic images and such-like, but since these were written in Syriac or Sabean languages they have not survived. The chief work extant which reveals Thābit's involvement in esoterics is the *De-Imaginibus*, which was also translated into Latin and had considerable influence in western Europe right down through the Renaissance.

Thābit made some contributions to the development of scientific geography, which had begun by his time to become a very serious matter for the Islamic world which was still stretching its extent from what is now Senegal well across to the Philippines. It never occurs to us that our maps may all be upside down, but the earliest Muslim maps did have south on top ! The Muslim geographers could rely on both Chinese and Greek cartography, the Indians being as far as we know still limited to mythological notions about the *dvīpas* or continents. The emphasis, however, was not so much on cartography as such but on the much more philosophical issue of the relation of climate to types of human civilization. In the Islamic context this is probably best known in Euramerica from the work of Ibn Khaldūn (d. 1406). Al-Farghānī (d. 820) had already done some pioneering work, and Thābit only tries to improve on that. Instead of attempting anything radically new, in whatever field he touched Thābit tried to improve the old. Given their equipment and background, the calculations of such Arab astronomers as al-Battānī, al-Farghānī, Thābit and others were amazingly close to the results of a modern geocentric model.

Thābit is one of those who did not achieve the fame of such as al-Kindī, al-Rāzī or al-Fārābī; but even as he was influenced by those who came before him, so he influenced very many of those who came after him. As was the case with al-Rāzī, so with Thābit and the other Arabic scientists of the ninth, tenth, and eleventh centuries when Baghdad was the intellectual, literary, scientific and philosophical center *par excellence* such as Nālandā and Loyang had been in previous cycles of history : it is only modern stereotypes that have classified them as scientists or philosophers, for most of them were both of these more or less together.

4. al-Junayd

Like most of the intellectual elite in the Islamic world, Junayd (d. 910) came from a famous family, in his case a family famous for heroism in Arab history. Junayd's father was glass merchant and Junayd himself was known as a merchant of raw silk. In Islamic society of that time, and perhaps rather generally, it was not unusual for Ṣūfīs to adopt a trade so that they would not have to be dependent on others; and also evidently bacause as in the case of Ch'an Buddhist and Benedictine and Basillian monastic practice, manual labor can be dedicated to service of the Divine just as acceptably as intellectual or artistic work. Certainly to say the least tenth century Baghdad, where Junayd resided all his life, must have been a marvellous place to live since trade with virtually the whole of Eurasia passed back and forth—and not only Ṣūfīs but monks of all persuasions travelled free of charge along with the traders.

Fakhry presents Junayd with some sense of historical continuity within the Ṣūfī tradition :

> Abu'l-Qāsim al-Junayd is regarded in the *Ṣūfī* tradition as one of the foremost pioneers and is universally venerated by orthodox and heterodox doctors alike, from al-Sarrāj and al-Qushayrī to al-Ḥallāj and Sa'īd b. Abi'l-Khayr. His teachers included al-Muḥāsibī, al-Saqaṭī (d. 870), and Abū Ḥafs al-Ḥaddād (d.873) and, despite his moderation, he venerated al-Bisṭāmī (d. 874), the extravagant votary of divine union...His influence on the subsequent development of *Ṣūfism* was very great. And, although he was diffident and dispassionate by nature, his profound sense of the unity and transcendence of God reached its culmination in the most exuberant expression of passion for union with God, of which al-Ḥallāj (d. 922) eventually became the symbol. It is noteworthy that his disciples included, in addition to this extravagant lover of divine union, some of the most orthodox adepts of theology and *Ṣūfism*, such as al-Ghazālī, who singles him out as one of his chief spiritual masters.[1]

Junayd started his education in law at a rather early age. It was probably this grounding that gave him a better balance between sterile orthodoxy and sensationally exotic doctrines and practices. There is the anecdote from his own writings that he was warned by his uncle not to become too friendly with the Mu'tazilites, and likewise he was definitely impressed by his uncle's counsel, "May God make you a traditionalist who is a Ṣūfī, and not a Ṣūfī who is a traditionalist!" Junayd wrote of his study :

> I studied law according to the school of such authorities on ḥadīth as Abū 'Ubayd and Abu Thawr, and later I associated with al-Harith al-Muḥāsibī and Sarī ibn Mughallas. That has been the reason for my success, because our knowledge must be controlled by going back to the Qur'ān and the Sunna. Whoever has not learned the Qur'ān by heart and has formally studied ḥadīth, and has not learned law before embarking on Ṣūfism, is a man who has nothing to lead.[2]

Corbin writes of Junayd's avoidance of extremes :

> The spirituality of Junayd is conditioned by bi-polarity between the Sharī'ah (the letter of the divine law) which changes from prophet to prophet, and the Ḥaqīqah (the truth that is spiritual and permanent). Junayd is opposed to the extremism that absorbed some Ṣūfīs of his own time in that they, from the ontological supremacy of the Ḥaqīqah over the Sharī'ah, concluded that the Sharī'ah was useless and therefore to abrogated, and that the excess of the Ḥaqīqah permitted them to neglect the Sharī'ah or even to disregard it.[3]

Junayd's chief teacher in the Ṣūfī heritage was Sarī al-Saqaṭī, Junayd's own uncle, who, having been a merchant for many years, renounced the world as a result of his own shop miraculously escaping a devastating fire. Later in Baghdad he had many disciples besides his nephew. He taught in a definitely Socratic manner, by asking questions rather than by harping on dogma. Needless to say there is an abundance of colorful anecdotes about the relation between uncle and nephew typical of Ṣūfī intuitive tradition, with vivid emphasis on the inadequacy of merely rational top-of-the head opinions in the face of profounder "wisdom of the heart". This uncle al-Saqaṭī became the founder of the Ṣūfī School of Baghdad.

The Baghdad school's main topic was Tawḥīd, unification, and used a richness of symbolic expressions that were not common among the Ṣūfīs of Syria and Khorasan. They, as Iraqis, were also noted for their eloquence. Indeed Junayd himself recorded the saying that "Syria is the home of chivalry, 'Irāq of eloquence and Khorasan of sincerity."[4]

Concerning the controversial question of Neo-Platonist influences on Ṣūfism, Abdel-Kader writes :

> In fact, when we study the Rasā'il (letters) of Junayd, we find what seems to be Neo-Platonic elements. To give a few examples only : The theory of the pre-existence and post-existence of the soul before and after life in this earthly body, as the reason for the longing of the soul in man to return to its origin. The nature of the "first separation from God" and of the "second separation" after mystical union, the deep search into the problem of essence and attributes, and of reality. God is the only reality, we are but phenomenal. Human attributes are only impressions (rasm) and ephemeral, mirroring faintly God's attributes, which are eternal.[5]

Al-Kindī and others before Junayd had access to materials translated first into Syriac by Christian Neo-Platonists, and indeed had direct contact with some of those translators. And it is difficult to think that even those non-Christian philosophers who fled to Iran/Persia when Justinian closed the Platonic Academy left nothing behind. Though in many other contexts we have mentioned these themes, it might be re-emphasized that the chief channel through which all this influence had flowed was John Philopon, who is usually classified as more of an Aristotelian than a (Neo-) Platonist; nevertheless, his Neo-Aristotelianism was more on the order of what may be found in Iamblichus and Porphyry and for the most part his roots are really in Proclus, the chief of the later Neo-Platonists. As a matter of fact, there is much even in Ibn Sīnā that is really Neo-Platonist, even though he is usually thought of as a prince of the long line of Muslim Aristotelians.

Neo-Platonic influence is very obvious in Ibn 'Arabī, Suhrawardī, and many others, although the extent of such influence is still a matter of controversy as concerns the earlier period before the time of Junayd and al-Ḥallāj. As Abdel-Kader notes, there are some unmistakable parallels if not direct influences in Junayd also. He also claims that the possible references and/or allusions are remarkably free of Christian coloring, so that "What we find appears to be a sum of pure and classical Neo-Platonic ideas, not blended with any other elements so characteristic for the later evolution of Neo-Platonism in Eastern Christian thought."[6] But in spite of obvious indirect influence, Junayd evidently had access to no actual texts of Plotinus.

Abdel-Kader puts very heavy stress on the theism of Junayd as opposed to what we have long since designated as the panpsychism of Plotinus : "Al-Junayd's idea of God shows no influence whatever of the Greek philosophy. His faith in God is purely Islamic; God all-present, creating, preserving, active, victorious, ever near to man, is the idea of God in the Qur'ān... No external philosophical influence can be assumed as an explanation of this development."[7] The question then naturally arises, given this radical difference (which of course is shared by Christians to a very great extent), by virtue of what were the Ṣūfīs attracted to such views as are inherent in the Neo-Platonic tradition ? The answer is basically simple : the emphasis on unity. Of course the Qur'anic tradition always intended the unicity of God rather than any panpsychism, much less pantheism. Nevertheless, the references in the Qur'ān are not systematic in the philosophical sense but given ecstatically and rather at random. So it was only natural that the Neo-Platonic unitive way did give an at least apparent support to the Qur'anic revelation. As Abdel-Kader writes : "The contact of the early Muslim mystics with Neo-Platonic philosophy made possible the development of a mystical system in Islam, with its discipline and its terminology, thus giving the opportunity for the emergence of mystical schools around the personalities of the early and later Ṣūfī thinkers."[8]

Fakhry gives us the following overview of Junayd's teachings and the further development of Islamic mysticism :

Conscious of the hazards inherent in mysticism, al-Junayd declared mystical knowledge to be circumscribed by the Koran and the Traditions. This did not bar him, however, from defining clearly the conditions of mystical union, which he fully understood though he never experienced. The starting point of his mysticism is the divine covenant (*mīthāq*) God concluded with man (Koran 7, 171) before creating him. Man's intellectual and mystical vocation consists in the progressive apprehension of his essence as an idea in the divine mind prior to his creation in time, and the abysmal difference between his essence and God's. This isolation of the eternal from the temporal (*ifrād*) is for al-Junayd the token of the genuine recognition of God's unity (*tauḥīd*), as indeed of any genuine knowledge of God. However, such knowledge is not by itself capable of bringing man to his final goal whereby he is lifted above the precepts of the law and brought so close to God that "he is reduced to dust, killed, buried, and later, if it pleases Him, resuscitated." Once this isolation of the temporal from the eternal has been completed and the creature has been reduced to his primordial condition as an idea in the mind of God, man becomes dead unto himself and alive unto God and this, as al-Junayd has put it, is the essence of the mystical experience.

Those two concepts of isolating the human from the divine and the reduction of man to his original condition of not-being or preexistence in the mind of God are symptomatic of the gradual maturation and sophistication of *Ṣūfism*. Having grown out of the ascetic ideal and the need to inject a new sense of inwardness into the ritualism of worship, *Ṣūfism* now felt the urge to break loose completely, to soar aloft into the vast spaces of spiritual experience.[8]

Although al-Ḥallāj is counted as a pupil of al-Junayd, he nevertheless strongly disapproved of al-Ḥallāj's excesses. The emphasis lies in Junayd's teaching of 'sobriety' whereas Ḥallāj was of those who affirmed 'intoxication' as the way to *fanā*' and *baqā*. Although all Ṣūfīs centered their whole Way on *tawḥīd* (the assertion of God's unity or unicity), some went to extremes more than others, whereas especially in his older and more mature days Junayd seems to have avoided those extremes. Hujwīri wrote of Junayd and his school :

> Al-Junayd and his followers prefer Sobriety to Intoxication. They say that Intoxication is evil, because it involves the disturbance of one's normal state and the loss of sanity and self-control; and, inasmuch as the principle of all things is sought, either by way of annihilation or subsistence, of effacement or affirmation, the principle of verification cannot be attained unless the seeker is sane....
>
> My teacher, who followed the doctrine of al-Junayd, used to say that Intoxication is the playing-ground of children, but Sobriety is the battle-field of struggle and death of men. I say, in agreement with my teacher, that the perfection of the state of the man who has been Intoxicated is Sobriety.[10]

In his intensive scholarly modesty Junayd was prudent even to the point of timidity, whereas Ḥallāj, like Bisṭāmī, was far more outspoken, especially on points that might be taken as heretical. But this is a major aspect of Junayd's Way. For in the stages of the mystical path, prudence, stability and harmony of the whole come after the various stages of ecstasy and dejection and should not be taken as lack of ardor. The greatest saints in all faiths have not been people floating in a cloud of incense as some iconography has depicted far too many of them. Rather they have an uncanny *sense of reality* such that without calculation or deliberation they know immediately what are the essential factors in any situation, and especially in dealing with people they have the capacity to penetrate hypocrisy in a liberating way. When one meets such a person, all efforts at deception, even for the sake of being 'polite', are discarded as useless weapons in the house of a friend.

All Ṣūfīs meditate, and Junayd, like Bisṭāmī or Ḥallāj, is no exception. But meditate on what? There is a constant danger in meditation as may be seen, for example, in the decadent cycle of the Neo-Taoists or in the Zen monasteries of the later T'ang Dynasty. If meditation becomes completely subjective and introspective to the exclusion of all structure, pathology is always a very real risk, or else meaningless infatuation with one's own psycho-physical delicacies and sensitivities, which then may be taken as spiritual states though they certainly are not. Whether some Ṣūfīs less well known had already got caught in that trap or not, Junayd gives a marked remedy : meditation should be on the primordial Covenant. Even Ḥallāj had that maturity—a neat warning lest we misinterpret Ḥallāj, by the way. This primordial Covenant is conceived by Junayd as the declaration of love anticipated which God Himself had made in our name. Thus it only remains for us to rediscover and to recover in ourselves this pure Word of acquiescence to the Divine Will; and the way to do that is simply to submit to a rigorous but progressive detachment from all memory, intelligence and will in order eventually to attain "the annihilation of That on which we think".

Junayd teaches that thanks to an amorous predilection for divine providence there are men invested even with the secret of revelation and admitted to an experiential taste of the successive stages of the prophetic vocation. Concerning the relation between the prophetic and the mystical vocation, on the one hand one can simply distinguish them as types on par with each other in excellence but different in function, the mystic emphasizing the upward path of the soul whereas the prophetic emphasizes the message given by God (often unwanted!) to His chosen ones. The avatār and/or Bodhisattva constitutes perhaps a third type wherein God Himself comes down in self-manifestation "to restore *Dharma*". Nevertheless there are always those, especially in Islam, who claim that the prophetic is higher than the mystic vocation—so much so that it is extremely dangerous to admit that the mystic could ever approach the state of prophethood much less attain to it by his own merit. In the distinction between the Bodhisattva state and the full Buddha-hood that according to the *Lotus Sūtra* is latent in all of us we might find a similar parallel, although the trend towards syncretism, especially in Chinese Buddhism, tended to diminish the distinction whereas in Islam through the many centuries to come we shall see this difference exaggerated. In short, Junayd here is treading on the same dangerous ground as Ḥallāj.

One of the highly controversial points not only in the face of ultra-orthodox rigidity but also among Ṣūfīs themselves was concerning the nature of human love for God. Could love of the undefinable, purely non-physical Deity on the part of man have anything resembling physical passion or even human affection? This is a point much debated in Christian mysticism ranging from, for example, Bernard of Clairvaux's allegories on the highly erotic *Song of Songs* in the Old Testament to the bizarre antics of such as Jacapone da Todi. And we do not have to look very far in the Ālvārs and Nāyanmārs, not to mention some forms of Tantra, to find some downright vivid eroticism focussed on the Divine. The key term here is *maḥabba*, which was spoken of by Qushayrī as

> ... a condition which man feels in his heart, too subtle to be expressed in words. This subtle spiritual state leads the worshipper to recognize the greatness of God, instills in him the desire, above all things, to please God, makes him unable to tolerate God's absence, induces in him constant excitement about the thought of God; he finds no rest without God and feels an intimate comfort in continual thought of Him.... If the lover were described as submerged in the beloved, it would be more adequate than if they were described as being together.[11]

In all heritages such extremes of the *bhakti* way have always been suspect by the ultra-orthodox, so it is not surprising that even Junayd suffered some persecution.

"For Bisṭāmī in his elevated state the ephemeral world took on divinity whereas for al-Junayd in his elevated state the ephemeral world did not exist."[12] For Junayd the state of the highest attainment was trans-worldly and undifferentiated, whereas that of Bisṭāmī was a sort of transformation or almost transfiguration. Thus Junayd in this regard might be closer to the Advaitin tradition and hence comparable perhaps to Padmapāda or even Vācaspati Miśra, whereas Bisṭāmī resembles more something in the Viśiṣṭādvaita tradition for which the world of creation is an embodiment of God and thus pervaded with His glorious and auspicious qualities.

The primary interest in Junayd is with the stages and states of the mystical life, the mystogogical path as the Byzantines called it. His *Dawā al-arwāḥ* constructs the first dynamic synthesis of the Qur'ān conceived as a manual of ascension towards God. Typical of Junayd is his distinction of levels of realization of the ultimate unicity : "Know that Tawḥīd is found in four stages in people. The first is the Tawḥīd of the ordinary people; the second is the Tawḥīd of those who are well versed in formal religious knowledge. The third and fourth stages are experienced by the elect who have esoteric knowledge (*ma'rifa*)."[13] *Mīthāq* is roughly equated with the final or esoteric realization of *tawḥīd* just prior to *fanā'* and *baqā*, entailing the realization by man of his place before God. Junayd wrote :

> In this state He has full possession of them and has destroyed their individuality and has removed their characteristics as we perceive it.
>
> This is because Existence after complete suppression of person is not the same as normal existence. The ultimate Truth of God is now refulgent and His Victory is complete.
>
> It is for this reason that we said, that when God granted existence to His worshippers, He caused, as it were, His desire to flow over them according to His Will.[14]

This could not by any means be interpreted in terms of any strict Advaita, in spite of some popular apologetics in comparative studies that Advaita and Ṣūfism are "exactly" the same. Rather perhaps Junayd here would be closer to Bhāskara or even Nimbārka since the difference between God and His worshippers is stressed perhaps more than even in Viśiṣṭādvaita.

Junayd uses the term *fanā'* only as a correlative way to *tawḥīd*, parallel with *Mīthāq* : "Both Mīthāq and Fanā' are different approaches to Tawḥīd, the former explaining the state of Return to God, the latter describing the way, method, training and successive steps to attain this state.... So in fact, the two theories are mutually complementary."[15] Junayd distinguishes three stages, thus making it clear that he is a 'gradualist' rather than a 'suddenist'—if we may interpolate those terms from Ch'an/Zen tradition, supposing that the way of 'intoxication' might be more similar than Junayd's 'sobriety' way.

> First : "The obliteration of attributes, characteristics and natural qualities in your motives when you carry out your religious duties, making great efforts and doing the opposite of what you may desire, and compelling yourself to do the things which you do not wish to do."
>
> Second : "The obliteration of your pursuit after pleasures and even the sensation of pleasure in obedience to God's behests—so that you are exclusively His, without any intermediary means of contact."
>
> Third : "The obliteration of the consciousness of having attained the vision of God at the final stage of ecstasy when God's victory over you is complete. At this stage you are obliterated and have eternal life with God, and you exist only in the existence of God because you have been obliterated. Your physical being continues but your individuality has departed."[16]

One does not have to look to any form of Buddhism, not even the great Bodhisattva Vow, for parallels since this looks very closely parallel with the Way designated under the Vow of Holy Obedience in Benedictine tradition, soon to be elaborated in the famous *Steps of Humility* by Bernard of Clairvaux. "*Fanā*' is not merely the cessation of self, like the Buddhist *nirvāṇa*, but...it includes the continuation of the worshipper's self in God"[17]—and in that respect Junayd may be closer to the Rām-ānuja tradition than to Advaita.

Balā' means the "veil" that still conceals the Deity even after individuality has been lost so that there is a painful longing for complete union, the remaining sense of separation sometimes being almost unbearable. This became extremely exaggerated in later centuries among both the followers of Caitanya and the Carmellites, and it was not unknown among the Ālvārs and Nāyanmārs still singing in South India during Junayd's time.

> They are consumed with longing for Him who has brought them Balā', and moan constantly in this second loss of their individuality... They grieve, suffering deeply as they seek after God.... This thirst for God is an anguish even more intense than the mourning for a beloved one.

> The soul accepts the spiritual burden with its implication of suffering, seeks for its cure, and is preoccupied with that divine revelation vouchsafed to it.... Though the soul has Balā', it is not rejected. How can it be hidden from God by a veil when it is, as it were, a captive bound before Him ? God has allowed the suppression of the individuality when man has Balā'. The soul no longer arrogates a degree of importance to its individuality but is amply satisfied with God's love and nearness. ...
>
> As a result, the soul derives spiritual pleasures from Balā' and is delighted with its Balā' with God, because it can enjoy propinquity with God and the wound of Balā' is soothed. The soul is not bent down under the burden of Balā' nor does it chafe at its spiritual load. Their experience makes heroes of them—because of the secrets revealed to them they stay conquered by God, awaiting His commands, that Allah may designate what shall be done.[18]

Not only Junayd but virtually all the mystics in all heritages have attested to this really *heroic* spiritual effectiveness.

There is the possibility of a two-level mode of operation in Junayd, one for esoteric personal practice and another for bublic teaching. Evidently Ḥallāj did not observe the needed prudence in regard to the latter, but Junayd did in realization that the masses need simpler forms of observance than those who have the freedom for total abandon to the interior life of renunciation. We are reminded of essentially the same sort of duplicity that had emerged in Chinese Buddhism also, and which had grown so wide that Tsung-mi had been puzzled by it so intensively that he tried to rationalize it by a sort of philosophy of history, claiming that the Buddha had taught different things for different people and periods in history.

There is a notion sometimes proposed that esoterics flourish during periods of "failure of nerve" and are "escapist". On the other hand there is also the counter-assertion that in times when materialistic values dominate the culture in general, such, mysticisms will spring up as "counter-cultures" and even in some instances may become the "creative minority" from which a whole civilization might recover its true identity and vitality.

But neither of these theories seems to fit the situation in Baghdad in its apogée. Rather it appears that excellence in esoterics develops largely *in concomitance*, parallel with and right along with, or even in dialectical interplay with, the other types of philosophy, from empirical science through realism and idealism, and from heresies on the extreme of rationality to heresies on the opposite extreme of intuitionism.

Although Junayd had the typical way of expressing himself, as almost all mystics in all traditions do, in aphorisms and metaphors rather than in architectonically constructed *summas* such as we later find in Ibn Sīnā and Ibn Rushd, the comprehensiveness of his heritage left him free to range as widely as he wished. That Junayd systematized the Ṣūfī tradition enough to incorporate within it (rather than in opposition to it) the more limited 'orthodox' views of such as al-Ash'arī is evidence that he was indeed a structured philosopher and not merely a charismatic religious figure or even an ecstatic mystic who had no philosophical grounding. Ṣūfī ways and thinking may have seemed inordinately unorthodox to his contemporaries, but Abdel-Kader remarks that Junayd joined

> ...the many wild mountain streams of Ṣūfism into a firm and constant river-bed. He, in fact, has jointed and united Mysticism with Orthodoxy. He is thus rightly called the "Shaykh al-Ṭarīqa", the "Master of the Way". Through him, we may say, Ṣūfism reached fulfillment.
>
> For this Junayd has been accepted and praised by all authorities in Islam, Mystics and conservative Orthodox alike. They have called him the "Scholarly Ṣūfī", the "Chief of the Community", the "peacock among the divines". Even traditionalists like Ibn Taymīya and Ibn al-Qauuim, who were very anti-Ṣūfī, accepted his authority and appreciated his ṭarīqa and spoke highly of him.[19]

It may well be that in making Ṣūfism acceptable among the orthodox mullas, Junayd compromised somewhat its vivid mission; but on the other hand, scholar that he was, it may be equally argued that rather, without compromising any basics of Ṣūfī tradition, he proved that it was not so heretical as some extremists among the literalists would like to assert.

It might be said that Junayd's spirituality was too deep and too mature to be sensational. Rather, as Abdel-Kader puts it in conclusion, "...he was a harmonious personality. He was a teacher in the full sense of the word, and he was a true friend. We imagine that he was a man serene, unpretentious and of good cheer, radiating something of his inner life towards those who surrounded him."[20] Junayd had the opinion that the best period of Ṣūfism was behind him and that it had already declined in merit and excellence by the end of his life. Indeed at the time of his death he was rather unhappy about these trends. It is unfortunate that he could not have foreseen the later flowering of the very best of Ṣūfī heritage in Rūmī, Jīli, Jāmi, Sirhindi and others.

5. al-Ḥallāj

One of the most controversial topics in all of Ṣūfī literature, but particularly with al-Ḥallāj (857-922), is the relation between Ṣūfism and Advaita Vedānta and other forms of Hinduism, but also between Ṣūfism and Mahāyāna Buddhism, as well as whether or to what extent Ṣūfism has Neo-Platonic roots. But perhaps it is better not to think of Ḥallāj as specifically a Ṣūfī (though he certainly was that) but, as Apollonius of Tyana, Mani and Mazdak had been in their eras, as a high syncretist, both incorporating and transcending all secularism (perhaps very much like the early founders of the Bahai faith in more recent times). Certainly with Ḥallāj we do have a monist in an extremely monistic mood, in fact about as near to Advaita metaphysics as anyone could come, and, at least in manner of expression, outstripping most of his Byzantine, Syrian, and Coptic Monophysite Christian contemporaries, even those involved in the Hesychast controversy. The earliest stages of the *bhakti* movement in South India in the classical Tamil heritage manifest some similar characteristics. Although there is strong evidence that his heritage mostly goes back to Neo-Platonism and Hermetic tradition, Ḥallāj can also be made out as much more 'conservative' in his almost total dependence on and obedience to the Qur'ān itself.

One may correctly view Ḥallāj's martyrdom in a way that is more in imitation of Christ than a following of the Prophet Muḥammad. Discarding all possible animus between Christians and Muslims still persisting in the world today, historically one gets the increasing impression that whereas Ḥallāj may have gotten something of yogic technique from India, and although indeed he justifies his way from the mentions of Jesus in the Qur'ān itself, there are other traits which seem to have come from contact with Syrian Christians and possibly also Manichaeans. Thus again we should like to inquire Socratically whether he should be taken merely as an eminent Ṣūfī as such, or as a sort of successor to Mani and Mazdak : a synthesizer of the basics of all that was available in Eurasia at the turn of the century around 900 A.D.

Ḥallāj is certainly pre-eminently outstanding in the history of Islam as well as in the history of Ṣūfism in a way comparable not so much to Śaṅkara as to Vācaspati Miśra. The Ṣūfīs before Ḥallāj expressed their experiences in cruder forms with less realization of the dialogical import of their theological boldness. Ḥallāj, however, not only had intensive experience but knew what he was talking about in its full implication in psychology, theology and philosophy in general.

Virtually everyone treats Ḥallāj as a very colorful and independent character, extreme in his ways and yet not necessarily at the furthest extreme of some Ṣūfī ways. Fakhry gives us this introduction :

> When al-Basṭāmī was accused of laxity in the performance of his ritual duties, we are told, he resorted to the expedient which other *Ṣūfīs* also employed : affected madness. This device apparently saved his life as well as the life of numerous fellow *Ṣūfīs*.
>
> There was one ninth-century *Ṣūfī*, however, who was not willing to resort to this dodge, and the price he paid for his extravagances was very dear. Al-Ḥusain b. Manṣūr al-Ḥalāj was born around 858 in a small town called al-Bayḍā, not far from the eastern shores of the Persian Gulf. His

> *Ṣūfī* teachers included al-Makkī (d. 909), al-Tustarī (d. 986), al-Shiblī (d.945), and al-Junayd, four of the greatest figures in the whole history of *Ṣūfism*. It was apparently al-Junayd who induced al-Ḥallāj to wear the woollen garment (*ṣūf*). He served as his spiritual director for twenty years but was aware of the hyperbolic strain in his character and eventually broke with him because of his arrogance, we are told.[1]

As an example of his hyperbolic strain, Fakhry relates how Ḥallāj remained immobile in a mosque for a whole year! Unappreciative observers are reported to have remarked, "This man in his folly is out to rival God in his capacity for endurance." Further, Ḥallāj would sleep either standing or squatting, and then for only about an hour at a time. Al-Junayd reproved Ḥallāj for his misunderstanding the way of 'intoxication', but to no avail. Instead Ḥallāj broke with the monastic orders and began public preaching, even becoming involved in dangerous political causes.

Fakhry explains the change which Ḥallāj experienced during his third pilgrimage to Mecca :

> The change appears to have been marked by a clearer and firmer sense of his identification with God, with whom he now entered into a more intimate personal converse, as it were. This condition of personal communion with the I-Thou is what he called the "essence of union" (*'ain al-jam'*), in which all the actions, thoughts, and aspirations of the mystic are wholly permeated by God. But, according to him, this union did not result, as it had in the case of al-Basṭāmī, in the total destruction or nullification of the self, but rather, in its elevation to joyful and intimate communion with the Beloved.[2]

While an intense love for and intimacy with God is characteristic of most if not all Ṣūfīs, few would go so far as to publicly exclaim (without feigning madness) the famous words *ana al-Haqq* (I am the Creative Truth). The charge of blasphemy against Ḥallāj was inevitable given his active temperament, but evidently there were political aspects also in his final condemnation.

Although the official charge against al-Ḥallāj was his claim to be God and to have the authority to free the pious of the ritual prescriptions of the Islamic law, political sedition was a decisive factor in his final torture and execution. As regards the charge of self-deification, it is noteworthy that when confronted with statements he had made and in which he spoke on behalf of God in the first person, he defended himself on the ground that this practice was perfectly compatible with the *Ṣūfī* doctrine of "essence of union", a mystical condition in which it is God who writes or speaks through the mystic, who is simply His instrument. But his accusers, especially the vizier Ḥāmid, would not hear of such theological subtlety, and although he had been ordered to be whipped and decapitated by the caliph, in an excess of zeal the vizier ordered him to be whipped, mutilated, crucified, decapitated, cremated, and his remains scattered to the four winds. Nothing like this had ever happened in the whole history of Muslim piety.[3]

Of course the career of Ḥallāj served as a warning to others, even though his "crucifixion has been looked at by the Sunni Ṣūfīs as the height (*mi'rāj*) of saintship; and many beautiful utterances are ascribed to al-Ḥallāj while on the stake."[4] According to Fakhry, "The great figures in the history of post-Ḥallājian mysticism, such as al-Ghazālī and Ibn 'Arabī, addressed themselves primarily to the task of systematization of synthesis."[5]

In consonance with the *nirguṇa* problem in Advaita Vedānta, and as the primary evidence of the monist tendency of the epoch, we could follow Ḥallāj's treatment of the attributes of Allah; but here his mysticism varies only in subtle details from that of his Muslim contemporaries, notably those involved in the Ash'arite-Mu'tazilite controversy, and the difficulty all non-literalist interpreters had in the face of the ultraorthodox Sunni Mutakallimūn. His epistemology largely only reiterates the *ascesis*, since for all great mystics nothing is really known except through and in the Vision of God as the only perfect Knower. With his theodicy and eschatology too, the *via negativa* is the key to the whole situation.

The doctrine of human nature is one topic which is universal and never becomes obsolete. If one could overlook (or look through rather than at) Ḥallāj's theological technicalities, one might find, as for example Iqbal did in the first part of the twentieth century, quite a bit of spirit in common between Ḥallāj and Nietzsche and Kierkegaard. By Ḥallāj's time a controversy had emerged out of varying interpretations of the Qur'ān as to the degree to which human action is predestined and under the complete omnipotence of God, and the extent to which it is free or capable of becoming free—the doctrine of providence, in short, over against the doctrine of human responsibility. Evidently the key to this problem for Ḥallāj lies not so much in dialectical juggling of arguments as in the human heart itself. Massignon writes :

> In summary, the Qur'ān makes the Heart the principle of knowledge (science) and of awareness (conscience) since nothing is retained in it in an irreversible and irremedial dissipation of its resources (gestures, sensations, etc. included) man cannot get complete control of himself except in his *taquib*—in the inner resources of his heart...
>
> Hence, what one can say is that the Qur'ān itself poses the fundamental problem of the 'Science of the Hearts' and of the purification of the Act of Faith ...
>
> Ḥallāj attempted to describe this last operation : the ultimate envelope of the heart, beyond the *nafs*, the concupiscible appetite, is the *sirr*, the latent personality, the implicit consciousness, a profound subconscious level, a secret cell immured in every (human) creature; the "inviolate virgin".
>
> Even though God should never visit the *sirr*, or even an angel, or even (the holiest) man, this latent personality of man would remain informed (of its own nature)...
>
> Whenever man accepts renunciation of this ultimate envelope of the heart, God will make it fecund, and will make it penetrate the *damīr*, its explicit definitive personality, its legitimate personal pronoun, the right to say 'I', the right which united the saint with the source even of the divine Word, His own *Fiat*.[6]

This last is like St. Paul's "now no longer I, but Christ in me" or like the *ātman*-Brahman equation. Of course Ḥallāj must be classed with the grace philosophers, like the Amida Buddhists, rather than with those, like orthodox Theravāda Buddhists, who depend on effort and faith alone.

Rather than mysticism and politics being poles apart, in the case of Ḥallāj they went hand in hand, but also in the case of the Hesychast controversy in Byzantium and of Ch'an Buddhism in the period of transition between the T'ang and Sung Dynasties, not to mention the little heeded social and political implications of Śaṅkara's reforms—all not too long distant chronologically from Ḥallāj's own time. Just as an orthodox Christian cannot ignore the dogma of the Church as the Body of Christ and no true Buddhist can neglect the *saṅgha*, so also no Muslim, whether Sunni, Shī'a or Ṣūfī, can ignore the concept of Islam as universal brotherhood-in-unity of all mankind under the one God Allah. The Ṣūfī orders in Islam played and continue to play a role no less significant than the monastic orders in both Byzantine-Russian and Latin Christianity, not to mention the Buddhist monastic system in all of East and Southeast Asia.

As we have long since seen in the case, for example, of John Philopon, the *ex nihilo* controversy in Christian and Islamic theology and cosmology constituted a matter of bitter dispute and a rather marked difference between those heritages and the Indic and Sinic world-views wherein the question really never arose since these things were considered to be beyond man's capacity to know with certainty and therefore were treated mythologically, poetically, or simply as a matter of awe and wonder. Another radical difference which cannot be easily ignored is that of the fiat-once-and-for-all Creation idea in the Judeo-Christian-Islamic traditions as distinct from the view of vast cosmic cycles of involution and evolution in the Indic traditions. Since Ḥallāj did get some sort of training in yoga while in India, we wonder whether closer examination of the text might reveal some hints of his awareness of these differences. Moreover, the question might be mooted whether mystical traditions find more compatibility with the eternalist and cyclist views than with the unique fiat views, since the former are obviously more compatible with monistic pantheism and the latter only with transcendental theism of the prophetic rather than the mystic type.

Ḥallāj is one of those rare figures whose philosophy was demonstrated as much by his life as by his writings. He really was a philosopher in the full sense, given his historical milieu, and not merely an erratic, naive mystic. He is not "just another Ṣūfī" on the very long list of those who have become famous for the beauty of their literary remains and similar reasons; but in the line of Mani and Mazdak, Ḥallāj is really a pivotal intercultural figure, syncretistic withall, and perhaps another of these missing links in our chain of communications whereby we can get some hints of how it is that there have been so many parallel developments in the history of ideas all across Eurasia.

Kaśmir, which is the only part of India we are certain Ḥallāj visited, was definitely a stronghold of the Vijñānavāda heritage from Śāntarakṣita, Kamalaśīla and Dharmottara. There were also Śaiva thinkers who had preceded Abhinavagupta's Kaśmir Śaivism, which was primarily an attempt at incorporating the dynamism of the Buddhist heritage into Hindu orthodoxy. During this epoch Kaśmir was as intellectual center of very high calibre, attracting scholars and thinkers from all directions—and also exporting them, not only to Tibet but far and wide around Eurasia. By the time of Ḥallāj Islam had made some initial inroads on India, including Kaśmir. The first raids were carried out as much as a century and half before Ḥallāj's visit. Moreover, he was not unique among Iranian or Arab Muslim intellectuals in his travel, al-Mas'ūdī and Abu Zaid Ḥasan having made their sojourns around 916, only ten or so years after Hallāj's visit.

Ḥallāj was searching for ways to go to China, which, however, was in a difficult position since the Central Asian peoples were making increasingly heavy bargains with the decadent T'ang Dynasty. By this time they had become almost as advanced in their civilization as the Chinese and the Persians themselves. Incidentally, many of those were either Manichaeans or Nestorian Christians. The Turkish race was then enjoying a considerable apogée thanks largely to increased bargaining power with the falling T'ang Dynasty as well as with their western neighbors in Iran. They also capitalized considerably on the trade along the centuries-old silk routes between China and

Byzantium, for Byzantium was very avid about Chinese goods. Not only exotic goods travelled the silk routes but also wandering monks of various faiths, including Mahâyāna Buddhists, Nestorian and Monophysite Christians, and more recently a few Ṣūfīs.

The abiding influence of Ḥallāj in this Central Asian area is pivotal for any cultural history from well before the Muslim expansion right down to the time of the eastern Europeans' preference for the sea routes for trans-Eurasian commerce and communication. Indeed, there is evidence of definite cults evidently honoring or even reverencing Ḥallāj as a sort of prophet or Bodhisattva, although the variations of these cults range from extreme reverence to fear of him as a satanic magician. Massignon writes that Ḥallāj "established not only the definitive orientation of ideal Turkish poetics, but also he may have been even the source of the inspiration for the eventual Turkish conquest of Constantinople..." So, to say the least, Ḥallāj was much more of a charismatic prophet than a completely other-worldly escapist or 'oriental mystic'.

Like many of the Ṣūfīs after him, Ḥallāj wrote most of his thoughts and meditations in poetic form. According to universal acclaim, it was definitely he who set the style for Ṣūfī poetry which still survives and is positively cultivated from North Africa to the Philippines. But he was much more than merely a literary figure. This is not the place to consider again what constituted a philosopher around 900 A.D. But certainly if several centuries later Giordano Bruno is called a philosopher, then surely there can be no objection to giving that name to al-Ḥallāj Manṣūr.

6. al-Rāzi

Although no less a philosopher than others who contributed to the emergence and development of Islamic scholasticism, Abū Bakr Muhammad b. Zakariyā al-Rāzī (864?-933) has been accepted almost exclusively as a scientist and physician. The stereotype of Rhazes (as he was known in Latin Europe) as a physician only goes back very far in medieval Europe. But fortunately many historians have begun to break through that image, including Henri Corbin, whose study of the Ismā'li tradition within Islam along with other varieties of Iranian Muslim esoterics has enabled him to see al-Rāzī in a new light. Corbin observes that it is very likely that al-Rāzī and al-Ḥallāj were not only acquainted but may even have been friends.[1] This is significant because of the notion that mysticism and science have nothing whatsoever to do with each other, not only in the present but historically. This prejudice needs some re-evaluation not only in the historical perspective but also by a more critical review of Sorokin's observations of a "sudden enlightenment" experience, usually in youth, of most geniuses including many if not most famous scientists of recent times.

In his early life al-Rāzī was a jeweler, money-changer and/or lute player according to different accounts. Evidently the divisions of such occupations were not as sharp in his time and milieu as now since both the music and the jewelry probably had to do with his interest in ulchemy. At the age of forty he forsook alchemy because experiments gave him some trouble with his eyes; so he went in search of physicians and took up the study of medicine himself. In the course of time he opened a hospital in his native city of Ray, later moving to Baghdad and opening another hospital there. Later he returned to his native place and began teaching. Traditional lore reports that his students were organized into different 'circles', each progressively closer to the Master. Though he had many students, some of whom became rather famous, he never gave up his medical practice. Eventually he went blind, evidently from cataracts, but he refused to be treated since "he had seen so much of the world that he was fed up": but other more sober accounts simply say he knew he would die soon anyway, which he did.

Al-Rāzī's famous treatise on measles and smallpox had a notable history in Latin Europe, continuing to be popular there until as late as the eighteenth century. His *Kitāb al-Hāwī* known as the *Continens* was "the most voluminous medical work ever written in Arabic."[2] It was translated into Latin along with the works of Ibn Rushd and was held in higher esteem than the works of Hippocartes and Galen. Psychosomatic and Psychological aspects receive heavy emphasis in al-Rāzī's medical practice, due no doubt to his reliance on Galen, who also had stressed the emotional and other psychological aspects of health and therapy.

Alchemy in its long history was concerned not only with chemicals and the esoteric search for the philosopher's stone and the attempt to synthesize gold and such like things that later earned it a bad reputation, but was concerned also if not primarily with spiritual matters, indeed the total transformation of human nature. This applied as much to the Muslim alchemists as to the old Roman and the Chinese brands of alchemy long before it became a common if not a basic science closely associated with medicine in the Islamic world. Nasr mentions three categories of alchemists, namely those concerned with the inner, those concerned with the outer, and those concerned with both types of transformations. He says that al-'Irāqī belongs to the first, al-Rāzī to the second, and Jābir to the third. Although most of his philosophical works have been lost according to Nasr it can be demonstrated that "his denial of the necessity of revelation is directly connected to the transformation he brought about in the domain of alchemy".[3] Al-Rāzī considered himself as a disciple of Jābir (Gerber), but in alchemy as in medicine and philosophy he was such an original pioneer thinker and scientific experimenter that one could make a very strong case that with him alchemy in Islam had already become scientific chemistry.

The following summation of al-Rāzī's place and value as a thinker is a very bold statement, but it is not made by an overzealous modernist but by a scholar of the first rank :

> Al-Rāzī had no organized system of philosophy, but compared to his time he must be reckoned as the most vigorous and liberal thinker in Islam and perhaps in the whole history of human thought.
>
> He was a pure rationalist, extremely confident in the power

> of reason, free from every kind of prejudice, and very daring in the expression of his ideas without reserve.
>
> He believed in man, in progress, and in God the Wise, but in no religion whatever.[4]

Everyone acknowledges that al-Rāzī's rationalism was quite thorough and complete both in his scientific work and in his philosophy. Indeed, he can be classed as an experimental empiricist.

> Al-Rāzī's exaltation of reason is best expressed on the first page of his *al-Ṭibb al-Rūḥānī*. He says : "God, glorious is His name, has given us reason in order to obtain through it from the present and future the utmost benefits that we can obtain: it is God's best gift to us...By reason we perceive all that is useful to us and all that makes our life good—by it we know obscure and remote things, those which are hidden from us...by it, too, we succeed to the knowledge of God, which is the highest knowledge we can obtain. ...If reason is so highly placed and is of such an important rank, we should not degrade it; we should not make it the judged while it is the judge, or controlled while it is the controller, or commanded while it is the commander; on the contrary, we should refer to it in everything and judge all matters by it; we should do according as it commands us to do."
>
> Even the most rationalistic mind could not exalt reason so clearly and so highly. There is no place for revelation or mystic intuition. It is only logical reason which is the unique criterion of knowledge and conduct. No irrational force can be invoked. Al-Rāzī is against prophecy, against revelation, against all irrational trends of thought.[5]

Al-Rāzī's rejection of prophecy, a horror to the ultra-orthodox Sunni theologian even today, may have been due to the influence of Brahmanism; but whether that might have been Mahāyāna instead is not a matter to quibble about since by the tenth century the difference between them had been so much narrowed. But it is of extreme importance in our wider perspective that even philosophical ideas did travel along with commercial goods and scientific information, and increasingly so throughout these centuries.

For al-Rāzī all men equally have a disposition for knowledge; they differ only in their mode and extent of cultivation of this faculty. Where he might have received this idea could also be a matter of speculation, for Aristotle did not believe this but held that some are born naturally fit to be slaves rather than intellectuals. However, this was a very common teaching in Mahāyāna Buddhism during this epoch and indeed had even become a cornerstone of most Mahāyāna schools. Such a doctrine can also be found in Mencius and his Neo-Confucianist interpreters, but the likelihood of influence there is not so great.

Al-Rāzī's philosophy divides into the famous Five Principles: Creator, Soul, Matter, Time and Space. Here there is the likelihood of influence from Zurvanite and Manichaean sources, or more likely, Mazdakite sources.

> Al-Rāzī's philosophy is chiefly characterized by his doctrine of the Five Eternals. Al-Bīrūni says that "Muḥammad ibn Zakarīya al-Rāzī has reported from the ancient Greeks the eternity of five things; God, the universal soul, first matter, absolute space, and absolute time, on which he founded his doctrine. But he distinguished between time and duration by saying that number applies to the one and not to the other, because finiteness attains numerality; and, therefore, the philosophers have defined time as the duration of what has a beginning and an end, whereas duration (*dahr*) has neither beginning nor end. He said also that in Being these five are necessary : the sensible in it is the matter formed by composition; it is spatial, so there must be a space ; alternation of its modes is a characteristic of time, because some precede and others follow, and it is by time that oldness, and older and newer and simultaneous are known; so time is necessary. In Being there are living things, so there must be soul; in it there are intelligibles and their constitution is absolutely perfect; there must be then a creator, wise, omniscient, doing things as perfectly as possible, and giving reason for the sake of Salvation."[6]

Al-Rāzī says that God knew that the Soul (the panpsychic or cosmic Soul, not the individual *jīva*) would get mixed up in matter and material pleasure and thus would experience alienation. God also planted intelligence in the Soul so that it would never forget its divine origin and true nature. Thus al-Rāzī's theodicy is of the rationalist Leibnizian type : it is the best of all possible worlds, a completely evil world and a completely good world being impossible, evil being defined as a not-necessary attachment to, but not necessarily a mixture with, matter. Of course such a position generated endless controversy on the part of the ultra-orthodox and no doubt among those unrecorded thinkers who were as radical as al-Rāzī.

With regard to Soul, Badawi has condensed al-Rāzī's views very succinctly as follows :

> God, according to al-Rāzī, has not created the world through any necessity, but He decided to create it after having at first no will to create it. Who determined Him to do so ? There must be another eternal who made Him decide this.
>
> This other eternal is the soul which was living but ignorant. Matter, too, was eternal. Owing to its ignorance, the soul was fond of matter and formed figures from it in order to get material pleasures. But matter was rebellious to forms; so God intervened in order to aid the soul. This aid was that He made this world and created in it strong forms wherein the soul could find corporeal pleasures. God then created man and from the substance of His divinity he created the intelligence of man to awaken the soul and to show to it that this world is not its real world.[7]

Whether there is influence or not, this sounds very much like the basic pattern in Kaśmir Śaivism, that of Abhinavagupta, for example, who was virtually al-Rāzī's contemporary. Since al-Ḥallāj, a friend of al-Rāzī, travelled most likely in Kaśmir and the surrounding area, there is at least the possibility of influence. However, essentially the same pattern is common not only in most of the Purāṇas in India but also in the Gnostics and Manichaeans and others influenced directly by the syncretisms of the later Roman Empire, especially Neo-Platonism and Neo-Pythagoreanism.

This concept of the co-eternity of both soul and matter gained al-Rāzī a great reputation as a protagonist to be refuted by scholastics of all three faiths. And there are many points which could be considerably clarified, such as how it could be that matter could be "rebellious" since as such it cannot do or be anything, at least according to the traditional Aristotelian heritage, without mixture with forms and the operation of all the four causes. Given the established position stemming back to Philopon, one wonders whether al-Rāzī here is just a critical genius in his own right or again whether he might have been influenced here and elsewhere by Mahāyāna or Kaśmir Śaivism. For one could easily read into this statement a doctrine of *māyā*. It is knowledge (*vidyā*) that gives the soul deliverance from attachment to matter; and although that knowledge must be acquired by the individual mind, there is a sense in which it is given by God. But even more radically like the Kaśmir/Balkh heritages, knowledge is rather a removal of ignorance than an addition of information.

In other words salvation for al-Rāzī is a matter of awakening or enlightenment rather than a matter of faith or grace; and again this sounds very Indic rather than Qur'anic, even though dialectically it also sounds remotely Socratic. We know for certain that, like al-Kindī, al-Rāzī was an admirer of Socrates—the Hellenistic Socrates rather than the Socrates of modern European philologists. Given that al-Rāzī was a friend of al-Ḥallāj, that he was familiar with those parts of the *materia medica* derived from India and/or China as well as the Indian influence on Muslim mathematics during his own lifetime, and given his independent spirit, again the thesis of Śaiva or Mahāyāna influence looks very attractive.

Matter according to al-Rāzī is co-eternal with God, so that he denies the *ex nihilo* dogma. It is composed of atoms, which have volume, and qualities such as heaviness, levity, darkness and luminosity "are to be explained by the more or less vacuity which is within matter. Quality is an accident which is attributed to substance, and substance is matter."[8] The difference between al-Rāzī's atomism and that of the classical Greeks could be accounted for by influence from the critiques of the atomistic concept by the Mahāyāna Buddhists who may have influenced al-Rāzī's teacher, who came from Balkh, which was still a stronghold of Mahāyāna Buddhism.

Al-Rāzī's concept of time is not the same as Aristotle's concept but an absolute time "predating (as a precondition) all motion". Likewise, al-Rāzī's space is not the same as Aristotle's place concept but "the void (*khalā*), capable of harboring matter or of not harboring it, and capable of serving as a metaphysical naught in discussions of ontology".[9] This sounds very much like a slightly altered version of the Mahāyāna critique of Vaiśeṣika, and this becomes even more compelling as the rest of his system is unfolded so that we can at least suggest a parallel even if there is no direct influence. Goodman continues with other contrasts with Aristotle :

> His matter is not Aristotelian matter but atomic, indivisible particles, capable like time and space of being treated as absolute, indeterminate, eternal—and at the same time usable in a contingency argument for the existence of God. Rāzī's Soul is far from being an Aristotelian soul, for it contains an element of irrationality and passion capable of becoming the model of a process which is neither natural nor voluntary in the Aristotelian sense of those terms. For Rāzī's nature is not Aristotle's nature...but a sequence...in which chance and whimsy are at work as well as the reason of a thought which thinks itself; and thus radical change, creation of a sort, is possible.[10]

As for theology, Badawi gives the following reasons for al-Rāzī's rejection of prophetic revelation :

1. Reason is sufficient to distinguish between good and evil, useful and harmful. By reason alone we can know God, and organize our lives in the best way. Why then is there need for prophets?
2. There is no justification for privileging some men for guiding all men, because all men are born equal in intelligence; the differences are not because of natural dispositions, but because of development and education.

3. Prophets contradict one another. If they speak in the name of one and the same God, why this contradiction?[11]

Al-Rāzī, however, did not stop there. He was a severe critic of the religions known to him, including Christianity, Judaism and Manichaeanism. His method is simply to play each against the others in such a way that they tend to cancel each other out. He even sounds quite modern in some of his criticisms.

> He denies especially the miraculousness (*i'jāz*) of the Qur'ān, either because of its style or its contents and affirms that it is possible to write a better book in a better style.
>
> He prefers scientific books to all sacred books, because scientific books are more useful to men in their lives than all sacred books. Books on medicine, geometry, astronomy, and logic are more useful than the Bible and the Qur'ān. The authors of these scientific books have found the facts and truths by their own intelligence, without the help of prophets. Science is drawn from three sources : reasoning, according to logic; tradition, from predecessors to successors according to sure and accurate testimony, as in history; and instinct which guides man without being in need of much reasoning.
>
> After this negative criticism, he goes on to say that it would not even be reasonable of God to send prophets, because they do much harm. Every nation believes only in its own prophets and vehemently denies those of others, with the result that there have been many religious wars and much hatred between nations professing different religions.[12]

Badawi's claim for al-Rāzī within the world of Islam could perhaps be extended to include the whole of Eurasia in the tenth century : "These ideas of al-Rāzī were most audacious. No other Muslim thinker was so daring as he."[13] However, we know much less about the scientists in India and China during al-Rāzī's time; in both cases they seem to have been virtually ignored by the philosophers of their own time and subsequently still do not receive any attention in traditional textbooks on Indian and Chinese philosophy.

As to al-Rāzī's moral philosophy, his own writings include the *al-Ṭibb al-Rūḥāni* and the *al-Sīrat al-Falsafīyyah*, the latter being a sort of *apologia pro vita sua* and the former being a more systematic treatise on ethics as such. In both of these moderation is the norm he claims to have followed and advises others to follow. In order to follow that counsel he claims that he himself declined patronage from affluent monarchs and avoided a military career, finding the medical profession much more compatible with his model, Socrates. Since moderation demands rationality, he puts reason above all other guides. It alone can make judgments about the passions and self-knowledge and even about how to balance pleasure, which he defines as a "return to nature", and pain, which he says is not wholly evil and depends on the cause, which reason alone can tell us. But reason must balance the virtues as well as control the vices, and it is only by reason that we can know the difference between virtue and vice, much less classify and systematize the different virtues which under certain circumstances conflict with each other. Thus al-Rāzī is not completely puritanical even about telling lies; the motive is what, rationally, makes the differences.

Concerning death, al-Rāzī is rationally detached. There is no use in getting upset about the inevitable. Our attention should be devoted to cultivating the present life to the best of our ability. If there is reward after death, that is the only way to earn it; and even if there isn't still one's time here will not have been wasted if others benefit. So why worry, since worrying about death can be worse than death itself!

According to the traditional image al-Rāzī looked to philosophy as a "way of life" and not as an academic profession. One might almost call him *neo-hellenistic*. He cultivated the lives and examples as well as the technical teachings of the philosophers, notably Socrates. But emphatically not in the same mode as the other *Falsafah* philosophers who were, as Goodman puts it, already hampered from originality by their "hide-bound conservatism". He was by no means merely an admiring "cultivator of the ancients", as were most of his Byzantine contemporaries, for example. Goodman writes : "In no sphere of his philosophical endeavor was Rāzī's spirit of independence more clearly manifested than in his ethics. For both in principle and in practice (which Rāzī avers to have modelled not upon the example of "*the* philosophers" but upon the pattern of his theory) Rāzī was an Epicurean."[14]

Al-Rāzī rejected outright the asceticism that had been ascribed to Socrates, who in Hellenistic tradition had become confused with the Cynic Diogenes. Rāzī knew that Socrates had gone to war, begat children, attended the theater, ate well and drank wine, as we know from Plato's *Symposium*, all with moderation and under rational control. Given his limited information about Socrates, al-Rāzī was much more impressed with the mature philosophic Socrates than with the youthful experimenter with every sort of doctrine and practice. The temptation is very strong with all interpreters to read into al-Rāzī's rational moderation something of the Golden Mean ethics of Aristotle; but Goodman warns us against that stereotype. For the Aristotelian type of moderation is not based on a calculus of pleasure but on a sort of logically calculated deontology of practical reason. Even though one might well read Stoicism from Galen into that picture, Goodman avers that al-Rāzī was an Epicurean.

First and foremost philosophy for al-Rāzī was the Platonic Socrates' search for truth, and not a matter of juggling of definitions in the 'peripatetic' fashion. As an open enquiry there is no necessity of positing a metaphysical dogma about the unity of all virtues. Rather, by way of concrete examples from his medical practice, he teaches that one should judge each individual situation on its own estimated long-term results. Goodman observes that "thus ethics has returned, by a long and circuitous route, to the hedonic base which it had been Plato's purpose, and after him that of Aristotle to transcend. The Socratic 'tendance of the soul' has become a 'spiritual physic'."[15]

Al-Rāzī defines vice not as excess of virtue as Aristotle did, much less as the depravity of human nature and disobedience to the revealed Will of Allah as was the case with some 'fundamentalist' Muslims in his environment, but simply as the free reign of desires. Goodman even claims that "the nerve of his ethical argumentation is prudential, hedonistic, or utilitarian—all three of which are merely different aspects of the hedonistic point of view, varying only as the subject under consideration is treated in terms of safety, pleasure, or profit ...."[16] Moreover the calculation of pleasure must be not only in the hierarchy of intellectual and spiritual pleasures over merely physical ones but in terms of long-lasting vs short-lived pleasures. He did not go along with the Platonic doctrine that virtue must be sought beyond the pleasure-pain experiential nexus. Hence, "the strictly *hedonic* practical conclusion is that to maximize pleasure one must be modest in one's desires and this precisely is the conclusion which Rāzī follows."[17]

The Stoics looked to Reason as almost a God, and certainly as a metaphysical principle that pervades and provides for cosmic order, firm conformity to which is the secret of virtue, requiring even heroic resignation to the inevitable when that providential order so dictates. Such is not al-Rāzī's conception of human rationality :

> Reason, moreover, as Rāzī treats it in the ethical context, must *earn* its keep : it is a means to an end and anything but the end itself of Rāzī's ethical hierarchy : Reason is praised for the advantages it brings, its many profits and benefits, its capacity to save us from harm, provide for our defense, and secure our supremacy over all creation. Reason must *earn* the authority it holds over human life (contrast the attitude of the democratic Rāzī here with that of the aristocratic Plato, for whom reason held authority in the soul and in the state as its just and due desert). Rāzī makes no bones about the fact that the standard by which the works of reason are judged is utilitarian (that is to say, hedonic), for he has little sympathy with the Platonic love of mathematics (the more abstract the better) and condemns mathematical studies as useless. Aristotle's notion of a life purely devoted to speculation for its own sake is as alien to Rāzī as the Aristotelian analysis of pleasure as a by-product of the completion of an activity done for its own sake. Thus in Rāzī's ethic there is a vice unknown to Plato's and Aristotle's ethics and one which could not be conceived in an ethic where reason was the ultimate ethical arbiter : i.e. the excess of the rational soul, over-intellectualism, excessive concern with the things of the mind.[18]

And as for those who are excessively romantic even in their

art of enjoying their miseries, he counsels again that this is only trying to compensate one excess with another, which is not a rational way to live. Vices are also basically a matter of the hedonic calculus. This stinginess, anxiety, excessive enthusiasm, ambition, social climbing, excessive intellectual appetite, are to be closely watched, not because they are inherently evil but simply futile. Goodman makes the bold rhetorical statement that "thus pleasure becomes the judge of reason, not reason of pleasure."[19]

Even from the most strictly theological point of view al-Rāzī remained a devout Muslim. But he interpreted the Qur'ān and the *ḥadīth* in terms of giving pleasure to God. Admittedly it is in a sense our duty to praise God; but evidently, according to Rāzī, God must be capable of enjoying our praise, and that rather than the duty is the motive he counsels.

We should be reminded that Epicurus himself and most of his school were definitely abstemious or even definitely ascetic in their "gardens", which were more like monasteries; moreover, they encouraged scientific studies as the best occupation of the mind, as affording the maximum 'pleasure' in the long run. Also there is a lot of Stoicism intermixed with this Epicureanism. For example, in terms of moral training al-Rāzī counsels "that we should inure ourselves to losses by considering the objects of our affection as already lost, and we should practice for hardships we may never have to undergo by forcing ourselves to accept privations by way of disciplining (N.B. *not* mortifying) the body and the soul."[20] In many cases it is not just abstemiousness that is called for but positive discipline in a way commensurate with Stoic fortitude. The search for tranquillity as such is also more commensurate with the Stoic ideal than with the Epicurean even though in different modes this idea was common to both.

Rāzī's hedonism is so refined that he never praises pleasure as such; and although his asceticism is "extra-philosophical", nevertheless "formally his philosophy is hedonistic; its asceticism is evident only in its material aspect."[21] There is a lot of hedonism in the Qur'ān itself, for instance the almost constant reference to Allah as "being pleased" or "taking pleasure" in showing mercy or in rewarding the good and punishing iniquity, or "being displeased" when His words are not heard or heeded. Thus there is no conflict between al-Rāzī's being Muslim and being hedonist, even though the Qur'anic hedonism is based on a system of rewards and punishments whereas the Epicurean system is based on a calculus of intrinsic values.

It remains to attempt some speculations about al-Rāzī's thought in comparison and contrast with his Eurasian contemporaries. As to his interest in the sciences, his Japanese contemporaries might be most puzzled since they had not received this heritage through the Chinese; or even where in the Kośa school something of, for example, the doctrine of atoms had come through in the text of Vasubandhu's *Abhidharmakośa*, somehow it did not fascinate them so much as the aesthetic appeal of the more esoteric varieties of Buddhism. Though having had al-Rāzī's medical expertise might have enhanced their prestige among the aristocracy at the court, al-Rāzī's aloofness to political and military matters might have challenged their patriotism. Though al-Rāzī might have found something in common with the Neo-Confucianist rationalistic condemnation of the superstitions that had come in the wake of the popularization of Buddhism, certainly his hedonism would not have pleased them very much.

As to his Indian contemporaries, notably the second generation Advaitins, al-Rāzī might criticize them for not paying more attention to the scientific achievements of India in previous centuries. His realistic attitudes would have challenged their metaphysical speculation about the various ways of interpreting *māyā* and all that is entailed by that, unless they might have come to some minimal common ground in terms of what we have termed the argument from contingency. But with the Kaśmir Śaiva school there might have been slightly greater understanding mutually in terms of hedonism as well as in their attempts at reconciling permanence and change both in the empirical world and in terms of metaphysical principles. And given al-Rāzī's broad-mindedness, he might have found their brand of theism somewhat more compatible than the Advaita 'acosmism' which needed adjustment in order to make it appear more or less theistic. Nevertheless, he might have asked Advaitins, Śaivas, Buddhists and many of his other contemporaries why they were not doing something to relieve human suffering in a practical way instead of indulging in such terribly sophisticated logistics of possible points of view and counter-refutations of all and sundry.

As for the Latin West, the ninth and tenth centuries were not very fertile in philosophy, much less in science. Rather we cannot but regret that al-Rāzī's influence did not arrive there until several centuries later. He might have encouraged them to look beyond or behind Boethius and Augustine to the Stoics and Epicureans, which he did not find incompatible with Islam except in some details; thus they should likewise be able to reconcile those teachings with Christianity. But such was not to happen until the High Renaissance.

As a humanist al-Rāzī would have welcomed increased intercommunication with Byzantium in spite of the military encounters and open hostility between Islam and the Second Rome, both of which were supposedly claimants to world domination or at least, in Toynbeean terms, to universal state status along with China (or what was left between the fall of the T'ang Dynasty and the amazing rescue job of the Southern Sung). Again he might have wondered why so many became so much entangled in ecclesiological controversies and theological disputes and pronouncements of anathema instead of furthering what they had achieved in the physical and medical sciences.

Certainly al-Rāzī was not the brilliant dialectician that, for example, Vācaspati Miśra was; and certainly he was not the "oriental mystic" that even his friend al-Ḥallāj was. A great soul, a very human person concerned about the well-being of his patients almost more than about his philosophy, original and semi-heretical, rationalist and humanist—almost all who know of him in his Islamic milieu nominate him among the greatest and boldest minds of all times. We simply but emphatically add, and of all places.

7. al-Ash'arī

As a gatherer of a cycle of development, or as an initiator of a new cycle, or as a more full and adequate embodiment of the monist spirit of the era, it may be debated whether al-Kindī or al-Ash'arī is more representative. But certainly they do go together in a *yin/yang* way like Plato and Aristotle, Confucius and Lao Tzu, Chu Hsi and Lu Ḥsiang-shan, Bonaventura and Aquinas, Ibn Rushd and Ibn Sīnā, and so on. But most of all al-Ash'arī must be seen in opposition to the Mu'tazilites :

> Ash'arism is the name of a philosophico-religious school of thought in Islam that developed during the fourth and fifth/ tenth and eleventh centuries. This movement was "an attempt not only to purge Islam of all non-Islamic elements which had quietly crept into it but also to harmonize the religious consciousness with the religious thought of Islam." It laid the foundation of an orthodox Islamic theology or orthodox *Kalām*, as opposed to the rationalist *Kalām* of the Mu'tazilites; and in opposition to the extreme orthodox class, it made use af the dialectical method for the defence of the authority of divine revelation as applied to theological subjects.[1]

Though the Mu'tazilite rationalists originally were only attempting "to put Islam and its basic principles on a rational foundation" and provide a means to give some kind of consistent interpretation of Islamic principles, with the introduction of Greek influence "they began to apply the Greek philosophical methods and ideas to the interpretation of the *basic* principles of Islam as well".[2]

> They made reason the sole basis of truth and reality and thus identified the sphere of philosophy with that of religion. They tried to interpret faith in terms of pure thought. They ignored the fact that the basic principles of religion are, by their very nature, incapable of logical demonstration or rational proof. The basic principles of Islam deal with supersensible realities and, as such, they must first be accepted on the authority of revelation. The Mu'tazilites, in their zeal to

> judge everything by reason alone, destroyed the personality of God and reduced Him to a bare indefinable universality or to an abstract unity. This idea of an abstract, impersonal absolute God could not appeal to the ordinary Muslims. The orthodox section of the people reacted strongly against the Mu'tazilite rationalism and began to consider the Mu'tazilites to be heretics.[3]

Nevertheless, al-Ash'arī (873-941) was himself a member of the Mu'tazilite movement until the age of forty, having studied under the famous scholar of the Baṣrite school, al-Jubbā'i.

> After that there happened a sudden change in his mind and one day he went to the Mosque of Baṣrah and declared : "He who knows me, knows who I am, and he who does not know me, let him know that I am abu al-Ḥasan 'Ali al-Ash'arī, that I used to maintain that the Qur'ān is created, that eyes of men shall not see God, and that the creatures create their actions. Lo! I repent that I have been a Mu'tazilite. I renounce these opinions and I take the engagement to refute the Mu'tazilites and expose their infamy and turpitude."[4]

The cause of al-Ash'arī's extreme reaction to the Mu'tazilites is not clear but apparently it was the result of a revelatory dream.

For those still thinking (if any such there be) that only Christians or only this or that sect has a corner on piety, we submit the Preface to al-Ash'arī's *Ibānah* :

> Praise to God ! the One, the Almighty, the Glorious, the only One to whom Unity is ascribed, the Magnified in praise, whom the attributes of human beings do not adequately describe. He has neither adversary nor rival, and He is the Creator and the Restorer. The Doer of what He wills. He is too exalted to possess consorts or children, too holy to associate with the genera of creation or things corrupt. He has not any form capable of expression, nor is a definition of Him by any means of a simile possible. He has always had the attributes of primacy and power, and He will always continue to be knowing and cognizant. His knowledge embraces

> created things. His will is fully realized in them, and the secrets of things are not far from Him. The vicissitudes of passing time do not alter Him nor does fatigue or weariness overtake Him in the creation of anything He creates, nor does exhaustion or loss of power touch Him. He creates things by His power, directs them by His wish, compels them by His strength, and reduces them by His might : wherefore the proud submit to His power, the lofty are subject to the strength of His Lordship, doubters are cut off from a sure foundation in the knowledge of Him, to Him the necks of man submit, and the prudence of the discreet is confounded in His kingdom. By His award the seven heavens arose, the extended earth is fixed, the firm mountains are established, the "fertilizing winds" blow, the clouds pursue their journey in the celestial atmosphere, and the seas observe their bounds. He is a compelling God, to whom the strong do homage and the exalted bow, and the worlds render Him their duty whether they will or no.[5]

But it is not piety alone that is involved here. Some of the points, such as having no rival, submitting to His power, the operation of His Word, etc., strongly suggest influence from both Hindu and Christian sources. The purity of the transcendence of God is as vigorously defended as in the Jewish tradition; the preservation of the attributes of knowing and cognizance suggests likeness to Śaṅkara ; the doctrine of creation (*ex-nihilo* is to be implied) suggests likeness to his Christian contemporaries; his denial of consorts could be taken as a refutation of Vaiṣṇava and Śaiva mythology; and "having children" is a reference to crude interpretations of the Christian Incarnation. On the other hand, all of these could have been indigenous developments.

Though al-Ash'arī was not by any means ignorant of Christianity and even wrote two books about it, having gained his information largely from the *Apology* of Timothy, the Patriarch of the Syrian Church, he evidently applies his fatalistic arguments to the Crucifixion of Jesus and the Fall of Adam without any alteration of his views from Saint Paul's doctrine of freedom. But then there have been many Christian theologians who held virtually the same views. At least he was aware that the doctrine of the Incarnation did not mean literally that God should (in the manner of the Greek gods) have a human son, but that it was a matter of the finite manifestation of the infinite *Logos*. The Jahmiyyah had been considerably influenced by this conception of the Word, whether they accepted the Incarnation or not. To this al-Ash'arī objects, not because this is trying to patch up an old tradition with more sophisticated ideas, but because he cannot conceive of God's Will, Word, or anything else as created within a finite encompassing. Anything, in other words, that in any measure can be taken as compromising God's absolute transcendence, His uncompromised and uncompromising *pāramārthika* conditions (if indeed we may even speak of God's "condition"), is rejected by him.

From this must be drawn the conclusion that God has an uncreated Word. Since every being must receive the command to *be* from Him, and since the Qur'ān must be accepted as the eternally true "speaking" of God, there is only the possibility that God "caused" it in a different mode than he did with finite things, for otherwise there would be an infinite regress of words depending on words. Al-Ash'arī further points out the absurdity of asserting that the Word as a Book and the Word as a Person in any sense could ever be identified. This bother about the Qur'ān is perhaps disturbing to the modern rationalist because it involves a fresh apology for Revelation. Tillich's apology for this mode of truth is perhaps pertinent but needs enlarging, for we find the same sort of arguments in Śaṅkara's dealing with the Pūrva-Mīmāṁsā. The Veda is also asserted to be eternal. It is true on the other hand that the Buddhists never went quite so far in divinizing their canon; they are the rationalist humanists of Indian civilization. But the point remains a challenging one for all theists of any brand : If there is God, then there must be some way for His communicating to men the nature of His being, will, excellence, etc., and if this *communicatio Dei* is to be taken as separate from His own eternal nature, then troubles arise. For somehow in His self-communication there must be a "not departing from the Unity", in the Taoist phrase.

In the *Luma'* al-Ash'arī seeks the resolution of the difficulty by emphasizing the will :

> The proof of the eternity of God's speech is also the proof of the eternity of God's willing. For if His willing were temporally produced, it would have to be produced by God either in Himself, or in another, as is self-subsistent. But God cannot produce it in Himself, because He is not a substrate for produced things; and He cannot produce it as self-subsistent, because it is an attribute, and an attribute cannot subsist in itself—just as God cannot produce it in another, because this would make it necessary for that other to be willing by God's willing. Therefore, since it is impossible to allow these attributes of which one would have to be realized if God's willing were temporally produced, it is certain that God's willing is eternal, and that by it God has ever been willing.[6]

Śaṅkara might deny the distinction between willing (*sankalpa*) and being (*satta*) and deny the refutation of the self-subsisting, analogically relating all self-subsistence into a single identity of all self-subsistence in such a manner that the dependent attribution involved is reflexively returned, as it were, to the self-subsistence of Brahman/Allah. Erigena might assert that the Trinitizing of the Personality of God makes possible the reflexivity implicit in Śaṅkara (which al-Ash'arī does not like and virtually denies) so that the identity is preserved, while the going-forth of the Word and the Return of all things and ideas, including even the idea of Willing, to the Father through the operation of the Holy Spirit still allows the dynamic as well as the static principles their proper integrities. In short, does al-Ash'arī, as Śaṅkara, fall into the same trap of "jumping off" at every finite point into the illicit Infinity of God's essence? The answer probably lies in the point that al-Ash'arī insists that that is the wrong way to state the issue : God *remains* in his own absoluteness, whether this is "infinite" or "essence" or whatever; and anything that suggests a compromise with that is simply untrue.

Rather than being merely a reversion to orthodoxy, al-Ash'arī's conversion might be taken as a *neo*-orthodoxy already arising. It seems that the chief reason for his conversion was a conviction of the shortcomings and limitations of human reason. Still, according to Watts, "al-Ash'arī's method of argument consists in confronting the *a priori* ideas of his adversaries with hard fact; he is a realist arguing with romantics."[7] And yet he was much motivated by his dreams, or visions, in which the Prophet himself appeared to him three times. The first stage (the first dream) represents a conversion away from random philosophical speculations; the second, a determination to study only the tradition (*ḥadīth*) and the commentaries on the Qur'ān; the third, a reinstatement of reason as a *servant* of revelation. Al-Ash'arī appeals to *ijmā'*, the commonality of agreement among the faithful, in a way that is foreign to the old Greek spirit or to the Indian or Chinese (although they appealed to "authority" in a different sense), but in a manner that became the basis for scholasticism, Islamic, Jewish and Christian until Kant. This apparently became more characteristic of the Sunni tradition, which changed little after its final formulation with him, while the Shī'as carried on more of the rationalistic traditions, although often that was in turn balanced by a large place for allegory and symbolism. Whether al-Ash'arī's acknowledgments of the limitations of reason are of the same sorts of attempts at exposition of the *via negativa* found in the Christian Neo-Platonists, the Śunyavāda, and in the Vedānta, or whether they are matters rather founded on a "wrong" retreat from rational construction of system, it is not easy to discern.

In the Hindu tradition the words *darśana* and *vidyā* both have the root meaning of "seeing", and in Christianity many saints were spending their entire lives in trying to gain a supernatural vision of God, or at least of some saint, visions especially of the Blessed Virgin being not uncommon. From the Mu'tazilite standpoint the Beatific Vision cannot be a matter of literal seeing simply because God is above time and space and corporeal existence. But to completely deny every possible sense of "seeing" God is to put a limitation on His power and even run the risk of denying Him "reality", not to mention disregarding the word of the Qur'ān. Al-Ash'arī distinguishes between the capacity of human vision to reach God and the capacity of God to reach the sight of man, and the settlement of distinction leads him into further distinctions between vision before and after death. As discernment from the heart, he insists that "sight" is more than mere knowledge. It is not very common these days to philosophize about the Beatific Vision. Nevertheless it is interesting to note that the Mu'tazilites had carried their rationalism far enough to deny this *Visio Dei*, which seems to have been almost blasphemy to al-Ash'arī.

Of course this seeing could not be of the *nirguṇa*-Brahman, but this does not mean that some visions of God are not valid. The *saguṇa*-Brahman in Vaiṣṇava and Śaiva iconography is very richly portrayed indeed, and Byzantine iconography reveals a genuinely spiritualized imagination as does that of Japan and China in this same century. While the trappers and traders from Byzantium were making great profit from furs and slaves, the monks who were civilizing Russia were becoming famous for their visions, as were also the Nestorian monks of Armenia. And, of course, in Tibet where the Tantra was developing, the science of the inner lights and visions of deities was highly developed indeed. In almost all traditions already quite a canon had begun to come into formulation whereby to distinguish valid from invalid visions, far antedating the classical work of Saint John of the Cross on that subject.

Al-Ash'arī refutes the interpretation given by the Mu'tazilites, the Jahmiyyah and others concerning God's being "seated on the Throne". These take this metaphorically and interpret it as a symbol of God's power. They also assert under this heading the doctrine of His omnipresence, and al-Ash'arī must reconcile this doctrine with his own emphasis on transcendence. Al-Ash'arī argues that the assertion of God's having hands and face cannot be taken metaphorically since what the Qur'ān says cannot be denied or altered, even though this makes it difficult to make no compromise with the anti-anthropomorphic bias of Islam in general. The more rationalistic interpreters wanted to simply allegorize the mention of hands to mean God's graces. As for al-Ash'arī, we must simply take this as one of those curiosities into which theologians will sometimes allow themselves to be led.

In dealing with the attributes of God, al-Ash'arī refutes those who asserted that God's knowledge *is* God. In his refutation he comes close to Śaṅkara's insistence on the ultimate convergence of knower, knowing and known, and in another argument even very nearly duplicates his doctrine of *nāmarūpa*; all "names", even the name of "knower", are only ascribed to God; they are not essential to His being or even to His knowing and willing, etc. Again, Ash'arī is just as anxious as Śaṅkara to defend the *nirguṇa* from the corruption of descent into relationality. In the *Luma'* it becomes more clear that the real issue for Ash'arī is not the attributes as such but the old puzzlement about the relation of reason to revelation. Al-Ash'arī simply insists that if the Qur'ān says that God is seeing, knowing, etc., that is all that needs to be said on the matter; interpretation is merely a matter of coordination of the texts.

God, as completely transcendent, cannot have an "other". This is based on texts in the Qur'ān as well as on reason. And yet if He is to "have" attributes, He must have them either in some mode of identity with Himself or else in some pseudo-mode or a quasi-other, or else by some third mode of "thusness" wherein attribution and essence are reincluded in an interreciprocation that transcends the either/or,/both/and manner of thinking and knowing, this manner being appropriate to man's condition but unnecessary to God's being and knowing. This third mode was already known to the Buddhists but evidently was not adequately understood until Duns Scotus among the Jewish, Islamic and Christian scholastics. McCarthy presents al-Ash'arī's position and its difficulty as follows :

> In man knowledge is an accident, but God's knowledge cannot be an accident. On the other hand,—and this creates the real difficulty—Ash'arī did not hold that the divine knowledge is identified with the divine essence, that God *is* His knowledge. This is explicitly denied . ... In the *Luma'*, then, we find both elements of the classic phrase in which Ash'arī's doctrine on the divine attributes was summed up : "They ere not God and they are not other than God."[8]

Out of this "impossible other" the Christian view shows the irreducibility of the ultimate Triad, notably in Maximus, Erigena and Photius. The Advaitin, however, considers all modes as *adhyāsa*, superimposition—with the possible exception of deliberately "allowing" symbolic attribution to the *saguṇa*-Brahman for the sake of pious devotion—thereby further reducing this possible triadizing tendency to pure Identity by equating "I-knowing" with "Thou-knowing" and "That-knowing", thus dissolving the difficulty found in the Buddhist *Trikāya* which leaves a strange gap between the Triad and the Zero (*Śūnya*). At any rate, whereas al-Āsh'arī should be expected to stress the Thou, it seems that he is caught in the That !

In this perspective al-Ash'arī also deals with the divine will. The problem is essentially the same structurally : man wills, or apparently wills; God wills, or is necessarily considered to will by man. What is the relation between these ? Does God will his own knowledge ? Does He foreknow what He will will ? Or does He only know what He has willed after it is willed ? Does this go on in endless interreciprocation, or is there some point of convergence of willing and knowing in God ? And above all within this context, even more than the problem of man's ignorance, how is it that man has the capacity to disobey ? Or is that only apparent ?

It is in this context that al-Ash'arī comes into his doctrine of predestination, which it seems to us is no less rigoristic than the Calvinistic sense. Al-Ash'arī's inference that God not only foreordains acceptance of the faithful and rejection of the unbelievers but even creates the unbelief and sins of men is merely a logical deduction from the treatment he must give to the doctrines of Guidance, Error and 'Sealing'. Al-Ash 'arī writes :

> We hold that there is no Creator but God, and that the deeds of the creature are created and pre-ordained by God, as He said (in Koran 37,94) : "He has created you and what you make"... we hold that God helps the faithful to obey Him, favors them, is gracious to them, reforms and guides them; whereas He has led the unfaithful astray, did not guide or favor them with signs, as the impious heretics claim. How-

ever, were He to favor and reform them, they would have been righteous, and had He guided them they would have been rightly guided. ... But it was His will that they should be ungodly, as He foresaw. Accordingly He abandoned them and sealed their hearts. We believe that good and evil are the outcome of God's decree and preordination (*qaḍā' wa qadar*) : good or evil, sweet or bitter, and we know that what has missed us could not have hit us, or what has hit us could not have missed us, and that creatures are unable to profit or injure themselves, without God.[9]

Fakhry comments on this as follows:

In this vindication of the omnipotence of God and the powerlessness of the creature, al-Ash'arī simply reaffirms the koranic concept of the God-Despot, whose decrees are both irreversible and inscrutable. At the back of this polemic, however, is the view of the Mu'tazilah that man is the "creator of his deeds," and consequently a fully free and responsible agent. The concept of a co-creator with God, according to al-Ash'arī, amounts to polytheism and involves a radical curtailing of God's absolute power. Despite these strictures, he does not concur with the Traditionists in their claim that man does not play any part whatsoever in the drama of moral activity. In his doctrine of *al-kasb*, or acquisition of the merit or demerit for the deed done, al-Ash'arī seeks a way out of the moral dilemma of responsibility, without sacrificing the omnipotence of God. Voluntary actions, in his view, are created by God, but acquired by the human agent or imputed to him. Creation differs from acquisition in that the former is the outcome of "eternal power," whereas the latter is the outcome of the "created power" of the agent, so that the same action is said to be created by the one and acquired by the other. Stated differently, man acquires the credit or discredit for the deed created by God, since it is impossible that God should acquire it in time, while He is its author eternally.[10]

Although there cannot be any activity willed and performed by man which God does not will, nevertheless the goodness of

God is not compromised by al-Ash'arī, although this goodness seems to be more of the order of the *Pāramārthika sat-cit-ānanda* of the Vedānta, above the limited attributes.

The attribute of willing involves the further difficulty of the relation between the *stasis* of God—as may be seen in Maximus and even in Aristotle to some extent and vividly in Sāṃkhya—wherein alone can reside perfection since all motion in some sense involves some mode of perfection toward which or away from which or cyclically around which the motion proceeds and/or returns, and the *dynamis* of God whereby God may not be considered as omnipotent without having a will to move things and therefore must generate motion within Himself. On this matter of motion al-Ash'arī does not accede to the Aristotelian Unmoved Mover idea so much as he inclines to the idea that all motion is outside of God, almost in the sense of Śaṅkara's *adhyāsa* doctrine. But this question of motion and the necessary "other" involved in any motion may be mposing an issue on al-Ash'arī which really is not his concern. For the answer again lies in his emphasis on predestination. He is more concerned with the problem of whether God wills disbelief and disobedience and such like. And the answer to this is largely in his doctrine of the Providence and Justice of God rather than in trying to probe into questions that are God's own concern and not man's.

The question of disbelief is another manner of attempting to arrive at a norm for determination of orthodoxy. Infidelity is the false attempt to resist the Unity. It cannot, of its own falsity, succeed. If it could, then God would have to be accused of injustice. In other words, all human ethics is to be referred back to God's Will. Violation of an oath, if violated because of impossibility of fulfilling it, must be thought of as due to God's fore-ordaining that impossibility; but if not because of this, the offense is really against God rather than against the fellow human to whom the oath was made. For from His Will there is no shelter nor shade.

If God is taken to be omnipotent, omniscient, just, merciful, etc., it follows that man must be subject to this, and if he is not, then he must become *like* God in these respects, the hiatus of man's weakness being left as a sort of "negative mystery" which only God could possibly explain. Otherwise one is led into the impossible inference that if man is weak then God must have some weakness also. Certainly it is at least a necessary proposition that man is less capable of explaining God's nature and will than God is of determining man's nature and will. Freedom ? Man's freedom lies only in obedience to what God freely wills for the inherent good of both.

It may well be that in the ethical sphere, where we are necessarily thrown back on the inscrutible Will of God, the same laws of opposition and contrariety do not apply as do in dealing with existents. There is movement and change involved, which perhaps al-Ash'arī himself does not see so well as his Buddhist contemporaries. Nevertheless, he anticipates much of what becomes a major issue in all scholasticism, namely the possibility of limitation by impossibility as such even on the part of God. It is indeed not easy to remove this difficulty because the whole antithesis of possibility and impossibility is a distinctly human manner of thinking, to which God alone could possibly supply a "valid third". This, of course, is prayer, about which most philosophers do not speculate sufficiently. Al-Ash'arī does have something to contribute here, but whether it is adequate by comparison with some of the Buddhist and Hindu methods of contemplation one must judge for oneself.

As the chief authority in all things political and theological for the Sunnis, the greatest importance we must attach to al-Ash'arī is not in his particular views about such themes as predestination and attributes, but in his establishing the definitive relation between the authority of the Qur'ān and the orthodox tradition (*Sunnah*). Nevertheless it must not be thought that al-Ash'arī remains the last word in determining orthodoxy. Islam still remains as divided as Christianity or Buddhism, and one could no doubt demonstrate parallel lines of division in all traditions down through history.

As a general estimate we offer the summary of Fakhry :

> The historical significance of al-Ash'arī's "reform" lies not in the elaborateness of his solutions of the theological problems raised by the Mu'tazilah, but rather in his willingness to exploit their dialectical method, and, *ipso facto*, to

> moderate the claims of the Traditionists and antirationalists to whom he was temperamentally drawn. If his theological position, expressed in the classic formula of *bilā kaifa* (ask not how) must be described as agnostic, it is nonetheless to be clearly distinguished from the blind agnosticism of the religious bigot who will entertain no questions whatsoever. For his was the qualified agnosticism of the earnest seeker who ends up by asserting, rightly or wrongly, the inability of reason to plumb the mystery of man in relation to God, or of God in relation to man.[11]

Within the framework of the extremes that had already arisen within Islam and in the wider ecumenical perspective, al-Ash'-arī is perhaps the model "orthodox" thinker. Between the possible extremes of naive, non-thinking text-worship and self-asserting humanistic rationalism; between sheer vacuity in the place of personal Deity and foolish deification of the attributes as actual hypostases having the full power and essence of the Godhead; between sheer evaporation into blank *anirvacanīya* (unknowability, inexpressibility, incommunicability) and existentializing knowledge into a gnostic self-sustaining divinity in-itself wherein the truly personal nature of God is lost sight of in fascination with man's capacity for the esoteric and pseudo-mystical self-realization—at least between these extremes al-Ash'arī is the true man of the Middle Way.

8. Saadia

Whether a man does his principal work in the fury of combat, in the flurry of ordinary busy-ness, or in flight from the world may be a key to both his character and significance. Saadia (882-942) worked about equally in each of the three modes. The Gaonate of which Saadia ben Joseph is perhaps the most illustrious example lasted from 600 to 1050, the plural *Geonim* meaning Excellencies, Illustrious Ones, or more exactly and prosaically, the heads of the Babylonian Talmudical academies of Sura and Pumbeditha. Although he never voluntarily retired from the world, Saadia's major philosophical work, *The Book of Beliefs and Opinions*, was written while he was banished from the Gaonate to Baghdad.

When his great literary productivity is contemplated, it would seem Saadia must have been born writing. Nothing is known of his childhood or education, but when he was twenty he composed a Hebrew dictionary, "Agron", and when he was twenty-three he wrote his first known polemical work against Karaism and other heresies in defense of traditional Judaism. A dispute over the calendar as it affected the timing of the Passover and other Jewish holidays brought Saadia into strong alliance with David ben Zakkai, the political leader (Exilarch) of the Jewish community in Babylonia. Although Saadia was an outsider in Babylonia, his strength of character and scholarship caused David ben Zakkai to appoint him Gaon of the Sura academy in 928. Saadia began to exercise his spiritual office with great diligence and success, but his forceful initiatives may have occasioned some envy on the part of the Exilarch or his advisers. At any rate, a rupture occurred between the Gaon and the Exilarch, and after a bitter contest Saadia was forced to retire to Baghdad for several years. According to the sources, "Saadia refused to confirm the terms of settlement of a will which would greatly benefit the Exilarch."[1] The opponents were reconciled in 937 but were not destined to enjoy their reconciliation very long, for the Exilarch died in 940 and Saadia in 942.

Saadia's situation is closely analogous to that of Philo of Alexandria in a different cycle of civilization, coming to the rescue of his community in the face of Caligula, and writing in Greek rather than in Hebrew as Saadia was writing in Arabic. There is probably no Jewish thinker who had greater influence since the time of Philo, unless it be Moses Maimonides who himself was much influenced by Saadia as were virtually all other Jewish scholastics in the intervening period. "Maimonides disagreed with his philosophical views in many fundamental points, but states 'were it not for Saadiah the Torah would have well-nigh disappeared from the midst of Israel'."[2]

> Saadiah belonged to the school of the Mu'tazilites but it is evident that he was also influenced by Aristotelianism, Platonism, and Stoicism. He, in turn, influenced Jewish Neoplatonists, such as Baḥyā ibn Paqudah, Moses ibn Ezra, and Abraham ibn Ezra. Jewish Aristotelians such as Abraham ibn Dā'ūd also borrowed some of his ideas.[3]

Saadia's popularity endured until about the time of Maimonides, who in his *Guide to the Perplexed* attacks the *kalām* tradition, never mentioning Saadia by name but obviously referring to him. Though that classic began to overshadow Saadia's work, Maimonides' opponents still relied on Saadia.

As for parallels, Saadia might be closer to the ritualistic aspect of the Pūrva-Mīmāṁsā than to the Vedānta. Certainly he was not an adept at *hatha yoga*, although as one exercising *niṣkāma karma yoga* he commands our respect and even marvelling as to how he was able to accomplish so much institutionally and still carry on at the scholarly and spiritual levels. Thus he might be better compared to his Neo-Confucian contemporaries or to Photius than to his Hindu or Buddhist contemporaries, although both Saichō and Kūkai also had that *śakti* or charisma of founding institutions and dealing with governmental patronage, and Śaṅkara also did found the order of monks which still carries on his work.

Saadia can be identified as the "first medieval Jewish philosopher", though the term "medieval" might more accurately be replaced by "neo-orthodox". Nakamura in Parallel Developments lists six characteristics of medieval ways of thinking, but Saddia seems to fit only two of these in any really clear-cut sense :

(1) "The absolute authority of traditional religions". Religious authority is accepted by Saadia as the complete basis for life, but that does not mean that it cannot be questioned, clarified or defended by reason. (Reason is perhaps best regarded as a part of, rather than apart from, religious authority of the moderate variety.) The big questions all have rational answers, according to thinkers like Saadia. Some parts of Torah are, according to Saadia, rationally defensible apart from revelation.

The minutiae of the rest of Torah do not have *detailed* rational defenses; otherwise there would be no need for revelation.

(2) "In the realm of social relations and in repressing scientific evaluations of the world, religious orders were extremely influential." Religious orders in general and asceticism in particular were repugnant to Saadia because religion is seen by him to be applicable to the whole of Jewish life and not only to those who have taken themselves out of the world. The self-segregated holiness of a monastic order would involve a contradiction of terms for Saadia. Holiness is obedience in the world or else it is nothing.

(3) "The absolute sacredness of religious scriptures was stressed. Scholarship was no more than the deduction from, and elucidation of, the fundamental dogmas of religions. ... Free thinking was not permitted, heretics were punished, skepticism was abhorred." This applies to Saadia with qualification, for Saadia's reliance on Scripture is complemented by his reliance on reason.

(4) "The tendency of thought was generally otherworldly. Religious life was regarded as noble, secular life as vile and mean." The tendency of Saadia's thought was otherworldly in its emphasis on rewards and punishments in the next life. However, secular life was "vile and mean" only if lived outside the proper moderating influences of human reason and divine commandment.

(5) "As for social structure, a feudalistic hierarchy of status was accepted by the common people and was enforced by authority." Some fairly rigid (and from time to time vigorously disputed) hierarchies held sway in Saadia's world, but these were probably not nearly as highly graduated or sharply differentiated as were the secular and religious hierarchies in medieval Europe under many emperors and popes.

(6) "Cultural life was limited to the upper classes; common people hardly participated in it." If Saadia had been concerned only with the upper classes he would not have taken the pains to put the Hebrew Scriptures into the Arabic vernacular of the Babylonian Jews. Of course the better educated always form a cultural elite in their societies whether they in-

tend to or not, no matter how hard they work to lift people to enlightenment.

In Saadia we find another attempt to exalt God into a position impregnable to any compromise by human attribution of what is not proper to Him. Saadia's insistence on the Unicity of God almost entails the reduction of this to sheer identity. He does not allow sufficient relatedness of this sheer identity for any knowing of it apart from prophetic revelation, as quite distinct from the Beatific Vision or the dawn of *jñāna*. Above all attributes except omniscience, omnipotence and living, God for Saadia is in such a position that all the usual Aristotelian categories fall away as readily as they do with Erigena. Thus he must distinguish between the essential and the active attributes of God (as al-Ash'arī also must do) in a way that very closely corresponds to Śaṅkara's dealing with the relation of *nirguṇa* to *saguṇa*-Brahman. The finite categories fail to define God and they have no ultimate validation except in God. Saadia will not even allow that Moses had really seen God, only that he had seen His Glory. As for the Creator Himself, there is no means whereby anybody might see Him.

It must be remembered, however, that Saadia is careful to guard this mode of the ignorance about God both from the difficulty of the agnostic and from falling into ignorance of everything—a constant danger that misguided mystics are always faced with—by insisting on a valid field for the discipline of logical abstraction according to the Aristotelian pattern. This applies without question in the realm of nature, as it does with Erigena and Śaṅkara also; but the question of the extent to which some other canon is needed when one is speaking of God vexes Saadia considerably.

Saddia is less grandiose than Erigena and depends less on paradoxes, and he does not allow so freely the concept that God creates things in bringing Himself into manifestation. In a sense he is at once more Semitic, leaving the nature of God in a position beyond questioning and reach of either metaphysical speculation or mystical vision, and more Aristotelian, reducing all things by purely logical demonstration back to the necessity of some First Origin. Nevertheless, in the end, like Śaṅkara and Erigena, Saadia appeals to Scripture : "Before the mountains were brought forth, or ever Thou hadst formed the earth and the world, even from everlasting to everlasting Thou art God."

Saadia was influenced by the Mu'tazilites and himself can be typified as a Jewish Mu'tazilite. And as such one can well argue that there is a very radical difference there between his 'monism' and that of the post-Śaṅkara Advaitins—if Saadia may be called a monist for the simple reason that he founds everything else on the Unicity of God as a necessary presupposition. We may recall that the Creator concept does not figure so prominently with the Advaitins as it does with the Vaiṣṇavas, who do not appear on the scene in full voice until somewhat later. Saadia no doubt would find it strange to learn that for most of the Advaitins the idea of the creatorship of God, as *Iśvara* belongs to the *saguṇa*-Brahman. As for the three most essential attributes of God in Saadia, namely life, power and wisdom, we have a triad not entirely different from the *sat-cit-ānanda* of all varieties of the Vedānta, although the extreme Advaitins can hardly justify any attributes in any sense at all except by an oblique way for the sake only of praise. Most of the non-Advaitins insist that as soon as that *sat-cit-ānanda* is admitted, the strict Advaitin interpretation of the "One only without a second" *vākya* in the Upaniṣads is very much compromised, since they all insist that attributes belong to *saguṇa*-Brahman, not *nirguṇa*-Brahman, and since they minimize the role of *saguṇa*-Brahman to the greatest possible extent. The more moderate of them, however, get around that problem in a way not entirely dissimilar from the way that Saadia does. He simply believes that plurality of attributes by no means entails plurality in the essential nature of God, because all possible attributes are united in His nature; moreover, he admits that when we speak of such things, since our language is limited, we speak of them as plural out of convenience and not because they lack what we might call 'inter-identity'.

The *ex nihilo* argument, as might be expected, figures very prominently in Saadia's system, and the related arguments from design and from contingency likewise. Indeed, the *ex nihilo* sets the pace for virtually everything else, in common with most of the Jewish, Christian and Islamic scholastics. The Trinitarian view is usually, as it were, appended after the *ex nihilo* creatorship of God is established, so that in basics the similarities are no doubt greater than the differences between the three Abrahamic heritages.

In typical Mu'tazilite fashion, Saadiah opens the body of his work with a discussion of creation. He maintains that the world was created in time, that its creator was other than itself, and that it was created *ex nihilo*. He presents four proofs for creation, the first based on Aristotelian premises, the other three drawn from the *Kalām*. In the first proof, invoking the principles that the world is finite in its dimension, and that a finite body cannot possess an infinte force, Saadiah concludes that the force preserving the world is finite and consequently that the world itself must be finite, i.e., must have a beginning and an end. In the second proof, on the basis of the fact that that which is composed of two or more elements must have been put together at some point in time, Saadia argues that the world, which is composed of various elements, must have been created at some point in time. In the third proof, Saadiah argues that the world is composed of various substances all of which are the bearers of accidents. Since accidents originated in time, the world itself must have originated in time. The fourth argument is taken from the nature of time. Were the world uncreated, time would be infinite. But infinite time cannot be traversed, and hence the present (or any other finite) moment could never have come to be. But the present clearly exists, and hence time cannot be infinite. It follows that the world must have had a beginning.[4]

One variant of the *ex nihilo* issue deserves some special attention since later Bonaventura will treat it favorably, with many in between taking differing positions in regard to it, namely the question whether instead of making the world out of nothing God make it out of Himself, on the analogy that the world is like the light emanating from the sun, whereas God is self-luminous like the sun. This is basically Neo-Platonist inheritance but the same mataphor is quite common also in Mahāyāna and Vedāntic texts and becomes basic in Kaśmir Śaiva tradition, which was already emerging in Saadia's century, and will become very basic among the Vivartavādins following after Padmapāda's interpretation of Advaita. Husik relates Saadia's view :

> It is unlikely, he says, that an eternal substance having neither form, condition, measure, place or time, should change into a body or bodies having those accidents;or that wise being, not subject to change or influence, or comprehensibility should choose to make himself into a body subject to all of these. What could have induced a just being who does no wrong to decree that some of his parts should be subject to such evils as matter and material beings are afflicted with? It is conceivable only in one of the two ways. Either they deserved it for having done wrong, or they did not deserve it, and it was an act of violence that was committed against them. Both suppositions are absurd. The fact of the matter is that the authors of this opinion to avoid the theory of creation *ex nihilo* went from the frying pan into the fire. To be sure, creation out of nothing is difficult to conceive, but this is reason why we ascribe this power to God alone. To demand that we show how this can be done is to demand that we ourselves become creators.[5]

Saadia holds that God created the world not out of need or even of necessity but out of His own free will. Here we have a general parallel with the various interpretations of the *līlā* concept in the *Brahma Sūtras*, though the strict Advaitins try to minimize that lest they thereby admit that the whole *māyā* concept has its grounding in Īśvara/Brahman Itself. But most of the Vaiṣṇava theists, especially Viśiṣṭādvaitins, have a similar interpretation : it is not that God is like some cosmic magician just playing with reality as though it were a toy (although some extreme *bhaktas*, notably in the later Chaitanya heritage, almost indulge in that view, at least as a sentiment); rather, pretty much as Saadia puts the matter, out of His own free will God creates the universe. However, there is one aspect of this that constitutes a difference, for "in creating the world, God wished to benefit His creatures by giving them the opportunity of serving Him through the observance of His commandments."[6] This moralistic aspect is not so strong in the Vaiṣṇavas, and is almost completely absent in the Advaitins as well as the Vaiśeṣikas. The basic emphasis there is on the *bhakti* aesthetic enjoyment of service to God devotionally and in pure affection, spontaneously enjoying His beauty and that of His creation as an expression of His *ānanda* attribute, rather than in conformity with any strictly moralistic code. The Mīmāṁsā was moralistic in the ritualistic sense, but it did not have the Creator-God doctrine in the same sense as the others. As for the Chinese and Japanese views then current, the contrasts are much greater since the Creator-God idea is almost absent there, even though in the Amida cult the ideas of grace, salvation and enjoyment of selfless service in affectionate *bhakti* devotion are very strong.

Man, to Saadia, is a composite of body and soul. The soul has three essential faculties : appetitive, which controls growth and reproduction: spirit, which controls the emotions; and reason, which controls knowledge. Here we recognize the old Aristotelian formula of vegetable, animal and rational souls functioning very much as *tamas*, *rajas* and *sattva* in Sāṃkhya. "The soul cannot act on its own and is therefore placed in the body, which serves as its instrument," which reminds us of the Sāṃkhya, since indeed *puruṣa* does not act on its own, not being active at all, but only observes the actions of *prakṛti* in which the *guṇas* operate. But there is a difference since it is the soul that is active, even though it cannot act on its own but only 'through' the body. Saadia may have had some disagreement with the Platonists and the Advaitins who in effect thought of the body as a prison for the soul rather than its instrument.

Concerning the classical theodicy question of why God expects man to undergo suffering in the world in order to gain virtuous merit, Saadia gives the classical answer, namely that God thereby—and by inference we gather that Saadia, like Leibniz, thinks it could not be otherwise—gives man the choice between obedience and disobedience and the opportunity to win his own reward. He is in accord with the Mu'tazilites over against the Ash'arites in putting the greater stress on man's freedom than on God's predestination. Saadia was perhaps more of a libertarian in that sense than even Peter Damien, who was almost his contemporary, and indeed might have found more fellowship with Rāmānuja's predecessors than with the Advaitins. Some more extreme Augustinians might not like his admitting that God's knowledge has no necessary causal power, but that is the way he attempts to resolve the paradox that God may even have foreknowledge of man's choosing disobedience rather than obedience and thus become not only worthy but deserving of punishment. Ultimately Saadia believes the theodicy difficulties can best be understood in the light of rewards and punishments in the afterlife. The whole issue of the destiny and nature of man to Saadia depends on his eschatology, including the doctrines of resurrection, the Messiah and redemption.

Whereas Saadia puts the emphasis on the revealed *commandments* of God, Śaṅkara and Erigena point to the superessential Goodness of God which is above affirmation and negation and all oppositions from the human standpoint. If Erigena is more like Spinoza, paradoxically Saadia is more like Kant. For the former do not separate the moral and the ontological so sharply, while the latter seem to fall back very heavily on the argument that though it is out of God's Goodness that he gives being to creatures and grants revelation, still this revelation is not so much the knowledge of what He *is* as of what *they must do*. According to Saadia, God could not have made His creatures happy without giving them commandments and prohibitions. Thus he is more in agreement with al-Ash'arī than with Śaṅkara and Erigena to whom the moral field is more a matter of aesthetic preparation for the consummate mystical enlightenment wherein all things are seen "in God" although He is somehow above them. But the Semitic temperament takes away that *somehow above them* and replaces it with a *necessarily* with such emphasis that the "all things in God" is all but cancelled out.

In short, Saadia's vision is essentially prophetic, not mystical. One even gets the impression that Saadia is more truly Jewish than Philo in his emphasis on the rule of the prophets and on the absolute difference between God and man. Whether that is due to the fact that Saadia was more free to travel throughout the Near East strengthening the again-exiled Jewish community, or whether it is simply because the temper of the age, along with the beginnings of Islam, called for an emphasis on revelation to top the ladder of the mystical path mapped out by the Alexandrian and Byzantine schools, or whether he had been influenced, in spite of his inadequate information about Islam, by the Islamic fervor for the transcendence of God and the completely subordinate role of the Prophet, it is not easy to judge.

Saadia did not intend to construct independent philosophical system; rather his purpose was

> to provide his fellow Jews with spiritual guidance in the face of the confusion which the multiple sects and religious disputes of the tenth century had created among the people, and to combat heretical views. ... Saadia believed that it was a religious obligation to provide a rational basis for the Law, in order to dispel doubts and refute views at variance with those which he accepts. Saadiah's importance lies in his being the first medieval Jewish philosopher to attempt to reconcile the Bible and philosophy, reason and revelation.[7]

Typical of scholasticism in all traditions, *The Book of Beliefs and Opinions* is basically polemical and consists largely of dialectical examinations and refutations of other works. In other words, systematic doubt was not discouraged but posed as a means of clarifying distinctions; but this had long since become standard all over Eurasia so that we may speak in that sense of scholasticism as just that balancing of opinions and doubts before coming to a more comprehensive *siddhānta*. In short, Saadia is simply in the current of his time.

Saadia states in *The Book of Beliefs and Opinions* that he intends to identify the causes of uncertainty and confusion in order to remove them, but the reader must also bear his responsibility : "If, now, the scholar and the student will pursue (an unbiased objective) course in the perusal of this book, then he that strives for certainty will gain in certitude, and doubt will be lifted from the doubter, and he that believes by sheer authority will come to believe out of insight and understanding."[8] At the outset Saadia explains the causes of uncertainty. In their sensory perceptions, men make mistakes either (a) because they do not know well enough what they are seeking or (b) because they lack thoroughness in their quest. In the things of the intellect, confusion may arise either (a) because the seeker does not know the methods of evidence, (b) because, although he knows the methods of correct reasoning, he jumps impulsively (or falls lazily) to conclusions without sufficient warrant, or (c) because "the seeker does not know what he is seeking".

> When, now, I considered these fundamentals and the evil resulting therefrom, my heart was grieved for my species, the species of rational beings, and my soul was stirred on account of our people, the childern of Israel. ... I saw, furthermore, men who were sunk as it were, in seas of doubt and overwhelmed by waves of confusion and there was no diver to bring them up from the depths nor a swimmer who might take hold of their hands and carry them home.[9]

Doubtless Saadia saw himself as the dedicated "diver" or strong "swimmer" who could save the confused. In a world created by a reasonable God, faith and reason together in the hands of such a rescuer could overcome all doubt and confusion.

God alone, according to Saadia, deserves to be regarded as the Evident Truth. Since He "verifies with certainty unto rational souls the existence of their souls" and the correct apprehension of objective knowledge, "uncertainties are thereby removed from them and doubts disappear". In a finite world protected by God from ultimate uncertainties, there are really only a finite number of questions which are matched exactly by an equivalent number of answers. But men and women are temporal creatures and hence need time to overcome their uncertainties.

> We maintain that the very fact of being created entities necessitates their entertaining uncertainties and illusions. ...However by the power of the intellect, which they possess, they do, in the course of time, continually refine and purify these until the uncertainties depart from them and the pure essence is extracted dissociated from any doubt.[10]

Why, then, are there skeptics and heretics who remain stubbornly attached to their doubts and errors? Saadia enumerates nine reasons. Eight of these have to do with human weaknesses. The last is perhaps of most concern to Saadia : problematical verses in the Bible, unanswered prayers, unpunished evildoers, in short, the issues of theodicy.

Like Aquinas three centuries after him, Saadia believed that the process of religious reasoning is time-consuming and difficult, so God, "exalted and magnified be He, afforded us a quick relief from all these burdens by sending us His messengers through whom He transmitted messages to us, and by letting us see with our own eyes the signs and proofs supporting them about which no doubt could prevail....[11] However, Saadia regarded revelation as an exterior catalyst for natural insight. Aquinas thought it was an absolute necessity because of the mysteries which lie beyond the realm of reason; but Saadia, according to Rau, "knew no mysteries of faith".[12]

Saadia lists four sources of knowledge: (1) the five senses; (2) the intuitions of the intellect which spring up "solely in the mind of a human being" and consist of such notions as "approbation of truthfulness and disapproval of mendacity"; (3) logical necessity which produces strong conclusions, "which, unless they are accepted by the individual as true, would compel his denial of the validity of his rational intuitions or the perception of his senses"; and (4) authentic tradition including the books of prophetic revelation.[13] The most philosophically interesting part of Saadia's epistemology is perhaps that devoted to tradition. Tradition can be flawed in two ways: when the one who hands it on has a false impression, or when he is duped by deliberate misrepresentation. It is not likely that in a large community everyone will have the same wrong impression; nor could the fact of a conspiracy to suppress or distort the truth be kept forever from the masses. "When, therefore, a tradition is free from the above mentioned two flaws, there is no third means of invalidating it."[14] Saadia writes:

> I deem it proper also to call to mind the following details that lend color to the validity of tradition. For example, were it not fact that men felt satisfied in their hearts that there is

> such a thing in the world as authentic tradition, no person would be able to cherish legitimate expectations on the basis of the reports he receives about the success of a certain commercial transaction, or the usefulness of a specified art. ... Nor would he heed the warnings about the dangers of a certain road, or the announcement of the prohibition of a certain act. (However,) without such expectations and apprehensions he would fail in his undertakings.[15]

Some aspects of Saadia's epistemology seem remarkably modern and sophisticated, for example, the idea that just because a theory "explains" a fact which we can deny only by denying our senses does not make the theory true. "We must inquire whether that precept might not be sustained by some other hypothesis than the one" put forth.[16] However, in the same passage Saadia shows he is very much a man of his time. He rejects certain theories of the Milky Way by uncritically reiterating the view that earth must be the center of the universe because God's crowning creation, man, has been placed upon it.

Saadia's method of argument against certain materialists who believed the world to be eternal is typical of this philosopher at his best. Saadia points first to the materialists' inconsistency in relying only on their senses, since neither the materialists nor any other group have in reality sensed—that is, perceived by their senses—the *lack* of a beginning (or end) of the material world. But even if their thesis could be established by the senses, a fundamental problem would remain. "Now would that I knew by means of what sense they could reject all knowledge outside that of sensation! Is it by sense of sight or that of hearing or something else?"[17] What a "modern" refutation of empiricism! If the sense-less is non-sense, then the theory of this is itself nonsense, since it cannot be sensed or proved empirically.

When Saadia considers the question of how to avoid falling back into sin, his answer is that one should think up reasons for holding this world in contempt. "Let a person remind himself of his condition of impotence, misery, exertion, and disillusionment, of his eventual death and the decomposition of the parts of his body, of the vermin and the putrefaction that are destined for him."[18] So far Saadia could have been laying down guidelines for meditation in a Buddhist monastery. In the Abrahamic religious tradition he continues to advise contemplation

> of the accounting he will have to give for his conduct and the torments to which he will be subjected. ... The result of such reflection would be contempt for this world, and once all mundane things are held in contempt by him, his sins would be included in the totality of things to be abstained from and his resolve to abandon them would be intensified.[19]

But Saadia does not completely depreciate the physical conditions under which man must live. "The body of man contains no impurity in and by itself."[20] The pains by which the soul is afflicted while connected with the body are due either to man's failing to take normal precautions in extreme conditions or to God's imposing suffering "as a discipline in order that He might, in return therefore, requite the soul with good".[21]

Because God is completely just, the thriving of the righteous and the wicked side by side—or, what is worse, thriving of the wicked in the very presence of those who suffer innocently—must eventually end. Heaven and hell are the means by which God the Judge must settle accounts fairly, finally and permanently. Therefore, to one who objects that perpetual hell-fire seems to imply a mercilessness and cruelty which are not consonant with God's nature, Saadia answers that

> just as it is necessary for God to use the strongest stimulant to arouse in men the desire to do good, so must He employ the strongest deterrent to keep them from doing evil. ... That is why God made the torment of the hereafter limitless, employing the strongest possible deterrent, that leaves no loopholes for anyone.[22]

So, on Saadia's assumptions, limitless torment must have appeared completely rational to him. Furthermore, the tormented are under no obligation to worship God both because they are in too great a state of suffering "and also because such service might bring about transfer from their state".[23]

Saadia concludes *The Book of Beliefs and Opinions* with a very carefully worked out treatise, Treatise X: "Concerning how it is most proper for man to conduct himself in this world." One might suppose that the oneness and unity of God would have to be reflected by the oneness and unity of each of his creatures, for example, by the unity of the good man or the unity of the whole fabric of the good man's conduct. Matters are not quite so simple, claims Saadia. "Inasmuch as the Creator of the universe, exalted and magnified be He, is essentially one, it follows by logical necessity that His creatures be composed of *many* elements, as I have made clear in the foregoing."[24] What is true of the earth and all that is in it, and even also of the heavens, applies as well to the tendencies exhibited by man. "So, too, man's conduct in the course of his lifetime cannot logically be based on just a single trait."[25] To attempt to do so is irrational, unnatural and perhaps ultimately idolatrous. God would not have implanted the desire for many things in us had he wanted us to desire one above all. (God, we assume, is no "thing".) Each of man's likes and dislikes has its distinctive role which must be honored. Solomon found all striving to be vanity, not because any of the things striven for were unworthy but because "any act practised exclusively constitutes a distortion". Exclusive devotion to wisdom or to mirth or to wealth is, therefore, a striving after wind. The list in Ecclesiastes is illustrative only, so Saadia seeks to make it more nearly complete. There are, he says, thirteen principal human pursuits, namely abstinence, eating and drinking, sexual intercourse, eroticism, the accumulation of money, the begetting of children, development of the land, longevity, dominion, the nursing of revenge, the acquisition of wisdom, worship, and rest.

In short, whatever is one-sided is wanting. "The only proper type of conduct consists of the combination of all these classes of activities."[26] Treatise X might be characterized as an autonomous ethic, general (if not secular), rational, humanistic and somewhat independent of any particular religion, whereas Saadia's more specifically religious ethic is theonomous and as dependent on revelation as the pious are upon active obedience to God. Saadia's religious ethic must stress the rewards and punishments of the afterlife. Treatise X tends to emphasize man's practical and balanced needs in this life ; however, the otherworldly emphasis is sometimes ringingly clear : "The righteous servant of God, therefore, loves the life of this world merely because it serves as a stepladder by means of which he reaches and ascends to the next world, not for its own sake."[27]

That Saadia gave Ecclesiastes a reading which almost confuses the Preacher with Aristotle is true (the Preacher is called "Koheleth" in Hebrew and "Ecclesiastes" in Greek and is equated by Saadia and tradition with Solomon). The complex background of Ecclesiastes is such that an Aristotelian or at least Greek reading of it is by no means completely off the mark. Atkins writes :

> All commentators stress the relationship of Ecclesiastes to Greek, Egyptian, even Chaldean, inquiries and conclusions upon the meanings of life, or else its dependence upon them. The resemblances cited prove at least how the shadows which lie across so many quests and so many conclusions are confined to no region and darken all time. Koheleth did not need Gautama to teach him the weariness of life, or the Greek tragedies to teach him the inexorableness of fate.[28]

But we should avoid an overly enthusiastic paralleling of Gautama's resignation and Koheleth's, for "what resignation there is in Ecclesiastes is an irritated resignation."[29]

For the Preacher and Saadia moderation in all things, including wisdom and the pursuit of happiness, is desirable. Proud theoretical wisdom must fall. Practical wisdom, chastened, limited, but nevertheless worthwhile, remains. Rankin writes that "a knowledge of the world will keep a man safe from the destruction that attends the rash and impetuous. That is why Koheleth gave advice to shun extremes, excesses, and enthusiasms. His wise man is a conformist who will do nothing overmuch, neither overrighteous nor overwise."[30] Though the most prominent side of the little book of Ecclesiastes is its shadow side, Saadia, in his dependence on the more optimistic confidence of Jewish traditionalism and Greek rationalism, chooses to highlight the more hopeful aspects of wisdom. Some of the seeming inconsistencies of Ecclesiastes vanish if we concede with Saadia that the book does not claim that every single act or activity is *completely* vain. Rather Saadia hears the Preacher saying, "If you seek any one thing exclusively for itself, you will forever chase the wind."

Saadia insists that there is one life hereafter and no life previous over against the metempsychosis of Hinduism, Buddhism, the Platonists and Neo-Platonists, Neo-Pythagoreans and Gnostics. Though some Jews have accepted metempsychosis, he rejects it forthright. He does acknowledge a condition after the departure from the body while the soul is awaiting the General Resurrection; but always the primary stress is on the moral implication of the soul's single existence and its facing its Creator, who alone can take pity or condemn it. Saadia makes the usual apologetic that the atoms that had composed the body in this life will be kept in reserve, as it were, until the resurrection, at which time they will be recomposed. The doctrine of the General Resurrection is now largely regarded as a curiosity, rightly or wrongly, but it did condition the minds of a rather large number of people (and still does in some places). The only claim that Christians have had here as distinct from Muslims and Jews is that Christ is believed to have anticipated the General Resurrection and opened the way, so to speak, in actuality and not in hope only. Saadia is indeed vexed with the problem of how a soul will regain its body if, for example, a man has been eaten by a wild beast which is later killed and eaten by another man—one must not laugh ; his belief is so secure that he really is perplexed about this. The time and place of the great event also concern him poignantly. The faithfully departed will be brought back to life in order to witness the restoration of the Jews to their Promised Land. But again, this is dependent to an almost exclusive degree on the moral conduct of the individuals and the nations. Thus the final emphasis is on ideal human conduct in *this* life.

Whether Saadia's criticisms of the Christian Trinity are conclusive is perhaps a matter of one's predilection. His chief charge seems to be that the Christian Trinitarian doctrine entails anthropomorphism. The doctrine of the Incarnation gives an existential link between God and man, but difficulties arise simply in an effort to keep the Godhead in Christ uncorrupted without compromising the manhood (as may be seen in Nestorius). However, this combination seems repugnant to Saadia though he did hold to the hope of a Messiah, not believing that Jesus had been that. One wonders what he might have said about the similar concepts in Hinduism and Mahāyāna Buddhism under the names of Kalki Avatār and Maitreya Bodhisattva, not to mention the Islamic Mahdi concept. Certainly this short focus on the future contrasts decidedly with the Confucian glorification of antiquity and the Greek notion that we have descended from a Golden Age in the long-forgotten past.

Saadia ends on a note of humility rather than of exaltation as is the case with Erigena. After a discursus on the word "good", he concludes, "Finally, there is included in this group the recognition on the part of the virtuous servant of God that he can never be completely free from error, so that he might be humble before his Master." But with both Śaṅkara and Erigena the conclusion is quite otherwise. True enough, man may not neglect his karmic duties. But not all rules apply to all men, and the monk stands in the best stead, provided, of course, that he lives up to his calling. Still for all three, as much as for any philosophers since the Stoics and Epicureans and their contemporaries, philosophy has bocome a Way, not a mere body of rules for the investigation of nature or even a canon for right speculation about first principles.

9. Ikhwān al-Ṣafā

The Ikhwān al-Ṣafā or Brethren of Purity (fl. tenth century), centered at Baṣra, was a society of seekers after truth who were "held together by their contempt for the world and its allurements and their devotion to truth".[1] Evidently we do not know even today who they were individually except for the following five : Abū Sulaymān al-Bustī (known as al-Muqaddasī), Abu'l-Hasan al-Zanjānī, Abū Aḥmad al-Nahrajūrī (alias al-Mihrajānī), al-'Aufī, and Zaid b. Rifā'a. Their *Rasā'il Ikhwān al-Ṣafā* or

Epistles of the Ikhwān al-Ṣafā is not the work of any one member but a collaborative effort of various writers. The *Rasā'il* is comprised of fifty-two epistles which divide the full range of knowledge into three classes : mathematics, physics, and metaphysics.

> Mathematics included ...the theory of numbers, geometry, astronomy, geography, music, theoretical and practical arts, ethics, and logic. Physics included matter, form, motion, time, space, the sky, generation, corruption, minerals, the essence of nature, plants, animals, the human body, the senses, life and death, microcosm, pleasure, pain, and language. Metaphysics was subdivided, as should be expected, into psychorationalism, being, macrocosm, mind, great years, love, resurrection, and causality. Theology included the beliefs of the Ikhwān al-Ṣafā, friendship, faith, divine Law, prophethood, call unto God, the incorporeals, polities, the structure of the world, and magic.[2]

Thus their *Rasā'il* or Encyclopedia attempts to include all knowledge and to give an interpretation to the efforts of the whole human intellectual and spiritual quest. Such was also the case with the Chinese Encyclopedias of the same epoch. It is somewhat strange that we have nothing similar in India, even though it might be said that Vācaspati Miśra's commentaries are virtually of that nature. Even Byzantium had scarcely anything comparable, and probably the nearest thing to it in Latin Europe was the by then almost forgotten work of Isidore of Seville.

A related work, *al-Risālāt al-Jāmi'ah* (*Comprehensive Epistle*) was intended for the most advanced members of the group and constitutes a sort of compendium handbook. It discards much of the scientific information found in the unabridged text and puts more emphasis on the esoteric training and discipline as well as allegorical and symbolic interpretations of various key verses in the Qur'ān—a trait that was quite common all across Eurasia but seems to have been most obvious in the Neo-Platonic heritage ever since well before Philo and in the works of Origen and the Greek Gregorys and Maximus Confessor (who influenced Erigena to such a great extent).

The Ikhwān had common sources to great extent with al-Fārābī, but there is no evidence of awareness of his work or of him as a person in the text. As to al-Kindī, evidently they were vaguely aware of his work but did not take him very seriously. In fact it is rather their habit of taunting the 'Aristotelian' *Falsafah* as mere jugglers with syllogisms and imitators of texts they did not necessarily comprehend with any depth of wisdom. Philosophy or wisdom for the Ikhwān is "to behave *Godlike* as best as a human being can" or "love for science added to knowledge of the essence of all beings".[3]

> Their aim, however, is not that of an Ibn Rushd or even a Thomas Aquinas, because here again the Ikhwān give a connotation to the word "philosophy" which differs greatly from the rationalistic, syllogistic meaning given to it by the Aristotelians. Instead, they identify philosophy with *ḥikmah*,in opposition to the great number of Muslim writers who use philosophy as being almost synonymous with purely human wisdom and *ḥikmah* as wisdom which has its ultimate source in the Revelations given to the ancient prophets. Philosophy for the Ikhwān is "the similitude as much as possible of man with God". It is "the means which again draws the elite of men or the angels on earth near to the Creator Most High." Its use is the "acquisition of the specific virtue of the human race, that of bringing to actualization all the sciences which man possesses potentially. ... By philosophy man realizes the virtual characteristics of his race. He attains the form of humanity and progresses in the hierarchy of beings until in crossing the straight way (bridge) and the correct path he becomes an angel..." One may easily see that there is a more intimate connection between this conception of philosophy and the Pythagorean-Socratic aim of purification of the soul of man than there is with Peripatetic logic.[4]

Their meetings were secret and were intended only for their own initiates. Age played an important role in the division of membership according to hierarchical groups, initiation being encouraged at the age of fifteen while the age of fifty was normal for entering the last most advanced group. They had a 'missionary' spirit and even cultivated the art of emotional appeal to the masses. They were very syncretistic, incorporating not only Shī'ite trends in their theology but much of Greek philosophy and many other elements besides. Technically they had no particular political doctrine of their own, although they are often listed as constituting a 'utopian' community. But their overt intention was preparation for the Heavenly Utopia or Paradise in the life hereafter. Nevertheless part of the training for that included scientific knowledge, for which they became quite famous, rivalling in a way the scientific information shared by al-Rāzī and Thābit ibn Qurra and even the later al-Bīrūnī. In ethics they had dualistic trends, not pretending to rise above the duality of Good and Evil, but quite the opposite, they may well have been influenced by some form of Zoroastrianism. Eventually they had the hope, as most newly inspirited movements do, of winning the entire world to their way.

The Ikhwān insisted that celibacy was the ideal and that (generally not unlike the Confucian idea of the same period) *example* will always outweigh precept and promulgated principles.

> The Ikhwān al-Ṣafā touch at a thorny problem in education. They believe that neither the pupil may benefit from the tutor, nor the tutor may benefit from the pupil, unless there is a kind of intimacy between them. We know for certain that some kind of a reserved friendship is very useful in this respect. But the Ikhwān al-Ṣafā overshoot themselves and speak frankly of "the desire of grown-up men for boys" as an incentive for effecting real education. Furthermore, they mention explicitly that such manners belong only to nations which esteem science, art, literature, and mathematics, like the Persians, the peoples of Mesopotamia and Syria as well as the Greeks. Nomads, who as a rule have no interest in science, art, etc., lack this desire.[5]

Whereas the *Symposium* of Plato and some of his other works besides the *Timaeus* had little influence in Latin Europe until well into the Italian Renaissance, the Ikhwān did cultivate Platonic love as exposited not only in the *Symposium* but also in the *Laws* as an essential component of education, since it is true that seldom does the student learn very much from a teacher who is really not a guru who has affectionate care for his students. In return his students become imbued or infused with his spirit or even infatuated. Evidently there was nothing like the actual worshipping of a guru as an incarnation of some deity or other as in Hindu India; but, within some restrictions, something of that intimate relationship between teacher and disciple was not uncommon in their secret celibate societies.

Although the Ikhwān had their secret meeting places for the sake of enjoyable company, the contention that it was a political society or a subversive movement within Islam has evidently been exaggerated. Rather the text itself reveals no more than "a sense of spiritual solidarity with like-minded persons everywhere, which idealists have always felt or longed for and whose expression is always particularly intensified by a sense of alienation from existing political powers and methods."[6]

> The evidence could not be more clear. The Ikhwān rejected and ridiculed all forms of denominationalism and factionalism. They regarded religious sects as the expression of human ignorance and deficiency (which required the adaptation of the universal message of religious faith and law to the limitations imposed by particular cultural circumstances) and sectarianism as an expression of the lust for power. They expressly state that the injection of politics into religion (no matter how necessary their collaboration may be) is the cause of religion turning from its true goal to the quest for worldly dominance.[7]

Nevertheless one of the major needs in the world at large today is a restudy and re-evaluation of Islamic law and political theory, which in the long run may hold some better hopes of giving the world a more integrated and peaceful political order than the present system of so-called "international" law based on the philosophies of Grotius, Vitoria and Suarez, all three of whom were woefully ignorant of the non-European world and put no restrictions on the plunder and exploitation and alienation of the colonial system.

As for religion, the Ikhwān were perhaps somewhat like the Quakers or the Gandhians in our own time, being Non-conformists as far as the established institutions are concerned, but being in their own way profoundly religious. The masses have difficulty in conceiving of abstract metaphysical principles and therefore do need the symbolic forms that religions provide. While this may be holding a "double standard", it certainly is based on very universal experience all down through the centuries in every culture and civilization. Perhaps the greater need is to provide in the educational system for gradual transfer from these symbolic and mythological forms to the metaphysical and philosophical forms of truth.

> The Ikhwān al-Ṣafā were not satisfied with any of the existing religions; they, nevertheless, urged everybody to select one of them. To have a defective religion is better than to be a disbeliever, since there is an element of truth in every religion. Everybody should be left free to embrace the religion he chooses; he may also change his religion, perhaps often too, though he is expected to look for the best religion in his time. He should refrain, however, from contradictory opinions and false doctrines : a wise man does not embrace two contradictory religions at the same time.
>
> There should be no compulsion in religion; compulsion should be effected only through the laws. This is so because religion is a self-conviction felt in the heart. The laws of religions, on the contrary, are social orders, to abide by which is necessary for the maintenance of security and welfare of the community.[8]

With all their marvellous tolerance of other faiths, the Qur'ān is still always their final appeal, though they may have had their own interpretation of it.

As for metaphysics, as was the case with virtually all the Abrahamic scholastics, the interest was in the theological implications of that discipline; even so, it included the following fields : (1) *Form and Matter* : This is essentially the basics of the Aristotelian system as filtered through the Neo-Platonism of Iamblichus, Porphyry, Proclus and no doubt John Philopon, although they did retain the perspective, somewhat as may be found in Erigena and the others influenced by the Byzantine heritage, that all the actual physical forms are only exemplars of the perfection which exists only in the realm of spirit.

(2) *Space and Time* : As regards space and time, their view was that both are not realities; space is more objective, since it is related to bodies which have dimensions : it is the vessel which holds the contained. Time has no independent existence. It cannot be conceived of except in connection with moving bodies. Now, if space is the outer surface of the world and time is the reckoning of the rotations of the spheres, space and time would be unthinkable prior to the spheres themselves. These views led some to think that they believed in the eternity of the world. They were aware of this accusation and tried to defend themselves against it.[9]

(3) *Causality and Motion*: Causality is the Aristotelian four causes, and motion is essentially the Aristotelian view, including disagreement with the arrow paradox of Zeno of Elea.

(4) *Number* : As might be expected, here the Pythagorean theory of numbers is adopted.

> The science of number (*'ilm al-'adad*) is considered by the Ikhwān as the way leading to the grasp of Unity, as a science which stands above Nature and is the principle of beings and the root of the other sciences, the first elixir and the most exhalted alchemy. It is, moreover, the first effusion (*faiḍ*) of the Intellect imprinted upon the Soul and the "tongue which speaks of Unity and transcendence". No wonder, then, that the *Rasā'il* always compare the relation of God to the world —or, metaphysically speaking, of Being to existence—as that of One to the other numbers. In the more esoteric *Risālat al-Jāmi'ah*, it is implied in one place that Being (*al-wujūd*) corresponds to one, and the Infinite, or the Divine Essence, to zero. Zero, therefore, symbolizes the Divine Ipseity, which is above all determinations including Being.[10]

Thus they realized that numbers do have qualities and are not merely mechanical devices for measuring quantities. Number is also important as a designation of the hierarchy of Being, a theme that can be followed later on through Byzantine transmission in such as Nicholas of Cusa and probably in Raymond

Lull and many connected with the Caballa in the Italian Renaissance if not even down through Descartes, Leibniz, Swedenbourg and eventually Whitehead. Needless to say, something like this can also be found in some sub-varieties of Tāntric tradition. Also, some of the geometrical designs commonly found in Islamic art may well be the fruits of the Ikhwān's contribution, since many of them very closely resemble the famous Śrī Yantra as well as some of the famous mandalas now associated with Tibetan and Nepalese Buddhism.

(5) *Being and Emanation* : Here we are again confronted with the familiar *ex nihilo* controversy but in the more or less Neo-Platonic form, probably filtered through Philopon's "corrections" of Proclus' views. It is especially noteworthy that the emanations are considerably extended far beyond the simple formula of Plotinus himself and as such should provoke a fresh investigation into the relations between Byzantium and Baṣra in the tenth century, for although there was conflict there was also communication so that we might well expect some parallel developments. But at the other end of the geographical spectrum, as it were, comparison with Kaśmir Buddhism and the then nascent Kaśmir Śaivism might also constitute an extremely fascinating study, although without any as yet demonstrable lines of communication being open until after al-Bīrūnī (d. 1048). Comparison with Udayana (d. 1050) might also prove very stimulating.

The creation of the Universe, beginning with the Creator, descending through the multiple states of Being, and ending with the terrestrial creatures whose final link is man, is outlined in the following manner :

1. Creator—who is one, simple, eternal, permanent.
2. Intellect (*'aql*)—which is of two kinds : innate and acquired.
3. Soul (*nafs*)—which has three species : vegetative, animal, and reasonable.
4. Matter (*hayūlā'*)—which is of four kinds : matter of artifacts, physical matter, universal matter, and original matter.

5. Nature (*ṭabī'ah*)—which is of five kinds : celestial nature and the four elemental natures.
6. Body (*jism*)—which has six directions : above, below, front, back, left, and right.
7. The sphere—which has its seven planets.
8. The elements—which have eight qualities, these being in reality the four qualities combined two by two :

   Earth—cold and dry
   Water—cold and wet
   Air—warm and wet
   Fire—warm and dry
9. Beings of this world—which are the mineral, plant, and animal kingdoms, each having three parts....

The Ikhwān describe the production of the "great chain of Being" in the following manner :

"The first thing which the Creator produced and called into existence is a simple, spiritual, extremely perfect and excellent substance in which the form of all things is contained. This substance is called the Intellect. From this substance there proceeds a second one which in hierarchy is below the first and which is called the Universal Soul (*al-nafs al-kullīyah*). From the Universal Soul proceeds another substance which is below the Soul and which is called Original Matter. The latter is transformed into the Absolute Body, that is, into Secondary Matter which has length, width and depth."[11]

Although by no means unique to the Ikhwān, the principle of hierarchy figures very prominently in virtually all aspects of their world-view. Indeed, it is difficult to find any country or civilization in the tenth century where this principle did not apply. Their hierarchy of hierarchies remains only implicit in the Vedāntic philosophies for the most part, and is almost exclusively applied to the merely human realm in Japan and China, although it could be duplicated among the Ikhwān's Byzantine contemporaries, not to mention the heritage of Erigena in Latin Europe (even though that was considerably 'flattened' by Peter Damien). Of course the hierarchy of the Ikhwān is reversible : evolution and involution, *yin* and *yang*, *sparśa* and *vimarśa* are there just as much as in any other system of the tenth century, although this is more obvious in the influence of Neo-Platonism and Neo-Pythagoreanism.

Nasr reminds us that the symbolism of love (*'ishq*) is also used by the Ikhwān in a way that is more often associated with Ṣūfī tradition :

> According to them, the whole world seeks the Creator and loves Him. In fact, the Creator is really the only Beloved (*ma'shūq*) and the only object of desire (*murād*). They make the power of yearning (*shawq*) the very cause of the coming into being of things and the law governing the Universe. It was through *shawq* for Allah that the Universal Soul brought the outermost sphere of the Universe, the *Muḥīt*, into existence. The *Muḥīt* in turn rotated to form the sphere below it, this process continuing all the way down to the sphere of the moon.[12]

Nasr goes on to suggest that "there is a striking resemblance between the three cosmic tendencies of ascent, descent, and horizontal expansion described by the Ikhwān and the three Hindu *guṇas*."[13] Of course an extended comparison with the Sāṃkhya three *guṇa* scheme would need some qualification since the classical Sāṃkhya was atheistic or at least non-theistic (although in the seventeenth century Vijñāna Bhikṣu revived interest in the Sāṃkhya by virtue of his theistic interpretation). Also the radical dualism of *prakṛti* and *puruṣa* is much more marked in the Sāṃkhya than in the Ikhwān's cosmogony and cosmology. Here we might mention instead Udayana, who was a refiner of the Vaiśeṣika system which was mildly but definitely theistic and had a system of categories, matter and causation that was scarcely less scientific than the Ikhwān's system. Nevertheless, in the emanational aspect of the Ikhwān's view, the four levels of matter constitute a fascinating parallel to the three *guṇa* scheme, with *Mahat* corresponding to Original Matter.

(6) *Macrocosm and Microcosm* : Here the Ikhwān simply followed the teaching of Democritus of Abdera (d.c. 370 B.C.) "which treated of man as a reduced model of the universe, and of the universe as the enlarged copy of man."[14]

(7) *The Individual Soul and Its Fall* : The Ikhwān had their own distinctive symbolical and allegorical interpretation of this with a relatively optimistic attitude towards the prospect of redemption. "The body is only the workshop of the soul, a temporary house, a shell, a mount necessary for a journey. Once the body is forsaken by the soul it becomes again a heap of solid matter akin to the constituent elements of the earth. But the body is as necessary for the soul as is the womb for the development of the foetus."[15]

The *Rasā'il* was the result of accumulated scientific speculation and systematization of many centuries. We do not know how much they added that was really their own, but this compendium was certainly representative of the scientific fields of medieval period at least in the Islamic world. As such it had incorporated not only the Hellenistic and perforce Byzantine sources, but also much of Indian sources and some Chinese as well. It would be many centuries before we find anything really comparable in Latin Europe. The following areas are treated :

(1) Arithmetic

(2) Geometry : This was recommended as good not only for practical application but as "good for the soul". Euclid is there of course. There are two kinds of geometry : "*ḥissīyyah*, tangible, sensible, or common plane and solid geometry which helps man to acquire skill in crafts; and '*aqlīyyah*, intellectual or rational, namely : analytic and descriptive, which enables man to be versed in theoretical sciences."[16] This latter disciplines the soul through the mind thinking in terms of pure forms which are close to the purely spiritual realm. In Sanskrit terminology the *ḥissīyyah* would be operative at the *prātibhāsika* level and the '*aqlīyyah* high in the *vyāvahārika*, the *pāramārthika* level perhaps being left for the purely theological.

(3) Music : Here there is again the Pythagorean heritage. The Ikhwān were fully aware that music is of such a primordially universal nature that other animals besides man can be moved by it. It is not entertainment but a truly spiritual art.

(4) Cosmology

(5) Sphericity of the Earth

(6) Geography and Meteorology

(7) Physics and Chemistry

(8) Mineral, Vegetable and Animal Kingdoms : There is here evidently a highly controversial topic for interpreters, some claiming that the Ikhwān virtually anticipated the evolutionary views of Darwin and Spencer. Nasr comments :

> The chain of Being described by the Ikhwān possesses a temporal aspect which has led certain scholars to the view that the authors of the *Rasā'il* believed in the modern theory of evolution... However, the divergence of the Ikhwān from modern theories of evolution should be clear. First of all, according to the *Rasā'il* all changes on earth occur as acts of the Universal Soul and not by an independent agent acting within bodies here on earth. Secondly, according to the Ikhwān this world is a shadow of another world more real than it, and the "idea" of everything in this world actually exists in the other, so that there is no question of a species changing into another, because the "idea" of each species is a form which is beyond change and decay.[17]

Further, the scientific interests of the Ikhwān generally should be seen in the following perspective :

> In the deepest sense, what separates all these ideas of the Ikhwān from their modern counterparts is that for the Ikhwān the hands of God were not cut off from creation after the beginning of the world—as is the case with the deists. On the contrary, every event here "below" is performed from "above" by the Universal Soul, which is God's agent. Consequently, the purpose of the study of Nature is to see these "vestiges of God"—the *vestigia Dei* as the medieval Latins used to express it—so that, thanks to the analogy existing between the Universe and man, the soul through this knowledge of cosmic realities can come to know itself better and ultimately be able to escape from the earthly prison into which it has fallen. "Thy soul, oh Brother, is one of the pure forms. Use your efforts then to know it. Thou willst succeed probably in saving it from the ocean of matter to raise it from the abyss of the body and deliver it from the prison of Nature."[18]

All across Eurasia in this epoch astronomy and astrology were seldom separated, although the separation of the two was not completely strange to the Ikhwān. Needless to say, the Ikhwān used the signs of the Zodiac, and they had no doubts about the geocentric nature of the universe much less of the solar system. However, for that age their astronomical science was as advanced as any. Nasr notes that in some relatively minor points of disagreement with the ancient Greek astronomers, the Ikhwān followed al-Farghānī, who had also made some connections between that science as such with certain verses in the Qur'ān. Calendar calculation of course was rather universal, so it should not be surprising that the Ikhwān have their own system based, as were all the other systems, on cycles, the greatest cycle being 36,000 years. Although most of this system can be traced back to the Chaldeans, the Ikhwān definitely state that in at least one detail they are knowledgeable of, if not indebted to, the Indian system :

> The conjunction of the stars at the end of the 36,000 years marks a cycle from the time when the planets have reunited together at the first degree of the sign of the Ram to the time when they come back to this point after the lapse of this time. The tables of Sindhind [that is, those of the Indians], call this lapse of time a year of the disposition of the world.[19]

This is just another of those numerous tags upon which we build our hypothesis of ever-present and more or less constant interchange between the various civilizations of Eurasia.

Somewhat as one finds in the Hindu *Purāṇas*, the Ikhwān also had a more or less mythical notion of the origin of the continents and how they were separated from the waters. In accordance with or from influence by the astrological factors, not only do the cycles include geological phenomena such that "mountains become seas and seas become mountains", but the cycles of human civilizations :

> It is by these primary and intermeditate causes that the domination of the world passes from one people to another that cultures as well as desolation may be transported from one quarter of the earth to another. All these events happen by virtue of the power determining the conjunctions which occur in regulated times and circumstances.[20]

As with virtually all systems up to that time, any sharp division between these 'natural' sciences and metaphysics and theology was virtually unknown. This remains perhaps the chief reason for marvelling at the Ikhwān, that they seem to have preserved and cultivated a marvellous harmony between the interior, the exterior and the superior sciences—a triad which comes to full blossom later in Bonaventura.

On the topic of Light, leading into the topic of the Vision of God, we find not only an amazingly detailed account of the refraction of 'white' light into different colors, but also a hierarchy of kinds of lights, ultimately culminating in a hierarchical pattern of transformations of the various elements, ultimately not only in the spiritual light which transforms human nature but in the nature of God Himself who—quite scripturally and almost non-figuratively—is called the "Light of Lights". Thus here we have something adumbrating a sort of Whiteheadian 'process' dynamic of an organismic type rather than a fixed and unchanging dualistic order of spirit and matter, body and soul, God and world. Many of the metaphors are quite universal, such as the fact that we seldom see light as such but we rather see other things through it; and the purer the light is the more nearly are we able to see spiritual reality, including the level of the Universal Soul, incorporating, as it were, in a Grand Body of Light, all the individual souls.

By the permeation of 'light'—in the modern world we might say "vibrations" extending through the long spectrum of which visible light and "brain waves" constitute only very small windows, but arranged in a hierarchy of harmonics such that when there is no static the harmony of microcosm and macrocosm is at its best—there is a vital continuum of degrees of freedom as purity of light is perceived or becomes the medium whereby the soul becomes increasingly sensitized to the more etherial ranges of Being, such that the ultimate Simplicity, which is divine, is really inclusive of the lower realms, or at least is related to them by a sort of 'magnetic' attraction, dynamically and not merely by static structures.

Freedom comes only with salvation, and that comes only by degrees according to this view rather than by a sudden enlightenment of being twice-born once and for all. Of course there is the paradox that such freedom comes only as one submits everything to God and the Revelation, so that apparent freedom, especially the rebellious assertions of freedom, remain perhaps the lowest form ; but spiritual freedom is of a higher order, embracing everything beneath it in the hierarchy. The Ikhwān nevertheless were in their own way quietly rebellious against the literalistic sort of submission to the law, but conceived of a Higher Obedience that was not constraining but liberating not only for themselves but for others if not for the whole of society. Moreover, these matters are not to be treated as subjects for bickerings and juggling of syllogisms but as a matter of meditation and contemplation.

> Man should thus meditate on his original home and awaken from his ignorant sleep, and desire fervently to return to his celestial abode announcing finally *Labbaika Labbaika* at Thy orders to the call of God, "But oh! thou soul at peace! Return unto thy Lord content in His good pleasure !" And so multiplicity returns again to Unity, integrating in this process the whole of Nature and bringing everything to the Source from which nothing really ever departs.[21]

As always we should review what is *not* in the *Rasā'il*, almost global in scope as it is, in application of our favorite *pramāṇa, anupalabdhi.* There are only remote parallels with the *pāramitās* of Mahāyāna, with the *kośas* of the Vedāntic systems, with the *satkāryavāda-asatkāryavāda* controversy in the various Hindu systems, and with the *saptabhangavāda,* the multiple-valued logic of Jainism which was still holding its own in the tenth century. Although one might investigate organization of their more or less communal society in relation to the *vinaya* rules of Buddhist *saṅgha,* and although the Ikhwān did counsel celibacy for all who could embrace it, nevertheless they did not in any strict sense constitute a monastic order. It would be difficult to find even in the Ikhwān anything quite resembling the nascent and developing Neo-Confucianist system of integration of education and politics, even though there is the insistence that the Calif like the Chinese Emperor should rule by virtue of his charismatic example rather than by mere enforcement of a legal system. One could go into almost unlimited detail in regard to the *nirguṇa-saguṇa* controversy in relation to the Ikhwān's roll in the Ash'arite-Mu'tazilite controversy. However, the Ikhwān seem not to be so much involved in that topic as in the nature of man in the microcosm-macrocosm relation, somewhat disdaining the merely theological squabbles which deal disproportionately with the vain attempt to define the undefinable.

In conclusion, Fakhry gives the following characterization of the Ikhwān al-Ṣafā :

> Despite their regard for Pythagoras, "the Sage," whom they do not tire of praising or paraphrasing, the Brethren are not loath to glean their teaching from every possible quarter, since their motto is to not leave any source of knowledge untapped and to encompass in their doctrine the positive aspects of all creeds. Accordingly, not only Greek philosophy, but Persian and Indian scientific and literary lore, Jewish and Christian Scripture, both canonical and apocryphal, Ptolemaic and post-Ptolemaic astronomy, as well as a fair sprinkling of astrological and magical legends, are brought together in this massive, though often ill-organized, verbose, and repetitious compendium of Arabic learning in the tenth century. A puzzling feature of this compendium is that, despite the undoubted reliance of its writers on other Islamic philosophers and theologians, hardly any of them are mentioned by name. Thus al-Rāzī, who reflected definite Pythagorean sympathies ; al-Kindī, whose concept of the creation of the world in time they made their own, despite the fact that it was ill-suited to their Neo-Platonic purposes ; the Mu'tazilah, whose view of free will they adopted, notwithstanding its obvious incompatibility with their astrological belief in the influence of the stars on earthly phenomena, etc., are not explicitly mentioned by the author or authors of this compendium.
>
> Once all this has been said, however, it must be noted that the Brethren occupy a unique position in the history of Islamic thought. Unlike the professional philosophers, from al-Kindī to Ibn Rushd, or the theologians, from Wāṣil to al-Ash'arī, the Brethren sought earnestly to break down the barrier between philosophy and dogma and to bring metaphysics and

science from the inaccessible heights of pure speculation down to the market place of active, practical concern.[22]

10. al-Fārābī

Al-Fārābī (870-950) became known as the "second teacher", the first teacher being Aristotle himself. But in spite of his extensive use of Aristotle, which he derives from al-Kindī, al-Fārābī remains pretty much a Neo-Platonist, and much of his effort is directed towards reconciling Plato and Aristotle as well as integrating them into Islamic tradition. For an initial introduction we may note the following from Fakhry:

> The first systematic exposition of Neo-Platonism in Arabic is undoubtedly the work of the first outstanding logician and metaphysician of Islam, Muḥammad b. Tarkhān al-Fārābī, better known in classical sources and among the Latins of the Middle Ages as Abū Naṣr (Latin : Abunaser).
>
> Our authorities are unanimous in bestowing the highest praise on al-Fārābī, chiefly as the leading logician and expositor of Plato and Aristotle in his day. According to an early source, he studied logic with a Christian scholar, Yuḥannā b. Hailān in Baghdad, but soon outstripped all his Muslim contemporaries; he refined the study of logic and completed the subtler aspects that al-Kindī had overlooked.
>
> Of al-Fārābī's life we know only that he came from Fārāb in Transoxiana and that his father was a captain of Persian, or probably Turkish, origin. He is said to have grown up in Damascus, where he devoted himself to reading philosophical books at night by the "watchman's torch," while working as a garden keeper by day. He was subseqently drawn to Baghdad where he met the leading teachers of his day, such as Mattā and Yuḥannā, and they initiated him into the study of logic. After a journey into Egypt, he returned to Aleppo in

northern Syria; shortly thereafter, in 950, he died at the age of eighty. ...

Not only in logic, but also in physics, metaphysics, and politics, al-Fārābī's contribution entitles him to a position of undoubted pre-eminence among the philosophers of Islam. He is particularly commended by one of the earliest historiographers for his masterly exposition of the philosophies of Plato and Aristotle. These two works, together with his *Enumeration of the Sciences*, are the most comprehensive general introduction to Aristotelianism and Platonism in Arabic, and they far surpass in quality and completeness any parallel works of that period.[1]

And Madkour presents the following as the Conclusion to his study of al-Fārābī:

We can now conclude that al-Fārābī's doctrine is so fully harmonious and consistent that its parts are completely interrelated. From the one, the First Cause, al-Fārābī gets on to ten intelligences from which the two worlds of heaven and earth have flowed. His spheres are moved by the managing intelligences, and nature with its generation and corruption is subjected to these intelligences. The soul is governed by one of these intelligences which is the agent intelligence. Politics and ethics are no exceptions, for happiness pursued by men is but the communion with the celestial world. His "Model City" only aims at this end.

This doctrine is at the same time spiritualistic and idealistic for al-Fārābī reduces almost everything to spirit. His God is the Spirit of the spirits, his astronomical spheres are governed by celestial spirits, and the prince of his city is a man whose spirit transcends his body. This spiritualism is rooted in ideas and concepts, and is given wholly to speculation and contemplation. The One is the Idea *par-excellence* and is the Intellect that intellects Itself. The other beings are generated by this Intellect. Through speculation and contemplation man can commune with the celestial world and attain the utmost happiness. No spiritualism is so closely related to idealism as that of al-Fārābī.

> Although al-Fārābī's doctrine is a reflection of the Middle Ages, it comprises some modern and even contemporary notions. He favours science, advocates experimentation, and denies augury and astrology. He so fully believes in causality and determinism that he refers to causes even for those effects which have no apparent causes. He elevates the intellect to a plane so sacred that he is driven to its conciliation with tradition so that philosophy and religion may accord.[2]

Al-Fārābī's materials included Hippocrates and Galen, most of Aristotle, several dialogues of Plato, Euclid and Ptolemy, Plotinus and Prophyry, the Byzantine text and commentaries of such as John Philopon who was the chief Christian commentator on Aristotle after Alexander of Aphrodisias, and no doubt a goodly portion of Proclus' work on Plato. But al-Fārābī was much more than merely a translator or transmitter. He wrote commentaries on many works, and it was in these commentaries that new ideas were expressed. By no means is it necessary to write individual specialized essays for new ideas, as though they descend from heaven finished and polished and perfectly packaged—as seems to be the modern secular bias; and often as not they turn out to be not so new at the core after all, whereas every seminal notion in a great classic does have the power of eliciting far more than it explicates. At any rate, Mahdi epitomizes the character and purpose of al-Fārābī's basic works as follows:

> Although al-Fārābī wrote commentaries on Euclid's *Elements* and Ptolemy's *Almagest*, the mathematical art to which he devoted particular attention was music. He wrote extensively on its history, theory, and instruments; and it is significant that his chosen art was the practice of music rather than medicine. Unlike the expository and didactic style of his mathematical writings, his specialized writings on natural science are for the most part polemical : against Galen's interpretations of Aristotle's views on the parts of animals; against John Philopons' criticism of Aristotle's views on the eternity of the world and movement; against the physician al-Rāzī's views on matter, time, place, and atoms; against the theologian Ibn al-Rāwandī's account of dialectic,

> which was the method used by the theologians in natural science; against the doctrines of the theologians in general concerning atoms and vacuum; and finally against the scientific claims of astrology and alchemy.... Al-Fārābī's intention was not primarily to defend the doctrines of Aristotle against his critics, but rather to clarify the questions at issue, to ascertain the assumptions, coherence, and relevance of the arguments against Aristotle's natural science, and to determine whether they are based on genuine differences between Aristotle and his opponents or merely on a misunderstanding or misinterpretation of Aristotle, overconfidence in the theoretical implications of certain experiments, or eagerness to support a religious doctrine. Al-Fārābī's openness regarding the foundations of Aristotle's natural science was restrained, however, because of his awareness of the decline of scientific learning since Aristotle's time and the overwhelming odds against free scientific inquiry in the new religious environment.[3]

Besides considerable influence in Latin Europe, in the Islamic world al-Fārābī had a definite impact on the Ikhwān al-Ṣafā, al-Mas'ūdī, Miskawayh, and al-Āmirī. "Ibn Sīnā seems to have known his works intimately and Ibn Rushd follows him in the essentials of his thought."[4]

For al-Fārābī logic is the first essential, and the training of character follows soon after that. In either case, "Philosophy is studied primarily to obtain a knowledge of God as the Creator and Efficient Cause of all things, the One, Immovable."[5] In logic al-Fārābī is most concerned with the typical Aristotelian scheme of universals and categories as handed down through Porphyry and Iamblicus. The difficulty of the manner in which composition of these takes place concerns him very much, and the sense in which the universals are therefore 'made' or whether they are already 'there'. As an Aristotelian he inclines toward the former view for the most part, although when it comes to the first principles he admits that these cannot be mediated or demonstrated. These first principles are those of contradiction, causality, and the excluded middle; they must simply be taken as self-evident.

The categories are still the ten of Aristotle : substance, quantity, quality, relation, place, time, action, passion, posture and having. But al-Fārābī sees in them a descending order, the first four being taken as absolutely simple, action and passion being derived from them, time and place being derived from substance and quantity; 'having' occurs between two substances, relation between any two of the others, although it does not follow that mere juxtaposition of things entails relation between them, for there are orders in the relatively elastic range of necessity. One spoken word does not necessarily entail other spoken words; nonsense is also possible, and there is a difference in degree between the causal relation between father and son and, say, the flight of Muḥammad from Meccah to Medinah and the setting up of the Abassid Califate. In short, we are already beginning to see a keen appreciation of the dynamic balance between identity and difference, equal and unequal, similar and dissimilar, One and many. But he did not stop with mere reflection on this 'balance'. Is it descriptive of quantity as a category, or essential to its existence as a part of the structure of the world and of thought? Moreover, does the Sung Neo-Confucianists' treatment of the *I Ching* give a better way of handling this quantity-quality relation nexus ? Likewise concerning the opposites : are contraries mutually exclusive, or does the presence of one merely entail the absence of the others? Al-Fārābī replies that a distinction must be made :

> If we deal with the science of something which happens to have a contrary, then that science is not identical with that of its contrary. The science of the Just is not that of the Unjust, the knowledge of White is not the knowledge of Black. On the other hand, if we deal with the science of something insofar as it has a contrary, then this science is one with that of its contrary, because in this sense the two contraries are really and truly two relatives.[6]

But we must distinguish between opposites and contraries (did his Chinese contemporaries understand this as clearly as he?) : "Opposites and contraries differ and must be distinguished one from the other. Opposites are two things which cannot exist in the same object at the same time and in the same respect, as the quality of father and son. Opposites are a part of relatives proper. Contraries are odd and even, affirmation and negation, sight and blindness."[7]

As to the old difficulty which all encounter who are limited to the Indo-European language group (which some claim Chinese and Japanese languages avoid by omitting the copula altogether) as to whether existential sentences involve a true subject and predicate, al-Fārābī says :

> If 'man' is considered from the natural and objective viewpoint, the judgment is without a predicate because the fact of existence is one with man and cannot be distinguished from him, while the predicate denotes distinction from the thing to which it is referred. From the logical point of view, the judgment has a predicate, because it is made up of the two terms which may be either true or false.[8]

This reminds us of some of Rāmānuja's logical arguments against Śaṅkara's monistic logic which collapses all predication back into the Single Subject, concerning which no discourse would then be possible, not even the possibility of designating it as *anirvacanīya,* indescribable. Or again, is it not like what we find in Chang Ts'ai for example, who would not allow that the Supreme Principle must remain in undifferentiated continuum but must be manifest by the operation of *yin* ('predicate') and *yang* ('subject').

According to al-Fārābī, "Universals do not exist in act, that is, they are not things existing in themselves, but they exist only in individuals, and their existence is accidental in the sense that they are subject to the existence of individuals. That does not mean, however, that universals are accidents, but merely that their existence in act can take place only per accident."[9] No doubt he is trying to guarantee the transcendence of Allah, who can have no true attributes, although in another sense He must be taken, if one is to integrate Aristotle into the tradition of revelation, as the Universals, as well as the creator of things about which rationalistic philosophers must formulate objective propositions in such a way as to demonstrate that as individuals they are only creatures and not subordinate or subsistent imitators of the Creator. Nevertheless, he cannot admit that universal can be self-existent without reference to the individuals because that would deny the reality of the things which the Creator has made and thereby run the risk of denying the Reality of the Creator who made them. The spirit of Islam demands the objective study of nature as the best way to approach the proper understanding of the Author of nature—in spite of the Ash'arites' arguments. Science, in other words, has full freedom, for perhaps more than in early medieval Christianity no otherworldliness is considered necessary as concomitant with the Faith.

In his definitions in regard to Being, this background of the Ash'arite-Mu'tazilite controversy should be even more clear :

> The most universal concept is Being and what is co-extensive with Being itself. ... Being cannot be defined, for it is self-evident, fixed in the mind, precedes all other concepts and is the simplest of all. It is the simplest, because to define a concept is to analyze its content, and Being having the least content, resists all efforts to resolve it into simpler thought elements. To try to define it by words serves only to make our mind attentive and directed to it, and not to explain the concept which is clearer than the words by which it is defined.... Just as in the demonstration of a proposition it is imperative that the judgments be coordinated in order to arrive at an ultimate judgment-principle, in like manner in the definition of a concept, it is necessary that the concept be resolved into other simpler concepts until one arrives at the simplest and most universal concept, which is Being.[10]

This Aristotelian manner of arriving at a concept of Being by way of ultimate abstraction seems not so comparable to the manner in which Shao Yung and his fellow Neo-Confucianists treated the Supreme Ultimate, for they did not so much follow the way of abstraction into universals, but (more after the manner of Plato, whose synchronological representative is Psellos) assumed the Tao and were interested in its self-differentiation and cyclic return to itself. However, as we follow al-Fārābī's divisions of Being, we see closer parallels. The first division is the classic Aristotelian distinction of potential and actual, corresponding not too remotely to *yin* and *yang*. This follows the still more basic distinction of necessary and contingent Being, which resembles to some extent the Tao or *li* considered in itself and as manifest in the myriads of things.

The quibble—or is it merely that since it takes so much space in the philosophical literature of Western Europe from Plato and Aristotle right down to the present—over the distinction between essence and existence for the most part seems to have been absent in most of the Confucianist tradition, no doubt for reasons largely semantical. Al-Fārābī nevertheless thought it was a real distinction and an important one, probably largely as a means of clarifying the relation between the mode of God's self-existence and the manner in which it must be said that the existence of things is dependent on their essences, which analogically depend directly on the Being of God, counter-balancing the purely abstract logical construction of particulars and universals, which analytically must be broken down into the singularity of Being which underlies them also before their full significance can be seen. Al-Fārābī writes :

> A real distinction occurs here and that existence is one thing and essence is another. If essence and existence were one thing, then we should be unable to conceive the one without conceiving the other. But in fact, we are able to conceive essence in itself. If it is true that man has existence by essence, this would be like saying that to conceive man's essence is to imply his existence. ... If existence should enter into composition with the essence of man like one entering into the essence of two, this would mean that it is impossible to conceive perfectly the essence of man without his existence as a part of the essence. Just as the essence of two would be destroyed by taking away a unity from it, so would the essence of man be destroyed by taking away existence from it. But this is not true, because existence does not enter into composition with the essence of a thing, for it is possible to understand the essence of man, and not to know whether it exists in reality. On the other hand, if there were no distinction between essence and existence in created beings, then these could be

> said to exist by their essence. But there is one being alone whose essence is His very existence, and that is God.[11]

Here al-Fārābī is closer to Anselm or to Rāmānuja than to Aquinas, who in a sense is committed necessarily to the same convergence of essence and existence in God but whose exaggerated objectivity would commit him still to retain the formal distinction between them, even within the nature of God. For al-Fārābī, God's nature remains so far beyond our ken that we can only acknowledge that all distinctions must disappear in His Being, which is so exalted that even to attribute omniscience, omnipresence, life, seeing, hearing, etc., may be done only permissively and descriptively, not necessarily.

Concerning the principle of causation al-Fārābī writes : "Whatever exists after having not existed, must be brought into being by a cause : nothing (not-being) cannot be the cause of being."[12] There is nothing unusual about this; only the boldest purveyors of paradox have ever dared to think otherwise. But his application turns toward the mystical : "In the world of created things we do not find either produced impressions or free choice unless it is the result of a cause. Man cannot do a thing without relying on external causes, which are not of his choice, and these causes rely on the order, and the order on the decree, and the decree on the judgment, and the judgment comes from the commandment. And so everything is decreed."[13] Here al-Fārābī is only trying to apply Aristotle to the necessity of affirming the doctrine of predestination as it had come down to him through the orthodox and not-so-orthodox theologians who had preceded him.

On the knowability of God al-Fārābī differs very little from the Christian scholastics. Specifically he writes :

> It is very difficult to know what God is because of the limitation of our intellect, and its union with matter. Just as light is the principle by which colors become visible, in like manner it would seem logical to say that a perfect light should produce a perfect vision. Instead the very opposite occurs. A perfect light dazzles the vision. The same is true of God. The imperfect knowledge we have of God is due to the fact that He is infinitely perfect. That explains why His infinitely

> perfect being bewilders our mind. But if we could strip our nature of all that we call matter, then certainly our knowledge of His being would be quite perfect.[14]

And as for the existence of God, al-Fārābī offers the traditional proofs ; from motion, from efficient cause, and from contingence.

> In this world there are things which are moved. Now every object which is moved receives its motion from a mover. If the mover is itself moved, there must be another mover moving it, and after that, still another and so on. But it is impossible to go on to infinity in the series of movers and things moved. Therefore there must be an immovable mover, and this is God....
>
> In contemplating the changeable world, one sees that it is composed of beings which have a cause, and this cause, in turn, is the cause of another. Now in the series of efficient causes it is not possible to proceed infinitely. For if A were the cause of B, B of C, C of D, and so on, here A would be the cause of itself, which is not admissible. Therefore outside the series of efficient causes, there must be an uncaused efficient cause, and this is God....
>
> Now that which begins to exist must owe its existence to the action of a cause. This cause, in turn, either is or is not contingent. If it is contingent, it also must have received its existence by the action of another cause, and so on. But a series of contingent beings which would produce one another cannot proceed to infinity or move in a circle. Therefore, the series of causes and effects must arrive at a cause that holds its existence for itself, and this is the first cause (*Ens Primum*).[15]

Al-Fārābī balances the *via affirmativa* and the *via negationis*, both of which must lead directly Godward of their own necessity, although, no less than the Byzantines and the Buddhists, he puts the emphasis on the latter as more nearly final : "We can have some knowledge of the nature of God by means of a twofold process : first, by exclusion (*via remotion*) by which we remove from God whatever implies defect, as limitation, dependence, mutability; and second by preeminence (*via eminentiae*), by which we attribute to God in an infinite degree all perfections, such as goodness, wisdom, etc."[16] This latter way had not been so prominent up to this century. It is especially curious that Rāmānuja takes the same way out of the impasse of a too strict application of the logic of identity and of the *via negativa.* The Chinese generally were not so inclined to superlatives, and Psellos likewise preserves a certain classic reserve: but at least it seems that their tendency is also pretty much in this direction, analogizing from what is good on earth to what must be in a supreme degree good in heaven. And certainly St. Anselm uses this sort of procedure very vividly, surrounding his more famous ontological argument with all sorts of superlative praises—or really launching into a sort of *turīya*, the fourth condition which was becoming the primary focus in the late Upaniṣads. And while Abelard remains adroitly dialectical, St. Bernard of Clairvaux never spares this *via aminentiae* in his discourse on the Love of God.

Nevertheless, superlatives or not, the Simplicity of God remains the ultimate *vidyā* :

> God is simple because He is free from every kind of composition, physical or metaphysical. Physical composition may be either substantial or accidental. It is substantial if the composite substance consists of body and soul, of matter and form. Now, an infinite being cannot be a substantial composite of matter and form, because this would mean that God results from the union of finite parts which would exist before Him in time, and therefore be the cause of His being. Nor can an accidental composition be attributed to the infinite, because this would imply a capacity for an increase in the perfection, which the very notion of the infinite excludes. Therefore, there is not and cannot be any physical composition....
>
> Neither can there be that kind of composition known as metaphysical, which results from the union of two different concepts so referred to the same real thing that neither one by itself signifies the whole reality as meant by their union. Thus, every contingent being is a metaphysical composite of essence and existence. Essence, as such, in reference to a contingent

> being, implies its conceivableness or possibility, and abstracts from actual existence; while existence as such must be added to essence before we can speak of being as actual. But the composite of essence and existence in a contingent being cannot be applied to the self-existent or infinite being in whom essence and existence are one. Therefore, there is no composition of essence and existence in God.[17]

Al-Fārābī was no doubt again arguing primarily against the Ash'arites who insisted that God and His attributes are distinct though perhaps inseparable. Al-Fārābī argues that all attribution, all logical operations, all truth, all being, essence and existence—all this is transconverted into the singular Simplicity of God, thereby also gainsaying the extreme Mu'tazilites who deny attribution to God altogether. On the larger stage we shall find Rāmānuja doing almost the same thing although everything leads out from and back into God, and is in the meanwhile being sustained and pervaded by God, He still remains superlatively above our complete comprehension; but this does not mean that He remains completely unknowable, which is what Śaṅkara would have to admit if he were completely consistent. Psellos to a great extent does the same thing in his manner of reconciling Plato and Aristotle.

For the Viśiṣṭadvaitin (Rāmānuja) there are only three bodies essentially, although Rāmānuja's philosophy of embodiment is progressive so that each evolute of matter is the further embodiment of the spiritual principle just above it, while the whole is also a direct embodiment of the Lord. But for al-Fārābī : "There are six kinds of bodies: the celestial, the rational animal, the irrational animal, the vegetable, the mineral and the four elements."[18] But on the score of God's relation to the world there is still the *ex nihilo* to contend with :

> When people say that God created the world, they simply mean that God produced the world out of matter by clothing it with determinate form. The world is certainly God's work, and though it comes after Him as a world form, yet it is equal to Him in time, or eternal, insofar as He could not begin to work on it exactly in time. The reason for this is that God is to the world exactly what a cause is to its effect. Since the

> cause in this case is inseparable from the effect, it follows that He could not, in a given moment, start making it. For, if He could, that would simply imply imperfection on His part while He had been trying to achieve His goal. This, of course is incompatible with the absolute perfection of God.[19]

On the question of good and evil, the following :

> God's providence is exercised over things. Hence, whatever happens in the world is not to be attributed to chance. Evil is under divine control and is united to corruptible things. That evil exists in the world is good accidently, because if it did not exist, a great deal of good in the world would never come about.[20]

At first glance this might look more like a Taoist or Zen manner of treating good and evil paradoxically on par, realizing that there is the Higher Neutrality from which they may both be observed; or, if one's conditioning has been otherwise, it might appear to be rather the modern utilitarian doctrine that the 'greater' good is to be chosen even though it may at least appear to include the 'lesser' evil. But historically this would be completely inaccurate, for the Muslim doctrine, both orthodox and heterodox, must somehow acknowledge that Allah has for reasons of His own—usually considered to be for the sake of corrective punishment, not retributive as found to a great extent in St. Anselm—ordained both good and evil in the world, while He Himself remains above them both, not allowing any finite creature to share in such a condition (at least not until the General Resurrection, when all will be balanced out).

As a Muslim al-Fārābī must guarantee that the soul as a creature of God is a real entity, not by any means equal with God but nevertheless sharing with Him the universality of spiritual (non-material) nature :

> The spirituality of the soul is demonstrated by its specific operations, which are intellection and volition. The operation of a being is according to the nature of the being itself (*actio sequitur esse*). Now intellect and will may attain to the abstract and immaterial; therefore, the soul itself must also be

> independent of matter.... *Omne agens sibi simile*, which means that the effect must resemble its cause, for the soul can give to its operations only what it has itself. Therefore the spiritual operations of the soul give us true knowledge of the nature of the soul itself.[21]

Al-Fārābī's teaching on immortality is not completely clear though, like Ibn Rushd, whom he influenced considerably, he probably held that the psycho-physical is broken up at death; but the passive intellect, as the cosmic or even the divine knower or contemplator within, never suffers difference of growth and decay and therefore is inherently immortal. It is therefore not a matter of what survives after death but what never suffers from corruption in its contact with the world of matter.

In ethics al-Fārābī represents a great synthesis indeed. He not only incorporates all of Plato's *Republic* and Aristotle's *Politics* but also the Islamic theories. Al-Fārābī is not concerned only with the individual but with man in society and the model state :

> Man needs the help of his fellowmen to attain the perfection proper to his nature. Unlike the brute, man is not equipped by nature with all that is necessary for the preservation and development of his being. It is only through society that he finds complete satisfaction of his physical, intellectual and moral needs. Hence, it follows, that society is natural to man....
>
> Just as the world is one harmonious whole ruled by the highest authority of God; just as the stars and the sublunar world are linked up and follow one another; just as the human soul is one in different powers; just as the human body is an organized whole moved by the heart; in like manner the state is to be regulated and patterned after these noble models....
>
> In the model state there must be a hierarchy of rulers coming under the control of a supreme head or prince. This prince, head of the model state of the whole earth, must possess certain traits : great intelligence, excellent memory, eloquence, firmness without weakness, firmness in the achieve-

> ment of good, love for justice, love for study, love for truth, aversion to falsehood, temperance in food, drink and enjoyments, and contempt for wealth.... All these must be found in one man alone placed in charge of directing the complicated machinery of the state. In case all these traits cannot be found in one man alone, then inquiry should be made to determine whether there are two or more who possess the required traits jointly. If there are two, they should both rule the model state. If there are three, then these three should rule. If more are needed then more should rule.[22]

These last statements are probably made in an effort to reconcile the Shī'as and the Sunnis, who were still bitterly quarrelling over the right of succession, the former contending that it should be hereditary, kept within the lineal descendents of the Prophet, the latter insisting on election by popular vote (which was becoming increasingly awkward as the territory to be governed increased so rapidly and so extensively).

When al-Fārābī points to the opposite of the model state, one wonders which states he had in mind as examples :

> Opposed to the model state are : the ignorant state, the perverted state and the mistaken state. The ignorant state is the state that has no knowledge of true happiness, and it very often exchanges it for health, wealth and pleasure. Thus it is the ignorant state which has for its end the enjoyment of eating and drinking, sensual pleasures, amusements and games; it is the ignorant state which has for its end the seeking of praise and the making of name; it is the ignorant state which believes in false liberty by which everyone can do as he pleases; it is the ignorant state which pursues imperialism as a national policy, namely the will of conquering people and nations by fire and sword....
>
> The perverted state is the state that maintains a conduct similar to that of the ignorant state, even though it knows what is true happiness and perfection....
>
> The mistaken state is the state that has wrong ideas about God and happiness.[23]

Of course the theocratic ideal was uppermost in all the world during the tenth century, and al-Fārābī perhaps sees clearly into its necessity :

> The goal of the model state is not only to procure the material prosperity of its citizens, but also their future destiny. The souls of the citizens of the ignorant state are devoid of reason, and will return to the material elements as sensible forms in order to be reunited again to their beings, animals, plants....
>
> In both the perverted and mistaken state, the ruler alone is to be held responsible, and he will be punished accordingly in the world hereafter; and the souls which have been led into error share the fate of the citizens of the ignorant state. On the other hand, the good souls will enter the world of pure spirits and the higher their knowledge in this life, the higher their position after death.[24]

It seems that al-Fārābī was perhaps the first to envisage a truly world state, embracing all of humanity. He sees this as necessary, evidently equally from his interpretation of the Qur'ān and the Greek philosophers. The lesser units, graded down to the local level are recognized as equally necessary, not merely from the aspect of political necessity but for the sake of the completion of human existence. Perfection at all levels is the aim. Rightly or wrongly, al-Fārābī was not yet in a position to envisage a universal democracy. The rule of the many must include the infidel, and how can God bless such a regime.

From Plato al-Fārābī derives and puts almost exaggerated emphasis on the philosopher-king, who must also be lawgiver and Imām, guide of the faithful in the name of the Prophet. By this time there was considerable dispute about the nature of the Imāmate. The Shī'as tended to regard the Imām as a virtual Incarnation to whom should be rendered honors and esteem in the style of the "oriental despot"; but the Sunnis put all the authority in the Qur'ān itself and not in the person or persons who were entrusted with actualization of Muḥammad's Vision. Just as the Sung Neo-Confucianists' theory was pretty well embodied in the person of Wang An-shih, and the Western

European medieval ideal came close to being realized in St. Louis of France, so the Islamic ideal came close to full realization in the person of Akbar. In short, for al-Fārābī, the ruler, like the Buddhist Bodhisattva, must turn the Wheel of the *Dharma*.

11. Abhinavagupta

During the period under review the cults of Vaiṣṇavism and Śaivism developed into full-fledged philosophies, a process which for Śaivism culminated in the philosophy of Abhinavagupta (fl. c. 991-1015). One very important feature in the emergence of Śaivism which influenced Abhinavagupta's philosophy is its rejection of the *Vedas* or *Upaniṣads* as necessary scripture. It appeals rather to the *Āgamas* and the *Purāṇas*, just as Vaiṣṇavism also increasingly appeals to the *Purāṇas*. In Kaśmir the term *Āgama* designates not only the texts but the tradition emanating directly from Śiva through a chain of disciples, the combined transmission of which is designated as the *Āgamaśāstra*. In contrast to the theoretical and contemplative emphasis in the classical "six systems", the *Āgamas* tend toward activity; and infused with the *bhakti* attitude toward a chosen Deity, there emerges an increasingly more personalized theism which emphasizes Śiva's lordship and His Will to rescue souls from *saṃsāra*.

Originally Kaśmir Śaivism had a dualistic world view and was known as the Pāśupata sect, the Pāśupata doctrine being first preached by Śrīkaṇṭha. With the coming of Vasugupta (early ninth century) idealistic monism is introduced based on pure *advaita tatva*. Though Kallaṭa did much to promulgate it, this new monism never really caught on with the masses in Kaśmir who remained attached to the older dualistic form.

There are two branches of Kaśmir Śaivism, which are sometimes united ; the writings of one are revered by the other. The first is Spanda (Vibration) which was founded by Vasugupta and his disciple Kallaṭa. Its more ancient work which tradition imputes to Śiva and which was revealed to Vasugupta is the

Śivasūtra. The *Spandakārikā*, another capital text, is attributed to Vasugupta or to Kallaṭa. The Pratyabhijñā branch was inaugurated by Somānanda, who wrote his *Śivadṛṣṭi* in the early tenth century. Other important writers preceding Abhinava were Udayākara, Utpala and Rāmakaṇṭha. Far from unique, Abhinava was, however, the most celebrated of Kaśmiri philosophical writers in this era. His works may be divided according to their emphasis on Tāntric training and practice, on aesthetics, and on philosophy, these three fields of intensification also being three stages in his biographical development. Abhinava's *Paramārthasāra* has been suggested as one of the most important works in the entire post-Śaṅkara field. It constitutes a hundred verses as an adaptation of the *Adhārakārikā* of Śeṣamuni. Technically it may be regarded as a derivation from the *Sāṃkhya Kārikās* relegated to a theistic form.

Mahadevan gives us this summary of Kaśmir Śaivism and its major branches:

> There is a form of Śaivism, popularly known as Kāshmir Śaivism, which is a kind of monism or non-dualism. The names by which the system is known are: *Trika*, *Spanda* and *Pratyabhijñā*. The name *Trika* primarily refers to the trible principle with which the system deals, viz. *Śiva-śakti-aṇu* or *pati-pāśa-paśu*. Though the other schools of Śaivism also accept these three categories, Kāshmir Śaivism regards the individual soul and the world as essentially identical with Śiva, and so the three, according to it, are reducible to one. The term *Spanda* indicates the principle of apparent movement or change from the state of absolute unity to the plurality of the world. And the expression *Pratyabhijñā*, which means 'recognition' refers to the way of realising the soul's identity with Śiva.[1]

Both branches affirm the identity of the three principles (God, the soul, and the world) and of the relative and the absolute. A remarkably original doctrine in comparison with classical Śaivism, one of its basic tenets is the identity of the individual soul, when in its perfect state (*bhairava*), with the Lord (Paramaśiva or Bhairava). In its state of impurity, however, it is not conscious of this true state of identity. In order to obtain the consciousness of the supreme reality (*mokṣa*), one must purify oneself by means of intense contemplation or self-absorption away from all finite thought. The world is not an illusion but a theophanic manifestation of Śiva, whose evolution via the feminine element (*śakti*) is sensibly unrolled in the same manner as in Sāṃkhya. In that respect, as well as in its role of cultivation of *bhakti*, Kaśmiri Śaivism is very closely related to the Liṅgāyata sect.

The creation theory of this system is known as *ābhāsavāda,* which sees the universe as consisting of appearances which themselves are real in so far as they are aspects of the ultimate reality.

> In the ultimate Reality, the entire manifested variety is in perfect unity, an undifferentiated mass just as the variegated plumage of the peacock with its beautiful, rich colour lies in a state of undifferentiated mass in the plasma of its egg. This is called in this system the analogy of the plasma of the peacock's egg (mayūrāṇḍarasanyāya).

> The underlying principle of all manifestation is *Cit* or pure Universal Consciousness. The world of ever-changing appearances is only an expression of Cit or Saṁvid. All that appears in any form whether as an object or subject or knowledge or means of knowledge or senses, all that exists in any way is only an *ābhāsa*—a manifestation of the Universal Consciousness. ... So *ābhāsa* is manifestation or appearance in a limited way. Every kind of manifestation has some sort of limitation. Everything in existence is a configuration of *ābhāsas.*[2]

However, Śiva in all His aspects has Consciousness as His attribute, not that He is Consciousness as the Vedāntins maintain. In his *Paramārthasāra* Abhinava writes:

> Just as in a clear mirror, varied images of city, village etc. appear as different from one another and from the mirror though they are non-different from the mirror, even so the world, though non-different from the purest consciousness of Parama Śiva, appears as different both in respect of its varied objects and that Universal Consciousness.[3]

The world as manifested is, then, held to be real under this system. Even before Somānanda the pantheistic overtones were relatively uncomplicated; but in the course of time, by virtue of refutations of other systems, with Utpaladeva and Abhinavagupta these pantheistic tendencies become increasingly qualified.

By the time of Abhinava there are three basic ways of realizing this grandiose vision of the theophanic universe: (1) *Sambhavopāya* or the way of Śiva as the knowing subject; (2) *Śāktopāya* or the way of *Śakti* (Energy); and (3) *Aṇavopāya* or the way of the individual. The first method relies upon the practice of *nirvikalpa* undifferentiated thought; the second, upon the three-fold practice of mantra, yantra and tantra; the third upon effort and activity. This system puts most emphasis on direct transmission of enlightenment—that is, attainment of *siddhi* and candidacy for *jīvan-muktihood.* Intellectual comprehension is radically insufficient to this attainment ; rather, *dīkṣā* (process of initiation), which imparts spiritual knowledge and removes innate ignorance, is a necessary component of this liberation process.

The actual working out of the manifested world is closely connected with *Śakti,* the Power of Śiva. *Śakti* is often thought of as the feminine aspect of Śiva, of which there are many modes. Mahadevan lists the five most basic modes as follows:

> (1) *chit-śakti,* the power of intelligence or self-luminosity, which means that the Supreme shines by itself without dependence on any other light and even in the absence of all objects; (2) *ānanda-śakti,* the power of independence (*svātantrya*) which is bliss or joy, and by virtue of which the Ultimate Reality is self-satisfied ; (3) *ichchhā-śakti,* the power of will or desire, the wonderful power of the Lord to create; (4) *jñāna-śakti,* the power of knowledge by virtue of which the objects are brought together and held together in consciousness ; and (5) *kriyā-śakti,* the power of action which is responsible for the actual manifestation of objects and their relations. By these powers the supreme Śiva in his aspects as Śakti manifests himself as the universe. He manifests himself by his own free will (*svechchhayā*) and in himself as the substrate (*svabhittau*).

> That is, there is nothing other than Śiva. If the universe appears as if different, such appearance is a delusion. With the opening out of Śakti, the universe appears; and when Śakti closes herself up, the universe disappears. *Sṛishṭi*(creation) and *pralaya* (dissolution) alternate : and this process is without a beginning.[4]

The Will of Śiva figures prominently in this system as distinct from most other systems of Hinduism, which is an indication of influence from Kaśmir Buddhism or even (given the syncretistic features of Abhinava's aesthetics) from Islam. The doctrine of Grace is also definitely present under the umbrella of the term *śakti-nipāta,* which indicates the descent of Divine Grace. The Will of Śiva is much more emphatic than human effort in the attainment of *mokṣa*, which Abhinava describes in one passage as follows: "When thus the imagination of duality has vanished, and he (the released soul) has surmounted the illusive *māyā*, he is merged in Brahman, as water in water, as milk in milk. When thus through contemplation the group of elements has been resolved into the substance of Śiva, what grief, what delusion can befall him who surveys the universe as Brahman?"[5]

Within the Pratyabhijñā school as developed by Abhinava the distinctions between Śaivism and Advaita become manifest. The pivotal difference lies in the *māyāśakti* concept, which replaces the illusoriness of the empirical world with the theophany theme. The realization of theophany is such that, given the proper discipline, the individual soul achieves once more its original state of complete identification with Paramaśiva and the external world is rightly viewed as a transparent manifestation of Śiva's marvelous power. Many interpreters agree that Abhinava represents an attempt to get beyond the dichotomy of realism and idealism ; others, however, believe his to be an idealistic philosophy. The three aspects of reality are not ignored, namely *abheda* (unity), *bhedābheda* (unity dominating over differentiation), and *bheda* (differentiation); yet these all remain subordinate to a monistic view of the universe.

Paramaśiva is not the same as the Brahman of the Vedānta, but is theistic; transcendent, yet available to anyone willing to undergo purification. For Abhinavagupta, purification can come through aesthetics as well as asceticism, for the aesthetic mode affords a *sense of identification* which may even be made more difficult by the merely ascetic mode of *sādhana.* It is not like Southern Śaivism, a *bhakti* cult. Rather, one affirms constantly higher identifications until one realizes that it is Śiva who is working the identity of oneself with Himself. In this process of identification or recognition of levels of Unity, Śiva is not just *sat-cit-ānanda* as in strict Vedānta systems, but the Good, the Beautiful, and Love or Wisdom. In the *Paramārthasāra* the Mahāyāna term *prajñā* is incorporated into this syncretistic Śiva, unifying by his magic (*śakti*) the many, as real, with Himself, also real. The ultimate is not knowledge as in Advaita, nor Consciousness in the sense of Vijñānavāda, but God, the Lord, Śiva who has unlimited attributes in contrast to Advaita's denial of attributes altogether. Since this tradition gives a sense of importance to the individual, wherein every human being is capable of the realization of his or her identity with Śiva, as he (or she, as *Śakti*) really *is* Śiva, it is evident that Abhinava's use of the term *ātman* is semantically quite different from what is found in the Brahmanical system or in Mahāyāna Buddhism. Singh gives us this summary comparison/contrast of Advaita and Śaivism :

1. *Cit* or *brahman* is only *prakāśa* (light) or *jñāna* (knowledge). It is *niṣkriya* (inactive).	*Cit* is both *prakāśa* and *vimarśa* (light and activity). Therefore it has both *jñātṛtva* (knowledge) and *kartṛtva* (doership). Generally speaking, it has five-fold activity.
2. Activity belongs only to *māyā* or *avidyā*. Īśvara assumes activity only when He is affected by *avidyā* or *māyā*.	Maheśvara has *svātantrya.* Therefore activity belongs to Him. *Māyā* is not something which affects Maheśvara or Śiva. *Māyā* is His own *Śakti* by which He brings about multiplicity and sense of difference.
3. *Māyā* is *anirvacanīya* (indefinable).	*Māyā* being the *śakti* of the Divine is perfectly real.

4.	*Māyā* being indefinable is loosely associated with Īśvara and is, in the last analysis, unreal. *Māyā* seems to play the role of a separate principle. Śaṁkara's nondualism is, therefore, exclusive.	*Māyā* is *Śiva-mayī* or *cinmayī* and is thus Śiva's own *śakti*. It is not a separate principle. Therefore, Śaiva nondualism is inclusive and integral.
5.	In the case of the empirical ego or *jīva* also, the *ātman* is inactive. All activity belongs to *buddhi*, the product of *prakṛti*.	Even in the case of *jīva*, the five-fold activity of Śiva never ceases.
6.	The universe is *mithyā* or unreal. Manifestation is only *nāma-rūpa* and cannot be regarded as real in the true sense. Śaṁkara's non-dualism is exclusive of the universe.	The universe is *śiva-rūpa* and therefore real. It is a display of the glory of the Divine. *Ābhāsas* being the ideation of Śiva cannot be false. Śaiva philosophy is thus inclusive of the universe and real non-dualism.
7.	In liberation, the universe is annulled.	In liberation, the universe appears as a form of Śiva-consciousness or real I-consciousness.
8.	According to Śaṁkara Vedānta, *avidyā* is removed by *vidyā*, and when this happens, there is *mukti* or liberation. *Vidyā* is the result of *śravaṇa*, *manana*, and *nididhyāsana*.	According to non-dualistic Śaiva philosophy, there are two kinds of *ajñāna*, viz., *pauruṣa ajñāna* which is inherent in the *puruṣa* or *aṇu*, and *bauddha ajñāna* which is intellectual. By *Vidyā* only *bauddha ajñāna* can be removed; *pauruṣa ajñāna* will still remain. Such a person will be landed only in blank abstractions, he will not realize *Śivatva* or divinization. *Pauruṣa ajñāna* has also to be removed. This can be

> removed only by *śaktipāta* which comes about either by the *dīkṣā* (initiation) imparted by a self-realized *guru* (spiritual director) or by direct divine grace.[6]

The usual list of *pramāṇas* does not figure so importantly as in most other systems, especially the Nyāya-Vaiśeṣika with such as Udayana, Abhinava's contemporary. One may raise the query whether in this system the controversy about theories of causation is important or not since speculatively Śiva is the one cause of everything. "Only the light of consciousness possesses an independent existence, and the insensible things themselves have reality only in so far as they are in that consciousness. 'Existence is but consciousness'."[7]

The point can be made that every "I-saying" is an assertion of existence; but actually only Śiva has the right to say that. Therefore every "I-saying" is really Śiva's saying, though things-in-themselves are not aware that His "saying-I" is the reason for their existence. This involves Abhinava in some very knotty problems; but he is not concerned with the origins and nature of such ignorance but with the remedy that human beings should seek. This is the discipline of self-purification by such means as meditation on one's personal identity with Śiva. "The entire universe which extends from Śiva to the earth, whether it be subject or object, is refulgent with the Spiritual Light and vibrates with Paramaśiva who consists in a mass of light (*Prakāśa*), is beatitude supreme (*ānanda*) and who transcends the universe all the while that He is also immanent in it."[8] In this paradox of transcendence and immanence, consciousness is only a veil on the reality of things as Śiva-in-manifestation; nevertheless this veil is rather transparent so that he who really opens his eyes can see through it instead of merely looking at it. The key terms here are *tirodhāna-śakti* or *apoha-śakti*, whose connotation is that Śiva withholds complete self-manifestation and gives only enticingly partial self-manifestation in order to increase our appetites for it.

There is a double aspect to the activity of Consciousness, first as the limiting energy (*tirodhāna-śakti*) which sustains objectivity, and secondly as the expression of itself. We see that the universe is only obscurely derived from pure autology. The Self in its infinite liberty determines in its self-enjoyment the erroneous belief that it is only partial and deprived of plenitude. It appears in consequence as a non-self. When the subject and object appear, full subjectivity disappears. Nevertheless, the Subject remains and eternally underlies that dualism, since in reality nothing is there to limit or differentiate it. "The Self...is the supreme Subject, although it is necessay that we do not in the least imagine that this is a subject opposed to an object, for (in this system) Consciousness is presented as the perfect identity of subject and object."[9] The second aspect to this activity of Consciousness involves *anugraha-śakti* (Grace) in its self-revelation. The universe is absorbed in this act. The term *vimarśa* has a much richer connotation in the Śaiva systems since ultimately it connotes the manner whereby Śiva works 'redemption' by withdrawing His external manifestations in the involutionary cycle back into Himself, destroying creation in a sense, or at least our attachments to externalities.

The real nature of the Divine is veiled by the play of *māyā* and her *kañcukas* (coverings), a term unique to Śaiva schools. Singh makes the following points concerning *māyā* which are closely in line with the text of the *Paramārthasāra*, whose poetic format somewhat obscures these technical points.

> *Māyā* is derived from the root 'mā', to measure out. That which makes experience measurable. i.e., limited and severs 'This' from 'I' and 'I' from 'This' and excludes things from one another is *Māyā*. Up to Sadvidyā, the experience was Universal; the 'This' meant 'all-this'—the total universe. Under the operation of *Māyā*, 'this' means merely 'this' different from everything else. From now on starts *Saṅkoca* or limitation. *Māyā* draws a veil (āvaraṇa) on the Self owing to which he forgets his real nature, and thus *Māyā* generates a sense of difference.
>
> The products of *Māyā* are the five *kañcukas* or coverings. We may note them briefly :

(i) *Kalā.* This reduces the sarvakartṛtva (universal authorship) of the Universal Consciousness and brings about limitation in respect of authorship or efficacy.

(ii) *Vidyā.* This reduces the omniscience (sarvajñatva) of the Universal Consciousness and brings about limitation in respect of knowledge.

(iii) *Rāga.* This reduces the all-satisfaction (pūrṇatva) of the Universal and brings about desire for this or that.

(iv) *Kāla.* This reduces the eternity (nityatva) of the Universal and brings about limitation in respect of time, i.e., division of past, present, and future.

(v) *Niyati.* This reduces the freedom and pervasiveness (svatantratā and vyāpakatva) of the Universal, and brings about limitation in respect of cause and space.[10]

Through this play of *māyā* Śiva becomes the individual subject, *puruṣa* or *aṇu* (literally, a point). "*Puruṣa* does not merely mean the human person, but every sentient being that is thus limited."[11]

Abhinavagupta intended the *Parātriṃśikalaghuvṛtti*, also referred to as the *Laghu* (short) *Vṛtti*, to be a brief summary or compendium of his whole philosophy. It is a commentary of only thirty-six *ślokas* and consists primarily of explanations rather than new contributions. The nature of the unequalled or transcendental form of Śiva and His energy (*śakti*) is examined in the first four *ślokas*. In five through eight, Abhinava gives a resume of the play of these *śaktis* of Śiva, and this is followed by an account of emanation as a production of the unequalled form of Śiva. Finally he speaks of this *śakti* as the "original vibration of the Heart of Śiva". The purpose of this work is to explain the way of deliverance (*mokṣa*) as a perfectly "logical" procedure. In that context, *sādhana* retraces the stages in the emanational process in the cosmos until the undifferentiated 'heart' is reached. Instead of the usual term *jīvanmukta*, this tradition uses the term *kaulisiddhi*, all of the powers (*siddhis*) of Śiva having been made available to the yogī who follows this path to the end.

This is a magico-mysticism, and the distinctions become somewhat blurred between the magic and the mysticism, the religion and the philosophy. The powers (*siddhis*) can become an obstacle to final realization, and we must be warned not to belittle the *siddhis* as they are indeed a manifestation of Śiva as Bhairava. Yoga having taken such an esoteric bent at this time, what is remarkable is that Abhinava manages to read into these esoterics his systematic metaphysics, so that Padoux can claim for him that he fully affirmed something remarkably like the classical pattern of emanations and involutions in Neo-Platonism in its many sub-varieties. "This, the universe, existing empirically, is in its own nature, profoundly in essence pure Being, emitted by Him (Śiva) but never separated from Him and dissolving in Him in order not to be more than a latent state until the complete reabsorption of all manifestations back into Himself."[12]

In his *Hymns*, as in the *Paramārthasāra*, Abhinava writes with full aesthetic profundity and clarity, often engaging in plays on words in order to bring out their *dhvani* import, whereby what is at first read as a 'mere' metaphor contains an actual truth manifested in several levels. This text was obviously written not for general consumption even in Abhinava's own time but for his inner circle of intimate disciples. Also clearly illustrated in the *Hymns* is the *bhakti* spirit with which Abhinavagupta was infused as in the manner of Rāmānuja and Bonaventura. Underlying the *Hymns* is the perspective of cosmic time in which there are vast cycles of creativity and of involution, with the vast nights of *pralaya* in between. According to some scientists working on astronomy and cosmogeny, the Cosmic Cycle theory still has a lot to say for it over against the Big Bang theory, since there may have been many 'Big Bangs', each beginning the vast cycles all over again. In the modern world the philosophies of Teilhard de Chardin and of Aurobindo have already done something like this, and it may well be that the 'Systems' philosophy of Ervin Laszlo and others now being applied in the social sciences, if extended sufficiently, may incorporate something like a *Neo*-Kaśmirian perspective, no longer marvelling only at the tremendousness of the Himalayan landscapes but at the vastness of the external cosmos, which could be called a theophany under any one of the religions of man.

We should approach Abhinava's *Hymns* through a parallel with those of his Śūfī contemporaries and Southern Vaiṣṇava Ālvār saints as well as with Byzantine hymnology such as that of Symeon the New Theologian. All of these involve a consciously controlled masterful technique which conceals as it reveals the profundity of the subtle truth therein. In India the tradition of writing such hymns goes back to antiquity and therefore constitutes the very heart of the soul of Indian civilization. With Yājñavalkya of the *Upaniṣads* as typical of the classical period, it is not surprising that Abhinava should also practice this art, since such creations compose a very real aspect of reality itself. But with his special talents we find an unusual innocence and spontaneity, even a sense of humor which hides the profundity of the themes. Abhinava shows himself to be no mere pundit grinding out arguments designed to compete in sophistical debates, but a true artist who has surpassed mere scholasticisms and dialectics in a *bhakti* spirit, filled to overflowing with love of the divine, or with divine love itself.

The following selections are from Abhinava's fifteen stanzas on consciousness :

1-2. This One whose essence is the immutable Light of all the clarities and of all the darknesses, in which clarities and darknesses reside, He is the Lord indeed, the innate nature of all beings; the multitude of things is really no other than his own energy.

3. And energy is not to be supposed to be other than non-separated from Him, indeed from the essence of Him. The two are eternally identical as fire is inseparable from its capacity of burning.

4. He, the God Bhairava, has for His characteristic that of maintaining the entire universe as it is reflected, thanks to this energy (*śakti*), in the mirror of His own Self.

5. She, the supreme Goddess, is adorned with an intensity of consciousness of the essence of Him whose plenitude in all that exists does not increase or diminish.

6. This God is eternally adorned with pleasure of enjoying Himself with this Goddess; omniscient, He sustains the

simultaneous fashion of the diverse emissions and reabsorptions.

14. In reality no differentiation really exists in Paramaśiva, for these two, bondage and liberation, are both not separated from the Essence of the Lord Supreme.
15. Thus enters one into contact with Bhairava, the innate nature of everything, which reposes on the lotus of the trident form by His *śaktis* : knowledge, subtle activity, and will.[13]

The best comparison for the *Hymns* is probably the *Shāhnāmeh* of Firdausi, a contemporary of Abhinava, which may be the best book of its kind of all time, the theme of this book of praise being the declaration that every name ascribed to God is a theophany. Of course there are other similar works listing all the holy names of Viṣṇu. The *Granth Sahib*, a sacred text of the Sikhs, represents a turning point for this kind of literature in the sixteenth and seventeenth centuries.

Abhinavagupta might have had Kālidāsa (mid-sixth century) in the background for his aesthetics, and there is the suggested influence of the Buddhist grammarian Candragomin (seventh century); but a more definite influence was the poet Bhāmaha who in the mid-eighth century wrote a long metric work on philosophy. Abhinava's most famous source was Lollaṭa (early ninth century), who expanded the theory of *rasa*. Abhinava also referred frequently to Ānandavardhana, who elaborated on the theory of *dhvani* as the "soul of poetry". Other writers who influenced him include Rudraṭa, Śaṅkuka, Bhaṭṭanāyaka, Bhaṭṭatauta, Bhallaṭa, and Jayanta Bhaṭṭa.

It was the religious significance of aesthetic experience and his deep concern with Tāntric ritual that intensified Abhinava's interest in the drama. His greatest achievement in literary criticism was the equating of imaginative experience with *ātmānanda* or mystic ecstasy. In fact, he is the first known writer in India to deal with issues of religion in literary terms and vice versa.[14] His theories concerning literature arrayed with the concept of *rasa*, which becomes the focal point for the development of his terminology which comes to dominate Sanskrit poetics.

Abhinava was the first author to link, in a complex and serious manner, religion and poetics, and later authors all followed his lead. His very phrases were copied, even in contexts where his views are not being propounded. His terminology became standard to the point where it is not possible to pick up any book on literary criticism after the twelfth century and not come across expressions like : *hṛdayasaṃvāda* (sympathetic imagination, rapport), *tanmayībhāva* (complete identification), *carvaṇā* (aesthetic relish), *alaukikacamatkāra* (extraordinary artistic beauty), *sādhāraṇīkaraṇa* (universality) and so forth, all of which are for the first time carefully elaborated by Abhinavagupta. What is even more interesting is that later philosophers, especially in the school of Kashmir Śaivism, began to use these same terms in their works on philosophy. ...Not only are his own students, like the brilliant Kṣemarāja for example, ... won over, but even orthodox Advaitins from the South, such as Madhusūdansarasvatī, many years later, use his terminology.[15]

Essential to the comprehension of how *rasa* is evolved and how it works is the term *vibhāva,* literally sources. Thus *ālambana-vibhāvas* indicates the characters (in a play), i.e., Śakuntalā and Duṣyanta. The *uddīpana-vibhāvas* indicates the setting, i.e., the spring flowers, the bees, etc. More problematic of the *vibhāvas* as elements of the stage are the *vyabhicāribhāvas*, the *sthāyibhāva* and *rasa.*

Vyabhicāribhāvas are emotions that accompany the primary feelings of the character. They are liable to change and are not inherent to the character's personality. Examples are joy (*harṣa*), longing (*autsukya*), etc., all of which belong exclusively to the characters. Duṣyanta's longing for Śakuntalā is not shared by the audience. Now the *sthāyibhāva* (*rati*, there are eight or nine of them) is a state of mind which, because it is more deeply felt, dominates all other emotions. It belongs to both the character and to the spectator. The difference is this : Once the character experiences the *sthāyibhāva,* he has reached the height of emotion. But the spectator can go farther, and in a sense deeper. For when "love" is awakened in him, it is not like the love that the original character felt. The spectators do not fall in love with Sītā. This *sthāyibhāva*

> *rati* is transformed (*pariṇata*) into an extraworldly state (*alaukikāvasthā*), and this is what is called *rasa*.[16]

The list of *rasas* is equivalent to the number of basic human emotions, though there are some aestheticians who wish to leave out certain accepted ones like *śānti* and *bhakti*. *Rasa* requires an intensely personal state of mind on the part of the author, performer and the audience, and it makes their common sharing of the same experience possible. Abhinava, in dealing with the problem of how *rasa* is achieved, gives this statement :

> In the course of our ordinary life, we acquire a certain proficiency (*pāṭava*) through long practice (*abhyāsa*) in inferring people's mental moods (*cittavṛtti*), i.e., their basic emotions (*sthyāyyātma*) from observing certain signs (*liṅga*) consisting in causes, effects and accompanying elements (*sahacāra*). In watching a drama (or reading a poem—*adhunā*), a garden, or a glance, i.e. ordinary causes (effects, etc.) lose their ordinary characters of cause etc. and take on the essential nature of the function of awakening a permanent emotion (*vibhāvanā*), the function of leading the spectator to a recognition of this permanent emotion (*anubhāvanā*) and of adding color (to the emotions in question—*samuparañjakatva*). And so they acquire the non-ordinary names of *vibhāvas* etc. Now it is through these things called *vibhāvas* etc., precisely in order to proclaim the fact that they are dependent upon the *saṃskāras* (latent impressions of their nature as a cause etc...., when they, by assuming a leading or subordinate role, attain a unity, a joining, a fusion (*yoga*) in the mind of the spectator, that an emotional situation (*artha*) whose essence consists exclusively in aesthetic pleasure (*carvyamāṇataikasāra*) is brought to the state of aesthetic relish (*carvaṇā*) which is a form of consciousness (*saṃvedana*) free from worldly obstacles (i.e. worldly preoccupations). It is not something that is objectively existent (*siddhasvabhāva*) (for) it exists only for the duration of aesthetic relish (*tātkālika eva*) and does not persist for any time after the aesthetic emotion. It is completely different from the permanent emotions. It is *rasa*.[17]

Abhinava insists that *rasa* is not something "certain" (*niyata*). It is the subjective element in poetic utterances which makes possible the introduction of a unique and highly subjective vocabulary which can effectively express the individual's response to poetry. Abhinava agrees that "the perception of beauty is the soul of poetry". He writes : "In literature the aesthetic relish (of the suggested sense) through the verbal paraphernalia (of a drama) is like (the blossoming) of a magic flower: it is essentially a thing of the present moment which does not depend on past or future time.[18]

Abhinava often makes the distinction between poetry and philosophy. "For poetry, as Abhinava never tires of telling us, is not philosophy. The Sahṛdaya's heart is often said to 'melt' (*dravati*) whereas the heart of the 'scholar' has become hardened and encrusted by his readings of dry texts on metaphysics."[19] The audience for poetry is a restricted one. As one of his learned commentators put it : "The person fit for (appreciating poetry) is the one whose state of being a sahṛdaya (i.e. sympathetic responsiveness) has reached its highest pitch. This only applies to some people, not to all, for we find that Mīmāṃsakas and Vedic scholars are simply not sensitive to literature.[20] In describing poetry Abhinava often used the simile of a woman in love : poetry, being like a woman in love, should be responded to with equal love. Or poetry is like fire, while the reader is like dry wood; or "good poetry is like a clean cloth dipped into pure water : the cloth quickly absorbs the water. When we know all this it becomes fairly easy to predict what Abhinava will regard as the goal of poetry : delight, with a nod in the direction of intellectual refinement."[21]

There is a story from mythology of how dance came into drama. Some of the other gods had produced a play, and knowing that Śiva is patron of the fine arts, they presented it before him. He was so pleased that he began to dance his great dance of cosmic destruction. This he repeats at the end of each grand cosmic cycle. Mythology aside, there were some aestheticians who thought that dance should not be included in drama, maintaining that it does not elicit the same meaningfulness as poetry and prose. Bharata, Abhinava's persuasive forerunner, offers this retort ; "Dance does not require any meaning. It has been created for the simple reason that it is beautiful. It is in the very nature of things that all people find dancing beautiful."[22] This coincides well with Abhinava's insight that poetry and all literature have no other goal than delight. In fact, Abhinava has only scorn for the academic and intellectualistic pursuit of art.

There is similar scorn for the relegation of art to everyday experience. His terminology seeks to communicate art in terms of something slow and meditative. It is for this reason that comparisons with religious states are often made, as our everyday life is most inadequate in preparing us for an aesthetic experience. One way of distinguishing poetry from everyday life or even from prose is by the requirement that *anaucitya* (impropriety) is *apratīta* (not perceived, not felt). Abhinava clarifies this insight :

> *Anaucitya* means that which obstructs the delight of those who experience rasa, because this experience is the all-in-all of rasa. What pleasure can there be in a reference to the love making of the highest god, which can only produce shame and horror in the mind of the reader, just as would a description of the love-making of one's own parents. (And yet), although the love-making has been described, nonetheless, because of the genius of the poet, the heart is so engrossed in the poetry that it does not stop to consider whether it is proper or improper. Just as when a man is genuinely courageous but happens to be fighting an improper battle, we might well laud him at the time, but would cease to do so if we consider at a later time the correctness or incorrectness of his behaviour. The same is true here.[23]

Abhinava coins the term *ad-bhuta-puṣpa* (like a never-fading flower) to make the point that great art must endure the test of time. Probably intercultural meaning is likewise an important criterion. Besides immediacy, repeatability, and endurability as positive characteristics of good art, he also laid down strictures or should-nots for good art.

What of the relation of drama to the 'real' world ? The experience of *rasa* removes our consciousness from that 'real' world until we re-emerge from the encapturing drama, in time. What is involved in this experience is the borderline between *māyā* as illusion and *māyā* as the action of *śakti*. Too much actuality, so to speak, will spoil the aesthetic effect.

> At another level, Abhinava compares the actor to the *Paramātman*. He retains his identity (just as the *Ātman* never gives up its self-luminosity) and yet manages to so engross people that they feel they are watching the original character. The spectator is thus like the *Jīva*, liable to illusion. So we come back once again to the fundamental notion of the real world and the world of shadow. Anything that takes us out of this dream world of literature, anything that comes between us and this lovely sub-creation of *māyā* is to be avoided. The delicate web must not be shattered.[24]

Abhinava would not sanction ultra-realism then. Dharma should avoid actual current events, perhaps with the exception of the comic effect as satire by deliberate anachronism.

There is in Abhinava's aesthetic theory a good basis for closing the assumed gap between art and theophany. The similarities and differences between aesthetic experience and mystical experience has often served as the context for an exposition of Abhinava's aesthetics. He himself often made parallels between them, though the aesthetic experience is no more than a reflection of the bliss that comes from resting in God or of the supreme bliss that is Śiva's alone. Masson and Patwardhan present thirteen similarities between aesthetic and mystical experiences, or between *rasāsvāda* and *brahmāsvāda*, as found in Abhinava :

> (1) There is no pain in drama, for everything is blissful when we attain the state of *rasa*. This is equally true of any higher ecstatic experience.
>
> (2) During an actual dramatic performance, we forget the self.
>
> (3) We have no hope of material gain from art. The same is true on the religious level, since to become seriously religious in India generally means abandoning one's acquired wealth.
>
> (4) Both experiences are *alaukika*.
>
> (5) Both experiences are *ānandaikaghana*.

(6) In both cases, the distance between the subject and the object is removed. Thus Abhinava stressed that *rasa* is not objective.

(7) Time and space disappear for the duration of the experience. We are not conscious of our surroundings during a drama, or at least we ought not to be, according to Abhinava.

(8) During both experiences there is total immersion. In the case of *samādhi* there is *vyutthāna,* which could correspond (perhaps forcibly, however) to leaving the theatre and re-entering ordinary life. We have all certainly experienced the curious feeling of being let-down, even of depression, upon leaving a theatre.

(9) In both cases, special preparation is necessary : music and dance in the theatre, and perhaps one might include *bhajans* and other paraphernalia of *bhakti* in the case of religion.

(10) In both cases, what appears is not something that is "created" anew, but something that is "manifested", or "suggested". *Rasa* is not "produced", it is "suggested". So also, the identity of the *ātman* and *Brahman* is only a question of removing ignorance (i.e. nothing "new" is to be acquired). In *Vedānta* the term *abhivyakti* is often used for this process, just as both Ānanda and Abhinava use the same expression for *rasa.*

(11) In *Vedānta, avidyā* is removed by means of *śravaṇa, manana,* etc. In *rasaniṣpatti,* Abhinava emphasizes how the *vighnas* must be removed before *rasa* can manifest itself.

(12) In both cases there is a sense of rest (*viśrānti*), of having reached the goal (cf. the Vedāntic expression *kṛtakṛtya*) beyond which there is nothing to be accomplished.

(13) In the aesthetic experience, Ānanda (and Abhinava) make light of the "means" that have brought it about, especially of the *vācya* sense, which is compared to a lamp which is useful for illuminating objects, but which is not the goal of our efforts. Similarly, in *Vedānta,* Śaṅkara speaks of the *upāyas* as being similar to a raft which we leave behind after our destination has been reached.[25]

We should keep in mind the inwardness and religious orientation of virtually all Indian aesthetics. Sneh Pandit makes a strong appeal that in the Indian field there may lie some remedy for what Ortegay Gassett has rightly called "the dehumanization of art".[26]

12. Genshin

Genshin (942-1017) is remembered both in connection with the Pure Land and as a patriarch in the Tendai. The Tendai was founded in Japan by no less than Saichō, but split between Ennin and Enchin. Genshin follows in the Ennin line after Ryōgen (912-985). But Genshin also belongs to the *bhakti* tradition devoted to Amida Bodhisattva, which comes into full flower with Hōnen (1133-1212) and Shinran (1173-1262). The Pure Land denomination had its first beginnings in Japan as early as 640. There was some confusion right from the outset in Japan between the Tendai and the Pure Land traditions, which had been fairly separate in China. Genshin sought to bring the Pure Land practice and discipline in Japan closer into conformity with the Chinese models during the Sui and T'ang Dynasties. It was on Mt. Hiei, the traditional stronghold of Tendai, that the Pure Land began to emerge with the career of Ryōgen, the teacher of Genshin. Thus Genshin was "at once a Tendai doctor, a Pure Land aspirant, and a Mahāyāna mystic. He constantly strove to embrace all of these positions and integrate them into a teaching that be both true and practical."[1]

Genshin joined the monastic community on Mt. Hiei when he was only nine years old. He was ordained at the age of thirteen when he became a disciple of Ryōgen, whose fame rested on the fact that he wrote the first distinctively Japanese work on the Pure Land Buddhist way. In spite of his youthful genius, Genshin did not compose the *Ōjōyōshū* until he was over forty. This work won him genuine fame by virtue of its favorable reception by the head abbot of the T'ien-t'ai sect in China. Incidentally, he was also a great artist, some of his paintings gaining him a very high reputation along with his poetry.

Politics and institutional religion still being inseparable in Japan, he was promoted to the rank of Gonshō Sōsu (provincial Vicar General), one of the highest offices of his time. His death day is still celebrated as a festival at Yokawa near Mt. Hiei.

The *Ōjōyōshū*, Genshin's best known work, is a systematization of all that was available to him. It comprises 80,000 Chinese characters divided into ten chapters, first three of which deal with the miseries of *saṃsāra* and the hoped-for pleasures and delights of the Heavenly Pure Land. Among Genshin's contemporaries one might look to Peter Damien or the Ṣūfī al-Ṭūsī, but comparisons and parallels on that theme are very numerous. Genshin was

> ... one of the first Tendai monks to declare that his goal was birth in the Pure Land of Amida. He presented the reasons for this desire in his famous treatise, the *Ōjōyōshū* (Essentials of Salvation), which became the first Japanese theological study on Pure Land as well as a foundation for the development of Pure Land schools in Japan.
>
> The *Ōjōyōshū* represented a departure from earlier Japanese Pure Land devotion in that it was strongly influenced by the writings of Shan-tao. The work actually consisted of an apologetical compilation of all available references in the Buddhist scriptures to Pure Land faith, relying most heavily upon the writings of Chih-I. Although it was a theological treatise written in Chinese script, it became very popular among the aristocracy and in fact, has been a best seller throughout Japanese history up to modern time.[2]

The form of the work for the most part is that of an extended annotated anthology. This is typically medieval in that text-and-commentary was the basic and indeed almost the exclusive method of philosophizing all across Eurasia beginning long before 800 but extending even down to the eighteenth century in many areas. Moreover, it is in these commentaries that original ideas are always suggested or even argued and debated at great length. Thus even though originality did not become a virtue necessarily until very recently, it was not absent. Although much of the *Ōjōyōshū* is apologetics for his particular manner of using and interpreting the *nembutsu,* there are discussions of Mahāyāna metaphysics involved at many turns.

In the *Ōjōyōshū* there is very little if any of the doctrine that *saṃsāra* is *nirvāṇa* which had emerged in some of the Śūnyavāda texts. Rather, as part of the general trend in these centuries from 800 to 1300 there is a considerable elaboration of a hierarchy of heavens, purgatories and hells—six of them in Genshin's scheme. The only variation on this universal theme is that this cycle is still associated with metempsychosis. We are reminded that it is very difficult to obtain a human birth in the first place, and in a sense even more difficult to merit another, much less to gain the eventual Western Paradise. Even the *devas* (gods or angels) are also subject to *saṃsāra* (though the historic Śākyamuni Buddha and Confucius were very sceptical about the existence of such supernatural beings).

Genshin counsels against insisting on uniformity for everyone and rather advises that each should follow his own way in accordance with his individual *karma*; indeed, his *karma* will normally determine which cult he may choose to follow. Many moderns contemptuous of medieval societies may rightly not condone many of the superstitions ; but feudalistic orders, which were very universal during the centuries under review, did allow and even encourage a lot of colorful pluralism. Everyone according to his state and station in life or occupation even wore different costumes and each was expected to follow his or her code of ethics and pattern of piety according to a very highly pluralistic set of standards.

The manner of doing *nembutsu* reminds us poignantly of the theme of *bhakti* and especially *prapatti* in Rāmānuja's way, which had its roots in both Yāmuna's teachings and the Ālvārs' and Nayanmars' poetic expressions of ecstatic devotion, these latter being contemporaneous with Genshin. This *prapatti* (total surrender, or "taking refuge" in Amida) is expressed by Genshin in passages like the following:

> Take refuge in Him single-mindedly. Throw yourself, your knees, arms, and forehead, to the ground and venerate Amida Buddha far off in the West. Consider not the quantity of your practice, but just be sincere of heart.

> One verse or many, one time or often, you must only be sincere. Do not consider the quantity of your practice. Even if you perform no other works, by means of this your praise, and in accordance with your aspiration, you will surely attain to rebirth. As the *Lotus Sūtra* verse tells us, 'If with a glad heart you sing out and praise the merit of a Buddha, even with so much as a single tone, without fail you will finally perfect Buddhahood.' If by one sound, how much more so by constant praise! If to Buddhahood, how much more so to rebirth![3]

Andrews interprets this and other passages like it as indicating a new level of systematic synthesis of the general Mahāyāna doctrine of the transformation of human nature into Buddhahood in this life as virtually equivalent to meriting rebirth in the Pure Land of Amida, thus comprising a merger of Pure Land with Tendai teachings.

Genshin classifies the Bodhisattva Vows as four-fold thus :

1. However innumerable beings are, I vow to save them ;
2. However inexhaustible the passions are, I vow to extinguish them;
3. However immeasurable the Dharmas are, I vow to master them;
4. However incomparable the Buddha-truth is, I vow to attain it.[4]

Even so, Genshin warns that these distinctions are to be taken only from the phenomenal (*samvṛtti* or *vyāvahārika*) point of view since they still involve duality. His *bhakti* and *prapatti* are to take him and his followers all the way through to the *pāramārthika* or *nivṛtti* level of reality beyond all dualisms, and are not merely ancillary aids. Genshin urges the aspirant "to realize that ultimately there are no beings to be saved, no passions to be extinguished, no Dharmas to be mastered, and no Buddha-truth to be attained, even though we and others are indeed *not* saved, *are* filled with passion, and so forth."[5] But perhaps almost uniquely Genshin requires vows governing all levels, thus hoping to avert the contradiction found in the Śūnyavāda *sūtra* literature about *saṃsāra* being *nirvāṇa*, for then it turns out that instead of contradiction we are confronted with a dilemma. As Andrews continues : "Both the relative and the absolute vows are necessary. He who takes only the former falls into the false views of selfhood, and he who takes only the latter, into that of nihilism."[6]

According to Andrews, Genshin's teachings were not elitist but egalitarian :

> The basic injunctions *Ōjōyōshū* are severe and difficult, often enjoining the most exhalted of Mahāyāna teachings. Yet without actually rescinding these demands, Genshin often provides some sort of accommodation for those incapable of fully meeting them. As we have seen... *all* beings can find salvation in the Pure Land, and Genshin continually concerns himself with the salvation of the most lowly.[7]

This note of spiritual democracy is worth investigating very thoroughly since it can be argued that this appeared in Japan long before it did in any other part of Eurasia; and if democratization of the hierarchy of spiritual attainments is an index of 'modernity' as is too often asserted, then Japan entered 'modernity' several centuries before Western Europe and even somewhat before India. Nevertheless, it is not as strong in Genshin as it later is in Hōnen and Shinran who are definitely 'protestant' in this respect.

Genshin outlines a method of contemplation of the Buddha-nature beginning with the phenomenal perspective as transitional (gradually, not suddenly) towards the higher contemplation of the Buddha-nature as such in its ultimate self-existence (*sva-bhāva*). The focus is evidently exclusively on Amida rather than on Śākyamuni Buddha. Genshin's description of the cosmic Buddha-nature with all sorts of florid embellishments symbolizing various degrees and forms of infinity with the Chief Buddha in the center and thousands of lesser buddhas surrounding Him, is more familiar to us in Tibetan art than in Japanese and certainly represents just the opposite trend from the reserved, restrained simplicity of Zen art. And there are references to all sorts of supernatural powers, radiances, spiritual lights and spiritual eyes as distinguishing marks of any Buddha.

No doubt one needs a guru even more at the higher stages since it is axiomatic that the higher we climb the farther we may fall. The next stage goes on in or up to the contemplation of the *Trikāya* nature of the Buddha, but with typical emphasis on the *Dharmakāya* at the expense of the *Nirmāṇakāya* and *Sambhogakāya* aspects of Cosmic Buddhahood. Some structuring is still present here also, however, since it is pointed out that this Ultimate includes all the less-than-ultimate Buddhas and other realities. However, even the *Dharmakāya* is still a form of body, of embodiment, although of the highest and most subtle conceivable type.

This being still not the highest contemplation, like Dante's *Paradiso,* we have yet still higher to climb; and as we do so, we get into distinctions that are rather difficult for modern secularists to understand due to lack of practice and experience, for it transcends even the realm of causation :

> Thus the triple Buddha-bodies of all Buddhas of the ten regions and of past, present, and future, all the dharmas countless as dust, the Dharma-ocean of perfectly harmonious, immeasurable merits of all Buddhas, in short, all the countless Dharma-realms, are replete in Amida's one body. Yet, it neither proceeds by causation nor exists spontaneously, is neither one nor different, neither actual nor illusory, neither existent nor non-existent. Pure in original nature, neither mind nor words can fathom it.[8]

Genshin's attempt to describe the indescribable is a sort of collage, according to Andrews, from the *Amitābha Contemplation Sūtra* the *Heart Contemplation Sūtra*, the *Golden Splendor Sūtra*, the *Bodhisattva Nembutsu-samādhi Sūtra*, as well as the *Prajñāpāramitā Sūtras*.

For those who are not strong enough to go up this straighter, steeper path, Genshin also provides a more accessible, indirect path that is much easier. Indeed, there is a way even for those with the least aptitude :

> If there are those who are incapable of contemplating (*kannen*) the Buddha-marks, while dwelling on taking refuge in Him, on His coming to welcome them, or on their own rebirth,

> they should single-mindedly call and reflect (*shonen*) on the Buddha. ...Whether walking, standing, sitting or lying, while speaking or while silent, whatever you may be doing, always keep the thought (*nen*) in your breast like a starving person thinking of food or a thirsty person seeking water. Bow your head, raise your hands, or lift up your voice calling the name, but whatever your outer acts may be, keep the thought constantly in your heart. Reflect ceaselessly, and sleeping or waking forget it not.[9]

Genshin advocates exclusive focus on Amida, though any other worthy Bodhisattva or Avatār may do, the principle being to tame the jumpiness of the "monkey-mind" and to gather the multiple things that distract into a single focus—"centering down", as the Quakers call it.

Genshin insists on three requisites : sincerity, deep faith, and dedicating merit in aspiration for rebirth. This he inherits from Shan-tao, emphasizing that Shan-tao taught that the Bodhisattva aspect of the practice included all of the nine grades of beings in existence and not merely one's friends or even all of mankind only. Such perspectives have begun to revive in the twentieth century with such as Teilhard de Chardin and Sri Aurobindo, although even in them one would no doubt find limitations to Shan-tao's claims.

The best *nembutsu*—or *prapatti* in its minimal form, which merges smoothly with simple *bhakti* and *parabhakti* and *paramabhakti* in Viśiṣṭādvaita — always emphasizes selfless devotion without any expectation of earthly benefit. In St. Bernard of Clairvaux, for example, one may also find a hierarchy of motives for devotional surrender and adoration. Nevertheless, benefits from such *nembutsu, bhakti, prapatti, dhikr, japa* should not be overlooked, even quite aside from the promise of heavenly reward after physical death. Genshin lists four major benefits:

1. The benefit of annulling evil karma and producing good
2. The benefit of receiving the protection and assistance of Buddhas and other spiritual beings

3. The benefit of seeing Buddhas
4. The benefit of being reborn into the Pure Land on death.[10]

Andrews notes that "Genshin's overall position regarding the relation of nembutsu to other practices...is that nembutsu is superior for rebirth, but that other practices are also effective when used together with nembutsu."[11]

The theme of concern for ordinary people might not seem so significant for the modern secular reader unless it is seen in historical perspective. For classically all through the centuries Buddhism had been (and admittedly at its best still is) basically a monastic movement with special codes adapted for the laymen. Evidently Genshin was struggling (but did not see the way, as later Hōnen and Shinran did) to abandon the monastic core-basis altogether in a sort of 'protestant reformation'. He was apparently puzzled how to make the proper adjustment to remove the great gulf between what was supposed to be not just the code for the monastic *saṅgha* but the standards set by the Buddha himself in an age that was more enlightened altogether, and the lesser code adapted to the later periods which had become degenerate —which the Japanese called *mappō* and which is essentially the same as Kali Yuga in Hinduism in which it is expected that things for several thousand years will get progressively worse until the final arrival of Kalki Avatār or Maitreya Bodhisattva, or like the Messiah in Judaism or the Second Coming of Christ in the Christian world or the coming of Mahdi in Islam. Or again, how to bridge the gap between what had come to be considered the 'secret' teachings of the Buddha to be handed down by oral tradition, and the recorded teachings which were meant for the masses. Both of these gaps were given as explanation of the differences in the Buddhist *sūtras* by Chih-i and most of the Nara Japanese Buddhists before Genshin could hardly escape the necessity of trying to puzzle it out for himself, no doubt having found that the previous ways of bridging the gaps had not been adequate either in theory or practice since essentially what had happened was that the monastic code had become so relaxed that the laity had no ideals to look to as models.

Various levels of interpretation of the same practice and for the same ultimate purpose was evidently the best solution Genshin could puzzle out, the common purpose and goal remaining the attainment of the Western Paradise after death through the grace of Amida and/or by strenuous effort. In short, all have the same practice but not all have or really need the completion of the 'third eye' of wisdom that is ascribed to all Buddhas and Bodhisattvas. Everyone without exception should do the *nembutsu,* but each interpreting it according to his or her own level of understanding.

Genshin lists the various *sūtras* he recommends for use along with the *nembutsu* and arranges them in a definite order, each having a different major purpose:

1. For instruction on contemplation of the Pure Land and for the rewards of the nine grades of beings, the *Amitābha Contemplation Sūtra*
2. For Amida's vows and a description of the Pure Land, the *Larger Pure Land Sūtra*
3. For the Buddha-marks and the benefits of contemplating these, the *Buddha Contemplation Samādhi Ocean Sūtra*
4. For the Buddha-marks and the characteristics of the Dharma-body, and for the merits of nembutsu-*samādhi,* the *Seeing All Buddhas Samādhi Sūtra* and *Bodhisattva Nembutsu-samādhi Sūtra*
5. For the method of practice, the above three *sūtras* (of 3 and 4), the '*Sūtra on the Ten Practices for Rebirth into Amitābha's Land*' and the *Śāstra on the Ten Bodhisattva Stages*
6. For daily recitation, the *Smaller Pure Land Sūtra*
7. For a general presentation (of nembutsu practices) together with a *gāthā* (in praise of Amida and the Pure Land), the *Vasubandhu Pure Land Śāstra*
8. For (among Chinese works) the method of practice, the *Great Concentration and Insight,* and Shan-tao's *Amitābha Buddha Nembutsu-samādhi Contemplation Method* and *Hymns to Rebirth*

9. For the interpretation of miscellaneous problems, the T'ien-t'ai *Ten Pure Land Problems*, Tao-ch'o's *Collection on Sukhāvatī*, the Fa-hsiang School *Standard Interpretations on the West*, and Huai-kan's *Interpretations on the Multitude of Pure Land Problems*
10. For records of those who have been reborn into the Pure Land, Chia-ts'ai's *Pure Land Treatise* and the '*Records of Felicitous Rebirth*'.[12]

Concerning these, Andrews reminds us that the first two are the most important as setting the best standard, while the others are largely for those who can't yet quite reach those higher standards. Andrews also notes that those in number eight above are virtually original with Genshin (except the *Great Concentration and Insight*), as well as those in nine and ten, since he must have brought them back from China himself and introduced them. But after him they were adopted as standard along with his own *Ōjōyōshū*, not only as canonical but as especially useful as a way to survive in this *mappō yuga*.

The Heian period as a whole was culturally a high-tide time in Japanese history ; however, increasing political unrest affected even the monastic institutions so much that the monks forgot all about the Buddha's teaching of non-violence and some monasteries, notably on Mt. Hiei, became virtually citadels of armed might. Here we might again recall the theory of *mappō* or the philosophy of history, not a belief in a finite event of the 'fall' of man as in the Abrahamic heritages, but as belief in successive cycles or aeons in which there had been and will continue to be decline of the *Dharma* so that people could no longer live up to the standards set by Śākyamuni, and the earth would have to await the messianic coming of Maitreya Bodhisattva. Hence *nembutsu* is the remedy until that supernatural event of the far distant future.

Genshin's roots were in both the Pure Land and T'ien-t'ai/ Tendai heritages in both Japan and China. Those were not necessarily the most systematic types of Chinese Buddhism, but the purer versions of such as Vijñānavāda Yogācāra which had been so heavily reinforced by the work of Hsüan-tsang had evidently virtually died out in the chaos between the fall of the

T'ang Dynasty and the rise of the Southern Sung. Nevertheless, Genshin did go back to the most systematic sources available to him even among the Chinese developments, including for the T'ien-t'ai the attempts of Chih-i at making sense out of the proliferation of miscellaneous *sūtras* and teachings and practices that had emerged since Sanskrit Buddhism had first entered China more than six hundred years before Genshin's time, with Shan-tao as the comparable root-source for the Pure Land heritage.

Although the hagiographies make the most of Genshin's virtues, it seems this virtuousness did not carry with it the ability to reconcile rival subsects within the Tendai tradition. Later on there were still further subdivisions and attempts at reconciliation and unification of the old divisions ; but typically in the histories of religions and also of philosophy seldom if ever were these attempts successful. Instead of reforming and reuniting the old, these attempts rather become new movements or sects. "There were no solid scriptural bases for the differences between these schools and transmission became esoteric from master to disciple. ...The Tendai sect thus gradually splintered into fragments and reflected the general worldly atmosphere of Heian society during its days of decline."[13] Nevertheless, Genshin's universalism made Tendai "the 'mother sect' of the three single-practice movements of the Kamakura Period : Pure Land (Amida), Nichiren (*Lotus Sutra*) and Zen (meditation)."[14] In addition to the indebtedness of Hōnen and Shinran, another important influence was on Kakuban (1094-1143), whose semi-tāntric Shingon sect also adopted Genshin's method of *nembutsu*. Likewise in the mid-twelfth century Shōshin continued the practice as advocated by Genshin, although that came by ties with Hōnen's Pure Land movement.

Systematic mystical theology, which Genshin is doing, is one of the most difficult of all fields to work in, no less for the reason that there are always those who insist that spiritual things cannot be systematized since the spiritual is by definition beyond or above system. The absence of logic and epistemology in the sense that is found in his contemporaries like Udayana in India or Ibn Sīnā in Islam or Psellos in Byzantium makes one wonder what difference if any it would have made had Genshin had access to some of the works of Dignāga, Dharmakīrti and others. Certainly the absence of training in the technical formalities of logic did not hinder him from being remarkably logical in his classification schemata.

In his encouragement of a pluralism of practices according to specific need and stations of the individual along the mystagogic path, in his position between extreme dogmatic assertions and complete amorphous openness such as later Rinzai Zen tried to encourage in Japan as it had already done (to its own peril) in China, and in his balance between extreme aestheticism and extreme asceticism, Genshin seems to take a middle ground all the way round.

13. Simeon the New Theologian

Simeon the Neo-Theologicos (d. 1022) is one of those Byzantine thinkers who has not received due recognition until relatively recently for the simple reason that the ultra-orthodox considered him on the borderline of heresy because of his mysticism. In his chapter entitled "The Last Flowering of Byzantine Orthodoxy", Pellikan makes it clear that, technically, those like Simeon who were called "new" theologians did not necessarily introduce anything new but reaffirmed the 'old' theology which had all through the centuries been considered precariously near to heresy.

> The task of articulating a new theology of the spiritual life, including the doctrine of God as light, was undertaken by Gregory Palamas more than three centuries after Simeon. Yet it was Simeon who acquired the title of "the New Theologian". Following Byzantine custom, he himself employed the title "the Theologian" to refer either to John the apostle (hence the title "John the Divine") or to Gregory of Nazianzus (often identified simply as "the Theologian"). The appellation "the New Theologian", as applied to Simeon, "was first used to distinguish him and compare him" in relation to the other two; for "one of the reasons why St. Simeon was called "Neo-

> Theologicos" was probably the fact that like St. Gregory of Nazianzus he had also written Theological Orations on the Holy Trinity." Gregory Palamas, in one of his very few explicit references to Simeon, called him "the New Theologian" and spoke of the miracles made visible in his life. Even though there appears in fact to have been little literary or intellectual connection between Simeon and Palamas, it does seem accurate to identify the latter as the one who took the personal mystical experiences of Simeon and gave them a "theological rigor" they had not had before.[1]

It is true of course that Latin Scholasticism also had its semi-heretical strains of Christianized Neo-Platonism; but seldom if ever did that gain ground enough to become a major issue, as it did in the Hesychast controversy.

> Formally and technically, orthodox monasticism always claimed to be at least as subservient as any other part of church life to the authority of the fathers and of the dogmatic tradition; this never changed. What changed was that, beginning in the eleventh century and climaxing in the fourteenth, there developed within Byzantine monachism a method of theologizing called "Hesychasm", which found in its practices of devotion and prayer a new resource for Christian doctrine. It had long been recognized by the Greek theologians that "practice is the basis of theory", and that the discipline of Christian devotion, like the discipline of Christian worship, provided a foundation for that vision of God which was the highest contemplation. Even the critics of the Hesychastic spirituality practiced by the monks on Mount Athos would have to agree with the principle enunciated by the synod that defended such spirituality : "The matrix of prayer is silence, and prayer is the manifestation of the glory of God."[2]

Simeon's contemporary Michael Psellos was a Hellenist almost completely, classically a humanist, with only peripheral interest in mysticism at all, not to mention mysticism of the quietist sort—which was really a kind of yoga, with particular postures, breathing exercises and mantra like chants, such as still survives on Mt. Athos, and such as Simeon actually practiced. This was really more in the heritage of Origen, Pseudo-Dionysius and Macarios of Egypt than of Gregory Nazianzen, whom Psellos so constantly consulted and cultivated. Hesychasm was strictly a monastic tradition. Such "confinement" was too much for Psellos, whose attitudes were more in public administration and what were considered as "secular" studies by the ultra-pious monks.

Within the monastic discipline the stages of spiritual advancement were very definitely marked, not only by a specialized vocabulary but also by different social positions in the community and often with different garb. The Ikhwān al-Ṣafā (the Brethren of the Purity) also had a similar structure and function as also the Buddhist *saṅgha*, especially in the Tendai/T'ien T'ai and the Ch'an/Zen communities. Needless to say, these things could become so ritually externalized that they could lose their true meaningfulness. Simeon was among those who continually insisted that although affirmation of all the Church's teachings must be mandatory, nevertheless intensive personal experience is really all that ultimately matters. If that experience is truly authentic, Simeon taught, then any and all could become equal to the saints and apostles—a teaching suggestive of the heritage from the *Lotus Sūtra* and other Mahāyāna teachings that guarantee not only that all creatures here below in *saṃsār* have at least potentially the Buddha nature but that they can become Bodhisattvas just like Amida or Maitreya. One gets the impression that those in this heritage had more reverence for and cultivation of the Holy Spirit than was generally the case in the Latin heritage, since it is by the operation of the Holy Spirit that anyone could have virtually, if not actually, the same relation with the Father as the Christ did.

As Simeon said in one of his hymns, not only had the believers become members of Christ, but Christ had become their member as well : "Christ is my hand and Christ is my foot,... and I am the hand of Christ and the foot of Christ." So intimate was this assimilation to Christ that every generation of the church had the same relation to Christ that the apostles had. Nor was the assimilation merely something to be expected in heaven; it was "not only after death, but also now in this present life."[3]

And again :

> "Do not," Simeon admonished his brethren, "try to describe ineffable matters by words alone, for this is an impossibility. ...But let us contemplate such matters by activity, labor, and fatigue.... In this way we shall be taught the meaning of such things as the sacred mysteries." Love in action was the most appropriate vehicle for the articulation of a truth that defied positive verbal formulation.[4]

In Simeon's case the method was essentially a matter of classifying the ways that we may know about God without ever "prying" into the incomprehensible mysteries of direct knowledge of His nature or direct familiarity with Him. Simeon insisted that we must know God "through his effects". Thus the intensity of the *via negativa* releases proportionately the mind and the soul, in detachment, for investigation of nature as the transparent mirror of the divine glory.

This reminds us of the Prajñāpāramitā/Śūnyavāda insistence that all the *dharmas* are 'empty', i.e., of any *svalakṣaṇa*, self-validating principle, and therefore must be treated at the secondary *vyāvahārika* level. This necessity of operating "at the second level" is a guard of orthodoxy against those mystics—and Simeon was accused of being such a mystic—who, like al-Ḥallaj and some Advaitins, claimed to have penetrated the "Cloud of Unknowing" and achieved *fanā* and mystical union with God, obliterating the *difference* which is an illusion covering His supreme Unity. Some modern apologists claim that this *via negativa* and the necessity of operating at the second level was one of the reasons why "Christian" Europe got ahead in the natural sciences; however, when this *via negativa* was most strongly asserted—and this applies to the Zen and Advaita traditions as well—the sciences were most neglected. We can readily suggest that Simeon might have felt more at home with Abhinavagupta, for example, than with his Latin Christian contemporaries; and we must not forget that similar things are to be found not only in many of his Muslim contemporaries but in Ibn Gabriol or Ibn Paquda, the Jewish Neo-Platonists who were his contemporaries.

Simeon never went beyond the pale of strict adherence to the Church's dogma; nevertheless, he does not try to minimize *theosis*, for such a doctrine was not beyond orthodox teaching but rather had quite a long history therein long before Simeon's reaffirmation of it.

> The end result of mystical union was deification, as Eastern theologians had been teaching since the early centuries. From those theologians Simeon learned to quote the biblical statements, "You are gods" and "You become partakers of the divine nature," applying them to the definition of salvation as deification. Echoing these passages, he spoke of "receiving the reward of the vision of God, becoming partakers of the divine nature and becoming gods." For Simeon, as for his tradition, the deification of man was the consequence and the counterpart of the incarnation of God in Christ. In one of his vision God said to him : "Yes, I am God, the one who became man for your sake. And behold, I have created you, as you see, and I shall make you God."[5]

Augustine had very little if any influence in Byzantium, being virtually unknown and not regarded very highly by those few who did know about him. The Augustinian view in Byzantine eyes over-exaggerated the Fall of Adam over against the Image of God that remains undefiled and the heritage of Christians as "new creatures" comparticipating in the divinity of the Christ through the operation of the Holy Spirit.

Light was to Simeon more than a metaphor and even more than a symbol, but a sort of *pratīka* as in the Vedāntic tradition especially as interpreted by Yāmuna, Simeon's contemporary, and Rāmānuja after him, i.e., something like an embodiment or almost first hypostasis. Modern apologists might well make more of this than they do since virtually everything we know by virtue of light (or vibrations of an electronic nature which are very closely related, harmonically, to the vibrations in the light spectrum). But we have long since seen that the association of light with divinity has been quite universal.

> The spiritual theology of Simeon was summarized in his doctrine of the vision of God as light. Although men were blind as a result of sin and could not see the divine light, the cleansing gift of salvation made it possible for "the pure in heart" to see God, as the Sermon on the Mount promised, and to see him truly. The way to acquire the vision of God was through acts of thenksgiving and love. What was seen by "the saints, both the ancient ones and those who now have spiritual sight," was no mere "form, image, or representation, but the formless light." "A great radiance in the heavens...exceeding the light of day" came upon Sergius of Radonez during his nocturnal vigil. From such passages as I John 1 :5, "God is light," it was evident that this light was God himself, the entire Trinity; Maximus Confessor had taught that the true light was the same as God. There was no other way for anyone to come to know God except by the vision of this true light. The supreme manifestation of the light on earth was the transfiguration of Christ, when "his face shone like the sun, and his garments became white as light." What shone here was "the light of the deity" rather than a sign or symbol. Even this emphasis on the identity of the light with God and on the reality of the vision had to be qualified by the reminder that God was transcendent; for the heavenly light, being divine, did not have "an appropriate name of its own." Simeon did not formulate a systematic treatment of the relation between transcendence and the identity of God with the light, but the principle components for such a systematization were present in his thought.[6]

Simeon is in full continuity with others such as Paul of Latros (d. 956) and the other Simeon called the Studite (949-1022 ?) from his association with that famous monastery, all of whom thought and practiced in terms of the 'uncreated' Light.

Tatakis points out that Nicétas Stéthatos, a disciple of Simeon, had stressed the theme of interior illumination as the heart and key to Hesychasm as the chief feature that distinguished (and still does according to some, including Nicholas Berdyaev) the Greek from the Latin Church. Thus it is not correct to look to Simeon as an innovator, but really as a continuer or renewer of this heritage. But within that heritage the claim can be made as Simeon did claim, that no one is truly a Christian until and unless this transformation from interior illumination leading toward divine perfection has at least begun. Thus, instead of considering Hesychasm as heretical or nearly so, the Hesychasts made the counter-claim that those who were merely indulging in dogmatic polemics and ornate oratory and ceremony for the sake of the external and sensational show were anything but orthodox in the best sense. Psellos might insist that pomp and ceremony without contemplation does become empty; but contemplation without exterior manifestaion is, at the other extreme, merely a variety of spiritual self-indulgence.

Simeon's retort to accusers was essentially the same as others even among his Eurasian contemporaries, including a wide spectrum from Peter Damien to Ryōnin : If you disagree, that is because you yourself need to become more spiritual, then you can recognize spiritual people. Whenever a saint has arrived at seeing the spirit, it is no longer he who speaks and writes, but it is the spirit which works and speaks in and through him, which suggests the *jīvanmukti* ideal emphasized by Abhinavagupta and the Bodhisattva ideal in most varieties of Mahāyāna Buddhism.

Simeon stresses the transformation of human nature that is supposed to take place by the operation of grace, resulting in *theosis*. The transformation is manifest by the capacity for unlimited givingness (*arapśtike*). How then to come into such a realization ? According to Simeon not by ascetic practices so much as by acts of thanksgiving and love. Here he might feel more accord with Ryōnin than with many of his other contemporaries. Ascetic though he must have been, his asceticism does not prevent him from writing poetry of a very high quality. In that he might also be compared with several of his Zen contemporaries or perhaps even with the Ālvārs who were the prime source for Rāmānuja's philosophizings in the Sanskrit tradition, or with Ṣūfīs who were 'quietists' theologically but poetically produced some of the world's most beautiful and refined verse.

As was the case with al-Ghazālī a century later and St. Bonaventura two or so centuries still later, 'secular' philosophy contained too many temptations; thus Simeon was rather intensively engaged in the supra-philosophical realms of mystical realizations. Indeed so intensive was his penchant for mystical immediacy that he left the famous Studite monastery and entered the community of St. Mamas of Constantinople where he became the chief guru. John Climacus and other ascetics were his chief models. Though he was ignorant of the secular sciences, nevertheless he was very erudite (unintentionally, as it were) as far as familiarity with Greek Patristic field is concerned.

For Simeon all the expertise in delineating steps on the mystical path is useless; it is a sort of all-or-none matter of direct experience. The Holy Spirit's visitation transforms everything, and the human all-too-human being is restored to the freedom that Adam had before the Fall. The sacraments are not so important in themselves as is the actual experience of the spiritual light. One might almost assert that he was a sort of Byzantine Quaker in this respect. Nevertheless, a certain *ascesis* does emerge in his works which is remarkably Zen-like : one must empty out all that is finite from one's mind, soul and spirit so that perfection is to become a blank white card ready to receive the appearances of the Holy Spirit. But for this, as in Zen tradition and Hindu also, a guru or spiritual guide is absolutely essential. In fact Simeon asserts that this is all that is needed.

The fruits of this spiritual attainment are peace and joy. Everything else becomes secondary. For instead of ordinary or merely human intellect, the divine or inner light, which is really life itself, leaves no gap between the self and truth, for ultimately they are one and the same. As Tatakis succinctly puts it : "The Spirit does not reason; It *sees*."[7] Instead of an exaggerated frenetic ecstasy, the person who achieves this saintly state suffers no variations of mood or temperament. One is reminded here of the *kṣānti-pāramitā* linked intimately with *dhyāna-pāramitā* as essential underpinnings of *prajñā-pāramitā*. Thus God for such a saint becomes not just an object of loving devotion but actually a loving Person whose love and compassion flow unhindered through the saint so that others benefit automatically in his presence.

One wonders whether Simeon was witnessing to levels and kinds of direct experience seldom if ever achieved in our modern secularized world (though there are some reports that some remnant of the tradition still survives on Mt. Athos); but no doubt in the secular world of Byzantium it might have been talked about but little practiced. For it must not be forgotten that Simeon was a monk and not a modern secular university professor. It might be said of Michael Psellos that he was a philosopher by choice and a theologian only by necessity, whereas Simeon is a theologian by choice and only in spite of himself a philosopher. Simeon is another of those trans-worldly, trans-historical contemplators whose heritage nevertheless does have a history—Neo-Platonism.

14. Miskawayh

Although he had his early training and work in the relatively advanced sciences of his day, and although as a *Falsafah* he did have the full heritage of the Greek tradition in metaphysics and logic and therefore might even be compared in a measure with his Byzantine contemporaries, Miskawayh (936-1030) turned mostly to ethics. Like so many of his contemporaries, Miskawayh was also a poet; and though he is most remembered as a moralist, he was also an historian—indeed, another polymath typical of his era, although somewhat outstanding as such. In his specifically Iranian milieu Miskawayh is contemporary with Ibn Sīnā and comes immediately before al-Baghdādī and al-Ghazālī. In Persian circles he is known not by his Arabic name Miskawayh, but as Ibn Māsuyeh. Miskawayh had yet another name also, abu' Ali al-Khāzin. There is an on-going controversy whether properly he should be listed as Ibn (son of) Miskawayh or simply as Miskawayh. This is of some importance since according to the traditional account he was a convert to Islam, having been a Zoroastrian Magi (*majūsi*), but this might have been true of his father rather than of himself.

The first part of Miskawayh's *al-Fauz al-Aṣghar* deals with the proofs for the existence of God, the second with the soul and its modes, and the third with prophethood. Following al-Fārābī, he therein is trying—as indeed we know that most of his Byzantine contemporaries were doing following after John Philopon—to reconcile Plato and Aristotle, and of course Plotinus. Our curiosity is aroused as to whether (and if not, why not) he was aware of the efforts of Photius in the same direction. But also the question arises why it is that Ibn Sīnā's works were translated into Latin but Miskawayh's were not.

Miskawayh develops the Aristotelian argument of motion, i.e., the notion of God as the Prime Mover, quite fully as his favorite argument for the existence of God, though of course he adds to it the attributes according to the Qur'anic tradition as his predecessors had long since done. Following Plotinus and Porphyry almost exclusively, but also as an effort to reconcile Aristotle with them, he identifies the first hypostasis in the emanational scale with the Aristotelian Higher Intellect, or First Intellect, describing that as "eternal, perfect in existence, and immutable in state, because 'emanation is connected with it in a continuous way eternally, the source of emanation being eternal and wholly generous' ".[1] But of course this perfection is somewhat relative, being inferior to the Perfection of God but superior to the things below it in order of being.

As to his version of the emanation doctrine, Fakhry notes in particular that whereas in the Arab Neo-Platonist tradition stemming from al-Fārābī and others the Active Intellect or First Reason was listed as the tenth intellect, Miskawayh treats it as the first emanation—obviously affirming a position closer to Plotinus than to Aristotle. Fakhry says that "as though unaware of the incompatibility of the emanationist and creationist theses he proceeds to add that God has created everything from nothing."[2] We wonder whether, as we have seen in the early Byzantine manner stemming from Origen and others, he simply sees no reason for all the fuss about it—as indeed later on even Bonaventura will do, saying that God created everything *ex nihilo* but *ab se ipso*, out of nothing but from out of Himself.

As for the Soul, the second hypostasis in Plotinus' system, Miskawayh complains that Aristotle had been too brief on this subject, so he depends heavily on the commentators Alexander of Aphrodisias and Thamistius. As might be expected, he puts heavy emphasis on the unity of the Soul in spite of the multiplicity of the impressions it receives through the senses and its other faculties. In a way that may be modernized by substituting "energy" or "being energized" for "motion", he follows the idea that the soul is essentially motion.

> This motion is of two kinds: one towards intelligence, the other towards matter; by the first it is illuminated, by the second it illuminates. But this motion is eternal and non-spatial, and so it is immutable. By the first kind of motion, the soul comes near to intelligence which is the first creation of God; by the second it descends and comes out of itself. Therefore, the soul comes nearer to God by the first motion, and goes farther by the second. The first leads to its salvation, the second to its perdition.[3]

Nevertheless the Soul preserves its own degree of perfection, in the same sense that a perfect sphere has its own perfection of geometrical form even though to depict it as such involves us in radical imperfection. Nature itself is like that imperfection which we experience in symbolizations—a strange mixture or mirroring of the ultimate perfection of God. It is from that radical imperfection that the concept of space is derived since it involves embodiment which can never, as contingent being, be perfectly perfect.

This emanational view for the theist has its difficulties, since although it explains the human being's alienation from God as being relatively far down the scale, it does not explain at the same time God's omniscience and omnipotence (which, for example, Peter Damien stressed above the emanational order). This distancing from God as a result of the long chain of emanations between God and ourselves is the reason for our weakness and changeability. Here a Hindu theologian might argue that his concept of Brahma-Śiva-Viṣṇu, being frankly symbolic but profoundly so, preserves a balance in regard to this problem better than the Judeo-Christain-Islamic scholastics.

It is only natural to affirm that the 'end' towards which all things move from potential to actual, or towards actualization, is God. Later on Bonaventura will put heavy emphasis on the argument, perhaps implicitly criticizing Aquinas for putting more emphasis on the Prime Mover argument. By analogy with causation by a magnet and causation by the more common pattern of, say, kicking a ball with one's foot or pushing towards a conclusion in an Aristotelian deductive syllogism, although both are to be affirmed of God, the magnet pattern seems to hold the preference. Evidently Miskawayh thought it had further merit in that it is perhaps the best way to bridge the usual gap between ontology and ethics. For 'happiness' (*sa'ādah*) is indeed the chief human good, as Aristotle had stated as a commonplace that was without question universally. But of course Aristotle had not been explicitly theistic in this statement as all the scholastics were. But it is simple enough to make the transition: Man cannot achieve that happiness except through "the realization of the viceregency of God (and) the place which man occupies in the cosmic evolution by virtue of his specific attribute of rationality".[4] In other words, we might well infer, ethics is simply a matter of removing the obstacles for God's 'magnetic' power to bring man back to the Center, wherein only is Rest.

We might say that the prophet is like the Bodhisattva, as contrasted with the mystic or Arhat who allows himself to be completely absorbed by the attraction of God. Rather, becoming 'magnetized' himself (or herself) the prophet or Bodhisattva returns or is sent as an auxiliary force to draw the unmagnetized order of beings and souls nearer. Thus it might be said that as in Plotinus and Kaśmir Śaivism, in this variety of scholasticism evolution is counterbalanced by involution. For just as everything has come forth from God 'out of nothing' but at His behest, so all things and souls must return towards Him in order to achieve their true well-being or happiness.

The majority of interpreters put more emphasis on Miskawayh's ethics than on his Neo-Platonic metaphysics. This judgment may in part be due to the fact that the chief treatise in which this field is exposited, the *Tahdhīb al-Akhlāq* (*Cultivation of Morals*), was written in Arabic rather than in Persian. Evidently the contents are not so strictly Qur'anic in listing and treating the virtues as direct commands of the Almighty but rather as patterns of conduct consciously to be cultivated in a more or less humanist way. "The aim of this work, as the author states in the introduction, is to cultivate in us those moral traits that render the performance of virtuous actions congenial or spontaneous."[5]

Basically Miskawayh believes that the soul is radically different from the body since it can judge what is good spiritually and what is good for the body. Man therefore is different from the other animals in his capacity for voluntary actions based on deliberation and reflection. Indeed, instead of positing that the virtues are there simply as commandments of God, he rather says, according to Fakhry, that "virtuous actions are defined as those 'which ensue upon man's will and initiative, in those matters for which he was destined by the Creator,' and evil actions are defined as those voluntarily undertaken, 'but (which) hinder him from attaining those desirable ends'!"[6] Fakhry calls this the "teleological" account of good and evil.

In Miskawayh we find the three-fold ordering of the faculties of the Soul: "(1) the rational or angelic, lodged in the brain; (2) the appetitive or bestial, lodged in the liver; and (3) the passionate or leonine in the heart."[7] Miskawayh is not a dualist but a triadizer, as is evident not only in division of the faculties of the Soul but in his ordering of the virtues and the corresponding vices which are parallel with those faculties, e.g., science or wisdom, temperance balanced with liberality, and courage. Justice, Aristotle's fourth, is not independent of the others but occurs if and only if all the others are in balance and harmony—a theory that may be worth considering in our own time since we perhaps too often demand "justice at any price" as an end in itself to be obtained by any means whether or not other virtues are present.

Although Miskawayh is almost completely Aristotelian in his dealing with justice (*'adl*), nevertheless justice for Miskawayh is a "shadow of divine unity, the true equipoise". Likewise kingship in his view, different from Aristotle's, is a divinely ordained institution, so that the king is really the "deputy of God". In regard to the relation between justice and altruistic love, Miskawayh was somewhat emphatic in pointing out that justice has to be maintained by fear and even in some cases by force, whereas altruistic love, based on voluntary and spontaneous affection, is a natural source of unity and needs no compulsion to evoke it much less to provoke or enforce it. As Badawi puts it, "Affection, thus, is the sovereign ; justice is the viceregent."[8]

In the second chapter of his *Tahdhīb al-Akhlāq* Miskawayh deals with the age-old and perpetual problem of whether or to what extent human nature is by nature good or bad and whether it can be changed or not. He believes, against the views of the early Greeks, that human nature can be changed, thus reinforcing a basic theme that had been developing in Byzantine and Taoist forms and in some brands of Mahāyāna Buddhism for centuries. But he also takes up the views of the Stoics of Galen, which parallels closely the varieties of views found in classical Confucian philosophy, that whether humans are by nature good, bad, mixed, or neither, *education* is the key to proper rectification and development. Miskawayh follows up this discussion with the opinion that "the existence of the human substance depends on God's will, but the amelioration of it is left to man on man's will."[9] From this we infer that he was probably much more open to Mu'tazilite views than to the views of al-Ash'arī.

The essential part of Miskawayh's ethical thinking follows after his schematizings, which have been propaedeutic. In other words, he is not just a "moralist" preaching some particular set of virtues, but is interested, in good Aristotelian tradition, in working towards a systematic philosophical definition of the good. In this he was indebted to Prophyry's commentary on Aristotle's *Nicomachaean Ethics*, a work which has been lost although it can be virtually reconstructed from Miskawayh's *Tahdhīb al-Akhlāq*. In Miskawayh's interpretation of the mean between extremes there is a metaphysical Neo-Platonic underpinning, as it were, for the mean must be in relation to ourselves and not merely an objectified calculation of the middle between extremes. The mean, he says, is like the Soul itself as having Unity or participation in the metaphysical One whereas the extremes belong to the Many. And the rational judgment locating the mean between extremes is a function of the divine code rather than a matter of unaided human reason alone.

Following the Greek medical tradition, Miskawayh affirms that healthy body is essential to spiritual health and happiness; and, as might then be expected, he further affirms that happiness is available in this life and not only in the life hereafter. Achievement or attainment of the higher virtues carries with it no guarantee of permanence, so cultivation of the moral life must be preserved even after excellence is attained. Miskawayh would therefore not agree with such as Abhinavagupta's ideal of the *jīvan mukta* whose attainment of *theosis* not only carries with it permanence and exemptions from obligations altogether but even the duty of pretending to be other than a saint in order to spread his merits and miraculous benefits secretly among the commonality; and likewise no doubt he would have serious doubts about the "sudden Southern" school of Ch'an Buddhism for similar reasons.

Miskawayh goes on to discuss the philosophy of love and friendship:

> A striking passage in this part is about two kinds of love: (a) love of man for God, and (b) of disciple for master. The first is too high to be attained by mortal beings, and is reserved only for a few. As to the second kind of love, Miskawaih draws a parallel between the son's love for his parents and the disciple's love for his master, and says that the latter is nobler and more generous, because masters educate our souls and by their guidance we obtain real happiness. The master is a "spiritual father and a human lord; his goodness for the disciple is divine goodness, because he brings him up on virtues, feeds him with high wisdom, and conducts him to everlasting life in eternal blessing."[10]

This sounds very much like the Hindu concept of the guru, although it was also in practice among Ṣūfīs. Nevertheless, although there may be passages in the Qur'ān which might lend support for that concept of the guru being superior to parents and having such powers, they must have been intended differently than the guru concept in Hindu heritage and tradition. At any rate, loyalty and reliability constitute the true test of friendship; and, again following Aristotle, Miskawayh affirms that all human beings need such friendship in a very basic way since man is a social animal (and therefore cannot manage with machines alone, or with machine-like people either).

Fear, and especially fear of death, concerns him considerably; but at first sight he seems to express something more like the Stoical attitude than the strictly Aristotelian. At any rate, this as other fears can be eliminated or transcended by gaining a complete understanding of the immortal and incorruptible nature of the soul. Miskawayh does affirm *sādhana* although not in any extreme ascetic form, since what he calls "voluntary death" is an affirmation of that spiritual condition wherein atrophy of the passions has been achieved and the body is brought into control by moderate self-denials and detached discipline, which might be a moderate affirmation of the *fanā'* ideal of the Ṣūfīs.

We wonder whether, in spite of lack of concrete evidence historically, there might have been some Buddhist or even Hindu influence, since Miskawayh considers ignorance as a root cause of suffering and sorrow and almost comes to treat it as the chief evil in itself. As with the other evils, he prescribes a rational Stoical attitude, since what he intends is simple ignorance of the true nature of authentic happiness, which need not depend on earthly possessions or the other lesser goods that capture our imagination if we are not well informed about the higher goods.

Ansari points out that "Miskawayh is the greatest representative of philosophical ethics in Islam. *Sa'ādah* for him is the central and basic problem."[11] *Sa'ādah* may be defined as "the ultimate end or ideal of human life". Obviously almost everything will follow in its proper place once one has achieved clarification of that. But to arrive at an adequate definition of that ultimate end or ideal is not so easy, even given the historical background of Miskawayh. *Sa'ādah* involves "all rational activity, philosophical or scientific", and even art is not excluded from its domain. "Every activity of the soul, whether individual or social, in the family or in the state, falls equally within its orbit. *Sa'ādah* is the object of ethics, no less of politics, of economics (the science of the household), or of any other social science."[12] There is difficulty in finding any English equivalent to the term *sa'ādah*. Ansari points out that the word "happiness" is inadequate since it does not include "prosperity, success, perfection, blessedness and beatitude" as well as naively a "good feeling". Likewise the more commonly used word "well-being" does not quite carry the proper semantic weight without special qualification since, explicitly, "*sa'ādah* primarily means the attainment of some desirable end or good, involving happiness or pleasure as a necessary concomitant. But in the widest sense the end or good expands to embrace the whole life and becomes the ideal or the end of all the activities of the soul."[13]

It should be interesting to investigate whether or to what extent this concept of *sa'ādah* has similarity with the Chinese concept of *li* (or possibly *jen*) and/or the Indian concept of *dharma*. Certainly in their historical development they came to have similar all-embracing ethical connotations and include all the particular virtues and patterns of *sādhana*. They are not necessarily simply equatable with "the Good", but rather more with the dynamics of human excellence-and-duty as embodiment of the principle of law or lawfulness. Certainly in their cultural heritages they are the absolute frame of reference, even the inner dynamic upon which a whole civilization spins, as it were, or ceases to function. And upon further examination it might be that Miskawayh's *sa'ādah* has a similar semantic weight and is not merely a translation of the Platonic, Aristotelian, *areté or kalos k'agathos* ideal. For Miskawayh seems to intend something more than the Greek ideal. Ansari reports that the Greek idea of the 'Good' is such as to be intrinsically or even ontologically self-existent, independent of human affairs; and by contrast, *sa'ādah* is dependent on human exemplification and cultivation. Nevertheless, as such *sa'ādah* (perhaps like *li* and *dharma*) does really exist, and human good, all human virtues, and all human efforts at virtue, are intimately related to it. Of course *li* and *dharma* are not necessarily theistic in the technical sense, although the theistic varieties of both Śaivism and Vaiṣṇavism reinterpret it in a theistic sense.

For Miskawayh, as for Plato and Aristotle, the perfection of proper function is the key to happiness. Here is one of Miskawayh's arguments :

It is its distinctive functions for which any being is created.

> since only it and no other being can best perform its specific functions and serve its particular purpose. This is a universal law which governs everything in the heavens and on the earth, in nature and in art. A thing is good if it serves its own special purpose and serves in the required way. And it is perfect and *sa'īd* in the proportion in which it achieves its purpose. ...If a horse fails in the performance of its specific function, to that extent it lacks the element of horseness and falls short of its perfection. No matter then, if such a horse is treated as an ass.[14]

And as for man : "The distinctive function of man may be easily found, says Miskawayh, to consist in the proper exercise of reason. The *sa'ādah* of man, therefore, consists in the perfection of his reason."[15]

Miskawayh is a humanist of the most commendable sort, commendable in that respect with his Neo-Confucianist and his Byzantine contemporaries. It might be of some interest in this perspective to review in the Chinese context the relation between *li* and the concepts of *li* and *yung*, substance and function, as well as the later similar thinking in Latin Scholasticism which in Miskawayh's own time was beginning to take shape under Pope Sylvester and Thierry of Chartres. The humanist interpretation of *sa'ādah* is further heightened by Miskawayh's emphasis that although other creatures do conform to a certain sort of *sa'ādah*, their conformity is more a matter of the inexorable law of nature, whereas man's *sa'ādah* is achieved by voluntary activity.

Reason is of two different kinds, theoretical and practical, the first dealing with the pure activity of thought or cognition intrinsically, while the second is instrumental and deals with the accidentals rather than the essence of *sa'ādah*. Ansari writes:

> The reason why theoretical perfection is the ultimate *sa'ādah*, superior to and more valuable than moral perfection, lies deep in the philosophy of Miskawayh. It is more valuable because here reason is directed to itself. Its activity is pure and has no reference to anything except itself. It is exposed to least interruption and affords the highest pleasure. It is least

> dependent on foreign support and external expedients. In pure activity of thought reason enjoys that peace and tranquillity which in the practical life of restless pursuit one cannot attain. Here reason takes possession of the most perfect and exact knowledge, and the objects of its contemplation are immutable and eternal realities. Here reason returns to its source and imitates its perfection. Here one is most God-like in his actions, only the pure contemplation can make possible the closest imitation of the Divine Being. This is the end of philosophy (which Miskawayh defines as the imitation of God). Only pure activity of thought raises man above the limitations of his humanity, and unites him with the Eternal Being.[16]

But the theoretical and practical aspects of *sa'ādah* are no more separable than Aristotle's form and matter. Thus moral perfection is "not only the means to the realization of ultimate happiness, but also a factor contributing to its completion."[17]

The chief requirement for *sa'ādah* is completeness of development of all one's potentialities—which may also be said of any Islamic society or government. Moral and practical perfection are virtually synonymous and deal with both private and public functions and activities. Certainly here he proves himself a true Muslim, not allowing any disparity between ethics and politics, which may be distinguished only for the sake of logical convenience but not separated in practice. Moreover, the notion that ethics is merely a personal matter—a notion that has become rather popular in the modern secularized societies—is impossible since inherently and inevitably moral perfection must necessarily relate us to others. No man can live completely to himself.

According to Miskawayh, the really virtuous man can never be completely miserable since his goods (one might now say his values) are not limited to such as fame and fortune, or beauty, power, influence, joy in one's family, friendship, health, etc., even though these are indeed good in their own way and at their own level. In other words, they are not indispensible even though they are natural additions to the completeness of *sa'ādah*—so much so that he seems not to make any dichotomy between the spiritual and the material goods but treats them in a sort of hierarchical continuum. Ansari writes :

> To sum up: the highest or the ultimate *sa'ādah* consists in the contemplation of intelligible realities, and of the most real being, God, and in effecting a union with Him in contemplation. Moral *sa'ādah* is the necessary condition of the ultimate *sa'ādah* and also its complement. The 'Goods' of the body and fortune are necessary to a fair degree for perfect *sa'ādah*. The pleasures of the body are necessary diversions. *Sa'ādah* itself is the most pleasant activity, and provides for the best and purest pleasure.[18]

On the question of whether perfect *sa'ādah* is attainable in this life—a theme which was very controversial between the Advaitins and the Kaśmir Śaivites on the one hand and the Rāmānuja school of Vedānta on the other over the interpretations of *jīvan mukti* vs *videha mukti*—Miskawayh is evidently caught in the discrepancy between the classical Greek views and the specifically Islamic concept of the afterlife and the Final Judgment. Being dissatisfied with the views of both Plato and Aristotle, he attempts a third position :

> Thus for Miskawayh the fundamental distinction from the point of view of ethics does not lie between this world and the next, but between a life of contemplation of the intelligibles and a life occupied with the sensibles. It is wrong, therefore, to ask the question :Is *sa'ādah* perfectly realisable in this or the next life? Do away with this bifurcation, and you have the correct answer. Perfect *sa'ādah* is realisable only in a life of contemplation of the intelligibles, and it can be attained in this life and the next. However, the perfect *sa'īd* does not turn away from the world, but abiding at the higher level of spiritual and intellectual activity he takes interest in the affairs of society, its organisation and well-being.[19]

Ansari posits the opinion that Miskawayh himself was not satisfied with this accommodation.

In Miskawayh there is a qualified claim that the perfect man has perfect knowledge. This suggests something like the Jaina goal of omniscience, as well as the controversies in the Byzantine heritage over the nature of the omniscience of the God-man Jesus, or again the characteristics of the *jīvan mukta*, or still again the claim of omniscience of the original Buddha and the extent to which the Bodhisattvas also participate in that omniscience. In Miskawayh, however, it is comparatively moderate by virtue of his qualification that this 'perfect' knowledge is not to be literally interpreted but rather that it is operative by virtue of the perfect man's capacity to think in terms of universal essences rather than limiting concrete particulars. Ansari writes:

> The ideal man of Miskawayh has perfect knowledge of all that exists. This becomes possible for him because he looks at things in their universal essence, not as particulars; and he who knows the universal, knows the particular also. He contemplates those intelligibles which are eternal and immutable. In so doing the soul shakes itself free from all the finite limitations imposed on it by its embodiment, and is united with the Intelligence. The part becomes one with the whole, the effluence with the fount. Contemplation is self-realisation and self-transcendence. United with the Intelligence the soul reflects the forms of all the beings that are there in the Intelligence, and thereby becomes a world in itself, a microcosm.[20]

This unitary experience is more characteristic of Ṣūfī mysticism than of systematic humanist Islamic philosophy; and yet there is no evidence that Miskawayh himself claimed to have experienced such self-tarnscendence or perfect knowledge. Rather he conceives of this level of perfection as merely a characteristic of the activity of the Aristotelian Higher Intellect.

Such a contemplative state for Miskawayh by no means entails inactivity or lack of social concern, much less the affirmation of the hermit life which had become rather common in Latin Europe by the eleventh century as well as among Taoists in China and individual yogīs in India. Miskawayh objects to the way so many ascetic renunciates become dependent on others for their sustenance. Somewhat like the Neo-Confucianists' argument against Buddhism, he argues that such people are more concerned about their own spiritual well-being than about the welfare of others, whether spiritual or material or cultural. In short, their renunciation falls short of their high ideal of becoming selfless since selfishly they serve themselves but fail in the basic virtues of altruism and concern for the social order of human existence. Cultivation of the God-given rational faculties according to his system is greater than any mortifications no matter what the motive might be. Thus he would take issue not only with the extreme Ṣūfīs of his time but also with the Byzantine Hesychast monks and most Śaṅkara Advaitin swamis and Ch'an/Zen monks. Ansari writes :

> On the contrary his ideal man is most active, ceaselessly striving after his perfection and the perfection of his family and of society at large. He longs for the company of pure souls; friendship is an enviable virtue for him. In Miskawayh's ideal man the Neoplatonic indifference to society is replaced by an Aristotelian ideal of active social life.[21]

The ideal is not for everyone but is ordinarily acquired by philosophers, prophets or *imāms*. Ultimately perfection is a matter of grace, but effort is still required of all of us, and even extra effort is expected of the privileged classes so that others in the whole of society may share in their merits.

Miskawayh was also an historian of considerable merit. He was so honest about his history writing that he underwent some spiritual *sādhana* before attempting to write historical works lest self-interest mar unprejudiced reportings of what actually happened. In that sense he was very scientific and critical as well as philosophically interpretative. Badawi summarizes Miskawayh's view of the function of history and the duties of the historian :

> History is not an amusing tale about the royal personages, but a mirror of the politico-economic structure of society in a particular age. It is a record of the rise and fall of civilizations, nations, and states.
>
> In order to realize this end, the historian should scrupulously guard himself against the common tendency of mixing

up facts with fiction or pseudo-events. He should not only be factual but also critical in collecting his data.

Above all, he should not be content with the mere descriptions of facts, but, with a philosophic insight, should interpret them in terms of the underlying "human interests," their immediate causal determinants. In history, as in nature, there is no room for chance or accident.

History, thus, is no longer a collection of static and isolated facts, but a dynamic process of creative human hopes and aspirations. It is a living and growing organism, whose structure is determined by the basic ideals and the ideals of nations and states. It not only binds together the facts of the past into an organic whole, but also determines the shape of things to come. The very title of his monumental work, *Tajārib al-Umam* (The Experiences of the Nations) is itself suggestive of its aims and method, which, in the words of Leon Caetani, are "much akin to the principles followed by Western and more modern historians."[22]

For some reason Ibn Sīnā did not have a high opinion of Miskawayh, nor did al-Tauḥīdī, who is nevertheless our best source for biographical details. Miskawayh also dabbled in alchemy (or was it a more serious occupation about which Tauḥīdī and Ibn Sīnā did not have enough information). There is a report, perhaps not unbiased, that his contemporaries blamed him for his miserliness and hypocrisy, and that his interest in alchemy was from desire for wealth rather than science. This seems to have been somewhat true in his youth, but his moralizings evidently were the voice of experience later on since he did not experience a moral transformation as a result of applying to himself a fifteen-point code of ethics. Although Ibn Sīnā and al-Tauḥīdī did not think highly of him, M'd Iqbāl did all he could to vindicate Miskawayh's achievement, regarding him as one of the "most eminent theistic thinkers, moralists and historians of Persia."[23]

15. Ibn Sīnā

Ibn Sīnā (980-1037) has long been well known in the Latin West under his Latinized name Avicenna as a philosopher, physician and scientist. However he still needs to be delivered from the stereotype that he is of value only in so far as he contributed to Latin Scholasticism and relocated in his proper position in world history. According to Rahman, Ibn Sīnā's system "has dominated the Muslim philosophical tradition right down to the modern era when his place is being given to some modern Western thinkers by those who have been educated in modern universities. In the *madrasahs* run on traditional lines, ibn Sīnā is still studied as the greatest philosopher of Islam."[1] And the following from Fakhry's introduction :

> Ibn Sīnā's high standing in the history of Arab Neo-Platonism does not rest on his originality. An autobiographical tradition points out his debt to al-Fārābī, whose *Intentions of Aristotle's Metaphysics* unraveled for him the secrets of that work, which he read forty times and almost memorized, we are told, without grasping its sense. His cosmology, his psychology, his theory of the intellect, his theory of prophecy, etc., despite the refinements they make on al-Fārābī's parallel doctrines, are essentially variations on similar themes. ...
>
> The literary output of Ibn Sīnā was truly voluminous and his treatises far outstrip in comprehensiveness anything earlier philosophical authors such as al-Kindī and al-Rāzī ever produced. Moreover, he surpasses all his predecessors, even the great al-Fārābī, in the fluency of his style and the thoroughness with which he dealt with questions that often were only sketched perfunctorily by his predecessors. His fluency and thoroughness account perhaps for the fact that he soon superseded al-Fārābī, his acknowledged master, and became before long the champion of Islamic Neo-Platonism, which al-Fārābī had in fact founded. ...[2]

Ibn Sīnā wrote both in Arabic and in Persian, and that both in the sciences and also in verse. He was the first to describe several drugs and diseases, such as menengitis. His method included very scientific and one might even say modern case histories carefully recorded. Beyond this calling, he was also a philosopher. How strange it should be that we have now to look into entirely different sources in order to put him together, as though he was a sort of historical humpty-dumpty who got broken up into bits and pieces by historians, even without a fall. Thus, some treat only his metaphysics and theology, and others only his scientific works, or only his literary works. However, Ibn Sīnā's utterly astounding versatility as one of the world's most widely-based polymath philosophers is relatively peripheral to his essential role in the *Falsafah* or 'Aristotelian' tradition. In this aspect he may be placed in close sequence with the Ikhwān al-Ṣafā and al-Fārābī.

Ibn Sīnā's striking and premature intellectual formation probably became a source of the many controversies arranging around his philosophy, as many envious contemporaries sought to alienate many persons from his entourage. It is also likely that the political tension between the dynasty and the professional concurrence of thinkers who received patronage therefrom constitutes a principle source of conflict. Ibn Sīnā was indeed a precocious genius, for "by the age of eighteen he had mastered logic, physics, and mathematics, so there was nothing left for him to learn except metaphysics".[3] In adulthood his principle works are *Kitāb al-Shifā'* and *Kitāb al-Najāt*, the former being a giant encyclopedic work and the latter being an abridgement of it.

Ibn Sīnā's place of origin was Balkh, where Buddhism survived the longest after the Muslim conquest. He seems to make quite a point of learning 'Indian numbers' from a local merchant who used them commercially. Perhaps this merchant, whether he was Hindu or Buddhist, may have taught him yoga and other things through oral tradition. For many centuries Balkh had been a center of intercultural exchange. His family was of Ismā'īlī persuasion, thus Ibn Sīnā was able to cultivate the works of the Ikhwān al-Ṣafā, Aristotle and Euclid.

The most likely communication might have been with Kaśmir, where Vijñānavāda Buddhism with its advanced logical expertise and its metaphysics derived from the *Prajñāpāramitā* literature was still flourishing, and Abhinavagupta's synthesis of that with traditional Śaivism was in full flower. Nevertheless, this proximity in time and space should not tempt us to a hasty and careless syncretism, since although there are syncretistic trends in Abhinavagupta, that is certainly not the case with Ibn Sīnā. In spite of the great architectonics of his cosmology and psychology and ontology, he remains strictly theistic rather than pantheistic or panpsychic, as distinct from the Kaśmir schools.

Although Ibn Sīnā is known as perhaps the greatest systematic philosopher in Islam, this is balanced by his realization of the spiritual/esoteric needs of the "wandering soul". Fakhry writes :

> A mystical strain in Ibn Sīnā's thought, which has remained latent in his earlier and more speculative writings, appears in *al-Ishārāt*, and a group of highly pictorial treatises, such as *Ḥayy b. Yaqzān*, *The Bird*, *On Love*, *On Prayer*, and *On Fate*. ... The allegorical idiom of some of these treatises and the *Ode on the Soul* reveal an obvious preoccupation with the problem of philosophical expression, which Plato himself betrays in the highest flights of his philosophical fancy. This preoccupation, both in Plato and Ibn Sīnā, involves more than the special problem of the use of allegory or myth. It is the outward expression of a spirit of dissatisfaction with the discursive forms of philosophic exposition and the urge to transcend or bypass them by evolving a new idiom that is more consonant with the Soul's vision or aspiration because it is more elusive and less direct.[4]

The *Kitāb al-Ishārāt wa'l-Tanbīhāt* (*Book of Directives and Remarks*) is almost a summa philosophica since it proceeds very systematically from elementary logic through philosophy of nature and psychology, theology, and esoterics in one comprehensive compass. Though the themes in this work may be traceable to the Neo-Platonist version of Aristotle, there is a marked independence from Plotinus' hypostases, though Ibn Sīnā writes freely of the 'celestial' soul as well as of the 'terrestrial' soul. The doctrine of Providence is much more prominent in his doctrine of creation than is so with Plotinus ; and there are other distinctive features which are more Islamic than Hellenistic, though as ever the age-old distinction between the passive or potential intellect and the active intellect or intelligence is not excluded. In this synthesis, the concept of recompense of individual souls by rewards of spiritual delights and horrible punishments takes a premium place. Ibn Sīnā may be interpreted as holding that the truly purified soul may even bypass the agent intellect and come into the unmediated enjoyment of Pure Being as such, as the source of all the intelligibles.

In *al-Ishārāt* Ibn Sīnā takes magic for granted as indistinguishable from science. This was true also of later Islamic writers like Ibn Khaldūn, and also of Nicolas of Oresme, Raymond Lulle, and Paraculsus. Goichon[5] in introducing *al-Ishārāt* distinguishes between *ḥikmah* (wisdom) and *falsafah*, applying the former to this work and the latter to the Aristotelian or Greek tradition or *Weltanschauung*. This distinction resembles that between *darśana* and *tattva* in Sanskrit terminology. *Al-Ishārāt* is then philosophy in the larger more inclusive sense, rather than as commentary on the Stagirite corpus. Under the term *ḥikmah* Ibn Sīnā's esoteric and exoteric works may be perceived in terms of a systematic unity.

Ibn Sīnā's esoteric works have only recently become known to Euramericans, and they were never Latinized. These esoterics were cast usually (as was the *Ikhwān al-Ṣafā* and other similar works) in a highly stylized literary form so that they could be enjoyed by all at the popular level but studied carefully for their true contents by philosophers, scholars and savants of other sorts. Scientific information thereby found good company among the Ṣūfīs and other mystics since in Islam, and especially in Iranian Islam, there was not anything like the early twentieth century mutual contempt between scientists and mystics. Also for Ibn Sīnā there exists no gap between logic and metaphysics, since both are dealing with being, essence and substance, universals and particulars or relatives, and so on until one finds that logic involves at least the categories. Though Ibn Sīnā is interested in logic as a tool, i.e., a necessity for practical use in his scientific researches, he emphasizes not only the desirability but the necessity of logic for anyone who would undertake any mystical *sādhana*. Thus in his perspective the gap between the esoteric and the exoteric really does not exist as it does in the modern secularized Euramerican perspective, at least until the last quarter of the twentieth century when the gap is beginning to diminish.

These visionary works rely on a symbolic language which functions to reflect in a lower order of existence a reality belonging to a higher ontological status. Nasr writes :

> These narratives are the records of the intellectual visions of the author described in a symbolic language which itself constitutes an integral aspect of the visions and which is not simply an allegory more or less made up by the author. In these narratives Ibn Sīnā has a vision of the Universe as a vast "cosmos of symbols" through which the initiate seeking Divine Knowledge, or gnosis (*ma'rifah*), must travel. The cosmos, instead of being an exterior object, becomes for the gnostic (*'ārif*) an interior reality; he sees all the diversities of Nature reflected in the mirror of his own being. Thanks to the transformation of the physical and astronomical elements of the Universe, the traveler (*sālik*) on his journey toward gnosis is able to realize the progressive interiorization of the cosmos within himself until finally he ascends above and beyond the "cosmic crypt" itself.[6]

Although we have designated this aspect of his work as "esoteric", this should not mean that it is unsystematic or amorphous like some Zen practices which depend only on oral tradition. For example, in *al-Ishārāt* there is a systematic classification of types of mystics or 'knowers', which in a sense is more analogous perhaps to the *Prajñāpāramitā* of Kaśmir Mahāyāna or Kaśmir Śaivism nearby than even to the Gnostic or Hermetic tradition : (a) the *zāhid*, a *sādhaka* initiate who undertakes ascetic discipline, (b) the *'ābid*, one who has reached the intermediate state of total dedication and devotion, and (c) the *'ārif*, one who has reached the stage of union, illumination and ecstasy or *samādhi* whose sole aim is to become identified with Truth.

Evidently at this last stage one attains to *siddhi* or supranormal powers, including some knowledge of the future. But most of all one then sees the physical world as a sort of transparent veil, and everything becomes what may be termed the "sacramental" or "symbolic" universe, as indeed was the case with the Victorines in the next century and the Ālvārs and Nāyanmārs of Tamil India about the same time that Ibn Sīnā was writing. Even without any knowledge of the *jīvanmukta* ideal so prominent in Abhinavagupta's system we have a rather clear description of the capacity of a great saint or prophet to work all kinds of miracles. In this case, however, these are not necessarily the works of God by divine intervention but simply the exercise of the 'higher powers' or *siddhis* as existing within the human order. Ibn Sīnā condemns 'black' magic as much as he recognizes that even 'white' magic is not supernatural but simply natural in a special sense. In a word, the psychic must be brought into the service of the spiritual or pneumatic.

In regard to the position of man in the whole of creation, Ibn Sīnā affirms the principle that everything naturally tends towards its own perfection and that love (*'ishq*) induces this movement. Indeed this is a double movement, descending into the depths of the lowest degrees of creation and evoking a return to its source, so that Ibn Sīnā uses the term 'circulation' to express the grand design. Nasr relates that in his *Risālah fi'l-'ishq* Ibn Sīnā considers love as the very cause of existence. Ibn Sīnā writes :

> Every being which is determined by a design strives by nature toward its perfection, i.e., that goodness of reality which ultimately flows from the reality of the Pure Good, and by nature it shies away from its specific defect which is the evil in it, i.e., materiality and non-being,—for every evil results from attachment to matter and non-being. Therefore it is obvious that all beings determined by a design possess a natural desire and an inborn love, and it follows of necessity that in such beings love is the cause of their existence.[7]
>
> Because It (Absolute Good), by Its very nature, loves the Being of what is caused by It, It desires to manifest Itself. And since the love of the Most Perfect for Its own perfection is the most excellent love, It has as Its true object the reception by others of Its manifestation, and this is most properly Its reception by those divine souls which have reached the highest degree of assimilation to It.[8]

Nasr adds :

> The sympathy between the microcosm and macrocosm is itself a manifestation of the love of God for His own Perfection and for all of creation. What attracts the various beings to Nature and to each other, and the pure soul of man toward the celestial Intelligences, is an expression of the sympathy of God for Himself, a sympathy which is the very reason for the manifestation of the Universe.

The microcosm/macrocosm problem was universal in the ninth through the twelfth centuries. In China there is the virtually materialist version with Chang Tsai and Shao Yung; in India, the post-Śaṅkara Advaitin interpretation of the *ātman*-Brahman equation presupposes it; and probably the most vivid version of it can be found in Ibn Sīnā's contemporary in Kaśmir, Abhinavagupta. In Islam it received a definite theistic interpretation, either as a qualification or as an addition-at-the-top, with the consideration of the distinction between the psychic levels wherein the equation operates and the specifically spiritual or prophetic level which remains transcendent to that as to every cosmic relation. However, there were some like the extreme Ṣūfī al-Ḥallāj who tended to minimize that, while the Ash'arites exaggerated it to the extent of holding all mysticism in suspicion if not abeyance.

Ibn Sīnā approaches this problem somewhat in a 'scientific' way through the science of medicine as he learned it from Hippocrates and Galen, but probably also from Indian materials through his correspondence with al-Bīrūnī and through the work of previous scientists who had brought in the so-called Arabic number system and improvements in astronomy. The notion that the whole universe is 'alive' may need some radical qualification, but Ibn Sīnā held what was then the prevailing view all across Eurasia. As Nasr writes, "The study of the human body by Ibn Sīnā is not that of dead matter to which life has been added":

> Modern medicine is based on the conception of the universe as a conglomeration of dead matter out of which, by some unexplainable process, life may become evolved in forms. To

> Avicenna the whole of the universe is the manifestation of a universal principle of life, acting through the instrumentality of forms. Or, again, in modern medicine, the forms are the source of life; to Avicenna they are the product of life.[10]

Although the general tendency among secular scholars and scientists might be to disregard his "metaphysics of medicine" (as Nasr terms it), surely there is something to be said for the revival of a thorough phenomenological re-examination of many modern theories which tend, for example, to kill the disease instead of strengthening the patient so that he can throw off the disease naturally. But the further hypothesis that probably needs re-examination is not only the psychosomatic organized wholeness of the human system-of-systems but the possible relations of every individual not only through genetics but through 'psycho-electronic' harmonies and disharmonies—relations indeed with who knows how much of the macrocosmic universe that surrounds us, not to mention the immediate environment.

Ibn Sīnā's theoretical approaches in the area of psychology show a definite influence from Aristotle. He wrote a commentary on Aristotle's *De Anima*, which has received much attention even today as fresh translations illustrate. Concerning the Muslim adaptation of Aristotle, the details of the differences between the two are considerable, though often subtle. Rahman characterizes the *Kitāb-al-Najāt* in this way :

> The treatise in its main teaching is basically Aristotelian and incorporates the later Peripatetic developments of the doctrines of Aristotle. Besides Aristotelianism, however, there are strong Neo-platonic currents which are most evident in Avicenna's conception of the soul-body relation.
>
> But although Avicenna's main ideas are no doubt taken from his predecessors, it would be incorrect to suppose that there is nothing new in his work. The formulation of many of the arguments of the treatise is the work of Avicenna : the fine and sometimes complicated differentiations by which these arguments are worked out are genuine Avicennian characteristics. The development of the doctrine of the grades

of abstraction emanates from Avicenna himself. The theory of prophecy built upon the few words of Aristotle is also his original contribution and is, indeed, a proof of his highly intelligent mind, responsive to every suggestion. Avicennian also for the most part are the arguments for the immortality and the immateriality of the soul.[11]

As to parallels and comparative reflections, let us point out that the Aristotelian system may be roughly analogized to the Sāṃkhya-Yoga, the prototype of Indian systems, according to the following schematism :

vegetable soul	*tamas guṇa*
animal soul	*rajas guṇa* (including most of the faculties of perception and action)
rational soul	*sattva guṇa* (but only in the sphere of *prakṛti* and including *manas*, *buddhi*, and *citta* within the lower range)
passive intellect	*antaḥkaraṇa*
active intellect	*antaryāmin*, *sākṣī*

This could be worked out in considerable detail, *puruṣa* being equated with Allah. We could also point out parallels between Ibn Sīnā and Vaiśeṣika, Ibn Sīnā's contemporary Udayana, for example, especially because of its emphasis on logic and its theistic basis. To attempt a rapproachment with Advaita would require several adaptations if not definite discrepancies such as one finds indicated in the refutations advocated within Advaita by Yāmunācārya or later by Rāmānuja or Mādhava.

As in Sāṃkhya-Yoga, even the rational soul, at least in its lower reaches, not to mention the vegetable and animal souls, is still within the natural psycho-physical and not necessarily spiritual level of reality. Concerning the soul, Nasr summarizes :

> The human soul stands between the earthly and heavenly worlds. Its felicity lies in uniting itself with the Intellect and in leaving the sensible world in favor of the Intelligible. This is its entelechy and deliverance. As the Universe is generated by God's contemplation and intellection of Himself, so does

> it become integrated in its Divine archetype in the act of intellection within man which results in the return of the sensible world to the intelligible one. Ibn Sīnā describes the human soul as a wanderer in this world who has lost his home and forgotten his original abode. It is for him to remember once again from where he came and to return once again to his original dwelling place.[12]

Against Plato, Aristotle, and Plotinus, Ibn Sīnā disagrees with the idea of the pre-existence of the soul and with metempsychosis. Here there could be no sharper contrast with his contemporary "third generation" post-Śaṅkara Advaitins who affirm the doctrine of *ekajīva-vāda*. For although the soul does not perish after death, just as it does come into existence individually along with its individuated body, it definitely preserves its individual identity after death. One chapter of Ibn Sīnā's *Kitāb al-Najāt* is a detailed series of arguments in support of this philosophy of individuation.

The ultra-orthodox Sunni, or more strictly the specialists in *Kalām* or thinking limited to exegesis of the Qur'ān only, had simply considered Allah as the cause of everything directly without any causal classifications. But the Muslim 'Aristotelians' had to reconcile this view with the four causes of Aristotle as before them Philopon and other Byzantines had done (long before the Latin Scholastics ever thought of such a scheme). Controversies about causation in the various schools of Indian philosophy by this time had been summarized, for example, by Vācaspati Miśra and his disciples and were beginning to get the attention of Rāmānuja's immediate predecessors, not to mention such as Udayana and Abhinavagupta, Ibn Sīnā's more immediate contemporaries. The Aristotelian heritage was reconciled by Ibn Sīnā with the Islamic view as follows, according to Nasr :

> The Peripatetic analysis of causality did not correspond in every respect with the Islamic spirit which is based on the reintegration of all multiplicity into Unity and the absorption of all particular causes into the Universal and Transcendent Cause. Yet, by considering the interrelatedness of natural

> events and studying the immediate in the light of the ultimate purpose of things, the Peripatetic notion of causality did find a place in the Islamic world view. Although not in conformity with the essence of that tradition, Ibn Sīnā's notion of causality was not completely opposed to the Islamic perspective, because it sought to demonstrate the interrelatedness and final purpose of things and consequently the unicity of Nature and the meaning of its existence. It is always the degree in which a science of Nature is capable of demonstrating this unicity that it is capable of being in conformity with the Islamic perspective and able to be integrated into it. It was this underlying intuition of the "unicity of all that exists" in the Aristotelian philosophy of Nature which, despite its syllogistic and rationalistic character and its placing of intermediate causes between God and the world, permitted the integration of many of its cosmological elements into the Islamic world view.[13]

Whether Ibn Sīnā belongs to the camp of those who consider all of nature as a theophany in the same sense that most Neo-Platonists do and certainly not a few Ṣūfīs even in Ibn Sīnā's own lifetime did, might be debated; but he does consider quite systematically the manner whereby the principle of entelechy is universally at work. What Ibn Sīnā is attempting is really a fascinating synthesis between panpsychism as far as Nature is concerned, especially in regard to motion, and strict theism as far as Being is concerned. But within that perspective he retains the Aristotelian notion that circularity of motion entails perfection such that no potentiality is retained, and likewise in regard to the 'uncorruptability' of the heavens.

Incidentally we might raise the query whether in the modern world we have not retained too much of this notion that nature is perfect and perfectly ordered, and that therefore if our experiments do not turn out right something is wrong with the experiment and not with nature. Charles Sanders Peirce may have been one of the first to suggest that this may not be so; and Teilhard de Chardin and Aurobindo had a grand vision of how, somewhat as St. Paul says, the whole of creation is groaning in its radical imperfection. That perspective, by the way, might be more compatible with the Vedānta than with the Aristotelian Scholastic theory.

In tracing Ibn Sīnā's adaptation of the *genesis* and *phthora* dynamic of Aristotle to the Qur'anic heritage, Nasr reminds us that Aristotle retains the classical and at that time universal notion of the four elements within the material or sublunary world. These are always transformable, the changes of form being just that and not a matter of change of essence. These things are so fixed in the Aristotelian tradition that they constitute nothing particularly distinctive for Ibn Sīnā, who made no fundamental alterations in them except the constant qualification of denial of the eternity of matter in his adaptation of the Aristotelian system to his Qur'anic theism.

Above the factual matters there remains in Ibn Sīnā the sense of awe and wonder: and, though a strict systematist, he also had this variety of mysticism, which has not been adequately appreciated in Euramerica until rather recently. And that mysticism extends to thinking of the whole of nature as still completely contingent on the nature of God. Versatile polymath that he was, being at home in virtually all the then-known sciences, he nevertheless never forgot to regard them as marvels of the works of Allah.

Not only was Ibn Sīnā a scientist and philosopher, but he was a litterateur of much merit, perhaps in part by virtue of his cultural milieu wherein Persian letters flourished alongside Arabic literary works in merit and esteem. Whether or not there was some theory of systematic aesthetics behind his prolific creative verse, we do know that Ibn Sīnā did scholarly analyses of the aesthetic theories of Aristotle, as evidenced in his commentary on the *Poetics*. Done more within the perspective of studies of the Greek classics rather than in that of Islamic philosophy or Arabic literary theory, this work is nevertheless a veritable gold mine of historical information on the history of the Aristotelian tradition.

Concerning the famous controversy about 'imitation' and 'representation', Dahiyat has given us a very complete explication from which we can excerpt the following four-point summary :

The concept of mimesis, according to Avicenna's interpretation, acquires the following characteristics :

1. The presentation of vivid images which have their objective basis, and which are not intended for conviction or (rhetorical) persuasion but primarily for psychological pleasure and imaginative assent.

2. The use of figurative language including metaphor, simile, and syntactical and rhetorical devices. The mimetic aspect of poetry lies as much in the form of the speech as in its sense or meaning.

3. There is a definite preference for the "icastic" type of mimesis which consists in presenting a precise and objective image of a thing since this means a combination of pleasure and learning. In "phantastic" mimesis, however, there is still some pleasurable effect which results from the contemplation of the manner of the image.

4. Dramatic mimesis is most effective since it combines word with gesture, but even here the emphasis is laid upon the mimetic aspects of language which have precedence over the outward dramatization which Avicenna calls "the player's art," i.e., *hypokrisis*.[14]

Poetry, according to Ibn Sīnā, appeals to the imaginative faculty: "The imaginative is the speech to which the soul yields, accepting or rejecting matters without pondering, reasoning or choice. In brief, it responds psychologically rather than ratiocinatively, whether the utterance is demonstrative or not."[15] However, one should not get the impression that this distinction is intended to lower the estimation of the importance of poetry, for it is not just pleasure (*lidhdhah*) that is involved but also wonder (*ta'jīb*) which Aristotle himself said is the beginning of philosophy.

Somehow the *Poetics* of Aristotle got appended to the *Organon*, as though it were really a part of Aristotle's logic. This influenced the interpretation of it among most Muslim commentators, including Ibn Sīnā, who nevertheless noted the discrepancy between matter of fact objectivity in the sciences and the manner of presenting truth in drama and poetry. The text of Ibn Sīnā's commentary sounds surprisingly modern because it was done from a remarkably universal level of reality. Indeed, this commentary would serve as a fascinating textbook for an aesthetics course even today. In our historical survey of many philosophers we should again be reminded that few of them neglected aesthetics, even though modern Euramerican historians of philosophy tend to neglect reporting this.

Although we are relatively de-emphasizing Ibn Sīnā's influence on Christian Scholasticism in order to restore him to his rightful place in the global or planetary perspective, we should not underestimate another stream of influence that is easy to overlook or neglect, namely his influence on Jewish Scholasticism and on Jewish philosophy even in the modern world. Rosenthal says of Muslim-Jewish relations in philosophy and theology in the age of Ibn Sīnā :

> Judaism was faced with the same problems as Islam due to essential similarity. Sectarian and heretical attack on the meaning of Scripture had to be warded off with the same arguments often. Apart from at least partially similar internal problems, there was a good deal of religious controversy. The Muslim charge of falsification of Scripture had to be met. The Muslim claim to possess the true revelation in absolute perfection through Muhammad, the seal of the prophets, raised the awkward question of the immutability of the will of God, for the Jews could not admit that Revelation was limited in time and imperfect in character, that Muhammad had superseded Moses.[16]

The similarities and parallels between the ideas of Ibn Sīnā and Maimonides are historically the fruit of the same cultural climate. They both draw on Philo of Alexandria, for example, as a source of inspiration.

> Yet, allowing for a parallelism in attitude and therefore in reaction, there can be little doubt that in some important concepts Jewish thought owes a good deal to Avicenna's Islamic interpretation of Greek and Hellenistic ideas. Even in the matter of the Divine Law, Avicenna may have helped Maimonides to see the fundamental difference between the Torah of Moses and the Laws of Plato more easily, and at the

same time to appreciate the character of the Torah as the Ideal Constitution.[17]

Ibn Daud and Maimonides agree with Ibn Sīnā and the Averroists, both Muslim and Christian, that it is the active intellect rather than the passive or potential intellect which is the part of the soul that is immortal. Similarly, in regard to the identification of the active intellect with the Holy Spirit concept, the parallels are close. Man, according to both traditions, can by virtue of his God-given rational faculties rise to the point of contemplation of the marvels of creation and even to contemplation of the Being and Majesty of God, and seek divine perfection. But when it comes to human society, the Mosaic Law or the Qur'ān is absolutely necessary.

Maimonides has very close parallels with the interpretation of al-Fārābī that God is Necessary Being in whom existence and essence are identical; but on this point Ibn Sīnā is much more explicit than al-Fārābī, as is the case with Maimonides himself and later on with Spinoza. Likewise in terms of the problem of the attributes of God, the parallels between Ibn Sīnā and Maimonides are close enough that the commentators on Maimonides could not ignore it, although in some details they followed Ibn Rushd where the latter criticizes Ibn Sīnā. In regard to the concept of prophecy likewise, it is well known that Ibn Sīnā never compromised the superiority of the prophets above the mystics and philosophers. And while Maimonides carried this out still more explicitly than Ibn Sīnā, the parallels are unmistakable. As to the division of philosophy into the practical and theoretical, it is generally acknowledged that Ibn Sīnā was not only the first to follow this Aristotelian division but was the first to include prophecy under the category of the practical philosophy. This too was followed by Ibn Daud and later by Maimonides and others.

As for Ibn Sīnā's influence in Latin Europe, we offer the following summary by Rahman :

> Ibn Sīnā's works were translated into Latin in Spain in the middle of the sixth/twelfth century. The influence of his thought in the West has been profound and far-reaching. ...Ibn Sīnā's

influence in the West started penetrating palpably since the time of Albert the Great, the famous saint and teacher of St. Thomas Aquinas. Aquinas' own metaphysics (and theology) will be unintelligible without an understanding of the debt he owes to ibn Sīnā. No one can fail to observe ibn Sīnā's influence even in Aquinas' later and bigger works like the *Summa Theologica* and the *Summa contra Gentiles*. But the influence of the Muslim philosopher in the earlier formative period of the Christian Saint is overwhelming; he is mentioned by the latter, e.g., on almost each page of his *De Ente et Essentia* which is, indeed, the foundation of Aquinas' metaphysics. No doubt, ibn Sīnā is also frequently criticized by Aquinas and others, but even the amount of criticism itself shows in what esteem he was held in the West.

But the influence of ibn Sīnā is not restricted to Aquinas, or, indeed, to the Dominican Order or even to the official theologians of the West. The translator of his *De Anima*, Gundisalvus, himself wrote a *De Anima* which is largely a wholesale transportation of ibn Sīnā's doctrines. Similar is the case with the medieval philosophers and scientists, Robert Grosseteste and Roger Bacon. Duns Scotus and Count Zabarella, the finest of the late medieval commentators of Aristotle, also bear testimony to ibn Sīnā's enduring influence.[18]

Just as more knowledge of Ibn Sīnā's broad polymath interests as a major humanist philosopher in the highest sense, including his correspondence with al-Bīrūnī, should serve to minimize tension in India between Muslims and Hindus, so now in Southwest Asia more awareness of his Jewish influence might ease tension between Muslims and Jews in the Holy Land. In the twentieth century al-Ghazāli has somehow gained more popularity in India, Indonesia and Malasia than Ibn Sīnā. Nevertheless as youth throughout the whole of the Islamic world, inculding the USSR, begin to regain their pride in their own heritage, and even perhaps regain the leadership in science and technology, the fresh re-study of Ibn Sīnā may produce some remarkable results, for a very vibrant Neo-Scholasticism is emerging in Islam which is as critically important as that in France and Euramerica in general.

16. Ibn al-Haitham

Ibn al-Haitham (965-c. 1040), who in his several roles and brilliant intellect is somewhat comparable to Roger Bacon, is one of the most controversial figures in the whole history of Islamic philosophy. He is lauded, not unjustly but sometimes perhaps too romantically, for being far ahead of his time in almost all of the sciences as they were known and practiced in the eleventh century. But the ultraorthodox still wonder about him : Is he heretical ? Is he a sceptic ? Or, as might also have been the case with Raymond Lulle after him and even Roger Bacon, who may have at least indirectly been influenced by him, was he a mystic? (We hopefully have been relieved of the inordinate prejudice abroad in the twentieth century that mysticism and science are necessarily at polar odds.)

Typically of his time, his studies and experiments and researches were not limited to any specialization but covered the full range of fields then available from physics through optics to medicine and what might today be called psychology. He also wrote on logic, ethics, politics, poetry, music and theology, though many of his writings are not extant. He is reported to have been a person with sufficient self-confidence not to compromise his ambitions unnecessarily, so he managed to get patronage from the Fāṭimid Calif al-Ḥākim, who though "whimsical and inclined to be cruel, was a patron of learning". Al-Ḥākim had founded a library that was a chief rival to that at Baghdad. This may have been one of the reasons why al-Haitham moved to Cairo, in addition to political instability in Iran due to the invasion of the Seljuk Turks.

Characteristically one of the first things that al-Haitham did after shifting to Cairo was to make a detailed scientific study of the annual inundation of the Nile River, with the result that he drew up plans for building a dam—at the present site of the Aswam Dam, as a matter of fact ! Of course such projects were not unknown in China; but evidently this was very unusual in the Islamic world of that time. Given the skills available such a dam was not feasible then; however, the idea was his originally. Due to fear of punishment or even execution by al-Hākim, al-Haitham pretended madness so that instead of the death penalty for not completing the project, howsoever impossible, he suffered imprisonment and confiscation of all his books and property, including his scientific instruments. He was not released from prison until after al-Ḥākim's death in 1021. It was during the next twenty years that he did his best work—but completely independent of political patronage! Hence he became associated with the then rather newly established Al-Azhar University (which is evidently the oldest university in the world with an unbroken record). But as a trade, he became a copyist, making fresh manuscripts in his fine calligraphy of classics like Euclid's *Geometry*.

Ibn al-Haitham's work on optics, for which he is best known, influenced Witelo, Pekham, Roger Bacon, Leonardo da Vinci and Kepler. His work on the function of the eye was the most advanced anywhere until well into the Renaissance. His best known work in this field has been preserved in Latin although the Arabic original has been lost. In this work he opposed the theory of Euclid and Ptolemy that the eye sends out rays (like a flashlight) to the object of vision. He also experimented rather extensively with refraction of light; and we are informed that "in certain experiments he approached the theoretical discovery of magnifying lenses which were manufactured in Italy centuries later"—although one must add that China had been in the lead for some time; and since his home was near the silk routes, perhaps that is where he got some of his ideas. He provided his own mathematical formulas for refraction of light in different media after discarding the methods of Ptolemy, and he realized the difference in speed of light through different media. In these matters he definitely influenced even Witelo, Kepler and Descartes.

According to Nazir Ahmad[1] if only Ibn-Haitham's fellow-workers and students had been as alert as he, they might even have invented the art of photography since al-Haitham's experiments with convex and concave mirrors and his invention of the "pinhole camera" whereby the inverted image of a candle-flame is projected were among his many successes in experimentation. One might likewise almost claim that he had anticipated much that the nineteenth century Fechner did in experimentation with after-images. Although he did not arrive at twentieth century knowledge of sensitivity to different colors in different parts of the retina, it seems that he was well on the way to that since he was certainly aware of the phenomenon of refraction of light and likewise was fully cognizant that the lense of the eye does alter what enters it. There is some evidence that he even knew something about what we now call rods and cones in the retina. How much he knew about the optic nerve might also surprise many ultramoderns who like to claim that no 'true' science ever developed outside of or before modern Europe's advances.

In his *Treatise on the Influence of Melodies on the Souls of Animals,* al-Haitham shows that the camel's pace could be hastened or retarded by the power of music. Other examples of the effect of music on animal behavior include horses, reptiles and birds. All through the nineteenth century domination of Cartesian notions about soul and machine and man and animal it was assumed that music was a distinctly human phenomenon. But more recent experiments have certainly vindicated al-Haitham many times over.

Although al-Haitham's fame has been due largely to his work in the sciences, he was equally well grounded in metaphysics, logic and medicine. Indeed, he made summary-commentaries on several of Aristotle's works as well as on Galen. According to Nasir, Ibn al-Haitham made considerable advances over the previous work of al-Rāzī, especially in matters of experimentation and induction. Nasir further says that al-Haitham "used both syllogism and induction as essential and has analyzed these two phenomena in considerable detail. He has also pointed out a few weak links in the logical theories, especially in their inductive aspects. One of the prime indices of Ibn al-Haitham's genius is that he regards induction as a built-in part of quest for knowledge."[2]

Against the popular stereotype that inductive logic did not become operative anywhere in the world before Francis Bacon, we have full justification that not only he but several other Muslim scientists not only used it functionally but even criticized Aristotle's lack of it. Indeed, al-Haitham had virtually direct influence on Roger Bacon in this and other matters.

> The philosophical development of the great Arab physicist ibn Haitham (Alhazen) proceeded from scepticism to a kind of criticism. The evolution from scepticism to his own ideological synthesis he owed to al-Fārābī. The Latin translations of some of ibn Haitham's books written during his empiricist and sceptical periods were instrumental to the development of Roger Bacon's ideas. In addition to this, Western science profited by ibn Haitham's detailed research on optics. He really marks the beginning of physics as well as that of the movement of empiricism in the West. In the origination, his role is even greater than that of al-Rāzī. Ibn Haitham explained the role of induction in syllogism. He criticized Aristotle for the meagreness of his contribution to the method of induction which he regarded as superior to syllogism. He considered it to be the basic requirement for true scientific research.[3]

Ibn al-Haitham's sophistication in observing the relation between perception and conception or, more specifically, between visual sensation and comprehension through immaterial sense-agents is very marked and reaches a genuine philosophical level of epistemology. Detailed investigation might even lead to a claim that he had almost anticipated Leibniz's stress on the "petits perceptions"—the minimal limit of detailed sense perceptions, especially in the perception of time. But it might be more apposite to compare this theme with the controversy already being argued in great minutiae in India over the distinction between *savikalpa pratyakṣa* and *nirvikalpa pratyakṣa*, differentiated and undifferentiated perception. In short, al-Haitham put much more stress on philosophical conceptualization than on mere sense perception as such. Incidentally, perhaps a little echo of Buddhist psychology has entered (howsoever indirectly) when he says that every sensation is a sort of 'suffering', and that what we call pain is only exaggerated perception, there being really no qualitative but only quantitative difference between pain and ordinary sensation.

Evidently none of his specifically philosophical works is extant, and therefore much is left to inference and conjecture. Various adventures with inadequate teachers and radical dissatisfaction with materials he found in the old texts—not to mention the petty theological bickerings of the various sectarian divisions in the Islam of his time—led him deep into philosophical, systematic doubt, so that he is often considered to have been a sceptic outright. But that conclusion may be exaggerated unless it is intended in the higher sense that philosophical inquiry must never be dogmatic but always open to revision.

As a philosopher of the physical sciences he believed that reality is an external entity which depends, for its being, both on the sensuous and intellectual faculties of man. He explains this by assuming that Reality comes to us garbed in a material form, registers an impact on our senses, is given form by the intellect, and through a process of logical deductions, becomes converted into concepts. In this definition it is presumed that Reality is neither objective nor subjective, but subjective-objective, a theory which is widely accepted in the present-day realm of philosophy. Unlike objectivists, Ibn al-Haitham does not regard Reality as an objective and subjective entity at the same time. In other words, Reality is a unitary entity which has two facets: one is that of appearance or externality and the other of interiority. In the modern philosophical terminology these aspects are termed objective and subjective respectively.[4]

Though Qur'anic at heart to say the very least, al-Haitham was deeply indebted, howsoever critically, to Aristotle for logic and philosophical method. Nevertheless, according to an account recorded by Moses Maimonides, after his death al-Haitham was accused of heresy and hence many of his most definitely philosophical works were burned.

Ibn al-Haitham believes that Reality can be gauged by philosophy alone; he, consequently, regards philosophy as the foundation-stone of all knowledge. Since he conceives logic to be the spirit of philosophy, he regards Aristotle's writings on logic as the guiding torchlight. It should be worth while to adumbrate that, because Reality can be visualized through philosophical knowledge only, he rigorously emhasizes the importance and the utility of the latter. He has often tried to

> prove that through the acquisition of philosophical knowledge, man is seized by two guiding principles: sacrifice for the sake of truth and practice of justice. ... An aesthetic interpretation of the foregoing would imply that the acquisition of philosophical knowledge results in the conceptualization of Reality, which is another name for Beauty and, thus guided, man's aesthetic sense is vivified and animated; this results in the sole acceptance of Reality, since such an aesthetic sense demands Beauty only and a mind attuned to Beauty therefore shuns the negative of life—ugliness, sin, evil, and falsehood—as a matter of habit. Rectification or justice is the basis of Beauty according to the Qur'ān and on this analogy we may equate the way of justice with the beauty of action. It is because of this that Ibn al-Haitham regards goodness and real success latent in the way of justice.[5]

And concerning al-Haitham's ethical thinking, Nasir writes :

> The ethical system of Ibn al-Haitham demands consideration on three points : (i) beautification and perfection of morality are not possible without quest for knowledge; (ii) truth, knowledge, and realization of self depend for their acquisition on (a) a clear and thorough understanding of theology, (b) acquirement of good through noble deeds and (c) the avoidance of the evil; and (iii) the main object of beautification and perfection of morals is to enjoy a happy, eternal life in Paradise in the thereafter.[6]

As with Christian ethicists, for example Symeon the New Theologian his Byzantine contemporary, al-Haitham must claim that revelation has afforded a higher basis for ethics than the Greek merely speculative systems. There is no evidence whatever to the effect that al-Haitham ever dreamed of not being a true believing Muslim. Indeed, among his other writings there is also a work on prophethood in which there is even a highly developed system of philosophic criteria whereby to discern true prophethood from false claimants.

Ibn al-Haitham wrote the following about his search, dedication and expectations :

I constantly sought knowledge and truth, and it became my belief that for gaining access to the effulgence and closeness of God, there is no better way than that of search for truth and knowledge. I studied in considerable detail the beliefs of various sects, thoughts, and theological systems, but I failed to gain anything which could point the way to Reality. At last I was led to the conclusion that Truth can only be discovered by the formulations of theories, the content of which is sense and the form of intellectual equipment. I found such theories present in the logic, physics, and theology of Aristotle, who has discussed the various aspects of the Primary Cause, the particular, the partial, and the general. He has further analyzed the terminology of logic and has divided it into primary kinds and has afterwards discussed the meanings of words which are arranged by means of words, and these formulate the speech of the purport of the "Known".

...When I discovered what Aristotle had done, I became engrossed in my desire to understand philosophy wholeheartedly. There are three disciplines which go to make philosophy: mathematics, physical sciences, and theology. I further discovered that duality and controversy are natural to human beings, and man is mortal; so that, while in his youth man can ponder over the principles which govern his existence on earth, he cannot do so when he grows old. So I thought over these three philosophical disciplines so far as my ratiocinative and intellectual faculties could allow me and summarized and explained them and their branches, and complicated problems connected with them. This is the month of Zil-Haj in the year 417 A. H. As long as I live, I shall keep myself pressed into the service of these disciplines to the best of my capacity. I have three objects in adopting this view: first, to be of service to those who are in search of Truth; second, that the disciplines which I have been able to understand to some extent should be extended and studied; and, third, the knowledge that I possess may turn out to be the wherewithal of my old age.[7]

Ibn al-Haitham might be called the first of the "moderns" in that he rejected the book authorities when they disagreed with his experimental and inductive methods. He was very critical of those who simply tried to patch up old systems by still more fanciful calculations rather than re-examining the basic presuppositions of the theories themselves. His science was almost purely that, unencumbered by the hoary definitions of the ancients, which lends an almost 'positivistic' note to his method.

It is philosophically significant that al-Haitham in all of his amazing originality in scientific experimentation by no means conforms to the stereotype that all 'medievalists' were merely scholastics buried in their superstitions and syllogisms. Certainly in our own era philosophers delving into philosophy of science should hope to be as well versed in actual experimental science as al-Haitham was in his own time; but also, if we had more scientists with as much philosophical awareness and concern for ethics, aesthetics, politics and theology as he had, we might not ever have allowed the technological revolution to bring about the degree of dehumanization of modern civilization that has transpired in recent years.

17. al-Bīrūnī

Al-Bīrūnī (973-1048) is important as another missing link in the network of intercultural communications in the early medieval period. His cosmological theories and many other aspects of his work also deserve our attention as profoundly significant for philosophy both in the modern technical sense and in the broader sense then current of being the all-inclusive discipline which demanded a polymath perspective on everything.

> Every one of al-Bīrūnī's writings, of which about one hundred eighty are known, is of value since he was both a great scientist and scholar. His *India* is the best account of the Hindu religion and of the sciences and customs of India in medieval times. His *Chronology of Ancient Nations* dealing with the calendar and festivities of different nations is unique. His *Canon of al-Mas'ūdī* dedicated to Maḥmūd of Ghazna's

> son, Mas'ūd, holds the same position in Islamic astronomy as the *Canon* of Avicenna does in medicine while his *Elements of Astrology* was the standard text for the teaching of the *Quadrivium* for centuries. He also wrote outstanding works on physics, mathematical geography, mineralogy and nearly every branch of mathematics, astronomy and astrology. No one in Islam combined the qualities of an outstanding scientist with that of a meticulous scholar, compiler and historian to the same degree as al-Bīrūnī. His only misfortune as far as his later influence is concerned was that his works were never translated into Latin. In the East he has always been respected as both a scientist and scholar.[1]

Al-Bīrūnī was born near the city of Khwarazm. It was at Khwarazm rather than at Baghdad or Baṣra that al-Bīrūnī received his scientific training, which is perhaps the reason that he remained unknown outside of Persian circles until he was discovered by Sachau and others in the late nineteenth century. This part of Central Asia had been for several centuries a cross-roads for virtually all the religions and philosophies known in Eurasia up to Bīrūnī's time, so that even from childhood he already had a more global perspective than many if not most of our present-day erudite scholars and philosophers who remain, sometimes willingly, ignorant of all that is not Western. Khwarazm was a cross-roads region for trade, communication, rivalries and assertions of contradicting identities for Turkish, Chinese, Persian, Scythian, Indian, Bactrian, Parthian and other peoples, and had been ever since the days of Alexander the Great. Bīrūnī was familiar not only with Persian, Arabic and several local dialects but also with Syriac, Greek, Hebrew and Sanskrit. Indeed he was perhaps the first Muslim to become proficient in the Sanskrit language, which he used extensively in his reading and reporting not only scientific materials from India but the different traditional systems of Indian philosophy.

Bīrūnī was a great admirer of al-Rāzī. Although credited with being good Muslims, they were both somewhat unorthodox. Whether through the influence of Patañjali yoga, out of vocational choice, or, as was the case with some others in the scientific field who had preceded him, as a result of association with Ṣūfī discipline, he remained celibate all his relatively long life. He was rather sensitive, but with a sense of humor withal, about his poverty before and also after he secured patronage. He wrote the following satirical verse :

> A wise man of by-gone times has said :
> 'The importance of a man lies in his smallest things.'
> I on my part also speak like a wise man, saying :
> 'The importance of a man lies only in his two dirhams.'
> If he has not his two dirhams with him,
> His bride does not care for him,
> In consequence of his poverty he is despised,
> So that people's cats piss at him.[2]

After the conquest of Khwarazm by Maḥmūd of Ghazna, Bīrūnī having been attached to the person of Maḥmūd, accompanied him in his conquest of India. Maḥmūd raids, which were scarcely more than that, had the intention deliberately not of conquest but of extracting for the greater glory of Islam every type of wealth and booty, from gold and jewels from the temples and food supplies from the villages to manuscripts and books (which Maḥmūd probably encouraged Bīrūnī to confiscate in the name of Allah the Merciful). There are conflicting records about Maḥmūd's attitude towards Bīrūnī, but given Maḥmūd's extremely stormy temperament, all accounts are probably true. Indeed, the relation between the two must have composed a fascinating continuous drama of personal affection between direct opposites, neither approving the other's ways but each indispensible to the other.

Bīrūnī was appreciative but objective and sometimes even beneficially critical of the ways of the paṇḍits and the puritanical Brahmanical pujārīs and their privileges in the caste system. Whether or not he merely wandered as a sanyāsī or sādhu, Bīrūnī did travel rather widely in India, perhaps even visiting the South where Advaita was no doubt stronger.

> He stayed in India for nearly ten years, teaching the Graeco-Muslim sciences, learning Sanskrit and other local dialects, making astronomical observations and studying all aspects of

> Indian life. But for his researches and studies, the Islamic world and the Arabic-knowing people of the time, especially, might have remained ignorant of the achievements of India in the spheres of science and philosophy in the ancient times. His studies are relevant for us in India even today, for his work on India, namely *Kitāb Taḥqīq mā li-'l-Hind* (completed in 421/1030, shortly after the death of Maḥmūd), is a comprehensive, scientific guide to India of the ancient period. The merit of the work lies in its comparative study of the Indian, Greek, Iranian, Islamic as well as Ṣūfī thought, in all of which al-Bīrūnī was proficient. The work represents the *summum bonum* of knowledge of an educated man of the time on India and is a mirror of universal knowledge, excluding the Chinese.[3]

The question remains as to what brands of philosophy in India he had access to, and according to which interpretation. Post-Śaṅkara Advaita was the new development, especially in the South. Bīrūnī could possibly have met some disciples of the famous Kaśmir Śaiva Abhinavagupta; but he also could have come into contact with those who were beginning to work on Nyāya logic in the way that was later to emerge as Navya (New) Nyāya. Contact with Nyāya would seem most likely since it was, along with Vaiśeṣika, most closely linked with the achievements in the natural sciences which constituted Bīrūnī's chief interest. Nevertheless, internal evidence indicates that, aside from the more traditional lore in the *Itihāsas* and such as the *Vāyu Purāṇas,* what he presents as truly Indian philosophy is none of these but overtly Sāṃkhya-Yoga. We do not know where this was best holding its own without the Advaitic overlay (for Bīrūnī seems not to have indulged in the controversies about the nature of *māyā* at all). Perhaps he studied with some Mīmāṁsā pundit at Mathura or Vrindaban.

Maḥmūd raided Somnāth and pillaged its very beautiful and rich temple which was devoted to Śiva. The chief feature—abhorrent as the devil himself to the pious Muslim—was and is the phallic Śiva Lingam. Bīrūnī's detailed account of the city and the temple gives us some clue as to the sort of Hinduism he had contact with : orthodox, ritualistic Śaivism, not necessarily of the philosophically inclined sort, but fanatically devout, at best probably reinforced by Mīmāṁsā but more likely simply carrying on ancient rituals without much interpretation. However, he must have had more contact with Vaiṣṇavism, or else he found that more compatible, since he has a whole chapter on Nārāyaṇa/Viṣṇu.

Bīrūnī's acquaintance with Buddhism is limited to popular lore about Mt. Meru, which is a Mahāyāna re-intrusion of Hindu mythology into Buddhist humanism. One may still meet well-educated Hindus who doggedly believe that Mt. Meru is there somewhere in the everlasting snows and that some day someone will discover it—but if they do they will go straight to heaven or into permanent *samādhi* and no one else will ever know about it. However, the absence of adequate information about philosophical Buddhism constitutes an historical puzzle. For if it is true that Buddhism disappeared from India as a result of Muslim fanaticism, then Bīrūnī no doubt would have recorded that, as he did, for example, concerning the destruction of the temple at Somnāth. Rather, then, we have to account for the disappearance of Buddhism in these areas by virtue of some other cause, or else perhaps we need to check very carefully whether Buddhism of any brand had ever been very strong, although certainly Jainism had been, at least in Gujarat and Rajasthan.

As for Bīrūnī's scientific information, Ujjain, for example, had been a center of scientific research, and perhaps there was some activity in Rajasthan where the desert skies encourage astronomical studies naturally. But Kaśmir at this time seems to have been the chief center for mathematical studies as well as, thanks to Tibetan counter-influence, the more esoteric aspects of astrology.

The great book by Bīrūnī on India is without doubt unparalleled in Islam during that epoch.

> The scholar who studied man most objectively, and in a way provided the kind of materials upon which Ibn Khaldūn could base his general observations of human history, was al-Bīrūnī, whom we have already met as an astronomer. Al-Bīrūnī made a study of both Islamic and Indian society; it

> was about the latter that he wrote his memorable *India*, a work that is without question one of the most scientific and objective studies of man and his society made in medieval times, at the time when, in the Western world, such studies did not pass beyond the level of chronicles.[4]

It has remained a source for almost everything that has been written subsequently on the religions and philosophies of India, Bīrūnī therein having put in sharp relief the harmony which could be made between Neo-Platonic-Pythagorian philosophy and the wisdom of India as well as certain conceptions in Ṣūfism.

Al-Bīrūnī does not accept anything without a good measure of scientific thoroughness, doubting assertions in which discrepancies are evident and treating hypotheses only as such—a manner of proceeding not much known in Latin or at least not widely used until Roger Bacon at the earliest and for the most part only slowly adopted after the Italian Renaissance. Herein Bīrūnī was also more advanced than his Byzantine contemporaries, although the Chinese by this time were beginning to revive scientific researches which had fallen into neglect towards the close of the T'ang Dynasty and during the chaotic interregnum before the establishment of the Southern Sung Dynasty.

In the preface to his book on India Bīrūnī sets forth his critical method. It constitutes a document in itself that cannot quite be equalled in the history of European civilization at least until the time of Vico. True enough, one might find some parallels in Byzantium with Michael Psellos' *Chronographia*, but even then the scope is much more limited and the method is certainly not as scientifically critical. Even in China one has to wait almost until the time of Ku Yen-wu for such honesty in checking empirical evidence against hearsay or mythological beliefs; and once again the scope is not intercultural. One has to look to Ibn Khaldūn for anything quite comparable in both scope and method; and even there, Ibn Khaldūn's fideism often tempts him to color his information in religious overtones that are virtually lacking in Bīrūnī's reportings.

Bīrūnī was not bound to any particular heritage but openly and scientifically took in all avilable sources, sorting and sifting them and attempting to deduce from their discrepancies and from his own personal inductive observations what must most probably be the best opinion possible. This method he applied to every discipline he was concerned with, from comparative religion to cosmology.

> In his method of treatment of a subject, of a scientific problem, al-Bīrūni strictly followed the scientific metod. His mind was free from any theological or mythological prejudices, and he kept his mind open. Again, he was not a 'traditionalist' in the sense that he did not look upon the 'ancients', or the Greek philosophers and scientists, as the final authorities on a subject nor their views as the final word. Thus, from his early youth he objected to certain concepts held by Aristotle, and praised certain other views of his. Again he did not adhere to certain views of Ptolemy and was critical of his findings in geography. In this respect he was a very outstanding thinker of his time, for there were many among the astronomers and geographers who followed these Greek philosophers without questioning their authority, among whom the most outstanding example was that of Ibn Sīnā (Avicenna).[5]

If intelligent use of empirical method is a sign of modernity, then certainly it is obvious that al-Bīrūnī is already very modern.

Al-Bīrūnī had the theory that the planetary orbits are elliptical rather than circular as the Aristotelians dogmatically asserted. This is recorded in his correspondence with Ibn Sīnā. And Bīrūnī definitely proposed a heliocentric model of the universe, though the actual work in which he exposited this theory is now lost. As for geology, although popular opinion has the notion that this is distinctly a very modern Western science, Bīrūnī had many empirical observations to record, quite scientifically, as well as some very salient theories about the relation of natural resources to the development of civilization, a theme which is still highly controversial in the post-Toynbeean perspective.

As for geography, in our own time too many teachers of philosophy are ignorant of what has been developing in the more advanced aspects of that discipline, including, for example, the geography of ideas, which, although too few writers seem to be adequately aware of this, is inseparable from the history of ideas. Bīrūnī did have that perspective, and one wonders whether Ibn Khaldūn was not here deeply indebted to him. Admittedly the Muslims needed better geography for purely practical purposes since their knowledge of the world had increased tremendously as they had by Bīrūnī's time stretched their rulership from Spain and West Africa to the Philippines. But they were also interested in the relation of types of culture to types of climate and other similar theories. Bīrūnī also carefully checked the methodological and quasi-mythological notions of the geography of India with his own personal observations and geological speculations, such as the notion that in former epochs the sea covered the Ganges-Indus plain leaving India as really a large separate continent.

In what one might now without undue exaggeration call his philosophy of the social sciences, Bīrūnī warns us against propaganda as perversion of truth. He is aware of the difficulties involved in intercultural studies and seems uneasy lest he has distorted the truth in his reportage of Brahmanical Hinduism. But even more than that he seems to be fully aware of the need for a definite *methodology* in making such studies since bias even in gathering information is almost inevitable while evaluations are as necessary as they are risky.

Bīrūnī's philosophy of history took a definitive form very much like that of the later and now better known Ibn Khaldūn, and appeared in the background of most of his works. Bīrūnī's conviction was that in the course of each period humanity lapses into corruption and materialism leading always to self-aggrandizement until some great disaster destroys that civilization. God will then send a new prophet in order to inaugurate a new period of human history. Bīrūnī's philosophy of history sounds very much like a syncretistic mixture of the Kalki Avatār notion, the Maitreya Bodhisattva (sometimes regarded as the Cosmic Buddha), the Mahdi concept in Islam (especially Shī'a and probably even more so among the Ismā'īlīs), the Second Coming in Christianity and the concept of the Messiah in Judaism. Geographically as well as historically this syncretism was almost predictable since all of these traditions had their representative communities in the region whence Bīrūnī came and where he did his work. This notion of the rise and fall of empires reminds one of the classical Chinese philosophy of history wherein there is initial vitality, flourishing, decadence and corruption, and final collapse, after which a new cycle begins.

By comparison with even the most advanced theories current in Byzantium and Latin Europe, Bīrūnī's perspective on the time-span of the age of the world, its cycles and eras (not to mention the specifics about the different calendars specifically compared), is certainly far in advance, even though he may be, through no fault of his own, lacking in information about China. That Bīrūnī's philosophy of history was undergirded with a sort of theodicy should not lead us to ignore it since even in our own time the popularity of such as Teilhard de Chardin has demonstrated the need of such a perspective. By Bīrūnī's time there had been no completely secular or materialist theory of the history of human civilizations and cultures which did not include some sort of entelchy in it; nor had there yet been an effort to include more than Judeo-Christian-Islamic cultures and civilizations in this perspective, except rather weakly in some Byzantine works which give, nevertheless, only passing notice to Zoroastrian Persia and Brahmanical India.

Nasr gives us his interesting speculation about al-Bīrūnī vis-a-vis modern science :

> If the idea of bringing Alhazen or al-Bīrūnī into the twentieth century could be realized, then the most probable reaction of these men to modern science would be that of surprise at the position that quantitative science has come to occupy today. Alhazen and al-Bīrūnī were able to practice a kind of science which may be called "progressive," while still remaining within a "nonprogressive" world view, because for them all *scientia* was subordinated to *sapientia*. Their quantitative science was only one interpretation of a segment of Nature, not *the* interpretation of all of it. The matrix of their world view remained immutable, even while they were pursuing their study of the world of becoming and change. The

> surprise felt by medieval Muslim natural scientists, if faced with modern science, would not arise from recognizing the "progress" of ideas which they had begun, but from seeing the complete reversal of relations. They would see the center of their perspective made peripheral, and the periphery made central; they would be astonished to learn that the "progressive" science, which in the Islamic world has always remained secondary, has now in the West become nearly everything, while the immutable and "nonprogressive" science or wisdom which was then primary has now been reduced to almost nothing.[6]

Most sources treat one aspect or another of the work of this omnivid genius, but few bother to treat him as a philosopher as such. He did not get translated into Latin so he is still just beginning to be known by Euramericans, Sachau's famous *Alberuni's India* having been a typical Victorian grandiose ambition which evidently fell into neglect. The correspondence between Ibn Sīnā and al-Bīrūnī attests that al-Bīrūnī was not only the founder of geodesy, a mathematician and astronomer of the highest caliber, a geographer and a linguist, but also equally a philosopher. This is another case where modern categories have done much mischief by stereotyping. Even within the Islamic field it may be well to recall that, for example, al-Rāzī, among many others, was also not only a scientist but a philosopher.

Bīrūnī has some insights that still might be helpful in general comparative philosophy, especially in regard to the similarity between the Greek and Hindu world views. Within the history of Islamic thought Bīrūnī is relatively unique, there being no one quite so open to Muslim-Hindu dialogue until the time of Kabīr, Nānak and Dārā Shikoh. We have given more importance than most current interpretations to Bīrūnī's intercultural, indeed almost trans-cultural, orientation and interests in hopes that others will bring out a more complete study of these philosophical intersts, since the study of Bīrūnī has too readily got into the stereotype that he was a scientist not much interested in philosophy. Nothing could be further from the truth.

18. Udayana

Udayana (975-1050) is co-founder with Gaṅgeśa of the Navya Nyāya or *new* school of logic. Chronologically this parallels similar developments in the Islamic world after al-Fārābī. In Latin Europe logic or dialectics really begins traditionally with Abelard a century later, although Fulbert of Chartres and others could be named as worthy predecessors. In China, in direct opposition to the subjectivistic intuition of Ch'an Buddhism and even in implicit opposition to the *bhakti* cults of the Pure Land and T'ien T'ai traditions, Chang Tsai is a somewhat comparable figure; and no doubt one can find a similar figure in Japan as much opposed to Eisai's "zanny" Ŕinzai Zen as Udayana was to the subjective idealism of Vijñānavāda Buddhism and the extremes that Vācaspati Miśra had gone to in trying to vindicate Śaṅkara's non-theistic monism.

Chemparathy gives this introductory estimate of Udayana :

> Scholars are almost unanimous in declaring Udayana to be one of the greatest of Indian philosophers. In the Nyāya-Vaiśeṣika school itself, to which he belongs, he occupies a singular position of authority and renown. Flourishing at the period of transition from the Older Nyāya to the New (Navya-Nyāya), he shines as an unrivalled master of the former and an inspiring herald of the latter. His importance in the history of Nyāya-Vaiśeṣika can be gauged by the attitude towards him of later writers, from his own school as well as from other schools. While he became for his own school a recognized authority who is often referred to by the mere title of Ācārya, his style and method of argumentation seem to have had a remarkable influence upon the followers even of the other schools. For example, Śrīharṣa,... despite his having been a bitter opponent of Udayana, discloses in his works a style and method of argumentation that betray the influence of the author of the Nyāyakusumāñjali. Similarly, Madhusūdana Sarasvatī, one of the greatest of the later exponents of the Advaita Vedānta, as well as Rāmādvayācārya, the author of the Vedānta Kaumudī, not only quote often form his works, but also seem to have imitated his style and method of argumentation.[1]

Udayana's fame rests primarily on his rational theism. The Buddhist Jñānaśrī whose arguments against theism Udayana attacks, was also a brilliant dialectician and controversialist, and his position was even more anti-theistic than Dharmakīrti's.

> ...Though Vātsyāyana, Uddyotakara and Vācaspati... were sturdy champions of the cause of theism, yet the most staggering blow to the Buddhist position was dealt by Udayana who in his *Nyāyakusumāñjali* vindicated theism in a very efficient manner. Udayana is well-known for his trenchant logic and his work is looked upon as the most cardinal text on this subject. History tells us that Jñānaśrī, a most formidable Buddhist dialectician, refuted theistic arguments in his *Īśvarabhaṅgakārikā*. Udayana who came after him had enough confidence in him to meet the arguments advanced by Jñānaśrī and declared in a most emphatic way that he rescued theism from the clutches of the Buddhist critics. The work of Udayana led all later Nyāya-Vaiśeṣika writers under a deep debt of gratitude who all derived inspiration from his outstanding work. Even the great Gaṅgeśopādhyāya, who set forth a most masterly defence of theism in his *magnum opus*, *Tattvacintāmaṇi*, followed in the foot-steps of Udayana.[2]

According to Chemparathy, Udayana was so successful that after him there was scarcely any Indian philosopher who was not a theist in some sense or other. In the wider world there was a general trend in the same direction, the chief exceptions being the pioneer Neo-Confucianists such as the Ch'eng brothers and Chou Tun-i. One could speculate as to whether this was due to the influence of Islam. But quite aside from extraneous influences, Udayana's inheritance in the Nyāya-Vaiśeṣika system is enough to account for his working out the inherent theism sufficiently to have a permanent impact on Indian philosophy. One might speculate, nevertheless, that he may have hoped that some Muslims might read his work and mitigate their attitude that all Hindus were *dhimmīs*, infidels; and on the other hand, one wonders likewise whether he could have been secretly motivated to convince even the most orthodox Mīmāṁsakas, Advaitins, and Sāṃkhyan philosophers that they did not have to convert to Islam in order to become theists.

Udayana's "dialectics" was not motivated by any merely speculative dilettantish intellectualism but rather by a deep philosophically religious conviction and devotion. In fact he offers his expertise in logic and all the rest of his talents as merely an unworthy offering of worship to the Lord with a fervor comparable to that of Rāmānuja (who chronologically could have been influenced by Udayana although we have no record to that effect). Comparison with Augustine here is indeed quite apt, although perhaps comparison with the ardency of Peter Damien could be invoked as a parallel even within Udayana's own lifetime, not to mention Michael Psellos, also his contemporary.

There are some irreducible differences between Udayana's views and those of the Advaitins, even though some of them try to claim that Udayana is also an Advaitin-at-heart. The claim is made because they tend to ignore differences of all kinds as unreal and therefore to be overlooked. Chemparathy writes:

> It is, indeed, true that among the opponents the Vedāntins are less often mentioned or refuted in his works than the Mīmāṃsakas, Sāṃkhyins or Cārvākas. This is especially remarkable in the Nyāyakusumāñjali where only once the view of a Vedāntin, namely Bhāskara, is mentioned together with the views of some others concerning the factor that determines a new creation after dissolution. That he did not enter into controversy with the Vedāntins on the Īśvara doctrine itself may be accounted for by the fact that these—even the Advaita Vedāntins—admit an Īśvara, though in a manner different from that taught in the Nyāya-Vaiśeṣika school. With regard to the alleged predilection of Udayana for Vedānta as shown in the last section of the Ātmatattvaviveka, the following observation may be made. While pointing out in that passage the gradual ascent in the path of the worship of the Supreme Soul, the author indicates the superior position of the Vedānta compared with the Pūrvamīmāṃsā, Cārvāka, Sāṃkhya etc., in as for as some Vedāntins teach Brahmā to be of nature of pure, self-illuminating consciousness. But it is to be noted that in the concluding lines of this passage he exhorts his reader not

to enter the city of liberation (*mokṣanagaram*) by these "side-gates" or "inferior entrances" (*apadvāram*), but, having avoided (*vihāya*) them, to enter by the "front-gate" or "main entrance" (*puradvāram*), by which he, no doubt, means his own system. In conclusion, with regard to Udayana's attitude towards Vedānta, we may say with G. Kaviraj that, "though professedly a Naiyāyika, he had the highest regard for Vedānta in its most rigorous and unfalsified form", but in no case can it be said that he was a staunch believer of Advaita.[3]

The work in which Udayana's rational theism is put forth, namely the *Nyāyakusumāñjali*, has received the greater share of attention among modern apologists and exponents among Indologists and philosophers, which emphasis again is very welcome as a refutation of the popular notion among superficial critics of Indian philosophy (especially Christian missionaries) that it is all so 'monistic' that even the concept of a personal Godhead gets absorbed back into the great amorphous *nirguṇa*-Brahman, but also welcome as a warning to neophytes who are trying to escape theism altogether and therefore look to Buddhism or Hinduism for reinforcement of their objections to "the God idea". Usually such rebellions, however, are dialectically very healthy and may indicate a transition from superstition and shallow sentiment to a genuine, philosophically sound rational theology of some sort or other.

The *Ātmatattvaviveka* is perhaps equally important with the *Nyāyakusumāñjali*. This work is divided into four different heads covering the four basic tenets of virtually all Buddhists—Udayana is not concerned here with the popular religious Buddhism that had virtually abandoned these basic things in their *bhakti* cults to Amitābha and Avalokiteśvara and other Bodhisattvas, even in their Indian roots, not to mention the Chinese and Japanese versions of them.

Kṣaṇabhaṅga, that is, everything is momentary, *Bāhyārthabhaṅga*, that is, there does not exist any external reality (this is from the Yogācāra point of view), *Guṇaguṇibhedabhaṅga*, that is, a substance is not different from the mere collocation

> of its attributes, and *Anupalambha*, that is, the world is nothing but void. These four are the problems which prevent the existence of Ātman as it is ordinarily accepted in common parlance, according to Udayana. So he divides the work under these four sections and refutes them one by one boldly.[4]

After making thorough refutations of these, Udayana adds his own proofs for the existence of a real permanent Self in a fifth section. According to Miśra, "There is no other work on the subject so far known to me in our philosophical literature which so strongly has refuted all the main theories of the Buddhists against the existence of the Ātman as an independent and separate entity."[5] One should not get the impression that vindication of the permanence of the *ātman* should be taken in the Advaitic sense of undifferentiated identity with *nirguṇa*-Brahman. For Udayana's metaphysics, true to his roots in Nyāya and Vaiśeṣika, is realistic and not idealistic or nihilistic. For Udayana there is no discrepancy between a realist metaphysics and spirituality, as is likewise the case for the Aristotelian scholastics, especially, for example, with his contemporaries al-Fārābī and Ibn Sīnā.

Udayana's *Nyāyapariśiṣṭa* is a commentary on the *Nyāya Sūtras* of Gautama. It was done after Vācaspati Miśra's work on Nyāya logic but it is not known to what extent it was written in refutation of Vācaspati's views since only the fifth chapter of it survives. This work does show the continuity, historically, of the controversies between the Buddhists and the Nyāya-Vaiśeṣikas and with the Mīmāṁsakas long after Śaṅkara is reputed to have settled such controversies once and for all by incorporating them into his *Brahma Sūtra Bhāṣya*.

Udayana's *Nyāyanibandhi* is a critique or refutation of Vācaspati Miśra's *Tātparyaṭika*. Herein the standard ritual observances of the Brahmin who follows in practice and not in theory only the *Dharma-śāstras* quite faithfully are prescribed for expiation of 'sins' and rectification of past *karma*. As is the case with the theories involved in the *Nyāya Sūtras*, the ultimate goal is described as *apavarga* rather than as *mokṣa* or *nirvāṇa*. Since the goal is the absence of hindrances to happiness (in the neo-Aristotelian sense), in the ethical dimension we may have a closer parallel to the realist variety of Neo-Confucianism, which did sanction pleasurable enjoyment so long as human dignity and altruism are not compromised, this alongside the Aristotelian scholastics in Islam and Christianity and as opposed to the Ch'an, Ṣūfī and Neo-Platonist tendency to disparage pleasure altogether. In a way that reminds us of the 'higher Epicureanism' of al-Rāzī and similar trends even in the 'scepticism' of Ibn Ḥasm, the pleasures that are permissible are arranged in a hierarchy from the gross sensual pleasures to the highest enjoyment of spiritual serenity, the intellectual pleasures mediating between the extremes. Thus it is that logic comes into focus, for it is only reason that can distinguish that hierarchy.

We are beginning to see an increasing number of books dealing with the technicalities of logic as such in regard to both the old Nyāya school and the new or Navya Nyāya. For example, in his *A Modern Introduction to Indian Logic*, S.S. Barlingay treats such technical topics as judgments, propositions and functions; theories of negation, nonexistence and contradiction (these being much more sharply distinguished in both the old and especially the Navya Nyāya logic than in modern Euramerican textbooks); problems of universal and particular; logic of relations (which traditionally, as we have observed in dealing with Vātsyāyana and Praśastapāda, is a very strong point in Nyāya-Vaiśeṣika thinking); theories of inference, elements of induction, and formal and informal fallacies—all of these being interpreted in modern symbolic notation so that Barlingay is no longer writing apologetically but making strong recommendations that Nyāya and Navya Nyāya do have something vital to contribute to the modern world. For the most part his focus is on the Nyāya experts previous to Udayana, such as Uddyotakara and his refutation of Dignāga. He emphasizes the importance in the historical perspective of Udayana's *Kiraṇavālī*, which is basically a commentary on Praśastapāda but which became the basis for Gaṅgeśa's brilliant innovations which we shall be treating in comparison with the Parisian logicians of the same period such as Buridan, Nicholas of Autrecourt and Nicholas of Oresme.

Needless to say, by Udayana's time, as was also the case with the Muslim Aristotelians and the Byzantines, there had developed a very sophisticated technical terminology. The following from Barlingay's study should attract the attention of those in twentieth century circles following after Bertrand Russell's entanglement in the controversy about whether a class of a class is just another class or not, for Udayana does deal with this problem also.

> The theory of Universals, after taking a drift in the connotative direction, develops in a very interesting way on one point. Following Udayana the logicians still maintained that only that attribute which is present in more than one individual is *Sāmānya* or Universal. But there are some characteristics which are possessed by only one individual. To distinguish such characteristics from *Jāti* the *Nyāya* logicians use the word *Akhaṇḍopādhi*. It is defined as a special characteristic which can be treated on par with *Jāti* or *Sāmānya—Jātitulya-dharma-viśeṣaḥ*.
>
> Another interesting point in this connection is recognition of *Upādhi*. This concept is introduced to do away with the concept of class of classes or *Vaijātyam*. The concept of class of classes raises several logical paradoxes. It is interesting that the *Nyāya* logic does not accept the class of classes as a class at all, but merely regards it as *Upādhi*, which has connotation but which has no extension. If we believe that the class of classes is also a class then it leads to a vicious circle or infinite regress (*Anavasthā*). Udayana states that a class of class should not be regarded as *Jāti* or class as it leads to infinite regress. To avert such difficulty notions like the class of classes and the like are called *Upādhis*. In the theory of Indian logic if there is a pot it is characterised by potness (which inheres in all pots). Potness is, thus, a Universal or indicates a class of all pots. But potness has another characteristic, *potness-ness*; this characteristic also characterises all pots, and so, by definition, it also becomes a universal or a class. But if this is recognised as class it would lead to infinite regress. For potness-ness-ness also will have to be regarded as a class: and this would go on ad infinitum. Further if both pot and potness become members of the same

> class then a member and a class of these members would stand on the same level. To avoid such difficulties, *Vaijātya* or the class of classes is not accepted as class (*Jāti* or *Sāmānya*) but is merely treated as *Upādhi*. *Upādhi* simply has meaning. It does not exist.[6]

It should be possible to find similar things in Ibn Sīnā's logical works also; but as for Latin Europe, we have to wait another century for Roscelin and Abelard to find anything quite comparable.

Udayana's *Nyāyakusumāñjali* has been more popular than his other works, though in a technical way the others may have been more astute and intellectually brilliant. This more definitely theological work has enjoyed popular appeal through the centuries right down to the present, at least in non-Advaita-dominated areas. For there is something primordial in human nature evidently—and this is manifest historically much more dramatically, we submit, than psychologically or sociologically —which wants to believe in a Highest Deity which is approachable in devotion and according to reason as well as in ethical matters, thus completing the triad *bhakti*, *jñāna* and *karma*. So perhaps this text did fill a need historically which his other works did not fill in quite the same measure.

In the *Nyāyakusumāñjali*, in keeping with the perpetual tradition of all Brahmanical schools, Udayana makes an appeal to the *Upaniṣads*, but not interpreted in the same light as Śaṅkara. In either case, however, the bases are there and one can do eclectic work in them to vindicate almost everything. Udayana says of his work : "This logical dissertation of God, which may be called his contemplation, constitutes verily His worship in as much as it follows the hearing (śravaṇa) of the śruti."[7] Udayana states that the ultimate aim of the work is in the approachability of God for benefits; but also an appeal to the universality of theistic belief and practice, even in cases, like the Jaina heritage, where this is officially denied. "Udayana does not emphasize any particular form of Īśvara for worship. What he asserts is that every school of thought does believe in the Supreme object of worship and it is, therefore, that he holds that even the schools of Cārvāka, Sāṃkhya, Mīmāṁsā, Bauddha,

Jaina and so on, who are in a way atheist, do believe in the existence of Īśvara in some form or other."[8] Udayana quotes the *Gītā* in support of this basic argument : "O son of Kuntī ! those who being full of faith and belief, worship other gods also worship me alone and none else, though their way of worship is different and not according to the proper method." (IX. 23)

The *Nyāyakusumāñjali* was written to answer objections to postulating an eternal Īśvara.

> The objections are : (1) absence of a supersensuous means to prove the existence of life after death, (2) possibility of even otherwise (that is, without admitting the existence of Īśvara) carrying out the means to prove the existence of another world, namely, sacrifice, (3) presence of proofs to prove His non-existence, (4) His not being regarded as the means to right knowledge, even if His existence is admitted, and (5) absence of proofs to demonstrate His existence.[9]

In his refutations of others' views Udayana deals with usual fallacies but leaves the heaviest burden on the refutation of the *regressus ad infinitum* argument against God as Creator (since of course Creator of Creator of Creator would still be just Creator Supremely). But there are also the 'positive' proofs. All these are separate from the argument from *śruti* (scripture), which Udayana does accept, although not as fanatically as some Mīmāṁsakas or Vedāntins or some of his Muslim and Christian contemporaries. His proof in reference to the function and structure of atoms is especially fascinating, though it may not have any possibility of re-statement in the twentieth century context. Udayana comes very close to what Rāmānuja later affirms, that all of creation is the *embodiment* of God, no matter how we conceive that embodiment to have come about. In this treatment of the attributes of the God whose existence (although really assumed much in the manner of Anselm) is to be proved, this similarity comes perhaps even closer. The notion of God as having a Will was not in the original Nyāya-Vaiśeṣika system, nor was the conception of the material world as the embodiment of God. Bhattacharyya writes :

> During cosmic rest (*pralaya*) the ultimate units of the universe i.e., atoms, lie separated from one another and when God creates, they are made active so that they are conjoined and dyads etc. are produced. Udayana here points out that divine volition generates motion in these atoms. Thus, Udayana clearly asserts that the atom serves the same purpose in regard to God, which a physical body accomplishes in regard to the embodied soul. In other words, the atom may be looked upon as the physical apparatus of God. It must be remembered here that the Naiyāyika does not believe in any physical organism of God. Udayana's suggestion, that the atom may be conceived as the divine body, is only to meet the contention of the opponent that *kṛti* is understood only with reference to a physical body.[10]

Since Udayana was a Northerner and Yāmuna and Rāmānuja were Southerners in India, influence there is really unlikely. Certainly no Muslim would think of Allah as having any embodiment since this would compromise His transcendental unity quite as much as having a consort of avatārs or incarnations would. Perhaps, then, it was just sheer original thinking on Udayana's part that led him to this position. The matter of having a Will does suggest possible, although by no means necessary, Muslim influence, or barring influence, certainly parallels, as may be seen by a cursory examination of Ibn Sīnā's theology, for example, or even more saliently in the work of Miskawaih, who was also Udayana's contemporary.

As a faithful interpreter of the Nyāya-Vaiśeṣika school, Udayana is obliged to reject the *pramāṇas* of *arthāpatti* and *anupalabdhi*, since according to that tradition they are both reducible to inference (*anumāna*); but even so, one senses that in his dealings with the traditional arguments in their favor, they might be useful in the realm of ordinary experience though they are not (any more than any other *pramāṇa*) directly applicable to the existence of Īśvara except indirectly by analogy. Incidentally, here again we cannot but be impresssd by the fact that in each case Udayana gives full scope to his captive opponent until the very termination of each point. In other words, one can easily be confused if the division between *pūrvapakṣa* and *siddhānta* is not kept clearly in mind.

Although scripture is accepted, Udayana's emphasis is always on inference as the key *pramāṇa* for the Nyāya-Vaiśeṣika system and such of the apparent intellectual gymnastics involves reducing the other *pramāṇas* to this *anumāna*. As a matter of fact, the whole text of the *Nyāyakusumāñjali* is remarkably free from scriptural quotations. But even inference does not give us absolute certainty, so Udayana falls back on direct experience (one is almost tempted to invoke William James and John Dewey as modern apologists in that context; but of course there are also among Udayana's contemporaries many in the Augustinian tradition and many Ṣūfīs also who have the same 'empirical' proof). What faculty, then, makes this direct perception possible ? For all the known faculties of man deal with perception of finite things, not with an eternal, omniscient, uncaused-Cause sort of transcendent Deity who has no body or embodiment. Udayana answers by putting a distinctive interpretation on the function of *manas* as an inner sense which cannot operate outside the human body but which does extend to God-knowledge. In short, he puts very heavy stress on the results of *tapasyā* on the part of yogins whereby one may gain access to that supra-sensible knowledge of the nonmaterial Deity. The same motif can be found quite readily even in the arch-humanist Michael Psellos, not to mention Miskawaih or such Japanese Buddhists as Genshin.

> Thus, in Udayana's view, Īśvara's existence can be known from sacred scriptures (*śrutiḥ*), from inference (*anumānam*) and, in rare cases, through direct perception *sākṣād darśanam* or *pratyakṣam*). The three means of cognition of the Supreme Being were already recognized by the Upaniṣadic thinkers and by later philosophers, and Udayana himself has referred to them in the opening prose passage of his Nyāyakusumāñjali. But since the last type of cognition of Īśvara is a personal experience limited only to a privileged few, our author does not propose it to his adversaries as an argument for his existence.[11]

There is a bit of the theology of grace in the background of

Udayana's philosophical faith, especially in the poetic flourishes; however, he does not for a moment capitulate to intuitionism but works very hard to present a completely rational approach to and exposition of the problem involved.

Udayana answers objections from the other schools in good scholastic form as the *ad contra* or *pūrvapakṣa* arguments are classified and listed quite systematically, in a way that the Ch'an Buddhists, especially the Rinzai of his time, would consider unnecessary and even bothersome (the Neo-Confucianists themselves objected to the Ch'an Buddhists that, claiming to be supra-human, they had allowed infra-human or even anti-humanistic neglect of moral as well as intellectual responsibilities : a mere shrug of the shoulders proves nothing at all, for even a dog can wag his own tail). In replying to the objections, Udayana begins with the Cārvāka view. Curiously enough we do not know of any outright Cārvākas of that time, just as in the Muslim, Judaic and Christian worlds there were no materialists that we know of. As once there was a parallel in the Axial Age between the Cārvākas in India and the materialists like Democritus and Leucippus in Greece, so their possible position was never forgotten down through the ages as a challenge to still mature thinking since their position had validly been posited as a rebellion against even cruder views based really on superstition rather than on rational theology.

According to Udayana, rationally there needs to be some intelligent explanation of the law *karma*, and this is better explained by the *adṛṣṭa* than without it. So the Cārvākas really ought to admit that much; then it should not be irrational to admit that the *adṛṣṭa* needs an Īśvara to "keep it going". And Udayana makes this point regarding inference :

> As to the argument that inference is not at all a means to right knowledge, it is said that the Cārvākas cannot but accept inference as a pramāṇa for the obvious reason that when they say that inference is not a pramāṇa, it itself is nothing but inference, which they accept as correct. So inference is also a means to right knowledge.[12]

Correspondingly, Udayana disposes of the age-old argument that body and soul or mind are identical with equal ease :

As regards the identification of physical organism with Ātman it may be said that if it were so, then a person, in his old age, could not have remembered what he had seen in his childhood, for the obvious reason that the physical organism changes from time to time and does not remain static. Hence it is necessary to believe in the existence of 'adṛṣṭa', 'paraloka' and Ātman and also in the eternal omniscient Īśvara.[13]

Next Udayana considers the Mīmāṁsā view that the Law of *Karma* is inexorable and therefore automatic, needing no Deity or Person or Power to govern it; and that therefore the Vedic rituals must be done perfunctorily as having opposing power *ex opere operato*. This position has a remarkably close parallel among the determinists or predestinarians in Islam who had the same belief about the unquestionability of the Qur'ān and therefore its *ex opere operato* effect if properly chanted. To such a view Udayana (like Ibn Ḥasm) opposes a healthy 'pinch of salt' scepticism :

> To this Udayana holds that Veda itself is not self-valid. It is non-eternal and as such, it cannot be the source of right knowledge unless its author is believed to be an infallible being. Such a person is Īśvara. From the Nyāya-point of view Udayana goes on arguing that there is no self-validity of Veda because all right knowledge depends upon some cause and as 'Śabda' is non-eternal, and Veda being 'śabda', it is also non-eternal. Thus, through the agency of Veda world-custom and usage will not be established. Again, nor can Kapila and others be ever regarded as giving a start to the world-process in the beginning of the creation, because one does not possess perfect faith in Kapila who is quite different from Īśvara; nor can we be sure that the saṁskāra produced by yogic powers always give valid results. . . . Hence, holds Udayana that there is an eternal and omniscient Īśvara.[14]

Udayana is probably well informed about the variety of Buddhist views that had developed in India, not to mention China, Southeast Asia, Tibet, Korea, Japan and Central Asia also, since his native place was not far from Nālandā or Bodh

Gaya, ground hallowed in antiquity by the presence of Lord Buddha there in person, whose arguments (if modern scholarship is justified in its restoration of the historical humanist that Śākyamuni Buddha Gotama really was) were much closer in many respects to Udayana's philosophy than to the Buddh*ism* which Udayana refutes. It is not completely clear which school of Buddhism is involved, though Udayana mentions by name the Saugata, which supposedly holds that there is not any *pramāṇa* that proves the existence of Īśvara since it is not possible to prove the existence of any bodiless being, much less one who is a doer (*kartṛ*) in the physical world without becoming embodied. The structure of the argument suggests that the idealist Buddhists were not who Udayana had in mind but rather perhaps one of the earlier classical schools before the division between the Mahāyāna idealists and the Theravāda realists, such as the Sautrāntika school. The fact that Udayana places this Buddhist or Saugata view next to the Cārvākas also suggests that he had the earlier if not the earliest schools of Buddhism in mind, which were so close to the Sceptics that Hindus often confused them with each other. At any rate, Udayana presents the *argumentum ad ignorantium* : absence of usefulness of any ordinary *pramāṇa* does not prove the non-existence of anything at all, since non-existence and absence are two quite different modes of negation. Thus the Saugatas have proved nothing at all and are left in complete agnosticism, which is worse than the scepticism of the Cārvākas. As Miśra puts it : "Hence because one does not get the perception of Īśvara, it is not possible to deny his very existence."[15]

There is the additional point, which sounds like a later possible objection to the Thomistic view (derived largely from Ibn Sīnā), that Īśvara, being perfect (in *actu*, without any potentiality), could not really be a Creator or have any "will" since such would involve unfulfilled desires and/or intentions, which would be contrary to His Perfection. Udayana's position is that, "as to the argument that Īśvara is without any aim, it may be pointed out that, no doubt, He has no personal aim to realize, but there is no doubt as doing good to the created beings is his aim (bhūtānugraha). So the existence of Īśvara cannot be denied."[16]

In accordance with the pattern set by tradition many centuries before Udayana, the Jainas come next for refutation. Although classical Jainism was definitely atheistic, the goal of the Jaina yogī is omniscience. It might be said of the Jainas that they believe that there is no God, but man must become divine ! But for a God to be omniscient would imply that, as with the Buddhist argument, He would have to be a Doer, engaging in the finite *pramāṇas* like any finite knower like ourselves. Moreover, we could not know God's omniscience without being or becoming a part of it, and that in such a way that God-knowledge would be its own *pramāṇa*, but in such a way that it would be inaccessible to us as long as we remained only human after all. Therefore omniscience may indeed remain a goal for human endeavor; but to assert it as known to us already as existing in a Deity is to assert too much since we would have to be omniscient ourselves in order to know whether God is omniscient.

The Sāṃkhya system was the chief concern in Udayana's earlier work and evidently it remains so in this *Nyāyakusumāñjali*. Again we are confronted with what may be called the argument from agnosticism or the absence of definitive proof for or against the existence of God. Udayana's argument is readily identifiable as the argument from design, which is easy to find, for example, in Psellos and Ibn Sīnā. Udayana retains the classical analogy of the pot and the potter :

> Udayana says that like the creator of a pot there must be a creator of the universe, as the universe is also a product like the pot. This 'kartṛtva' is not possible in ordinary beings. Hence, the creator of the universe is Īśvara. Prakṛti cannot be the cause of the creation, because it is 'jaḍa' and as such, it is not possible for it to be the doer. A doer must be a conscious being . . . Besides, there are Vedic injunctions like 'pray to Īśvara' (Īśvaram upāsīta), which also support the existence of Īśvara. The entire universe is kept in its place through the effort of Īśvara. Even the destruction of the universe is possible only through His effort. From all these various proofs it is evident that there is Īśvara.[17]

Udayana's emphasis all through the *Nyāyakusumāñjali* has not been just the refutation of others' views but the demonstration of his own personal faith. This comes out very vividly in the beautiful verse-prayer with which he concludes the work, thus seasoning his *jñāna* with the *rasa* of *bhakti* in a way that is almost in anticipation of the work of Rāmānuja and Śrīkaṇṭha.

> O Kind and Compassionate Lord! those in whose hearts Thou canst find a place are indeed as hard-hearted as rocks or iron, though repeatedly their hearts are washed by the overflow of water in the form of ethical and Vaidic teachings; still in time Thou with Thy mercy wilt take them away across the ocean-like saṁsāra which is full of miseries, because even in the act of opposing Thy existence, they have very sincerely thought of Thee.[18]

Miśra adds the comment, "What a generous and merciful heart Udayana had even for his enemies!"

Udayana's place in the history of Indian logic needs much more emphasis than our textbook reports allow since he is pivotal between the old traditional Nyāya logic and the emergence of Navya Nyāya with Gaṅgeśa and others. And one wonders whether the interpretations of Udayana's system have accorded adequate credit to the realistic metaphysics that underlies and permeates very consistently all of his thinking. The time when one must be apologetic about any system of Indian philosophy that is not mystical or at least idealistic has at last begun to fade. Although Udayana is certainly not a radical pluralist, the pluralistic emphasis has its proper proportions even in his theology—perhaps instead of pluralism the designation "particularism" might be better. This would mark him off in direct contrast to Advaita; for even though we do not have anything in his system that gives an explicit estimation of *māyāvāda*, we may infer that he would definitely be in opposition to it.

Finally, if we look back to Udayana from the Viśiṣṭādvaita position of Yāmuna and Rāmānuja, again historically Udayana appears to be in a transitional position. We might even assert that Viśiṣṭādvaita, which criticizes Nyāya-Vaiśeṣika for its excessive pluralism, might be taken as only a temporary compromise with what later emerges not only in Navya Nyāya but also in Mādhava as really radical revolutions in the history of Indian philosophy which have until very recently received woefully inadequate attention, again due to lack of historical perspective.

Out of the ninth century monism gradually theism dominates (or in the Buddhist systems, Buddhology, Bodhisattvas and theology of grace) and then an increasing number of attributes are ascribed to God (or Tathatā, Allah, Īśvara, Nārāyaṇa, Śiva, etc.) until by the time of Rāmānuja and Śrīkaṇṭha a plethora of attributes—the more the better !—is used in lyric paeans of praise. This obtains by and large all across Eurasia.

19. Atīśa

The context in which Atīśa (Dīpaṁkara Śrījñāna, 980-1052) worked gives reinforcement to our insistence that the "parallel developments" in the history of philosophy were not accidental but definitely the result of intercultural and constantly increasing trans-Eurasian communications. For example, in 972 forty-four Buddhist monks went from India to China; and the following year one Dharmadeva, a monk from Nālandā, was formally received by the Chinese Emperor with great honors, in spite of the fact that Neo-Confucianism had begun to prevail. In 982 the Chinese Emperor commissioned a board of translators with three Indian scholars at the head. They translated more than 200 volumes between 982 and 1011—during the lifetime of Atīśa, who very well could have known at least some of them or known of them by virtue of common roots at Nālandā. We also have comparable information about Chinese Buddhists continuing to come to India on pilgrimage, at least up to about 1036 when there was a marked decline (we might conjecture because of the advance of Muslim control over the routes of communication and the destruction of Buddhist centers in North India).

As Tibet grew in strength and began even to threaten China and indeed almost anticipated the Mongols in expansion through Central Asia, the Chinese as early as 787 had made an alliance with the Calif of Baghdad against the Tibetan power.

Although our information is terribly sketchy about the increase of Muslims in China itself, we may well infer that cordial relations persisted perhaps right down to the Mongol conquest. Indeed, it is not unlikely that some of the advances in the several sciences during the Sung Period might have been because of this opening of communications between China and the Islamic world. Although communications between North India and China and between China and Tibet waned in the latter half of the eleventh century, every channel between South India and Southeast Asia and Southern China was not only open but increasing in commerce and trade and perforce in ideas and monk-philosophers.

It is difficult to believe that Atīśa with all his contacts in Southeast Asia and India as well as Nepal and Tibet could have been unaware of this background environment. Indeed, the most likely conclusion is that Atīśa studied at Palembang in Suvarṇadvīpa, which had been a rival to Nālandā as center for Buddhist studies for many centuries. Suvarṇadvīpa is Sumatra, Java and the islands of eastern archipelago, where Tāntric Buddhism was if anything stronger than in India, Tibet or Nepal. Atīśa was not the only one who wandered quite widely as Buddhist monks are supposed to do, but as one about whom and from whom we have more concrete information he symbolizes this "wider world".

As for Buddhism in India, after the patronage of the Pala Dynasty there was a major crisis when that Dynasty was replaced by the Sena rule, and that in turn was threatened very seriously by the Muslim invasion or raids on the temples and monasteries. The Buddhism that did survive there as long as it did was very different from what Hsüan-tsang (d. 664) had found and described. Tantra, in short, had come to dominate what continued to be called Buddhism, but that was a far cry from the original teaching and example of Śākyamuni Buddha. To a great extent the same was true of China. By 1197 when a Tibetan monk visited India he found most of the temples woefully neglected and most of the monasteries empty; even at Nālandā he had to flee from a Muslim onslaught. However, when Atīśa had been there in 1040, Nālandā was still thriving. But from his time on we have very few records about Buddhism in India except from Tibetan sources, and these are not too reliable since they are largely based on rumors filtering into Tibet from weary pilgrims.

The charisma of Śāntarakṣita, Padmasambhava and Kamalaśīla in Tibet was far over-shadowed by that of Atīśa Dīpaṁkara, who came to be regarded as an incarnation of Mañjuśrī, the Bodhisattva of wisdom, and was worshipped as such. One reason for this is that after the initial work of Śāntarakṣita there had been a violent persecution of Buddhism in Tibet, and it was the work of Atīśa that revived the *Dharma*, though the ground had been laid for his success by the translations that had accrued; also, the Tibetan alphabet had made literary and general cultural advance possible, while material prosperity had been augmented by military and political expansion. Dharmapāla of eastern India had also laid the groundwork for Atīśa's success, though he did not acquire the same charisma either.

Atīśa was really a reformer and not only a transmitter or translator. However, the organizational aspect of his reforms was carried not so much by himself as by his disciple 'Brom Ston-pa' who persuaded Atīśa not to return to India according to his original plan but to travel around Tibet to get more familiarity with conditions in the various monasteries, some of which, thanks to the influence of Kamalaśīla and others, had a solid foundation in Buddhist metaphysics and epistemology, even though in the meanwhile laxity had set in and there was critical need of fresh inspiration. Thus western as well as central Tibet came under the influence of his reforming zeal. Even so his activities were not limited to institutional work since he continued to work also as a translator and became known as one of the chief transmitters of the Sanskrit tradition into Tibetan language—fortunately for posterity since as is well known many texts lost in Sanskrit have been preserved in Tibetan.

Śāntarakṣita had attempted to interpret classical Vijñānavāda epistemology in a way that converts from the Bon Shamanism religion in Central Asia and Tibet could understand; however, this had become miserably corrupt, and Atīśa's chief mission was to clean up these practices. Not that he rejected Tantra outright; rather he had been trained in that tradition but had progressed in it to the highest stages, which are virtually identical with the best of the Śūnyvāda or Vijñānavāda heritages and are often even today equated with Advaita *sādhana*, namely, the achievement of desirelessness and selflessness. Atīśa knew the Tāntric *sāstras* very well, and never did he completely reject the higher level attainments and more refined practices of that school, although it appears that even there he did not think they were necessary.

> Without ever formally denying their scriptural authority and even taking active part in the composition and translation of some of the Tāntrika treatises, he concentrated in his own teachings on the fundamentals of Mahāyāna Buddhism in its classical or pre-Tāntrika form and he insisted that an insight into the real significance of the Tāntrika practices meant the recommendation of some forms of intense meditation on the phenomenal world being unreal, any attachment to which, therefore, meaning only misery for the living beings. Rather than making any allowance to the coarse practices then enjoying the sanction of the tantras, Dīpaṁkara himself put the strongest emphasis on moral purity, asceticism and the method of meditation.[1]

Atīśa found a very similar situation in Nepal and again recommends a cultivation of traditional Mahāyāna :

> An important work of Atīśa in Nepal was his composition of a Buddhist book named *Charyaṣagraha pradīpa*. Through this work, written for the cause of the Nepalese Buddhist ideas, Atīśa tried to expose and denounce the evil aspects of Tāntric Buddhism rampant in the Nepalese society....
>
> ... He explained the methods and purposes of meditation for the Nepalese Buddhists; he described the special meditation-posture called the 7-fold worship (saptangapuja) for them. He showed the importance of recognized and classical teachings of Mahāyāna.

Certainly four philosophical systems of Nepalese Buddhism, Svabhāvika, Aiśvarika, Karmika and Yātnika, are the products

> of this period. Before his visit to Nepal, no attempt to systematize the Buddhist philosophy had been made so far.[2]

Everything points to Atīśa beings a reformer who, although qualified as a Tāntrika, was profoundly committed to restoring the *saṅgha* to its purer original Mahāyāna form. It is not impossible that he might have had some contact also with Burmese Theravāda which also might have influenced his zeal for reform.

One of the most crucial activities that Atīśa engaged in during the first three years of his residence and work in Tibet was the composition of the independent original work *Bodhi-patha-pradīpa*. This was done specifically at the request of one of his disciples who said that "since there was disagreement on points of doctrine between various scholars in Tibet, the Master should compose a treatise which would serve as an antidote for it. The Master composed the *Bodhi-patha-pradīpa*."[3] Basically it is a Śūnyavāda text based on Nāgārjuna and Chandrakīrti rather than on Tāntric sūtras; but it has heavier emphasis on the Mahāyāna doctrine of universal compassion than is for the most part overtly manifest in the works of those two *ācāryas*. In illustration of this Chattopadhyaya gives some citations from it :

> ...The first thing to do is to establish empathy with all living beings, inclusive of the three kinds of beings with degraded births suffering from birth and death, etc. Look at all living beings suffering from miseries and arrive at the firmest determination to work with the resolution of never turning back from the liberation of all living beings from the miseries that are born of miseries.
>
> ... Do not be anxious to attain quick enlightenment for yourself. Live up to the end of the *saṃsāra* for the sake of even a single living being. Purify the boundless and unthinkable number of *kṣetra-s* and live for the emancipation of each individual by name that exist in all the ten directions.
>
> ... Persons (*puruṣa*) are to be known as belonging to either of the three types : inferior (*adhama*), mediocre (*madhyama*) and superior (*uttama*). The characteristics of each are very

> clear. Therefore I shall write the distinguishing features of each. By the *adhama puruṣa* is to be known one who in one's own interest acts in every way for the worldly pleasures only (*saṃsāra sikha-mātra*). One who, indifferent to the pleasures of birth (*bhava-sukha*) and by nature opposed to sinful acts, works for oneself alone is to be known as the *madhyama-puruṣa*. One who always wishes to remove the sufferings of others by his own sufferings is the *uttama-puruṣa*.[4]

Atīśa realized that this would be a vade mecum sort of manual or enchiridion for virtually all and sundry people, so deliberately he omitted the complex dialectics of validating each point by argument and counter-argument and final resolution in full scholastic style which had been current in India for a long time already.

It is doubtful whether Atīśa had a system of philosophy as such, especially since as reformer his moralizings seem to have been remembered most. But on the other hand they are not mere moralizings but actual instruction in *sādhana* such as one finds, for example, in Byzantine Neo-Platonism even with Psellos and certainly with Symeon the New Theologian, and among his Ṣūfī contemporaries, and for that matter with Peter Damien as fellow-reformer. Behind the *ascesis* Atīśa recommends is the systematic metaphysics and epistemology of the same type and genre as that found in Śāntarakṣita and Kamalaśīla and their immediate successors.

The mirror metaphor figures so prominently in Atīśa that one soon realizes that he and Abhinavagupta have very much in common; the world is not just *māyā* in the Advaita Vedānta sense, but *pratibimba* (reflection). In other words, nothing in human experience has its *svabhāva*, its true and eternal essence. But then Atīśa is indeed a Buddhist and not a Vedāntist. The reason why we can't grasp any *svabhāva* of anything is not just because it is inaccessible, but because there is no substance since everything is always changing. At best we may empathetically become aware of processes of cause and effect.

> The self as well as all the living beings are clearly seen (as reflections are seen) in a vast mirror (*maṇi-darpaṇa*) on a day

with clear sky. Why do you have the delusion about the difference between yourself and others, in the way in which the child is deluded by its own reflection ?

One who sees permanence in reflections is like the animal fighting (its own) shadow (reflected image). Firmly meditate on the *maṇḍala-cakra*. With the knowledge of this, the *yogi* does not stay there (i.e. at the stage of mistaking reflections as real).[5]

One may find traces of influences from Kaśmir Śaivism when, as frequently, Atīśa stresses the 'dirt' metaphor: and other familiar metaphors take their place, such as that of crossing the stream and cleaning the mirror.

The teaching that nothing has any *svabhāva* (substantial, self-authenticating, permanent existence) should be very familiar :

As it is well-explained (in the scriptures), *prajñā* is that knowledge which is the realisation of the intrinsic nature of the void (*svabhāva-śūnyatā*),— of the *skandha-dhātu-s* and of the *āyantana-s* being unborn (*ajāta*).

That which exists by nature cannot come into being. Again that which is by nature non-existing is like the sky-flower Both (alternatives), implying fallacy (*doṣa*), both are unreal (literally, belong to the category of non-being).

Things (*bhava*) can be born neither of themselves, nor of others, nor of both. These cannot be without cause either. Hence, they are by nature natureless (*svabhāvena niḥ-svabhāva*).

Again, the nature of all things (*dharma-s*), examined either as unities or as compounds, cannot be determined. Therefore, it is certain that they are void....

Therefore, the nature (*svabhāva*) of everything is unsupported (*anālambana*, lit. not proved by any *pramāṇa*). So to meditate on the void (*nairātmya*) is to meditate on *prajñā*.

The nature (*svabhāva*) of everything, as seen by *prajñā*, is invisible (i.e. *prajñā* sees no *svabhāva* in anything). This *prajñā* is demonstrated by logic. Therefore, meditate on *prajñā* without any doubt (*vikalpa*, delusional thought).[6]

The above is from his *Bodhi-patha-pradīpa.* Atīśa closes this with the counsel that the truly celibate monk who follows this path should not meddle with the 'lower' Tantra, even though even that is allowed for those who have not chosen the celibate path—provided they are under the close supervision of an adequate guru.

Once at a Benedictine monastery the monk showing the area open to non-monks pointed to a certain door, saying, "Once you pass that door (i.e., when you enter the novitiate within the enclosure) only the Devil follows you !" For it is axiomatic that although in the *saṅgha* more advanced achievements are possible, so also the temptations are even stronger, though of different sort. One of the greatest temptations mentioned by Atīśa is one that has begun to affect secular societies and counter-cultures as well as individuals in the monastic vocation : Is any one really above the law ? Is anyone exempt, by virtue of higher achievements in any field, from the normal duties of everyday life ? No doubt there were not a few Indian and Tibetan super-gurus in his own time who were claiming to be great Bodhisattvas who, being emancipated, could do anything they pleased and get by with it. And in Kaśmir Śaivism the *jīvanmukti* ideal is so exaggerated that supposedly anyone who has achieved that level of attainment is obliged to do odd things in order to conceal his super-normal powers (*siddhis*) and thus helps people secretly. Even the great Śaṅkarācārya is accredited with some strange acts contrary to strict monastic regularity as demonstration that he had achieved that level of freedom that included exemption from all obligations, i.e., conformity to the rules is observed only for the sake of setting a good example for the masses. One need not reiterate the odd antics of some Rinzai Ch'an monks of this period. Atīśa says : "Your *dharma* will be miscarried if in spite of claiming to be aloof from *karma* you remain involved in it and, moreover, if you do not guard against fall in both the lives (i.e. in this life and in the next). Such miscarried *dharma* will be *dharma* only in name. Therefore, friend, do not think in that way. Jewels once lost by the blind are not recovered."[7]

In several sections entitled "The Sayings of Atīśa" Chattopadhyaya has given us some of Atīśa's more down-to-earth ordinary but universal maxims, such as avoiding retailing the faults of others and keeping one's own virtues secret and hidden, avoidance of bad company, exercising compassion on all living beings, avoiding garrulousness and gossip, and in general keeping the goal of the Great Enlightenment constantly in mind. Further :

> Friends, desire cannot be satisfied as thirst cannot be quenched with salt water. It is vain to try to satisfy the desire....
>
> Happiness, prosperity and friendship of the present are but momentary. Discard these in the way you throw out the spittle. The future lives longer than the present one. Save that wealth (viz. *puṇya*) : that alone will provide you when you make the jouney to the next world. One will eventually have to abandon everything and depart. Nothing will go with one. Therefore, have no craving. Love the lower people. Do not injure or insult them.
>
> Love the enemy and the friend equally; have no partiality. Have no jealousy for those with good qualities but have respect for them and cultivate their qualities in you. Do not examine the faults of others; examine those of your own and leave those in the way in which you shed off your poisonous blood. ...
>
> Have the same feeling for the living beings as the parents have for their son. Have always a smiling face. Avoid anger and speak softly with a loving heart. Be careful of your words. and speak simply, for too much of unnecessary words are bound to contain errors....
>
> There is no sense in getting tired with useless actions. Everything being determined by past actions, nothing happens by mere wish. Therefore, keep yourself free and be happy. Listen! For a noble person death is better than shameful acts. So, be straight and steady. The pleasures and pain of this life are but results of the actions of the past lives. Therefore, do not blame anybody for these.
>
> All happiness comes from the blessings of the *guru*. One must, (therefore), be grateful to him. You cannot control others unless you can control yourself. Therefore, control yourself first. You cannot help others to be successful without

> (yourself) attaining *abhijñāna*. Therefore, work hard for the *siddhi*. One will have to leave savings behind. This is sure. Therefore, do not accumulate sin in the name of wealth.
>
> Enjoyment and distraction have no substance. Therefore, enrich yourself with *dāna*, the (only) wealth. You will thereby become beautiful in this life and happy in the next. Always uphold *viśuddha-śīla*. Anger is specially powerful in the *kali-yuga*. Therefore, protect yourself with armour (*varma*) of forgiveness. Do not lag behind under the influence of laziness. Kindle the fire of courage for attaining *siddhi*.
>
> Human life is being wasted by distractions. Therefore, care for meditation. Truth is not realised under the spell of ignorance. Therefore, be careful of the meaning of truth. Friends! Do not sink into the mire of *saṃsāra*. Reach the dry land of *mokṣa*. Try to understand properly the precepts of the *guru*. Meditate on *saṃsāra* as but the river of misery.
>
> These are not empty words. You should listen to these with care and place these in the depth of your heart. If you act thus then you will make yourself as well as others happy.[8]

Atīśa also warns that mere ascetic appearance and performance of Brahmanical sacrifices amount to nothing unless the interior renunciation is quite complete. Such counsel can be found even in the *Dhammapāda*; but by Atīśa's time it was equally common to all traditions and not only those originating on Indian soil. Even Neo-Confucianism at its best under the term *ch'ung* also puts very heavy emphasis on the completeness of one's interior integrity or sincerity.

There is an obvious lack of science in Atīśa by comparison with, for example, Ibn Ḥazm, who was also relatively ascetic in his personal life. Although a sense of system, no doubt absorbed from his translating activities, is not absent it certainly is not as overt as what one finds, for example, in Ibn Sīnā, who also was not ignorant of esoteric *ascesis*, or in Udayana or Vācaspati Miśra who had preceded him by almost a century. The absence of logical treatises is somewhat of an anomaly since it is difficult to believe that in his training he was not exposed to the best of it as formulated by Dharmakīrti several centuries before him, especially when we have learned that some of his contemporaries in India were experts in logic. And we have no concrete evidence that he knew mathematics and astronomy, but it is difficult to believe that he was ignorant of these disciplines since virtually all *sādhakas* trained in the higher Tantra are expected to know astrology with a high degree of expertise.

Atīśa has a special place in our catalogue as one of the few known connecting links between India, Southeast Asia and Tibet. There is still some doubt about his historical identity behind the legendary lore that has accumulated around his rather remarkable charisma. For that matter, we still do not have a really clear picture of the history of Buddhism in Tibet, even in these centuries when Tibet was a major power in Central Asia, invading China and threatening to become the chief rival of Islam for hegemony in that area. But this much is quite clear : Atīśa is certainly the major figure in the formation of the Tibetan canon after the work of Śāntarakṣita, Kamalaśīla and Padmasambhava. It is encouraging that interest in Tibetan matters has finally begun to get out of fascination with the esoterics of that "forbidden roof of the world" and is settling down to factual historical analysis and translation of the classical texts, many of which have survived in the Tibetan language where the Sanskrit originals have been lost.

20. Ibn Gabirol

Since Ibn Gabirol (c. 1020-c.1057) was a keen-witted controversialist, he was often accused of vainglory and pride, or at least of self-esteem that was somewhat inordinate. Like so many intellectuals of his era, he was dependent on patronage; but evidently he did not always get along well with his patrons since he insisted on keeping his independence of mind and spirit, regardless of their opinions and predilections and prejudices. His health was never good, and he had a skin disease which disfigured his face and was very disturbing. Husik notes his place in the Jewish intellectual tradition: "With Gabirol the scene of Jewish intellectual activity changes from the east to the west. Prior to the middle of the tenth century the centre of Jewish learning was in Babylonia. ...The long line of Spanish Jewish worthies continued almost five centuries, constituting the golden era of Jewish literature and making of Spain the intellectual centre of all Jewry."[1]

There is a definite strain of mysticism in Ibn Gabirol's verse, which resembles the Sūfī poetry of his time. He did write some lyric love poetry, but of course in that typical Spanish manner wherein human love can lead to the love of God. Some of his poems are nature poems and are woven around the usual themes of the seasons. In others he proposes an ethics based on personal introspection, perhaps reflecting some of the more esoteric lore of Jewish mysticism. Not only in China but in India also some of the most definitely philosophical work with original content and even themes not in the canonical text was cast into poetic form; for most philosophers of that time everywhere did write poetry as well as prose. Shlomo Pines writes of Gabirol:

> Following convention, especially that of the great Arab pessimistic poets, he emphasizes the contrast between himself and the society in which he lives, frequently voicing complaints against time, i.e., fate, and his inability to find his place among his fellows, involved as they are in mundane matters and temporal successes. Nonetheless, he was alive to the impulses of youth and while he composed few love poems those few are powerful lyrics. An erotic note is sounded in his description of his relation to poetry, which he portrays as a desirable young girl. Primarily, however, he mourns his inability to enjoy the pleasures of the world and of love, finding refuge from these afflictions in wisdom and in God.
>
> In his "wisdom poetry" he depicts himself as devoting his life to knowledge in order to prepare his soul to rejoin the "Source of Life" on its release from its bodily prison. Knowledge has two aspects consisting both of the effort of the intellect to scale the heights of the heavenly spheres and of the soul's introspection. At first pleading with God to let him

> live, the poet soon begins to deride the world and time, regarding them as valueless and insignificant obstacles on the way to eternity. From the height of his identification with the infinity of the Godhead and of eternity, he regards with disgust the trials of the world below, the illusions of the senses, and the weakness of the flesh.[2]

His devotional poetry is definitely theistic but never becomes sentimental, so that unlike the work of Judah Halevi—not to mention so many in the *bhakti* tradition in other parts of Eurasia—he never addresses God with the lover-beloved metaphor. As for Gabirol's philosophical poetry, his major poem, *Keter Malkhut* (*The Kingly Crown*), has essentially the same content as his more famous major prose work *Mekor Ḥayyim.* The metaphor—or as it is called by the Vedāntic commentators, the *pratīka*—of Light plays a prominent role. The attributes are said to be inseparable from the essential nature of God, and we focus on them because we know no better way of expressing exaltedness of an infinite nature.

Ibn Gabirol's famous *Mekor Ḥayyim* or *The Source of Life* was translated into Latin as *Fons Vitae* and thus had considerable influence later outside of Spain. The *Mekor Ḥayyim* was never translated into Hebrew, and the Arabic original was lost. It survived only in the twelfth century Latin translation by Johannes Hispalensus (Hispanus) and Dominicus Gundissalinus, and Ibn Gabirol became known as Avicebron to the Latin scholastics. Some thought that he was a Muslim while others thought he was a Christian, for he does not use Jewish terminology or quote religious texts. Among the Christian scholastics he influenced was no less than Thomas Aquinas, although with reservations and 'corrections'. He enjoyed a greater favor among the Franciscans, who saw something in Avicebron's work that was kindred to Augustinianism, to which they were devoted in opposition to the Aristotelianism of Aquinas and other Dominicans.

The *Mekor Ḥayyim* was written in the form of a dialogue between student and master. Its most outstanding doctrine is that of universal matter. Pines gives this overview :

> Gabirol's cosmological system generally has a neoplatonic structure but with modifications of his own. The first principle is the First Essence, which can be identified with God. Next in order of being are the divine will, universal matter and form, then the simple substances, intellect, soul, and nature, and finally the corporeal world and its parts. Gabirol holds that all substances in the world, both spiritual and corporeal, are composed of two elements, form and matter. This duality produces the differences between various substances, but, according to some passages, it is specifically the forms that distinguish one substance from the other, while according to others, it is matter. Matter is the substratum underlying the forms : forms inhere in it. All distinctions between matter and forms in the various substances stem from the distinction between universal matter and universal form, the most general kinds of matter and form, which, according to Gabirol's account of being, are the first created beings.[3]

In Gabirol's philosophy of matter and form we might expect just another typical scholastic version of the adaptation of the Aristotelian system to the Abrahamic faiths. But Gabirol was opposed to the Aristotelian system in that he posited a more etherial universal spiritual matter, thus graduating the hierarchy of emanations and avoiding a latent dualism between spirit as completely transcendent and matter as substantíal combination of pure matter and form. This arouses our curiosity since it resembles or is parallel to the concept of *cid-ākāśa* in the Hindu and Mahāyāna systems. Pines writes: "Hence, as opposed to the Aristotelian views, spiritual matter exists, and it is found in all incorporeal substances."[4]

But for the rest, for the most part his system follows fairly closely the Neo-Platonic pattern of emanations. Husik gives this summary:

> When we speak of Gabirol as a Neo-Platonist, we mean that the essence of his system is Neo-Platonic. He is not a dualist, but a monist. God and matter are not opposed as two ultimate principles, as they are in Aristotle. Matter in Gabirol is ultimately identified with God. In this he goes even beyond

> Plotinus. For whereas in Plotinus matter occupies the lowest scale in the gradation of being as it flows from the One or the Good, and becomes equivalent to the nonexistent, and is the cause of evil, in Gabirol matter is the underlying substance for all being from the highest to the lowest, with the one exception of the Creator himself. It emanates from the essence of the Creator, forming the basis of all sabsequent emanations. Hence the spiritual substances of the celestial world, or, to use a more technical and more precise term—since spirit is not located in heaven or anywhere spatially—the intelligible world, have matter underlying their form. In fact, matter itself is intelligible or spiritual, not corporeal. Corporeality and materiality are two different things. There are various gradations of matter, to be sure; for the prime matter as it emerges from the essence of the Creator pervades all existence from highest to lowest, and the further it extends from its origin the less spiritual and the more corporeal it becomes until in the sublunar world we have in the matters of its particular objects, corporeal matter, i.e., matter affected with quantity and magnitude and figure and color. Like Plotinus, Gabirol conceives of the universe as a process of gradually descending series of existences or worlds, as the Kabbalistic writers term them; these cosmic existences radiating or flowing out of the superabundant light and goodness of the Creator. The two extremes of this graded universe are God at the one end, and the corporeal world at the other. Intermediate between these are the spiritual substances, Intelligence, Soul and Nature. Man as a microcosm, a universe in little, partakes of both the corporeal and intermediate worlds, and hence may serve as a model of the constitution of the macrocosm, or great universe.[5]

The hierarchy, we infer, is not just a simple one but is structured on a scale of harmonics, as it were, so that higher resonate in the lower but the lower do not necessarily but only potentially resonate in the higher. Pines emphasizes the term "mediation" in the patterning according to proportionality—actually "proportionailty" is a key to very much of scholasticism of all varieties. Husik continues :

> His system still has a strong flavor of Pantheism, and moreover his identification of the Will of God with the Wisdom and the Word of God, and his hypostatization of the latter as in a sense a being distinct from God, reminds us strongly of Philo's Logos, which became the Logos of Christianity, the person in the trinity. This is the reason why William of Auvergne, bishop of Paris in the thirteenth century, regarded Avicebron as a Christian. And these same reasons were no doubt adequate to estrange Jewish readers, as Abraham ibn Daud expressly tells us about himself, though his terms are general.[6]

Gabirol's ethics is naturally geared to this pattern of *sādhanā* which is quite universal, namely, retracing the proportional levels back through knowledge of the operation of God's Will in the world and in oneself—but not completion of the Beatific Vision in this life evidently, for he does not follow such extremes as the Hesychasts and some Ṣūfīs claimed regarding complete union with the Divine, for "The First Essence, i.e., God, cannot be known because it is infinite and because it lacks any similarity to the soul. Nevertheless, its existence can be demonstrated."[7]

Ibn Gabirol was soon forgotten as a philosopher and remembered only as a poet in the Jewish community, but "the Christian scholastics of the thirteenth century made Gabirol their own and studied him diligently. His fundamental thesis of a universal matter underlying all existence outside of God was made a bone of contention between the two dominant schools; the Dominicans, led by Thomas Aquinas, opposing this un-Aristotelian principle, the Franciscans with Duns Scotus at their head, adopting it as their own."[8] Ibn Gabirol's Neo-Platonism also influenced some Kabbalistic writers, but with Maimonides Aristotelianism will replace Neo-Platonism as the dominant intellectual force.

21. Ibn Ḥazm

Ibn Ḥazm's father was a vizier to the Umayyad caliph, which entailed troubles when the Berbers of North Africa caused much trouble to the Spaniards, so that finally Ibn Ḥazm (994-1064) had to leave his beloved Cordova and renounce politics altogether. However, the various dynasties in Indonesia, India, Iran, Iraq, Egypt, the Maghrib, as well as in Spain, although frequently in political conflict, never interfered with the religious and cultural unity of the Islamicate. Communications were completely open all across the Islamic realms, even uniting areas which have since then been separated by modern nationalisms.

> Unlike many other scholars, Ibn Ḥazm was born in a castle and grew up in the midst of power and pelf. He was brought up under the supervision of the cultured ladies of the period, and also received education from them. He thus picked up the most refined and simplest Arabic, and studied Arabic poetry, literature, Qur'ān, Ḥadīth and Tafsīr with the ladies of the ḥarem. According to Ibn Khallikān : "No man of learning was to be found like him. He united in himself brilliance, a powerful and quick memory, graceful soul and religious devotion. Nobody composed verses extempore like him."[1]

Like virtually the majority of scholastics in Judaism, Christianity and Islam down through the centuries, Ibn Ḥazm was not infrequently under suspicion of heresy. As a result of censorship even more of his books would have been completely obliterated except that some of them were taken to the East; but also the fact that his works had been proscribed only aroused greater curiosity about them so that they were considerably in demand in some quarters.

Ibn Ḥazm evidently developed a critical faculty such that he did not allow himself to be limited to any particular school or sect but became somewhat eclectic. Even after returning to public life his fortune did not improve because his family had been proteges of the previous dynasty which was now definitely out of favor. Thus we have another addition to our list of those who had difficulty with patronage. He did gain some respite from such troubles by obtaining temporary patronage from the ruler of Majorca, who is described as a man of considerable cultural talents. However, even there he fell into disfavor because of his Zahirite convictions. He was not very successful in gaining many converts, and lost face in a debate with a famous jurist. The result was that he had to return to Spain. But there he was far from popular, and the report of his misfortune indicated that he was "chased out of every town and village in which he tried to secure a footing."[2] Thus he died in relative oblivion after finally finding asylum on what was left of his family's estate.

Ibn Ḥazm rejected all forms of analogy (or tried to) both in interpreting Islamic law and also in Qur'anic exegesis. Thus he is remembered as a 'literalist', and as such a comparison with his contemporary Peter Damien might be rewarding. Fakhry writes:

> In a tract entitled *Kitāb al-Ibṭāl*, Ibn Ḥazm inveighs against the use of analogy (*qiyās*), independent judgment (*ra'y*), preference (*istiḥsān*), imitation (*taqlīd*), and causal interpretation (*ta'līl*), and asserts the exclusive validity of the literal method as the only one rooted in the explicit statements of the Koran, the Traditions, or *ijmā'* (consensus).[3]

The possible comparison with Peter Damien becomes even more vivid when we learn that he brushed aside all the scholastic commentaries and went back to the Qur'ān itself and the *ḥadīth*, deeming all the speculation about God's attributes, predestination, essence, etc., as beyond the proper range of human ambition, man's role being purely and simply total submission to revelation. Fakhry writes:

> Ibn Ḥazm's polemics are thus leveled at liberal and conservative theologians of the Mu'tazilite and Ash'arite varieties alike and amount in fact to a repudiation of the validity of applying any of the methods of scholastic theology to questions of jurisprudence or dogma. In this repudiation, Ibn Ḥazm is simply content to cling to the authority of Scripture

and resists any attempt by others to draw him into theological discussions.[4]

Others were also "returning to the source" : the Neo-Confucians were going back to the Confucian classics as such: and likewise, the ascendency of the Vedânta even in its several sub-varieties was really a neo-orthodoxy by way of critique and rejection not only of philosophical Buddhism and Jainism but also Nyāya-Vaiśeṣika and Śāṃkhya-Yoga as well. However, the rejection of scholasticism only stimulated still more scholastic controversies, so that these neo-orthodox trends only led to what we have generally designated as "exfoliation and elaboration" in the transition between the "monism in many moods" of the ninth century and the full-flowering of the "great summas" of the thirteenth century.

According to Ibn Ḥazm there are the following sources of knowledge :

(a) Sensory perception (*shahādat al-ḥawās*), that is, observation or sensory evidence.

(b) Primary reason (*badīhat al-'aql* or *awwal al-'aql*), that is, a priori reason without the use of the five senses.

(c) Proof (*burhān*), which goes back, either closely or remotely, to the evidence of the senses or to primary reason.[5]

However, he did believe that man has six rather than five senses, the sixth being "the soul's knowledge of primary things" such as axioms or the laws of valid reasoning.

As was typically the case with most educated Muslims of his era, although he did not have access to the Greek original texts, he was by no means ignorant of the sciences as inherited from the Greek classics, such as the works of the Milesian and Eleatic schools, Euclid and Ptolemy, and of course Plato and Aristotle and Alexander of Aphrodisias' interpretations of Aristotle. But he rejected Heracleitus in favor of the ontology of the Eleatics, even denying the validity of the 'notion' of motion. Time and space are created by God and are therefore limited. At first it may seem curious that he did not admit the indivisibility of atoms; however, his view was probably tempered by his

Zahirite position theologically, since he believed that indivisibility of the atom entailed a limitation on God's omnipotence much as Peter Damien believed.

In cosmology of course he stressed the createdness of the world over against the classical Greek view of the enternity of the world. In ethics, although he was not ignorant of the Greek classics, the 'pagan' view was qualified by his assertion that philosophy alone, i.e., in the 'pagan' sense, was not enough, for the role of revelation through the prophets is essential. In epistemology likewise, he insists on the crucial importance of revelation, and with that, in accordance with his Zahirite leanings, the literal sense of the Qur'ān must be accepted, although consensus (*ijmā'*) is also crucially important for interpretation (no doubt he would not admit that there are outright contradictions involved, but that was true of Christians, Jews, many Vedāntists and not a few Neo-Confucians).

As for his treatment of the attributes of God, he is very close to the Ash'arite position that God's essence is unique and has nothing to do with the attributes ascribed to Him, much less with the ninety-nine names by which we may invoke God or give praise and thanks to Him. Consistent with his other affirmations of the exaltedness or complete transcendence of Allah, Ibn Ḥazm says that reason (rationalist though he is in other respects) is incapable of knowing God in this life. In so far as we may know God in this life, it is by the sixth sense; mere disputation is not enough, especially for the masses, who are incapable of thinking 'dialectically'. Although apparently he was less astute in his critical studies of the Qur'ān, he even anticipated some of the so-called "higher criticism" of the Bible which did not become effective in Latin Europe until well after the sixteenth century. Although he claimed that argumentation would not necessarily lead anyone to God unless aided by conformity to revelation, he had such a proclivity for argumentation that sometimes he lost favor even with those who otherwise agreed with him.

Needless to say, Ibn Ḥazm did not question the belief that revelation had been closed with the recording of the Qur'ān. Muḥammad was the last of the prophets and there will be no others. But as such he believed—and that in a way that is becoming less common among modernizers who have turned against Euramerican colonialism and exploitation—that Islam has a unique mission in the world of human history, for it is not a religion for any particular "chosen" people but for all mankind.

Ibn Ḥazm's work on love, *Ṭaub al-Ḥamāmah*, is actually for the most part a commentary on Plato's *Symposium*. The key passage in that work Corbin renders thus; "Certain adepts of philosophy have thought that God created each spirit as having a spherical form, but later He divided that into two parts, placing each half in a different body"—so that they have ever since been trying to get back together. "The secret of love is the reunion of these two members into their initial totality. The idea of the pre-existence of souls is also here affirmed expressly by a *ḥadīth* of the Prophet."[6] There is also a book by Ibn Ḥazm on *Characters and the Comportments*. This is in the form of a personal journal or diary in which have been jotted down his meditations, observations ond judgments about people and life in general. It is really a sort of autobiography, revealing not only a lot about its author but also about life in Andalusia during the eleventh century when Cordova was at the height of its magnificence.

The most significant book by Ibn Ḥazm is the theological work *Religions and Sects* in which he treats of the different religions known to him. This book is quite voluminous and is justly considered to be the first systematic treatment of the history of religions, whether in Arabic or any other language. It is an exposition not only of the different sects and religions known to him but also of the wide range of attitudes of which the human spirit is capable in the presence of religious reality. It is evidently from his own attitude about this wide variety that some have called him a sceptic since he has some doubts about them all.

Ibn Ḥazm was very conversant with the Bible as well as with the Qur'ān. It is a pity he did not have access to *śruti* and *smṛti* of other faiths, for his omnivorous mind no doubt would have taken all in tow, and that, no doubt, with an almost Voltarian scepticism. Ibn Ḥazm expresses doubt about the Arabic language being anything special by reason of the Qur'anic revelation being recorded in that language since other revelations had been given in other languages. Knowing that the Prophet Muḥammad was actually illiterate, he even has questions about the orthography of the Qur'ān itself. And he points out that whereas Muslim custom requires five prayers per day the Qur'ān explicitly mentions only two. Thus we have some concrete examples of what some authorities have referred to as his amazing capacity, not unlike that first of Erasmus and later of nineteenth century German scholars, for what has come to be termed "higher criticism" even of "holy writ". Tritton points out that to a great extent his "scepticism" is largely a matter of commonsense, or, as he puts it, "pedestrian good sense."[7]

Even the best of arguments can be countered with counter-arguments, and then counter-arguments against those counter-arguments, until the original proposition has long since been forgotten and one becomes interested only in victory over the opponent, truth or no truth. Thus, even when Judeo-Christian-Islamic scholasticism was really coming into its own, Ibn Hazm warns against excessive use of such scholastic method. His motive for this warning is fascinatingly ethical rather than intellectual: he says that he only intends to deflate the false pride of his opponents, who might be tempted to think they know more than they really do as a result of victory in a battle of empty words. It seems that there is at least some remote parallel between his method and that of the Śūnyavādins or even of some varieties of Advaita such as that of Vācaspati Miśra which were still operative in his own time, namely, the confidence that if all possible views were refuted by counter-refutation, the truth would shine forth of its own accord.

Whether behind his linguistic expertise Ibn Ḥazm was somewhat of a 'yogī' must be left to speculation, although he does seem to be writing out of experience rather than mere "book-learning" when he discusses the difference between *rūḥ* and *nafs*, the former perhaps being equated with the *sukṣma śarīra*, the subtle body sometimes exaggeratedly referred to as one's "astral" body. Since he was as educated as anyone in Cordova in that century, no doubt he was fully conversant with esoterics; but he was by no means primarily concerned with it but rather was able to keep it in its own place in the totality of human experience. Even so, he is fully aware that the grosser body (*sthūla śarīra*) is a hindrance to the *rūḥ* or spiritual body and to the cunning of reason itself. Thus we may surmise that he shows a remarkable detachment from things which might be classified as in the *prātibhāsika* or even *vyāvahārika* levels, since, having access to the *pāramārthika* level, he can play with what other unenlightened humans still treat as sacrosanct. If so, then we might find in him some fascinating parallels with Abhinavagupta who was his contemporary and who also worked largely in the aesthetic medium rather than merely in the academically intellectual.

Among Ibn Ḥazm's opponents there was the saying: "We seek refuge with Allāh from the sword of al-Ḥajjāj and the tongue of Ibn Ḥazm."[8] Al-Ghazālī admired him for his book on the Names of Allah; but one al-Maqqarī was of the opinion that "but for his evil genius, doctrine, and bitter criticism of the savants of the past, he would have been unique in the world of history."[9] Other opinions express similar sentiments, for often his wit probably exceeded his wisdom.

22. Chou Tun-i

Chou Tun-i (1017-1073) had a busy official career, but his philosophical achievements place him very high in the intellectual history of Chinese civilization. Others have compared Chou-Tun-i to Aristotle, Thomas Aquinas, Leibniz (whom no doubt indirectly at least he influenced since it was most likely his interpretation of the *I-Ching* that Leibniz followed enthusiastically) and Herbert Spencer. The short but loadstone treatise which Chou wrote explaining his Diagram of the Supreme Ultimate is a classic that should be a part of everyone's standard education alongside the *Tao Te Ching* and the *Bhagavad Gītā* and other seminal texts. Here we cannot but give it in full along with Chou's Diagram.

Diagram of the Supreme Ultimate

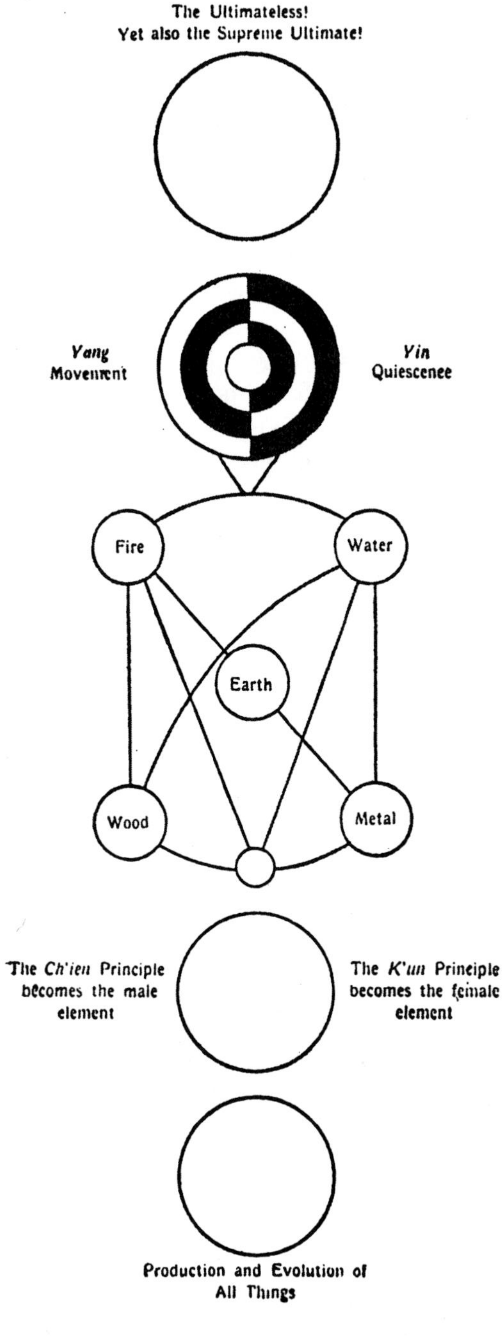

The Ultimateless (*wu chi*) ! And yet also the Supreme Ultimate (*t'ai chi*) !

The Supreme Ultimate through movement (*tung*) produces the *yang*. This movement, having reached its limit, is followed by quiescence (*ching*), and by this quiescence it produces the *yin*. When quiescence has reached its limit, there is a return to movement. Thus movement and quiescence, in alternation, become each the source of the other. The distinction between *yin* and *yang* is determined, and their Two Forms (*liang yi*) stand revealed.

By the transformations of the *yang*, and the union therewith of the *yin*, water, fire, wood, metal, and earth are produced. These five ethers (*ch'i*, i.e., elements) become diffused in harmonious order, and the four seasons proceed in their course.

The Five Elements are the one *yin* and *yang*; the *yin* and *yang* are the one Supreme Ultimate; and the Supreme Ultimate is fundamentally the Ultimateless. The Five Elements come into being each having its own particular nature (*hsing*).

The true substance of the Ultimateless, and the essences of the Two (Forms) and Five (Elements), unite in mysterious union, so that consolidation ensues. The *ch'ien* principle becomes the male element, and the *k'un* principle becomes the female element. The two ethers (i.e., the *yin* and *yang*) by their interaction operate to produce all things, and these in their turn produce and reproduce, so that transformation and change continue without end.

It is man alone, however, who receives all these in their highest excellence, and hence is the most intelligent (of all beings). His bodily form thereupon is produced, and his spirit develops consciousness. The five principles of his nature react (to external phenomena), so that the distinction between good and evil emerges and the myriad phenomena of conduct appear.

The sage regulates himself according to the mean, correctness, love, and righteousness, and takes quiescence as the essential, thus establishing the highest standard for mankind.

Hence the sage's "virtue is one with that of Heaven and Earth; his brilliance is equal to that of the sun and moon; his course is in harmony with that of the four seasons; and in his relation to good or bad fortune he is in harmony with the spirits." The superior man, by cultivating these (sagely virtues), enjoys good fortune, while the petty man, by violating them, incurs bad fortune.

Therefore it is said : "The Way (*Tao*) of Heaven is established by the *yin* and *yang*: the Way of Earth is established by softness (*jou*) and hardness (*kang*); the Way of man is established by love (*jen*) and righteousness (*yi*)." And again : "By tracing things to their beginning and back again to their final issue, (the *Book of Changes*) comes to know the meaning of life and death." Great indeed is the *Changes*. Herein has been expressed its fullest (meaning).[1]

The Neo-Confucian application of this basic schematism was much more limited than what it can be in our own time. In a global synthesis of philosophical developments up to the eleventh century, it should be integrated with such things as the Aristotelian categories, the *pramāṇas* of classical Indian philosophy, the three *guṇas* of classical Sāṃkhya and its medieval elaborations, and with the categories of Vaiśeṣika. The modern Marxist dualism of conflict is quite different from this pattern of *harmonious polarization.* Needham asserts that Chou Tun-i and Chu Hsi after him considered the whole of reality as organic in a sort of proto-Whiteheadian sense, every part harmoniously integrated with all the rest, and no one part in supreme control or limited by any other part as long as it functioned and developed naturally.

In his *Ways of Thinking of Eastern Peoples*, Nakamura notes the Chinese fondness for schematic diagrams :

.. In explaining the genesis of the universe he (Chou) did not resort to abstractions of the Indian variety but introduced such concrete empirical principles as "*yang* and *yin*" or "man and woman".... Diagrams for explaining metaphysical theories are not found in Greece or in India where such theories were rather set forth in complicated series of sentences. The

> same tendency can be observed in the use of diagrammatic genealogies depicting the descent of doctrine from master to pupil, while in India the same material is presented in dry prose.[2]

Concerning the origin of the Diagram of the Supreme Ultimate in the Taoist school, Carsun Chang says that Chou Tun-i only "revised it and put it in its present form".[3] Wing-tsit Chan does not deny the likelihood of heavy Taoist influence; rather he claims that by bringing the *yin-yang* philosophy into Confucianism (thus *Neo*-Confucianism) Chou "discarded the fantasy and mysticism of Taoism. The diagram had been used by Taoists in their attempt to obtain elixir for immortal life, but Chou Tun-i used it for rational philosophy."[4] Chan says that even though it appears that Buddhist and Taoist influence is not absent, "neither Buddhist nor Taoist influence changed its (Chou's) fundamentally Confucian character."[5]

The ultimate merit of this cosmology is its continuing relevance and potential for wider applicability in the modern framework. Needham writes :

> Modern minds have become accustomed to thinking (or consciously not thinking) in these terms : the world is full of poles and centers, magnetic fields, cells and their nuclei, centers of social control in time of peace and war. But they are all secondary to the organisms of which they form part, not superior to them....
>
> When one takes a further look at this pithily expressed system of nature, one cannot but admit that the Sung philosophers were working with concepts not unlike some being used in modern science. No doubt the idea of two fundamental forces was an ancient generalization based on the two sexes of so many species, man included, and the Sung thinkers may have done little more than tabulate its consequences; yet the more one reads them, the more one feels that they really did attain to an inkling of the deeply rooted aspects of matter which appear later in the West as positive and negative electricity, as protons and electrons, as the components of all material particles.[6]

Needham could well have mentioned north and south magnetic poles, clockwise and counter-clockwise spirals or vortices in the northern and southern hemispheres (affecting everything from ocean currents to what happens in our bathroom lavatory drains), the relation between acids and bases, and bi-lateral symmetry in many biological organisms, as well as such polarization in social and historical phenomena and, as we have seen many times, philosophies. (Martin Gardner's *Ambidextrous Universe* could be taken as a twentieth century commentary on Chou Tun'i's philosophy of polarization).

It is interesting to note that instead of treating Chou Tun-i as a scientist as Needham does, Hou Wai-lu, writing from the early Maoist point of view, characterizes him as superstitious and idealist and only concerned with esoterics. This seems rather strange since Chou-i's 'dialectic' could be taken as a precursor of Hegelian and Marxist dialectics. Indeed, in the controversy between Chairman Mao and Liu Shao-ch'i it seems that Chairman Mao proved more Chinese and Liu more the orthodox Western Marxist. For popular consumption Liu claimed that "two makes one" (thesis-antithesis-synthesis) and thus society would evolve dialectically until contradictions no longer existed. But Chairman Mao claimed that "one makes two" (everything polarizes). Thus, while antagonistic contradictions (those which result in conflict) will disappear, non-antagonistic ones (those between correlative phenomena, e.g., producer and consumer) will not.

According to Chou Tun-i, whose source is the *I Ching*, we do not find completely pure *yin* without some mixture of *yang* nor any pure *yang* without some *yin*. Hence we have the harmonius polarizations of correlatives rather than the conflict of opposites. Then come the traditional five agents which pertain to *ch'i*, which is roughly equivalent to the *prakṛti* of the Indian tradition. In some contexts one gets the impression that the five *ch'i* are comparable to the *prāṇas* (breaths) of Indian yogic practice. The ch'i renders the abstract principle (s) (*li*) manifest by virtue of embodiment. One of the most basic early controversies in the history of Neo-Confucian philosophy is that concerning the nature of the relation between *li* and *ch'i*. But certainly there is never the one without the other. Fung writes :

> Opposed to *ch'i* is another key concept, that of *li* or "principle".... As used in Neo-Confucianism, *li* is a designation for the immaterial and metaphysical principle or principles that underlie, yet transcend, the physical universe. ... Often it is used as a synonym for the Supreme Ultimate. Hence when Chou Tun-yi speaks...of "oneness", referring thereby to the Supreme Ultimate, it would seem that he also has in mind *li* or Principle; whereas when he speaks of *yin* and *yang*, he has in mind forces which, for him, pertain to *ch'i* or matter.
>
> This apposition between *li* and *ch'i*, so important in later Neo-Confucianism, thus seemingly begins with Chou Tun-yi. It was not until Chu Hsi, however, that it was to become fully elaborated.... We see that all things of the physical universe are derived from a "oneness", which is the Supreme Ultimate; the later, therefore, though a transcendent principle, is at the same time regarded as actually being *within* all material things. In Chou's own words: "The myriad-fold constitutes a oneness, and the single reality divides to be a myriadfold."[7]

Taken in isolation this schematic relation between transcendence and immanence is fascinating enough; but historically one may well ask whether it does not represent a parallel transition from the monistic tendencies of the ninth century to more panentheistic (or even panenpsychic) views in Europe and India, i.e., from Scotus Erigena to the beginning of the School of Chartres, in Byzantium from Photius to Psellos, in India from Śaṅkara to Rāmānuja, as well as the transition from al-Ḥallāj and al-Kindī to Ibn Sīnā and al-Ṭūsī—all of whom might agree with that dictum, "The myriad-fold constitutes a oneness, and the single reality divides to be a myriad-fold." The problem of embodiment, in other words, has assumed priority over the problem of transcendence, and the *via affirmativa* has begun to be emphasized as much as the *via negativa*. Whether in Japan the same basic transition was present might be questioned; but although the differentiation may not be so explicit, one can still claim that Genshin and Jōkei were no longer so basically monistic as Saichō and Kūkai.

Curiously enough, Chou Tun-i did not explain the relation between the Supreme Ultimate and the classical Confucian concept of *li* or even the relation between those and the virtue of *ch'eng* (sincerity), though he did write about these individually. That was the great contribution of Chu Hsi later on. In the famous controversy between Chu Hsi and Lu Hsiang-shan over the interpretation of the Diagram the key point was whether this Supreme Ultimate out of which the polarizations emerge is an "Ultimate of Nothingness" (obviously the *Śūnyatā* of Mādhyamika) or something of a more 'substantial' nature. We could compare this with Rāmānuja's argument that the Advaitins must either admit that *Śūnyatā* should replace their concept of *nirguṇa*-Brahman or else they must admit attributes.

Concerning the five-element theory, Carsun Chang reports the following summary :

> The five-element-theory is an old and complicated one.... The Chinese expanded the signification of the five elements until they embraced all the phenomena in the universe. The following table shows the wide scope of the five elements in representing the different aspects of nature :

Wood	East	Spring	*Jen*	Liver	Blue
Fire	South	Summer	*Li*	Heart	Red
Earth	Middle		*Hsin* (Honesty)	Spleen or Stomach	Yellow
Metal	West	Autumn	*I*	Lungs	Black
Water	North	Winter	*Chih*	Kidneys	White

> Thus, the five element theory may be applied in the following fields : (1) moral values, (2) ge ography, (3) seasons, (4) physiological organs, (5) colors. The theory of the five elements was developed so elaborately that it can explain any aspect of the life of nature. It was invented by the School of *Yin* and *Yang*, and later was adopted by the Taoists and Confucianists. Chou Tun-i, basing his thought on this tradition, applied the theory in its conventional sense.[8]

Carsun Chang goes on to say of Chou that he was the founder of a new philosophy comparable to Descartes, Spinoza and Leibniz in modern European philosophy;[9] we might rather suggest Peter Lombard's *Sentences* or even Bādarāyaṇa's *Sūtras* as the more apt comparison.

Chou Tun-i was a complete philosopher and not only a 'scientist' intrigued by the esoterics of natural phenomena. We might profit as much in our present-day world situation from his ethics as from his 'natural' philosophy, although in the Neo-Confucian philosophy there was no gap between the realm of nature, the realm of man, and the realm of value. Chou's other important work, the *T'ung Shu* (*Penetrating the Book of Ch .nges*), is traditional in its concern with ethical matters, teaching, like Li Ao and Han Yü, *ch'eng* (sincerity). Needham writes regarding *ch'eng* :

> ... The *Chung Yung* also says 'Sincerity is the Tao of heaven; to apply oneself to sincerity is the Tao of man', indicating that it transcends the (merely) human sphere. Heaven has *ch'eng* because it faithfully follows its true nature and does nothing against its Tao. Thus we come to the realization that *ch'eng* is achieved when every organism fulfills with obsolute precision whatever its function may be in the higher organism of which it is a part, and here again we have a state of affairs that is quite familiar to modern philosophers of organism.[10]

The term *ch'eng* is perhaps better translated as integrity or authenticity, or even perfection—perhaps with the Mahāyāna *prajñāpāramitā* in the background, this ancient Confucian/Taoist term now being infused with that new richness as the nearest Chinese equivalent to this ultimate ideal in the Mahāyāna *sūtras*.

Chou's philosophy of human nature at first looks terribly conservative and traditional : following Han Yü and Li Ao, he takes his inspiration from Mencius rather than Hsün Tzu, asserting that human nature is essentially good. But on second look there is a very significant difference, for Chou gives the traditional ethical view a metaphysical underpinning. It is the Diagram of the Supreme Ultimate, the Diagram of Differentiation, that guarantees this goodness—which differentiation he affirms, like Rāmānuja, rather than rejecting it as *māyā* (illusion) as was the case with Śaṅkara. The same point seems to apply to Chou's interpretation of *ch'eng*, sincerity or authenticity : "The successive movement of yin and yang constitutes the Way (Tao). What issues from the Way is good, and that which realizes it is the individual nature."[11] In other words, *ch'eng* is not just a matter of moralizing, but a matter of allowing the inherent natural values to become operative without hindrance, functionally. It seems that greater security and stability in the external world has perhaps restored great confidence in the world and in man and his ability to effect change in it. One might point to Psellos' further development of Photius' humanism as providing a suggestive parallel; and although Peter Damien might not agree with such confidence, certainly Berenger of Tours, if not Fulbert of Chartres, might have no major objection.

If everything is thus so metaphysically rosy, how come evil ? This seemingly eternal problem is still there. Fung writes : "Chou's theory is that though man's nature is originally good, its manifestations in actual conduct do not always accord with the mean; conduct of this sort we then call evil."[12] Chou writes :

> ...Righteousness, uprightness, decisiveness, strictness, and firmness of action are examples of strength that is good, and fierceness, narrow-mindedness, and violence are examples of strength that is evil. Kindness, mildness, and humility are examples of weakness that is good, and softness, indecision, and perverseness are examples of weakness that is evil. Only the Mean brings harmony. The Mean is the principle of regularity, the universally recognized law of morality, and is that to which the sage is devoted. Therefore the sage institutes education so as to arrive at the Mean and to rest there.[13]

Chou's suggestion that all evil is a deviation from the Mean is one of the two essentially different approaches to the problem of evil found in Neo-Confucianism. It is essentially a monistic approach, as it were, in that it claims that all evil is essentially one insofar as it is a deviation from the Mean. This solution was to be adopted by Wang Yang-ming (1472-1529). It was, however, rejected by Chu Hsi. He distinguished two essentially different kinds of evil : inappropriate action or emotional response, and action or emotional response which was not in accordance with the Mean. An example of the former would be to feel joy rather than sorrow upon the death of one's father. Such a response is completely inappropriate, and by no stretch of the imagination could joy be seen as an improper degree of sorrow. An example of the latter would be to feel sorrow upon the death of one's father, but to an insufficient degree. In spite of such a dualistic view of evil, Chu Hsi explains the existence of both monistically, i.e., both are due to *ch'i.* The two different types arise, however, because of two essentially different ways in which *ch'i* affects *li.*

Chou's views on a second major problem for Neo-Confucian moral theory are also important. What exactly are the implications of the claim that human nature is good ? If virtue is in some sense innate, what is the status of moral education ? Is it even necessary ? Whatever attraction towards Taoism Chou might have had or influence he might have received, he proves himself a traditional and orthodox Confucian when he insists upon the necessity of socialization. Only a Taoist would suggest that men are best left alone to develop naturally. According to Chou, one can become a sage through learning. He writes :

> The essential way is to (concentrate on) one thing. By (concentrating on) one thing is meant having no desire. Having no desire, one is vacuous (hsü, being absolutely pure and peaceful) while tranquil, and straightforward while in action. Being vacuous while tranquil, one becomes intelligent and hence penetrating. Being straightforward while active, one becomes impartial and hence all-embracing. Being intelligent, penetrating, impartial, and all-embracing, one is almost a sage.[14]

Nevertheless, in the end the whole matter and means to sagehood is comprised simply in the all-encompassing virtue of *ch'eng*, sincerity. As Fung writes: "By this Chou means to say that *ch'eng* or sincerity is the original condition of man's nature, and that the sage is a sage precisely because he has succeeded in returning his nature to this original condition. This doctrine... had already been enunciated two centuries earlier by Li Ao. Beginning with Chou Tun-yi, it was generally accepted by all the Neo-Confucianists."[15]

Almost in a sociology of aesthetic taste, Chou Tun-i recorded his love of flowers, having made a study of which flowers which famous person had favored most:

> Among all kinds of loveable plants... on land or in the water, the Ch'in Dynasty poet, T'ao Yuan-ming, adored the chrysanthemum. After the T'ang Dynasty, most people turned to the peony. I myself love the lotus because it grows out of the shiny mud and yet is not defiled, and because it lives in the pure and rippling water without appearing like a too fascinating and seductive lady. It has a system of tubes inside and is straight outside. Without branches or spreading vines its scent comes from afar. And how pure is that fragrance! It is stately and unsullied. It is better to look at it from a distance than from too near—like a lady's petticoat. I consider the chrysanthemum to be a hermit among plants and the peony a flower signifying riches and power. But the lotus is a flower with a noble character. Alas! Where is a lover of the chrysanthemum like T'ao Yuan-ming? Who will love the lotus as much as I? Most people love only the peony![16]

This preference for the lotus and the allegorical and metaphorical virtues attached to it, typical all through both in Hindu and Buddhist literature, is another indicator of the influence of Buddhism on Neo-Confucianism.

Applying our favorite *pramāṇa*, we must ask what can be found historically in Chou Tun-i's contemporaries that is *not* present in his thinking. Muslim and Christian theologians will complain that the Supreme Ultimate or the Ultimate of 'Emptiness' is scarcely the equivalent of the transcendent Allah or God the Father, although those in the Neo-Platonic emanationist tradition might concede much similarity. Others might consider

Chou's non-anthropomorphic 'naturalism' a relief, since much of the energy of Christian, Jewish and Islamic scholasticism had been devoted to the technicalities of revealed theology to the neglect of the study of nature. (Many centuries later this becomes a major issue between the Jesuits and the Dominicans; and even with all of his enthusiasm for the *I Chang* and things Chinese, Leibniz still had reservations about the absence of "revealed" religion in the Confucian world-view.)

From the Indian point of view three comments can be made. (1) Chou does not take into account the involutionray cycle of cosmology. Although he might have done so by asserting that the famous Diagram can be read both ways, evidently he intended it only in the evolutionary mode. Thus he does not consider the possibility of *pralaya* which is so deep-seated in the Hindu world-view and is often implicit in Mahāyāna Buddhism. (2) Admitting that he was influenced by at least two varieties of Chinese Buddhism, it is somewhat strange that the *mappo* concept is not very explicit in his work (although the idea of tracing the degeneration of Confucian *dharma* since Mencius does have a remote parallel). (3) Chou is another Chinese philosopher who fails to see any necessity for a logic such as had developed with Dignāga and Dharmakīrti and was attaining ever greater sophistication in the Navya Nyāya school. Although Hsüan-tsang did bring some Nyāya texts and pre-Dignāga Buddhist logical texts with him from India and had even translated them, the technicalities of the terminology that he had to invent for the purpose were so abstruse that no one could understand them; and even today specialists in Chinese language of that period find them quite puzzling and difficult. Most Neo-Confucians were adept at arguing in sorites, so it cannot be asserted that Chinese scholars, whether Taoist, Buddhist or Confucian, were illogical. Their constant concern was not with the development of sophisticated tools for the analysis of argumentation but (as one might say nowadays) with the phenomenological search for the pre-logical basics; and reason for them increasingly became, not a matter of juggling refutations of refutations, but a metaphysical principle whereby the mind of man should operate in harmony with the cosmic order of nature.

23. Shao Yung

Shao Yung (1011-1077), Chou Tun-i and Chang Tsai constitute a sort of triad of semi-scientific or at least realist if not semi-materialist philosophers in the early Southern Sung period of Chinese history. Shao Yung is often listed as "a predecessor of Chu Hsi". This is the traditional and almost universal attitude, somewhat parallel with the relation between Ibn Ḥazm and Ibn Rushd, even though both deserve credit in their own light. As with Chou Tun-i, whether Shao Yung was really a Taoist or a Taoizing Neo-Confucian seems to be debatable. But the point is that he did have a system, and this system was definitely advanced for his era.

Although most of Taoism had become what is termed 'religious' Taoism, philosophical Taoism was revived in the Southern Sung alongside of Neo-Confucianism; and it was this, not the popular cult, that influenced Shao Yung. He became an initiate under Li Chih-ts'ai, this line of transmission going back at least to the Taoist Ch'en T'uan (c. 906-989). Shao was somewhat of a recluse, his cottage being something like what in India now is called an āshram, where people, even of notoreity and high position, come for meditation, counsel and religious retreats. Tradition ascribes to him the usual ascetic practices of indifference to cold and heat and abstemiousness even in his manner of sleeping. He was a strict vegetarian, as we might expect. He began his ascetic or abstemious ways even in his youth, being among those who gradually grow spiritual realities instead of undergoing some traumatic conversion or "sudden" enlightenment.

According to tradition Shao Yung's last words were : "You must leave the road ahead of you wide open. Otherwise you will not let other people walk on it." He wrote the following poem about himself:

> Character same as the pine-tree and—
> Literary style as splendid as the poppy:
> Caliber as great as a mountain or river;
> Sentiment as fine as the wind or the moon.
> My face and physical shape are borrowed from you (Heaven).

After toying with the ball (the world, the Supreme Ultimate).
I come and go as I please.[1]

The following is from Shao's essay *The Man Mr. Nameless,* a sort of autobiographical piece:

> When he was ten years old, he studied in his home village, and exhausted what there was to know about the village. From ten to twenty per cent of his crudeness was removed. When he was twenty years old, he studied in the district and learned everything about the district. From thirty to forty per cent of his crudeness was taken away. From thirty years of age, he studied in his county, and knew all there was to know about his county. Then his crudeness was reduced to fifty per cent. At forty he studied the ancients, and knew all about them. His crudeness was reduced to twenty per cent. When he was fifty years old he became a student of Heaven and Earth, and knew all about Heaven and Earth. Then his crudeness was down to zero.[2]

Then he describes his relations with "people from all directions" who came to visit him, all of them more or less suspicious of his character because they did not know anyone quite like him. So they began to call him Mr. Nameless—a designation not uncommon among Hindu yogīs even today, but in this instance more in line with Taoist theory and practice. One is reminded of the parable of the arrow in flight ascribed to the historic Śākyamuni Buddha : it leaves no trace of where it has been and is useful only in so far as it hits the target at which it has been aimed; that is how the true *sādhaka* should live. Shao's goal was to be like the Nameless Tao or the Supreme Ultimate, knowledge of which cannot adequately be contained in any human finite mind. Of course the ultra-orthodox Confucians naturally considered Shao as very unorthodox if not a little odd.

Needham gives us this introductory overview of Shao Yung:

> Shao Yung, who in characteristic Taoist fashion refused all official responsibility, was an original but fanciful thinker. His *Huang Chi Ching Shih Shu* (Book of the Sublime Prin-

ciple which governs all Things within the World) was partly composed of elaborate diagrams in which cosmological and ethical ideas mingled, but which were found to be so hard to understand that they were replaced by a descriptive account from the hands of his son and another philosopher. Shao Yung also wrote an interesting philosophical dialogue, *Yü Chhiao Wēn Tui* (The Conversation of the Fisherman and the Woodcutter), in which he spoke of the uniformity of natural phenomena, the finiteness of 'forms' (*hsing*), and the infinity of 'matter' (*chhi*); adding his views on the hexagrams. ... Shao Yung retained the Tao as the name for the universal principle of Nature, but gave a very high place to 'number' concevied in a Pythagorean way; the Tao first makes numbers, then forms, and then fills these with matter. This was associated in him with a strong tendency to metaphysical idealism, ...and in this sense he was not on the main line of Neo-Confucian development, which could rather be described as dualistic realism. ... According to him, the two primary manifestations (*liang i*) of the Tao were motion (*tung*) and rest (*ching*); the former generated the Yin and the Yang, the latter generated two entities newly introduced by Shao Yung namely, softness (*jou*) and hardness (*kang*). Earth was a mixture of these while Heaven was a mixture of Yin and Yang. The four generated entities were called the four secondary manifestations (*ssu hsiang*), and each of them could exist in two qualities, strong or weak. With the eight components thus available Shao Yung derived, in a more or less arbitrary and fanciful way... all kinds of phenomena. One can at any rate remember that this was in the +llth century, and what is worth noting is the extremely concrete and physical nature of his world-picture. Motion and rest, and to a lesser extent softness and hardness, were taken over as basic conceptions by the Neo-Confucians. Shao Yung fully believed in the Indian idea, introduced with Buddhism, that there were periodical world-catastrophes in which the world was dissolved into chao and then remade anew. One medieval notion, very clear in him, is that of the microcosm and the macrocosm, and there seems no reason to attribute it to any but indigenous sources.

> Perhaps the most interesting idea of Shao Yung's from the point of view of the history of science was embodied in his expression *fan kuan,* or 'objective observation'. In science, he said, 'there are often things which one cannot understand. One must not attempt to "force" them (into a scheme), for "forcing" them brings in one's self (and one's prejudices), and thus one loses the (objective) principles, and falls into artificial constructions.' It is only unfortunate that Shao Yung did not bear this wisdom more in mind in the construction of his own theoretical schemes. Another useful emphasis of his was on the general community of observers; we are not restricted, he said, to personal observations, but can use the eyes of all men as our syes, and their ears as our ears, and thus we can form a connected body of understanding of Nature.[3]

The judgment of Shao Yung as a fanciful thinker may also apply to Ibn Ḥazm; moreover, this judgment is made only *post facto.* Again and again, even though we do it, we should continually try not to "read history backwards". In a couple of centuries essentially the same remark can be made about Roger Bacon, and still later about figures like Paracelsus. Certainly a lot of modern secular prejudices tend to interfere with empathetic historical interpretation. For example, magic, science and mysticism all across Eurasia did not get separated from each other until very much later; and even then in our own time they are threatening, as it were, to re-emerge together.

The numerology which Shao Yung developed is not unlike that which may be found in the mystagogical works of Maximus and those who followed him in Byzantium. Shao's great interest in 'number' suggests some indirect influence from Neo-Pythagoreanism, although intriguing games with numbers are so universal that one should not be surprised if they are discovered independently of influence. (Actually, if reinvestigated, these number games might be found to be rather significant after all from the standpoint of 'pure' mathematics even today.) Although virtually all Chinese philosophers had been influenced by the *I Ching,* Shao Yung was to make number as such the basis of his philosophizing, claiming that mathematics holds the key to all reality, including cycles of all sorts. Of course such things were not unknown in Greece, if not in Babylon and Egypt long before that, and in India since remote antiquity. Carsun Chang dubs Shao Yung "the Chinese Pythagoras"; however, closer parallels can probably be found in his contemporary Ibn Hazm as well as in al-Bīrūnī and in the Ikhwān al-Ṣafā.

Chan summarized Shao Yung's world-view in the following paragraph :

> Shao's fundamental concepts are three. First, there are the supreme principles governing the universe. Second, these principles can be discerned in terms of numbers. And third, the best knowledge of them is the objective, that is, viewing things from the viewpoint of things. In holding that all things have principles in them, he is not different from other Neo-Confucianists. To this concept, he devoted his major work, the *Huang-chi ching-shih shu* (Supreme Principles Governing the World). However, while he followed the same pattern of cosmic evolution in the *Book of Changes* as most other Neo-Confucianists did, that is, the evolution from the Great Ultimate through yin and yang or negative and positive cosmic force, to the myriad things, he added the element of number. To him universal operation, or Change, is due to spirit which gives rise to number, number to form, and form to concrete things. The whole process works according to principle and is nature. Man is the most intelligent of the products of natural evolution, but like all other things he is governed by numbers.[4]

Chan qualifies the claim that Shao was the first to found his philosophy on number as such, since the concept of numerology was of course aleady present in the *I Ching* and even in the *Lao Tzu* and in Yang Hsiung. But Shao was the first to "base his whole philosophy on it and build a system of numerical progression."[5]

Shao Yung had a tendency to classify everything in groups of fours. Chan spells out more explicitly how Shao's schemes of fours work :

> Thus there are the four heavenly bodies (sun, moon, stars, and zodiacal space), the four earthly substances (water, fire, earth, and stone), the four kinds of creatures (animals, birds, grass, and plants), the four sense organs (eye, ear, nose, and mouth), the four ways of transforming the world (by truth, virtue, work, and effort), the four kinds of rulers, the four kinds of Mandate of Heaven, and so forth.[6]

Shao did not intend it as a static manner of thinking but a dynamism so that progressions from four to sixty-four (in the hexagrams of the *I Ching*) can be devised, hopefully in a way that predictions can be made. Parenthetically, it may be that Giordano Bruno comprehended what is afoot here more profoundly and comprehensively than anyone else, for he schematizes not only in terms of monads, dyads, triads, quadrads, etc., but goes right on down to decads, which then, as a realization of the 'metaphysics' of the decimal system, goes on to infinity, God and God alone being the Infinity of Infinities. Thus it might even be claimed of Bruno that in a sense he almost anticipated Einstein in replacing the traditional categories by dimensions. Historically it may not be an accident that this should be considering Bruno's sources: Raymond Lull, and behind him Ibn Ḥazm, and eventually behind him Hindu mathematics, which directly or indirectly also influenced Shao Yung.

Shao Yung's elaborate diagrams suggest the many Renaissance geniuses as well as the more contemporary mandalas of Tibetan Buddhism. Unfortunately Shao's diagrams are now lost, although they have been speculatively more or less reconstructed. Proper use of the diagrams does not have to be seen as a matter of necromancy and superstition (not only was Leibniz intrigued by them but Karl Jung used them freely in his psychotherapy). Paradoxically their merit and their limitation lies in their universal applicability.

Shao's sense of time cycles is rather remarkable by comparison with what was believed to be the age of creation in Latin Europe and in Byzantium. Once again one may suspect Indian influence since such grand cycles of time sequences are found in almost all of the *Purāṇas* as well as in Jaina literature (although Jaina influence is not very likely). Shao believed less in involution as well as evolution. This idea that the world, much less the whole universe, will be destroyed someday was completely foreign to the traditional Chinese mind, so the obvious inference is Buddhist influence. No other Neo-Confucian philosopher emphasized the idea of cyclic change as much as Shao; thus we may pair Shao Yung, the philosopher of cycles, with Chou Tun-i, the philosopher of polarization.

Shao's interpretation of "the observation of things" suggests the *ko wu* "investigation of things" which beginning with Chu Hsi becomes so controversial. This capacity of man to observe and investigate nature for the sake of knowledge-as-such as an essential prerequisite for wisdom inevitably becomes involved in those other two classical if not perennial themes of philosophizing in China, namely, *hsing* and *ming*, human nature and destiny, and likewise the controversy concerning the proper relation between *li* and *ch'i* (the Chinese counterpart of the Latin and Arabic scholastic controversy about universals). As a scientific humanist, Shao puts stress on the concrete particulars rather than on any abstract realm of Platonic Ideas. He specifically states that everything has its own *li*: thus "the observation of things" is not just a matter of the internal subjective function of the mind (Wang Yang-ming interpreted *ko wu* to mean observation of the function of the mind) but the very objective factual knowledge of the actual things in the world. It is in this context that he extolls objectivity, whether or not he followed his own advice. Shao writes :

> What I mean by the observation of things does not mean observing them with the eye. No, it is not observation with the eye, but observation with the mind. Nor is it observation with the mind, but observation of them in the light of their own Principles. There is no creature in the world that does not have its own Principle (*li*), nature (*hsing*), and Destiny (*ming*). What I mean by Principle is something that can be known only after it has been completely penetrated. What I mean by Destiny is something that can be known only after (our minds) have reached it. These three kinds of knowledge

> are the real knowledge of the world, and even the sage cannot go beyond them. Anyone who tries to go beyond them is not what I call a sage....
>
> The sage's ability thus to synthesize the qualities of all things lies in his ability to observe objectively. By such objective observation I mean an observation of things not made in terms of self, by which I mean the observation of things in terms of those things themselves. When one is thus able to observe things in terms of those things, how can the self then be interposed between them?[7]

As with most mathematical minds in all ages, Shao Yung does not rate the senses very highly as sources of knowledge. Indeed the senses tend more to distract us than to enable us to think. Reason holds the key to reality. Carsun Chang looks to Spinoza as the best comparison in this context, but we could as well point to Ibn Sīnā or even to some precursor of Moses Maimonides, to whom Spinoza was so deeply indebted.

Given his sense of the vast extent of time sequences, one would expect Shao to have a realistic metaphysics of substantial time; but rather he has a very relativistic conception of time which parallels Dignāga's way of proving the unreality of time. But Shao does not call time illusory; instead he merely warns that most of our thinking about time is too subjective. Shao writes:

> What is past and present is like day and night in this world. If one looks at the present from the present, this present is called present. If one looks at the present from the future, this so-called present is also the past. If one looks at the past from the present, this past is past. If one looks at the past from the past itself, this past is present. Therefore, we know that the past is not itself the past, and the present is not itself the present. The so-called past and the present originated in a subjective point of view. It is quite possible that before the past of thousands of years ago, or after the future of many thousands of years ahead, mankind did, or will, relinquish the subjective point of view.[8]

Over against some of his scholastic contemporaries, Shao Yung, like many Renaissance geniuses in Europe who were also interested in esoterics and mathematics, was decidedly a humanist, and in this respect he might be compared to his Byzantine contemporary Psellos (though Psellos did not sanction esoterics and emphasized logic instead). Thus Shao writes, not merely echoing the implicit limited classical humanism of Confucius, but a humanism that has incorporated all that China had developed in Confucianism, Taoism, and Buddhism (and perhaps under cover quite a bit of Nestorianism and Manichaeanism as well) :

> Man, too, is a creature (like other creatures), and the sage, too, is a man (like other men).... But man is the most perfect of creatures, and the sage is the most perfect of men.... How is this ? It means that he (the sage) is a person able by means of his own single mind to observe a myriad other minds, by means of his own single body to observe a myriad other bodies, by means of a single (external) object to observe a myriad other objects, and by means of a single generation to observe a myriad other generations. It also means that he is one able with his mind to represent the meaning of Heaven, with his mouth to represent the words of Heaven, with his hands to represent the labors of Heaven, and with his body to represent the functions of Heaven. It means too that he is one able to possess knowledge of the seasons of Heaven above, to have a complete grasp of the principles of Earth below and between these, to have a complete grasp of the qualities of things, and to comprehend clearly the affairs of men. In addition, it means that he is one able to supplement and carry onward (the activities of) Heaven and Earth, to come and go with creative and transforming influence, to pass to and fro between past and present, and to reach the inner and outer aspects of current affairs.[9]

And the key to all of this is man's capacity of observation. Here we should recall that the school of Śaṅkara and many others in India put the *sākṣī* (observer) consciousness at the junction-point of human and divine existence. Ultimately perhaps the whole cosmos is only a sort of partially crystallized prismatization of Consciousness in the process of observing itself, and man's capacity to observe all this is therefore the ultimate reality itself.

The reason that Shao Yung was not so popular in later generations was partly due to the fact that, since he was strongly influenced by Taoist teachings, Chu Hsi did not consider him so important, although Chu Hsi was very much influenced by Chou Tun-i in spite of Chou's non-Confucian influences. But Shao's unpopularity was also due to the one unpardonable 'sin' for anyone who would claim Confucian identity of any sort : he failed to make any commentary on the classics dealing with *jen* (humanity) and *yi* (righteousness).[10] Shao's contemporary Hsieh Liang-tao wrote of him : "He had insight on the principle of progress and retrogression of the universe ond the rise and fall of all things...but had not devoted himself to the task of studying things on the lower level (human affairs) before penetrating things on the higher level."[11] One may recall Karl Marx's remark that Hegel had looked on the world as though standing on his head, and his own job was to put him back on his feet ! Another reason why Shao did not have much historical influence is because he followed the Taoist ideal of complete detachment from public affairs, so he gained very few disciples.

24. Chang Tsai

In the official biography we find the following concerning Chang Tsai (1320-1077) :

> (Chang) Tsai read this book (the *Doctrine of the Mean*), yet found it not wholly satisfactory. So he turned his attention to Buddhism and Taoism, into whose doctrines he delved for several successive years. Yet here too he failed to acquire the (desired) understanding, so again he turned from them to the Six Classics (of Confucianism).... Having discoursed with the two Ch'engs about the important principles of Neo-Confucianism, he came to acquire self-confidence and said : "This Truth of ours is self-sufficient. What need, then, to

search elsewhere ?" And with this he completely discarded his heterodox learning and accepted orthodoxy.[1]

Such a patter of development as outlined here for Chang Tsai is not uncommon in any culture; indeed, seldom does one come to mature understanding of one's own heritage until there is an 'other' with which to compare it and perhaps with which eventually to synthesize it in a neo-orthodoxy. The above passage could apply to almost any of the most important Neo-Confucians, but apparently they rarely had significant acquaintance with the great Buddhist treatises on logic, epistemology and metaphysics. Too often their contact was only with cultic popular-religion Buddhism.

Like most Neo-Confucians, Chang first rejected and finally attacked Buddhism. Neo-Confucians were particularly critical of Buddhist monasticism. They were appalled that people would be encouraged to attempt to escape their social responsibilities by renouncing familial and societal ties and joining a monastery. A basic Confucian criticism of such action was that it was the result of a selfish desire for personal salvation. The Neo-Confucians insisted with Mencius that human beings were essentially social beings who had innate tendencies towards an altruistic fiulfillment of duty without regard for personal benefit. As Confucians, the duties they particularly had in mind were those towards the members of one's own family. Thus monasticism was not consonant with filial piety and as such was unnatural and to be condemned. Chang's criticisms followed similar lines, but he criticized the Buddhists to some extent on philosophical grounds as well : "The Buddhists do not understand destiny decreed by Heaven and think that the production and annihilation of the universe are due to the elements of existence (dharmas) created by the mind. They regard the small (human consciousness) as the cause of the great (reality), and the secondary as the cause of the fundamental. Whatever they cannot understand thoroughly, they regard as illusion or error. They are indeed (summer insects) which doubt the existence of ice."[2]

Chang Tsai's final mature work is the *Cheng-meng* (Correcting Youthful Ignorance). Like Chou Tun-i and Shao Yung, Chang derives many of his ideas from the *I Ching*. Its emphasis on The

Great Harmony (*t'ai ho*) is quite different from the concept of necessary conflict that seems so deeply ingrained in so much of the Western European heritage. Thus from Chang's *Correcting Youthful Ignorance* :

> The Great Harmony is called the Way (Tao, Moral Law). It embraces the nature which underlies all counter processes of floating and sinking, rising and falling, and motion and rest. It is the origin of the process of fusion and intermingling, of overcoming and being overcome, and of expansion and contraction. At the commencement, these processes are incipient, subtle, obscure, easy, and simple, but at the end they are extensive, great, strong, and firm. It is *ch'ien* (Heaven) that begins with the knowledge of Change, *k'un* (Earth) that models after simplicity. That which is dispersed, differentiated and capable of assuming form becomes material force (*ch'i*), and that which is pure, penetrating, and not capable of assuming form becomes spirit. Unless the whole universe is in the process of fusion and intermingling like fleeting forces moving in all directions, it may not be called Great Harmony.[3]

Essentially Chang Tsai presents a philosophy of *ch'i*, the basic "stuff" which fills the universe, from which all things arise and into which they eventually return. Chang writes :

> As the Great Vacuity, material force is extensive and vague. Yet it ascends and descends and moves in all ways without ever ceasing. This is what is called in the *Book of Changes* "fusion and intermingling" and in the *Chuang Tzu* "fleeting forces moving in all directions while all living beings blow against one another with their breath." Here lies the subtle, incipient activation of reality and unreality, of motion and rest, and the beginning of yin and yang, as well as the elements of strength and weakness. Yang that is clear ascends upward, whereas yin that is turbid sinks downward. As a result of their contact and influence and of their integration and disintegration, winds and rains, snow and frost come into being. Whether it be the countless variety of things in their changing configurations or the mountains and rivers in

> their fixed forms, the dregs of wine or the ashes of fire, there is nothing (in which the principle) is not revealed.[4]

What we have here is Chou Tun-i's interpretation of the phenomenon of the *yin/yang* polarization but with the concept of ranges of solidification or of materialization—in other words, the concept of energization as the polar dynamic of materialization —rather than a more static concept of matter found in but a single state.

Again Chang writes in his *Correcting Youthful Ignorance* : "If yin and yang do not exist, the One (the Great Ultimate) cannot be revealed. If the One cannot be revealed, then the function of the two forces will cease. Reality and unreality, motion and rest, integration and disintegration, and clearness and turbidity are two different substances. In the final analysis, however, they are one."[5] This *one* he sometimes described as the Great Harmony (*t'ai ho*), which he characterized for the most part in terms of the "wandering Air" (*yeh ma*) or the Ether(s). This theory of the ethers in their microcosmic/macrocosmic relations may sound too 'medieval' to most of us, but if one has some inkling of the effectiveness of the breathing exercises of hatha yoga, one may begin to have some notion of its importance. The wole of the cosmos is conceived, in an almost Whiteheadian sense, as varying degrees of condensation of the primordial *ch'i*.

Chang Tsai lays more stress on the "manying" of the one than was the tendency in the ninth century. But his equation of the *ch'i* with the Void shows him still closely linked with the "cultivators of emptiness" who had preceded him. "The Great Void (*t'ai hsü*)," he writes, "in which no shapes exist : such is the Ether in its original essence." The Void is not to be confused with the idea of the vacuum, for Chang is quite explicit : "There is no non-existence." "What constitutes a single object, yet has two embodiments, is the Ether. Being single, it has spirituality (*shen*); being dual, it has transforming force (*hua*)." In the cosmological framework, Chang speculates as follows :

> In its original state of great Vacuity, material force is absolutely tranquil and formless. As it is acted upon, it en-

> genders the two fundamental elements of yin and yang, and through integration gives rise to forms. As there are forms, there are their opposites. These opposites necessarily stand in opposition to what they do. Opposition leads to conflict, which will necessarily be reconciled and resolved. Thus the feelings of love and hate are both derived from the great Vacuity, and they ultimately result in material desires. Suddenly to bring into existence and promptly to bring to completion without a moment's interruption—this is indeed the wonderful operation of spirit.[6]

The problem of the other which is so prominent here has its marked parallels in Rāmānuja, al-Fārābī, Psellos to some extent, and in Anselm and many others. In general this emphasis illustrates our thesis that the stricter monistic tendency of the ninth century comes into a self-othering, so to speak, in the eleventh century and this expands to an all-encompassing comprehensiveness by the thirteenth century.

Chang Tsai's identification of T'ien, *wu* and *yu* with *ch'i* is almost as revolutionary as Marx's turning Hegel's Dialectic "back on its feet" by asserting the primacy of matter which has within itself the *śakti* of cultural and historical development. We wonder whether any Chinese philosopher, even Wang Ch'ung, went so far as this. Chang's equating of the Great Void and *ch'i* makes it a dynamic ultimate rather than the static Absolute Brahman of the Advaitins. In this respect he may be closer to Abhinavagupta's efforts at reconciling the ontology of Śaiva 'Vedānta' with the dynamism of Buddhist *kṣaṇavāda*.

Although the relation between *ch'i* and *li* was not fully worked out until Chu Hsi's enlargement and synthesis of what had preceded him, in Chang Tsai we have the seminal concept of the inseparability of *li* and *ch'i*. That is to say that orderliness pervades all reality; we cannot know anything about this ultimate orderliness except through its manifestation-in-concretion. Thus Chang insists :

> According to principle nothing exists alone. Unless there are similarity and difference, contraction and expansion, and

> beginning and end among things to make it stand out, it is not really a thing although it seems to be. To become complete (to attain individuality), a thing must have a beginning and an end. But completion cannot be achieved unless there is mutual influence between similarity and difference (change) and between being and non-being (becoming). If completion is not achieved, it is not really a thing although it seems to be. Therefore it is said, "Contraction and expansion act on each other and thus advantages are produced."[7]

Chang is often characterized as a monist, and it is true that for him all things are essentially the same insofar as they are composed of *ch'i.* However, such a characterization can be somewhat misleading, for Chang neither ignores nor downplays individuality. He is certainly not a monist in the strict Advaitin sense, rejecting all difference as illusory. He maintains that every individual is just that *unique* in its own right, *different* from everything else. Certainly we have come a long way from the monistic tendencies of Li Ao. Specifically Chang writes :

> The Great Vacuity of necessity consists of material force. Material force of necessity integrates to become the myriad things. Things of necessity disintegrate and return to the Great Vacuity....[8]
>
> No two of the products of creation are alike. From this we know that although the number of things is infinite, at bottom there is nothing without yin or yang (which differentiate them). From this we know also that the transformations and changes in the universe are due to these two fundamental forces.[9]

Chang cannot reject differences as illusory because ultimately they are all manifestations of the fundamental differences between *yin* and *yang*. Although these are two aspects of the *same* reality *ch'i,* nevertheless they are *two*. Thus Chang's monism is a qualified one and he is perhaps more comparable to his Viśiṣṭādvaitin contemporary Yamunācārya. We may say that in Chang we find a dynamic harmonization of identity and individuality which suggests a comparison with Abhinavagupta. Chang Tsai says not only that the undifferentiated *ch'i* becomes individuated and manifests in the virtually infinite number of individuals, but that the Undifferentiated is not some mystical Absolute or Idea-beyond-our-comprehension (in Abhinavagupta's case, the Parama Śiva). Again, almost equally in China, India, Persia, Arabia, Byzantium and Western Europe monistic doctrines were uppermost in the ninth century; but by the eleventh, in the West through the growing influence of Aristotle, in China through the Neo-Confucian revival, and in India through the reassertion of the indigenous Dravidian elements against the Vedic Sanskritic elements, this reassertion of difference becomes the dominant note.

Chang Tsai has attracted a good deal of attention in the People's Republic of China on account of his "materialism". The orthodox Maoist interpretation of Chang is given by Hou Wai Lu : "Like Liu Tsung-yüan he accepted matter as the primary substance of the universe. He considered birth and death as a process of condensation and dispersion of matter. He emphatically pointed out that development and changes in the universe are a result of contradiction within matter itself, the result of the 'interaction' between the 'two extremes' of positive and negative forces and not by any external cause."[10] For the history of philosophy it may be that much depends on whether one is dependent more on the history of religions than the history of science. One may easily concede too much to the stereotype prejudice that there was little in science until the Italian Renaissance that was philosophically significant. But since the work of Sarton, Needham and an increasing number of others working on the history of the sciences in other civilizations than that of modern and postmodern Euramerica-*cum*-Russia, such a stereotype is not as welcome as once it was taken for granted without question.

For Chang there is a harmonious transition from ontology to psychology through the application of the same sort of metaphysics to human nature. For man is not a creature in necessary conflict with nature but simply the highest and greatest embodiment of the *ch'i*. "The Heavenly endowed nature in man is comparable to the nature of water in ice. It is the same whether the ice freezes or melts. Water's reflection of light may be much or little, dark or bright, but in receiving the light, it is the same in all cases."[11]

In ethics Chang is best known as author of the extremely influential *Western Inscription.* According to Chan, "Just as Chou Tun-i's short essay on the diagram of the Great Ultimate has become the basis of Neo-Confucian metaphysics, so Chang's 'Western Inscription' has become the basis of Neo-Confucian ethics. Ch'eng I was not exaggerating when he said that there was nothing like it since Mencius."[12]
Since it is both brief and basic, we present it in its entirety :

> Heaven is my father and Earth is my mother, and even such a small creature as I find an intimate place in their midst.
>
> Therefore that which fills the universe I regard as my body and that which directs the universe I consider as my nature.
>
> All people are my brothers and sisters, and all things are my companions.
>
> The great ruler (the emperor) is the eldest son of my parents (Heaven and Earth), and the great ministers are his stewards. Respect the aged—this is the way to treat them as elders should be treated. Show deep love toward the orphaned and the weak—this is the way to treat them as the young should be treated. The sage identifies his character with that of Heaven and Earth, and the worthy is the most outstanding man. Even those who are tired, infirm, crippled, or sick; those who have no brothers or children, wives or husbands, are all my brothers who are in distress and have no one to turn to.
>
> When the time comes, to keep himself from harm—this is the care of a son. To rejoice in Heaven and to have no anxiety—this is filial piety at its purest.
>
> He who disobeys (the Principle of Nature) violates virtue. He who destroys humanity is a robber. He who promotes evil lacks (moral) capacity. But he who puts his moral nature into practice and brings his physical existence into complete fulfillment can match (Heaven and Earth).

> One who knows the principles of transformation will skillfully carry forward the undertakings (of Heaven and Earth), and one who penetrates spirit to the highest degree will skillfully carry out their will.
>
> Do nothing shameful in the recesses of your own house and thus bring no dishonor to them. Preserve your mind and nourish your nature and thus (serve them) with untiring effort.
>
> The Great Yü hated pleasant wine but attended to the protection and support of his parents. Border Warden Ying brought up and educated the young and thus extended his love to his own kind.
>
> Shun's merit lay in delighting his parents with unceasing effort, and Shen-sheng's reverence was demonstrated when he awaited punishment without making an attempt to escape.
>
> Tsang Ts'an received his body from his parents and reverently kept it intact throughout life, while Po-ch'i vigorously obeyed his father's command.
>
> Wealth, honor, blessing, and benefits are meant for the enrichment of my life, while poverty, humble station, and sorrow are meant to help me to fulfillment.
>
> In life I follow and serve (Heaven and Earth). In death I will be at peace.[13]

The suggestion that "Heaven is my father and Earth is my mother" should not be misread. Chang is not to be interpreted as suggesting that the universe is under the guidance of anthropomorphic deities. The Neo-Confucian tradition consistently rejected theism. Rather, the *Western Inscription* should be viewed as an extended analogy and an attempt to base an entire social and political philosophy upon the model of familial duties. Such an approach is characteristic of the Chinese tradition, but uncommon elsewhere.

The family, of course, is a hierarchy in which distinctions are natural and proper. Thus the theme of love-with-distinctions is also characteristically Confucian. There are, however, other themes in Chang Tsai's ethical philosophy which are less orthodox :

> By enlarging one's mind, one can enter into all the things in the world (to examine and understand their principle). As long as anything is not yet entered into, there is still something outside the mind. The mind of ordinary people is limited to the narrowness of what is seen and what is heard. The sage, however, fully develops his nature and does not allow what is seen or heard to fetter his mind. He regards everything in the world to be his own self. This is why Mencius said that if one exerts his mind to the utmost, he can know nature and Heaven. Knowledge coming from seeing and hearing is knowledge obtained through contact with things. It is not knowledge obtained through one's moral nature. Knowledge obtained through one's moral nature does not originate from seeing or hearing.[14]

This expansion of mind is suggestive of the Buddhist meditative technique of immeasurable contemplation. Here the meditator concentrates in turn upon love, compassion, sympathetic joy, and equanimity. He systematically widens the circle of beings towards which he feels such emotions until all sentient beings are included. It is not clear that such egalitarian tendencies are compatible with traditional Confucianism. And again :

> One's nature is the one source of all things and is not one's own private possession. It is only the great man who is able to know and practice its principle to the utmost. Therefore, when he establishes himself, he will help others to establish themselves. He will share his knowledge with all. He will love universally. When he achieves something, he wants others to achieve the same. As for those who are so obstructed themselves (by selfishness) as not to understand this principle of mine, nothing can be done.[15]

The reference to universal love is an allusion to Mo Tzu's *chien ai*, which traditional Confucians had consistently rejected since love of all beings without distinction is not natural and therefore is not the way to run society, for without subordination there can be no organization. Here again was a point of difference between orthodox Confucianism and Buddhism of the *Lotus*

Sūtra heritage; for if everyone equally can become a Buddha, then everyone is deserving of the same respect and honor. Hence by invoking Mo Tzu, Chang is in effect attempting to synthesize Buddhist and Confucian teachings.

Fung suggests that for Chang Tsai the emphasis was on attaining the proper state of mind for performing the daily round of duties rather than on some ultimate mystical or transcendental end, howsoever alluring. Then as reward one may say with Chang, "In life I shall serve unresistingly, and when death comes, I shall be at peace." Chang's traditional Confucian view on the influence of the sage is comparable to the Hindu *jīvan-mukti* ideal such as that propounded by Abhinavagupta; if anyone truly achieves sagehood the whole world will be benefited for many ages to come.

Chang Tsai's very great influence on later Neo-Confucianism is indicated in the following by Tang Chün-i :

> In Chang Tsai's doctrine of the mind, emphasis is placed on its void character, and this void is derived from the Supreme Void whereas the concept of reason is made secondary. The Ch'ēng-and-Chu school substituted reason for void and assumed nature as the manifestation of the cosmic reason. Chang says that apart from oneself there is a universe with which one ought to enter into a union. While Ch'ēng Hao says, "Every activity of the universe is an activity of myself," and "The universe and onself are not two, and there is no point of talking about their union," Lu Chiu-yüan says, "The universe is my mind and my mind is the universe." And finally, Wang Shou-jēn says that man's intuitive knowledge (*liang-chih*) is the cosmic reason, and that the *liang-chih* of one single man is the *liang-chih* of the universe and of all things. If Chang Tsai had not established for the mind an objective cosmic basis, these philosophers after him would not have been able to elevate the human mind to the same high level as the heavenly mind. And, if one did not comprehend what Chang Tsai called the void of the mind, one would not be able to grasp what the Ch'ēng-and-Chu school called reason, or what the Lu-and-Wang school referred to as the original mind that is one with the cosmos and all things.[16]

An historical approach to Chang Tsai's interpretation of the Supreme Void should be the best since it stems back at least to Kumārajīva in the Chinese Mahāyāna heritage and in the Taoist tradition can be traced much further back.

25. Bahya Ibn Paquda

Like Ibn Gabirol, Bahya Ibn Paquda (fl. 1050-1080) is remembered as a literary figure influencing Spanish letters and as a philosopher. He was a Jewish Neo-Platonist and author of the first systematic philosophical work on ethics in the Jewish tradition (although some might claim that for Saadia or Gabirol). His *Duties of the Heart* was written in Arabic in 1040 and became very popular. No other works by Bahya are known, but that one little classic has evidently enjoyed a reputation perhaps comparable to the *Imitatio Christi* in recent years. It was translated not only into Hebrew but into virtually all the vernaculars of Europe. Vajda[1] says that this is another instance where the book has eclipsed the author. It is fairly certain that he did not have access to the works of al-Ghazālī, contrary to some opinions; but there are common traits between his world-view and that of the Ikhwān al-Ṣafā, and he was no doubt influenced by the Ṣūfī tradition. Vajda says that actually Bahya is quite eclectic in his sources and not a slave to any set tradition.

Bahya Ibn Paquda wrote his *Duties of the Heart* basically as a rebuke to the ritualistic rabbis of his time who were more concerned with outward observances and obligations than inward and truly spiritual concerns. Still Bahya's 'way' sought a balance between reason, revelation and tradition; hence we infer that he was still within the bounds of orthodoxy and was only trying to make the dry bones come to life again. Theologically he, like all the Abrahamic philosophers of his era, put primary emphasis on God's unity and existence; but also God's wisdom, power and goodness figure in his perspective, and that in such a way that marvelling at the wonders of nature as the manifestation of these attributes is prominent in his writing.

According to Bahya, science (*'ilm*), in classical style, is divisible into two parts or members : exterior science, and "the science of the duties of the heart", or interior science. All of the duties of the heart are founded on reason, and include :

> ... To believe in a Creator who formed the universe *ex nihilo*; to profess His absolute Unity exempt from all participation; to obey Him in our heart to discover Him by contemplation of His creatures; to become abandoned to Him; to humble oneself before Him and to fear Him; to live in the conviction that He is informed of all our acts and of all our thoughts; to love those He loves, and to hate those He hates, by cultivating the sentiments which do not lead us into exterior distractions by any act.[2]

Such a list is classic in the sense that it could be paralleled in virtually every one of Bahya's contemporaries in Eurasia.

To say the least, the *Duties of the Heart* is not concerned with mere sentimental piety; rather it is a full-blown scholastic work of the highest order, systematically planned and systematically incorporating some very thorough scholarship. In the technical terms of Catholic tradition this should be termed as an exercise in ascetic theology. What emerges in this work is a sensitivity to the interior life consciously cultivated and an exploration into the depths of human nature such as most modern secularists have lost, lacking any conception of these disciplines of inward control. Yet 'yoga' as interior discipline is by no means limited to the esoterics of Hindu or Zen methods but may be found in all traditions if only one does proper research with an open mind.

In his view of man as microcosm, Bahya has an attitude toward human nature which reminds us of the Renaissance Platonists later such as Pico della Mirandola, marvelling at man's basic superiority to the other creatures on earth. In this human reason figures as the most important faculty, since that faculty gives man not only means of knowledge of the physical universe but of discovering God and His attributes and our obligations toward Him. Nevertheless, man is limited in two dimensions : body and soul. In the soul itself there are two opposite tendencies or properties, namely concupiscence and reason. Vajda compares Bahya in these matters with Hujīri, who attributed the creation of what we commonly know as 'civilization' to the lower faculties, the higher having an almost strictly supramundane function, being reserved for more rigorously ascetic selfless disciplines leading to God.

Reason, Bahya says, is a subtle substance and is a stranger in the gross body. As a Neo-Platonist he stresses the view of the soul as 'imprisoned' in the body, but the emphasis is more on the higher possibilities of human capacities than on the imprisonment since the body is seen as necessary in order to facilitate the exercise of the disciplines necessary to spiritual attainment. As with the Ikhwān al-Ṣafā, for Bahya reason is that which governs not only human ascesis or *sādhanā* but also the cosmic process of emanation itself; and it is this perspective that the usual dualism of matter and soul is transported into a larger perspective. Submission or obedience is interpreted not as an onerous burden in a context of struggle and conflict, but as a rational means of freeing reason to perform its natural function, which is to lead man to knowledge of the Law first, and then reasonable rather than fanatical conformity to it. Rational obedience is like a seed, the Law is like the earth in which it is planted, and the divine assistance is like fertilizing rain.

Whether Bahya ever achieved satisfaction in regard to the problem of providence and free will is somewhat doubtful. What he does seem to lean toward is that all the realm of nature known externally is strictly determined; but as one gets further into the interiority of motivation, into rational submission to the Law which is already determined, then increasingly one finds some spark of freedom. It is classically true with virtually all spiritual guides that the most interior is the most superior, so that freedom comes with 'elevation'. But elevation entails greater submission and obedience to God, so that one gains more freedom as one surrenders all freedom one has won, for such (rational) submission/surrender is intensively of more value than freedom. For Bahya, once the love of God is aroused, zeal takes the place of the notion of freedom, and aesthetic delight in singing His praises creatively crowns all the previous moralizings—which was also true of the many Ṣūfīs who could well have influenced him. Love of God comes after one has reached the highest submission rationally to the Law. But such *bhakti* entails all sorts of delicate virtues not easy to practice, especially in the hurly-burly of worldly affairs. The chief of these virtues is constant recollection or permanent remembrance or awareness of the presence of God, and a sort of rational fear of losing that sense of communion. Again we might remember Rāmānuja's metaphor that such love of God should be like a steady small stream of oil feeding a vigil lamp.

The Unity of God necessarily entails the governance of the universe by Him. Thus, as one might say, at the risk of accepting predestination and denial of freedom, Bahya teaches *tawakkul* or abandon—which is perhaps close to *prapatti* in the then-emerging Rāmānuja tradition. Vajda writes :

> Concerning Tawakkul, Bahya gives a definition that is quite complex. The indispensable foundation of this attitude is the confidence that He to whom we abandon ourselves will not only accomplish what He has promised, but that He will also do, out of His generosity and benevolence, much more than He had engaged Himself to accomplish. From that confidence is born the tranquillity of the soul and the assurance that the object of our confidence will do whatever He knows is best and most salutary for us.[3]

Here we find the generosity of undeserved grace such as one finds in Vaiṣṇava and Amida Buddhist traditions. *Maḥabba* or love of God is the key to the virtue or practice of surrender. Through love of God one becomes disinterested in both this world and the next. The best spiritual guides generally and not alone Bahya counsel detachment even in regard to spiritual things. Some even go so far, as we have long since seen in the Bodhisattva vow, to counsel deliberate transdescendence—almost renunciation of renunciation; but others say not so, since it will happen any way.

Concerning penitence, the Judeo-Christian sense of guilt and remorse and constant moralizing about it seems to have a slightly different flavor than found in other traditions. In

Hinduism and to some extent in Buddhism and Jainism also, the emphasis generally is a concern with accumulation of good and bad karma, or rather the quest to be delivered from both in order to cease the endless round of causation. Indeed that is the secret all the way through to the *pratītyasamutpāda* and the Śūnyavāda concept of the Middle Way. Hence penance and *tapas* are more common than penitence. In the Confucian milieu, although there are exceptions, it is a matter of rectification, of self-rectification in order to seek restoration of one's original (good) nature; thus it is basically a humanistic ideal rather than one provoked by Fear of Judgment and the Wrath of the Lord. Hence, as Wing-tsit Chan is fond of saying, "we prefer to negotiate" ! For those coming from Chinese or Indian backgrounds it may be difficult to understand that *sin* is the problem, and sin is basically defined as disobedience to the Revealed Law. This needs emphasizing in contrast to the classical Buddhist emphasis not on sin but on ignorance and suffering. Of course there are many exceptions to this generalization about penitence. For example, although in Peter Damien we find almost an excessive scrupulosity, the Christian humanism of Michael Psellos is so rounded out and leavened with classical Apollonian grace and cultivation of excellence that the problem of penitence scarcely figures at all. For Bahya, penitence is reparation rather than abject emotional begging for mercy. Hence penitence for Bahya is basically a "return to obedience". Utter sincerity is the requirement of true penitence. Thus he too might be curious about all the fuss over "guilt feelings" since he is not interested in 'feelings' at all but in factual and actual wrongs done and in actual ways of recompense and rectification.

Zuhd means renunciation, detachment, abstinence, ascesis. "It is the submission of the passions of the soul, voluntary abstention even from the object of the ascesis. It is in this sense that one has said, 'An ascete is he who can accomplish something—and leave it behind'."[4] Ascesis is practiced by the faithful because the law and reason recommend it for the greatest possible good of the soul in the present and in the life to come. Bahya does sanction the special asceticism of the anchorites, the hermits and prophetic ascetics, the solitary 'yogīs', who renounce not only the passions and seek to control desires but even renounce society completely. Nevertheless, for Bahya it is really necessary only to satisfy the ordinary virtues of the average sort : goodwill, discretion, humility, sincerity, and frequent association with the pious—nothing sensational at all, no miracles, no astral body, no secrets of astrology, no psychic tricks. Extremes are discouraged since the Law is sufficient if followed sincerely. Likew se asceticism should not be a matter of discouragement of all joy, for just as the Law does prescribe fasts and proscribe certain practices, so it does provide and even enjoins feasts and times of rejoicing. But the over-all counsel is that it is not the actual deeds so much as the abiding attention and recollection of God's constant Presence that is the main thing, all else being only means to maintain that constancy whether in adversity or even in ecstasy.

In spite of his learning in the Jewish canon, Bahya's thoughts are very much moulded by his Islamic milieu. For example, he does not omit a reference to the definitely Muslim doctrine of *jihād*, and that closely connected with the literature about *zuhd*. But he takes it in Muḥāsibī's interpreration in which the true *jihād* is against passions in one's own life and soul. Of course Bahya had the chosen nation/people concept. We have long since dilated on this aspect of so many peoples. Certainly the Chinese had it, and were profoundly disturbed by the Mongol invasion because of it, although they interpreted that event as merely the loss of the Will of Heaven, which they recovered. Brahmanical India was also shocked by the inroads of Islam on their "twice-born" prerogatives, while the Muslims considered it their divinely appointed chosen-people mission to deliver these idolaters from all that was contrary to their revelation, never realizing that the Hindus also believed in their Vedas as revelation. We have to wait really for Akbar in the sixteenth century before we find any gesture historically toward a larger tolerance and accommodation to these "chosen people" claims—but even Akbar thought he had a special revelation of his own! Needless to say, it would be difficult to universalize the claim to uniqueness of the Jewish prophetic revelation in the face of all the other similar claims. But that much can be observed, that each tradition seems to need the *sense of uniqueness* howsoever difficult it may be to reconcile conflicting claims.

On the whole Bahya Ibn Paquda gives a more prominent place to reason than many of his Muslim predecessors and contemporaries, even in the economy of the interior life, although his intellectualism is far from a mere cold calculation such as happened to some extent among the later thirteenth and fourteenth century logicians at Paris and in the Navya Nyāya school. Rather the Mu'tazilite and Ṣūfī influences give a more humane, warm-hearted flavor to his thinking. Reason is the binding thread that keeps the pieces together so that they form one whole garment, as it were. Reason naturally, as inherently part of man's God-given nature, guides him to realize the advantages of the virtues and of observing the Law, whose purpose itself after all is not the strengthening of reason so much as the regulation of the human tendency to go to extremes. Reason, in short, is the instrument *par excellence* in Bahya's method and approach to the contemplative vocation

26. Ch'eng Hao and Ch'eng I

With Ch'eng Hao (1032-1085) and Ch'eng I (1033-1107) we have one of those rare occasions in the world history of philosophy where two brothers became major philosophers. One other such occasion was with Asaṅga and Vasubandhu in the Indian Mahāyāna Buddhist tradition. Ch'eng Hao and Ch'eng I also represent two different lines of development in the Neo-Confucian movement. Ch'eng Hao influenced Lu Hsiang-shan, the major proponent of idealistic Neo-Confucianism, and may be said to have inaugurated the idealistic school of Neo-Confucianism, while Ch'eng I influenced Chu Hsi, the major proponent of rationalistic Neo-Confucianism, and may be said to have inaugurated the rationalistic school of Neo-Confucianism. Nevertheless, the Ch'eng brothers philosophized on the same themes and agreed on very many points. Indeed, many of the sayings in *The Complete Works of the Two Ch'engs* wherein we find their views are not clearly attributed to one of the brothers as opposed to the other. Still they can be definitely distinguished in their respective idealistic and rationalistic trends and can be said to have established that dual pattern in the development of Neo-Confucianism, i.e., the Lu-Wang School or *Hsin-Hsüeh Chia*, School of the Study of Mind, and the Ch'eng-Chu School or *Li-Hsüeh Chia* School of study of Principle.

Ch'eng Hao and I were nephews of Chang Tsai, friends of Shao Yung, and studied with Chou Tun-i. These five together are sometimes known as the Five Masters of early Sung philosophy. The brothers were quite different in temperament. "Ch'eng Hao was warm, always at ease, tolerant, agreeable, understanding, amiable, and never angry for as long as twenty years. Ch'eng I, on the other hand, was stern, grave, straight, not hesitating to shout at people..."[1] Ch'eng I says of Hao : "From the time when, at fifteen or sixteen, he heard Chou Tun-i discourse on the Way, he got tired of preparing for civil service examinations and arduously made up his mind to seek the Way. Not knowing the essential steps, he drifted among the various schools of thought and went in and out of the Taoist and Buddhist schools for almost ten years. Finally he returned to the Six Classics (of Confucianism) and only then did he find the Way."[2] According to reports Ch'eng I was so punctillious in his exemplary decorum that one cannot but sympathize with those in the court, including the party of Wang An-shih, who were eventually responsible for his demotion, criticizing this as proper but excessive. Concerning Ch'eng I's unruffled comportment, there is the anecdote that while crossing a river in a boat a heavy wind blew up. Most of the passengers were terribly disturbed, fearing the worst, but Ch'eng I remained undisturbed. After they had all reached the other shore safely, one fellow-passenger asked him what was his secret. His answer was very benevolent : "I simply keep my mind under control." But sensing his dignified Confucian pride, a Zen monk who had also been in the boat incisively said : "Not enough! Leave your mind on the other shore!" and disappeared before the Master could catch him for further instruction. This anecdote may be taken as an illustration of the importance of Ch'an Buddhism as the counter-foil for the Neo-Confucian synthesis.

It remains to the credit of the Ch'eng brothers that they were the first ones to establish *li* (principle) as aprimary concept for Neo-Confucianism. The concept of *ch'i* (material force) in the *li/ch'i* pair had already been well established, especially by Chang Tsai. Nevertheless, *li* would not be given its fullest exposition until Chu Hsi. As Chan explains :

> As conceived and understood by the brothers, principle is self-evident and self-sufficient, extending everywhere and governing all things. It cannot be augmented or diminished. It is many but it is essentially one, for all specific principles are but principle. It is laid before our very eyes. Man and all things form one body because all of them share this principle. To be sincere is to be sincere to it, and to be serious is to be serious about it. In short, it is one and all. It is identical with the mind and it is identical with the nature. All things exist because of it and can be understood through it. It is universal truth, universal order, universal law. Most important of all, it is a universal process of creation and production. It is dynamic and vital.
>
> It can easily be seen that to the Ch'eng brothers this principle means both natural principles and moral principles, and both general principles and specific principles. They were not much concerned with abstract reality, for they were primarily interested in the meaning of principle for man. Thus they turned Neo-Confucianism from speculation on cosmology to concentrate on the problems of principle and human nature, thereby making Neo-Confucianism truly a School of Nature and Principle (*Hsing-li hsüeh*).[3]

Carsun Chang parallels this move from the cosmological speculations of Chou Tun-i, Shao Yung and Chang Tsai to the ethical and epistemological concerns of the Ch'eng brothers with the transition from Thales, Anaximander, Pythagoras and Heraclitus to the concern for human knowledge, nature, virtue and action on the part of Socrates and the Sophists.[4]

For Ch'eng Hao *li* does not exist apart from things, while for Ch'eng I *li* does exist apart from things. This is one of the themes where the brothers apparently differ and upon which there has been much discussion and debate. While Ch'eng Hao apparently made little distinction between the physical and metaphysical, Ch'eng I's view is sometimes compared to Plato's distinction between the physical (*ch'i*) and metaphysical (*li*).

In Ch'eng Hao we have something of the distinction that was also springing up in the Muslim and Christian scholastics between the *universalia ante rem, in re* and *post rem*—there is nothing at all of the complete dualism of the Cartesian sort or even of the sort that Mādhava soon advances. According to Ch'eng Hao :

> 'The operations of supreme Heaven proceed without sound, without smell.' Its essential character is said to be 'change' (*yi*); its Principle (*li*) is said to be the Way (*Tao*); its functioning is said to be 'spirituality' (*shen*); what it allots to man is said to be his 'nature' (*hsing*); the following of this nature is said to be the Way (of man); cultivation of this Way is said to be (moral) 'instruction' (*chiao*). ... There are many affairs, great and small, yet it is merely said that 'such is the impossibility of repressing the outgoings of sincerity (*ch'eng*).' Penetrating high and low, there is nothing more than this. In 'what is above shapes,' it is *Tao*; in 'what is within shapes,' it is instrument (*ch'i*). Though we are forced to express ourselves in this way, instrument is (really) also *Tao* and *Tao* is also instrument. Once we grant *Tao* to be present, it may then no longer be (specifically) associated with the present or the future, the self or the non-self.[5]

This qualified identity of means and end, of principle and instrument, reminds us rather vividly of Rāmānuja's *tattva-hita-puruṣārtha* triad: principle, means, and end are really one and the same from the *pāramārthika* point of view in such a way that man in the operationally necessitated world which manifests God's wonder-working play (*līlā*) partakes of the same structure analogically without compromising his individuality analytically.

As for ethical philosophy, Ch'eng Hao followed Mencius rather closely in his interpretation of *hsing* and *ming* (nature and destiny). Evil does not belong intrinsically to human nature, but good and evil are regarded as the products of the ethers (*ch'i*) prevalent at birth. He follows the old Taoist metaphor that like water, human nature will seek its own level. Man should therefore seek original nature, which is quiet and peaceful like a tranquil lake. As to spiritual cultivation, the Ch'engs seem to have incorporated much of the Buddhist methods of contemplation, but again linked them integrally with the Confucian virtues, especially *jen* and *ching*. Thus Ch'eng Hao:

> The student must first of all understand the nature of *jen*. The man of *jen* forms one body with all things without any differentiation. Righteousness, propriety, wisdom, and faithfulness are all (expressions of) *jen*.
>
> (One's duty) is to understand this principle (*li*) and preserve *jen* with sincerity and seriousness (*ching*), that is all. There is no need for caution and control. Nor is there any need for exhaustive search. Caution is necessary when one is mentally negligent, but if one is not negligent, what is the necessity for caution? Exhaustive search is necessary when one has not understood principle, but if one preserves *jen* long enough, it will automatically dawn on him. Why should he have to depend on exhaustive search?
>
> Nothing can be equal to this Way(Tao, that is, *jen*). It is so vast that nothing can adequately explain it. All operations of the universe are our operations. Mencius said that "all things are already complete in oneself" and that one must "examine oneself and be sincere (or absolutely real)" and only then will there be great joy. If one examines himself and finds himself not yet sincere, it means there is still an opposition between the two (the self and the non-self). Even if one tries to identify the self with the non-self, one still does not achieve unity. How can one have joy?...
>
> For our innate knowledge of good and innate ability to do good are originally not lost. However, because we have not gotten rid of the mind dominated by habits, we must preserve and exercise our original mind, and in time old habits will be overcome. This principle is extremely simple; the only danger is that people will not be able to hold on to it. But

> if we practice it and enjoy it, there need be no worry of our being unable to hold it.[6]

In Ch'eng Hao and in the Neo-Confucians generally there is not as much ascetic denial of the emotions as we find in the Taoists and Buddhists. Emotions should be regulated according to the proper occasion, but there is nothing wrong with them in themselves. Ch'eng Hao says: "The normality of the sage is that his emotions accord with the nature of all things, yet of himself he has no emotion." The important thing, in short, is the elimination of selfishness.

Sometimes it is a bit difficult to discern whether Ch'eng I believed that *li* and *Tao* are completely synonymous or merely so intimately related that it is difficult to distinguish between them without compromising their high level of abstraction. In his dealing with the concept of *li* one may see analogies if not definite parallels with the problem of universals in Islamic and Latin scholasticism about the same time. On the one hand Ch'eng I insists that *li* as such is independent of time and space and has no physical appearance in its own right; indeed, he almost associates it with the *Dharmakāya* or *Tathatā* concept in *Mahāyāna* Buddhism, but never openly, even though he indicates that in its own right (*suprarem*, as the Latin scholastics might say) it is "void and pure". Nevertheless, even though as such it is completely independent of human reasoning, it governs all particulars completely. Not only is the supreme *li* as the ultimate principle almost synonymous with the Tao, but every individual thing also has its particular *li*. In short, "*Li* is one but there is a diversity of duties", and "where there is a thing, there is bound to be a *li*—a Law".

In this as in many other respects, in spite of his more conservative manner, Ch'eng I is indebted to Chou Tun-i and Chang Tsai. But he rejects Mo Tzu's extreme, as he regards it, of excessive particularity without any generality, just as he rejects the elusiveness of esoteric Taoism and the vagueness of some interpretations of Ch'an 'emptiness'. Mo Tzu ran the risk of reduction to sentimentality because of lack of overriding principle; and his excessive pluralism leaves too much room for selfishness, in spite of his insistence on equality. For without *li* there is no order, and without order there is no propriety, and without propriety, society will degenerate into anarchistic barbarism. Therefore Mo Tzu was wrong. Even in these matters, ethics prevails over metaphysics.

In regard to *ch'i*, Chu Hsi did evidently seriously consider the concept of many series of *kalpas*, *yugas*, and/or other grand cycles of cosmic order of evolution and involution such as were taken for granted by the best of Buddhists and Hindus (notably Śaivism such as that of Abhinavagupta); but Ch'eng I did not see sufficeint evidence to support this view. In a sort of common-sense way, he observes that when fire is burning up wood, that is also the operation of *ch'i*; but when it has burned up all the wood, the *ch'i* is no longer there. It becomes exhausted in particular operations (even though ultimately it is always inexhaustibly operating from some source—perhaps the Tao in accordance with *li*). Likewise when two stones are struck together, sparks fly out and then disappear. That is also *ch'i* being exhausted in particulars. Therefore he rejects the Buddhist and Hindu concept of renewable ultimate cycles of creation. Ch'eng I, unlike Chang Tsai, "maintains that the Ether once dispersed reverts to nothingness and cannot condense again to form new objects. Such objects, he asserts, take shape only from newly produced Ether, quite unrelated to that already dispersed." The real relation between the *ch'i* and the ultimate source, whether considered as Prime Mover or as simply the Inconceivable (*pace* al-Fārābī and Anselm) which as mysteriously is Creator as much as Sustainer (*pace* Rāmānuja) or Destroyer (*pace* Nīlakaṇṭha) or Incarnation (Anselm and Rāmānuja).

Ch'eng I, while not disagreeing with Mencius, seems to have more closely integrated *hsing* and *ming* with *li*, and out of this coins the term *ts'ai* (capacity).

> Mencius is right when he says that the nature is good; neither Hsün nor Yang knew anything about it. It is because of his ability to understand the nature that Mencius has gained his unique position, exceeding that of the other literati. There is nothing in the nature itself that is not good; anything that is not good pertains to 'capacity' (*ts'ai*). The nature is the same as principle (*li*), which is uniform from Yao and

> Shun down to the man of little intelligence. But 'capacity' means the endowment of the Ether, some of which is clear and some turbid. Persons endowed with its clear elements are the worthies, while those endowed with its turbid elements are the stupid people.
>
> The nature derives from Heaven, while 'capacity' derives from the Ether. If the Ether is clear, 'capacity' is also clear but if the Ether is turbid, 'capacity' is also turbid. ... The case is like that of a tree: its (innate) crookedness or straightness is its nature, but its possibility of being made into the wheels or shafts of a carriage, or into the beams or pillars, clap-boards or rafters, of a house, is its 'capacity'. 'Capacity' may be either good or not good, but in the nature itself there is nothing that is not good.[7]

One may compare this *ts'ai* to the Aristotelian scholastic *potentia* or to the *hexis habitudo* in the Aristotelian system, or to Rāmānuja's distinction between *dharma* and *dharmin.*

Ch'eng I did not differ much from his brother on spiritual cultivation. He said: "Spiritual nature requires the application of earnestness (*ching*); the advancement of learning lies in the extension of knowledge." Such a classically simple statement is likely to go unnoticed until it is realized how profound such standards really are. Ch'eng I also counselled a primary emptiness of the mind as the key to proper attainments of all the positive virtues. However, he made a sharp distinction between the Buddhist sort of quiescence and his earnestness (*ching*).

> By speaking of quiescence one immediately falls into Buddhist doctrine. Not 'quiescence' but only 'earnestness' is the word that should be used. For as soon as one speaks of quiescence, the result is that 'forgetting' (of which Mencius speaks). Mencius says: "We must do something, and never stop and never forget, yet never help to grow." When there is this doing of something, then we do not forget, and when there is no stopping, then there is no (forcible) helping to grow.[8]

Nevertheless there is an important distinction between Ch'eng I and Ch'eng Hao on the theme of "investigation of things" (*ko wu*), which Chan explains:

> However, while Ch'eng Hao more or less concentrates on self-cultivation, Ch'eng I insists that self-cultivation and the extension of knowledge must be pursued at the same time. Here lies perhaps the greatest divergence between the two brothers. Ch'eng Hao said very little about the investigation of things. Ch'eng I, on the contrary, makes the investigation a cardinal concept in his system. Besides, for Ch'eng Hao, the investigation of things means to correct the mind of bad habits, but for Ch'eng I it means inductive and deductive study and handling human affairs, for, according to him, everything, however small, contains principle and is to be investigated. This is the rationalistic spirit that characterizes his whole philosophy and later that of his follower, Chu'Hsi (1130-1200), so that their school, called the Ch'eng-Chu School, may properly be called the Rationalistic School.[9]

The end result of such cultivation—which obviously should lead on to the systematic investigation of everything from astronomy to the nocturnal habits of butterflies, rather than the pathological bemoaning of 'sins', original, mortal and venial—would be a mind of this description: "The mind of a single person is the mind of Heaven and Earth: the Principle of a single thing is the Principle of all things; the cycle of a single day is the cycle of a whole year." Had we not seen already the practical counterbalances to this sort of opening of the realm of universal analogy, we should be cautious. But the Neo-Confucian Encompassing is one that does not transgress humility.

27. Wang An-shih

The philosophy of Wang An-shih (1021-1086) greatly influenced the subsequent developments in the Southern Sung, and therein lies his claim to historical significance even more than in his attempts at economic, political and educational reforms. In Wang's interpretation of Yao and Shun, provocatively different from the stereotype interpretations, lies his importance in the history of Chinese intellectual life. Even though the Ch'eng brothers' ideas finally prevailed, they did so only as a counter-attack against Wang's radical challenges. The fact that Wang's commentaries on the Confucian classics remained for a long time the standard text for the state examinations certainly is sufficient reason for not excluding him from any history of Neo-Confucianism.

For a general introduction to Wang An-shih, we note the following from Dun Li:

> Wang was soon promoted from a comparatively obscure position as magistrate of Nanking to that of Prime Minister. To the literary elite, however, Wang was no stranger. He had passed the imperial examinations with the highest honors, and his writings, both prose and poetry, had been widely acclaimed as the work of a true genius. He was said to have a photographic memory and a bad temper, never avoiding an argument or debate whenever he thought the issue involved was important. His personal life was frugal to the greatest extreme: he cared little for good food and good clothing, and it was even said that he seldom bathed. He had served with distinction as magistrate of Ningpo (modern Chekiang) before his appointment in Nanking. Once he sent a long petition to the reigning emperor urging sweeping reforms, but the petition was rejected and ignored. It was not until the accession to the throne of Sung Shen-tsung that he was given the opportunity to carrry out his reforms.[1]

Needham gives the following summary of Wang's achievements:

> Besides this upsurge of cultural activity, the Sung period also produced Wang An-shih, the second of the two great reformers in Chinese history. Unlike Wang Mang he never attained or desired the Emperor's Imperor yellow, but like him he took a lively interest in science and technology, and studied botany, medicine, agriculture and weaving.[2]

Thus Wang An-shih may well be rated alongside the other great polymath type of philosophers such as we need more of today. Needham continues:

> ..Mainly financial, they began with a reform of the Treasury, reducing embezzlement that went on and rationalizing the administration so effectively that he was able to save some forty percent of the national budget. Wang also abolished the system of transporting grain to the capital, establishing government warehouses in all large cities from which the grain could be sold directly instead. The taxes, which he based on new land surveys, could therefore be transmitted to the capital in cash. Government advances were instituted for farmers on the security of growing crops at cheaper than market interest rates while payments were allowed in lieu of forced labor. Introduction of luxury goods was restricted and any hoarding of commodities was heavily taxed. In addition to these measures, every ten families was grouped into one unit, and all members of that unit were responsible for the misdeeds of any one member. These units were also used as the basis for army conscription although large landowners had to furnish horses instead of men.[3]

Needham's judgment is that "although the reforms showed a surprising degree of original thought, they were too radical a departure from traditional feudal bureaucracy." And from de Bary *et al* we get this estimation :"...his approach was bold and visionary in the sense that he saw the problem of reform as reaching into virtually all spheres of Chinese life; and though few of his measures were new or highly original, his program taken as a whole was broader in scope and more diversified in character than anything attempted before or after (until Communist rule)."[4]

Lo Ssu-ting in his article entitled "Evolution of the Controversy between the Confucianists and the Legalists as seen from Wang An-shih's Reforms" goes all the way back to the time of Tung Chung-shu and briefly sketches the long and often obscure history of the Legalist tradition, coming rather quickly down to Liu Tsung-yuan (773-819). Wang An-shih himself is cited as often seeking "ideological weapons from the arsenal of the pre-Chin Legalists who had been advocates of reform...."[5] The chief spokesman for the opposition to Wang An-shih was Ssu-ma Kuang (1019-1086), who is described by Lo Ssu-ting as one of the "diehards of the big landlord class". We are reminded that the ideological work of the opposition was done by the 'political' group Ch'eng Hao (1032-1085) and Ch'eng I (1033-1107) and their predecessors and collaborators.

Wang An-shih was for *change*, and the traditionalist Confucianists were definitely not. Wang was not timid about stating his position in no uncertain language; thus he is quoted as insisting, "Natural changes need not be feared, ancestral ways need not be followed, and others' slanders need not be heeded."[6] Legalist or not, this is the heart of the conflict between Wang and his opponents and the cause of vascillation of opinions about him through subsequent centuries. Thus Ssu-ma Kuang, the leader of the traditionalist opposition, insisted that "Heaven changes not, likewise the Way changes not", thereby implying that "the laws decreed by the ancestors must not be changed". Wen Yen-po (1006-1097), another member of the opposition party, is quoted as writing, "The laws already established by nacestors must not be altered". To this Wang retorted, "The laws decreed by the ancestors are not worth observing. From ancient times, they have never been observed."[7]

The traditionalists were big landlords with many villages in their possession, whereas Wang's party belonged to the lower class, scarcely proletarians but "small and medium" landlords. Thus class contradiction did have a major role to play (whether or not Wang could be seen as a sort of social scientist of his time). As soon as he became Chancellor one of the first things he did was to promulgate a Land Reform measure to prevent the big landowners from adding even more to their possessions. At first this may seem unique and even modern; but it had been done before, and since then too long before Mao Tse-tung. But what Wang attempted was one of the most thorough and we might even say scientific projects in the whole of Chinese history if not in universal history until very recent times. That his revolution did virtually amount to a sort of pre-Leninist "dictatorship of the proletariat" could be claimed of Wang in the light of the fact that Ssu-ma Kuang and his colleagues accused him of "using the humble people to bully the aristocrats and unruliness to impair propriety,... seizing the wealth of the rich", and promoting measures for the welfare of the poor.[8]

The extent to which Chinese society then was in the stricter sense a "feudal" system might be debated since some investigators are beginning to wonder something like a capitalist system, including inflated currency and usury and all the rest of 'investment finance', had not already developed (what a pity that Marx himself or Lenin did not know more of the actual rather than the semi-mythological history of China inherited from Hegel). At any rate, Lo Ssu-ting comments on why Wang was not successful :

> The social crisis of the Sung dynasty stemmed from the feudal system itself. Wang An-shih, acting within the historical limitations of the landlord class, imagined that by taking the path of reform he could patch up the feudal system without touching its foundation. He was traveling down a blind alley. Even his Legalist thinking was not thorough, so he could not fully shake off the bonds of Confucianism. Moreover, his reforms were weaker in practice than they were in theory, suspended at times and resumed at others, applied strictly at times and slackly at others. In fact, they were never seriously enforced.[9]

Actually, realizing where his chief weakness lay, namely in the lack of adequate personnel, Wang did all within his power quite selflessly (in a way that not only Chairman Mao but also no doubt Mahatma Gandhi would have approved as meeting the requirement in the *Gītā* of *niṣkāma karma*), but before he could train a new generation of reliable and able youth to take over, reaction set in.

Like so many other reformers, Wang has been blamed by camps of both extremes. The 'radicals' blame him for not being rigorous enough, while the conservatives or 'reactionaries' blame him even for the downfall of the Northern Sung Dynasty. Lo Ssu-ting cites Lu Hsun :

> Without exception, the scholars of the Sung dynasty harped on Neo-Confucianism, holding Confucius in high esteem. Although there were a few reformers, such as Wang An-shih, who tried to enforce reforms for a time, they failed for lack of support Consequently, everybody continued to sing the old tune, which had nothing to do with social realities, until the end of the Sung dynasty.[10]

Lo also records the opinion of Li Tz'u-ming of the Ch'ing Dynasty :

> Wang An-shih's reforms in the Sung dynasty ended in chaos. This was a profound lesson to later generations. Anyone who attempted even a mild reform would meet a hail of opposition and be labeled "another Wang An-shih." So everybody remained mute and subservient, afraid to utter any opinion.[11]

The disapproval of Chu Hsi was largely responsible for the bad reputation heaped upon Wang An-shih in future centuries. During the Ming Dynasty, Chou Te-king, whom Lo describes as a reactionary follower of the Neo-Confucian school, dubbed Wang An-shih as "the meanest man in history".

Lo Ssu-ting notes that the famous Tai Chen (1723-1777) learned to criticize the Confucian classics by a restudy of Wang An-shih. Ts'ai Shang-hsiang, who did approve of Wang's attempts at reform, registers the opinion that perhaps one of the reasons why those reforms failed was that Wang tried too hard to make them appear as still in conformity with Confucian ideals.

According to Hou Wai Lu, if anything Wang's views on Nature erred, if at all, not in conforming too much to Confucian 'idealism' but to mechanist rather than dialectical materialism. Hou writes : "Wang An-shih's theory was that matter was the primary substance of the universe and that all things were composed of the five elements of metal, wood, water, fire, and earth. These five elements existed externally in the universe and were in constant motion."[12] If not direct influence, the similarity with Shao Yung's views are pretty clear, and also in the same nexus is Chang Ts'ai of the same century. Whether these were outright materialists as much, China in the period of the Northern Sung had achieved a level of scientific thinking scarcely rivalled elsewhere at that time except perhaps with Ibn Ḥazm and others in the Islamic world. Hou Wai Lu continues :

> There is change and motion in the universe because there are contending forces within it; in other words, there are contradictions. Wang An-shih said that motion in the material world follows definite laws (he used the term "the Way") and this does not change by man's will. If man knows the natural laws he can control the greatest and largest number of things. In Wang An-shih's opinions all things in the universe were determined by natural laws and nothing happened by accident. Althoug his history tends towards mechanism it deals a strong blow to idealism.[13]

Since Confucian China has such deep roots in the cult of ancestor veneration, Wang's opinions on that topic reveal his attitudes on almost everything else. Thus we cite the following statements from Wang's brush :

> The ancients were only slightly superior to the birds and beasts. The sages in their loathing of this state of things, made their laws and regulations, to emphasize and develop further the distinctions that should subsist between man and the brute creation...
>
> My own opinion is that responsible officials, in their efforts to deal with a disorderly situation, should advocate some positive method of improvement, and that they are either stupid or misled when they advocate a reversion to the ancient ways.[14]

Perhaps here is where another stereotype, even though it may have some limited historical validity, gets punctured. For by no means was China always looking to the past, except as a means of gaining perspective for the future (which is what the renaissances in all of human civilizations and cultures have done). Wang An-shih is by no means unique in debunking the perverse chauvinistic cult of antiquity which is only a pretext for clinging obstinately to recalcitrant and deadening conservatism. His message was conserve, yes; but *develop*.

28. Psellos

Michael Psellos (1018-1096) wrote theological metaphysics or philosophical theology, not merely 'dogmatic' theology as such. He is a philosopher of the very first rank in the whole of the global history of philosophy. And he is a humanist in the profoundest sense, dealing in what has come to be termed, ever since Leibniz at least, the "perennial philosophy".

Psellos had memorized the *Iliad* of Homer even as a child; and in his normal education he naturally encompassed all that was then known of arithmetic, geometry, astronomy and music, "all primarily in the form that had been developed by ancient Greece."[1] Psellos was not anything of the "near neo-Pagan" that later on Pletho was accused of being. Nevertheless, he was deeply indebted to the Greek Patristic literature, and he was fully aware of the adjustments that were necessary to reconcile Plato and Aristotle, and their Hellenistic interpreters, to the Christian "Dispensation". But he was not unaware of the "aberrations" that led even the great Origen astray, as he thought. "Admirer of Greek philosophy though he was, Psellos rejected as heresies such Platonic notions as 'recollection (*anamnesis*)' and 'transmigration of souls (*metempsychosis*)', which had been condemned by the church."[2]

With these reservations, Psellos is among those who see no harm but rather benefit in using syllogistic logic and other basics from the classical heritage; indeed, he says with profound feeling :

> My Plato!... I do not know how to bear the weight of such a word. Have I not long honored the divine cross above everything else ?... I may belong entirely to Christ, but I refuse to deny the wiser of our writers or the knowledge of reality, both intelligible and sensible. Interceding with God by

prayer according to my capacity, I will eagerly accept whatever may be granted to me.[3]

Psellos' teacher was one John Mauropus, a poet and rhetorician, who had virtually the same opinions, believing that if any of the 'pagans' should escape damnation through lack of the Christian Revelation it should be Plato and Plutarch. Psellos' student John the Italian was even more liberal in this attitude, risking condemnation as a heretic. Psellos himself anticipates Ficino by several centuries in seeing in Plato's *Phaedrus* a parallel to the Christian concept of the Trinity.

Psellos was fond of comparing and contrasting Plato and Aristotle, as almost every Byzantine philosopher sooner or later had done and continued to do right down to the time of the fall of Byzantium to the Muslims. Others that interested him were Pythagoras, Plotinus, Iamblichus and Proclus. Psellos was an eclectic, but with very strong Neo-Platonic leanings, although his Neo-Platonism had been filtered through the Greek Patristic heritage, including foremost Gregory Nazianzen whom he rated as superior even to Plato, Socrates, Isocrates of Thucydides. In matters of interpretation he was fully aware of the panpsychic tendencies in Neo-Platonism as a doctrine not very compatible with orthodox Christianity; while holding that the soul of man does have an inherent likeness to God, the Church looked somewhat askance at the notion that this likeness approached anything like identity. To Psellos this likeness means "the ability to make man divine, to lead him out of the material realm, to deliver him from passions, and to endow him with the ability to deify another—this is the most perfect likeness."[4]

Psellos does not condemn atheism as such nor so much argue against it but points to the inadequacy of those Pre-Socratics such as Democritus, Anaximines, Hippo and others who confuse the transcendental nature of God as Being, First Cause, etc., with the physical elements, deifying what is not worthy of worship, as it were. As to the apophatic way—the assertion that necessarily we must acknowledge the existence of God even though we may not define His nature—Karahalios gives a cursory review of the history of this *via-negativa* stemming back through

Proclus and others to Plotinus, and of course to Plato himself, and coming on down through Pseudo-Dionysius and Maximus Confessor, et al, as a sort of propaedeutic before introducing Psellos' own interpretation :

> God is neither the universe, nor above it, nor the limit, nor the region, neither the light nor life, neither Nous, nor the 'non-being', neither the One nor above that. All these names are nothing else but sufferings and travails of our soul; God is ineffable and super-ineffable and not only we do not know what he is, but we cannot even be precise about his ignorance for even his 'unknown' is incomprehensible to us.[5]

This suggests the Śūnyavāda of Nāgārjuna and his followers; and Psellos comes close to the Hesychast position. Psellos' contemporaries like Ryōnin in Japan, *bhakta* that he was, and the Ālvārs who preceded Rāmānuja (not to mention Rāmānuja himself whose very long life overlapped Psellos') would disagree rather seriously when he says that God is "above all words and understandings, for he is totally incomprehensible and inexpressible; it would be better therefore to be honored 'in silence' rather than to be magnified in marvellous utterances."[6] As with most of the best of the Śūnyavāda heritage so in Psellos too, after the supreme detachment has been achieved and *prajñā* (supreme wisdom) with it, there should be an opening of the divine compassion operating spontaneously and selflessly in the devotee; and, moreover, just as in the *Lotus Sūtra* and other Mahāyāna literature, not to mention in Psellos' Muslim contemporaries, even though we may not comprehend God's *ousia*, the whole world becomes a sort of theophany after the supreme detachment is achieved.

Although in the above passage, if taken in isolation from the rest of his system, one could almost call Psellos a Śūnyavādin, in treatment of the attributes of God one might see him rather as an Advaitin. For he hesitates to say that God is Being, since it is better to say that God is the Source of Being, and as such is the simplest conceivable, and is therefore prior to mind or any other describable essence, substance, function or what have you. Hence the best we may say is that, "If anything else is called one, it is not essentially so....Only God, therefore, is One."[7] Karahalios has quinticized this theme by filtering out from Psellos' voluminous works such expressions as the following : absolutely One, singularly One, unmixedly One, purely One and essentially One, above all simplicity, one simple essence, most original and exalted, One, absolute and simple.

So far we say Śūnyavādin or even Advaitin, but when we get to his exposition of the Trinity we find him closer, as a panentheist, to Rāmānuja. One wonders what Psellos might have said about the Mahāyāna *Trikāya* doctrine since that is not encumbered by the anthropomorphic terms "Father" or "Son" or the terribly ambiguous word "Spirit". Pelikan comments on Psellos' interpretation of Christian trinitarian monotheism as follows :

> Fundamentally, the Christian picture of God was set apart from all other views by its trinitarian monotheism. "The first thing" to be learned was "to worship Father, Son, and Spirit, one God." Psellos opened his compilation of philosophical and theological teachings, *Omnifarious Doctrine*, with a confession of faith in the Trinity, three hypostases and one divine ousia. True piety consited of the confession of the Holy Trinity and of faith in the evangelical message. One was faithful to God when, in harmony with the decrees of the ecumenical councils, one taught the trinitarian dogma as it had been handed down by the fathers on the basis of the New Testament. The term "monad" had been used by Plato, Aristotle, and Proclus; but in the context of Christian monotheism, as systematized by Dionysius the Areopagite, the divine monad was seen to transcend life and mind, and even being. In his statements about the Trinity, Psellos adhered to the strict line of orthodox Greek theology : he rejected the Filioque, taught that in the incarnation the nature of the Logos had been concealed in the flesh, and defended the doctrine of the homoousios on the basis of "the term 'humanity,' which is common" to several men and yet single in itself. Christian monotheism distinguished itself from Jewish and Muslim monotheism by its trinitarian character, and from Hellenism by its loyalty to the biblical doctrine of God as one.[8]

Incidentally, the debate with Islam was probably, more than

most previous writers on Byzantine thought have thus far been willing to admit, a definite factor in the formulation of Christian doctrine. We have long since speculated about the real possibility that the Iconoclast controversy was already a spill-over from the Islamic challenge, although it is not clear as yet whether the Hesychast controversy could be said to have the same characteristic. At any rate, Jewish, Islamic and Christian philosophers and theologians had in common the Greek heritage and the Biblical-Qur'anic, or the "Abrahamic", heritage; so all in all one may expect more in common than differences, except in the Trinitarian doctrine over against the purer forms of transcendental theism. Moreover, although the others had the Greek heritage at second-hand, as it were, the Byzantines never lost their pride in being, first and foremost, Greek.

Psellos denies outright that the world is 'besouled' or 'beminded' in the sense used by Plato or Aristotle, since such a doctrine would compromise God's omniscience and omnipotence and providence. Likewise, Plotinus' panpsychic tendencies would need some radical 'rectification' in order to become acceptible to Byzantine orthodoxy. Nevertheless, there is a sense in which the world is 'besouled' in so far as God the Holy Spirit permeates the world as its sustaining *arché* (principle), for, as Karahalios puts it, "there is nothing neither above him (God) nor under him that can be called an 'arché' in an absolute sense. Hylé—matter—and eidos—form—may perhaps be called 'principles of beings', but only in reference and comparison to the 'composite elements', that is, in a subsidiary sense."[9] In our wider perspective the likeness and similarities to Psellos' Neo-Confucianist contemporaries in their theme of the relation between *li* ane *ch'i* suggests itself. Again Psellos is treading a tight-rope between extremes, and in that sense is 'orthodox'. We may readily see that he would not agree with Chang Ts'ai with his realistic emphasis on the *ch'i* at the expense of the *li*; but on the other hand he might not agree with the predecessors of the idealist tradition of Lu Hsiang-shan, neglecting the *ch'i* in favor of the *li*. Karahalios further reports :

> God is the 'principle of all beings'. This 'principle or Cause' created *athroōs* (all at once) the Eidos—Form—and the Hylé—

> Matter which subsequently became, in a secondary sense, the principles of the elements. Out of the elements and out of their combination, we have the particular beings in a hierarchical scheme. "My opinion," Psellos goes on to say, "is that the cosmos is neither the hylé, the shapeless form, the unformed shape, nor the eidos; for this is not varied nor adorned. On the contrary, (I believe) that the cosmos is both of them.[10]

And further concerning Psellos' concept of matter :

> Hylé, so to say, is an immaterial thing, which to the senses is incomprehensible and only through the discursive reason understood or through reason only explained. It is the worst of all things, shapeless, formless, indefinable, essence without essence and existence without existence. If one were to remove all the accidentia from the bodies, what remains lastly is hylé.[11]

One is reminded of some Mahāyāna metaphysics about the 'emptiness' of the *dharmas* and the Vedāntic critique of the Vaiśeṣika and Jaina theory of atoms, as well as again the classical problem in Neo-Confucianism of the relation between *ch'ī* and *li.* The similarity becomes even more vivid when Psellos also calls matter "a phantom of a hypostasis, feigning everything while being nothing; plaything of existence, spectre and ever-fleeting shadow running to non-being"; and, "Hylé is pure shame, totally alienated (removed) from God, a non-being amongst the beings and a being amongst the non-beings." Karahalios reminds us that in spite of this "nothingness", *hylé* is also an 'echo of the Divine nature' in so far as it has the capacity of receiving from (*eidos*), and is not even deprived of the Good; indeed, it even has the ability to "testify to God's existence, affording an indirect way to knowing God as his 'last echo'".[12]

Still these do not constitute a definition of *hylé* for it is emphatically indefinable according to Psellos, just as in Mahāyāna and some varieties of Vedānta and in Kaśmir Śaivism *māyā* is indefinable. Psellos even challenges anyone to come up with an adequate definition since he claims that that is just not possible. The reason is that we never have experience of matter in its 'purity', but ever and always 'clothed' with *eidos*, form. But then, even though *eidos*, form, is compromised in its combination with matter, it is only in such mixture that we experience it also—though as a Christian Neo-Platonist Psellos wished that this were not so since the more that matter gets mixed with form the grosser it gets.

As to Psellos' conception of time, the whole matter hangs on the richness of possible meanings of the adverb *athroōs*, "all at once". Here we are confronted with the classical problem of whether in any sense we can speak of a 'timeless' time before Creation, a theme which is not avoided by Taoism, Mahāyāna Buddhism, or any other complete metaphysical system (although many modern scientists would simply ignore it, even though some are beginning to speculate that in the case of black holes and similar actual phenomena time as we know it in our local solar system may either be going in reverse or even have ceased to exist). Psellos says : "Time.. is nothing else but measure of movement. It is not a self-existing thing, nor a visible body, nor an incorporal entity (hypostasis) like nature, soul or mind; it is a thing found only in thought. This means that time is the inventiveness and name of man's mind."[13] In a commentary on Gregory Nazianzen's texts, Psellos also writes : "... time has been created athroōs, receiving its existence out of a timely duration . Thus time, being created athroōs, is not 'in time' and therefore it can be characterized as achronos—outside of time, like the universe."[14] And Karahalios further writes : "Time does not apply to the existing (i.e., existentially) but to the accidentia, like for instance, we ascribe movement to the bodies by the same analogy as we assign time to movement. And while movement is an inseparable activity of the moveable body, time is a measure of this motion. Consequently time does not belong to the real but to the contingent."[15]

Concerning the soul, Psellos says that habituation does not at all constitute the *ousia* of the soul but belongs to the accidental characteristics. The part-whole dialectic plays a rather pivotal role, as it does in the Vaiśeṣika tradition; but here the Greek terminology is even more convenient perhaps than Sanskrit for echoing the *iota* controversy in the Byzantine version of the Nicene Creed. Psellos says that the unity of the soul's *ousia* is not compromised by the parts since the whole is *homoousia*, whereas the parts are *homoiomerus*—identity of essence but analogous, assimilatable parts. In other words, wholeness as such is not such that all wholenesses are distinct, unassimilatable entities, but they are intimately related by their commonality of wholeness as such. We may here have something remarkable like the *samānādikaraṇa* relationship worked out in Viśiṣṭādvaita Vedānta wherein a substance as such or even an essence can still be itself in its own right in one respect but also serve as an attribute to another substance or essence in another respect, analogical relationalities being more intimate than mere connexity or commonality in a universal.

This may well be extended to the relation of the soul to God, both of them being so similar in characteristics that they can be considered—at least as far as the spiritual Image of God in us is concerned—as almost a *homoousia* but definitely a *homoiousia*. This radical similarity of soul to God constitutes the reason why both are ultimately indefinable short of a sort of anthropomorphic or even materialist hybris. In Psellos the likeness of the soul to God is carried to such an extent that not only are both by nature indefinable but they are approachable only through the *via negativa*. We have to assert out of necessity that something is there which is called "soul", but to say exactly what it is is as difficult almost as saying what God is. We may better say what it is not.

In Psellos there is a very important distinction between discursive reason (*dianoia*) and the still higher functions of the mind. Although at first it may seem enigmatic, *dianoia* lies halfway between *doxa*—opinion, rather than knowledge (*episteme*), as in Plato —and *Nous*, Mind in the metaphysical sense rather than the psychological sense.

> Thus the discursive reason, being in the middle of the cognitive powers of the soul, 'ascends and descends' either reaching high to the Mind or low to the doxa. On account of its peculiar place and function, it is likened to our soul, because it also occupies the middle order of the universe. It is through discursive reason that man's soul is 'led' to the contemplation

> of the Intelligibles, (i.e., the rational soul or *nous*); this contemplation constitutes the perfection of the soul.[16]

One wonders which terms Psellos would have selected if he had been writing in Sanskrit instead of Greek. For example, *manas* being the general undifferentiated word for "mind", would he have used that for *dianoia*; *or buddhi*, which has the governance of the senses and through *antaḥkaraṇa* integrates them into intelligible percepts; or *citta*, which embodies, as it were, the capacity of the higher intuitive contemplation; or even *vijñāna*, which includes the dynamic undifferentiated unity of intellect and will; or *sākṣī*, the observer consciousness. Relatively excellent though Greek is by comparison with Latin modern European languages, Psellos was striving for distinctions which he could perhaps have expressed better in Sanskrit.

In the Neo-Platonic tradition, Mind (*Nous*) constitutes the trans-human hypostasis along with One (*to-Hen*) and the Soul (*Psyché*); but Psellos is here not so much concerned with that as he is with man's mind. Thus even in metaphysical profundities he remains, we suggest, consistently a humanist. Noting that basically Psellos follows Proclus, Karahalios discerns the following 'levels':

> ...a) the imparticipable (unpossessed) Mind; b) the supramundane and c) the mundane. The Unpossessed Mind is identified by Psellos with the Creative Mind, who ... is called the Logos or Wisdom of God.
>
> The Unpossessed Mind is also called the First Mind; he knows only himself and he is simultaneously intelligence and intelligent. Further the Unpossessed Mind is eternal according to essence, power, and act; his knowledge is exactly like his essence; he knows everything in the present and he is outside of time, movement, mutation and syllogisms. The Unpossessed Mind, moreover, grants certain illuminations of his own existence which pass to those beings that come under him.[17]

The Supramundane Mind is sort of Janus-faced; without changing his *ousia* he knows both what is above and below himself, that is, both the intelligibles and the sensibles. Psellos further develops the functions of this Supramundane Mind in the Celestial Realms of the Angelic Hosts as well as the *Eidé* (the Pure Forms or Ideas)—not just the Aristotelian universals, but the full-blown metaphysics of that realm which no doubt parallels with the *Ālayavijñāna* of Yogācāra Buddhism or the *dharmas* of Śūnyavāda. Karahalios puts it this way:

> Since corporeity, extension, etc., do not apply to these intellectual Forms they find themselves both unified with each other and at the same time separated, like the 'contemplations in the soul'. Mind (man's mind) both embraces and is permeated by the Divine Eide, viz., pure forms of ideas like goodness, holiness, justice, sameness, etc. However, the sublimer Mind or superior Intelligence embraces these forms in a more universal and fuller degree, whereas the inferior possesses them to a lesser extent... (and in that degree diminish in power).[18]

As an alternative interpretation for the modern secular world, instead of asserting as in this Neo-Platonic heritage that these higher realms are substantial or essential as really ontological, we might take them as levels of *value*, somewhat as Max Scheler has done in his attempt at revindicating the *hierarchy* of values. This has been done at least by way of an apologetic in presenting the basics of Vedāntic tradition, and there is no reason why it might not be attempted in terms of Neo-Platonism, whether Jewish, Christian or Islamic. One might even suggest that what has happened in the secularization of the modern world is essentially the denial of universals in the medieval sense with the net result that they have come back in the guise of "values". Or, we have discarded (or so we thought) the angels, saints, Bodhisattvas, *ācāryas*, and the supramundane 'intelligences' only to almost deify 'natural laws' which serve the same function structurally in most modern secular systems as the 'intelligences' did in the older systems: and that in such a way that there is a sort of "scientific faith" (to paraphrase Santayana's quipping about "animal faith") that our merely human intellect, by virtue of the 'laws' of mathematics and logic, is intrinsically capable of understanding and even by which we, as it were, embody those laws of the universe.

A question inherited from Plotinus himself somewhat and certainly from Proclus and his Greek Patristic 'purifiers' is the relation of *Nous* (Mind) in the metaphysical almost meta-cosmic sense as one of the Hypostases to mind as a function of our human rational souls. Karahalios reports that Psellos himself asks the question, "Is mind really the eye of the soul as some philosophers contend it to be?", and his answer is an emphatic no:

> I say, having an accurate knowledge of it, that the mind is not the eye of the soul; for the eye is a serving instrument, moved by another agent...; the mind, on the contrary, has complete authority over the soul and leads it up to divine illuminations, drenching it with divine light and filling it with the immaterial eidé. ... (The mind) is not a dynamis of the soul; it is rather a primary and eternal essence, surpassing soul in power, in beauty and in all other order; it (the Nous) does not belong to the soul but rather fashions it after itself; it does not have its abode in the soul but within itself. ... The mind that exists in the soul is certainly subordinate and inferior to the First Nous, yet it is over and above the psychic essence which it illuminates. ... (One should not) take mind and soul as the same thing for the mind is immovable whereas the soul is self-moving; the former is eternal according to its essence and act, the latter, eternal only in essence while mutable according to its act. The mind exists always along with the superior (eidé) while the soul, because of its inner double dynamis, faces on both ends (directions) and sometimes turns to the better lot, sometimes to the worse. The mind, without being moved, possesses the *nooumenon*; the soul, on the contrary, cannot come to any conclusion unless it moves through syllogistic propositions.[19]

This last constitutes a very close parallel to the distinction in Sanskrit terminology between *buddhi* as belonging to *jīva* and *cit* as belonging to *ātman*-Brahman as one 'hypostasis' along with *sat* and *ānanda*. Even if we might have some difficulty in finding such a close parallel in Ibn Sīnā, no doubt it would be easy to find in al-Ṭūsī, who was also Psellos' contemporary.

Karahalios cites the following typical but crucial passage from one of Psellos' opuscula, "De Anima Celbers Opiniones":

> It is true that mind, according to Aristotle, may be called entelechy of the body and as such is inseparable from it, however, not according to its ousia, nor according to its acts which it holds from (its) association with the body, which are mostly practical. These acts are inseparable from the body, for, as soon as the body perishes, they perish along with it. And as the captain is the entelechy of the ship, ... the same way our soul, being the entelechy of our body, cannot exist apart from it. However, because it possesses certain separate acts from the body, and I mean acts regarding the intelligible eidé, to which (acts) the body not only does not contribute anything, but on the contrary, hinders them, it becomes evident that the soul must have a separate ousia, and as such is and is called nous.[20]

Psellos' Muslim contemporaries were faced with almost identically the same problem, interpretations varying from the almost purely Aristotelian position of Ibn Sīnā to the extremely 'meta-metaphysical' position in the mysticism of al-Ṭūsī. In the emerging variety of sub-schools of the Vedānta and Kaśmir Śaivism we find combinations like *jīv-ātman* and *cidākāśa* (i.e., *ākāśa*, finest 'material' elements, linked with Citta, Mind as the Supreme Reality common to both *ātman* and Brahman as *sat-cit-ānanda*). Likewise not all of the *ācāryas*, not even Abhinavagupta, are completely clear as to the relation of *manas* and *buddhi* as definitely psychophysical functions of the embodied *jīva*. The *ātman*/Self is quite capable, as the *manas* and *buddhi* are not, of complete identification with Parama-Śiva ultimately and transcendentally, even though as experienced empirically it is Sadāśiva which makes this identification not only operative but actual in the phenomenal world.

From a modern process orientation it might be asserted that in almost all of Euramerican tradition the radical mistake has been to assume spirit and matter, and soul and mind as well, as *ousiai*, as substances or essences instead of processes. In other words, we really should be thinking in terms of spiritua*lizaion* and materi*alization*. But Psellos remains emphatically a philosopher of *ousiai*, of distinct entities; and although *Pneuma* reaches far above our normal empirical grasp, Psellos is not a Buddhist: there is something, a Supreme Something, that is really *there*.

Karahalios warns us that in Psellos nothing is to be found like the *cidākāśa* or fiery, etherial or astral substance which in classical Neo-Pythagoreanism and Neo-Platonism (thanks to Heracleitus, no doubt) was supposed to be the actual link between *nous*/soul and body/*sōma*. Quite the contrary, *Pneuma* (Spirit) is completely free from influence on or by *psyché* or *nous*. In this higher realm it evidently may be said of Psellos that even he joins with those like Symeon the New Theologian and Peter Damien and abandons the Greek 'pagan' sources at this point (like Dante as he approaches those realms which are still closed off to Virgil so that he must go on alone) and finds St. Paul as his guide through the next etherial realms. In the Pauline terminology *Pneuma* is completely distinct from *psychê* and *sōma* and free from their influences. *Pneuma* is the Divine Principle working in us for Good. Thus *Pneuma* cannot be subordinated to any other order; rather, other orders have what order they do have as somehow derived from *Pneuma*. There are subtleties involved here which might determine the razor's edge between orthodoxy and heresy. Psellos writes:

> What could be lovelier than if a soul separated itself from nature and flesh as much as possible and conquered the hindering passions, then turning unto itself were to view clearly the whole psychical beauty; then, lifting up itself toward the more divine, were to contemplate the intellectual life possessing directly the loftier visions, then having superseded all power and activity were to stand on the extremest of its connate (akin) life, projecting the singularity of its nature... were to unite itself with the One, becoming straightway pneuma and mind and god?[21]

And again:

> It is necessary for him who intends to contemplate to first

> turn toward the soul; then through it toward the mind and through the mind toward the celestial and through them toward God. However, neither he who has made the return into the soul is deified, nor he who has returned to mind; the former has become a psychical man and cannot receive the things of the spirit; the latter has become intellectual but not yet god.[22]

In the wider comparative perspective the parallels are more evident than the differences. Even in present-day India, Advaitins use the metaphor that once you have reached the top by means of a 'ladder', you may kick the ladder back away since you will not need it again. The Mahāyāna Bodhisattva Vow is the one great exception, and even that had virtually ceased in the eleventh century to be seriously followed except by a few *bhaktas* like Ryōnin.

Spirit (*Pneuma*) is the longed-for goal primarily, and only remotely the means (*upāya*) of attaining the goal. It might be argued that here Psellos comes very close to the *Prajñāpāramitā* literature based primarily on the Śūnyavāda heritage: The ultimacies being scarcely attainable in this life, we have no alternative but to make the most of our here and now situation in the world, somewhat like Plato's own realization that rational choice of the "second best" is better than fanatical desperation in the pursuit of ultimacy and unblemished infinite perfection. Hence wisdom/*prajñā* is what must be cultivated, with *detachment*, rather than with a Promethian or Faustian thrust. The result is not tense ecstasy but, as Psellos himself puts it, "Spiritual is he who has acquired wings through the spirit and has ascended so much to the infinite ends of knowledge as much as he has descended to the abyss of sacred humility."[23]

Under circumstances such as those that prevailed among spiritualized intellectuals of the eleventh century, interior attainments must have been possible which in our modern technologized, exteriorized, frenetic struggle with the cosmos have been tragically lost. How to regain them ? Perhaps some new forms of a sort of neo-monasticism? Karahalios suggests however that even Psellos himself, having found monastic life too much of a restraint, never attained more than a dualistic orientation: spirit and body, soul and mind. Man to Psellos is inherently and inevitably caught (as later Kant will again remind us) in the antinomic situation of having citizenship in two worlds.

Psellos plays down the theme of *theosis* such as is found in the less Christianized forms of Neo-Platonism. He even denies that there is such a thing as the 'pneumatic body' surviving death, Spirit almost by definition being totally different from body or embodiment. This would also present a contrast with those varieties of the Vedānta which put stress on the *sūkṣma śarīra,* the 'subtle body', as well as with modern Theosophical and other speculations about the astral body. In other words, perhaps it may be said that Psellos stops short of esoterics and remains almost a Christian mystic, but certainly a disciplined Christian metaphysician, advocating the oria-contemplation and illumination, fully realizing that spiritual attainments cannot be produced by magic.

Psellos' philosophical anthropology or concept of the nature of man is historically of very great significance since, as with the concept of matter and form, it had much influence in Renaissance Italy later on. In all three of the Abrahamic heritages, Jewish, Christian and Islamic, speculation about the nature of Adam before the Fall left room for expounding quite freely on the most ideal possible notion of human perfection (many Euramerican philosophers who are somewhat biased against the Old Testament materials tend to overlook that freedom). Of course this idealization of a part is not unique to the Abrahamic heritages but is shared by Confucianists and Taoists who look back to the Yellow Emperor and the others in the period of the Sage Kings as well as by the Hindus who regard the present era as *Kali Yuga*. Nor is Psellos an exception to this pattern of using Adam as a symbol of perfect humanity.

Concerning the relation between the Image of God in man and his 'fallen' nature, for Psellos the Image (*Icon, eikon*) is nothing else but an illumination of God's own *ousia*. But in a certain sense all of creation partakes of that characteristic; so how is man different ? The answer is expressed by adding a prefix to the term *eikon* : *Kat-eikona*, which conveys that man over and above the rest of nature or creation has the potentiality as a result of intelligence and free will to do righteous works and even the innate power to imitate or liken himself to God. Thus man is created *en timēi*, created in honor. In all, then, Psellos is simply continuing in systematic consistency his use of Aristotle's distinction between potential and actual. Thus it cannot be said as some predestinarians have done and continue to do that man is, was, and always will be inherently good or bad by nature; rather man has been given the power to become not only good but saintly and sage-like, and to approach perfection by constant cultivation of this potentiality. This potentiality is never lost, even though it may be neglected. Thus Psellos in this regard is more like his fellow-humanists in China who insisted on selfless cultivation of the 'original nature' than like fellow-Christians (Peter Damien, for example) who put more emphasis on the Fall than on the Image. But in other respects Psellos' philosophical psychology is closer to Plato than to Aristotle since he believed that, along with the potentiality in the Image, God has implanted innately the *eidei*, the Ideas, the Forms, of everything that can be known.

The ideal perfect human soul is described by four basic characteristics or attributes, namely, *anarchos*, *athanatos*, *aiōnios*, and *aiholos*, i.e., without any external ruler, without death, everlasting through all ages, emphatically whole or everlasting. Again most of them if not all have been derived from Gregory Nazianzen; but as ever, Psellos breathes new life into them. In these terms Psellos is considering the ideal and perfect human nature that Adam is supposed to have had before the Fall, and which therefore all of us still have essentially by virtue of the Image of God in us, even though that might have become soiled even as a mirror gets dirty—but not broken, so that the potentiality of restoration of this Original Nature (again we could here invoke Neo-Confucianist terminology) is always possible. Indeed, it is our privilege, duty, and natural inclination to make every effort to remove the barriers to the realization of that original perfection.

Evidently Psellos put heavy emphasis on the aesthetic aspect of freedom. The soul that is truly free lacks all hindrances to contemplation of the Beauty of Perfection—perfection as such as well as perfection of the Image of God in the human soul. "Self-awareness of the Image" (more like the Vedāntic *ātma-*

vidyā than a function of the *ahaṅkāra* or *jīva*) is also called "contemplation of the dignity of man" such that, all hindrances being removed, the Glory of God shines through it as man praises unhindered his Divine Creator and Perfector. Historically this is no doubt one of the prime sources of Pico della Mirandola's famous classic essay "On the Dignity of Man" which echoes the same theme—quite the opposite of the gloomy picture of man among the Northern European theologians.

So far Psellos stays pretty close to the Biblical concept of human nature, although very much filtered through the Greek Patristic lenses. But as far as his philosophizing about man in his present state, Psellos is almost entirely Greek : man is a mixture. He is a mixture, that is, of body and soul, of mind and spirit, material cause and spiritual aspiration, rational and irrational, mortal and immortal, material and formal, inferior and superior. One is tempted in this respect to see Psellos and Chou Tun-i as virtually twins philosophically. In Psellos' own words :

> The soul and body interchange their particular traits, and the body lives on account of the soul, the soul suffers on account of the body. ... Since there has been a coming together of contraries, each one gains something from the other; the soul (gains) from the affections of the body where it is said for it (the soul) to desire, to act irrational, to have opinion, to remember and to think discursively; the body, on the other hand, (gains) from it the advantages of the soul inasmuch as we ascribe life and motion to it.[24]

This parallels many of Psellos' contemporaries, especially Muslims but also Neo-Confucianists and, if not extreme Advaitins, at least Abhinavagupta and in a sense the Jainas also. For example, *jīva* as the vitalizing principle is related to the body in its three-*guṇa* nature; even in the various varieties of Vedānta, only the *ātman* is above the psycho-physical nexus of our mixed condition in *saṃsāra*. *Ātman*, not *jīva*, would be equal to spirit (*pneuma*) in Psellos' system. One difference, however, that may be outstanding is that in the Vedāntic systems the distinction is made between the gross and subtle bodies. Nevertheless, it might well be that something like that may be found in Psellos' speculations about the body of Christ after the Resurrection, as is the case later on in Bonaventura. And something like it can be found in Psellos' contemporary Symeon the New Theologian in regard to his speculations about the body of Adam.

The question that naturally arises from the observation that man is a mixture is what to do about it. Some even among Psellos' Byzantine contemporaries, especially those influenced by the Quietist (Hesychast) controversy, would say that purification of the bodily grossness by ascetic discipline is the right way. But Psellos is a humanist; we can scarcely think of him as a martyr or a fanatic of any sort. He rather affirms the Greek ideal of the middle way and the avoidance of extremes :

> I do not abstain totally from hylé neither am I in every respect immersed in it. For I am a divine person, yet I live with a body. Neither does the totally earthly please me nor do I follow these (things) that force me into flight in the beyond of nature. Thus, here I am in the middle of extremes; yet I like 'nothing in excess'. But because I am in the middle of two extremes, of inferior and superior, I cleave to this (i.e., the earthly) while I prefer the others (i.e., that force me into the flight...). We are body and soul and sort of a mixture on the borderline of the better and worse nature.[25]

Psellos not only emphasized the changeableness of human nature by virtue of embodiment, but he even asserts that this combination of irrational body with rational soul is "a strange mixture of incongruous constituents". The incongruity lies in the fact that in a very real sense man is "a rational soul using a body".[26]

Psellos teaches that tireless and constant effort is needed *Philosophos* and *philotheos*, the love of wisdom and the love of God, are more than enough to constitute the basic and yet the highest discipline. Philosophy itself, in short, constitutes a *sādhana*. Psellos tried monastic life but he was not satisfied with that, his vocation being more in the realm of scholarly endeavors and public responsibility institutionally. Karahalios suggests that he justified this by appealing to Aristotle's dictum that man is a social animal: but what interests us here is that in this respect he would have been more at home with his Neo-Confucianist contemporaries than, say, with Atīśa or with Symeon the New Theologian (who was such a recluse that biographical information about him is extremely scarce).

Psellos was very much aware of the contradictions within the Bible and even of the impossibilities therein reported. He got around or through these by allegorical interpretation (which stems back at least to Philo of Alexandria). Thus he set the pace for Christian philosophy as such, whereas the Latin tradition often seemed opposed to such merging and tended in the more extreme cases to keep philosophy separate from 'divinity', even following the way that some Muslims had adopted of allowing or even promoting a "double standard" between the two fields. Psellos considered Plato as a precursor of Christ, which was nothing new in Byzantine heritage, anathema as it might have been with Jerome, Tertullian and Augustine. But he considered the logic of Aristotle as an indispensable propaedeutic for metaphysics, even though he thought Aristotle lacking when it comes to theology. Nevertheless he wrote commentaries on Aristotle's *Logic* and *Physics*.

Besides Psellos' philosophical works there are also his scientific works as well as his literary and historical efforts, all of which are remarkable. His encyclopedic works include such topics as grammar, metrics, rhetoric, arithmetic, geometry, music, astronomy, meteorology, physics, medicine, law, agriculture, divination and other aspects of esoterics, including of course astrology. Mathematical speculation is also typical of Psellos. He even speculated—fascinatingly like his contemporary Shao Yung in that regard—with symbolic numbers for such as health and sickness, death, the soul, intelligence, discursive reason, opinion and sensation. But it is as historian that Psellos occupies a place virtually next to none as far as Byzantine history is concerned. It is a pity that he did not have communication with those Muslim historians who were his contemporaries, like al-Bīrūnī, Mas'ūdi, or Miskawayh, whose information about wider perspectives across Eurasia was much more complete.

However he did share with them to a great extent somewhat of a Neo-Platonist (or Neo-Pythagorean) perspective about history on the grander scale. Thus Psellos was no less of a polymath than his contemporaries Ibn Sīnā and Ibn al-Haitham, or Vācaspati Miśra or Chou Tun-i; and, given this spirit, no doubt if he were alive today he would be advancing an at least post-Toynbeean and post-Marxist global perspective.

Perfection of the individual is perhaps the most essential theme for Psellos, who as a humanist *par excellence* offers a sharp contrast to the rigorism of such as Peter Damien and perhaps an implicit warningagainst the cult of 'sudden' enlightenment as found in some popular forms of Zen. It must be emphasized that by no means was Psellos a lone figure in eleventh century Byzantium. Even though he has been selected as perhaps the most representative of the basic trends and is perhaps the most comprehensive in his range of learning, it might be said that what is more important (as was the case with the Southern Sung Dynasty in the same epoch in China) is the nexus of cultural excellence of which he is at once the representative and also the stimulator and reinforcer.

29 Anselm

Unfortunately Anselm of Canterbury (1033-1109), Bernard of Clairvaux and Abelard were not direct beneficiaries of the renaissance of learning sponsored by Charlemagne around 800 A.D. The Carolinian renaissance was made possible by governmental centralization, so that when the empire was divided among Charlemagne's descendants, decentralization (feudalism) arose and all intellectual and spiritual leaders had to contend with the forces of disunity. Under these circumstances pockets of learning existed in connection with monasteries or cathedrals, but no general atmosphere conducive to the progress of culture was to be found. Leaders of vision and integrity, therefore, had an upstream battle most of the time. The two ultimately favorable factors in the European picture were the vitality of Muslim culture and the presence of the Church in many places as a potential resource for enlightenment and change.

Son of a Lombard (Italian) nobleman, abbot in France and archbishop in England, Anselm was international in a way that characterized other leading clerics of his day (which is perhaps too often overlooked by critics of a "parochial" Middle Ages). In 1060 Anselm entered the Benedictine monastery at Bec in Normandy, France, and became abbot there in 1078. Anselm's ecclesiastical life can be characterized by what we might call his "three refusals". First, since Anselm intended to reform the English Church, which involved securing freedom from secular domination, he refused to be consecrated as Archbishop of Canterbury until King William (son of William the Conqueror) both restored to the monastery the lands he had pillaged and recognized Pope Urban II against the antipope Clement III. Ill and fearing death, William acceded to Anselm's demands. Secondly, Anselm refused to pay the king money for his new office—"simony" is the technical term for payment made for ecclesiastical positions—whereupon William detained him from going to Rome to receive the mantle of papal approval. Then after a papal legate brought the mantle to England, Anselm did not allow William to invest him with it on the grounds that he did not owe his authority to the king but to the pope. The series of events in which this third refusal constituted one chapter is known as the "investiture controversy". In 1107 under the new king Henry I the investiture controversy was settled by a famous compromise in which the king renounced the right to invest bishops and abbots but they in turn did homage to him before their consecration. It is somewhat ironic that Anselm was canonized by Alexander VI, a pope who was elected to the papacy through bribery and would be a strong contender for the worst pope in history.

Anselm wrote his *Monologium* ("Monologue") in 1077 in response to questions posed by his fellow monks. When the monks requested further clarification, simplification and cogency in Anselm's reasoning concerning God's existence, he wrote the *Proslogium* ("Addition", "Sequel") which contains his famous "ontological argument" (Kant named it, without necessarily understanding it). While the *Monologium* was seen by Anselm as a work in which one "investigates what he does not know by silent reasoning within himself", the *Proslogium* was seen as issuing from one "striving to elevate his mind to the contemplation of God and seeking to understand what he believes".[1]

Whether Anselm was reflecting on the incarnation, the atonement, or the existence of God, his major intellectual and spiritual affinities lay with the Augustinian tradition. The intellectual and spiritual context for the development of his famous ontological argument is also the Augustinian tradition, for Anselm like Augustine believes in order to know rather than reasoning in order to be able to believe. "He who does not believe will not experience, and he who has not experienced will not understand." So his unique argument is intended to help strengthen the person predisposed through faith to accept it rather than the person totally outside the circle of theistic commitment and experience. The ontological argument, then, is designed to clarify what a perfect being is and not just that it abstractly must exist. The heart of the ontological argument is found in the second chapter of the *Proslogium* (here with headings by the translator) :

That God Truly Is

Opening Prayer O Lord, you who give understanding to faith, so far as you know it to be beneficial, give me to understand that you are just as we believe, and that you are what we believe.

Starting Point We certainly believe that you are something than which nothing greater can be conceived.

The Problem But is there any such nature, since "the fool has said in his heart : God is not"?

Step 1 However, when this very same fool hears what I say, when he hears of "something than which nothing greater can be conceived," he certainly understands what he hears.

Step 2 What he understands stands in relation to his understanding (*esse in intellectu*), even if he does not understand that it exists. For it is one thing for a thing to stand in relation to our understanding; it is another thing for us to understand that it really exists. For instance, when a painter imagines what he is about to paint, he has it in relation to his understanding.

However, he does not yet understand that it exists, because he has not yet made it. After he paints it, then he both has it in relation to his understanding and understands that it exists. Therefore, even the fool is convinced that "something than which nothing greater can be conceived" at least stands in relation to his understanding, because when he hears of it he understands it, and whatever he understands stands in relation to his understanding.

Step 3 And certainly that than which a greater cannot be conceived cannot stand only in relation to the understanding. For if it stands at least in relation to the understanding, it can be conceived to be also in reality, and this is something greater. Therefore, if "that than which a greater cannot be conceived" only stood in relation to the understanding, then "that than which a greater cannot be conceived" would be something than which a greater can be conceived. But this is certainly impossible.

Conclusion Therefore, something than which a greater cannot be conceived undoubtedly both stands in relation to the understanding and exists in reality.[2]

Although Anselm's argument has been called "many-faced" and "complex" it is stated simply and succinctly : *That being than which no more perfect being can be conceived must exist*, for if it did not then a more perfect being would be conceivable, namely, one that *did* exist. Actual existence is necessary to perfect being, and if one attempts to deny existence to perfect being one has really only denied existence to something less. Anselm elaborates how it is impossible (without inconsistency) to conceive that God is not. The fool can deny that God exists if he has in mind only "the word signifying what is thought", not "the very thing itself". "Accordingly, God can be conceived not to be in the first way, but not at all in the second."[3]

Further, For Anselm if God does not exist in such a way as to evoke sincere *worship*, it is not the ultimate God of religious devotion and theology. A perfect God must exist always, and a God worthy of worship in the highest conceivable sense must be eternal. God, according to Anselm's clarification, is not only supremely good and just but also real, eternal, and ultimately effective (though Anselm might prefer "self-sufficient", "absolute" or "that on which all else depends").

The "idea of God" contains an interesting ambiguity (related to the whole controversy about universals) which can be read between the lines of Anselm's argument. To us "idea" and "concept" are all but identical in meaning, due in no small part to the work of Abelard. "Idea" and "concept" may seem to be completely congruent so that there is nothing in "idea" that is not in "concept". But from Plato on "idea" carried an additional connotation : the objective pattern, structure, essence or nature of a thing which makes our definitions and knowledge accurate and, what is more, determines whether the thing is fully and perfectly itself or not. In short, "idea" in this second sense can mean "objective standard". Our subjective concept of God, Anselm seems to be saying, must match the objective standard of Godness or else it is an inadequate concept of its object, which he defines as "the very thing itself" and not just the word signifying it. Through reason, faith, intuition and experience all working together Anselm's argument becomes for him and likeminded individuals a pointer to the supreme Standard without which all human judgments lapse into a morass of relativism. We do make secure nonrelative judgments; therefore God (the Standard) *is*. One judgment the human mind can make is to decide that unless this standard is as real as the world it measures or the mind which conceives it, it is not truly *the* standard. Anselm's argument, then, might be viewed as a kind of matrimonial linking of man's highest concept with what *is* highest. Descartes went a step further to suggest that we could not even conceive of a perfect (infinite) being were there no such being to make our conception possible.

The ontological argument has been subject to various rejections, acceptances, criticisms, reinterpretations and misunderstandings, probably beginning with the monks who first read it and including the first critic of record, Gaunilo. The list of those who accepted the argument in one form or another includes Descartes, Leibniz, Hegel, Karl Barth, Anselm Stolz, and Charles Hartshorne. Eminent critics and rejectors of the argument, as they understood it, are Gaunilo, Thomas Aquinas, Kant, and Bertrand Russell.

Shortly after the ontological argument was first published the monk Gaunily pointed out that one might conceive of a most perfect island. Certainly it would be "more perfect" if it really existed, but that did not mean that it did exist and certainly could not cause it to exist. Of Anselm's "that than which a greater cannot be conceived" Gaunilo writes: "It must be made certain that this 'greater' is actually somewhere; and only then from the fact that it is greater than all things, will there be no doubt that it subsists in itself." In other words, it cannot be proved to exist by any process of elimination or deduction alone. It must be found 'greatest' by inspection or even by revelation. Copleston responds for Anselm that the "idea of even the most beautiful islands is not the idea of something which must exist : even in the purely logical order the two ideas are not on a par. If God is possible, i.e., if the idea of the all-perfect and necessary Being contains no contradiction, God must exist, since it would be absurd to speak of a *merely possible necessary Being* (it is a contradiction in terms), whereas there is no contradiction in speaking of merely possible beautiful islands."[4]

John Wyclif (1350 ?-1384) seems to expand the Anselmian emphasis on the perfection of God to include the perfection of his creation as well. Like Anselm, Wyclif was a realist in the classical sense of the term (unlike Anselm, he exalted the rights of secular lords over the clergy). God is will, he contended, but never arbitrary will. "In truth God willed the best; nothing better could be conceived, for had a better conception been possible God would have willed it instead of the existing universe."[5] This line of reasoning culminated many centuries later in "the best of all possible worlds" of Leibniz and its parody by Voltaire.

Thomas Aquinas thought the argument was an argument for God's self-evidence and did not directly know it in its original context in the *Proslogium*. Kant, one of the chief critics of the argument, seems not to have associated it with Anselm at all. What he criticized was Leibniz' version which excludes from consideration most of the *Proslogium*.

The Benedictine theologian Anselm Stolz has presented the radical thesis that Anselm had no idea whatsoever of proving the existenee of God. The ontological argument is not really an argument for God's existence (*Dasein*) at all but rather an argument for God's unique way of existing (*Seinsweise*), that is, absolutely and unchangeably. Thus the *nature* of God, according to Stolz, is indissolubly linked by Anselm to the *existence* of God. Anselm writes : "Therefore, what are you, O Lord, than whom nothing greater can be conceived ?" The answer weds the necessary existence of God to his nature : "You are just and truthful and blessed and whatever else it is better to be than not to be." Stolz argues that the textual evidence as well as the Augustinian tradition of which Anselm was a part indicate that Anselm presupposed the existence of God and only tried to show that it was a fuller kind of existence. Though Anselm himself says that he has proved that God exists, Stolz points out that he says he has proved only that God "truly is", which is a different thing.[6]

The Protestant theologian Karl Barth sees the ontological argument as an elucidation of faith. Indeed, according to Stolz, Barth discovered that "there is no trace of an ontological argument to be found in Anselm. Anselm always speaks as a theologian, and the rule of faith is his constant presupposition." Among Barth's significant contributions, Stolz says, is the clear insight that Anselm was concerned with the *way* God exists for faith rather than with a rational proof of faith, which is impossible in any case. Nevertheless Stolz faults Barth for neglecting the prayer form of the whole work, for "Anselm theologizes in prayer".[7] Unfortunately the modern prejudice is that logic and prayer must be kept completely distinct, and according to McGill, "People today so objectivize logic and so sentimentalize prayer that each can be seen as the negation of the other".[8]

Stolz regards the end of Anselm's whole effort in the *Proslogium* to be religious experience, joy. In Anselm's own words : "Therefore, that whole joy does not enter into the beatified, but the beatified wholly enter into that joy." "Let me find thee in love, and love thee in finding," Anselm prays at the outset of his argument, and at its conclusion he writes, "There is, then, so truly a being than which nothing greater can be conceived to exist; and this being thou are, O Lord, our God.... I thank thee, gracious Lord, I thank thee; because what I formerly believed by thy bounty, I now so understand by thine illumination."

Anselm's *Cur Deus Homo* illustrates more his doctrinal interests. Usually Anselm is regarded as setting forth an "objective" view of the atonement and incarnation of Christ while Abelard sets forth a "subjective" view. While Christ in the long tradition beginning with Irenaeus was believed to have been a ransom for sin paid to the devil, Anselm made a sharp departure from this tradition by regarding Christ as the God-man "satisfaction" not of the devil but of God Himself who is also the giver of the satisfaction. Satisfaction rests on the feudal theory that the higher the level of the offended the greater the payment required for the offense. Since God is infinite, the offense against Him must be infinite too. Since man is the offender he must pay an infinite satisfaction which, unassisted, he cannot do. Hence the need for the God-man, Christ, and the answer to the quetion *Cur Deus Homo* ? or "Why the Incarnation ?" or "Why did man need for God to become man ?"[9]

An important issue in the background of Anselm's major works is the status of universals. As a realist on the matter, Anselm holds that universals are real. Correspondingly, he assumes that individual members of the Trinity are no more real than the Trinity, the one God, just as individual men are no more real than the universal "mankind". Anselm saw preeminent reality to be in the one perfect God, so that all creatures have derivative or dependent reality. The essence (or universal "idea") of God necessarily includes His existence, but all other beings exist contingently; that is, they do not *have* to be, and their existence and nature depend entirely upon God. Once the chief "real" becomes so perfect and all-encompassing, everything else tends to become either unreal or an attenuated participation in or reflection of the real. When that happens, the Christian, Jewish and Muslim distinction between God and the world tends to break down. It may be the case that Anselm's vigorous piety saved him from flirting with the 'dangers' of pantheism or panentheism. Nevertheless, W. H. V Reade gives us this judgment concerning the status of universals in Anselm's thought : "Distressing as this may be to the historian of logic, the historian of philosophy will find in Anselm's very silences and omissions fresh reason for rejecting the once common opinion that medieval thinkers exhausted themselves for centuries in trying to defind the nature of universals. It is scarcely too much to say that Anselm does not care what they are, so long as the function of reason is not simply confounded with sensuous perception."[10]

Although Anselm is certainly best known for his ontological argument, Copleston cautions us to view his contributions in a broader context :

> It is clear, then, how erroneous it is to associate his name with the 'Ontological Argument' in such a way as to imply that St. Anselm's only contribution to the development of philosophy was an argument the validity of which is at least questionable. His work may have not exercised any very considerable influence on contemporary thinkers and those who immediately followed him, because of their preoccupation with other matters (dialectical problems, reconciling the opinions of the Fathers, and so on), but looked at in the light of the general development of philosophy in the Middle Ages he must be acknowledged as one of the main contributors to Scholastic philosophy and theology, on account both of his natural theology and of his application of dialectic to dogma.[11]

Another important caution is found in Evelyn Underhill's view of Anselm as primarily a mystic : "In spite of the vast influence and permanent value of his theological writings and his important ecclesiastical work, it is a mistake to regard Anselm mainly as a theologian or administrator. His real interest and the efficacious cause of his ceaseless labours was the personal passion of the mystic."[12]

30. al-Ghazālī

Al-Ghazālī (1059-1110) remains one of the world's greatest mystics, of the same rank at least as Plotinus, Augustine, Rāmānuja and Bonaventura. His mysticism was not of the type that leads to quietism (at this time the Hesychast controversy was still raging at Mt. Athos and in the Byzantine court); rather he remains in history and on the roles of the great philosophers. Above all al-Ghazālī's mysticism was not in opposition to the proper consideration of prophecy.

The comprehensive working out of a 'scientific' basis of the stages of the mysitc way as recorded by authorities in all faiths should be extremely valuable for psychoanalysts and others (although most are still blind to all but their own limited predispositions). Al-Ghazālī's patterning of the mystical path of ascent culminates beyond the mind. Here he is very close to the Victorines.

> Beyond the intellect there is yet another stage. In this another eye is opened by which he beholds the unseen, what is to be in the future, and other things which are beyond the ken of intellect in the same way as the objects of intellect are beyond the ken of the faculty of discernment and the objects of discernment are beyond the ken of sense. Moreover, just as the man at the stage of discernment would reject and disregard the object of intellect were these to be presented to him, so some intellectuals reject and disregard the objects of prophetic revelation. That is sheer ignorance. They have no ground for their view except that this is a stage which they have not reached and which for them does not exist; yet they suppose that it is non-existent in itself. When a man blind from birth who has not learnt about colors and shapes by listening to people's talk, is told about these things for the first time, he does not understand them nor admit their existence.[1]

The dialectical materialist may say to this, Therefore let us get better electronic telescopes in order to explore the universe with some measure more subtle than light. And no doubt al-Ghazālī would bless him. But he would quickly add, But after you have explored all that, there remains your self to be explored. For in describing his early search as well as in his systematic writings al-Ghazālī, no less so than Śaṅkara, Augustine, Bernard, Maximus and many others, emphasizes very pointedly the importance of self-knowledge and the vanity of relying solely on the authority of tradition. Though not quite in the same sense as God *is* already that which He knows, still man also must *become* that which he knows.

Al-Ghazālī classifies thinkers as follows:

(1) the Theologians (*mutakallimūn*) who claim that they are the exponents of thought and intellectual speculation;

(2) the *Bāṭinīyyah* who consider that they, as the party of 'authoritative instruction' (*ta'līm*), alone derive the truth from the infallible *Imām*;

(3) the Philosophers, who regard themselves as the exponents of logic and demonstration;

(4) The Ṣūfīs or mystics, who claim that they alone enter into the presence of God and possess vision and intuitive understanding.[2]

The third category includes the materialists, the naturalists and the theists. Thus it may readily be seen that al-Ghazālī lived in a period of great philosophical ferment; virtually all the varieties known today were present and he was well acquainted with them all. His mysticism, therefore, cannot be taken as an evasion in any sense (as may have become the case with the Chinese Buddhists of his century if the Neo-Confucianists' criticism be true).

Al-Ghazālī was, scarcely less than Ibn Sīnā, an encyclopedic mind acquainted with every known science of his time from mathematics to astronomy. Nevertheless, rather like Rāmānuja who regards logic as useful but not absolutely essential to the realization of the spiritual goal, al-Ghazālī takes logic as the instrument of *demonstration* rather than as the means of *proof* of the existence of God and the other matters subordinate to that (which, of course, includes everything, thereby to a great measure anticipating the difficulties in Ockham and perhaps even in Hume). In dealing with natural science, which for al-Ghazālī is by no means to be despised but which is subordinate to the higher reaches of divine inspiration—to the gift of prophecy, in short—logic is absolutely essential even though, for example, in the matter of causation, nothing is really and finally proved thereby. The first premises must come from elsewhere, although in the matter of extending their universal and particular applications, logic is necessary for the sake of manipulating concepts and especially for the sake of eliminating false arguments.

In his *Incoherence of the Philosophers* al-Ghazālī has listed twenty points wherein al-Fārābī and Ibn Sīnā have erred, but later he reduced these to three basic points:

> (a) They say that for bodies there is no resurrection; it is bare spirits which are rewarded and punished; and the rewards and punishments are spiritual, not bodily. They certainly speak truth in affirming the spiritual ones, since these do exist as well; but they speak falsely in denying the bodily ones and in their pronouncements disbelieve the Divine Law. (b) They say that God knows universals but not particulars. This too is plain unbelief; the truth is that 'there does not escape Him the weight of an atom in the heavens or in the earth.' (Qur'ān 34, 3) (c) They say that the world is everlasting, without beginning or end. But no Muslim has ever adopted any such view on the question.[3]

In the first we have a sort of neo-orthodoxy in which after the inrush of rationalism there is a slight swing of the pendulum back to the pseudo-center of rationalized tradition. The same may be said of the third proposition. In these al-Ghazālī has long anticipated the settlement of Christian orthodoxy on these points (he even influenced Bonaventura quite a bit) and in a way that may be another parallel to the neo-orthodox tendencies in China and India where the Buddhist 'rationalism' yielded to a slightly reformed and more sophisticated Neo-Confucianism and (Neo-) Hinduism. Neo-orthodoxy in full-flower will become the key-point of interpretation of the twelfth century, and al-Ghazālī is one of the pivotal figures in the transition toward this.

It must not be thought that al-Ghazālī's neo-orthodoxy is mere authoritarianism. He was uncompromising in his search and was not satisfied until he had reached something evidently approximating to the Beatific Vision. With al-Ghazālī it is not only a matter of the will as with Ibn Gabirol, or of faith as with Abelard, or of cultivated enlightenment as with Psellos, or even of ecstatic and selfless love of God as with Bernard of Clairvaux, but a matter of mystical immediacy that overflows all these, making available a sort of certainty which is rare among men—an actual instance, shall we say, of the Upaniṣadic ideal of the realization of the "that by which all else is known". Philosophy, then, becomes a way, a *tao*, whose purpose is primarily the removal of the obstacles to this *darśan*. Thus in the little work *The Beginning of Guidance* there is a sort of "return to simple piety" without the least naiveté (somewhat parallel to Fechner's experience in the modern era). Indeed, those who seek a reconciliation between piety and scholarship, science and religion, faith and culture, may well find a guru in al-Ghazālī.

Praise and prayer for Light are for al-Ghazālī at the apex of all that human enterprise is capable of. Why modern secular man has become ashamed of such professions is a great and very negative mystery indeed.

> O God, grant me light in my heart and light in my tomb, light in my hearing and light in my seeking, light in my hair and light in my flesh and light in my blood and light in my bones, light before me, light behind me, light to the left of me, light above me, light beneath me. O God, increase my light and give me the greatest light of all. Of Thy mercy grant me light, O Thou most merciful![4]

Historically one may read into this some revival of the Zoroastrian cult of Light, but that does not matter. We shall see what Râmânuja has to say about Light as the *pratīka* of Brahman, not to mention Bonaventura, Suhrawardī, and the Renaissance Platonist Pico della Mirandola.

Al-Ghazālī's *Ayyuha al-Walad* is another of those gems which needs almost to be memorized entire. Quite poetical in quality, it is addressed to a youth who is a seeker. After the invocatory prayer, it enjoins work, work of all kinds, but chiefly the work of prayer in the night as the chief feature of the way. The spirit which al-Ghazâlī got from the Ṣūfīs seems rather strange to the modern industrialized era; but until one has come into direct contact with such God-intoxicated men one's experience is still very limited indeed. This spirit was prevalent in the eleventh century and onwards for quite a season equally in Japan, India, Persia and Europe. The uplifting of *Eros* to its highest end which is the Vision af God and the purgation of the soul and spirit is a perpetual task of mankind. One may prefer the Stoic way of complete indifference to emotion; but al-Ghazālī's way is an alternative, or even the *yin* complement of the *yang* sort of discipline.

Our institutionalized monasteries scarcely have any conception of how literally this is still carried out in some parts of the world. Some even go to the extreme of discarding all their possessions and going forth either begging or living from nature, perfectly detached from life and death. Perhaps it is only when a culture can produce such renunciates that it may be considered as still having vitality. Hegel's view that war is necessary to prevent the people from becoming soft is by no means true. The monastic life is always the alternative to the army. In the best times of the most advanced cultures the education of youth included something at least resembling a monastic discipline from which one returned to the world only as a duty under obedience in detachment rather than embracing the world with selfish desire.

In general the *Ayyuha al-Walad* reminds us of Bhartṛhari or *Yogavaśiṣṭha* or some passages in the *Bhāgavata Purāṇa* as well as the exordia of the Carthusians, who also began to flourish about this time. The work closes with a radiant prayer in which we find zeal for the extinction of the ego in what the Ṣūfīs called *fanā'*, which is not to be confused with Buddhist *nirvāṇa* for that is done by dispassionate quietude whereas the Ṣūfīs found it in ecstasy. The beauty and music of al-Ghazālī's prayers is rivalled perhaps only by similar expressions of the school of Rāmānuja or the songs of Jacaponi da Todi.

Al-Ghazālī also wrote a little tract on the beautiful means of God (ninety-nine in all). This was a favorite theme among Muslims of all kinds and is historically interesting because about the same time a similar tract, either excerpted from or based on the *Viṣṇu Purāṇa*, began to be popular in India. It may well be that this sort of Islam had some indirect influence on Hinduism and on Rāmānuja's school in particular. However the cult of the Holy Names of Jesus, although Origen had recommended something like it, did not become popular in Western Europe until several centuries later. These things are significant not only as a matter of piety and in the frame of reference of the history and sociololgy of ideas but as an extension of the metaphysical difficulties of applying attributes to the attributeless Absolute.

In al-Ghazālī we find the same controversy coming into focus as is found in the Teṅgalai sect that followed Rāmānuja in controversy with the Veḍagalai sect, namely whether everything is literally dependent on complete surrender (*śaraṇāgati*) to God or whether there is still a region of effort, of independence, discretely and necessarily exercised on the part of man even though the surrender is made. The same polarity can easily be seen in European scholasticism, the Aristotelians for the most part inclining to the latter position, the Augustinians toward surrender and grace. Al-Ghazālī, contrary to the Aristotelians both before him (al-Fārābī and Ibn Sīnā) and after him (Ibn Rushd), was strongly bent toward the surrender school.

For al-Ghazālī the advancement of metaphysics and logic comes at a relatively subordinate level of the spiritual states. The spiritual stages themselves are the degrees of uncovering the Mystery of the Unity of God, so that, in typical Ṣūfī fashion, al-Ghazālī resorts to allegory even more than to the type of ontologizing analogy that is typical of the followers of Plotinus down through the centuries. It is the Ineffable that must be entered, and for those who have not so entered only hints *can* be given.

> Just as an ant, owing to its limited sight, will see the point of a pen blackening a blank sheet of paper and not the fingers and hand of the writer, so the person whose mental sight is not keen will attribute the actions to the immediate doer only. But there are minds which, with the searchlight of intuition, expose the lurking danger of wrongly attributing power to any except the all-powerful omniscient Being. To them every

> atom in the universe speaks out the truth of this revelation. They find it in trees, books in the running brooks, sermons in stones. The worldling will say: Though we have ears, we do not hear them. But asses also have ears and do not hear. Verily there are such ears which hear words that have no sound, that are neither Arabic nor any other language known to man. These words are drops in the boundless unfathomable ocean of divine knowledge: "If the sea were ink for the words of my Lord, the sea would surely be consumed before the words of my Lord are exhausted !" (Qur'ān XVIII, 109)[5]

Rūmi (d.1273) wrote a verse on the same theme, representing a poetical flowering of what in al-Ghazālī is still in metaphysical bud. Certainly one of the easiest things for a philosopher to get drunk on is this sort of allegory. Al-Ghazālī writes concerning *riḍā'*:

> ... *Riḍā'* or joyous submission to God's will is possible and is one of the highest to which souls of true devotees should aspire. People believe in the eccentricities of Cupid's votaries but give no ear to the ecstacies of the nature lovers of God. Perhaps they have no eyes to look at the manifestation of His Beauty; no ears to listen to the Music of his love, no heart to gaze at and enjoy His sweet presence. Perhaps they are proud of their learning and think too much of their good deeds but they have no idea of humble and broken hearts.[6]

One has to listen to such a devotee, singing ecstatically, singing and praising to exhaustion. For such is the fountain of history from which even emperors have drunk—Akbar is only one example.

In al-Ghazālī's *Alchemy of Happiness* we have primarily the themes of self-knowledge, knowledge of God, knowledge of the world as it really is, and knowledge of the next world as it really is. He begins with the axiomatic truth, ascribed to Muḥammed but familiar to us since Socrates, Zoroaster and Confucius, that he who knows himself knows God. On this theme of self-knowledge and knowledge of God, Śaṅkara had said that once all the falsehood of externals and merely logical speculations are removed, once the hurdle across the *māyā*/

Brahman ambivalence is surmounted, there is really no difference at all. Augustine teaches that one cannot know oneself except through the operation of divine grace which shows man both what he is and what he could and ought to be. Al-Ghazālī seems to mean both of these comprehensively as well as the removal of difference between God and man by Ṣūfī ecstatic experience. We also should not deny him the view that once one has known the woes of human existence, then by the logistic of contrariety one must perforce know what God must be. His statement of the question is universal: "But real self-knowledge consists in knowing the following things: What art thou in thyself, and from whence hast thou come? Whither art thou going, and for what purpose hast thou come to tarry here awhile, and in what does thy real happiness and misery consist?"

Al-Ghazālī starts as it were from the bottom, taking in Aristotle's psychology of the three souls and topping that with the Ṣūfī doctrine of the heart and the spirit. He acknowledges a certain reality of spiritual 'warfare' in the further advancement of self-knowledge, which also must include the realm of the angels and demons, leading toward the Day of Judgment (which of course he has no reason to doubt). But the culmination is still in reason :

> Similarly with man : the highest faculty in him is Reason, which fits him for the contemplation of God. If this predominates in him when he dies, he leaves behind him all the tendencies to passion and resentment, and becomes capable of association with angels. As regards his mere animal qualities, man is inferior to many animals, but reason makes him superior to them, as it is written in the Qur'ān : "To man we have subjected all things on earth."[7]

The rational soul is the seat of both knowledge and power—power over all the rest of creation, somewhat as in Rāmānuja's teaching that the beatified soul comes into a full sharing with God's nature in all respects except the power of creating and destroying the universe. For al-Ghazālī this entails three characteristics : (1) what others only see in dreams they see in their waking moments; (2) while others' wills only affect their own bodies, these, by will power, can move bodies extraneous to themselves; (3) the knowledge which others acquire by laborious learning comes to them by intuition.

Even astronomy is included in self-knowledge, for al-Ghazālī takes the doctrine of man as the microcosm quite seriously, a theme which had already been strong in both Chinese and Alexandrian tradition :

> Man has been truly termed a "microcosm" or little world in himself, and the structure of his body should be studied not only by those who wish to become doctors, but by those who wish to attain to a more intimate knowledge of God, just as close study of the niceties and shades of language in a great poem reveals to us more and more of the genius of its author.[8]

However, knowledge of the soul remains much more important, although the view of the whole situation leads to this conclusion :

> In truth, man in this world is extremely weak and contemptible; it is only in the next that he will be of value, if by the means of the "alchemy of happiness" he rises from the rank of beasts to that of angels. Otherwise his condition will be worse than the brutes, which perish and turn to dust. It is necessary for him, at the same time that he is conscious of his superiority as the climax of created things, to learn to know also his helplessness, as that too is one of the keys to the knowledge of God.[9]

Has he here anticipated Pico della Mirandola's "Essay on Man"? Is there anything here that is not still quite true in spite of all the technological advancement of the intervening centuries? Suppose we shall be able to break through the light barrier in the same way that we have broken through the sound barrier and are able somehow to harness the very forces of gravitation that hold the galaxies and spiral nebulae in their relativistic nodes of space time; shall we then know ourselves any better? Is there not still a case for piety?

Al-Ghazālī's doctrine of spiritual analogy is almost

the Thomistic *analogia entis* of the likeness of (spiritual) man to God, since for the Muslim, no less than for the Jew or the Christian, man is made in the 'image' of God (though the typical Muslim considered the Christian as risking anthropomorphism by virtue of his affirmation of the Incarnation of God in Christ).

> Not only are the man's attributes a reflection of God's attributes, but the mode of existence of man's soul affords some insight into God's mode of existence. That is to say, both God and the soul are invisible, indivisible, unconfined by space and time, and outside the categories of quantity and quality; nor can the ideas of shape, size or color attach to them.... So much, however, we can see, that as God is Ruler of the Universe, and being Himself beyond space and time, quantity and quality, governs things that are so conditioned, so the soul rules the body and its members, being itself invisible, indivisible, and unlocated at any special part. For how can the indivisible be located in that which is divisible ? From all this we see how true is the saying of the Prophet, "God created man in His own likeness."[10]

Al-Ghazālī warns that not all who cultivate self-knowledge will arrive at knowledge of God. There is a possible hiatus here that is to be bridged at all costs. Al-Ghazālī crosses it negatively, i.e., by describing six classes of unbelievers.

Knowledge of the world means *this* world, for al-Ghazālī is not of the *jīvan-mukti* school which holds that it is possible for a man to attain something resembling (if not actual) immortality in this life. Even the dialectical materialists will have to deal more directly with this problem sooner or later, for renunciation of the world, even at its minimum interpretation, has been one of the most powerful factors in shaping the destiny of mankind. What it means at bottom is not the acceeding to a romantic *êlan eternal*, although that is often a component, or giving in to a world-weariness, which is really a perversion of the true renunciation, but rather a shift of the basis of operation to a higher ideological level. There are always those who linger behind and try to patch up the old order; but even they very often yield one way or the other. Toynbee's *chrysalis* theory of the ideological relation of one culture or civilization to another is an illustration of this.

For al-Ghazālī the world is "like a table spread for successive relays of guests who come and go."

> Although we have said so much against the world, it must be remembered that there are some things in the world which are not of it, such as knowledge and good deeds. A man carries what knowledge he possesses with him into the next world, and though his good deeds have passed, yet the effect of them remains in his character. Especially is this the case with acts of devotion, which result in the perpetual remembrance and love of God. These are among "those good things" which, as the Qur'ān says, "pass not away".[11]

While he seems to capture some of Muḥammad's own severity on the personal score, al-Ghazālī comes closer here to the Neo-Confucianists who were facing the Buddhists on similar questions :

> Other things there are in the world, such as marria e, food, clothing, etc., which a wise man uses just in proportion as they help him to attain the next world. Other things which engross the mind, causing it to cleave to this world, and to be careless of the next, are purely a curse, and all which is in it is a curse, except the remembrance of God, and that which aids it.[12]

Music, for example, may be used to help attain the next world, for the highest aim of music is the experience of *fanā'*, extinction of egoitry in religious ecstasy. Dancing is included in music and is not discouraged as a means to ecstasy focussed on Allah.

Al-Ghazālī had already come to that condition where the beginnings of the 'science' of mystical theology had become almost a necessity. Well-acquainted with every extreme, he became very keen at discerning true from false mystical states, the chief criterion evidently being that of genuine spontaneity as against artificially induced conditions. Obedience to the master of the school is too often taken as the test of the genuineness of the spontaneity. Suppression of individual feelings, even to the point of death, was not considered extreme if the guru commanded it—another rather universal trend in the medieval era, from Cambodia to the British Isles, from Kamakura to Timbuktu, which the modern world thinks just will not do.

Concerning the love of God, not unlike St. Bernard to Clairvaux and the Tamil *bhaktas*, al-Ghazālī lists seven tests of its genuineness. Most of these are variations on the need of constant remembrance, usually maintained in the beginner by the constant use of the rosary. The seventh rather surprises us, for with the love of God comes hatred of the "enemies of God", as though God could have enemies. "The Prophet once asked God and said, 'O Lord ! who are Thy lovers,' and the answer came, 'those who cleave to Me as a child to its mother, take refuge in the remembrance of Me as a bird seeks shelter of its nest, and are as angry at the sight of sin as an angry lion who fears nothing.'"[13]

Al-Ghazālī is ranked as one of the greatest philosophical mystics of all time. In dealing with the classical metaphysical themes his basic problem is the question of the degree to which Being can and must be "divided" for the sake of our understanding without "departing from the unity". There are several possibilities in this regard. One is that we do it arbitrarily in order to come to an adequate understanding, trying meanwhile to keep the *pravṛtti* and *nivṛtti* in correct balance and harmony, having been given insight by grace or by dialectics into the structure of the whole; or else we must acknowledge that this structure of division and unification is inherently the nature of Being itself; or that there is something about the Being of God that is, as it were, a superabundance, overflowing into these divisions. This last seems to be al-Ghazālī's closest inclination, the corollary being that the 'otherness' involved in the 'divisions' is still of the same necessary Being. He resorts to the familiar and universal analogy of the sun and its radiation of light without diminishing itself so that even other bodies than itself can be channels of light without being destroyed in themselves. In other words, the 'other' is never other than the other of the One. The other belonging to the One, there can be no other than the One, itself at best its own othering. This 'overflow' is still the same necessary Being. Now the question is raised, is this othering really of the order of existence or of the order of intelligence, or is there any difference ? What, after all, is the relation of intelligence and existence ? We are right back up against the difficulties of the Vijñānavāda school of Buddhism again.

The Islamic philosopher, somewhat in contrast to the strict Advaitin but not in disagreement with the school of Rāmānuja or the Christian scholastic, must assert that the First Being as God is *living*. But this is not so simple since it involves also some form of assertion that the knowing, the knowledge, and the known are somehow one and the same. Al-Ghazālī proceeds basically on the analogy of the human soul, which knows this unity in itself through self-knowledge. From this the analogy to the absolute self-knowing of God is not so easy for many to make without a leap of some sort which the analogy rationalizes after the leap. It must be admitted, however, that al-Ghazālī was not bothered too much by this difficulty. It is possible to posit an "at least" argument : if this be true even in us, how much more so in God. This self-knowledge of the First is paradoxically both infinite and most simple—the only non-complex Being indeed, and one in which there is no diversity even though it may have comparison with infinite forms. Al-Ghazālī is not so clear, however, concerning the ambiguity latent in infinity. He still remains, as perhaps the Zen Buddhists of China did not, in the infinity which is in contrast to the finite, at least as far as the strict metaphysical structure is concerned (although in his mystical experiences he no doubt went further).

In al-Ghazālī we have a close analogy to the Vedāntic *sat-cit-ānanda* as Rāmānuja interprets it, i.e., not as an absence of attribution but as a superabundance of attributes and perfections in which He not only delights in Himself but further delights in imparting to His creation. But al-Ghazālī is more reserved than Rāmānuja on this point, for only God can be the perfect knower of Himself. For any Islamic philosopher, including even the most extreme Ṣūfī, to admit that God, who is so highly exalted above everything that can be known or experienced by man, could be perfectly known by anything less than Himself would almost amount to blasphemy. Whereas Ibn Sīnā and Ibn Rushd from there go on to the logical study of nature, not trying to close the gap, al-Ghazālī takes the Ṣūfī way of acknowledging the necessity of a mystical mode of knowing and experiencing that closes this gap.

As for the problem of evil, al-Ghazālī takes the position that evil is only privative. The Muslim philosophers before him had argued that Allah causes the evil and the good alike, the former for the punishment and/or correction of those who try to oppose Him and the good as reward for those who submit to His will ("Islam" means "surrender"). It will be remembered that Abelard had proposed the view that evil is relative in a graduated scale between the farthest wrongdoing and the *visio Dei.* The only evil is sin, not the contrary, for God could not create things evil in themselves and sin is a matter of the human will only. Ibn Gabirol also took a strictly voluntarist position.

Al-Ghazālī fits into the general pattern of our eleventh century by his inclusive comprehensiveness as contrasted with the sheer monism of the period just preceding. However, in a sense he begins to go beyond this into a rising above both via a mystical perspective—the *pāramārthika* in the sense which Rāmānuja takes that term rather than the Mādhyamika, i.e., an over-inclusive survey of the 'super-unitizing' of the Divine rather than elimination of all that is not sheer Unity which leaves the problem of illusion and error in a no-man's land, and that in such a way that whatever is said is expressed by way of demonstration rather than by analytical approach. As applied to the human soul, for example, in contrast to the assertion of complete identity with the Divine once all falsehood is removed, al-Ghazālī believes it to be completely spiritual in itself untrammelled by the limitations of finite existence even though sojourning therein. One might say that the Neo-Platonic elements prevail over the Aristotelian in him much more than in Ibn Sīnā, although still the interpretation of the Active Intellect is the fulcrum. In other words, he does acknowledge the validity of the way of abstraction; but one senses something else also at work, namely something very much like the old mystical *via negativa*, which must take us existentially through the stripping even of imaginative conceptions straight to the barren core wherein "intellectual"—the word has been degraded from its classical semantic weight—conceptualizations and images are equally discarded for immediate insight into the quiddity, the *tathatā*, the 'suchness' of whatever we are dealing with.

From this perspective al-Ghazālī surveys the function of the senses in laying the foundation from which this purely intellectual insight takes over and, as it were, springs into infinity. The senses are classified according to their capacity of reflexivity. The gross senses report nothing of themselves; the refined senses can check up on their operation; but the intellect alone can make the judgment as to what they have perceived, either in objective knowing of things or in self-knowledge. It must have a region of independence from them but without being completely divorced. In short, there is an over-inclusive relatedness of the Intellect whereby unavoidably both relation and non-relation may and must be operative and/or become demonstrable. Demonstration, in other words, must always counter-balance abstraction. This, of course, is not the case with a pure monist, who, having arrived at the height of the abstraction, is not concerned with the re-entry; he would rather stay "out there" and forget the world, even if he becomes evaporated into the void. The one risks burning up in the re-entry; the other, perishing in weightlessness in the lure towards the pure.

The knowledge of God remains an unfulfilled desideratum in this life for it would be an insult to the Perfection of Allah to expect that any but He should have it. Here there must always remain a painful yearning for God: "His Attributes, His Wisdom, His Actions can never be known to man as much as they are known to God Himself; the more man will know Him, the more will he yearn for Him."[14] Here is where the rationalism that gave Ibn Sīnā such confidence finds its limitations, and here is where the Ṣūfī in al-Ghazālī takes over, at least as much as is the case with St. Bernard against Abelard or Rāmānuja against the Advaitins, Buddhists and Jainas of his time, or the Japanese followers of Hōnen and Shinran against the Shinto legalism. According to al-Ghazālī there are four stages in the completion of the knowledge of God (insofar as that is possible in this life), the highest involving the experience of *fanā'* wherein the personality of one's own self is lost in the unity of God in a way that makes all else seem as mere dross, and even 'demonstration' involves some sense of loss.

For those (we trust there are none left) who would lump all "Eastern" thought into pantheism, Umaruddin has written the following concerning al-Ghazālī :

> His position is between the orthodox theologian who would divide God and his creation in two entities, and that of the pantheist who would deny the existence of everything except God. The universe has a being but only with relation to God. This is the meaning of the Qur'anic verse, "Everything perisheth except His countenance, His aspects." (88 : 28) It is difficult to determine exactly what al-Ghazālī means by 'aspect'. In any case it does away with pantheism and yet remains loyal to the mystical verity of the One-and-Onliness of God.[15]

The phase of transdescendence in the life of the mystic or prophet, correlating with the Bodhisattva Vow of the Buddhist ascetic, seems to have engaged al-Ghazālī considerably. When one realizes the influence of al-Ghazālī down through the centuries, one wonders if he had not really reached this Bodhisattva condition. Concerning the mystic and prophet from Umaruddin :

> "Muhammed of Arabia ascended the highest Heaven and returned. I swear by God that if I ever reached that point, I should never have returned." These are the words of the great Muslim Saint Abdul Quddus of Gangoh. In the whole range of Sufi literature it will probably be difficult to find words which in a single sentence disclose such an acute perception of the psychological difference between the prophetic and the mystical types of consciousness. The mystic does not wish to return, from the 'unitary experience'; even when he does return, as he must, his return does not mean much for mankind at large. The prophet's return is creative. He returns to insert himself to control the forces of history, and thereby to create a fresh world of ideals. For the mystic the repose

> of unitary experience is something final; for the prophet it is the awakening within him of world-shaking psychological forces, calculated to completely transform the human world. The desire to see his religious experience transformed into a living world-force is supreme in the prophet.[16]

Al-Ghazālī should be a reliable guide even today, avoiding the extremes of mystical evasiveness and prophetic fanaticism, but still having the Tao, that indefinable but altogether necessary charisma of becoming the voice of the *Weltgeist* as it moves through history.

His system of virtues puts al-Ghazālī almost in the lead of Abelard as one of the world's greatest casuists (if we may take that word in its original meaning of the right judgment of particular cases of morals according to established principles). He seems again to have had Tao that not only grasps the mean between extremes but infuses them with the *teh* that makes them effective in the world of men. He takes the Aristotelian four virtues of wisdom, courage, temperance and justice as a framework but in between weaves an arabesque of virtues, and vices for the sake of contrast and avoidance, which is as accurate as it is intricate. It is excellent theoretically, manifesting the 'demonstrative' way in ethics, even as it is practically efficient, giving a Rule which perhaps is applicable today. Within his own century as contrasted with the previous ones, this art of listing particular virtues and vices had become quite a common undertaking; Abelard and Rāmānuja may be taken as examples, in contrast to, for example, Śaṅkara and Erigena, to whom the only virtue is *Brahma-jñāna* and the only vice is non-transcendence of *māyā*.

Concerning the polarity of society and solitude, al-Ghazālī evidently considered solitude a concession to those who could not carry on sufficient contemplation in the round of worldly activity, but a valid one nevertheless since thereby is acknowledged the priority of man's duty to God. But it should not be carried out in sacrifice of one's duties to society. It seems a matter of the middle way.

In all, knowledge stays pretty much on top with al-Ghazālī, the highest knowledge being the immediate prophetic knowledge of the Will of God. Constant remembrance of His presence is forever the key to everything.

31. Ryōnin

Ryōnin (1072-1132) is the founder of the Yūzū Nembutsu sect of Japan which taught that there is an interaction between the *nembutsu* of one devotee and the *nembutsu* of others. Ryōnin is supposed to have received the *yūzū nembutsu* teaching as a direct revelation from Amida Buddha. It is very typical for each sect to make quite a fuss over the line of patriarchs or apostolic succession; but since Ryōnin himself and his faithful followers believed that he had a direct revelation from Amida, they did not need any apostolic succession to vindicate his and their charisma. As with many great *bhaktas* and socratic gurus, Ryōnin left very little behind in writing except the verses which embody the revelation from Amida.

His father was a local landlord of the lower aristocracy so that, given the heavy weight of the lower aristocracy in ecclesiastical matters, Ryōnin probably had some degree of class consciousness in his attitudes which would predispose him to the *nembutsu* practice rather than the Tendai, which had become a stronghold of "upperclass" Buddhism by that time, or the more rigorous Zen discipline (in so far as it was available as yet, for Eisai and Dōgen do not appear on the historical stage until about the time of Ryōnin's death). His mother was the daughter of a Shinto priest, which gives us just another hint of the increasingly syncretistic relationship between Buddhism, Shinto and even Confucianism if not Taoism also during the late Heian period. His brother had preceded him on Mt. Hiei and eventually gave him initiation to the novitiate.[1]

Most charismatic figures in the history of religions and often in the history of science and philosophy receive an ecstatic vision of their true vocation at a relatively early age, as Sorokin has demonstrated; but Ryōnin was already forty-six years old when he had a vision of Amida who "revealed the philosophy of the *yūzū nembutsu* as the pathway to salvation. At the same time, he was presented with a visual *maṇḍala* of Amida surrounded by ten bodhisattvas as the central image to be used for veneration while chanting."[2] Such *maṇḍalas* by this time had become relatively common in Japan as well as in Tibet. It is noteworthy that these *maṇḍalas* had become increasingly elaborate through the centuries, having originated as part of the halo or nimbus. This pattern of increasing elaboration and diversification, so obvious in art and architecture, is what has led us to the designation "exfoliation and elaboration", i.e., of the original inspirations of the basically monist and relatively monolithic systems of the ninth century. Such elaborations were by no means unique to Buddhism but can easily be discerned in Gothic architecture as well as in Dravidian architecture and iconography, and also in the styles of famous mosques in the Islamic world (notably Iran).

Throughout Eurasia visions such as those of Ryōnin were considered as very important, although not unusual. It is only very recently in Euramerica that they have come to be considered as pathological, oddly enough. Though devoted to Amida, Ryōnin's next vision was evidently of a Hindu deity, Bishamonten (Vaiśravaṇa), which reminds us of how in Tāntric circles by this time almost everywhere, but notoriously in Southeast Asia, Tibet, Nepal, and pretty much in China as well as in India itself, the difference between Hinduism and Buddhism became so blurred that they had become virtually indistinguishable (this being one reason often given for the disappearance of Buddhism as such from India). At any rate, the burden of this vision was that he should abandon his hermitage in accordance with the Bodhisattva vow to teach Buddhism to all suffering beings. The Emperor Toba became his disciple, vowing to repeat the *yūzū nembutsu* one hundred times a day. Needless to say, with imperial patronage Ryōnin's popularity increased. Among the places influenced by him was the Shūrakuji temple, which had originally belonged to the Shingon (esoteric) sect. This later became renamed the Dainembutsuji and became the headquarters for Ryōnin's successor, Gongen. Ryōnin seems to have been in contact with virtually all of the movements of his time. There must have been quite a bit of Shinto mixed in with his *nembutsu*, for at a second appearance Bishamonten "allegedly presented him with the names of eight million Japanese gods, who had vowed to recite the *yūzū nembutsu* daily."[3]

The Matsunagas give us the following concerning Ryōnin's practice and its meaning :

> *Yūzū*, derived from the *Kegongyō* (*Avataṃsaka sūtra*), denotes the intercommunicable relationship between existents, and in the form of the *yūzū nembutsu* is considered to be a practical application of the Kegon concept of *jiji muge* (the interrelationship of phenomena). The entire philosophy is summarized in the revelation Ryōnin received from Amida, as follows :
>
> One man equals all men,
> All men equal one man,
> One practice equals all practices,
> All practices equal one practice;
> This is *ōjō* (attainment) by Other-power.
>
> The ten worlds are within a single thought,
> And if the *yūzū nembutsu* is recited countless times,
> All virtues will be complete.[4]

Here we could invoke a long list of parallels even among Ryōnin's contemporaries, including Rāmānuja, Śrīkaṇṭha, al-Ghazālī and Bernard of Clairvaux. Thus fundamentally it remains true that it is not necessary to limit a seminal thinker or charismatic person merely to the history of religions simply because the *bhakti* or aesthetic element in his attitudinal nexus predominates—unless, of course, there is nothing else. But that is very seldom the case.

Nor is the ethical aspect missing in Ryōnin, for by using this *yūzū nembutsu* something can be done for the relief of human suffering and even suffering in general. If one's *tapas* is adequate, whether in the *bhakti*, *karma* or *jñāna* form, many philosophies, especially during the centuries under review, held that the whole of the universe will be purified. The Matsunagas write :

> Due to the interrelated nature of existents, man does not stand alone, but is inseparably united to the sufferings and

> fate of all mankind. Thus the action of a single individual, even though it may seemingly have invisible immediate consequences, ultimately affects the destiny of the entire society. In view of this vast interwoven network, the constant chanting of the *nembutsu* by one individual permeates and purifies the whole of society, just as the chanting of the group influences the life of the individual, for the individual contains within himself the totality of the universe and mirrors all other attributes of existence. If he is successful in purifying himself, he will in turn expurgate the universe reflected within him.[5]

These claims in some cases may be exaggerated, but the claims are so universal that there must be something there, and something very important, whether one calls it the power of intercessory prayer or uses some other designation. There are places where the practice of constant *japa* or *nembutsu* continues. At Mt. Athos, for example, where Byzantine tradition still survives, the so-called "Jesus prayer" is still effectively in force; and at Vrindaban and Varanasi the practice is still in force to the extent that people do it in shifts so that the chanting of the holy name never ceases.

Group or congregational practice in addition to private individual practice is important in Ryōnin's *nembutsu.* The theological claim—and who could disapprove it since in order for it to be effective it has to be done with such detachment in the spirit of praise that no reward is expected and therefore no experimental method will touch the inner essence of its significance—is that group practice is increased in intensity ten-fold geometrically as the number using it is increased arithmetically. But, like all *bhaktas,* Ryōnin depends implicitly on the grace of Amida. Needless to say, once the devotee is caught up in the spirit of devotion, all sense of *me* and *mine* should disappear, which is supposed to be evidence of grace at work.

Another point in the syncretic trend of Ryōnin's *bhakti* was derived from the Tendai concept of 3,000 worlds contained in one thought—the classical micro-macrocosm doctrine of the so-called "perennial philosophy" which is very strong in Psellos and by no means absent in Islam and Latino-Germanic Europe through Nicholas of Cusa and others right down to Hermann Lotze in much more recent times. But notably among Ryōnin's contemporaries it was especially strong among the pre-Chu Hsi Neo-Confucians and even in Lu Hsiang-shan. Again, the universality of this doctrine makes one suspect that those moderns who have lost this may be missing something of profound importance.

Ryōnin evidently made a major contribution to the development of devotional music, which suggests comparison with some of his Sūfī contemporaries or some of the famous Byzantine hymn writers or those who were further developing Gregorian plain chant so that it, like Gothic architecture, was becoming increasingly rich if not occasionally florid. We need not mention the Ālvārs and Nayanmars of South India, whose *bhakti* was developing karnatic music to a high degree. Unfortunately the global history of music has yet to be written.

32. Rāmānuja

In Rāmānuja (d. c. 1137) the monistic tendency of the ninth century has given way to a more comprehensive supra-monistic panentheism in which a dynamic harmony is achieved—a harmony of transcendence and immanence and mediation, of individuation and universalization, of logic, praise and social responsibility. There is scarcely anyone in the list of those who founded a system of philosophy who was more saintly than Rāmānuja. He was born in South India, went through the traditional training, was married, left home and family at a rather early age and became a monk. He worked mostly at Śrirangam (Trichinopoly) until the Muslims conquered that part of India. Then he fled to Melkote, a small mountain near Mysore, where according to tradition he discovered a very beautiful image of Viṣṇu in an ant hill and established a village which still remains pretty much as he planned it. He converted several kings of the region who had been Jainas mostly, and did many miracles. He returned to Śrirangam as soon as the Muslims allowed restoration of the traditional worship there. His death was of such a sort that his body may still be seen undecayed without embalming (or so it is claimed) in the temple at Śrirangam—the final test of sanctity according to traditions of all faiths. He had achieved a sort of resurrection-body long since, remaining behind after the pattern of a Bodhisattva for the sake of others. Finally allowed, he achieved *videha-mukti* and left the work for his disciples to carry on.

There is the famous story that when Rāmānuja received the mantra of initiation, he was warned that he must keep it secret. He asked what would happen if he spoke it to others and was told that he would be damned forever. Then he asked what would happen to those who heard it and was told that they would receive salvation there and then. Immediately he became bold as few Brahmins before or after him have ever done. He rushed to the top of the pagoda-like structure over the gate of the temple compound and proclaimed the mantra at the top of his voice so that all the multitude below could hear it, including many out-castes. Rāmānuja thus and in other ways introduced a new element of democracy into Hinduism, ever granting greater favors to his lower-caste devotees, who often had greater piety than his fellow-Brahmins.

For such reasons, and also because of his skill in logic and argumentation (although he did not like to engage in disputes), he was much persecuted by the followers of Śaṅkara and had to flee to North India, suffering much deprivation and barely escaping death at their hands. But after his return to the South his saintliness as well as his scholarship were so well established that he soon became recognized as the equal of Śaṅkara.

There can be no doubt that Rāmānuja's heart was primarily warmed by the Tamil *bhakti* tradition, with Nammālvār (Śaṭha-kopa) as his chief spiritual guide. Of course he owed much to his teacher Yāmunācārya, but he so far surpassed the teacher that all acknowledge him as the virtual founder of a new *sampradāya* (school or sect) which still flourishes. The school later became divided between the Teṅgalai and Vaḍagalai sub-sects, the former inclining more toward the Tamil tradition and emphasizing grace and surrender (the 'cat' theory : the mother cat carries her kittens to safety). The Vaḍagalai is for the most part more inclined toward the Sanskrit tradition, more strict about ritual observances, and less 'democratic' in general. They espouse the 'monkey' theory : the young monkey has to ride on the back or cling to the underside of the mother, so that effort is needed on the part of the *bhakta*. However, there is now after many centuries of quarrelling good feeling between them and some chance of reconsolidation. Although there has crept in through the centuries a lot of conservatism, this school seems to be squaring up most realistically with the modern world, for inherent in Rāmānuja's philosophy is a marvellous balance between the eternally vaild and the eternally changing. Indeed, to risk a summary generalization, it seems that this is his chief objection to strict Advaita, that *you can't live that way*! Rāmānuja called his system Viśiṣṭādvaita, qualified non-dualism, the nearest modern term being panentheism.

Constant remembrance of God underlies his systematic considerations. In most of the temples following his teaching this is guaranteed by an almost uninterrupted schedule of devotions ranging through all the emotions, using everything from flowers, incense, instrumental music and pieces of cloth to precious gems and priceless poetry often as not spontaneous. One of the most common practices is the constant repetition of the Holy Name *Nārāyaṇa* in a rhythmical pattern that becomes almost intoxicating. Rāmānuja believed that, as the *Gītā* says, one *becomes* that which one worships. No less than with al-Ghazālī, Rāmānuja combines systematic considerations and the tradition of ecstatic praise. Al-Ghazālī, al-Suhrawardī, Abelard, Anselm and Bernard of Clairvaux would all have found their equal in him, and no less their peer in humility, for he was the last to acknowledge that he was anything at all.

For Rāmānuja, God is necessarily and intimately related to His creation. He cannot be considered as without attributes; rather, to Rāmānuja God has the ultimate possible superfluity of attributes. The *nirguṇa-saguṇa* controversy engages him through many long arguments in the *Śrī Bhāṣya*, his commentary on the *Brahma Sūtras*. If one affirms the sheer *nirguṇa* as the extreme followers of Śaṅkara do, it is difficult indeed to speak of creation or even of the existence of the world; but if one does not in some mode affirm this Simplicity of God, one runs the risk of losing Him in the manifold. Rāmānuja tries hard to bridge this gap by constantly reiterating the good qualities. Even though his interpretation of the *nirguṇa* as meaning that there are no *undesirable* qualities in the Divine Nature is a sort of trick of textual interpretation, it does have the advantage of acknowledging the *accessibility* of God.

Everything is so intimately bound to the exaltedness and unity of God, which cannot be compromised by any 'other', that Rāmānuja admits that the closest analogy (and he is fully aware that it is only an analogy) is that the whole universe is His body. Of course if one forgets that this is only metaphorical one gets into difficulty; but then if one does not, the same difficulty (and the same way out of it) remains. For metaphor itself is only one sort of embodiment of meaning, even as meaning in turn is also an embodiment of That which must sooner or later be phenomenologically reduced to, and at the same time recognized as, the Single Component which we call Reality/Brahman. Nevertheless, this metaphor would be repugnant to all but the most heretical of his Muslim and Jewish contemporaries, for to them to say that God has a body in any sense is nothing short of blasphemy. But then they had to deal with emanation theory, and emanation is just half-a-jump from embodiment in the sense which Rāmānuja intends. As for his Christian contemporaries, in the doctrine of the Incarnation of Christ they had the *Exemplar* doctrine of embodiment which is quite compatible with what Rāmānuja teaches. Thus it might be said that Rāmānuja reconciles the extremes of Erigena and Abelard.

In regard to Rāmānuja's philosophy of embodiment, one must understand his doctrine of the *antaryāmin* (the "inner controller") and his version of the nature of mystical union, namely that the beatified soul is admitted to the privilege through the operation of extraordinary grace gained by adequate surrender (*prapatti*) to God as the *Parama Puruṣa*, the super-Personal Deity who so abounds in marvellous attributes that He shares all characteristics (though contrary to Śaṅkara, retaining His personhood and individuality) except that of creating and destroying the universe. God wills embodiment in order to relieve souls limited by finitude from bondage to blindness to their true nature, which is essentially spiritual and of the nature of Light, that nature itself being a qualified mode of the Lord's own embodiment. Therefore liberation (*mokṣa*) is deliverance from separation from God, but not complete absorption into Him or loss of identity in a transcendental blank.

One of the most vexing problems in comparative studies, both for those who demand precision of demonstrable experiential results and for those who are still within any single dogmatic tradition, is that of the rule of the Holy Spirit, or the *antaryāmin* in Vaiṣṇava tradition, the Active Intellect of the Aristotelians, the *Teh* of Chinese tradition, or the *sākṣī* observer-consciousness. A theme with many other variants in all traditions, including Jewish and strict Qur'anic Islamic traditions, it is the most difficult to discern and yet perhaps the most crucial *vidyā* or realization of all, for without it, according to all authorities, human enterprise comes to nothing. The further understanding of its role in nature and in the inner Being of God, and the linking of this with the reaches of the human mind, leads one into a sort of metaphysical vertigo; nevertheless it cannot be avoided, for there is something here that is all-important and not mere semantical quibbling. Rāmānuja goes into highly technical arguments which involve many references to scripture as well as appeals to experience and to reason. In essence perhaps it could be said simply that for him the *antaryāmin* is *that which is embodied* in all reality-in-manifestation, even in the invisible soul. This is near to Whitehead's "consequent nature" of God, and so may not easily be relegated to the closet of obscure medieval speculation. If something like Rāmānuja's position is not adopted, we have no organon, no logistic for making a unified study, and should rather engage ourselves in a full-time cultivation of 'emptiness' after the manner of extreme Mahāyāna or Rinzai Zen, although even they did not escape the necessity of admitting something which they termed the *Sambhogakāya* which enprinciples all of *māyā*, 'empty' though it be at the core.

There is a sense of realistic continuity in Rāmānuja's system which seems more marked than those of his contemporaries or even those of other Indian systems before or after him (unless perhaps with the Vijñānavāda, but without the risk of subjective idealism inherent in that). It is a sense of continuity not only through all the elements of nature, which are unified by virtue of their being degrees of embodiment of God, but also through the psychic and spiritual realms as well. It may be that some inconsistencies are involved in this matter of degrees, for in another sense Rāmānuja does not allow that there are degrees of intensity of God's omnipresence. The all-pervasiveness of the *antaryāmin* leaves little to be desired; after that vision is given, there is only praise till heaven opens and the soul is free for immortal destiny. It is said not only by Rāmānuja but by many others that then inconsistencies are melted together and problems are seen to have been pseudo-problems and are not so much solved as dissolved.

This most difficult problem of rightly distinguishing the balance or dynamic relationality between God and the individual or individuated soul was sharp in Islam also, ranging from the extreme Ṣūfīs who sometimes in ecstatic states would claim almost a superiority to God in *fanā'* or at least an obliteration of the difference between the self and God, and the ultra-orthodox to whom it was blasphemy to go so far as to suggest that man could ever completely know the will of Allah in this life, much less His nature. Within the Christian fold there was also quite a wide range between the Hesychasts of Mt. Athos in their extreme quietism and the jubilant armies of the *Miles Christiani* going on crusade against the 'infidel Turk' ! There was a very similar range of varieties in China and Japan, from extreme militant Legalism and Shintoism to escapist and quietist Zen. And the theory of the Active Intellect that al-Fārābī had introduced would continue to be a source of controversy for all parties from the palasades of Bukhara to the new citadels of learning at Cambridge and Oxford.

Identity and difference, like mirrors on opposite walls, equally reflect God's infinity of aspects, multiplying the images; but He remains the same. He can, radically, have no true 'other', for even that would be derived from His Unity. Nevertheless, each individual thing at its particular node, at its particular focus of the image, by its very preservation of its own identity, remains 'other than', but *somehow* inseparable from, the One who is One-only-without-a-second. How does Rāmānuja handle this "somehow"? He always writes with such confidence that it never occurs to him tnat there is any "somehow" there to explain. His only difficulty is in explaining what evidently was perfectly clear to him, that both comprehensively and in each individuality all Reality, every reality, follows the same rule: whatever is, is a glorifier of God in the same sense that every adjective is, so to speak, a glorifier of the noun it modifies—and both the noun and the adjective are *equally real.*

His arguments from logic alone are strong enough, but Rāmānuja turns, as anyone then must do, to scripture as his authority for the most part. The canon of Hindu scriptures was many times the size of either the Bible or the Qur'ān, but Rāmānuja handles them very intelligently. No less than with St. Bernard, the Victorines and al-Ghazālī, Rāmānuja is only trying to make a rational apologetic for the sake of his audience of what must be realized from beyond reason. In other words, *bhakti* and *prapatti* for him, contrary to Śaṅkara, take precedence over *jñāna* and *karma.* This does not mean that reason is not valid in its own designated area. Rāmānuja is trying to show that no matter what the topic may be, no matter where we begin, we are in the midst of an infinity of infinities of the 'overflow' of God's being. And we must swim, as it were, in the undertow of these all too cosmic currents until we realize that we are always both immediately and mediately in an unbreakable engagement existentially with the Source of all being to Whom all devotion, and all work as an aspect of that devotion, is due.

It might be argued nowadays that such a mystical foundation does not give an adequate basis for scientific research. Admittedly, Rāmānuja did not make any great advances in science such as Ibn Sīnā did, and today the most orthodox of his following are not encouraging influence from the West; nevertheless there is nothing inherent in his system to prevent the further scientific investigation of nature. Rather, much more than with strict Advaita, the Rāmānuja tradition offers more encouragement to science by allowing the aspect of difference in its own perspective. Moreover, all matter as the embodiment of God may and must be investigated as His manifestation, His *līlāvibhūti.*

Two basic doctrines of Viśiṣṭādvaita undergird its emphasis

on *bhakti* throughout, namely, the supremacy of the *personal* nature of the Godhead and the concept of creation as *līlā* (play). For Rāmānuja, true knowability implies personality; and being known as personal leads directly to worship, to *bhakti*, which, in being received, still further reinforces the personal relation to the personal nature—somewhat in the same sense that Whitehead teaches, viz., that God is the Supreme Appreciator, the faculty of appreciation being the highest characteristic of personality, and worship being the highest form of appreciation. The doctrine of creation as the "play" of the Creator undergirds the *bhakti* relation between the creature and the Creator by putting the primary focus on the aesthetic order, with its roots in love and its fruition in complete freedom. For Rāmānuja, all the rational arguments for the existence of God fail; but the concept of *līlā* remains of a super-rational order, and stands not as a 'proof' but as a truth of the apophatic order. The world is an expression of the Joy of the Lord, and such expression is *easy* for Him. It follows that the way of return to Him on the part of the creature should be one of ease and of delight, freely expressed towards the Ground and Source of Freedom.

Rāmānuja interprets *māyā* as God's alluring game or play, and gives the beginnings of a systematic consideration of the play idea as the foundation and reason for the creation of the world and the redemption of man. In Vaiṣṇavism laughter is seriously acknowledged as a form of devotion. It is as though Kṛṣṇa were bewitching all mankind, playing his flute alluring us on, singing, "Catch me if you can" while He dances out into the starry cosmic spaces leaving only traces of light upon which we must take our own half-mortal flight; or again, the least little glitter of whatever there may be in sub-atomic structure is another allurement that comes from Him, for He Himself is ineffably there: "Catch me if you can, but every plan remains my own. You are only man." And we shall give pursuit, though we shall never 'catch' Him, for it is He that is 'playing' with us!

On the score of ontology, there could be no meaning to devotion on the part of an unreal or indescribable (*anirvacanīya*) soul to a fictitious *Īśvara* who is only a symbolic portrayal of Being as such. Yet this is essentially what the Advaitin school believed. By long argument, Rāmānuja and his school abolish the whole concept of *māyā* as illusion and prove that individuation must be a distinct and necessary component of Being itself. It follows that true devotion, as the highest relation between the modes of individuation (both between themselves, and between each of them and the 'undifferentiated'), is also a necessary relation. For Rāmānuja, bliss (*ānanda*) is the innermost attribute of Being, and the common bond between the modes and the Ground. The other necessary attributes (*satya, jñāna, ananta*—truth, knowledge, infinity) are necessary because without them Being would be only a vacuum, a void (*śūnya*). Though *karma* and *jñāna* may lead to *ānanda*, they cannot reach it except by a transfer to another order; but *bhakti* leads directly into the heart of Being itself, since it is of the same order as that 'heart'.

Being itself cannot be impersonal. That view involves what Marcel calls the *fallacy of abstraction*. Being *is* Bliss : this is irreducible. All other attributes are enfolded within it, but as separable, distinct factors, constituting dependent orders of reality. But bliss/*ānanda*, though in a sense it remains an attribute as descriptive, as the irreducible and all-including attribute, is yet of the same order as irreducible Being. There is no more important key to the understanding of the whole of the Vedānta than this, and it is to Rāmānuja's credit that he seems to see its implications much more fully than the other *ācāryas*.

Upāsanā in its broad sense means simply remembrance or recollection in the technical sense as developed also within mystical theology in the West. But in the more restricted sense it indicates the technique of meditation which makes this remembrance or recollection possible. For Rāmānuja and all his school it is described by the metaphor of the flow of a steady stream of oil (Rāmānuja's favorite metaphor). It is a strange tragedy indeed that in the West the secularization of philosophy since Descartes has left this discipline to go its own way within the strictly religious field, although within that field it has continued to play a very important role.

In a word, the method for Rāmānuja is *affective meditation.* At first glance this looks very simple. But when one realizes that this had to be worked out against the strong stream of Śaṅkara's labored view that the method is that of *gnostic assimilation*, and that few of the *ācāryas* who followed after Rāmānuja linked *bhakti* with meditation at all but left it purely as the devotional expression of emotion as such, then it becomes clear what a high synthesis he was striving for. Śrīkaṇṭha is probably the only one of the major *ācāryas* who takes the same position as Rāmānuja on this point. Even Nimbārka, who is probably the closest to Rāmānuja in general, kept *bhakti* and *upāsanā* distinct from each other.

For Rāmānuja and his school, identity by *gnosis* with the Absolute, which eternally remains an absolute "Other", is inherently impossible. Otherness can be bridged only by *affection* —affection, moreover, which liberates one from all sense of frustration. *Gnosis* can give only an ingrowth of self-limitation which, intensified to the utmost, falsely seems to be a transcendence but in reality is nothing more than a dead-end beyond which none can go and from which none can escape once he is in it; but *affection* is a reciprocation from and within the boundlessness of the Other, who is not just a blank but an unlimited overplus of His own otherness, not just reducing all to Himself but rather embracing all within Himself by the re-enfoldment of grace as the free gift of His Being.

Not that knowledge does not have its place; far from that. For, as is the case with interpersonal relations on the purely human level, love and knowledge go hand-in-hand. Even in cases when love is "blind" an intuitive knowledge springs up within the love; else it is not true love but only sentiment. There can be no true remembrance of the Beloved that is not motivated by affection. How easily we forget those whom we do not love! and if we are in love, how the image of the Beloved lingers in all that we do. The completion of personality cannot be achieved without this sort of affective identification with an other; it becomes very deeply rooted in the subconscious mind and gives color to all that we do. This intuitive affective sense of identification for the followers of Rāmānuja is expressed in the term *sākṣātkāra*, a word that may be heard in almost any conversation of a serious nature among them even today, for it is the most basic concept governing their life and is the prime source of their healthy-mindedness.

It is a common saying that there are a lot of Advaitin philosophers in India, but very few truly realized Advaitins. Although it is possible, as perhaps in the case of Ramanamaharṣi of Tirunanamalai, to come into the absolute plenitude of Being by the Advaitic *sādhanā*, the likelihood of getting stuck in a complete withdrawal, in a complete blockage of all communicative Presence—even that of 'being present' to oneself—is very great indeed. For that matter, an examination of the Ramana's life story, at least from the outside, makes one wonder if even he had not been mad at one time and finally somehow came out of it.

Be that as it may, the basic necessity is the universalization of the identification; and this is obviously easier when the identification is conceived in terms of an *other*, and not the expansion-by-reduction of one's own self-awareness—especially in view of the fact that the atrophying of the affections necessary in the latter case can lead to untold complications. Moreover, the universalization is more natural when it functions by an analogical and anagogical enlargement by hierarchical ascent rather than by an ingressive intensification of point-consciousness in which all analogies are reduced to zero.

The concept of Brahman/God and the method of *sādhanā* are for Rāmānuja intimately connected. The affective aspect of the method is grounded on the Divine Mercy, and the necessity of attributes in the Divine Nature gives support for the *jīva's* approaching Him as Personal Presence. Quite the same doctrine may also be found in St. Bonaventura. Affection, love in all of its gradations, reaches beyond knowledge, for the essential reason that love is of the nature of God Himself; and the other attributes of divinity only follow after this. At the deeper level the method and the end are essentially the same—an emphasis that cannot be overstressed. Basically the method is meditation, contemplation, *upāsanā*. It is passing strange that such disciplines are no longer considered necessary to philosophers. Perhaps Spinoza was the last major figure to consider the *contemptus mundi* as essential for philosophy as such and not just a twirk in the mystical temperament.

The attainment of the state of *jīvan-mukti* is the Advaitic equivalent of what Rāmānuja and his school refer to under the metaphor of the continuous flow of oil. In other words, *dhyāna* for the Advaitin is absolute perfection as an ultra-phenomenal *gnostic* state while still in the world, while Rāmānuja denies that such perfection is possible in the flesh and interprets *dhyāna* as the perfection of *bhakti*. *Dhyāna* is the settling into the Presence, the harmonious immobility, the peaceful dwelling in oneness, in which love flows like the steady uninterrupted stream of oil. In *dhyāna* there is a re-inclusion of all of nature and life, all that has been left behind in the 'plunge', and the symphonic expansion of the Presence into wholeness. Most interpreters stress the aspect of intuitive knowledge here; and it cannot be denied that Rāmānuja does mean that also. But to us it appears that his primary stress remains on the affective aspect—indeed, not aspect, for to him meditative *vidyā* is affectional *by nature*, and not just 'intuitive'. Thus he says: "Meditation must become vivid like sense perception; it must be marked with a high degree of love; it must grow every day; and it should be done throughout life. It is denoted by *dhyāna*, *upāsanā*, and other terms; and it is more than mere knowledge of texts."

For Rāmānuja, contemplation is still of an Other, even though there may be a unitive (as affective) relation with that (Absolute and absolutely transcendent) Other. These higher states in all schools blur; and in the Advatin school, if we may use a strong expression, the blurring is taken as the basic principle: unitive *relation* there is none: only realization of the blur, total nondifferentiation, the complete erasure of both relation and related. Thus in the strict sense, for the Advaitin there can be no contemplation; there is only meditation and *samādhi*, or transcendence of personality and all that goes with it: a sort of evaporation into indescribability—which Rāmānuja and his followers ridicule as either meaningless or impossible.

For Rāmānuja, the internal relatedness of the world-and-souls and God is reciprocal. Not only is there nothing outside of God (world-and-souls are internal to Him), but He, in order to make this possible, is inherent to them (He is internal to them). Thus it is that *bhakti* means not only elevation but inwardness, as is also the case with Bonaventura. God's

Relatedness—that of Being itself—is so internally structured that our own very being is essentially caught up into it. Thus *upāsanā* is the reduction out of metaphysical falsehood (*avidyā*, 'beginningless' *karma*) back into and at the same time forward into, our own primordiality in Him. Hence it is not a matter of ideas or ideation, but a matter of *bhakti* which reaches beyond and beneath ideas and all forms of duality by re-linking the differences. Hence our term *unitive relation*, for relatedness is simply the ontology of affection.

It is both within and towards God as indwelling, an *antaryāmin*, that *bhakti* is both aroused and realized in its culmination, the other realizations (exaltedness, power, transcendence) being as it were a necessary parabola through which the devotion must pass. Thus the sense of egocentricity is dissolved, and the focus of the heart and mind is at once turned more deeply inward and more vastly outward. As the sense of awe merges into participation in existential harmony, one realizes that there is a seat of agency within oneself that has been at work all the time, but unconsciously : the Spirit groaning within our spirits, working toward the consummation of the creatures (to use St. Paul's language); the spiritual within the psychical, the God within, working to restore the 'image' of the perfect Godhead befouled by the fall (*avidyā* being the Hindu way of expressing this 'fall'). When this happens, 'sonship' is restored. Individuation is not broken down or dissolved, but the ultimate level of individuation, with its primary subordinate nodes, is brought into full focus : one realizes that he is only an individual echo (*ādheya*) of the Ultimate Individual (*ādhāra*) in which and out of which all individuals derive their dimensions in qualified identity. But the qualification of the identity is not only attributive; it is substantial also. It is the *antaryāmin* itself, as the Relatedness of Love, which inheres in the Absolute rendering it Personal and rendering ourselves capable of enjoying itself. Such an ultimate profundity, such a balanced harmony of dynamism and identity, is perhaps best realized by Rāmānuja, for all of the other *ācāryas* seem to stop short somewhere or warp the subtlety (and the profundity lies in the subtlety) by over-emphasis on one extreme or other.

For Rāmānuja the formal proofs for the existence of God fail. With revelation as the only 'proof', the crux of our knowledge of God lies (as we see with Bonaventura) in the mystical ontology of experience—difficult for the modern man because experience is generally considered to belong to the empirical realm, whereas ontology belongs to the realm of grace. Yet grace is 'understandable' only after it is experienced, and hence must be considered as a matter of mysticism and not of epistemology in the usual sense. It is only in this perspective that Rāmānuja's doctrine of the soul as the embodiment of God may be understood. Bonaventura's innateness of the idea of God in us is of the same nature as this embodiment, which is technically termed *apṛthak-siddha*. Again, Rāmānuja's doctrine that the soul is a mode (*prakāra*) of Brahman, it seems to us, is best understood in this light of innateness rather than in the usual cosmological order. Souls are modes of God in the sense not that they are undifferentiable from Him, but that His *presence* in them is their true Being and their foundation of knowing Him both objectively and subjectively. Things too are modes in the sense that their being cannot be truly known except in the common ontological root of the Divine Presence in them and the knower.

Behind the use of scriptures is always the doctrine of revelation, which is much suspect in our own time, not only because of the greater importance of what is considered as reason, but also because of the meeting of all traditions in such a way that we are tempted to say that since there have been so many 'revelations', all of which claim absolute authority, we cannot accept their rival claims and therefore reject them all as obsolete and of little use. But such a judgment is surely short-sighted. Would it not be better to accept all, and set about at systematic reinterpretations and the rebuilding of a comprehensive theology on a comprehensive basis ? The time for mere 'comparative' studies is past; we must go on to synthesis and integrally build—a job wherein once again philosophers must join in to keep the theologians awake, as Hegel suggests in his philosophy of religion.

As with all Vedāntic philosophers, the basic problem for Rāmānuja is that of release from the "merry-go-round" of *saṃsāra*, from spiritual bondage by virtue of limitations of the senses and the results of karma or the accumulated results of all past sins—this is the essential basic given, just as in all the Christian scholastics original sin is the basic orientation. In a word, the problem is that of salvation. Rāmānuja must, if he follows the scriptures at all, assent to the central teaching that *Brahma-vidyā*, the vision of the Absolute Reality, is the solution of the problem. But the interpretation of the nature of this 'vision' as well as the means to reach it is where he parts company with his predecessors (except, of course, his guru Yāmunācārya and behind him the Ālvārs). This Brahman for him is not only supremely the *personal* God, full of inexhaustible glorious qualities, but positively goes out to take the initiative in this business of salvation; hence the importance of the doctrine of grace. But on the side of the recipient of this grace, it would be strange if mere knowledge, of howsoever high an order, would be enough. Like all Augustinians in the West, Rāmānuja insists at every turn that the philosophical man is, *must* be, a *lover* of God. But as in the case of all types of love, all of which come direct from His essential nature, there are two essential aspects : the infatuated constant remembrance (*bhakti*) and the once-and-for-all falling in love (*prapatti*). Govindācārya has written : "The best means to salvation is God Himself. Even this is two-fold. One is by *bhakti* or loving Him with all the energy of one's own will; the other by *prapatti* or loving Him with all the force derived from God Himself when the aspirant has resigned his own will, and placed all his hope and confidence in the sweet will and dispensations of Providence."

It is best to study the *Brahma Sūtras* with the commentaries of Rāmānuja, Śaṅkara, Nimbārka, Mādhava, Vallabha, and Baladeva side-by-side if one is to appreciate the force of the arguments, just as it is best to study the commentaries on the *Sentences* of Peter Lombard side-by-side. One feels that in his *Śrī Bhāṣya* Rāmānuja is under more constraint than he would like and wrote it primarily to make his ecstatic way of devotion to Nārāyaṇa acceptable to the traditionalists. If Śaṅkara is closer to the Upaniṣads, Rāmānuja is the better interpreter of the "Lord's Song", the *Bhagavad Gītā*. One often feels that he is only dutifully faithful to the text of the *Sūtras* in the *Śrī Bhāṣya*, but in his *Gītā Bhāṣya* he finds more freedom to express his own thought and feeling. This is especially important in consideration of the fact that *prapatti* finds little if any place, strictly speaking, in the *Śrī Bhāṣya*; but in the *Gītā Bhāṣya*, *prapatti* as well as *bhakti* is extolled and enjoined. The typical attitude towards this discrepancy, if it be that, was expressed by Pundit Buberhampillai thus : "What does it matter if the *Sūtras*, which are only a Sage's wisdom, say nothing of *prapatti* ? The *Gītā* is the Lord's own words, and therefore of much greater authority. If the Lord Himself teaches *prapatti*, what more can you ask for ?"

For Rāmānuja, the Upanisads are not rightly understood until one has harmonized the texts that indicate complete transcendence (absolute otherness) and complete immanence. For him Śaṅkara's *nirguṇa*-Brahman is the result of the "fallacy of abstraction" (as Marcel somewhere says of Bradley's Absolute). Personalistic *sādhanā* is grounded in a Personal Absolute; and Personality entails not only attributes but an organic relation with the world and souls in it (panentheism). Rāmānuja teaches that God 're-enters' what He makes, making the world his own body, and that on different levels : the undifferentiated cosmos first; the gross world in second course, the *jīvas* at the end of the normal course; the *avatāra* to lighten the burden of the world and illuminate it with his splendor so that men may receive inspiration; and last, at the hands of men thus inspired, the *arcāvatāra*, the artistic embodiment in stone or metal, the product of Imagination which makes Him easily accessible to those who would begin their re-entrance back into Him in full but therefore imaginative enjoyment. And in both reciprocating movements, just as God is both remotely and immediately both giver and enjoyer of our enjoyment, so, both directly and indirectly, He Himself remains the meaning of all meaning. He is Himself also the enjoyed. Things-in-themselves are always things-as-enjoyed, for it is *bhakti* which incites the search for their meaningfulness and reinvests creatively, incarnatively, what it finds, inducing enjoyment of the whole never-ending spiral into non-limitation, into aesthetic freedom, which is Being in its ever-reduplicative, analogical fullness.

Kriyā concerns the social and moral obligations. Śaṅkara tends to the counsel that renunciation (*sannyāsa*) carries with it the neglect of these duties; but Rāmānuja is very emphatic on their continuance—and we should say wisely, on two accounts : for the sake of humility (for no one may presume to escape his human duties as long as he is in a human body—Bonaventura in many places stresses this) and also for the sake of the social order itself, which almost must be viewed as important to God. There is a typical story of a Carmellite monk who asked to be excused from manual work so that he could the more pursue his meditations, but who, when he was given the permission to do so on the proviso that he would not *eat*, left off his high ambition. It may be true that the mystic at the highest stages no longer needs the sacraments and rites as means of grace; but Rāmānuja and St. Bonaventura both teach that continued participation in them is best, not just for the sake of good example for the masses but also with a higher motive, namely that of *kaiṅkarya,* loving *service* and thanksgiving for grace already received, and humble devotion to what God has enjoined for all men.

Anavasāda, freedom from dejection, is certainly worthy of note. St. Benedict expressly condemns moroseness and mental depression in his Holy Rule; and Bonaventura, with the joyous St. Francis as his model, can see no room for it in the Christian system. But more than that, it is basically a moral matter, not a result of natural causation to which the psyche becomes a victim unwillingly. Hope, its opposite, is a virtue which can be deliberately practiced. The theist who allows himself to be plunged into an orgy of despair is giving affront to God; it is an abrogation of faith. One also thinks of St. Bernard's three principles of a good monastic community : *humilitas, humanitas, hilaritas*—the last being not the superficial excitement which the word has now come (symptomatically ?) to mean: not boisterousness, but the spirit of joyous willingness which naturally follows the spirit of devotional dedication of all activity to God, in the way of Victory. A good figure for this is the angel who rolled the stone away from the tomb of the Lord, "and *sat* upon it" as an antiphon in the Breviary Office for Easter says. Or, as Rāma and Kṛṣṇa were never weaklings but always victorious over all demons (dejection is a demon!), so the spiritual man partakes of their victories. Rāmānuja cites the Muṇḍaka

Upaniṣad (III : 2 : 4) : "The *ātman* cannot be attained by one devoid of strength."

The other extreme, *anuddharṣa*, emotional elation, is likewise to be avoided. Contemplation should lead to deep-seated quietude, as Rāmānuja points out by quoting the Bṛhad-āraṇyaka Upaniṣad (IV : 4 : 23) : "He who knows Him becomes calm, subdued, etc." The Southern tradition has for this reason always looked with some suspicion on Chaitanya and his followers. Religious ecstasy should be more than a matter of the emotions, and the focus should be on the will. Again St. Bernard, in his commentary on the ladder of humility in the Benedictine Rule, is quite explicit : *inepta laetitia* is a selfish condition and soon leads to a 'fall'. Only abiding joy is in the constant Peace of God, which "passes understanding". For Rāmānuja religious joy is always reinvested in praise; it never descends to mere sentiment.

In Rāmānuja we have a sort of counter-reformation at work still further liberating the orthodox from the ritualistic rigorism of the Pūrva Mīmāṁsā. Śaṅkara still divided practices from the elite from those for the masses, but Rāmānuja wanted liberation of all and sundry together democratically quite as much as the followers of St. Francis of Assissi and certainly more than the most liberal of the Neo-Confucians of his era. There are many stories wherein Rāmānuja favored his non-Brahmin disciples over his fellow-caste if only they were more zealous even in sweeping the pathway to the temple. Indeed, he came as near as any philosopher-reformer in any country of his period to abolishing class distinctions altogether. It is not surprising that one of the world's leading ex-communist humanists, M. N. Roy, turned to Rāmānuja in his later years as a possible model on which to build an indigenous humanism whereby violence and regimentation might be avoided.

There does remain a little tag of henotheism in Rāmānuja, which was a dominant tendency in all sects of his time. There continued to be a sort of friendly rivalry (which still persists) between the Śaivas and the Vaiṣṇavas while each appropriated all the theories ascribed to the other. This was possible because the Upaniṣads for the most part are quite neutral and are rich enough to promote the full gamut of theories which appeared in other parts of the world also. It might be said, nevertheless, that Rāmānuja's preference for Viṣṇu has some reason in it, for the Eternal Preservation in its inexhaustibility gives an indestructible foundation, uncreated in itself, which cannot be diminished or increased, and all of the finite and infinite orders come and go at His behest. One answer to the charge of henotheism is that to the philosophically minded these are only symbolic forms which the One God allows for the sake of understanding and approachability on the part of the devotee. Contrary to Hegel's teaching, the symbolic forms may and should still be used consciously and meaningfully even after concept of Pure Infinity has been understood.

Finally, the Vaiṣṇava saint simply leaves the body by yogic practice, permanently, when his work is done, having long since grown accustomed to treating the body as quite optional. It is a matter of sloughing off all the gross elements; only the subtle body and the *prāṇas* remain. But there is little in Rāmānuja and his school of the exaggerated asceticism that is supposed to characterize "Eastern" religiosity, quite as it did for that matter the early Christian monks of Egypt and the Syrian desert and medieval Latin monks like Peter Damien. *Bhojan* and *bhajan*, food and praise of God, are more likely to be the basic occupations of the Vaiṣṇava *bhakta*, although never is anything allowed that has not first been offered to God thankfully. The *economy of abundance* is presupposed.

33. Hugh of St. Victor

The key to understanding Hugh of St. Victor (1096-1141) is his ecstatic contemplation. Convinced of the ultimate vanity of the world and all that merely human knowledge can give, he exalts faith above reason, without destroying reason, to an extent seldom achieved in the history of human spirituality. Following upon the path opened by Pseudo-Dionysius (fl. 490), he uses symbols but is not limited by them; for the highest reach of the divine charity should itself lift the soul into the immediate contemplation of the Formless, perhaps even more directly than the way that some Japanese Buddhists found in Amida Buddha.

Hugh and Richard of St. Victor are the most prominent of the Victorines. Concerning the School of St. Victor we may note the following :

> The Augustinian house of canons at St. Victor in Paris was founded in 1108 by William of Champeaux.... The abbey survived until the French Revolution, but in the twelfth and early thirteenth centuries it was especially famous for its public school and for the distinction of the matter and canons who resided and taught there. From William, St. Victor derived high religious ideals, a leaning toward the conservative theological tradition of the school of Anselm of Laon, and an active interest in the work of other Parisian schools. Its masters mediated between the theological orthodoxy and strictness of the Cistercians—Bernard of Clairvaux was a friend to St. Victor—and the intellectual adventurousness of such secular masters as Abelard. St. Victor in the twelfth century combined Scholasticism and mysticism and exerted a most powerful influence upon the development of both philosophical and theological thought in that century.[1]

Hugh came to the Abbey of St. Victor in 1115 and directed it from 1133 until his death.

On the manner of God's being truly and supremely one, there is nothing essentially new in Hugh; still, one senses that he speaks from a valid mystical certainty that is rare in any century. In his *De Sacramentis* Hugh writes :

> Reason approved this and acquiesced, and said that He was one, not through the gathering of diverse elements lest He form a multitude, nor through the composition of parts lest He form a mass, nor through the likeness of many lest He appear superfluous plurality or an imperfect singleness. For every unity consisting in the likeness alone of many shows either imperfection in part, if the individual elements have too

> little, or a superfluous duplication in the whole, if all elements are perfect. And in all these there is not true unity....
>
> But God must be one, and essentially one, and immutably one and supremely one, for what is essentially one is truly one; what is immutably one, is supremely one. But what is good in both is better as both than as only the one, and it is good to be essentially one, and to be immutably one, and it is better to be both. But God is the highest good, and there cannot be lacking to the highest good a good which is better. And so it confesses its God and its author and its principle to be one for this is better, namely to be truly one, since it is so substantially, and to be supremely one, since it is invariably so.[2]

Hugh does not see the problem here which so vexed his Vedāntic contemporaries so that the followers of Śaṅkara and Rāmānuja and Mādhava were having a merry time arguing it with each other. For even these adverbs "essentially" and "immutably" and "supremely" are superfluous if we insist that the unity is self-subsistant, or else if they are asserted as necessary in order to demonstrate that there is a *that* which is one, the unity is necessarily, even by its own existence, qualified. Moses Maimonides, another contemporary, was also very much vexed by this problem.

Of course Hugh insists that in spite of this Unity there must also be Trinity. After laying the foundation in the unavoidable necessity of God's making Himself known, he concedes an unusual measure of difference of function appropriate to the different Persons of the Trinity :

> For the Father is called powerful, and the Father is powerful, and not the Father alone, because the Father is powerful and the Son and the Holy Ghost; not three are powerful, but one is powerful, because there is one power in one nature and in one substance. And the Son is wise, but not alone, because the Father is wise and the Son and Holy Ghost; not three are wise, but one is wise, because there is one wisdom in one nature and in one substance. And the Holy Ghost is called kind and good, and indeed the Holy Ghost is kind and good, but the Holy Ghost is not alone kind and good, but the

> Father is kind and good and the Son and the Holy Ghost; yet the three are not kind and the three are not good, but one is kind and one is good, because there is one benignity and one goodness in one nature and in one substance.[3]

Under his interpretation of the Christian doctrine of the Trinity it seems that Hugh has come very near to synthesizing the *prajñā* concept and the Aristotelian manner of dealing with the difficulty in positing a non-propositional knowledge. There is perhaps too much emphasis on a dualism of faith and reason, revelation and ratiocination, nature and grace, than we should like to see; but at least he does have some clear grasp or 'beholding' of the Ground *above* reason (but not contrary to it) which is almost the sole focus of most of Japanese Buddhism in the same period.

The appeal to miracles in Hugh is not too different from that in Ibn Sīnā; the appeal to reason is at least as strong as that of the other Aristotelians; the appeal to illumination is very similar to that found in the Ṣūfīs; and the ambivalence of the reciprocation of divine revelation and human aspiration is as vivid as in any contemplative of the twelfth century. It is seldom that we find all of these compacted together; but they are all there, harmoniously, in Hugh and his fellow Victorines. One is therefore challenged with the question whether the doctrine of the Christian Trinity, like the *Trikāya* of Mahāyāna, rightly understood, does not give an adequate ground for bringing all of these together in spite of the difficulties in other aspects. It is unfortunate that Ibn Rushd was not better informed concerning the true interpretation of it. The only alternative may be a more rigorous Mādhyamika such as that held by Nāgārjuna himself, yet even he found it necessary in the second focus to posit the *Trikāya* and the cultivation of the *prajñā-pāramitā* in order to avoid annihilist impasse which would be completely suicidal to anything any human could hold on to, or even let go of !

There is a constant triadic structuring in Hugh which is much closer to that of Peirce than the "dialectic" of Hegel and the Marxists. For each member of each triad is interreciprocally equal to the others. There are the basic factors of body, Spirit and God. The soul is, as it were, in the middle of them all. The first is experienced with the natural senses, the second by the exercise of rational judgment, the third by the eye of contemplation. This eye of contemplation is the key to the whole of Hugh's "way", for to him as to most of the Buddhist, Hindu and Islamic sages up to this time, philosophy is a *way*, even a way of salvation, and not merely a body of speculation. However, it is not easy to find a vantage point from which to get a critical appraisal of this manner. Is it any more after all than something like al-Ghazālī's reservations about the limitations of Aristotelian rationalism in the light of faith, or is it more than the *dhyāna* of Japanese Zen ? Hugh writes :

> Therefore, God can be believed, but by no means can he be comprehended. You say to me, "What shall I say ? What is God ?" I reply to you that what God is, is quite ineffable. "At least," you say, "what shall I think when I wish to think what God is ?" I say further that God is unthinkable, for whatever is said or is thought, is said according to something. For what cannot be said or thought according to something cannot be said or thought at all. What, therefore, will you say or will you think, when you wish to say or think that which is God ? If you think of earth, if you think of heaven, if you think of all that is in heaven and on earth, none of these is God. Finally, if you think of spirit, if you think of soul, this is not God. "I know," you say, "that this is not God, yet this is like God, and God can be demonstrated by his likeness."[4]

Whereas for most Augustinian Christians this likeness is sufficient basis for analogical proceeding, for Hugh it is not. He still discerns a definitely qualified difference in the likeness of the soul to its Maker even after the restoration of grace. God stands alone in His ineffable uniqueness, for above all that can be conceptually entertained. Hugh has here not only taken another step ahead of Anselm but may have been accepting the challenge of the Muslims also. For faith to him is *darśan*, open vision, not mere credulity.

Faith must not be asked to do work that is not in its own designated province. Where there are things that cannot be reached through faith Hugh does not discern so clearly, since the answer to that would imply some bit of God's own omniscience. But faith should at least put everything into the right perspective so that the creature will never be cherished before the Creator, the material before the spiritual, the irrational before the rational, or the rational before the super-rational. Just as the Aristotelians must, after Ibn Rushd, resort to some sort of two-truth theory of natural and super-natural, Hugh discerns the things that are beneath reason, contrary to reason, in accord with reason, indifferent to and above reason. It is only by faith that this place of reason can be seen; it is not reason that so discerns its own place. Hugh writes:

> From reason are necessary things, according to reason (there are) probable, above reason marvellous, contrary to reason incredible. And the two extremes, indeed, are not capable of faith. For those things that are from reason are certainly known and cannot be believed because they are known. But what are contrary to reason likewise cannot in any way be believed, because they are not susceptible of any reason, nor does reason at any time give assent to them. Therefore, things that are according to reason and that are above reason are alone susceptible to faith. In the first kind, indeed, faith is aided by reason and reason is perfected by faith, since the things that are believed are according to reason. If reason does not comprehend the truth of these things, yet it does not contradict faith in them. In those things which are above reason, faith is not added by any reason; since reason does not grasp what faith believes, and yet there is something by which reason is admonished to respect the faith which it does not comprehend.[5]

Further Hugh discerns a hierarchy of progressive approaches to certainty: "There are first the deniers, then the doubters, third the conjecturers, fourth the believers, fifth the knowers."[6]

Faith should lead to illumination just as salvation should lead on to sanctification. It is not merely a way of knowing but the opening of another level of Becoming. Only to God is rightly imputed Being; whatever 'being' beneath Him there may 'be' is entirely dependent on Him, as is Becoming, which God makes extremely elastic, as it were, and never fixed. This field of existence, though still subordinate to the essential nature of Deity, has a close resemblance to the essence of infinity in its character. The infinity of the divine essence, however, is homogenous whereas the infinity of existence, which is the realm of Process, is an infinity of levels. It is faith, the eye of contemplation, that allows this whole pattern to be seen. Ibn Rushd was struggling with the same problem in discerning the levels of the active intellect, the speculative intellect, the passive intellect and the material intellect. But even he, it seems to us, does not discern the "that by which all this is known", which remains the primary focus in Śrīharṣa, Honen, and Hugh.

Hugh lifts faith up to the level and rank of being itself a sort of sacrament and not merely the means whereby the sacraments are maintained and made the instrument of grace. For even faith also leads beyond itself, as everything but the inherently self-sufficient Trinity must do, until all difference between believer and believed is obliterated. Hugh writes:

> Those who see through faith see the image, those who see through contemplation see the thing. Those who have the faith have the sacrament; those who have contemplation have the thing. Faith, then, is the sacrament of future contemplation and contemplation itself is the thing and the virtue of the sacrament. ... If then, the highest good is rightly believed to be man's contemplation of his Creator, not unfittingly is faith, through which he begins in some manner to see the absent, said to be the beginning of good and the first step in his restoration; this restoration, indeed, increases according to increases of faith, while man is enlightened more through knowledge that he may know more fully, and is inflamed with love that he may love more ardently.[7]

The rest of the *De Sacramentis* is an application of this sort of understanding to all the particular sacraments of the Church. But it is more than a mere apologetic. To a certain extent Hugh has begun the science of the sociology of religion in trying to devise a typology of sacraments. The pity is that he was not sufficiently informed about rights, customs, ceremonies and sacraments in other traditions. And unfortunately there is still the need of a typology that will cover all cases without destroying reverence for any.

Comparable with Hōnen's zeal for achievement of the Pure Land of Amida, Hugh closes this work with a description of Paradise, which description does not differ very sharply from that promised by most varieties of Islam. The medieval mind did not differ so much in different parts of Eurasia in this respect. At least the ideal was established. Plato's *Republic* has been garnished considerably, and the Heavenly Jerusalem not only opens its doors to weary pilgrims but descends to earth in the fullness of glory and majesty. We are almost ready for Dante.

The *Didascalicon*, which is more like the encyclopedia of Isidore of Seville (d. 638), shows Hugh to be not by any means a mystic of the type that goes off into some private cloister and communes with his own feelings only. His learning is just about as wide as that of Ibn Rushd, and he makes good use of it. The chapter on meditation contains the usual triad of reading, consideration and contemplation as the basic scheme for meditation, which is universal enough. Likewise one is admonished to consider the circumspection of morals, the scrutinizing of the commandments, and the investigation of divine works. From the chapter on humility we may note :

> The beginning of discipline is humility, concerning which there are many documents, but these three especially pertain to the reader : the first, that he hold no knowledge, no scripture, as vile; the second, that with no one he presume to dispute; third, that when he becomes adept in learning he not become contemptuous of others. Many fail in this, because they wish to see wise men before their time. For from this they are corrupted by a sort of tumor of elation, so that they begin already to simulate what is not theirs and to grow ruddy over learning which they do not have, until they are farther from wisdom than those which have no learning, and they only think that they think.[8]

Perhaps we could turn to the Chinese for such humility which comes from the right pursuit of learning. But of course humility, like all other principles and virtues, also has its varieties. While the pursuit of any virtue may become a vice if not properly balanced by other virtues, there is also the argument that if one virtue is consistently followed all the others will sooner or later become involved.

The chapter on the Triple Intelligence follows the old triadic scheme of considering any topic from the historical or analytical, the allegorical, and the topological points of view. His treatment of this division follows the analogy of music: the theme is stated, the variations may be improvised upon it, and then, as the mystical level is opened, the full harmonization of the theme converts into contrapuntal praise. Why the mystical is universally so closely associated with the analogical is not easy to discern. Hugh does not necessarily subscribe to the view of universal analogy; but in the chapter on analogy, using mathematical examples, he comes rather close to this. The limits of analogy are the limits of ignorance itself. But analogy does make faith easier, whereby the soul may find a way across the gulf of uncertainty and come to (some approximation of) the knowledge of the Blessed Trinity, the source and sustenance and end of all things.

Mystical contemplation, the exercise of the practical virtues, and the provision of daily necessities correspond to the division of philosophy into wisdom, virtue, and necessity. This scheme may have given the medieval Eurasian world a more universal basis of unity than its fragmentation in the Renaissance era with its individualistic *virtuosi* from whose unbalanced explosiveness we in the twentieth century are only beginning to recover. Thus again we have an instance not of philosophy 'East' and 'West' but of 'medieval' and 'modern', if by 'modern' we mean the trend away from contemplation toward secularization and scientism.

Hugh of St. Victor achieved a high degree of synthesis between the logical and the symbolic, the dogmatic, the moral, and the ascetic aspect of wisdom, and handled very well the problems of filtering the elixir of wisdom out of the dross of dry erudition. In asking whether Hugh in any measure excells his contemporaries in other parts of the world we may be confronted with the old problem of evaluating types rather than excellence. His emphasis on reason is certainly less than that of Ibn Rushd, but his capitulation to the 'learned ignorance' of religiosity is not so complete as that of Hōnen, although his erudition falls behind that of Chu Hsi as does his relative lack of humanist social concern. Like Hōnen, Hugh of St. Victor remains mostly in the personal nexus and seeks escape from ego in flights of ecstatic contemplation rather than in political reform or social action. But his treatment of the traditional dogmas seems to have touched the Tao of genuineness and breathes an atmosphere of freshness of comprehension that is more than mere repetition of old dogmatic formulae.

34. Judah Halevi

Judah Halevi (c. 1075-1141) was born in Toledo, Spain, and received his early training in the traditional rabbinical lore. He early manifested some poetic genius, which culminated in a body of Hebrew poetry heavily influenced by Arabic styles then current. That Halevi was also a poet was by no means unusual since that was true of many of his predecessors in Spanish Jewry of that period as well as of most of the Spanish Muslim philosophers (Ibn Hazm, for example). But by profession he practiced medicine, in both Christian and Muslim circles. Instead of going to Meccah, of course he made a pilgrimage to Jerusalem; and there according to legend he was killed by an Arab horseman. Coming from a wealthy family in Muslim Spain, Halevi received the best of training in both Hebrew and Arabic letters from an early age and enjoyed a cultural atmosphere relatively peaceful. This was the period leading up to the time of Moses Maimonides and the famous Ibn Rushd (Averroes) when *Spanish* Islam produced such astute thinkers. Indeed, in Halevi's epoch Spain and Iran were the chief intellectual and cultural centers in the Islamic world.

The Book of Argument and Proof in Defense of the Despised Faith, which came to be known by the shorter title *The Book of the Kuzari*, is Halevi's chief philosophical work. It was the fruit of twenty years work, which Halevi says was sparked off by some questions from a Karaite; but Karism takes up only a minor part. It is surprisingly like the work of al-Ghazālī and Rāmānuja in that it is, among other things, an attempt at refuting Aristotelianism, that comparison or parallel being directly in al-Ghazālī's case and analogous to Rāmānuja's refutation of Advaita. This represents a rather universal factor in human aspiration and thinking through world history, namely that we are seldom satisfied with sheer intellectualism or *jñāna* without the human-hearted leaven of *bhakti* and the discipline of selfless *niṣkāma-karma* yoga. In modern Euramerican terminology, no philosophy can be considered complete until it achieves some balance between epistemology, aesthetics and ethics.

The *Kuzari* really must be seen as an apologia rather than a systematic work.

> The work is called the *Kuzari* after the king of the Khazars whose conversion to Judaism provides the literary framework of the work. After being told by an angel in a dream that, while his intentions were acceptable to God, his actions were not, the king, in an effort to discover how he should lead his life, invites first an Aristotelian philosopher, and then representatives of Islam, Christianity, and Judaism, to discuss with him their respective beliefs. This literary framework enables Halevi to compare the teachings of Judaism with those of Aristotelianism, Islam, and Christianity, in an effort to prove the superiority of Judaism.[1]

Halevi highlights the discrepancy between the highly personal God of the Old Testament with the God of the rationalist or 'Aristotelian' philosophers. He did not follow his predecessors but minimized the Greek sources in preference for the Biblical revelation. However, Aristotelianism was better known by Halevi than by most of his predecessors in Jewry, although his knowledge of this field was still rather indirect. It is quite likely that, like al-Ghazālī, he had what he knew of that heritage from Ibn Sīnā.

Halevi's treatment of the attributes of God is pretty much in line with what more recently has come to be termed "personalism", thus running the risk of anthropomorphism rather than the other more common extreme of pushing God off into a super-vacuum of indescribability and indeterminacy as was the current trend among the Aristotelian philosophers, most of whom were basically Neo-Platonists. Such personalism does not necessarily entail a commitment to exclusivism or ethnocentrism, but sometimes the fact that Halevi does not compromise the "chosen people" concept of the Jewish revelation has left him open to much criticism for his trend in that direction.

Of course with Halevi the emphasis remains on the prophetic tradition as distinct from the philosophical in the more restricted sense; but, as is the case for example with al-Ghazālī and Rāmānuja—and even with the Neo-Confucians, who did incorporate quite a bit of Buddhist metaphysics—Halevi does use deductive reasoning and some systematic metaphysics in his 'refutations'. As Aristotle himself noted, in order to refute philosophy one must philosophize. But deduction is by no means all of philosophizing. Experience is always the other side of the coin to any systematizing, even according to Aristotle himself. Even so, as in all the scholastics of the Abrahamic traditions, revelation is put above reason, taking that as the substitute for, or even the highest form of, experience. This sort of "two story" philosophizing—which has its parallels also in all the commentators of the Upaniṣads, who insist that the Vedas are the final authority even though the interpretations of those sacred revealed texts vary diametrically—was clear enough in Ibn Sīnā to provoke some discussion as to whether the prophetic type should remain outside the pale of philosophy in the stricter sense, or whether rather our concept of the typology of philosophy is incomplete without it, the prophet being rated above the mystic in the same way that the mystic is rated above the idealist. For Halevi,

> The prophet, because he experiences directly the presence of God, can become much closer to God than the philosopher who has an indirect theoretical knowledge of Him. The mission of the prophet is not to instruct men in eternal truths, but to teach them the deeds whose performance leads to the experience of God's presence. This is indeed the

> purpose of the Torah, Judaism being the only religion which seeks to instruct men in correct and righteous action, rather than speculative truths. The prophetic faculty is a faculty beyond ordinary human reason, and constitutes a generic distinction between the prophet and the ordinary man, parallel to the distinction between man and animals. This faculty is hereditary and unique to the people of Isreal. It is only through the intermediacy of Israel that the other nations can approach God, just as it is only through the intermediacy of the prophets that the people of Israel can come close to Him. This is the cornerstone of Halevi's doctrine of particularity of the people of Israel.[2]

As for the claims of Christianity and Islam to revelations, Halevi's attitude seems to be that their claims are not very authentic since they are of a rather second-water variety, derived from the Mosaic revelation, which therefore remains the real one which they both ought therefore to acknowledge as superior. We have long since made the observation that such ethnocentricity is by no means unique to the Jewish people. That was the basic motivation behind the emergence and development of Neo-Confucianism, for example, Buddhism being considered a foreign importation. And it became strong enough in Japan that Nichiren and others believed that the deliverance of Japan from the Mongols was evidence of their being a 'chosen' people. Then there were the Advaitins of India against whom Rāmānuja had so much difficulty in his equalitarian and virtually casteless teachings.

Somewhat as some modern Hindus regard Buddhism as merely another form of Hinduism, so, Halevi regards Christianity and Islam as mere offshoots of the Jewish revelation. As missionary religions they have spread over the world, but they have not really added to the original revelation and the real content of their message remains, indellibly, Jewish. Halevi puts much emphasis on the claim that the Israelites had the direct experience of encounter with God whereas the others were only relying on that experience second-hand. There is also the argument from analogy that just as the plant is higher in order of excellence than the mineral, and the animal than the vegetative, and man than the (other) animals, so the prophetic man is of a higher order than the ordinary man. The Christian might have objected to this by citing the New Testament doctrine that the Christian is likewise a "new creature" higher in dispensation if not in transformed nature than those of the Old Covenant. But then if a Hindu, say Śrīharṣa his contemporary, had reminded him that Brahmins are supposed to be also "twice born" that might have altered the picture considerably; and if a Neo-Confucian, especially some predecessor of Lu Ḥsiang-shan, had made his typical appeals to Mencius or human nature, that might have complicated things considerably more. But to cap it all off, if, for example, Ryōnin had brought in the *Lotus Sūtra* with its doctrine of spiritual equality of all men alike, then the claims to superiority on the part of them all might have been mitigated somewhat. We must hope that twentieth century humanity will develop greater degrees of humble mutuality instead of claims of uniqueness and/or superiority, since otherwise, how shall we have peace.

Several treatments of Halevi acknowledge the similarity to the work of al-Ghazālī, "from whom there is no doubt that he borrowed his inspiration".[3] Al-Ghazālī was almost twenty years his senior, and communications were completely open (more so than today as a matter of fact) between Spain and Iran/Baghdad. Neher[4] puts the similarity in terms of keeping religion and philosophy separate instead of trying to mix them, preserving the claim for religion that it alone can reach the "absolute" whereas philosophy always must deal with the relatives in that it is always involved in *controversies* between widely disparate views so that each philosophy contains only a small part of the truth. Husik says that "there is no doubt that skepticism in respect of the powers of the human reason on the one hand, and a deep religious sense on the other are responsible for the point of view of al-Ghazālī as well as Halevi."[5] Husik continues :

> In Judah Halevi the poet got the better of the rationalist. Not that Judah Halevi was not familiar with philosophical terminology as well as the ideas contained therein. Quite the contrary. He shows a better knowledge of Aristotelian ideas than his predecessors, and is well versed in Neo-Platonism....

> Revelation alone can make us wise as to certain aspects of God's nature and as to certain details in human conduct; and in these philosophy must fail because as philosophy it has no revelation. With all due respect therefore to the philosophers, who are the most reliable guides in matters not conflicting with revelation, we must leave them if we wish to learn the truth concerning those matters in which they are incompetent to judge.[6]

As a possible way toward understanding Halevi, Neher suggests a certain similarity to Pascal, for Halevi's way may validly be called "existentialist" in that it is the voice of direct and intensive religious experience. Neher adds that Halevi's existentialism is one of joy, not of anxiety as is so often the case with our twentieth century 'people of immediacy'. This is not to say that there are no dark moments, especially in his poems of lament. But those laments are not mere expressions of self pity but are always prayerfully directed to the Lord in hope. Religious joy for Halevi is not a matter of the fruits of asceticism, but rather of joyful acceptance of the revealed commandments of the Torah or Law. Neher claims that for Halevi revelation is the movement which comes from God to man, and observance is the inverse movement which goes from man to God. "By observance, each rite of the Law is inserted into a harmonious though complex rhythm whose pulsations animate time and space and the human organism."[7] Thus every act becomes a sort of prayer and (as we might add in the perspective of the *Gītā*) becomes livable rather than cataclysmic. That is the real purpose of the rituals : they facilitate encounters with the Almighty in a regulated *normal* way.

The *Kuzari* is relatively unique within its historical milieu in that most of the other works by medieval Jewish thinkers were more like anthologies or commentaries on other works, whereas Halevi's is an original essay throughout. The *Kuzari* "exercised a great influence on Judaism throughout history. It was particularly influential in kabbalistic circles in the 13th century, among the anti-Aristotelians in the 14th and 15th centuries. In more recent times it had a marked influence on Ḥasidism."[8] Like Ibn Gabirol, Halevi is almost more famous as a poet than as a philosopher. Modern Jews who have had difficulty maintaining their identity have found in Halevi great solace and strength, and a poignant longing for an existential purity of the Faith. But historically just as the pendulum swings back from al-Ghazālī to Ibn Rushd, so it also swings from Halevi to Maimonides—and keeps on swinging through history.

35. Abelard

Abelard (1079-1142) was both a theologian and a logician, though in all three Abrahamic heritages there were those who believed that there is a discrepancy there. He was also both a monk and a scholar; but throughout Eurasia then there were very few scholars or thinkers who were not monks, the Chinese Neo-Confucians being perhaps the greatest exception. That Abelard was (only) twice accused of heresy should not disturb us since sooner or later it was not uncommon in that era to have such accusations leveled against anyone who attempted anything new; and after all, these accusations usually did not amount to much, unlike the later violent purges and executions that developed in the Spanish Inquisition.

Much has been made of Abelard's colorful personality, such as this characterization from W.H.V. Reade: "With all his weakness, his vanity, his almost wanton pugnacity, there must have been in Abelard some quality of greatness, something that forbade men to gaze on him with indifference and pass by on the other side.... He was born to fascinate or to repel.... In vain he was driven into exile, for where the master was there was the school."[1] Abelard was born in western France. Instead of following a military career as his father wished, he wandered in pursuit of learning the arts of disputation wherever they thrived. At Paris he studied under William of Champeaux, a well-known teacher of the day, but soon came to disagree with William's extreme realism and proceeded first to set his teacher straight and then to establish a rival school. William understandably became an enemy, but by no means the most formidable enemy Abelard was to make.

While in Paris the brilliant young Abelard fell in love with his private pupil, Héloise, and a child was born to the lovers. Héloise's uncle insisted that the relationship be legitimized through marriage, to which the couple agreed, but Héloise wanted the marriage kept secret in order not to jeopardize Abelard's career. This angered the uncle, who in revenge caused Abelard to be set upon and castrated by a band of ruffians. Subsequently Héloise entered a convent on the urging of Abelard, and Abelard for a time ceased teaching and withdrew to the monastery at St. Denis. Héloise deserves some recognition as a thinker in her own right. In her assessment of her exact measure of responsibility for the heinous assault on Abelard she uses a bit of reasoning worthy of her teacher and lover : "You know Abelard, I was the great cause of your misfortunes; but yet I was not guilty. It is the motive with which we act, and not the event of things, that makes us criminal. Equity weighs the intention and not the mere actions we may have done."[2] Abelard and Héloise remained in communication, and their extant letters show their continuing devotion to each other.

Abelard accepted election as abbot in a remote monastery in Brittany; however, he was soon again embroiled in controversy and had to flee because of attempts upon his life. One of Abelard's problems with the religious authorities of his day was that he insisted on being both a monk and a teacher of secular arts, which conflict rose to such a point that he considered leaving Christendom altogether. In about 1135 Abelard went to the Mont-Sainte-Geneviève outside Paris where he worked on further drafts of his *Theologia* in which he searched for the sources of the doctrine of the Trinity and "praised the pagan philosophers of classical antiquity for their virtues and for their discovery by the use of reason of many fundamental aspects of Christian revelation."[3] Bernard of Clairvaux became alarmed about Abelard's lack of orthodoxy, as he saw it, and successfully recruited an opposition so that Abelard was resoundingly condemned in 1142. Abelard withdrew to the great monastery of Cluny in Burgundy, made peace with Bernard through the intercession of Peter the Venerable, and retired from teaching.

Abelard is perhaps best known for his proposed solution to

the problem of universals. W. T. Jones gives us this background and statement of the problem :

> The thinkers of the eleventh century were not metaphysicians but logicians. Rather than constructing all-inclusive systems, they devoted themselves for the most part to painstakingly thorough examination of two very technical problems—status of universals and the relation between the spheres of faith and reason.
>
> These were questions that had to be settled before the great synthesis of the thirteenth century could be undertaken. For, though everyone agreed that Christian truths were above reason in the sense that their truth was guaranteed by the Christian faith in revelation and by the authority of the canonical writings, it was desirable, if only for pragmatic reasons, to prove these truths by rational argument. The crusades as well as an expanding trade were bringing Western Christians into contact with infidels who found it easy to ridicule the simplicities of unreasoned faith. And, at home, heresy continued to divide the Christian fold.
>
> ... There was general agreement among philosophers that apart from revelation, men have but two modes of cognition—perception and reason. It was also agreed that what perception knows is particulars, that is, the various individual objects of the spatiotemporal world. Reason, on the other hand, knows universal truths.... But philosophers of the Middle Ages were not much interested in perception and its objects, for sense perception obviously cannot yield knowledge of God or any of the great truths of Christian religion. Hence, if men are to know these truths (in distinction from accepting them on the authority of faith and revelation) it must be by means of reason. Accordingly, the attention of philosophers of the Middle Ages was focused on the nature of reason and the status of "universals", as the objects of reason were called.[4]

The *universale ante rem* is the universal as Plato or the Platonists took it : the idea in the mind of the artist or engineer before he executes the work. The *universale in rem* is the universal in the thing executed, not easily perceived directly in the thing but abstracted through the reconstruction of its genus and species. The *universale post rem* is the universal thus conceived in the mind of the thinker who is trying to understand the true nature of things. This is relatively simple when the finite mind is dealing with things. But are these three types really the same universal at work ? This threefold structure is not so easily applied to ideas as such and the words signifying them without engaging us in a circularity that is hard to break through. If the universal arouses the word by which it is known, then what arouses the universal ? If the universal pre-exists in our minds and is only evoked by the perception of its particulars in the things, then what is to guarantee the connection between them as common to both ? It is another universal. Through an infinite series of universals must we admit a Universal of universals which is God, or at least the final nexus of universals in the Mind of God ? But even here, how do we know this except as another pesky universal ? Is there anything from the strictly logical point of view that is not of this structure ? Are negative Universals possible, or is negation in essence the denial of universality as such ? Since the words meaning "no" entail the power or at least the possibility of cancelling that of which a statement may be made, if God is merely a Universal of universals does the denial of His existence really cancel His existence, at least for the one making the denial ? Is there anything not subject to this process of universalization and function according to affirmation and negation ? And if so, how may we know that except by construction of further arguments which are necessarily (since Aristotle says so) still subject to the *sic et non* of human ratiocination ?

Abelard's embroilment in controversy with the orthodox over universals stemmed from the same argument which became part of his abiding contribution to the history of logic and metaphysics. He argued what seems a rather moderate, reasonable position today, that the universal ("man" or "mankind," for example) is neither a mere sound nor a transcendental "reality" making the individual real. We may summarize the positions on the question of universals as follows :

(1) *Nominalists* considered universals to have no reality except in the mind of man. A universal concept exists in the mind *after* we sense a similarity among ordinary objects; it has no

reality prior to or in things. Extreme nominalists denied *all* reality to universals.

(2) *Extreme realists* taught that universals exist *before* particulars, *in* particulars, and *after* particulars. (Plato seems never to have argued for the existence of forms/universals *in* things. Instead, particulars imitate or participate in their prototypical forms. Forms *in* things represents the Aristotelian adaptation of Platonism as usually interpreted.) "For the realist, universals exist in themselves and would exist even if there were no minds to be aware of them; if the world were exactly what it is now, with the one difference that it contained no minds at all, no consciousness of any kind, the existence of universals would be unaffected.... They would be available for discovery even if there were nobody to discover them."[5] In his attack on the nominalism of Roscellinus, the extreme realist William of Champeaux held "that the universal alone has real existence, that it is wholly and exhaustively present in each particular example of itself, and that the individuality of these examples is nothing but an accidental variation of the generic essence. The difference between you and me, for example, is only skin deep. Underneath the skin we are one and the same human being."[6] We moderns may be puzzled as to why Abelard ever needed to debate the exponents of extreme realism, for how could any reasonable person see a universal such as "man" or "being" as anything more than an empty abstraction, and the more abstract the emptier ? Imagine the consequences if instead of a paltry individual named Adam, Mankind appeared ! That is exactly how some of the extreme realists interpreted "Adam" in the Genesis account (they even have some support from twentieth century Biblical scholars as to the original meaning of the name "Adam"). Moreover, "if each individual man is a separate reality, it is difficult, if not impossible, to understand how all men could have sinned in Adam's sin. But if the universal 'man' is real, then anything that happens to the universal affects all the particulars subsumed by it.... So you and I, by virtue of being men, cannot help having corrupt wills."[7]

(3) *Moderate realists* thought that universals refer to the similarities actually *in* things and to the concept formed *after*

these similarities have been correctly inferred by the mind of man. Universals for moderate realists may or may not pre-exist; the question is somewhat open. But the emphasis throughout is more psychological than metaphysical. The universal exists *in* things as a real similarity among members of the same group recognized by the process of abstraction, and the universal exists *after* the thing as a correct psychological construct, but not as a separate metaphysical entity. Abelard was the first eloquent spokesman for this moderate realist or *conceptualist* point of view. "Abelard's treatment of the problem of universals involved shifting the emphasis from metaphysics to logic and psychology. Instead of trying to determine the ontological status of universals, he examined the process by which we arrive at universal concepts."[8] The extreme realists against whom Abelard did battle probably tended to think more metaphysically than psychologically or epistemologically and hence misread some of Abelard's efforts to establish the mentalistic viewpoint.

Instead of siding with the nominalists or the (extreme) realists, Abelard found a way between them: "If the universal is a concept, it follows that without the activity of human intellects there would be no universals. On this point, the nominalists were correct and the realists mistaken. But given the 'collective' activity of human intellects, a universal is a real entity with an objective reference. On this point, the realists were correct and the nominalists mistaken. The distinction of working out this medieval compromise belonged to Peter Abelard."[9] Abelard's intermediate conceptualism disclosed to his readers for the first time those abstractive psychological processes which enable us to talk about universals. Universals facilitate communication about particulars by gathering up their similarities and laying aside their individual uniquenesses. The similarities are objective in that the objects *are* alike, and subjective in that our minds can entertain *selected* aspects of the world without the whole buzzing confusion of similarities and dissimilarities being present in our heads at once. For Abelard, then, "a universal therefore exists in two ways: (1) It exists in the individual particulars as a common likeness, and (2) it exists in the human intellect as a concept formed as a result of the intellect's having focused its attention on the likeness."[10] By solving the problem thus, Abelard doubtless bequeathed other problems to his successors. We cannot anticipate here the history of this problem which remains an open question even today, but Copleston clearly shows the relevance of this nominalist/realist debate to the philosophy or science : "The scientist expresses his knowledge in abstract and general terms (for example, he does not make a statement about this particular electron, but about electrons in general), and if these terms have no foundation in extramental reality, his science is an arbitrary construction, which has no relation to reality. ... Scepticism would result."[11] We should add that Abelard was not an empiricist either in the Aristotelian or Thomistic sense, not to mention the emerging empiricism of the later nominalists. Rather he was concerned with the rightness of conceptualizations as expressed in language; he was a philosopher of language more than an empiricist.

According to Abelard's middle position of conceptualism, what the human mind conceives is pretty much *in medias res*, building up concepts as best it can between the extremes of attaching significance to the logical functions themselves and maintaining that that which they are about is the important thing. This is not peculiar to the area of Western Europe at this time. From Aristotle the same questions were vexing Jewish and Islamic philosophers. Also the Neo-Confucians were trying to find the particular unities analogous to the Supreme Ultimate and yet somehow individualized out of that same Supreme Ultimate (number as such had become important, for example, even though each number must be somehow a combination of the one and the many in varying degrees of balance between the *yin* and the *yang*). Rāmānuja is dealing with the same difficulties in his commentary on the first four sūtras of the *Śrī Bhāṣya*, in which he is essentially trying to show that Śaṅkara, like a trapeze artist with all too hypothetical wings, has tried to take off into infinity. Indeed, the systems of Śaṅkara (unqualified non-dualism), Rāmānuja (qualified non-dualism), and Mādhava (dualism) represent three different Hindu ways of relating the one and the many, Brahman and *māyā*, reality and appearance, the universal and the particular; and while the Nyāya-Vaiśeṣika emphasized a kind of conceptual realism, the Buddhists generally taught nominalistic theories.

For Abelard not only did universals exist as likenesses and concepts based on likenesses but in a third way :

> Theological considerations, as a matter of fact, required Abelard to hold that universals exist in a third way : as the ideal prototypes used by God as models when He created the world. For, not content (as a modern writer might be) with the *fact* that similarities exist among the individual particulars of experience, Abelard proceeded to ask in typical medieval fashion, "Why do these similarities exist ?" He arrived at the answer, "Because God created them similar." "But how did God come to do this ?" "Because He was working from eternal archetypes." So, in the end, he too turned to Platonism and to the Middle Ages' understanding of the *Timaeus*.[12]

The theological importance of the controversy over universals is easily illustrated by the Christian doctrine of the Trinity. According to the nominalist theory, the Trinity is simply Father, Son, and Holy Spirit—a collection of individuals with no real underlying unity; in short, polytheism or, more specifically, tritheism. In an extreme version of realism, on the other hand, the key principle of the Trinity would not be the individual members but the one Godhead. Pushed to its limit this emphasis on the single Godhead leads to a monism or mysticism at odds with Biblical and traditional Christianity. Orthodoxy, viewed generously, may be said to be the avoidance of oversimple extremes through paradox which holds diverse elements together in tension, while Christian heresies have tended either to exalt one of the three so as to lose the triune character of God, or else to emphasize the mystical unity so as to lose the three persons of the Trinity and the personal aspect of God entirely. Because the realists dominated the early part of the Middle Ages in Europe, and because extreme realism tends to become monism in one or another of its heretical forms, Abelard's criticism of universals as believed in by many of his predecessors and contemporaries was an important protection of orthodoxy, although most of the orthodox did not then appreciate his contribution.

Abelard is the chief one to make the transfer from ethics in the classical sense to arrive at a definition of the Good to the 'science' of moral theology. Although Tertullian had done something like this, in his little work bearing the title *Know Thyself,* Abelard was the first in Western Europe to make the sharp distinction between venial and mortal sin. This sort of development was also taking place elsewhere at the same time. The rationalist tendency in the Islamic philosophers had somewhat modified the rigorism of the doctrine of predestination in its application to the problem of whether God is the cause of evil or not. Rāmānuja showed much greater leniency towards defect in the sense that the Pūrva Mīmāṁsā had prescribed on the basis of its rigoristic doctrine in regard to the inexorability of the law of *karma*. Śaṅkara had taught that this is also within the realm of *adhyāsa* and that therefore the liberated soul, the *jīvan-mukta,* should be excused from the ritual observance prescribed by the old orthodoxy. Rāmānuja went further and taught that sufficiently ardent devotion, even on the part of the non-Brahmin masses, should be enough to gain the pardon and blessing of Bhagavan, "who takes delight in forgiving human defection." The Neo-Confucians also criticized the Buddhist monks for their ascetic excesses. Therefore it would appear that Abelard is only sailing well on the prevailing wind of the era. Indeed his expression seems to epitomize this aspect of the eleventh and early twelfth centuries. We might remember meanwhile that St. Bernard of Clairvaux is all the while peering over his shoulder, as it were, not so much censuring him for his leniency as vigilant lest his rationalism go too far and upset his own pious devotions.

That Abelard was a radical in his time cannot be denied; but this does not mean that he was not a sound and brilliant theologian. In his *Know Thyself,* instead of leaving the usual formulations of problems of conscience where we found them in St. Augustine and Pope Gregory, he is beginning to provide a schematic framework whereby the conscience can be instructed in its guidance of the soul. This revival of the spirit of Aristotle in the West must have been refreshing to some, although of course it was alarming to others who, like the followers of al-Ash'arī and the stricter rigorists in that tradition, were determined to stick to the "scriptures only" basis of operation. In spite of the traditional interpretation of the Fall of Adam, or the fall of Lucifer, as the source of *all* evil and imperfection, Abelard blatantly states, "Certain defects of merits of mind have no connection with morals." One can well imagine the effect among the ultra-pious, to whom salvation was the lot of only a blessed few who somehow could merit it in spite of the odds of "the world, the flesh, and the devil" which were so greatly against them.

Often the important thing is not the doctrine but Abelard's application of reason to it. He does not reduce ethics entirely to a system of logical propositions; there are real moral problems to be dealt with. But it is only by the application of reason to them that their often contradictory demands can be reconciled and ordered into a coherent pattern of life that not only *ought* but *can* be followed. Of course Abelard did not further extend his systematizing to include the relation between personal sins and sins of whole societies, for this comes much later for the most part, although traces of it can be found in Ibn Khaldūn and of course in Augustine, and later it has a wider development in Russian tradition in the concept of the *sobornost* and is found in most non-Buddhist philosophizing in China after Tung Chung-shu.

Only with great reservations in the little *Dialogue Between a Philosopher, a Jew and a Christian* does Abelard acknowledge that reason may have limitations. In this the Jew represents the Old Law based on the exclusiveness of the Mosaic revelation (comparable to the Mīmāṁsā) and presents a course of salvation that is highly rigoristic and ritualistic. The Philosopher represents the classical Graeco-Roman perspective with its ideal of the Golden Mean, the cultivation of the arts and the virtues, and the pursuit of happiness leading toward the *summum bonum*, something that is within human reach but not necessarily transcending nature or necessitated by anything beyond nature. One feels that Abelard is largely speaking through this character until well on toward the last dialogue where the arguments of the Christian begin to prevail. Here Abelard pulls together a scheme of virtues in addition to the classical temperance, prudence, fortitude, and justice which mediates the way to a *summum bonum* which is not less than a participation in the condition of Christ after the Resurrection. These are reverence, *beneficia*, veracity, *vindicatio*, magnanimity, humility, frugality.

It was difficult for Abelard's contemporaries to understand a man who would ridicule his teacher (the extreme realist William of Champeaux), but it was impossible to forgive a man who would risk upsetting the faith of the young by writing *Sic et Non*. Abelard's *Sic et Non* was a collection of seeming contradictions, not of scripture (which would have placed him where he never intended to be, outside the bounds of faith), but of the Church Fathers who though deservedly respected were nevertheless fallible. "Peter Abelard," wrote Bernard of Clairvaux, "is a persecutor of the Catholic faith and an enemy of the cross of Christ. Outwardly he is a monk but inwardly he is heretic."[13] Abelard's chief intellectual sin—unless pride to the point of arrogance is a candidate—was that he trusted reason as much as possible while Bernard trusted it as little as possible. But Abelard did not intend to produce sceptics. His theory in *Sic et Non* was: "By doubting we come to inquiry; by inquiry we discover the truth." Even his difference from the extreme realists was often more a matter of debate tactics than total rejection of all their fundamental theses.

Both Anselm and Abelard used and helped perfect (particularly Abelard) the dialogical and dialectical methods most fully synthesized into the method of Thomas Aquinas. "Dialectic remains for Abelard the *ars disputandi*, by which you sharpen your wits to detect fallacies, and learn to know a good argument from a bad."[14] As a logician/dialectician Abelard has been placed in the company of Aristotle, William of Ockham (the famous fourteenth-century nominalist), Leibniz, John Stuart Mill, George Boole, Gottlob Frege, Whitehead, Russell and Kurt Gödel. "Peter Abelard is sometimes called the father of Scholasticism. He created the format and rules by which philosophical debate was carried on during the later medieval period, reformulated the principles governing syllogistic inference, and made explicit the distinction between formal (logical) and factual truths."[15]

The outline of Abelard's *Dialectica* does not differ greatly from that of any treatise on logic from any medieval school:

genus and species, differentiae, quantity, relation, problems of perfection; relation of all and some and none; problems concerning providence and fate; modes of affirmation and negation; problems of causation; and finally the problem of definition itself, in which is opened the vexing scholastic problem of the relation between univocal, equivocal and other types of definition. One will not therein find more than is to be found in other lands where man has made the same attempts to find some way through his own necessary logical equipment in order to come to an adequate understanding of the relation of complexity. A comparison of Abelard and Gaṅgeśa should be appropriate since they were at least in comparable historical positions: both were 'modernizers' of a tradition that had grown hoary but little heeded largely for that reason. Although both were master technicians in their respective fields, they were well aware of the limitations of their techniques. However, if one is to benefit from these scholastic works one must have the patience to get inside the terminology and see the precision clearly, for therein lies the scholastic genius. Like the great cathedrals and abbeys, not only the vast exalted arches but the fine filigree in the ornamental sculptures manifest true genius if not indeed supernatural inspiration, just as the dialectical subtleties in Indian logic were paralleled by the intricate ornaments in Dravidian architecture.

It seems that Abelard's chief contribution is not so much in his manipulation of the nominalist-realist controversy as in his rediscovery that arguments are only arguments after all, and that they can be deliberately constructed and jostled against each other diacritically without running the risk of complete scepticism. Faith remains above these arguments. It is man's rational prerogative to manipulate arguments with the utmost sagacity and good judgment without becoming unduly engrossed with them. The philosopher is one who can argue against himself for the sake of the intellectual perfection of God with the same perspicacity that the saint must use in his dependency before the moral perfection of his Creator. It is out of this, from an inner compulsion rather than as a mere enlarging commentary of Porphyry, Iamblicus and Boethius, that his conceptualism develops. Logical functions within the grasp and management of the human intellect are not necessarily *onto*logical, and therefore are not ultimate in themselves. We arrive at universals by abstraction, but that does not mean that those things from which they are abstracted must be discarded. Thomas Gilby gives us this for conclusion: "Abelard founded no lasting school, but he left a lasting spirit. His character and work abound with the contrasts of a good debate; he was a linguistic philosopher, a poet, and a monk with a great love of the world. He confessed that he was bad at mathematics; it is said that he excelled at music. Indeed, he communicates a singing quality to topics ordinarily unmelodious. Few other Scholastics remain as readable and alive."[16]

NOTES

Jābir

1. Seyyed Hossein Nasr, *Science and Civilization in Islam* (Cambridge: Harvard University Press, 1968), pp. 258-59.

2. Ibid., p. 259.

3. Seyyed Hossein Nasr, *Islamic Studies* (Beirut : Librairie du Liban, 1967), p. 90.

4. Nasr, *Science and Civilization*, pp. 267-68.

Nara Buddhism

1. Daigan and Alicia Matsunaga, *Foundation of Japanese Buddhism* (Tokyo : Buddhist Books International, 1974).

2. Ibid., p. 29.

3. Ibid., p. 47.

4. Ibid., p. 48.

5. Ibid., p. 49.

6. Ibid., pp. 63-4.

7. Ibid., p. 64.

8. Ibid., p. 64.

9. Ibid., p. 75.

10. Ibid., p. 76.

11. Ibid., p. 76.

12. E. Steinilber-Oberlin, *The Buddhist Sects of Japan*, trans. by Marc Logé, Greenwood reprint, 1970, pp. 51-2.

13. Matsunagas, pp. 91-2.

14. Ibid., p. 94.

15. Ibid., p. 97.

16. Steinilber-Onerlin, p. 59.

17. Matsunagas, p. 137.

Rābi'ah

1. A. J. Arberry, trans., *Muslim Saints and Mystics*, p. 39.

2. Ibid., pp. 50-51.

3. Majid Fakhry, *A History of Islamic Philosophy* (New York : Columbia Universiry Press, 1970), p. 264.

4. Margaret Smith, *Rābi'a the Mystic* (Amsterdam : Philo Press, 1974), pp. 108-9.

5. Arberry, p. 51.

6. Smith, p. 112.

Liu Tsung-yüan

1. Hou Wai-lu, "Liu Tsung-yüan's Materialist Thought and Social Thought", Chinese Studies in Philosophy, vol. IV, no. 4.
2. Ibid., p. 43.
3. Ibid., p. 15.
4. Ibid., p. 21.
5. Ibid., pp. 40-41.
6. Ibid., p. 17.
7. Ibid., p. 18.
8. Ibid., p. 47.
9. Ibid., pp. 55-56.
10. Ibid., p. 59.
11. Ibid., p. 64.
12. Ibid., p. 72.

Śaṅkara

1. U. C. Bhattacharjee, *The History and Culture of the Indian People* (Bombay : Bharatitya Vidya Bhavan, 1964), p. 356.
2. Chandradhar Sharma, *Indian Philosophy: A Critical Survey* (London : Rider & Co., 1960), p. 241.
3. R. C. Majumdar, *The History and Culture of the Indian People* p. 355.
4. N. K. Devaraja, *An Introduction to Śaṅkara's Theory of Knowledge* (Delhi : Motilal Banarsidass, 1962), pp. 60-61.
5. Ibid., p. 62.
6. Ibid., p. 65.
7. V. M. Apte, *Brahma-Sūtra-Shānkara-Bhāshya* (Bombay : Popular Book Depot, 1960), p. xiii ff.
8. Devaraja, p. 182.
9. Ibid., p. 189.
10. Ibid., p. 191.
11. Apte, p. xv-xvi.
12. Ibid., p. xxx.
13. Ibid., p. xxx-xxxi.
14. Ibid., p. xxxi.
15. Jadunath Sinha, *A History of Indian Philosophy*, vol. II (Calcutta : Central Book Agency, 1952), p. 608.
16. Ibid., p. 609.
17. Ibid., p. 610.
18. Devaraja, p. 159.
19. Ibid., pp. 68-9.
20. Ibid., p. 119.
21. Ibid., p. 120.
22. Sinha, p. 611.

Padmapāda

1. Eliot Deutsch and J. van Buitenen, *A Source Book of Advaita Vedānta* (Honolulu : University Press of Hawaii, 1971), p. 242.
2. Surendranath Dasgupta, *A History of Indian Philosophy*, vol. II (Cambridge : Cambridge University Press, 1961), p. 104.
3. Ibid., pp. 104-5.
4. Ibid., p. 105.
5. Ibid., pp. 105-6.
6. Jadunath Sinha, *A History of Indian Philosophy*, vol. II (Calcutta : Central Book Agency, 1952), p. 204.
7. Ibid., p. 206.

Sureśvara

1. T. M. P. Mahadevan, *Saṁbandha-vārtika of Sureśvarācārya* (University of Madras, 1972), p. xiv.
2. R. Balasubramanian, *The Taittirīyopaniṣad Bhāṣya-vārtika* (University of Madras, 1974), pp. 93-94.
3. Ibid., p. 145.
4. C. Markandeya Sastri, *Sureśvara's Contribution to Advaita* (Sundari Samskrita Vidyalaya, 1971), p. 17f.
5. Ibid., p. 40.
6. Ibid., p. 72.
7. Ibid., pp. 39-40.
8. Ibid., p. 72.
9. Jadunath Sinha, *A History of Indian Philosophy*, vol. III (Calcutta : Central Book Agency, 1952), pp. 236-37.
10. Ibid., p. 264.
11. Guy Maximilien, *La Démonstration du Non-Agir* (Paris, 1975), p. 14.
12. Ibid., p. 15.
13. J. M. van Boetzelaer, *Sureśvara's Taittirīyopaniṣad- Bhāṣyavārtikam* (Leiden : E. J. Brill, 1971), p. 6.
14. Ibid., p. 6.
15. Ibid., p. 87.
16. Ibid., p. 92.
17. Balasubramanian, p. 47.
18. Sinha, p. 342.
19. van Boetzelaer, p. 49.
20. Ibid., p. 73.
21. Balasubramanian, p. 208.
22. Ibid., p. 209.

Saichō

1. Daigan and Alicia Matsunaga, *Foundation of Japanese Buddhism* (Tokyo : Buddhist Books International, 1974), pp. 139-40.

2. Ibid., p. 142.
3. Ibid., p. 143.
4. Hajime Nakamura, *A History of the Development of Japanese Thought* (Tokyo, 1969), pp. 40-41.
5. Matsunagas, p. 150.
6. Ibid., p. 161.

Han Yü and Li Ao

1. Chou Hsiang-kuang, *The History of Chinese Buddhism* (Allahabad : Indo-Chinese Literature Publications, 1956), pp. 157-58.
2. Wing-tsit Chan, *A Source Book in Chinese Philosophy* (Princeton : Princeton University Press, 1963), p. 454.
3. Ibid., pp. 451-52.
4. Carsun Chang, *The Development of Neo-Confucian Thought*, vol. I (New Haven : College and University Press, 1963), p. 111.
5. Fung Yu-lan, *A History of Chinese Philosophy*, vol. II (Princeton: Princeton University Press, 1953), p. 414.
6. Ibid., p. 417.
7. Chang, p. 108.
8. Fung, p. 419.
9. Chan, p. 458.
10. Chang, p. 104.

Theodore of Studium

1. Irénée Hausherr, *St. Théodore Studite l'Homme et l'Ascète* (Rome : Orientalia Christiana, VI, 1, 1962), p. 62.
2. Alice Gardner, *Theodore of Studium : His Life and Times* (London : Edward Arnold, 1905), p. 219.

Nicephorus

1. Davin Talbot Rice, *The Appreciation of Byzantine Art* (Oxford, 1972), p. 106.
2. Ibid., p. 107.
3. Stephen Gero, "Notes on Byzantine Iconoclasm in the Eighth Century", *Byzantion*, vol. 44, 1974, pp. 36-7.
4. Paul J. Alexander, *The Patriarch Nicephorus of Constantinople* (Oxford, 1958), p. 138.
5. Ibid., pp. 198-99.
6. Ibid., p. 199.
7. Ibid., p. 200.
8. Ibid., p. 200.
9. Ibid., pp. 205-6.
10. Ibid., p. 206.
11. Ibid., pp. 229-30.

Kūkai

1. G. B. Sansom, *Japan : A Short Cultural History* (London, 1946), p. 230.
2. Yoshito S. Hakeda, *Kūkai : Major Works* (New York : Columbia University Press, 1972), pp. 5-6.
3. Daigan and Alicia Matsunaga, *Foundation of Japanese Buddhism* (Tokyo : Buddhist Books International, 1974), p. 179.
4. Chou Hsiang-kuang, *The History of Chinese Buddhism* (Allahabad : Indo-Chinese Literature Publications, 1956), p. 155.
5. Yūkei Matsunaga, "Tantric Buddhism and Shingon Buddhism", *The Eastern Buddhist*, vol. II, no. 2, 1969, p. 5.
6. Hakeda, pp. 98-99.
7. Ibid., p. 99.
8. Ibid., p. 63.
9. Ibid., pp. 77-78.
10. Ibid., p. 74.
11. Jissho Kinoshita, *The Problem of Filial Piety in Japan* (University of Hawaii, 1968), p. 65.
12. Ryusaku Tsunoda *et al*, *Sources of Japanese Tradition* (New York : Columbia University Press, 1958), pp. 141-42.
13. Ibid., pp. 150-51.

Vidyānanda

1. K. K. Dixit, *Jaina Ontology* (Ahmedabad, 1971), p. 101.
2. Nathmal Tatia, *A Compendium of Vidyānanda's Satyaśāsanaparīkṣā*, 13.
3. Ibid., p. 14.
4. Ibid., p. 15.
5. Ibid., p. 17.
6. Ibid., p. 18.
7. Ibid., pp. 18-19.
8. Ibid., pp. 24-25.
9. Ibid., p. 32.
10. Ibid., p. 33.
11. Ibid., pp. 33-34.
12. Ibid., p. 34.
13. Ibid., pp. 34-5.
14. Ibid., p. 35.
15. Ibid., p. 36.
16. Ibid., pp. 37-8.
17. Ibid., p. 42.
18. Ibid., p. 44.
19. Ibid., pp. 46-7.
20. Ibid., p. 47.

Haribhadra

1. E. Obermiller, "*A Study of the Twenty Aspects of Śūnyatā*", Indian Historical Quarterly, 9, 1933, p. 174.
2. Ibid., p. 176.
3. Ibid., p. 177.
4. Ibid., p. 178.
5. Ibid., p. 179.
6. Ibid., p. 181.
7. Ibid., pp. 182-3.
8. Ibid., p. 186.

Vācaspati Miśra

1. Jadunath Sinha, *A History of Indian Philosophy*, vol. III (Calcutta : Central Book Agency, 1952), p. 258.
2. Surendranath Dasgupta, *A History of Indian Philosophy*, vol. II (Cambridge : Cambridge Univ. Press, 1961), p. 108.
3. Sinha, p. 264.
4. Ibid., p. 280.
5. Ibid., p. 203.
6. Ibid., p. 287.
7. Ibid., p. 205.
8. Ibid., p. 229.

Mu'tazilites

1. Majid Fakhry, *A History of Islamic Philosophy* (New York : Columbia University Press, 1970), p. 59.
2. Ibid., pp. 61-2.
3. A. E. Affifi, "The Rational and Mystical Interpretations of Islam," in *Islam—The Straight Path*, K. Morgan ed. (New York : Ronald Press, 1958), p. 151.
4. Mir Valiuddin, "Mu'tazilism", in *A History of Muslim Philosophy*, vol. I (Wiesbaden : Otto Harrassowitz, 1963), pp. 203-4.

al-Muḥāsibī

1. Abdel-Halim Mahmoud, *Al-Mohāsibī : un Mystic Musulman Religieux et Moraliste* (Paris : P. Geuthner, 1940).
2. Margaret Smith, *Al-Muḥāsibī : An Early Mystic of Baghdad* (Amsterdam : Philo Press, 1974).
3. Mahmoud, pp. 214-15.
4. Smith, p. 169.
5. Ibid., pp. 231-32.
6. Mahmoud, p. 236.

7. Smith, p. 242.
8. Mahmoud, p. 241.
9. Smith, p. 16.

Ennin

1. Edwin Reischauer, *Ennin's Travels in T'ang China* (New York : Ronald Press, 1955), p. 29.
2. Ibid., p. 29.
3. Ibid., p. 30.
4. Ibid., pp. 172-3.
5. Ibid., p. 30.
6. Daigan and Alicia Matsunaga, *Foundation of Japanese Buddhism* (Tokyo : Buddhist Books International, 1974), p. 164.
7. Ibid., p. 164.

al-Kindī

1. George Atiyeh, *Al-Kindī : The Philosophy of the Arabs*, p. 8.
2. Ibid., p. viii-ix.
3. Ibid., p. 19.
4. Ibid., p. 25.
5. Ibid., p. 28.
6. Ibid., p. 27.
7. Ibid., p. 30.
8. Ibid., p. 34.
9. Ibid., p. 40.
10. Ibid., p. 48.
11. Ibid., p. 57.
12. Ibid., p. 59.
13. Ibid., p. 59.
14. Ibid., p. 63.
15. Ibid., pp. 86-7.
16. Ibid., p. 113.
17. Ibid., p. 115.
18. Ibid., pp. 116-17.
19. Ibid., p. 118.
20. Ibid., p. 119.
21. Fehmi Jadaane, *L'Influence de Stoicisme sur la Pensée Musulmane* (Beyrouth, 1968), p. 21.
22. Jean Jolivet, *L'Intellect selon Kindī* (Leiden, 1971), pp. 155-56.

Erigena

1. René Martin, "Á propos d'une Remarque le Schopenhauer sur Jean Scot Érigène et la Philosophie Indienne", in *Jean Scot Érigène et L'Histoire de la Philosophie* (Laon, 1975).

2. Donald Duclow, "Pseudo-Dionysius, John Scotus Eriugena, Nicholas of Cusa : An Approach to the Hermeneutic of the Divine Names", International Philosophical Quarterly, no. 12, 1972, p. 264.
3. Jorge Gracia, "Ontological Characterization of the Relation Between Man and Created Nature in Eriugena", Journal of the History of Philosophy, no. 16, 1978, p. 156.
4. Ibid., p. 157.
5. Ibid., p. 157.
6. Ibid., p. 158.
7. Ibid., p. 160.
8. Ibid., p. 161.
9. Ibid., p. 161.
10. Ibid., p. 161.
11. Ibid., p. 161.
12. Ibid., p. 162.
13. Duclow, p. 276.
14. Gracia, p. 163.
15. Ibid., pp. 163-64.
16. Ibid., p. 164.
17. Ibid., p. 164.
18. Ibid., p. 165.
19. René Roques, *Libres Sentiers vers L'Erigenisme* (Rome, 1975), p. 40.
20. Erika von Erhardt-Siebold and Rudolf von Erhardt, *The Astronomy of Johannes Scotus Erigena* (New York, 1940), p. 56.

Bāyazīd al-Basṭāmī

1. A. E. Affifi, "The Rational and Mystical Interpretations of Islam" in *Islam—The Straight Path*, ed. Kenneth Morgan (New York, 1958), p. 170.
2. Ibid.
3. Ibid.
4. Ibid., pp. 174-75.
5. Ibid., pp. 175-76.
6. B. A. Dar, "Sufis Before al-Ḥallāj" in *A History of Muslim Philosophy* ed. M. M. Sharif (Wiesbaden, 1963) p. 343.
7. Ibid., pp. 342-43.
8. Majid Fakhry, *A History of Islamic Philosophy* (New York, 1970), p. 272.
9. Ibid., pp. 272-73.

Jayanta Bhaṭṭa

1. Satkari Mookerjee, "Jayanta Bhaṭṭa—The Author of the Nyāyamañjarī", Calcutta Review, no. 40, 1931, pp. 256-57.
2. H. G. Narahari, "Jayantabhaṭṭa : Poet-Philosopher of Kashmir", Aryan Path, 1966, p. 27.
3. Ibid., p. 25.

4. Ibid., p. 26.
5. Mookerjee, p. 254.
6. Ibid., p. 255.
7. Ibid., pp. 265-66.
8. Ibid., pp. 264-65.
9. Ibid., pp. 266-67.
10. G. N. Shastri, "The Doctrine of Sabdabrahman—A Criticism by Jayantabhaṭṭa", Indian Historical Quarterly, no. 15, 1939, pp. 441-42.
11. Ibid., p. 447.
12. Ibid., p. 454.
13. D. N. Shastri, *Critique of Indian Realism* (Agra : Agra University Press, 1964), pp. 339-40.
14. Ibid., p. 381.
15. Ibid., p. 401.
16. Ibid., p. 402.
17. Mookerjee, pp. 273-74.

Photius

1. H. S. Williams, The Historians' History of the World, vol. VII, p. 570.
2. Ibid., p. 570.
3. Earnest Barker, *Social and Political Thought in Byzantium* (Oxford, 1957), pp. 111-12.
4. Ibid., pp. 109-10.
5. Francis Dvornik, New Catholic Encyclopedia, p. 329.
6. J. M. Hussey, *Church and Learning in the Byzantine Empire* (New York, 1937), pp. 35-6.
7. Paul Lemerle, *Le Premier Humanisme Byzantin* (Presses Universitaires de France, 1971), p. 202.
8. Barker, p. 113.
9. Ibid., pp. 113-114.
10. Francis Dvornik, *The Photian Schism* (Cambridge, 1948), pp. 386-87.
11. Barker, p. 112.

al-Sarakhsī

1. *Cambridge History of Iran*, vol. IV, pp. 422-23.

Somānanda

1. Raniero Gnoli, "Śivadṛṣṭi by Somānanda", East & West, no. 8, 1957, p. 16.
2. Ibid., p. 17.
3. Ibid., p. 17.
4. Ibid., pp. 17-8.
5. Ibid., p. 19.
6. Jadunath Sinha, *A History of Indian Philosophy*, vol. III (Calcutta : Central Book Agency, 1971), p. 35.

7. Gnoli, pp. 19-20.
8. Ibid., p. 20.
9. Ibid., pp. 19-20.
10. Ibid., p. 21.
11. Ibid., p. 22.
12. Sinha, pp. 97-8.

Bhāskara

1. Jadunath Sinha, *A History of Indian Philosophy*, vol. III (Calcutta : Sinha Publishing House, 1971), p. 2.
2. Ibid., p. 3.
3. Ibid., p. 4.
4. Ibid., p. 7.
5. Ibid., p. 8.
6. Ibid., p. 11.
7. Ibid., p. 12.
8. Ibid.
9. Ibid., p. 13.
10. Ibid., pp. 19-20.
11. Ibid., pp. 21-22.
12. Ibid., p. 23.
13. Surendranath Dasgupta, *A History of Indian Philosophy*, vol. III (Cambridge, 1940), pp. 9-10.

Thābit ibn Qurra

1. Majid Fakhry, *A History of Islamic Philosophy* (New York : Columbia University Press, 1970), p. 29.
2. Seyyed Hossein Nasr, *Science and Civilization in Islam* (Harvard University Press, 1968), pp. 44-45.

al-Junayd

1. Majid Fakhry, *A History of Islamic Philosophy* (New York, 1970), pp. 265-66.
2. Abdel-Kader, *The Life, Personality and Writings of al-Junayd* (London, 1976), p. 5.
3. Henri Corbin, in *Histoire de la Philosophie*, vol. I, Pléiade series (Editions Gallimard, 1969), pp. 1162-63.
4. Abdel-Kader, p. 11.
5. Ibid., p. 12.
6. Ibid., p. 104.
7. Ibid., p. 114.
8. Ibid., p. 115.
9. Fakhry, pp. 266-67.
10. Abdel-Kader, pp. 93-4.
11. Ibid., p. 38.

12. Ibid., p. 32.
13. Ibid., p. 72.
14. Ibid.
15. Ibid., p. 81.
16. Ibid.
17. Ibid., p. 82.
18. Ibid., p. 85.
19. Ibid., p. 34.
20. Ibid., p. 51.

al-Ḥallāj

1. Majid Fakhry, *A History of Islamic Philosophy* (New York, 1970), p. 273.
2. Ibid., p. 274.
3. Ibid., p. 275.
4. Louis Massignon, "Al-Ḥallāj", *A History of Muslim Philosophy*, ed. M. M. Sharif (Wiesbaden, 1963), p. 347.
5. Fakhry, p. 277.
6. Louis Massignon, *La Passion d'al-Ḥallāj* (Paris, 1922), p. 28.
7. Ibid., p. 233.

al-Rāzī

1. Henri Corbin, in *Histoire de la Philosophie* vol. I, Pléiade series (Editions Gallimard, 1969), p. 1127.
2. Seyyed Hossein Nasr, *Science and Civilization in Islam* (Cambridge, 1968), p. 204.
3. Ibid., p. 268.
4. M. M. Sharif, ed., *A History of Muslim Philosophy*, vol. I (Wiesbaden, 1963), p. 448.
5. Ibid., pp. 439-40.
6. Ibid., pp. 441-42.
7. Ibid., p. 443.
8. Ibid., p. 444.
9. Lenn Evan Goodman, "Rāzī's Myth of the Fall of Soul", in *Essays On Islamic Philosophy and Science*, G. Hourani, ed., p. 35.
10. Ibid.
11. Sharif, pp. 445-46.
12. Ibid., p. 446.
13. Ibid.
14. Lenn Evan Goodman, "The Epicurean Ethics of Muḥammad Ibn Zakariyā' al-Rāzī", Studia Islamica, no. XXXIV, 1972, p. 6.
15. Ibid., pp. 8-9.
16. Ibid., p. 9.
17. Ibid., p. 10.

18. Ibid., pp. 10-11.
19. Ibid., p. 17.
20. Ibid., p. 20.
21. Ibid., pp. 21-22.

al-Ash'arī

1. M. M. Sharif, ed., *A History of Muslim Philosophy*, vol. I (Wiesbaden, 1963), p. 220.
2. Ibid., pp. 220-21.
3. Ibid., p. 221.
4. Ibid., p. 223.
5. *Handworterbuch des Islam,* trans. Klein, 19541, p. 37.
6. R. J. McCarthy, *Theology of al-Ash'arī* (Beirut, 1953), p. 32.
7. W. M. Watt, *Free Will and Predestination in Early Islam* (London, 1948).
8. McCarthy, p. 16f.
9. Fakhry, pp. 233-34.
10. Ibid., p. 233.
11. Ibid., p. 235.

Saadia

1. Encyclopedia Judaica, vol. 14, p. 546.
2. Ibid., p. 554.
3. Ibid., p. 549.
4. Ibid., p. 550.
5. Isaac Husik, *A History of Mediaeval Jewish Philosophy* (New York, 1969), p. 31.
6. Encyclopedia Judaica, p. 550.
7. Ibid., p. 549.
8. *The Book of Beliefs and Opinions,* Samuel Rosenblatt, trans. (New Haven : Yale University Press, 1948), p. xxviii.
9. Ibid., p. 7.
10. Ibid., p. 10.
11. Ibid., p. 31.
12. David Rau, "Die Ethik R. Saadja (The Ethics of Rabbi Saadya)", Monatsschrift für Geschichte und Wissenschaft des Judentums, vol. 55, 1911, p. 399.
13. *Book of Beliefs and Opinions*, p. 9.
14. Ibid., p. 157.
15. Ibid., p. 156.
16. Ibid., p. 23.
17. Ibid., p. 77.
18. Ibid., p. 222.

19. Ibid.
20. Ibid., p. 249.
21. Ibid., p. 250.
22. Ibid., pp. 344-45.
23. Ibid., p. 354.
24. Ibid., p. 357.
25. Ibid., p. 358.
26. Ibid., p. 399.
27. Ibid., p. 387.
28. Gaius G. Atkins, *The Interpreter's Bible* (New York, Abingdon Press, 1956), V, 23.
29. Ibid., p. 23.
30. Ibid., p. 19.

Ikhwān al-Ṣafā

1. Majid Fakhry, *A History of Islamic Philosophy* (New York, 1970), p. 186.
2. Omar Farrukh, "Ikhwān al-Ṣafā", in *A History of Muslim Philosophy*, M. M. Sharif, ed. (Wiesbaden, 1963), pp. 291-92.
3. Ibid.
4. Seyyed Hossein Nasr, *An Introduction to Islamic Cosmological Doctrines* (Cambridge, 1964), pp. 33-4.
5. Farrukh, p. 308.
6. Lenn Evan Goodman, *The Case of the Animals versus Man Before the King of the Jinn* (Boston, 1978), p. 43.
7. Ibid.
8. Farrukh, p. 309.
9. Ibid., p. 293.
10. Nasr, p. 46.
11. Ibid., pp. 51-2.
12. Ibid., pp. 53-4.
13. Ibid., p. 59n.
14. Farrukh, p. 296.
15. Ibid., p. 298.
16. Ibid., p. 300.
17. Nasr, pp. 71-2.
18. Ibid., p. 74.
19. Ibid., p. 80.
20. Ibid.
21. Ibid., p. 104.
22. Fakhry, pp. 203-4.

Abhinavagupta

1. T. M. P. Mahadevan, "Śaivism", in *The History and Culture of the Indian People*, vol. IV (Bombay, 1964), pp. 300-1.

2. Jaideva Singh, *Pratyabhijñāhṛdayam* (Delhi, 1977), pp. 17-18.
3. Ibid., p. 18.
4. Mahadevan, pp. 302-3.
5. Ibid., p. 304.
6. Singh, pp. 24-26.
7. Lilian Silburn, *Hymnes de Abhinavagupta* (Paris, 1970), p. 22.
8. Ibid., p. 24.
9. Ibid., p. 21.
10. Singh, pp. 12-13.
11. Ibid., p. 13.
12. André Padoux, *Paratrimsikalaghuvṛtti*, (Paris, 1975), p. 15.
13. Silburn, pp. 25-6.
14. J. L. Masson and M. V. Patwardhan, *Aesthetic Rapture* (Poona, 1970), p. 7.
15. Ibid., p. 4.
16. Ibid., p. 23.
17. Ibid., pp. 26-7.
18. Ibid., pp. 17-18.
19. Ibid., p. 18.
20. Ibid.
21. Ibid.
22. Ibid., pp. 19-20.
23. Ibid., p. 21.
24. Ibid., p. 36.
25. J. L. Masson and M. V. Patwardhan, *Śāntarasa and Abhinavagupta's Philosophy of Aesthetics* (Poona, 1969), pp. 161-62.
26. Sneh Pandit, *An Approach to the Indian Theory of Art and Aesthetics* (Delhi, 1977).

Genshin

1. Allan A. Andrews, *The Teachings Essential for Rebirth* (Tokyo, 1973), p. 56.
2. Daigan and Alicia Matsunaga, *Foundation of Japanese Buddhism* (Tokyo, 1974), pp. 216-17.
3. Andrews, p. 52.
4. Ibid., p. 54.
5. Ibid., p. 55.
6. Ibid.
7. Ibid., p. 56.
8. Ibid., p. 61.
9. Ibid., pp. 64-5.
10. Ibid., p. 86.
11. Ibid., p. 90.
12. Ibid., p. 103.
13. Matsunagas, p. 170.
14. Ibid., p. 256.

Simeon the New Theologian

1. Jaroslav Pelikan, *The Spirit of Eastern Christendom*, vol. II (Chicago, 1974), p. 261.
2. Ibid., p. 254.
3. Ibid., p. 257.
4. Ibid., p. 258.
5. Ibid., pp. 259-60.
6. Ibid., pp. 260-61.
7. Basile Tatakis, *La Philosophie Byzantine*, Bréhier series, no. 11 (Paris, 1959), p. 148.

Miskawayh

1. Abdurrahman Badawi, "Miskawaih", in *A History of Muslim Philosophy*, M. M. Sharif, ed. (Wiesbaden, 1963), p. 471.
2. Majid Fakhry, *A History of Islamic Philosophy* (New York, 1970) p. 211.
3. Badawi, p. 473.
4. Ibid., p. 472.
5. Fakhry, p. 211.
6. Ibid., p. 212.
7. Ibid.
8. Badawi, p. 477.
9. Ibid., p. 475.
10. Ibid., p. 476.
11. M. Ansari, *The Ethical Philosophy of Miskawaih* (Aligarh, 1964), p. 317.
12. Ibid., p. 319.
13. Ibid., p. 320.
14. Ibid., p. 323.
15. Ibid., p. 324.
16. Ibid., p. 325.
17. Ibid., pp. 326-27.
18. Ibid., p. 329.
19. Ibid., p. 330.
20. Ibid.
21. Ibid., p. 331.
22. Badawi, p. 479.
23. Ibid., p. 469.

Ibn Sīnā

1. Fazlur Rahman, "Ibn Sīnā" in *A History of Muslim Philosophy* vol. I, M. M. Sharif, ed. (Wiesbaden, 1963), p. 504.
2. Majid Fakhry, *A History of Islamic Philosophy* (New York, 1970), p. 147 ff.

3. Ibid., p. 149.
4. Ibid., p. 178.
5. Seyyed Hossein Nasr, *An Introduction to Islamic Cosmological Doctrines* (Cambridge, 1964), pp. 263-64.
6. Ibid., pp. 261-62.
7. Ibid.
8. Ibid., p. 262.
9. Ibid., p. 252.
10. F. Rahman, *Avicenna's Psychology* (London, 1952), p. 21.
11. Nasr, p. 259.
12. Ibid., p. 231.
13. Ismail Dahiyat, *Avicenna's Commentary on the Poetics of Aristotle* (Leiden, 1974), pp. 41-2.
14. Ibid., p. 34.
15. E.I.J. Rosenthal, "Avicenna's Influence on Jewish Thought", in *Avicenna, Scientist and Philosopher* (London, 1952), pp. 68-9.
16. Ibid., p. 80.
17. Rahman, pp. 504-5.

Ibn al-Haitham

1. Nazir Ahmad, "Ibn al-Haitham : His Life and Work" in *Ibn al-Haitham* (Hamdard National Foundation, Pakistan : 1965).
2. Naseer Ahmad Nasir, "Ibn al-Haitham and his Philosophy" in *Ibn al-Haitham* (Pakistan : 1965), pp. 85-6.
3. M. M. Sharif, ed., *A History of Muslim Philosophy* vol. II (Wiesbaden, 1966), p. 1372.
4. Nasir, p. 83.
5. Ibid.
6. Ibid., p. 84.
7. Ibid., p. 82.

al-Bīrūnī

1. Seyyed Hossein Nasr, *Science and Civilization in Islam* (Cambridge, 1968), pp. 50-51.
2. Maqbul Ahmad *et al*, "Al-Bīrunī, An Introduction to his Life and Writings on the Indian Sciences", Indian Journal of the History of Science, Nov., 1975, p. 99.
3. Ibid., p. 101.
4. Nasr, p. 231.
5. Maqbul Ahmad, "Al-Bīrunī as a Synthesizer and Transmitter of Scientific Knowledge", Indian Journal of the History of Science, 1975, p. 247.
6. Nasr, pp. 144-45.

Udayana

1. George Chemparathy, *An Indian Rational Theology* (Vienna, 1972), pp. 25-6.

2. G. Bhattacharyya, *Studies in Nyāya-Vaiśeṣika Theism* (Calcutta, 1961), p. xiv.
3. Chemparathy, p. 31.
4. Umesh Miśra, *History of Indian Philosophy* vol. II (Allahabad, 1966), p. 160.
5. Ibid., p. 161.
6. S. S. Barlingay, *A Modern Introduction to Indian Logic* (Delhi, 1965), pp. 89-90.
7. Miśra, pp. 175-76.
8. Ibid., p. 176.
9. Ibid., p. 180.
10. Bhattacharyya, p. 144.
11. Chemparathy, p. 137.
12. Miśra, p. 182.
13. Ibid.
14. Ibid., pp. 182-3.
15. Ibid., p. 184.
16. Ibid.
17. Ibid., pp. 186-7.
18. Ibid., p. 187.

Atiśa

1. Śrimati Alaka Chattopadhyaya, *Atiśa and Tibet* (Calcutta, 1967), p. 355.
2. Rajendra Ram, *A History of Buddhism in Nepal* (Motilal Banarsidass, 1978), p. 104 ff.
3. Chattopadhyaya, p. 344.
4. Ibid., p. 345 ff.
5. Ibid., p. 362.
6. Ibid., pp. 533-34.
7. Ibid., p. 542.
8. Ibid., pp. 537-39.

Ibn Gabirol

1. Isaac Husik, *A History of Mediaeval Jewish Philosophy* (New York, 1969), pp. 59-60.
2. Shlomo Pines in *Encyclopedia Judaica*, p. 237.
3. Ibid., pp. 240-41.
4. Ibid., p. 241.
5. Husik, pp. 64-5.
6. Ibid., p. 71.
7. Pines, p. 242.
8. Husik, p. 61.

Ibn Ḥazm

1. M. S. H. Ma'ṣūmī, "Ibn Ḥazm's Allegations Against the Leading Imāms", Islamic Studies, vol. VII, 1968, p. 113.
2. M. M. Sharif, ed., *A History of Muslim Philosophy* vol. I (Wiesbaden, 1963), p. 281.
3. Majid Fakhry, *A History of Islamic Philosophy* (New York, 1970), p. 349.
4. Ibid., p. 350.
5. Sharif, p. 282.
6. Henri Corbin, in *Histoire de la Philosophie*, vol. I, Pléiade series (Editions Gallimard, 1969), p. 1179 ff.
7. A. S. Tritton, "Ibn Ḥazm : The Man and The Thinker", Islamic Studies, vol. III, 1964.
8. Ma'ṣūmī, p. 114.
9. Ibid.

Chou Tun-i

1. Fung Yu-lan, *A History of Chinese Philosophy*, vol. II (Princeton : Princeton Univ. Press, 1953), pp. 435-38.
2. Hajime Nakamura, *Ways of Thinking of Eastern Peoples* (Honolulu, 1964), p. 104.
3. Carson Chang, *Development of Neo-Confucian Thought* (New York, 1957), p. 142.
4. Wing-tsit Chan, *A Source Book in Chinese Philosophy* (Princeton, 1963), p. 460.
5. Ibid., p. 462.
6. Joseph Needham, *Science and Civilisation in China*, Colin Ronan ed., p. 236.
7. Fung, pp. 444-45.
8. Chang, pp. 143-44.
9. Ibid., p. 158.
10. Needham, p. 217.
11. Chan, p. 466.
12. Fung, p. 446.
13. Chan, p. 468.
14. Ibid., p. 473.
15. Fung, p. 451.
16. Chang, pp. 139-40.

Shao Yung

1. Carson Chang, *Development of Neo-Confucian Thought* (New York, 1957), p. 161.
2. Ibid., p. 162.
3. Joseph Needham, *Science and Civilisation in China* (Cambridge, 1956), pp. 455-56.

traditions as varied as those of Arabia, India, China and Western Europe.

Although the present writer is not competent to speak authoritatively on the subject of Eastern thought, it would appear in general that the two pivotal points at which all these traditions were in contact are : (a) The valiant effort of the mind to lift the mystery surrounding man's experience of the divine, and (b) the deepening of religious feeling to the extent that it can no longer be penetrated by the light of reason. The former we call logic, the second mysticism. However, the unrelenting attempt, during the centuries under study, to overcome the antithesis between them is the principal goal of scholasticism, as the present volume illustrates in so many ways.

Majid Fakhry
Chairman,
Department of Philosophy,
American University of Beirut,
Lebanon

FOREWORD

The present volume of the *Global History of Philosophy* covers the period 800-1150 and the next volume will cover the period 1150-1350, which together are aptly designated by the authors as the Period of Scholasticism. By Scholasticism, in the broadest sense, should be understood the systematic attempt to bring into harmony the data of reason and those of revelation.

As far as the Islamic tradition is concerned, the two major schools of systematic theology (*Kalām*), i.e. the Mu'tazilite and Ash'arite, are adequately dealt with, and thus the dramatic confrontation between the first, rationalist and philhellenic, and the second anti-rationalist group, are highlighted. This volume, however, does not leave out the far more radical rationalist tendencies inherent in the writings of the great philosophers of the classical Islamic age, al-Kindi (d. ca. 866), al-Fārābi (d. 950), Ibn Sīna (d. 1037), and their Jewish successors, Sa'adia (d. 942), Ibn Gabirol (d. 1057) and Halevy (d. 1141). It also touches on the first broodings of the pre-Scholastic Latin philosophers and theologians of the ninth and eleventh centuries, i.e. Eriugena (d. 870), St. Anselm (d. 1109) and Abelard (d. 1142). This period is rightly referred to as pre-Scholastic, we believe, because it preceded the great period of Latin Aristotelianism, which to all intents and purposes, was a continuation of Arabic Aristotelianism. Prior to the introduction of Aristotelian Logic through the Arabic medium, the theologians of that period obviously lacked the intellectual tools for developing a scholastic system of the magnitude of later systems, such as those of St. Thomas Aquinas (1224-1270), Roger Bacon (ca. 1212-1292), Duns Scotus (1265-1308) and others. This was indeed the golden age of Latin Scholasticism, to be dealt with in Volume V.

The authors of this History should be complimented on their dedication to this difficult task of writing a global history which transcends the limits of space and time and isolates the fundamental trans-cultural, trans-national concepts common to

Head Office : 41-U.A., Bungalow Road, Delhi 110 007
Branches : Chowk, Varanasi 221 001
Ashok Rajpath, Patna 800 004
6, Appar Swamy Koil Street, Mylapore, Madras 600 004

First Edition : Delhi, 1984

ISBN : 0–89581–678–4

Printed in India
By Shantilal Jain, at Shri Jainendra Press,
A-45, Phase-I, Naraina, New Delhi 110 028 and published by
Narendra Prakash Jain, for Motilal Banarsidass Delhi 110 007.

Global History of Philosophy

VOLUME IV

The Period of Scholasticism

(PART ONE)

JOHN C. PLOTT

with

James Michael Dolin

Paul David Mays

MOTILAL BANARSIDASS

Delhi Varanasi Patna Madras

GLOBAL HISTORY OF PHILOSOPHY

4. Wing-tsit Chan, *A Source Book in Chinese Philosophy* (Princeton, 1963), p. 461.
5. Ibid.
6. Ibid.
7. Fung Yu-lan, *A History of Chinese Philosophy*, vol. II (Princeton, 1953), p. 466.
8. Chang, p. 165.
9. Fung, pp. 465-66.
10. Chan, p. 483.
11. Ibid.

Chang Tsai

1. Fung Yu-lan, *A History of Chinese Philosophy*, vol. II (Princeton, 1953), p. 477.
2. Wing-tsit Chan, *A Source Book in Chinese Philosophy* (Princeton, 1963), p. 515.
3. Ibid., pp. 500-501.
4. Ibid., p. 503.
5. Ibid., p. 505.
6. Ibid., p. 506.
7. Ibid., p. 515.
8. Ibid., p. 501.
9. Ibid., p. 506.
10. Hou Wai-lu, p. 47.
11. Chan, p. 509.
12. Ibid., p. 498.
13. Ibid., pp. 497-98.
14. Ibid., p. 515.
15. Tang Chün-i, "Chang Tsai's Theory of Mind and Its Metaphysical Basis", Philosophy East-West, vol. VI, pp. 114-15.

Bahya Ibn Paquda

1. George Vajda, *La Théologie Ascétique de Bahya Ibn Paquda* (Paris, 1947).
2. Ibid., p. 15.
3. Ibid., p. 68.
4. Ibid., p. 119.

Ch'eng Hao and Ch'eng I

1. Wing-tsit Chan, *A Source Book in Chinese Philosophy* (Princeton, 1963), pp. 545-46.
2. Ibid., p. 519.
3. Ibid.
4. Carson Chang, *Development of Neo-Confucian Thought* (New York, 1957), p. 185.

5. Fung Yu-lan, *A History of Chinese Philosophy*, vol. II (Princeton, 1953), pp. 510-11.
6. Chan, pp. 523-24.
7. Fung, p. 517.
8. Ibid., pp. 528-29.
9. Chan, p. 545.

Wang An-shih

1. Dun J. Li, *The Ageless Chinese* (New York, 1965), pp. 207-8.
2. Joseph Needham, *Science and Civilisation in China* (Cambridge, 1965), pp. 138-9.
3. Ibid.
4. Wm Theodore de Bary, *et al*, *Sources of Chinese Tradition* (New York, 1960), p. 465.
5. Lo Ssu-ting, "Evolution of the Controversy Between the Confucianists and the Legalists as Seen from Wang An-shih's Reforms", Chinese Studies in History, vol. IX, no. 2, p. 4.
6. Ibid., p. 7.
7. Ibid.
8. Ibid., p. 9.
9. Ibid., pp. 9-10.
10. Ibid., p. 10.
11. Ibid., p. 13.
12. Hou Wai-lu
13. Ibid.
14. H. R. Williamson, *Wang An-shih* (London, 1937), p. 375 ff.

Psellos

1. Jaroslav Pelikan, *The Spirit of Eastern Christendo m* (Chicago, 1974), p. 243.
2. Ibid., p. 244.
3. Ibid., p. 245.
4. Ibid., p. 247.
5. George Karahalios, *The Philosophical Trilogy of Michael Psellos* (Heidelberg, 1970), pp. 7-8.
6. Ibid., p. 9.
7. Ibid., p. 15.
8. Pelikan, p. 247.
9. Karahalios, p. 48.
10. Ibid., p. 49.
11. Ibid., p. 164.
12. Ibid., p. 165.
13. Ibid., p. 50.
14. Ibid.
15. Ibid., p. 51.

16. Ibid., p. 123.
17. Ibid., pp. 123-24.
18. Ibid., p. 125.
19. Ibid., p. 129.
20. Ibid., p. 133.
21. Ibid., p. 144.
22. Ibid.
23. Ibid., p. 145.
24. Ibid., p. 105.
25. Ibid., p. 106.
26. Ibid., p. 107.

Anselm

1. John Hick and Arthur McGill, eds., *The Many-faced Argument* (New York, 1967), p. 185.
2. Ibid., pp. 4-6.
3. Ibid., p. 7.
4. Frederick Copleston, *A History of Philosophy*, vol. II, part I (New York, 1962), p. 185.
5. Bernard L. Manning, "Wyclif" in *The Cambridge Medieval History*, vol. VII, p. 496.
6. *Many-faced Argument* pp. 183-206.
7. Ibid., pp. 183-84.
8. Ibid., p. 68.
9. Gustaf Aulen, *Christus Victor* (New York, 1951).
10. *The Cambridge Medieval History* vol. V, p. 796.
11. Copleston, p. 182.
12. *Cambridge History*, p. 782.

Ryōnin

1. Daigan and Alicia Matsunaga, *Foundation of Japanese Buddhism* (Tokyo, 1976), pp. 12-13.
2. Ibid., p. 13.
3. Ibid., p. 14.
4. Ibid., pp. 14-15.
5. Ibid., p. 15.

Hugh of St. Victor

1. David Luscombe, *Encyclopedia of Philosophy*, vol. I, p. 277.
2. Roy Joseph Deferrari, ed., *On Sacraments*, p. 50.
3. Ibid., p. 53.
4. Ibid., p. 55.
5. Ibid., p. 58.
6. Ibid., p. 168.
7. Ibid., p. 181.
8. Charles Buttimer, ed., *Didascalicon* (Catholic Univ. Press, 1939).

Halevi

1. *Encyclopedia Judaica*, p. 363.
2. Ibid., p. 364.
3. Isaac Husik, *A History of Mediaeval Jewish Philosophy* (New York, 1969), p. 152.
4. André Neher in *Histoire de la Philosophie* , vol. I, in the *Encyclopédie de la Pléiade* (Editions Gallimard, 1969).
5. Husik, p. 153.
6. Ibid., pp. 150-51.
7. Neher, p. 1025.
8. *Encyclopedia Judaica*, p. 365.

Abelard

1. *The Cambridge Medieval History* (New York, 1929), vol. V, p. 807.
2. Abby S. Richardson, ed., *Abelard and Heloise : A Medieval Romance* (New York, 1883), p. 25.
3. *The New Encyclopedia Britannica, Macropaedia*, 1, p. 10.
4. W. T. Jones, *The Medieval Mind* (New York, 1969), pp. 185-86.
5. *Encyclopedia of Philosophy*, vol. VIII, p. 194.
6. B. A. G. Fuller and Sterling McMurrin, *A History of Philosophy* (New York, 1955), p. 374.
7. Jones, p. 188.
8. Ibid., p. 195.
9. Ibid., p. 190.
10. Ibid., p. 196.
11. Copleston, p. 160.
12. Jones., p. 196n.
13. Ibid., p. 200n.
14. W.H.V. Reade in *The Cambridge Medieval History* (New York, 1929), p. 799.
15. *The Cambridge Medieval History*, vol. V (New York, 1936), p. 799.
16. Thomas Gilby in *The Encyclopedia of Philosophy* (New York, 1967), vol. I, p. 6.

INDEX

Typological Chart of Islamic Philosophers

John C. Plott with Paul D. Mays

TYPE	800 900	1000	1100	1200	1300
FALSAFAH	Abû Yûsuf Ya'qûb ibn Isḥâq al-Kindî (c. 801-c. 866)	Abû Naṣr Muhammad ibn Tarkhân al-Fârâbi (Alpharabius) (870-950) Yaḥia ibn 'Adî (d. 974)	Abû Ḥayyân al-Tauḥîdî (d. c. 1023) Ibn Miskawaih (Ahmad ibn Ya'qûb) (936?-1030) Abû 'Alî al-Ḥusain ibn Sînâ (Avicenna) (980-1037)	Ibn Bâjjah (Abû Bakr Muhammad ibn al-Ṣâyigh) (Latin: Avempace) (d. 1138) Abû Bakr ibn Tufayl (Latin: Abubacer) (d. 1185) Abû al-Walîd Muhammad ibn Aḥmad ibn Rushd (Latin: Averroës) (1126-1198)	Ibn Sab'în (d. 1270)
SCIENTISTS AND HISTORIANS	Jâbir ibn Ḥayyân (c. 722-815?) al-Farghani (d. 820?) Bishr ibn al-Mu'tamir (d. 825) Abû al-Hudhail (Hudayl) al-'Allaf (748-840) Mu'ammar ibn 'Abbâd al-Sulami (d. 842?) Abû Isḥaq Ibrâhîm ibn Sayyâr (al-Nazzâm) (d. 845) Muhammad ibn Mûsa al-Khwârizmi (d. 850?) 'Amr ibn Bahr al-Jâḥiz (d. 869)	Thâbit ibn Qurra (d. 901) al-Hamadânî (fl. 902) Abû 'Ali al-Jubbâ'î (849-915) Abû Hâshim 'Abd al-Salâm (861-933) Abû Bakr Muhammad ibn Zakariyâ al-Râzî (864?-933?) al-Mas'ûdî (d. c. 956) Ikhwân al-Safâ (Brethen of Purity) (founded c. 983) Muhammad ibn Yûsuf Kâtib Khwârizmî (d. 997)	Maslamah ibn Aḥmad al-Majrîṭî (d. 1007) Hamîd al-Dîn al-Kirmânî (d. 1017?) Abû 'Ali ibn al-Haitham (Alhazen) (965?-c. 1040) Abû Raiḥân Muhammad ibn Ahmad al-Bîrûnî (973-1048)	'Umar Khayyâm (c. 1038-1123) 'Ayn al-Qozât Hamadâni (d. 1131) Abû al-Barakât al-Baghdâdî (d. c. 1166)	Naṣîr al-Dîn Ṭûsî (1201-1274) Shams al-Dîn al-Shahrazûrî (d. c. 1281)
SÛFIS	Râbi'ah al-Adawiyah (d. 801) al-Muḥâsibi (d. 857) Ahmad ibn Khezrâyeh (fl. 865) Abû Yazid al-Bisṭâmi (Bâyazîd Bisṭâmi) (d. 874)	Abû al-Qâsim al-Junayd (Junaid of Baghdâd) (d. 910) al-Ḥusain ibn Mansûr al Ḥallâj (858-922) Hakaym ibn 'Isâ ibn Marwân (d. 944)	'Ali Hujwîri (d. c. 1063) Khwâjeh 'Abdullah al-Anṣârî (1006-1088)	Abû Ḥâmid Muhammad al-Ghazâlî (Latin: Alghazel) (1058-1111) 'Abd al-Qâhir al-Jîlânî (d. 1166) Aḥmad Yasavî (fl. c. 1166) Abû Najîb Suhrawardi (d. 1167) Aḥmad al-Rifâ'î (d. 1175)	Shihâb al-Dîn Suhrawardi (1144-1234) Ibn 'Arabî (1165-1240) Jalâl al-Dîn Rûmî (1207-1273) Ahmad al-Badawî (d. 1276)
ISHRÂQI (ILLUMINATIONISTS)	al-Tirmidhî (d. 898)	Ibn Masarrah of Spain (833-931) al-Wâsiṭî (d. 942)		Ibn al-'Ârif (d. 1141) Shihâb al-Dîn Yahiâ al-Suhrawardî (al-Maqtûl) 1153-1191)	Ibn Kammûnah (d. 1284)
LEGALISTS	Ḥunain ibn Ishâq (809-873)	al-Ṭaḥâwi (843-933)	Abû al-Ḥasan al-Mâwardi (c. 974-1058) Niẓâm al-Mulk Ṭûsi ('Ali Ḥasan) (1018-1092)		
KALÂM AND ULTRA ORTHODOX		Ibn Dâwûd al-Isfahânî (867-909) Muḥammad ibn Ya'qub Kolaynî (940) Abû al-Ḥasan al-Ash'arî (873-941?) al-Mâturîdi (853?-944)	Abû Bakr al-Bâqillânî (d. 1013) 'Abd al-Qâdir ibn Tâhir al-Baghdâdî (d. 1037) Ibn Hazm (994-1064) Abû al-Ma'âli 'Abd al-Malik al-Juwainî (1028-1085)		Fakhr al-Dîn al-Râzî (d. 1209)